FENN'S CHINESE-ENGLISH POCKET DICTIONARY

THE FIVE THOUSAND DICTIONARY

AND INDEX TO THE CHARACTER CARDS OF THE COLLEGE OF CHINESE STUDIES, CALIFORNIA COLLEGE IN CHINA, ORIGINALLY COMPILED BY COURTENAY H. FENN, M.A., D.D. WITH THE ASSISTANCE OF MR. CHIN HSIEN TSENG

REVISED AMERICAN EDITION

Based on the Fifth Peking edition, which included additions and revisions by George D. Wilder, B.A., D.D. and Mr. Chin Hsien Tseng

HARVARD UNIVERSITY PRESS
CAMBRIDGE, MASSACHUSETTS

Fourteenth Printing, 1976
Library of Congress Catalog Card Number 43-754
ISBN 0-674-30551-5
Printed in the United States of America

FOREWORD TO THE AMERICAN EDITION

In response to the urgent need of a handy pocket dictionary to aid the growing number of students in elementary Chinese in this country, the Department of Far Eastern Languages of Harvard University has undertaken to reprint this little dictionary by Dr. C. H. Fenn and Mr. Chin Hsien-tseng. Thanks are due to Dr. W. B. Pettus for giving prompt permission for the undertaking and for furnishing his own precious copies of the book in first-class condition for the reproduction. The necessary funds for this publication were furnished by the Rockefeller Foundation.

The urgency of the task has made it impossible to go into any extensive revisions or additions, aside from some corrections and the introduction of a few new terms which have recently come into general use. The chief features in this edition are (1) the rewriting of the pages on standards and styles of pronunciation and the exposition on tones, and (2) the marking of the neutral tone with dots and circles, making this the first Chinese-English dictionary in which such information is given. Mr. Min-yuan Wang was responsible for a part of the revision of the entries and the mechanical details in preparation for the reproduction, and Dr. Y. R. Chao was responsible for revising the introduction and furnishing the data on the neutral tones.

Cambridge, Mass.
October, 1942.

CONTENTS

FOREWORD

The compiler of this little book finds a very special satisfaction in the fact that he is giving to the public a thing the lack of which he has personally felt keenly for the more than thirty years of his sojourn in "The Land of Sinim". Of making of dictionaries there is no end, and there are already many pocket dictionaries upon the market; but the compiler of this latest of them all has never found one specially adapted to be the pocket companion, from his first day to his last, of the foreigner who comes to China, either for business or for missions; furnishing on the instant 98-100 of all the information he requires as to Chinese printed or written characters, or speech for every day use. The vocabularies have always been too large or too small, the translations too few or too many, the common combinations too numerous or lacking altogether, the information given as to the composition of characters and as to their relative frequency too meager, or hidden in out-of-the way places. The compiler of the book now before you believes that he has fairly overcome all these difficulties, and that all students and speakers of Chinese, except those wishing to acquire a strictly technical vocabulary in certain professional lines and those planning profound study of Chinese classical literature, will find in this little book all the requisites for ordinary conversation and reading.

The book was primarily intended as an Index to the Five Thousand Character Cards prepared by the compiler for the North China Union Language School for the use of its own students and any others who may feel the need of this great auxiliary to language study. After selecting and preparing for the press these 5000 character cards, with their abundance of convenient information as to the characters earliest met and most frequently used in the Chinese language, the compiler began on an Index. But why not make this a supplement, as well as a complement, to the Character Cards? The individual characters are not the thing which the student most frequently desires to use in speech and in ordinary reading The Chinese may be a monosyllabic language, but Chinese speech is largely dissyllabic, and the clustering of the most common combinations of characters in connection with them adds many fold to the usefulness of an Index. Therefore this Index, without adding greatly to its bulk, has become a most convenient pocket Dictionary. The cutting out of the second 5000 infrequently used characters found in most pocket dictionaries makes room for these useful combinations and saves many a long search.

The first column on each page gives, of course, the characters, with the various forms in which they may be encountered, also the Peking tone of each The arrangement of the whole is that of the Wade Romanization, not because it is ideal, but simply because its recognition is most nearly universal. The second column gives the Radical, the third, the Phonetic, with its number in Soothill's Dictionary. The fourth column gives the usual translations, common combinations, and indications as to whether the character when thus read is colloquial (俗) or literary (文), and whether it is used as a "Classifier", or Numerator" (C), or as a Surname (S). The fifth column gives other readings of the same character, under which further information may be sought. Thə sixth column indicates the group to which the character has been assigned in reference to the earliness of its occurrence in the Lessons of the Language School. The School's Character Cards are arranged in ten groups of 500 each, lettered from A to K. Groups A and B differ slightly from the others in that they include a few characters which would not occur in a list of the 1000 *most frequently used* characters, but which do occur in the Language School Lessons of the first year. Group P includes the Phoneties which are not used as characters.

Unless unconscious omissions have been made, this Dictionary Index includes all characters which occur in any of the Language School Lessons, Baller's Primer, Mateer's Mandarin Lessons, Kuan Hua Chih Nan, The Old and New Testaments, and the Blodget-Goodrich Hymnal.

A Radical Index and List of Radicals will be found at the end of the book, which is sent forth in the hope that, with others as well as the compiler, it may "meet a long-felt want."

Courtenay H. Fenn

Peking, June, 1926,

INTRODUCTION TO THE THIRD EDITION

The continued demand for Dr. Fenn's 5000 Dictionary proves that he and Mr. Chin have done their work well. The 5000 characters which form the basis for the dictionary have been selected in a scientific way. An actual count of the material studied and used by foreign students of Chinese during their early years in China has been made. The work is a "phrase dictionary"; the most commonly used phrases with their English equivalents have been selected and are given under each character. The radical of each principal character is shown, thus assisting students in learning to 'spell" Chinese characters according to their form, which is one of the most helpful ways of fixing them in the memory. This dictionary forms an index to Dr. Fenn's Character Slips, of which 5000 have been printed, classfied according to the order of frequency so that the most important may be learned first.

Experience shows that this dictionary meets most of the needs of students of spoken Chinese during the first years of their work on the language. No absolutely ideal vocabulary can be presented, because individual needs differ, but the basis of selection used in this dictionary has produced a time-saving compromise Unabridged dictionaries are necessary for research students and all students must secure technical vocabularies if their work deals with science, philosophy, politics, or religion. It is true that by the end of the second year, or in the third year, the students should begin to use the large standard Chinese dictionaries, such as the "Tz'u Yuan" (辭源), or "K'ang Hsi Tzu Tien" (康熙字典), but these are not used until the student has completed some such work as Brandt's Introduction to Literary Chinese and has plunged into the vast sea of Chinese literature, which offers to the Western student more of new and unexplored territory than does any European language he can learn, and which amply repays the years of effort required to secure a working knowledge of Chinese.

W. B. Pettus

California College in China
Peking.
January 12, 1932.

PREFACE TO THE FOURTH EDITION.

Experience has proved that the 5000 words which Dr. Fenn has included in his dictionary have been well chosen and well compiled. An increasing demand has necessitated a new edition. Dr. C. H. Fenn, ably assisted by Mr. Chin Hsien Tseng, has not only provided students with the most common words classified according to frequency, but has also made an excellent selection of the terms and phrases that are still in current use.

This small dictionary is now rated as one of the most acceptable for beginners. While unabridged and technical dictionaries are always required by advanced students, it has been found that a dictionary of this size and nature is most useful at the early stage of acquiring the language. The errata of previous editions have been carefully revised. One may rely upon this edition for the pronunciation of Peking Mandarin now coming into general use.

J. D. Hayes

College of Chinese Studies
Peking, China
April, 1936

PREFACE TO THE FIFTH EDITION

Those who have used this dictionary in the past may care to know how this present fifth edition has been changed from those of the past. Mr. Chin Hsien-tseng, has been engaged in the compilation and revisions of the book from its very inception with Dr. Fenn. He had been inserting the numbers under the radicals in the second columns of the text, and doing other mechanical work connected with a reprinting, when the writer arrived last April with leisure to assist.

In our collaboration on the work at the beginning we did not plan changes radical enough for us to call the reprinting a revision. But by request we inserted 150 phrases selected by the teachers in the College from the newer teaching material; we also deleted a few of the obsolete phrases, and corrected some errors copied from other dictionaries or revealed by recent discoveries and studies in things Chinese. We have occasionally rearranged the definitions of the basic 5,000 characters so as to bring root meanings first, and from page 101 onward we have put illustrative Chinese phrases immediately after the English meaning they illustrate, rather than leave them at the end of the list where the student not familiar with them would be at a loss from not knowing to which of several meanings in the definition they belong. We have also tried to make the book still more useful by adding General Information, giving the usual means for determining dates, and places, etc., met in general reading. In addition we have listed all of the 438 surnames in Po Chia Hsing not found in our text, and also have compiled two more unusual tables.

One of these, the "Chinese Ordinals", shows the many ways of indicating series numbers from one to 1000 by the use of well-known groups of characters and classic quotations; the other table gives the "Standard Methods of Showing Pronunciations, (including tones)", much like our diacritical marks, since Kang Hsi in 1716 A.D. These tables are unique so far as we know, and the latter is useful as a key to tone marks in the Bible, William's Dictionary, etc. We have inserted a list not only of the radicals but also of the phonetics with the numbers used in the text, after Soothill, calling it the "Phonetic Index". In this Index the letters under each character refer it to some one of the eight groups (A. a, B. b, *b*, C. c. D) arranged in order of importance as to number and certitude of derivatives, by J. F. Corta, S. J. and J, A. Colinas. S. J. in their recent Latin brochure "Phonetical Series P. Wieger". In consideration of these efforts we have been emboldened to add our names on the title page as revisers in this present edition.

College of Chinese Studies — Chin Hsien Tseng

Peking, April. 1940 — George D. Wilder

Key to Reference Numbers and Abbreviations.

N.B. Read last paragraph of Foreword on Page IV.

ALPHABETICAL INDEX pp. 1-659

1st column on each page gives character to be defined, sometimes linked by a line at the left with one or more other forms of the same character, and the number of its Peking tone.

2nd column gives the radical and its number.

3rd column gives the phonetic and its Soothill number.

4th column has the usual translations and other facts, as S,C, 俗,文.

5th column gives other readings of the same character under which more facts may be found in this book.

6th column shows frequency groups based on earliness of occurrence in the textbooks of 1926 by capital letters.

Thus capitals in last column show:—

A = 1st 500 group: B = 2nd 500; C = 3rd 500: D = 4th 500; E = 5th 500;
F = 6th 500; G = 7th 500; H = 8th 500; I = 9th 500; K = 10th 500;
P = the the remaining phonetics not found in the text.

IN THE TEXT. 4th Col. C means Classifier or Numerator; Chien[3] 減 means that the adjacent character in the first column is an abbreviated writing for the one above it.

S = surname either single or double, used only in the fourth column.
Su[2] 俗 = colloquial character.
Wen[2] 文 = literary character.

NUMBERS IN THE PHONETIC INDEX, pp. XIV-XIX, under the characters refer to page in the Dictionary, Digits and numbers on the four margins of the pages indicate Soothil list numbers. Letters under a character refer it to some one of the eight groups in the order of importance, A, a, B, b. *b*, C, c. D.

NUMBERS IN THE RADICAL INDEX, pp 659-695, (1) opposite each character refer to the page in the book: (2) the small numbers at the upper corner of a character indicate the first character under the radical to have this number of strokes in excess of the number of strokes in the radical; (3) Numbers in parenthesis at the top of a page show that radicals of that number of strokes begin in the column underneath. When they continue to another page it is printed without the parenthesis as "x strokes (con't)".

A dot (or a circle) before a character indicates that the character must be (or may be) pronounced without stress and without tone.

GENERAL INFORMATION

List of Radicals

1 Stroke

No.	Radical	Name	Meaning
1.*	一	I^1	One.
2.*	丨	Kun^3	Down stroke.
3.*	丶	Chu^3	A dot.
4.*	丿	P'ieh^1	Left stroke.
5.	乙	I^4	One, bent.
6.	亅	Chüeh^2	Hooked down stroke.

2 Strokes

No.	Radical	Name	Meaning
7.*	二	Erh^4	Two.
8.	亠	T'ou^2	Above, cover.
9.	人 *亻	Jen^2	Man (erect).
10.	儿	Jen^2	Man (going).
11.	入	Ju^4	Enter.
12.	八	Pa^1	Eight.
13.*	冂	Chiung^3	Borders.
14.*	冖	Mi^4	To cover.
15.*	冫	Ping^1	Ice.
16.	几	Chi^1	Table, stool.
17.	凵	K'an^3	Receptacle.
18.	刀 *刂	Tao^1	Knife.
19.	力	Li^4	Strength.
20.	勹	Pao^1	Wrap.
21.	匕	Pi^3	Spoon, ladle.
22.*	匚	Fang^1	Basket.
23.*	匸	Hsi^3	Box.
24.	十	Shih^2	Ten.
25.	卜	Pu^3	To divine.
26.*	卩 㔾	Chieh^2	Seal, stamp.
27.*	厂	Han^4	A cliff.
28.	厶	Szu^1	Private.
29.	又	Yu^4	Also; a hand.

3 Strokes

No.	Radical	Name	Meaning
30.	口	K'ou^3	Mouth.
31.*	囗	Wei^2	Enclosure.
32.*	土	T'u^3	Earth.
33.	士	Shih^4	Scholar.
34.	夂	Chih^4	Step forward.
35.	夊	Sui^1	Walk slowly.
36.	夕	Hsi^4	Evening.
37.	大	Ta^4	Great.
38.	女	Nü^3	Female.
39.	子	Tzu^3	Child, son.
40.*	宀	Mien^2	Roof.
41.	寸	Ts'un^4	Inch.
42.	小	Hsiao^3	Small.
43.	尢 兀 尣	Wang^1	Lame, crooked.
44.	尸	Shih^1	A corpse.
45.*	屮	Ch'e^4	A sprout.
46.	山	Shan^1	Hill.
47.	巛 川 巜	Ch'uan^1	A stream.
48.	工	Kung^1	Work.
49.	己	Chi^3	Self.

* See P. XIII for colloquial names.

No.	Radical	Name	Meaning
50.*	巾	Chin^{1}	Napkin.
51.	干	Kan^{1}	Shield.
52.	幺	Yao^{1}	Little, fine.
53.*	广	Yen^{3}	Roof, shelter.
54.	廴	Yin^{3}	Move on.
55.	廾	Kung^{3}	Folded hands.
56.	弋	I^{4}	Dart, to shoot.
57.	弓	Kung^{1}	A bow.
58.*	彐	Chi^{4}	Pig's head.
	彑		
	⺕		
59.*	彡	Shan^{1}	Feathery.
60.*	彳	Ch'ih^{4}	Left step.

4 Strokes

No.	Radical	Name	Meaning
61.	心	Hsin^{1}	Heart.
*	忄		
	⺗		
62.	戈	Ko^{1}	A spear.
63.	戶	Hu^{4}	Door, family.
64.	手	Shou^{3}	Hand.
*	扌		
65.	支	Chih^{1}	Branch, prop.
66.	攴	P'u^{1}	Tap, rap.
*	攵		
67.	文	Wen^{2}	Literature.
68.	斗	Tou^{3}	A peck.
69.	斤	Chin^{1}	Axe. catty.
70.	方	Fang^{1}	Square.
71.	无	Wu^{2}	Not.
	旡		
72.	日	Jih^{4}	Sun, day.
73.	曰	Yüeh^{1}	To say.
74.	月	Yüeh^{4}	Moon.
75.	木	Mu^{4}	Wood.
76.	欠	Ch'ien^{4}	Owe.
77.	止	Chih^{3}	To stop.
78.	歹	Tai^{3}	Bad.
	歺		
79.	殳	Shu^{1}	Pole-ax, kill.
80.	毋	Wu^{2}	Do not.
81.	比	Pi^{3}	Compare.
82.	毛	Mao^{2}	Hair.
83.	氏	Shih^{4}	Clan.
84.	气	Ch'i^{4}	Air, breath.
85.	水	Shui^{3}	Water.
*	氵		
	氺		
86.	火	Huo^{3}	Fire.
*	灬		
87.	爪	Chao^{3}	Claws.
	爫		
88.	父	Fu^{4}	Father.
89.	爻	Yao^{2}	Interwine.
90.	爿	Ch'uang^{2}	Frame, bed
91.	片	P'ien^{4}	A slip, strip
92.	牙	Ya^{2}	Tooth.
93.*	牛	Niu^{2}	Ox.
94.	犬	Ch'üan^{3}	Dog.
*	犭		

5 Strokes

No.	Radical	Name	Meaning
95.	玄	Hsüan^{2}	Dark, deep.
96.	玉	Yü^{4}	Gem, jade.
*	王		
97.	瓜	Kua^{1}	Melon.
98.	瓦	Wa^{3}	Tile.
99.	甘	Kan^{1}	Sweet.
100.	生	Sheng^{1}	Produce.
101.	用	Yung^{4}	Use.
102.	田	T'ien^{2}	Field.
103.	疋	P'i^{3}	Roll of cloth.
104.*	疒	Ni^{4}	Sick.

* See P. XIII for colloquial names,

No.	Radical	Name	Meaning
105.	癶	Po^4	Legs spread out.
106.	白	Pai^2	White.
107.	皮	P'i^2	Skin.
108.*	皿	Min^3	Dish.
109.	目 罒	Mu^4	Eye.
110.	矛	Mao^2	Lance.
111.	矢	Shih^3	Arrow.
112.	石	Shih^2	Stone.
113.	示 示 礻	Shih^4	Reveal.
114.	禸	Jou^3	Beast's track.
115.*	禾	Ho^2	Growing grain.
116.*	穴	Hsüeh^4	Cave, hole.
117.	立	Li^4	To stand.

6 Strokes

No.	Radical	Name	Meaning
118.*	竹	Chu^2	Bamboo.
119.	米	Mi^3	Kernels, rice.
120.	糸 *糹	Mi^4	Silk.
121.	缶	Fou^3	Earthen ware
122.	网 *罒 㓁	Wang^3	A net.
123.	羊	Yang^2	Sheep.
124.	羽	Yü^3	Quill feathers.
125.	老 耂	Lao^3	Old.
126.	而	Erh^2	And, yet.
127.	耒	Lei^3	A plough.
128.	耳	Erh^3	Ear.
129.	聿	Yü^4	Stylus.
130.	肉 *月	Jou^4	Flesh.
131.	臣	Ch'en^2	King's officers
132.	自	Tzu^4	Self, from.
133.	至	Chih^4	Reach.
134.	臼	Chiu^4	A mortar.
135.	舌	She^2	Tongue
136.	舛	Ch'uan^3	Opposed to.
137.	舟	Chou^1	Boat.
138.	艮	Ken^4	A limit, perverse or hard.
139.	色	Se^4	Colour.
140.	艸 *艹 [illegible]	Ts'ao^3	Grass, herbs.
141.	虍	Hu$^{1.3}$	Tiger.
142.	虫	Ch'ung^2	Insect.
143.*	血	Hsieh^3	Blood.
144.	行	Hsing^2	Go, do.
145.	衣 衤	I^1	Clothes.
146.	襾 *西 覀	Hsia^4	A cover.

7 Strokes

No.	Radical	Name	Meaning
147.	見	Chien^4	See, perceive.
148.	角	Chüeh^2	Horn, angle.
149.	言	Yen^2	Words.
150.	谷	Ku^3	Gully, ravines
151.	豆	Tou^4	Platter, bean.
152.	豕	Shih^{34}	Swine.
153.	豸	Chai^4	Footless reptiles.
154.	貝	Pei^4	Cowries, valuable.
155.	赤	Ch'ih^4	Red, bare.
156.	走	Tsou^3	Walk.

* See P. XIII for colloquial names.

157.*	足	Tsu^{2}	Foot, enough.
158.	身	Shen^{1}	Body.
159.	車	Ch'e^{1}	Cart.
160.	辛	Hsin^{1}	Pungent, acrid.
161.	辰	Ch'en^{2}	Time.
162.	辵 *辶	Cho^{4}	To run and stop.
163.	邑 *阝	I^{4}	City, district.
164.	酉	Yu^{3}	New wine, ripe.
165.	釆	Pien^{4}	To separate.
166.	里	Li^{3}	Hamlet; Chinese mile.

8 Strokes

167.	金	Chin^{1}	Gold, metal.
168.	長 镸	Ch'ang^{2}	Long.
169.	門	Men^{2}	Door.
170.	阜 *阝	Fou^{34}	A mound, plenty.
171.	隶	Tai^{4}	Reach to.
172.	隹	Chui^{1}	Short-tailed birds.
173.*	雨	Yü^{3}	Rain.
174.	青	Ch'ing^{1}	Nature colors, as blue, green, etc.
175.	非	Fei^{1}	Wrong, not.

9 Strokes

176.	面	Mien^{4}	Face, surface.
177.	革	Ko^{2}	Rawhide.
178.	韋	Wei^{2}	Leather.
179.	韭	Chiu^{3}	Leeks.
180.	音	Yin^{1}	Sound.
181.	頁	Yeh^{4}	The head, a page.
182.	風	Feng^{1}	Wind.
183.	飛	Fei^{1}	To fly.
184.	食	Shih^{2}	To eat.
185.	首	Shou^{3}	Head.
186.	香	Hsiang^{1}	Fragrance.

10 Strokes

187.	馬	Ma^{3}	Horse.
188.	骨	Ku^{3}	Bone.
189.	高	Kao^{1}	High.
190.	髟	Piao^{1}	Bushy human hair.
191.	鬥	Tou^{4}	To fight.
192.	鬯	Ch'ang^{4}	Fragrant sacrificial wine.
193:	鬲	Li^{4}	Three-legged incense caldron.
194.	鬼	Kuei^{3}	Spirits, of the dead.

11 Strokes

195.	魚	Yü^{2}	Fish.
196.	鳥	Niao^{3}	Long-tailed birds.
197.	鹵	Lu^{3}	Rock salt.
198.	鹿	Lu^{4}	Deer.
199.	麥	Mai^{4}	Wheat.
200.	麻	Ma^{2}	Hemp.

12 Strokes

201.	黃	Huang^{2}	Yellow.
202.	黍	Shu^{3}	Glutinous millet.

* See P. XIII for colloquial names.

203.	黑	Hei^{1}	Black.
204.	黹	Chih^{3}	Embroidery.

13 Strokes

205.	黽	Meng^{3}	Frog or toad.
206.	鼎	Ting^{3}	Tripod.
207.	鼓	Ku^{3}	Drum.
208.	鼠	Shu^{3}	The rat kind.

14 Strokes

209.	鼻	Pi^{2}	Nose.
210.	齊	Ch'i^{2}	Even.

15 Strokes

211.	齒	Ch'ih^{3}	Front teeth.

16 Strokes

212.	龍	Lung^{2}	Dragon.
213.	龜	Kuei^{1}	Tortoise.

17 Strokes

214.	龠	Yüeh^{4}	Flute, pipes.

Colloquial Names of Radicals

1	一	一橫
2	丨	一竪
3	丶	一點
4	丿	一撇
7	二	兩橫
9	亻	單立人
13	冂	三道框下缺
14	冖	禿寶蓋
15	冫	兩點水
18	刂	立刀
22	匚	三道框右缺
23	匸	三道框上橫
26	卩	硬耳刀, 單耳刀, 小耳
27	厂	偏廠兒, 禿偏上
31	囗	四道框
32	土	提土
40	宀	寶蓋
45	屮	牛艸
50	巾	大巾旁
53	广	偏上
58	彐	橫山
59	彡	三撇
60	彳	雙立人
61	忄	竪心
64	扌	提手
66	攵	反文
85	氵	三點水
86	灬	四點火
93	牜	牛字傍
94	犭	反犬, 犬猶
96	王	側玉, 玉字傍
104	疒	病廠兒
108	皿	皿墩
115	禾	禾木旁
116	穴	穴字頭
118	竹	竹字頭
120	糸	絞絲
122	罒	扁四
130	月	肉字旁,
	月	肉月
140	艹	草字頭
143	血	血墩
146	襾	西字部
157	𧾷	足路
162	辶	走之
163	阝	軟耳刀, 雙耳刀, 右耳刀
170	阝	左耳刀
173	⻗	雨字頭

Phonetic Index*

		10	20	30	40	50	60	70	80	90	100	110	120	130	140	
0		空 C 279	府 A 142	于 D 643	贊 C 542	厓 b 613	藋 D 268	廷 A 528	上 536	音 629	寅 164	業 D 621	不 423	肯 247	胥 b 190	0
1	一 216		將 A 44	余 643	生 D 445	佳 42	瞿 A 114	王 594	主 a 94	意 220	甘 238	丨 275	小 171	步 424	手 458	1
2	丁 a 525	巫 605	才 540	干 c 238	星 D 184	隹 105	雍 a 640	匡 b 270	青 82	章 A 14	其 A 39	子 D 584	少 440	歲 477	邦 *b* 383	2
3	亭 a 528	十 450	斗 533	旱 149	土 570	隺 b 561	羅 A 315	狂 *b* 270	責 548	戠 a 66	斯 480	孛 c 419	叔 462	足 556	那 353	3
4	宁 A 96	卒 D 556	千 63	幵 64 刑 185 *b*	去 D 117	隼 469	華 200	皇 A 206	立 297	竟 81	甚 444	予 643	肖 D 173	走 555	半 a 380	4
5	行 184	卓 88	乖 265	并 c 415	盍 156	雇 261	士 455	閏 233	妾 57	共 C 279	革 251	矛 331	貨 471	從 a 566	丰 137	5
6		朝 19	垂 D 106	平 c 415	寺 482	焦 A 48	壽 460	畺 A 371	新 182	巷 169	堇 a 75	務 610	止 68	徙 162	害 146	6
7	竹 94	埶 239	重 C 110	午 608	奎 320	翟 510	壬 a 226	玨 120	親 77	巽 197	莫 148	柔 b 230	正 D 28	疋 404	刼 41	7
8	工 D 276	寸 563	熏 b 195	牛 365	圭 272	蒦 a 215	任 a 228	全 B 118	帝 A 512	異 222	難 355	喬 649	延 624	定 526	夆 C 137	8
9		付 A 143	乎 197	先 a 176	卦 264		呈 D 29	金 74	音 536	暴 b 388	世 454	卜 423	此 D 588	是 c 453	逢 C 138	9
	9	19	29	39	49	59	69	79	89	99	109	119	129	139	149	

* Following Soothill, who omits Nos. 6, 9, 11, 59, 185, 656, and adds thirteen others, the actual total being 895, not 888.

A, a; B, b, *b*; C, c; D = groups based on importance, Corta and Colinas

	150	160	170	180	190	200	210	220	230	240	250	260	270	280	290	
0	乍 D 7	罷 221	吏 299	隋 476	考 *b* 245	度 568	折 B 22	到 501	旬 B 196	丂 52	朿 *b* 585	爲 596	名 *b* 344	彡 434	豦 A 113	0
1	羊 D 614	丩 84	布 424	右 639	孝 172	庶 D 464	析 b 160	制 70	勺 440	亟 33	夷 B 218	方 A 130	夗 c 592	参 D 25	象 *b* 169	1
2	善 b 435	爿 105	希 c 159	若 230	者 D 22	雁 632	斬 12	刃 C 227	匀 656	夸 264	弗 D 141	旁 A 384	宛 c 592	參 542	豖 94	2
3	鮮 177	壯 *b* 104	灰 207	匿 360	厂 149	尼 199	丘 *b* 86	力 297	勿 D 609	粤 371	鳥 361	於 643	舛 103	翏 D 303	羽 645	3
4	羔 244	片 411 肅 475	尢 594	有 638	原 b 651	虒 10	斥 73	另 313	忽 A 565	弓 278	島 501	敖 a 5	舜 *b* 469	彥 628	習 160	4
5	達 484	牙 D 612	尤 637		厭 B 627	虐 369	反 C 129	勹 385 a 勾 255 D	易 221	弱 230	馬 A 326	㫃 626	粦 a 309	豕 453	扇 *b* 436	5
6	美 426	丿 408	光 630	友 639	厄 b 371	虛 189	乃 354 朵 530 b	匋 A 504	昜 D 614	發 125	魚 642	斿 637	夢 337	家 *b* 41	舃 A 487	6
7	辛 182	厷 278	左 552	爰 652	危 598	盧 a 318	秀 188	句 D 113	湯 b 498	亞 a 612	穌 473	夕 163	歹 ·488	彖 573	乙 222	7
8	辟 a 401	丈 16	差 10	犮 374	广 626	慮 324	及 D 33	敬 b 81	舄 437	弔 516	魯 319	夜 *b* 621	死 481	豙 574	乞 40	8
9	幸 186	史 453	育 c 530	老 289	庄 103	斤 73	刀 500	匊 A 112	曷 156	弟 A 512	無 D 606	多 529	列 a 305	蒙 A 336	之 66	9
	159	169	179	189	199	209	219	229	239	249	259	269	279	289	299	

	300	310	320	330	340	350	360	370	380	390	400	410	420	430	440	
0	乏 127	留 A 314	麗 D 299	武 609	戉 *b* 654	𠂢 379	貇 247	袁 652	恩 565	光 269	敞 253	受 459	鐵 63	久 84	僉 D 63	0
1	也 620	己 D 34	北 391	戈 250	戊 611	昏 b 211	良 c 301	睘 a 88	㥯 631 惪 505	堯 617	段 b 572	愛 *b* 2	齊 B 39	以 219	欠 65	1
2	九 D 84	巴 D 373	它 a 532	癸 59	戌 190	畏 600 b 喪 (2)	郎 *b* 287	表 *b* 405	儿 227	八 373	股 629	憂 635	亦 223	坐 a 552	次 A 588	2
3	丸 592	色 431	旨 68	或 215	蔑 341	長 D 17	食 452	乇 533	兆 D 20	松 b 478	毆 A 216	爭 C 27	赤 73	介 A 56	入 232	3
4	執 67	邑 223	能 359	戋 540	咸 178	展 11	卽 *b* 33	宅 9	免 341	穴 195	殸 83	廾 278	赫 156	令 D 74	内 358	4
5	埶 222	龍 B 323	罷 375	伐 *b* 126	感 239	辰 B 26	鄉 166	毛 D 331	兔 571	分 D 134	㱿 35	井 *b* 80	川 102	陰 629	丙 A 414	5
6	㔾 55	黽 344	七 37	戎 C 234	幾 A 34	辱 231	旣 34	屯 D 577	毚 a 13	儿 32	爪 20	卉 210	州 *b* 89	念 D 364	火 214	6
7	卸 176	匕 399	化 201	戒 56	成 29	農 a 368	衣 216	心 181	兀 610	凡 128 凢 196	瓜 D 263	貴 B 395	巠 D 78	含 b 147	炎 D 624	7
8	卬 4	皆 c 54	弋 224	我 A 604	氏 455	民 c 343	褱 202	必 a 400	元 c 650	亢 D 243	孚 D 141	非 D 132	巤 357	令 a 313	粦 635	8
9	卯 331	鹿 D 320	式 454	義 b 221	氐 C 510	艮 D 247	襄 c 168	思 479	完 591	殳 461	妥 533	韭 84	人 226	侖 A 321	勞 b 288	9
	309	319	329	339	349	359	369	379	389	399	409	419	429	439	449	

	450	460	470	480	490	500	510	520	530	540	550	560	570	580	590	
0	秋 D 86	獄 648	奉 138	欵 269	樂 291	東 588	禾 154	水 467	父 143	夊 71	徵 28	帶 489	丹 492	同 A 581	商 509	0
1	大 485	莽 *b* 330	奏 *b* 555	失 449	朮 94	東 464	利 A 297	永 641	交 D 47	冬 578	敫 32	敝 400	母 350	咼 263	南 355	1
2	奇 C 38	天 523	春 b 107	夬 265	林 309	欶 464	委 D 598	丞 30	叉 639	夋 123	女 369	兩 301	每 334	高 D 243	岡 b 241	2
3	莫 D 348	夭 616	舂 111	央 C 613	樊 129	賴 285	歷 A 299	泉 119	桑 *b* 429	麦 c 312	奴 D 367	蔺 A 328	敏 343	喬 A 52	用 642	3
4	寮 A 304	癸 b 272	矢 453	朩 350	厤 326	東 b 578	示 455	求 A 86	發 D 89	复 B 142	如 231	爾 125	内 231	尙 439	甬 641 勇 641 C	4
5	夾 42	夫 B 139	知 65	本 395	未 D 599	東 C 60	祭 35	彔 c 320	畗 321	復 144	安 b 3	冊 549	禺 c 643	堂 *b* 499	庸 640	5
6	犬 119	关 a 119	疾 33	休 b 187	末 A 347	闌 A 286	宗 B 563	隶 490	殳 347	文 602	冂 87	扁 A 408	萬 593	當 A 497	備 392	6
7	吠 134	卷 a 117	矣 220	枲 443	桼 *b* 295	果 281	米 A 338	黍 38	皮 403 波 417 D	离 C 294	巾 74	侖 655	厲 b 298	掌 15	甫 c 142	7
8	戾 300	朕 507	侯 a 157	采 b 540	耒 292	巢 21	粲 543	乂 224	叉 8	支 425	市 455	舟 90	冋 b 87	賞 437	專 140	8
9	然 224	夫 398	疑 218	梁 300	朱 a 93	某 349	奥 D 5	爻 618	攴 66	攸 636	席 161	般 A 379	向 169	鬲 300	溥 426	9
	459	469	479	489	499	509	519	529	539	549	559	569	579	589	599	

	600	610	620	630	640	650	660	670	680	690	700	710	720	730	740	
0	冉 224	益 218	前 b 64	嚴 623	匚 131	凵 241	弁 360	建 A 61	臼 85	龠 C 306	何 155	谷 260	占 D 11	周 90	言 623	0
1	冓 B 256	血 175	月 654	咠 38	巨 A 114	凶 a 188	朔 472	兼 D 59	叟 B 473	與 D 645	司 C 481	容 b 233	后 158	豆 B 534	詹 11	1
2	角 120	而 125	朋 A 397	耶 b 620	臣 26	函 148	款 120	廉 b 307	舀 a 618	舁 194	古 B 259	各 251 客 254	石 452	豈 40	亨 153	2
3	解 55	需 190	且 D 57	聶 362	臤 58	卥 19	芻 D 98	彗 209	臽 180	兜 533	固 B 262	路 319	唐 b 499	登 B 506	享 C 168	3
4	皿 343	耑 101	助 96 宜 218	身 442	臧 b 544	鹵 319	豈 72	帚 90	兒 D 124	口 b 256	克 254	咎 85	尸 450	壹 216	孰 462	4
5	孟 b 337	肉 231	具 b 114	門 335 閔 343	乚 162	山 434	出 97	受 a 76	皃 332	品 412	胡 A 198	召 D 20	尼 A 359	豊 296	郭 b 281	5
6	盈 601	骨 260	耳 125	間 C 58	亡 D 594		屈 115	丑 92	皇 b 361	區 D 115	居 A 112	加 D 42	犀 160	豐 137	敦 B 576	6
7	盡 76	胃 601	取 116	開 C 177	㒳 b 595	缶 139	肀 37	尹 631	毀 209	桑 C 430	舌 441	告 244	尉 b 600	鼓 260	京 79	7
8	監 c 59	脊 34	最 560	鬥 534	芒 330	番 a 617	妻 b 37	君 a 123	舄 163	靁 310	合 154	台 490	戶 199	封 463	景 80	8
9	覽 b 286	僉 a 644	敢 239	叚 c 164	荒 b 205	屮 23	聿 649	倉 D 544	鼠 463	可 D 253	荅 A 483	㕣 626	吉 c 34	喜 A 161	呂 324	9
	609	619	629	639	649	659	669	679	689	699	709	719	729	739	749	

	750	760	770	780	790	800	810	820	830	840	850	860	870	880	
0	旨 219	員 D 649	齋 c 431	覃 a 495	婁 D 317	散 429	奄 C 626	曹 A 547	廛 *b* 13	惠 210	衆 110	賓 a 411	充 110	茲 A 584	0
1	官 B 267	吳 607	因 c 628	西 639	數 463	晉 543	番 D 127	寅 630	黑 152	目 351	爵 b 121	貫 268	㐬 313	奚 C 159	1
2	阜 139	五 607	㒳 b 276	酉 84	日 229	縣 179	畺 C 44	黄 D 205	曾 A 550	直 b 67	自 585	貴 D 272	育 647	鹽 36	2
3	師 449	吾 607	四 481	尊 a 562	且 a 493	昌 A 16	雷 *b* 292	廣 D 270	會 209	眞 D 24	息 *b* 160	買 *b* 327	敢 *b* 23	至 B 69	3
4	追 a 105	韋 a 597	奐 b 204	中 D 108	导 *b* 2	白 D 376	畾 C 292	申 443	更 248	盾 577	夏 165	賣 D 328	亥 D 147	屋 605	4
5	兒 188	冂 A 598	西 158	虫 111	亘 192 早 545	百 377	累 292	甲 43	曳 223	冒 332	首 458	見 D 61	云 656	臺 b 490	5
6	兌 574	面 342	要 *b* 618	風 *b* 136	明 344	帛 418	畐 140	單 491	車 23	肩 *b* 333	貝 392	頁 621	幺 616	糸 339	6
7	只 *b* 68	啚 400	票 A 406	蚤 D 546	冥 a 345	卑 D 391	苗 339	里 D 295	連 A 306	相 *b* 167	貞 b 24	頃 82	玄 192	系 163	7
8	保 386	亶 D 493	栗 b 299	蜀 463	昆 C 275	鬼 272	由 636	量 301	軍 123	算 475	則 548	厶 480	牽 63	䜌 D 321	8
9	肙 a 649	稟 316	罨 177	串 103	昔 161	田 524	曲 115	童 D 582	專 c 100	曼 A 329	嬰 633	允 656	畜 99		9
	759	769	779	789	799	809	819	829	839	849	859	869	879	889	

A Table of Pekingese Initial and Final Sounds

combined with

Chinese Characters

and the

Chinese Phonetic Letters (注音符號)

Initials 聲母

Ch - 之 ㄓ	Hs - 希 ㄒ	P' - 潑 ㄆ	Ts' - 疵 ㄘ
Ch' - 痴 ㄔ	J - 入 ㄖ	S - 私 ㄙ	Tz' - 疵 ㄘ
Ch -	K - 格 ㄍ	Sz - 私 ㄙ	W - 烏 ㄨ
(chi) 基 ㄐ	K' - 克 ㄎ	Sh - 尸 ㄕ	Y - 衣 ㄧ
Ch' -	L - 勒 ㄌ	T - 德 ㄉ	Yü - 迂 ㄩ
(ch'i) 欺 ㄑ	M - 墨 ㄇ	T' - 特 ㄊ	Ch - ㄐ, Ch'-ㄑ
F - 弗 ㄈ	N - 訥 ㄋ	Ts - 資 ㄗ	used before ㄧ
H - 黑 ㄏ	P - 薄 ㄅ	Tz - 資 ㄗ	and ㄩ only

There are still three other initial phonetic letters ㄪ—V, ㄫ—Ng, ㄬ—Gn, which were formerly included with the above 24, but because they are not used in Pekingese and the New Standard National Language, they are now omitted. The medial vowels, W, Y, Yü are included here as initials because they represent these vowels when they occur at the beginning of a word. Certain of the initials are sometimes used alone without any final, these are Chih ㄓ, Ch'ih ㄔ, Jih ㄖ, Shih ㄕ, Szu ㄙ, Tzu ㄗ and Tz'u ㄘ.

Finals 韻母

-A	阿	ㄚ	-Er	兒	ㄦ	-Iu	幽	ㄧㄡ	-Ui	威	ㄨㄟ
-Ai	哀	ㄞ	-I	衣	ㄧ	-Iung	雍	ㄩㄥ	-Un	溫	ㄨㄣ
-An	安	ㄢ	-Ia	鴉	ㄧㄚ	-O	痾	ㄛ	-Ung	翁	ㄨㄥ
-Ang	盎	ㄤ	-Iang	央	ㄧㄤ	-Ou	歐	ㄡ	-Uo	窩	ㄨㄛ
-Ao	奧	ㄠ	-Iao	腰	ㄧㄠ	-U	烏	ㄨ	-Ü	迂	ㄩ
-E	厄	ㄜ	-Ieh	葉	ㄧㄝ	-Ua	蛙	ㄨㄚ	-Üan	遠	ㄩㄢ
-Eh	也	ㄝ	-Ien	烟	ㄧㄢ	-Uai	歪	ㄨㄞ	-Üeh	月	ㄩㄝ
-Ei	危	ㄟ	-Ih*			-Uan	彎	ㄨㄢ	-Ün	允	ㄩㄣ
-En	恩	ㄣ	-In	音	ㄧㄣ	-Uang	汪	ㄨㄤ	-Ŭ **		
-Eng	哼	ㄥ	-Ing	英	ㄧㄥ	-Uei	威	ㄨㄟ			

* In Pekingese there are only four cases of this final i.e. Chih, Ch'ih, Jih, Shih; so the Phonetic Letters could indicate these four sounds independently without this final as ㄓ, ㄔ, ㄖ, ㄕ.

** There are but three cases of this final, viz, Szŭ, Tzŭ, Tz'ŭ and the Letters could indicate these three initial sounds by ㄙ, ㄗ, ㄘ, without this final. So it seems unnecessary to have Phonetic Letters for these two sounds—Ih and Ŭ.

XXII

STANDARDS OF PRONUNCIATION

The standard of Chinese pronunciation is that of Peiping. Some Western sinologists have experimented with the idea of constructing an artificial Mandarin which takes into account features of other dialects of the Mandarin group. For instance, the French scholars have always distinguished between dentals and gutterals before *i* and *ü*, e.g., *Chin* is differentiated into *tsin* 晉 and *kin* 金. The original, 1874 edition of S. W. Williams' *Syllabic Dictionary* makes the same distinction, besides retaining a fifth or entering tone and other features. Since the coming into general use of the Wade System, which is based on the dialect of Peiping, most writers on Chinese subjects in English and some others have consistently followed the pronunciation of Peiping as it is, without consideration of any other dialectal features. The standard of pronunciation in China has had a similar development. The official standard pronunciation embodied in 國音字典 *Kuo-yin Tzu-tien*, Shanghai, 1920, was also a constructed Mandarin, having among other Southern features an entering tone, and the distinction between *tsin* and *kin*, etc. Since 1932, however, the standard has also been changed to that of Peiping. The official publication superseding the *Kuo-yin Tzu-tien* is 國音常用字彙 *Gwoin Charngyonq Tzyhhuey*, Shanghai, 1932, of which probably a more accessible form is found in an appendix to the dictionary 辭海 *Tz'u Hai*, Shanghai, 1937, in the form of an index to about 9,000 characters. Besides using the National Phonetic Letters, these new publications also use a system of National Romanization, of which the most available form in this country is W. Simon's *Chinese Sentence Series*, London, 1942.

STYLES OF PRONUNCIATION

In Peiping, as elsewhere, there are variations of pronunciation according to class, education, occasion, mood, etc. Thus, 弄 is pronounced *lung*^{4} in the title of a piece of music, *nung*^{4} in average unaffected speech, *neng*^{4} in rather informal speech, and *nou*^{4} in the speech of children and illiterates. The greatest variation of pronunciation in Peiping occurs in words belonging to the entering tone of Ancient Chinese which ended in *-k*. Thus, 拍 *p'ɒk* >modern literary *p'o*^{4}, colloq. *p'ai*^{1}. Following is a list of finals in which such alternation occurs:

Literary	*e*		*o*			*u*		*üeh*
Colloquial	*ai*	*ei*	*ai*	*ao*	*ei*	*iu*	*ou*	*iao*
Example	窄	黑	白	薄	北	六	熟	脚

Which type is the usual one to use depends both upon the context or situation and upon the individual speaker. This dictionary has only space to record the variants for the compounds which are included here.

Characters used as particles, etc. usually have a strong form, or reading pronunciation, and a weak form, or spoken pronunciation. The most important of these are:

Character	着	了	麽	呢	的
Strong	*cho*^{2}	*liao*^{3}	*ma*^{1}, *mo*^{3}	*ni*^{1,2}	*ti*^{4}
Weak	·*che*, ·*chih*	·*le*	·*me*	·*ne*	·*te*

Because of the wide currency of the orthography used in H. A. Giles' *Chinese-English Dictionary*, it will be well to mention the chief points in which it differs from that of the present dictionary. The class of syllables *chio*, *ch'io*, *hsio*, and *yo* in Giles is definitely obsolete, and is now completely absorbed into *chüeh*, *ch'üeh*, *hsüeh*, and *yüeh* respectively. The distinction between syllables *i* and *yi* has no basis in the dialect and the two are combined here under the heading *I*, *Yi*, placed after *H*. In syllables listed here as *ko, ke; k'o, k'e; ho, he; o, e*, which have *-o* in Giles and *-e* in Chauncey Goodrich's *Pocket Dictionary*, the Giles orthography is recommended, but the actual pronunciation is always *-e*, there being however no ambiguity resulting from this orthography.

A graphical simplification adopted in this dictionary is the omission of diacritics over vowels in syllables like *ken*, *szu*, etc.

In this revised edition of **1942**, if a pronunciation of a character is added in the fourth (main) column without parentheses, it is to replace the one under which the character occurs.

TONES

A word in Chinese is what it is, not only through having such and such consonants and vowels, which form the initials and finals, but also through having a certain tone, or change (or no change) of pitch during the voiced part of the syllable. To the unsophisticated Chinese speaker, *ma*^{1} 'mother' and *ma*^{3} 'horse' are as different as *bad* and *bed* to an English-speaking person. If we divide the pitch of a person's voice into five points: 1 low, 2 half-low, 3 middle, 4 half-high, 5 high, we can describe a tone by naming its starting and ending pitch (including a turning point for circumflex tones). The four tones of Mandarin will then be as follows:

No.		*Chinese Name*	*English Name*	*Description*	*Pitch*
1	陰平(聲)	*yin*^{1}*-p'ing*^{2}*-(sheng*^{1}*)*	Upper Even (Tone)	High level	55:
2	陽平(聲)	*yang*^{2}*-p'ing*^{2}*-(sheng*^{1}*)*	Lower Even (Tone)	High rising	35:
3	上聲	*shang*^{3}*-sheng*^{1}	Rising Tone	Low rising	214:
4	去聲	*ch'ü*^{4}*-sheng*^{1}	Falling Tone	High falling to low	51:

When syllables are spoken in succession, changes known as tone-sandhi occur. There are two important rules of tone-sandhi in the Peiping dialect.

(1) A third tone followed by any tone except another third tone is pronounced without its final rise. This is known as the half-third tone. In *hao*^{3} *jen*^{2}, 'good man', for example, *hao*^{3} does not only start low, but stays low in pitch.

(2) A third tone followed by another third tone is pronounced high rising and thus indistinguishable from the second tone, as *hao*^{3}*-mi*^{3} 'good rice' is pronounced *hao*^{2} *-mi*^{3}.

A very important feature of the Peiping dialect is the neutral tone, or pitch of the atonic syllable, which, being unstressed, does not have one of the four regular tones. The notation for the atonic syllable is a dot before the syllable for compulsory cases and a circle for optional cases, that is, cases in which the syllable may or may not lose its stress and tone. The actual pitch of the atonic syllable varies according to the tone of the preceding syllable. After the first two tones it is half-low, after the third tone it is half-high, and after the fourth it is low.

It is one thing to know how a neutral tone is pronounced; it is another thing to know when a neutral tone is used. Particles, interjection, pronouns after verbs, and other 'empty words' which do not carry important concrete meanings in a sentence have the neutral tone. Except for particles, these are mostly optional neutral tones. More important than those just mentioned are fixed neutral tones in compounds, which have to be learned as such and cannot be reasoned out by rule. This is where it is important to record the actual cases in this dictionary. In this 1942 edition, all neutral tones in the compounds have been marked with dots or circles according as the neutrality is compulsory or optional. It should be noted however that the neutral tone occurring in the second of a three-syllable compound is usually left unmarked, as any syllable in this position tends to be weakened and thus ceases to present a lexical case.

An extreme case of the neutral tone is the suffix 兒 -(*e*)*r*, which is so weakened as to form one syllable with the preceding one. In such combinations, certain phonetic changes occur, of which the most important to note is that if the preceding syllable ends in -*i* (in a diphthong) or -*n*, the -*i* or -*n* is dropped, as 今 *chin*[1], p. 74 but 今 兒 *chier*[1]; 蓋 *kai*[4], but 蓋 兒 *kar*[4], p. 236. In this dictionary, an unmarked 兒 is always taken to be non-syllabic except under the main word *erh*[2] itself or when marked as 2. Only when it is both syllabic and unstressed is it marked with a dot, as under *nü*, p. 367.

Abstract of the Chinese Dynasties

The Five Rulers.	五帝	B.C.	2852	9	Rulers
Hsia^{4}.	夏		2205	17	“
Shang^{1} or Yin^{1}.	商 or 殷		1766	28	“
Chou^{1}.	周		1122	34	“
Ch'in^{2}.	秦		255	5	“
Han^{4}.	漢,前漢,西漢		206	14	“
Later Han^{4}.	後漢,東漢	A.D.	25	12	“
The Three Kingdoms.	三國				
Minor Han^{4}.	蜀漢		221	2	“
Wei^{4}.	魏		220	5	“
Wu^{2}.	吳		229	4	“
Western Chin^{4}.	西晋		265	4	“
Eastern Chin^{4}.	東晋		317	11	“
Division between N. & S.	南北朝				
Liu^{2} Sung^{4}.	劉宋		420	9	“
Ch'i^{2}.	齊		479	7	“
Liang^{2}.	梁		502	6	“
Ch'en^{2}.	陳		557	5	“
Northern Wei^{4}.	北魏		386	15	“
Western Wei^{4}.	西魏		535	3	“
Eastern Wei^{4}.	東魏		534	1	“
Northern Ch'i^{2}.	北齊		550	7	“
Northern Chou^{1}.	北周		557	5	“
Sui^{2}.	隋		589	4	“
T'ang^{2}	唐		618	22	“
The Five Dynasties	五代				
Posterior Liang^{2}	後梁		907	2	“
Posterior T'ang^{2}	後唐		923	4	“
Posterior Chin^{4}	後晋		936	2	“
Posterior Han^{4}	後漢		947	2	“
Posterior Chou^{1}	後周		951	3	“
Sung^{4}	宋,北宋		960	9	“
Southern Sung^{4}	南宋		1127	9	“
Yüan^{2} or Mongol	元		1280	9	“
Ming^{2}	明		1368	17	“
Ch'ing^{1} or Manchu	淸		1644	10	“
The Republic of China	中華民國		1912		

The Ming Dynasty—276 Years

DYNASTIC TITLE 廟號	ACCESSION A. D.	TITLE OF REIGN 年號	REIGNED YEARS
太祖	1368	洪武	31
惠帝	1399	建文	4
成祖	1403	永樂	22
仁宗	1425	洪熙	1
宣宗	1426	宣德	10
英宗	1436	正統	14
代宗 } 景帝	1450	景泰	7
英宗	1458*	天順	8
憲宗	1465	成化	23
孝宗	1488	弘治	18
武宗	1506	正德	16
世宗	1522	嘉靖	45
穆宗	1567	隆慶	6
神宗	1573	萬歷	47
光宗	1620	泰昌	1
熹宗	1621	天啓	7
莊烈帝	1628	崇禎	16

*Resumed government under new title after 7 yrs. captivity

The Ch'ing Dynasty (Manchu)—268 Years

DYNASTIC TITLE	ACCESSION A. D.	TITLE OF REIGN	REIGNED YEARS
世祖章皇帝	1644	順治	18
聖祖仁皇帝	1662	康熙	61
世宗憲皇帝	1723	雍正	13
高宗純皇帝	1736	乾隆	60
仁宗睿皇帝	1796*	嘉慶	25
宣宗成皇帝	1821	道光	30
文宗顯皇帝	1851	咸豐	11
穆宗毅皇帝	1862	同治°	13
德宗景皇帝	1875	光緒	34
	1908	宣統	3

* 乾隆 Lived three years longer.

° Empress Dowager more or less in power until 1908.

天干 or 十干 The Ten Celestial Stems.

天干		天干	五方	四時	五行	五星	五色	五味	五音	五臟
甲 乙	Chia^{4} I^{3}	甲乙	東	春	木	Jupiter	青	酸	角	肝
丙 丁	Ping^{3} Ting^{1}	丙丁	南	夏	火	Mars	赤	苦	徵	心
戊 己	Wu^{4} Chi^{3}	戊己	中	季夏	土	Saturn	黃	甘	宮	脾
庚 辛	Keng^{1} Hsin^{1}	庚辛	西	秋	金	Venus	白	辛	商	肺
壬 癸	Jen^{2} Kuei^{3}	壬癸	北	冬	水	Mercury	黑	鹹	羽	腎

地支 or 十二支 The 12 Horary Characters (Branches).

Branches		Animals	Zodiac	Hours	Directions
子	Tzu^{3}	Rat	Aries	11—1 a.m.	N
丑	Ch'ou^{3}	Ox	Taurus	1—3	NNE $\frac{3}{4}$ E
寅	Yin^{2}	Tiger	Gemini	3—5	ENE $\frac{3}{4}$ N
卯	Mao^{3}	Hare	Cancer	5—7	E
辰	Ch'en^{2}	Dragon	Leo	7—9	ESE $\frac{3}{4}$ S
巳	Szu^{4}	Serpent	Virgo	9—11	SSE $\frac{3}{4}$ E
午	Wu^{3}	Horse	Libra	11—1 p.m.	S
未	Wei^{4}	Sheep	Scorpio	1—3	SSW $\frac{3}{4}$ W
申	Shen^{1}	Monkey	Sagittarius	3—5	WSW $\frac{3}{4}$ S
酉	Yu^{3}	Cock	Capricornus	5—7	W
戌	Hsü^{1}	Dog	Aquarius	7—9	WNW $\frac{3}{4}$ N
亥	Hai^{4}	Boar	Pisces	9—11	NNW $\frac{3}{4}$ W

Reference Books for Dates,

For details of the dynasties and for exact dating since 841 B.C. see Hoang's *Concordance des Chronclogies Néoméniques, Chinoise Et Européene.*

Since the Christian Era see Ch'en Yüan's 中西回史日曆 *A Comparative Daily Calendar for Chinese European and Mohammedan History.*

For the century since 1849 see Gardner's "The Peerless 100-year Chinese-English Calendar".

For comparative dates of East Asiatic Kingdoms see Tchang's *Synchronismes Chinois.*

The Sexagenary Cycle

The Chinese cycle is sixty years. Each year is denoted by two characters; the first, a Celestial Stem; the second, an Horary character. They are taken in regular sequence, commencing with 甲子, 乙丑, 丙寅, etc., and as the least common multiple of 10 and 12 is 60, the cycle recommences in like order after 60 years.

The first cycle was set by Huang Ti B.C. 2697 and the system is continuous to the present, in groups of three cycles called respectively (上元, 中元 and 下元) The present cycle beginning 1924 is the third (下元) in the 26th group since Huang Ti and it is the 78th cycle. This group, from 1804 A.D. to 1983 A.D. inclusive, is found below.

The 26th Group of the Chinese Sexagenary Cycles 1804-1983. A.D.

三　元　甲　子　表

鼠 shu³	Rat	甲 1804 1864 子 1924	丙 1816 1876 子 1936	戊 1828 1888 子 1948	庚 1840 1900 子 1960	壬 1852 1912 子 1972
牛 niu²	Ox	乙 1805 1865 丑 1925	丁 1817 1877 丑 1937	己 1829 1889 丑 1949	辛 1841 1901 丑 1961	癸 1853 1913 丑 1973
虎 hu³	Tiger	丙 1806 1866 寅 1926	戊 1818 1878 寅 1938	庚 1830 1890 寅 1950	壬 1842 1902 寅 1962	甲 1854 1914 寅 1974
兎 t'u⁴	Hare	丁 1807 1867 卯 1927	己 1819 1879 卯 1939	辛 1831 1891 卯 1951	癸 1843 1903 卯 1963	乙 1855 1915 卯 1975

龍 lung^2	Dragon	戊 1808 1868 辰 1928	庚 1820 1880 辰 1940	壬 1832 1892 辰 1952	甲 1844 1904 辰 1964	丙 1856 1916 辰 1976
蛇 she^2	Snake	己 1809 1869 巳 1929	辛 1821 1881 巳 1941	癸 1833 1893 巳 1953	乙 1845 1905 巳 1965	丁 1857 1917 巳 1977
馬 ma^3	Horse	庚 1810 1870 午 1930	壬 1822 1882 午 1942	甲 1834 1894 午 1954	丙 1846 1906 午 1966	戊 1858 1918 午 1978
羊 yang^2	Sheep	辛 1811 1871 未 1931	癸 1823 1883 未 1943	乙 1835 1895 未 1955	丁 1847 1907 未 1967	己 1859 1919 未 1979
猴 hou^2	Monkey	壬 1812 1872 申 1932	甲 1824 1884 申 1944	丙 1836 1896 申 1956	戊 1848 1908 申 1968	庚 1860 1920 申 1980
雞 chi^1	Fowl	癸 1813 1873 酉 1933	乙 1825 1885 酉 1945	丁 1837 1897 酉 1957	己 1849 1909 酉 1969	辛 1861 1921 酉 1981
狗 kou^3	Dog	甲 1814 1874 戌 1934	丙 1826 1886 戌 1946	戊 1838 1898 戌 1958	庚 1850 1910 戌 1970	壬 1862 1922 戌 1982
猪 chu^1	Pig	乙 1815 1875 亥 1935	丁 1827 1887 亥 1947	己 1839 1899 亥 1959	辛 1851 1911 亥 1971	癸 1863 1923 亥 1983

Table of Rhymes

(used in telegrams and newspapers for days of month).

韻目 日期	上平	下平	上聲	去聲	入聲
一	東 tung^1	先 hsien^1	董 tung^3	送 sung^4	屋 wu^1
二	冬 tung^1	蕭 hsiao^1	腫 chung^3	宋 sung^4	沃 wo^4
三	江 chiang^1	肴 yao^2	講 chiang^3	絳 chiang^4	覺 chüeh^2
四	支 chih^1	豪 hao^2	紙 chih^3	寘 chih^4	質 chih^4
五	微 wei^1	歌 ko^1	尾 wei^3	未 wei^4	物 wu^4
六	魚 yü^2	麻 ma^2	語 yü^3	御 yü^4	月 yüeh^4
七	虞 yü^2	陽 yang^2	麌 yü^3	遇 yü^4	曷 ho^2
八	齊 ch'i^2	庚 keng^1	薺 ch'i^2	霽 chi^4	黠 hsia^2
九	佳 chia^1	青 ch'ing^1	蟹 hsieh^4	泰 t'ai^4	屑 hsieh^4
十	灰 hui^1	蒸 cheng^1	賄 hui^4	卦 kua^4	藥 yüeh^4
十一	眞 chen^1	尤 yu^2	軫 chen^3	隊 tui^4	陌 mo^4
十二	文 wen^2	侵 ch'in^1	吻 wen^3	震 chen^4	錫 hsi^2
十三	元 yüan^2	覃 t'an^2	阮 juan^3	問 wen^4	職 chih^2
十四	寒 han^2	鹽 yen^2	旱 han^4	願 yüan^4	緝 ch'i^1
十五	刪 shan^1	咸 hsien^2	潸 shan^3	翰 han^4	合 ho^2
十六			銑 hsien^3	諫 chien^4	葉 yeh^4
十七			篠 hsiao^3	霰 hsien^4	洽 hsia^4
十八			巧 ch'iao^3	嘯 hsiao^4	
十九			皓 hao^4	效 hsiao^4	
二十			哿 k'o^3	號 hao^4	
廿一			馬 ma^3	箇 ko^4	
廿二			養 yang^3	禡 ma^4	
廿三			梗 keng^3	漾 yang^4	
廿四			迥 chiung^3	敬 ching^4	
廿五			有 yu^3	徑 ching^4	
廿六			寑 ch'in^3	宥 yu^4	
廿七			感 kan^3	沁 ch'in^4	
廿八			琰 yen^3	勘 k'an^4	
廿九			豏 hsien^3	豔 yen^4	
三十				陷 hsien^4	
三十一	*			世 shih^4	

* This is an abbreviation of 三十一 i.e. 世, added for the 31st day, not a rhyme.

Appellations for the Months

1. 正　月; 端月, 元月; 靑陽, 三陽; 孟陽, 春王.
2. 二　月; 杏月, 如月; 中和, 花朝.
3. 三　月; 桃月; 上巳; 寒食.
4. 四　月; 槐月; 淸和; 麥秋.
5. 五　月; 蒲月; 榴月; 天中, 滿月; 端陽.
6. 六　月; 荷月; 伏月; 天貺.
7. 七　月; 桐月, 巧月, 中元, 蘭月.
8. 八　月; 桂月; 中秋.
9. 九　月; 菊月; 重陽; 菊秋.
10. 十　月; 梅月; 陽春; 小陽春.
11. 十一月; 冬月; 仲冬月; 長至; 葭月.
12. 十二月; 臘月; 嘉平; 淸祀.

The 24 Solar Terms

Approximate dates.			
February	5	立　春	Spring begins.
,,	19	雨　水	The rains.
March	5	驚　蟄	Insects awaken.
,,	20	春　分	Vernal Equinox.
April	5	淸　明	Clear and bright.
,,	20	穀　雨	Grain rain.
May	5	立　夏	Summer begins.
,,	21	小　滿	Grain buds.
June	6	芒　種	Grain in ear.
,,	21	夏　至	Summer Solstice.
July	7	小　暑	Slight heat.
,,	23	大　暑	Great heat.
August	7	立　秋	Autumn begins.
,,	23	處　暑	Stopping of heat.
September	8	白　露	White dews.
,,	23	秋　分	Autumnal Equinox.
October	8	寒　露	Cold dews.
,,	23	霜　降	Hoar frost falls.
November	7	立　冬	Winter begins.
,,	22	小　雪	Light snow.
December	7	大　雪	Heavy snow.
,,	21	冬　至	Winter Solstice.
January	6	小　寒	Slight cold.
,,	21	大　寒	Great cold.

The Surnames*

(which are not included in our 5000 Characters).

Single Surnames

甄	Chen^1
姬	Chi^1
祁	Ch'i^2
郟	Chia^4
靳	Chin^4
褚	Ch'u^3
璩	Chü^4
范	Fan^4
韓	Han^2
杭	Hang^2
郗	Hsi^1
嵇	Hsi^1
郤	Hsi^4
莘	Hsin^1
邢	Hsing^2
荀	Hsün^2
扈	Hu^4
霍	Huo^4
羿	I^4
芮	Jui^{34}
闞	K'an^3
郜	Kao^3
蒯	K'uai^3
夔	K'uei^2
龔	Kung^1
酈	Li^4
廖	Liao^4
藺	Lin^4
逯	Lu^4
宓	Mi^4
繆	Miu^4
逄	P'ang^2
鮑	Pao^4
卞	Pien^4
邴	Ping^3
濮	P'u^3
邵	Shao^4
厙	She^4
邰	T'ai^2
党	Tang^3
滕	T'eng^2
鈄	Tou^3
昝	Tsan^3
岑	Ts'en^2
鄒	Tsou^1
訾	Tzu^1
隗	Wei^3
鄔	Wu^4
庾	Yü^2
郁	Yü^4

Double Surnames

万俟 Mo^4-Ch'i^2 澹臺 T'an^2-T'ai^2 濮陽 P'u^3-Yang^2

* Refer to the Chinese Po Chia Hsing 百家姓 or Book of Surnames for a popular mnemonic list in rhyme of 438 Chinese family names out of the total 1458 names listed in the 人名大辭典.

A Chinese uses three methods of telling his name exactly.

(1) By quoting the 4 character line in which his name occurs.

(2) By giving a common phrase linking his name with another character as 千萬的萬

(3) By splitting or describing the character as Kung^1 (弓) Ch'ang^2 (長) ti (的) Chang^1 (張), or, Kan^1 (干) Kou^1 (亅) ti (的) Yü^2 (于)

Provinces

with Archaic Names and Capitals

	Modern name		Archaic names	Capital.	
1	河北	Hopei	冀, 幽燕	天津	Tientsin
2	山東	Shantung	魯, 山左	歷城	Lich'eng (Tsinanfu)
3	山西	Shansi	晋, 山右	陽曲	Yangch'ü (T'aiyüan)
4	河南	Honan	豫, 中州	開封	K'aifeng
5	江蘇	Kiangsu	吳	鎮江	Chenkiang (Nanking)
6	安徽	Anhwei	皖	懷寧	Huaining (Anching)
7	江西	Kiangsi	贛, 豫章	南昌	Nanch'ang
8	浙江	Chekiang	越, 淛	杭	Hang (Hangchow)
9	福建	Fukien	閩	閩侯	Minhou (Foochow)
10	湖北	Hupeh	鄂, 楚北	武昌	Wuch'ang
11	湖南	Hunan	湘, 楚南	長沙	Ch'angsha
12	廣東	Kwangtung	粤, 粤東	廣州	Canton
13	廣西	Kwangsi	桂, 粤西	邕寧	Yungning (Kweilin)
14	雲南	Yünnan	滇	昆明	K'unming (Yunnanfu)
15	貴州	Kweichow	黔	貴筑	Kueichu (Kweiyang)
16	四川	Szechwan	蜀	成都	Ch'engtu
17	陝西	Shensi	秦, 關中	長安	Ch'angan (Sian)
18	甘肅	Kansu	隴	皐蘭	Kaolan (Lanchow)

The Capitals under Different Dynasties

Dyn.	B.C.	Cap.	Present name
唐	2356	平陽	臨汾縣,山西
虞	2255	蒲阪	永濟縣,山西
夏	2205	安邑	安邑縣,山西
商	1766	亳	商丘縣,河南
殷	1401	殷	偃師縣,河南
周	1122	鎬	長安縣,陝西
	781	洛邑	洛陽縣,河南
秦	255	咸陽	長安縣,陝西
漢	206	長安	長安縣,陝西

Dyn.	A.D.	Cap.	Present name
東漢	25	洛陽	洛陽縣,河南
魏	220	洛陽	洛陽縣,河南
晋	265	洛陽	洛陽縣,河南
東晋	317	建康	江寧縣,江蘇
隋	589	長安	長安縣,陝西
唐	618	長安	長安縣,陝西
宋	960	汴梁	開封縣,河南
南宋	1127	臨安	杭　縣,浙江
元	1280	燕京	北　京
明	1368	南京	南　京
	1403	北京	北　京
清	1644	北京	北　京

Weights and Measures

Avoirdupois: A 斤 (lb.) consists of 16 兩 (ounces); below the 兩 in decimals follow 錢,分,釐,毫,絲,忽,微.

Corn measure: A 石 (tan[4]) has 10 斗 (bushels); a 斗 has 10 升 (pints), and in decimals follow 合,勺,抄,撮,圭, and 6 粟 make a 圭.

Measure of distance: 10 分 (lines) make a 寸 (inch), 10 寸 a 尺 (foot), 5 尺 a 步, (pace) 2 步 (or 10 尺) a 丈, 180 丈 a 里 li[3] (one third of mile).

Square measure: 100 方寸 make a 方尺, 25 方尺 a 方步, 4 方步 (or 100 方尺) a 方丈, 6 方丈 a 分, 10 分 a 畝 (Chinese acre), 100 畝 a 頃, 540 畝 a 方里.

Cubic measure: 1,000 立方寸 make a 立方尺, 125 立方尺 a 立方步, 8 立方步 a 立方丈.

Time measure: 15 分 (minutes) make a 刻 (quarter hour), 8 刻 a 時辰 (Chinese hour), 12 時辰 a 日 (day), 29 or 30 日 a 月, 12 月 (13 when there is an intercalary month 閏月) a year. Or, 60 秒 (seconds) make a 分, (minute) 60 分 a 點 (hour), 24 點 a 日 (day).

The Chinese Numerals

	Ordinary Style 小寫	Large Style 大寫	Business Style 碼字
0	零	零	0
1	一	壹 or 弌	〡
2	二	貳 or 弍	〢
3	三	叁 or 弎	〣
4	四	肆	〤
5	五	伍	〥
6	六	陸	〦
7	七	柒	〧
8	八	捌	〨
9	九	玖	〩
10	十	拾 or 什	十
100	百	佰	
1,000	千	仟	
10,000	萬 or 万	萬	
100,000	億	億	
1,000,000	兆	兆	

Chinese Ordinals

Certain groups of characters are used in lieu of numerals for enumerating articles, houses, classes, seniorities of persons, seasons, etc. These may be compared to our series of the letters, A.B.C., a.b.c., etc. Most of the groups of characters are used for numbering the volumes of works by literati. For instance if there is a set of four books the volumes are numbered with the four characters 元,亨,利,貞; this phrase being quoted from the beginning of the Book of Changes, 易經, you may know that the book marked with 利 is the 3rd. book of a set of four; if the work involves six volumes it should be marked with 六藝 Six Arts, eight with 八卦 Eight Diagrams, etc. The last two groups of longer series 百家姓 and 千字文 are ordinarily used by the pawn shops.

The following is a list of the common groups of characters with the respective numerals and the uses in each series.

Chinese Ordinals (Con't)

No.	Ordinals	Uses and explanations
1. a.	頭 t'ou²; 元 yüan²; 首 shou³; 魁 k'uei².	may be used for the 1st person among others in rank, position or success.
b.	全 ch'üan²	used for a work with only one volume. It means the whole thing involved.
2. a.	上 shang⁴, 下 hsia⁴.	used for a set of 2 books as 上冊, 下冊; for time as 上午, 下午; etc.
b.	前 ch'ien², 後 hou⁴.	used for 2 parts of a book as 前部, 後部; for dynasties as 前漢, 後漢; etc.
3. a.	上 shang⁴, 中 chung¹, 下 hsia⁴.	used for 3 decades of month, respectively as 上浣, 中浣, 下浣; for classes of society as 上等社會 upper circles of society, so 中, 下等社會 etc.
b.	孟 meng⁴, 仲 chung⁴, 季 chi⁴,	used for the month of a season, as 孟春, 仲春, 季春, three months of spring respectively; so of 夏, 秋, 冬 each.
4. a.	元 yüan², 亨 heng², 利 li⁴, 貞 chen¹.	used for a set of 4 books, qualities of goods, etc.
b.	伯 po² or 孟 meng⁴, 仲 chung⁴, 叔 shu², 季 chi⁴.	used for the birth of brothers as Confucius being the 2nd birth he is named 仲尼 Chung Ni. His eldest brother was named 孟皮 Meng-P'i. Lao Tzu is the 1st birth, named 伯陽 Po-Yang.
5.	宮 kung¹, 商 shang¹, 角 chüeh², 徵 chih³, 羽 yü³.	These are the 5 notes of the ancient Chinese musical scale, 五音; also used for a set of 5 books.

No.	Ordinals	Uses & explanations
6.	禮 li³, 樂 yüeh⁴, 射 she⁴, 御 yü⁴, 書 shu¹ 數 shu⁴.	These are six arts 六藝 propriety, music, archery, charioteering, writing and mathematics. Used for a set of 6 books.
7.	日 jih⁴, 月 yüeh⁴, 火 huo³, 水 shui³, 木 mu⁴, 金 chin¹, 土 t'u³.	These are the seven sources of brightness, 七曜 yao⁴, sun, moon and the five planets, used to indicate the seven days of a week as 日曜日 Sunday; 月曜日 Monday; so 火, 水, 木, 金, 土曜日
8.	乾 ch'ien², 坎 k'an³ 艮 ken⁴, 震 chen⁴, 巽 hsün⁴, 離 li², 坤 k'un¹, 兌 tui⁴.	These are the Eight Diagrams 八卦 which are used for a set of eight books
9.	上上,上中,上下; 中上,中中,中下; 下上,下中,下下.	These are the nine ranks 九等, used to classify the goods and to criticise the skill and ability of persons etc.
10.	甲 chia⁴, 乙 i³, 丙 ping³, 丁 ting¹, 戊 wu,⁴, 己 chi³, 庚 keng¹, 辛 hsin¹, 壬 jen², 癸 kuei³.	These are the 10 Stems 十干 or 天干, which are used for ten books in one set; for classes in school as 甲班, 乙班 class A. class B; for students grades as 甲等, 乙等; for qualities of goods as 甲種, 乙種; for additional numbers as 甲十五號, No. 15a; etc. See page XXVII

No.	Ordinals	Uses & explanations	
12.	子 tzu^3, 丑 ch'ou^3, 寅 yin^2, 卯 mao^3, 辰 ch'en^2, 巳 ssu^4, 午 wu^3, 未 wei^4, 申 shen^1, 酉 yu^3, 戌 hsü^1, 亥 hai^4.	These are the 12 Branches 十二支 or 地支 used for 24 hours of a day and for 12 vols. or 12 parts in a set of books as adopted in Kanghsi Dictionary; etc. See page XXVII	
15.	東 tung^1, 冬 tung^1, 江 chiang^1 ...... 删 shan^1	15 rhyming words of 上平	These 5 groups are used in telegrames and news papers for days of month. See page XXX
15.	先 hsien^1, 蕭 hsiao^1 肴 yao^2 ...... 咸 hsien^2	15 rhyming words of 下平	
17.	屋 wu^5, 沃 wo^5, 覺 chüeh^5, ... 洽 hsia^5	17 rhyming words of 入聲	
29.	董 tung^3 腫 chung^3, 講 chiang^3 ...... 豏 hsien^3	29 rhyming words of 上聲	
30.	送 sung^4, 宋 sung^4, 絳 chiang^4 ...... 陷 hsien^4	30 rhyming words of 去聲	
60.	甲 子 chia^4 tzu^3, 乙 丑 i^3 ch'ou^3, 丙 寅 ping^3 yin^2, 丁 卯 ting^1 mao^3..... 癸 亥 kuei^3 hai^4.	The Sexagenary cycle used in series of 60 years, months, days and time. See page XXVIII	
438	趙 chao^4, 錢 ch'ien^2, 孫 sun^1, 李 li^3	Book of Family Names 百家姓. It contains 408 single surnames and 30 double surnames.	
1,000	天 t'ien^1, 地 ti^4, 元 yüan^2, 黃 huang^2.	Book of 1,000 Characters 千字文. It has 1,000 characters, not one of which is repeated. The last two longer series are ordinarily used by the pawn shops.	

			A		
阿^{1} 啊^{1}	阜 170	可 699	An exclamation; an interrogative final	$a^{234}o^{1}$	C
腌^{1}	肉 130	奄 810	Filthy ｜髒 a^{1} tsa^{1} 俗	ang^{1}	C
阿^{2}	阜 170	可 699	Interrogative exclamation	$a^{134}o^{1}$	C
阿^{3}	阜 170	可 699	Exclamation of surprise, or doubt	$a^{124}o^{1}$	C
阿^{4}	阜 170	可 699	Initial particle; prefix ｜哥 Manchu brother ｜彌陀佛 Amida Buddha ｜媽 a nurse-maid	$a^{123}o^{1}$	C
			Ai		
哎^{14}	口 30	乂 528	Aiya! alas! dear me! ｜呀		A
挨^{1}	手 64	矣 477	To trust to; next to; in order ｜近 close to ｜次 in order	ai^{2}	B
唉^{1} 欸^{1}	口 30	矣 477	Exclamation of disgust or regret	ai^{3}	F
哀^{1}	口 30	衣 367	To grieve, pity; alas! ｜求 to entreat, implore ｜懇 ｜號 loud lamentation ｜告 report sadly ｜哭 weep, lament ｜哉 alas! ｜慟 mourn, extreme grief		C
獃^{12} 呆^{12}	犬 94	豈 732	Silly, idiotic	tai^{1}	F
噯^{1}	口 30	愛 411	Tone of disapproval ｜呀 excl. of surprise	ai^{34}	G

Ai

埃^{12}	土 32	矣 477	Dust, dirt 塵｜		D
挨^{2}	手 64	矣 477	To suffer anything ｜冷 suffer cold ｜駡 receive abuse ｜打 to be beaten	ai^{1}	B
矮^{3} 騃^{3}	矢 111	委 512	Low, short of stature ｜·子 a dwarf ｜人 ｜小 low, short, stunted		B
唉^{3} 欸^{3}	口 30	矣 477	Excl. of doubt	ai^{1}	F
噯^{3}	口 30	愛 411	Exclam. of surprise	ai^{14}	G
愛^{4}	心 61	愛 411	To like, love, delight in ｜惜 sparing of, to like ｜慕 fond of ｜財 covet wealth, miserly 親｜ to love and cherish 喜｜ delight in 可｜ lovable 憐｜ pitying love		A
噯^{4}	口 30	愛 411	Dear me!	ai^{13}	G
导^{4}	寸 41	导 794	Obstacle		P
礙^{4} 碍^{4}	石 112	导 794	To obstruct, hinder, to concern ｜難 difficult, inconvenient ｜不着 cannot concern 妨｜ hindrance 不｜事 no matter		D
艾^{4}	艸 140	乂 528	Mugwort, artemisia, over 50 years S ｜絨 moxa punk		E
隘^{4}	阜 170	益 610	A defile, contracted		K

睚^{4}	目 109	厓 50	To stare at fixedly │目	iai^{2}	K

An

安^{1}	宀 40	安 555	Quiet, rest; still; where? to pacify; to place; contented. S. │·置 place, establish │靖 peace, quiet │居 live tranquilly │居樂業 │放 put in safe place │∘分 contented with lot │息 quiet rest │歇 │息日 Sabbath │心 with intent; quiet │·徽 Anhui │然 quietly, tranquilly │民 pacify the people │·排 arrange, set in order │定 at rest, settled │∘慰 comfort, soothe, console │∘穩 steady, firm, sound │營 to encamp 平│peace		B
鞍^{1}	革 177	安 555	Saddle │·子		D
俺^{1,2,3}	人 9	奄 810	I, myself		F
唵^{1,3}	口 30	奄 810	To gobble up	nan^{3}	K
庵^{1}	广 53	奄 810	Buddhist monastery; small temple, cottage 尼姑│Buddhist nunnery │堂 山│summer retreat		E
鵪^{1}	鳥 196	奄 810	Quail │·鶉		F
諳^{1}	言 149	音 90	Skilled in; to recite │習 well versed in │練		G

按[4]	手 64	安 555	To lay hands on, press down; according to ｜·着 according to ｜ 照 ｜法 according to law ｜ 例 ｜本分[4] according to duty	en[4]	B
案[4]	木 75	安 555	A table, judge's desk; law-case ｜·子 ｜件 a case, an affair 公｜ ｜情 circumstances of case 命｜ case of murder or homicide 審｜ to hear or try a case		D
暗[4]	日 72	音 90	Dark, invisible, secret 黑 ｜ ｜中 in secret, by stealth ｜ ｜·的 ｜訪 inquire secretly ｜號 private signal ｜昧 gloomy, dark, obscure ｜地 dark place, underhand		C
岸[4]	山 46	干 32	Shore, bank; goal ｜路 riverside road, bund 攏｜ draw close to shore 上｜ go ashore		C

Ang

腌[1] 骯[1]	肉 130	奄 810	Filthy, dirty ｜髒 dirty 俗	a[1]	C
卬[2]	卩 26	卬 308	Great, high; I		K
昂[2]	日 72	卬 308	Rise high, raise, pompous ｜首 carry the head high ｜價 rising price ｜貴 high in price		E

Ao

熬[12]	火 86	敖 264	To boil, simmer; endure, watch ｜粥 boil congee, porridge ｜一｜ give it a boil ｜爛·了 cooked thoroughly		C

<table>
<tr><td>熬^{12}</td><td></td><td></td><td>| 湯 boil soup. | 藥 decoct
| 夜 to watch at night</td><td></td><td>C</td></tr>
<tr><td>敖^{2}</td><td>攴
66</td><td>敖
264</td><td>Pleased, proud S.
| 遊 to saunter, travel</td><td></td><td>I</td></tr>
<tr><td>廒^{2}</td><td>广
53</td><td>敖
264</td><td>Granary 倉 |</td><td></td><td>K</td></tr>
<tr><td>鰲^{2}</td><td>魚
195</td><td>敖
264</td><td>Huge sea-fish | 魚</td><td></td><td>K</td></tr>
<tr><td>襖^{3}</td><td>衣
145</td><td>奥
519</td><td>Outer coat
棉 | wadded coat
皮 | fur-lined coat
大 | great coat</td><td></td><td>E</td></tr>
<tr><td>媼^{34}</td><td>女
38</td><td>𥁕
606</td><td>Old woman 老 |</td><td>wen^{3}</td><td>I</td></tr>
<tr><td>傲^{4}</td><td>人
9</td><td>敖
264</td><td>Proud, arrogant, rude
| 慢 haughty, uncivil 驕 | proud</td><td></td><td>C</td></tr>
<tr><td>鏊^{4}</td><td>金
167</td><td>敖
264</td><td>Iron griddle 餅 |
| 燒 fry on griddle</td><td></td><td>K</td></tr>
<tr><td>奧^{4}</td><td>大
37</td><td>奥
519</td><td>Obscure, profound 深 |
|•妙 mysterious</td><td></td><td>E</td></tr>
<tr><td>懊^{4}</td><td>心
61</td><td>奥
519</td><td>To regret, angry | 悶
| 悔 to repent. | 恨 hate
| 惱 irritated, vexed</td><td></td><td>D</td></tr>
<tr><td>澳^{4}</td><td>水
85</td><td>奥
519</td><td>A cove, bay, dock
| 門 Macao | 洲 Australia
船 | a dock</td><td></td><td>F</td></tr>
<tr><td>鄂^{4}</td><td>邑
163</td><td>咢
243</td><td>Surname</td><td>o^{4}</td><td>H</td></tr>
</table>

Cha

<table>
<tr><td>扎^{1}</td><td>手
64</td><td>乙
297</td><td>To pierce; pull up
| 鍼 acupuncture in surgery
| 猛·子 to dive
| 破 prick a hole in | 透·了
| 傷 to stab</td><td>cha^{2}</td><td>C</td></tr>
<tr><td>紮^{1}
紥^{1}</td><td>糸
120</td><td>乙
297</td><td>To bind, tie up, wind | 綁
| 緊 bind up tight</td><td>tsa^{1}</td><td>G</td></tr>
</table>

Cha

喳[1]	口 30	旦 793	To lisp, twitter || answer call. Yes, sir	ch'a[1]	G
渣[1]	水 85	旦 793	Dregs, sediment, refuse | 滓 grounds, dregs		E
楂[1]	木 57	旦 793	A sour red fruit jelly 山 |		K
蹅[1]	足 157	旦 793	Walk in mud | 雨, | 泥	ch'a[3]	K
挓[1]	手 64	宅 374	Open, expand | 挱		K
蜡[1] 䄍[1]	虫 142	昔 799	Imperial thanks-giving for crops (蜡 also short for 蠟 la. wax)	la[4]	K
扎[2]	手 64	乙 297	| 掙 make effort, strain	cha[1]	C
札[2]	木 75	乙 297	A tablet, letter, superior's instruction | 文, 大 | 簡 | writing tablet		H
蚻[2]	虫 142	乙 297	A small cicada 螞·| grasshopper		K
炸[2] 煠[2] ⿰火乚[2]	火 86 減	乍 150	To fry in oil, scald in hot water | 糕 cake fried in oil | 肉丸 fry meat balls	cha[34]	D
閘[2]	門 169	甲 825	A water-gate, lock, 水 | ; barrier | 板 a lock, sill-board | 門 | 上水 to dam water		G
劄[2]	竹 118	合 708	To instruct, order |·子 write out, agree | 單 a contract for goods | 貨 住 | stationed at		G
⿰金⿰算刂[2] ⿰算刂[2]	金 167	算 848	To cut, chop fine | 草 | 刀 fodder knife		I

牐^{2}	片 91	千 24	｜板 Front boards		K
炸^{3}	火 86	乍 150	Fine coal 煤｜兒	cha^{24}	D
蚱^{3}	虫 142	乍 150	Cicada, locust ｜蜢 edible locust		G
詐^{3}	言 149	乍 150	Artful turn to talk 拿話｜人 beguile to confession	cha^{4}	C
眨^{3}	目 109	乏 300	To wink, blink ｜·巴眼兒 俗 ｜眼 in a twinkling	chan^{3}	E
拃^{3} 折^{3}	手 64	乍 150	A span, to span —｜ ｜—｜ measure by spanning	che^{2} she^{2}	I
乍^{4}	丿 4	乍 150	For the first time, suddenly ｜然 ｜見 see suddenly, at first sight ｜猛的 suddenly ｜聽 on first hearing.		D
咋^{4}	口 30	乍 150	Loud, coarse noise 山｜ ｜舌 put out the tongue		K
炸^{4}	火 86	乍 150	To burst, explode ｜破 ｜彈 a bomb, shell	cha^{23}	D
痄^{4}	疒 104	乍 150	Running sore, mumps 長｜腮		K
詐^{4}	言 149	乍 150	Artful, false 詭｜ artful, deceitful 訛｜ to cheat, extort	cha^{3}	C
榨^{4} 醡^{4}	木 75	乍 150	Press to extract oil, sugar, wine, to express ｜房 house for such press		F
柵^{4}	木 75	冊 565	A palisade, fence, railing ｜欄 railing, barrier		D

Ch'a

差^{1}	工 48	差 178	To err, differ; unlike; 相｜ discrepancy 二數之｜ remainder	ch'a^{4} ch'ai^{1} tz'u^{1}	A

Ch'a

擦¹	手 64	祭 515	To rub, brush, clean	俗	ts'a¹	A
叉¹	又 29	叉 538	Fold hands in bowing ｜手 ｜·子 a fork			A
扠¹	手 64	叉 538	To fork up, pitch out ｜·出·去 ｜腰 stand arms akimbo			H
插¹	手 64	千 24	To insert, stick in, meddle ｜關 bolt a door ｜嘴 interrupt, intermeddle			E
喳¹	口 30	旦 793	To whisper together 嘁嘁｜｜	俗	cha¹	G
皻¹	皮 107	旦 793	Rough skin; rough			K
查²	木 75	旦 793	To investigate, examine 訪｜ see also 察	S		B
⿰缶查²	缶 121	旦 793	找｜兒 Find fault		ch'a⁴	K
茶²	艸 140	木 484	Tea, ｜葉 tea leaves ｜壺 tea-pot ｜碗 tea-cup			A
搽²	手 64	木 484	To smear, paint, to rub on ｜粉			H
察² 詧²	宀 40	祭 515	Officially examine, investigate ｜出 discover ｜考 examine closely ｜看, ｜閱 ｜問 investigate			C
鍤²	金 167	千 24	A spade; large pin ｜·子 a pointed bar			G
岔³	山 46	分 395	｜·了氣·了 A stitch in the side		ch'a⁴	D
蹅³	足 157	旦 793	Walk in mud ｜泥		cha¹	K
差⁴	工 48	差 178	｜兒 A mistake ｜一點 not quite right ｜不多 almost, nearly correct		ch'a¹ ch'ai¹ tz'u¹	A
岔⁴	山 46	分 395	Fork of road ｜道, ｜路口 走｜了 taken wrong road		ch'a³	D

詫 4	言 149	宅 374	To brag, boast |·異 be amazed,			D
杈 4	木 75	叉 538	Fork of a tree | 枝			G
汊 4	水 85	叉 538	Fork of stream | 港			F
衩 4	衣 145	叉 538	| 褲 Outside pants, opening in clothes			H
刹 4	刀 18	利 511	Pagoda top, Buddhist monastery 上 | visit a temple			H
𦉜 4	缶 121	日 793	Potsherd 瓦 |		ch'a²	K

Chai

摘 1	手 64	啇 590	To pick fruit; select; take off | 果·子 pick fruit | 帽·子 take off hat 指 | criticize	俗	tse⁴	A
謫 1	言 149	啇 590	To reproach; fault	俗	tse⁴	K
側 1	人 9	則 858	Side, at the side | 歪	俗	ts'e⁴	F
齋 1	齊 210	齊 421	To abstain, fast; a shop; refinement 吃 | abstain from meat			F
斋 1	減					
齊 1						C
擇 2	手 64	睪 160	To select, pick out	俗	tse²⁴	D
澤 2	水 85	睪 160	Moist, slippery 恩 | kindness	俗	tse²⁴	F
責 2	貝 154	責 83	Reprove, punish	俗	tse²⁴	D
宅 2	宀 40	宅 374	A house, residence 住 | residence			E

翟²	羽 124	翟 57	A surname	ti²	K
窄³	穴 116	乍 150	Narrow, strait, mean, contracted; bigoted 丨小 narrow. confined 狹丨	tse⁴	A
仄³	人 9	人 429	Oblique tone 俗	che⁴ tse⁴	G
債⁴	人 9	責 83	A debt. 欠丨 be in debt 丨主 a creditor		C
寨⁴ 砦⁴	宀 40	寒 100	Stronghold, castle, corral, camp, military outpost, 營丨 barracks		F
豸⁴	豸 153		Fabulous monster		K
虒⁴	虍 141	虒 204	Uneven, rugged		P

Ch'ai

差¹	工 48	差 178	To send officially, a legate 丨遣 to send, depute 丨役 official servant, runner 丨·使 official employment	ch'a¹⁴ tz'u¹	A
拆¹	手 64	斥 214	To break open, pull down, destroy 丨信 open a letter 丨壞 break to pieces 丨毀 pull down, demolish 丨開 break or tear open	ts'e⁴	B
儕¹²	人 9	齊 421	Sign of plural, company, class		F
釵¹	金 167	叉 538	Hair-pin, womankind		I
柴²	木 75	此 129	Firewood, fuel 丨·火 S 劈丨 kindling		C

Character	Radical	Phonetic	Meaning		Alt. reading	
豺[2] 犲[2]	豸 153	才 22	Wolfish, cruel, truculent ｜狼 a wolf			F
跐[3]	足 157	此 129	To trample	俗	ts'ai[3] tz'u[3]	E
蠆[4]	虫 142	萬 576	Sting in tail 蜂｜			K

Chan

Character	Radical	Phonetic	Meaning		Alt. reading	
占[1]	卜 25	占 720	To divine by lot, foretell ｜卦 divine｜卜		chan[4]	D
沾[1]	水 85	占 720	Moisten, soak; receive favor ｜·染 saturated, infected ｜光 gain benefit from			G
粘[1]	米 119	占 620	To paste, stick on, adhere ｜貼 paste up or on｜·上		nien[2]	B
苫[1]	艸 140	占 720	Thatch, mat 在｜mourning for parents		shan[4]	B
霑[1]	雨 173	占 720	To wet; bestow benefit ｜潤 steeped in, imbued			E
氈[1] 毡[1]	毛 82	亶 768	Felt, rugs; rough｜·子 ｜房 Mongol tent ｜鞋 felt shoes			G
詹[1]	言 149	詹 741	To direct, oversee; verbose 謹｜take great care	S.		G
瞻[1]	目 109	詹 741	To regard with reverence ｜望 to look up to, look at			F
展[3]	尸 44	展 354	To unroll, open out, expand｜開 發｜to develop			D
搌[3]	手 64	展 354	To wipe away ｜·布 dish cloth			G
輾[3]	車 159	展 354	To turn over, revolve｜轉 水｜a water-mill		nien[3]	G

Chan

斬^3	斤 69	斬 212	To cut in two, sever ｜斷 ｜首 behead, decapitate ｜頭, ｜殺		D
眨^3	目 109	乏 300	To wink, twinkle 一｜眼之間 in the twinkling of an eye	cha^3	E
盞^3	皿 108	戔 332	A lamp-bowl, wine-cup C. of lamps		F
占^4 佔^4	卜 25	占 720	Usurp, take by force ｜便宜 take advantage	chan^1	D
站^4	立 117	占 720	To stand up, stand still, stop; a station. ｜·住 stop 車｜ R.R. station ｜立 stand up ｜·着		A
戰^4	戈 62	單 826	Terrified; to fight, contend 爭｜ ｜場 battle-field ｜船 war vessel ｜壕 trenches ｜車 tank ｜略 war strategy ｜法 tactics ｜區 war zone ｜敗 be defeated ｜勝 gain victory ｜鬥 fight and quarrel		C
暫^4	日 72	斬 212	Briefly, shortly, ｜時 ｜且 temporarily ｜住 stop for a while		C
棧^4	木 75	戔 332	A storehouse. godown, shop ｜房 客｜ lodging-house		E
蘸^4	艸 140	焦 56	To dip into, to soak ｜筆 dip pen in ink ｜手 dip the hand in		E
顫^4	頁 181	亶 768	To shiver, shake, unsteady	ch'an^4	E
湛^4	水 85	甚 104	To sink, soak deep, clear. S. ｜恩 under great obligation		I

綻^4 䘺^4	糸 120	定 138	Open seam, to rip, split. |裂 補| patch a rent		K

Ch'an

攙^1	手 64	毚 386	To support with the hand; to mix |扶 to assist |和 to mix; cordial, social |雜 to mix, blend		E
鑱^1	金 167	毚 386	To cut into; carve, chisel		I
毚^2	比 81	毚 386	Crafty hare. cunning, wily 犁| plow-share		K
饞^2 嚵^2	食 184	毚 386	To love good eating, greedy 口| |嘴人 a glutton		H
廛^2	广 53	廛 830	Market place, shop, |市		K
纏^2	糸 120	廛 830	To bind up, wrap; implicate |住 wind round |繞 |足 bound feet		D
躔^2	足 157	廛 830	Orbit, precedent, to revolve 日| |迹 follow precedent		K
禪^2	示 113	單 826	Meditation, Buddhist, zen |經 Buddhist scriptures |林 Buddhist temple	shan^4	H
蟬^2	虫 142	單 826	Cicada, broad locust |吟 cicada's chirp		I
蟾^2	虫 142	詹 741	A striped toad; moon |光 moonlight		K
產^3	生 100	生 41	To produce, bear offspring |生 bear a child, to produce |業 estate 田| products, estate		B

鏟^{3}	金 167	生 41	A spade, shovel; to dig 丨鉗 fire irons, shovel and tongs			F
諂^{3}	言 149	臽 683	To toady, fawn 丨媚 flatter			F
闡^{3}	門 169	單 826	To enlarge, explain 丨明	shan^{4}		I
顫^{4}	頁 181	亶 768	To shiver, shake, unsteady 發丨 寒丨 shivering with cold	chan^{4}		E
懺^{4}	心 61	韱 420	Regret, ritual 丨悔 repent 丨罪 repent, atone			K
讖^{4}	言 149	韱 420	Prognostic, prophesy 丨語 丨願 fulfill a vow 軍丨 military password 口號,口令			I
驏^{4}	馬 187		Barebacked horse 丨騎 ride bareback			K
[毚瓦]^{4}	瓦 98	毚 386	瓦丨 A jug for boiling congee			K
韂^{4}	革 177	詹 741	Trappings 鞍丨 saddle-flap			K

Chang

張^{1}	弓 57	長 353	To extend, publish; open; boast 丨着嘴 open the mouth 丨口 丨絃 draw a bow 丨狂 boastful, arrogant 丨羅 help, collect money 丨三李四 somebody 丨揚 spread abroad, display		S.	A
章^{1}	立 117	章 92	A section, chapter 丨·程 rules, plan, constitution 丨節 chapter & verse 典丨 classics; constitution		S.	C
彰^{1}	彡 59	章 92	To make manifest, exhibit 丨顯 to manifest 丨明, 丨揚			C

Chang

樟[1]	木 75	章 92	The camphor tree |·木 |∘腦 camphor		K
熚[1]	火 86	章 92	Flaming explosion; flash 炮| fire cracker		H
璋[1]	玉 96	章 92	A sceptre; jade stone		I
麞[1]	鹿 198	章 92	A kind of deer, roebuck |·子		I
長[3]	長 168	長 353	Old, senior; to increase, grow |見識 learn by experience |·進 make progress |瘡 have a boil |兄 eldest brother |老 an elder |毛 grow mouldy |輩 seniors, superiors |孫 double surname |·大 grow up |·得好看 good-looking |子[3] eldest son	ch'ang[2]	A
掌[3]	手 64	掌 587	Palm 手|; sole 脚|; paw, hoof; to rule, control |權 have authority |家 rule family |管 control, manage, preside |握, |理 same		B
鞝[3]	革 177	尙 584	Leather sole; patch 皮|		E
帳[4]	巾 50	長 353	A canopy; screen |·棚 a tent |房		D
悵[4]	心 61	長 353	Disappointed, vexed	ch'ang[4]	G
脹[4] 瘬[4]	肉 130	長 353	To swell up; dropsical 水| |飽 swelled with eating		F

Character	Radical	Phonetic	Meaning		
賬4	貝 154	長 353	An account, bill, debt |∘房 treasurer's office |·目 bills, debts, accounts | 本 account book | 單 bill, account 清| clear account 算| settle		B
漲3 4	水 85	長 353	To expand, overflow 水| |3潮 flood tide | 起 to rise as water |3價 rise in price		E
丈4	一 1	丈 168	Ten Chinese feet; an elder | 尺 measurement |·夫 a husband, manly man | 量 to measure land, etc.		B
仗4	人 9	丈 168	Weapons; to fight 打| |·着 to rely upon | 勢 depend on influence		C
杖4	木 75	丈 168	A staff, stick, 枴∘| a cane | 信 trust to | 打 to bamboo		C
嶂4	山 46	章 92	Chain of peaks 峰|		K
瘴4	疒 104	章 92	Malaria, miasma |氣		K
障4	阜 170	章 92	A screen, barricade ; to protect |礙 obstacle 保| barrier, defence		E

Ch'ang

Character	Radical	Phonetic	Meaning		
昌1	日 72	昌 803	Prosperous; shining, good |明 splendid	S.	F
娼1	女 38	昌 803	Singing-girl, courtesan |妓		F
猖1	犬 94	昌 803	Mad, violent |狂 wild, crazy behavior		K

Ch'ang

菖[1]	艸 140	昌 803	Calamus, sweet flag ｜蒲		K
閶[1]	門 169	昌 803	Gate of heaven (kept by Kuan Ti)		K
徜[1]	彳 60	尙 584	To and fro, irresolute ｜徉	ch'ang[2]	I
常[2]	巾 50	尙 584	Frequent, constant, usual S. ｜｜constantly, commonly ｜時 ｜見 constantly seeing ｜久 long time, in perpetuity 久長 ｜飯 common fare, pot-luck ｜性 persevering ｜人 common person ｜規 common custom ｜事 every-day affairs ｜識 general information, common sense ｜有 frequently occur 非｜ unusual		A
嫦[2]	女 38	尙 584	Name of goddess in the moon ｜娥		K
嘗[2]	口 30	尙 584	To taste, try; formerly ｜·一·｜ take a taste 未｜ never, in no case		A
長[2]	長 168	長 353	Long, excelling ｜∘久 permanently, also 常久 ｜·處 good qualities ｜·虫 snakes ｜工 continuous work ｜舌 talkative ｜生 long life ｜壽 ｜短 length, merits & demerits	chang[3]	A
償[2]	人 9	賞 588	To restore, indemnity ｜還 to pay back ｜債 ｜命 life for life		C

Ch'ang

<table>
<tr><td>塲[2]
場[2]</td><td>土
32</td><td>昜
238</td><td>Level area, arena
禾 | threshing-floor
打 | to thresh</td><td>ch'ang[3]</td><td>C</td></tr>
<tr><td>腸[2]</td><td>肉
130</td><td>昜
236</td><td>Intestines. bowels |·子
心·| heart, affections</td><td></td><td>E</td></tr>
<tr><td>敞[3]</td><td>攴
66</td><td>尙
584</td><td>High level land, plateau 高 |
| 心 disclose feelings
| 開 to open, leave ajar</td><td></td><td>D</td></tr>
<tr><td>廠[3]
厰[3]</td><td>广
53</td><td>尙
584</td><td>A shed, work-shop, yard |·子
車 | livery, garage 飛機 | airdrome
木 |·子 lumber yard 工 | factory</td><td></td><td>C</td></tr>
<tr><td>惝[3]
⿰忄敞[3]</td><td>心
61</td><td>尙
584</td><td>Alarmed, nervous, apprehensive</td><td></td><td>K</td></tr>
<tr><td>氅[3]
⿱敞鳥[3]</td><td>毛
82</td><td>尙
584</td><td>Down of crane, etc.
| 衣 crane-skin robe of Taoist priest 大 | overcoat</td><td></td><td>H</td></tr>
<tr><td>塲[3]
場[3]</td><td>土
32</td><td>昜
238</td><td>Open field
戰 | field of battle 市 | market
跑馬 | race-course 飛行 | airfield</td><td>ch'ang[2]</td><td>C</td></tr>
<tr><td>暢[34]</td><td>日
72</td><td>昜
236</td><td>Joyous; clear
|·快 happy, contented</td><td></td><td>E</td></tr>
<tr><td>倡[4]</td><td>人
9</td><td>昌
803</td><td>To lead, initiate | 始
| 言 speak first |[1] 優 actors
提 | to advocate</td><td></td><td>D</td></tr>
<tr><td>唱[4]</td><td>口
30</td><td>昌
803</td><td>To sing; call out
| 曲 sing songs | 歌
| 戲 theatricals
| 名 call the roll
| 本 song-book
| 片 phonograph record
| 詩 sing hymns</td><td></td><td>B</td></tr>
</table>

悵4	心 61	長 353	Disappointed, vexed, provoking	chang4	G
鬯4	鬯 192	鬯 653	Aromatic herbs, sacrificial spirits		K

Chao

着1	目 109	目 841	A move in a game	chao2 che2 cho2	A
招1	手 64	召 715	To hail, beckon, call |·呼 beckon, call, hail | 禍 bring on trouble | 災 |·惹 provoke, aggravate | 募 enlist, recruit | 勇 |·牌 sign-board | 生 invite pupils | 手 beckon |◦待 receive guests, usher | 帖 hand-bill, poster		B
昭1	日 72	召 715	Bright, glorious, illustrious; to show forth |、明 bright, manifest		G
酌14	酉 164	勺 231	Deliberate 俗	cho24	D
朝1 鼂1	月 74	朝 16	Dawn, early | 夕 morn and even	ch'ao2	D
嘲1	口 30	朝 16	Ridicule, jest	ch'ao2	H
着2 著2	目 109	目 841	Sign of present participle, to attain to |1 急 anxious. |·上 to add (salt, etc.)	chao1 che2 cho2 chu4	A C
⿰火着2	火 86	目 841	To set fire to, catch fire | 火 blaze up | 不着 will not kindle		E

Chao

找^{3}	手 64	戈 331	To seek, make up balance ｜着·了 found ｜錢 give change ｜尋 seek for 尋｜ ｜還 repay ｜門路 seek livelihood, openings ｜·補 supply deficiency ｜不着 cannot find ｜事 seek work, raise row			A
爪^{3}	爪 87	爪 406	Claws, talons; to clutch, scratch ｜牙 "tooth and nail"		chua^{3}	E
沼^{3}	水 85	召 715	Fish-pond, pool 蓮｜ water-lily, lotus pond			K
棹^{4}	木 75	卓 15	An oar; ｜槳 shade ｜船 scull a boat		cho^{1}	A
罩^{4} 箪^{4}	网 122	卓 15	A shade, cover ｜·子 ｜衣 cloak, hood 燈｜ lamp shade			E
召^{4}	口 30	召 715	To call, summon, cite ｜集 call together 蒙｜ the Christian "call."			D
詔^{4}	言 149	召 715	To proclaim, mandate ｜告 下｜ issue a proclamation			F
照^{4}	火 86	召 715	To illumine, enlighten, look after, according to ｜·着 according to ｜相^{4} to photograph ｜像 ｜·料 to look after ｜應			B
兆^{4}	儿 10	兆 383	An omen; a million ｜頭 an omen			D
趙^{4}	走 156	肖 124	Hasten to, visit	S.		G
笊^{4}	竹 118	爪 406	Bamboo ladle, skimmer ｜·籬			G
櫂^{4}	木 75	翟 57	An oar, to row a boat ｜船			K

Character	Radical	Phonetic	Meaning		Alt.	
肇⁴	聿 129	聿 669	To begin, initiate 丨興 丨端 original plan or institution			H

Ch'ao

Character	Radical	Phonetic	Meaning		Alt.	
超¹	走 156	召 715	To excel; save 丨乎 surpassing 丨越			E
吵¹	口 30	少 122	Clamor, din 丨人耳 deafen with noise		ch'ao³	D
抄¹	手 64	少 122	To seize, confiscate; copy out 丨寫 to copy 丨謄			C
綽¹⁴	糸 120	卓 15	Spacious, ample, abundant		ch'o¹⁴	G
朝² 晁²	月 74	朝 16	The imperial court, a dynasty, towards 丨前 face or go forward 丨陽 facing the south	S.	chao¹	D
嘲²	口 30	朝 16	Ridicule, jest 丨笑		chao¹	H
潮²	水 85	朝 16	The tide, moist, damp 發丨 丨熱 damp heat, muggy 丨流 tide; drift of opinion			C
巢²	巛 47	巢 508	A nest in a tree, haunt 丨窩 bird's nest 窩丨	S.		E
吵³	口 30	少 122	An uproar; to wrangle 丨鬧 to brawl 丨嚷		ch'ao¹	D
炒³	火 86	少 122	To roast, as coffee, fry 丨米 to pop rice			D
鈔⁴	金 167	少 122	Money, document, taxes, to copy 丨錢 paper money, cash notes			H

Che

Character	Radical	Phonetic	Meaning		Alt.	
蔗¹ 藷¹	艸 140	庶 201	Sugar-cane 甘丨			G
遮¹	辵 162	庶 201	To cover, hide, screen, protect 丨蔽 hide, conceal 丨掩			D

Che

鷓^{1}	鳥 196	庶 201	Partridge 丨鴣			H
螫^{1}	虫 142	赤 423	To sting, poison, poisonous 毒丨 丨虫 a poisonous insect		shih^{4}	F
着^{2} 著^{2}	目 109	目 841	Present participle, to attain to ·來·丨 just been or done		chao^{12} cho^{2} chu^{4}	A
折^{2}	手 64	折 210	To break in two, snap 丨扣 discount 丨斷 break off, sunder		cha^{3} she^{2}	B
摺^{2}	手 64	習 294	To fold, double up 丨·子 Chinese receipt book			D
轍^{2}	車 159	散 873	A rut, track; precedent 丨窩 a rut 丨眼	俗	ch'e^{4}	F
蜇^{2} 蜥^{2}	虫 142	折 210	To sting; a sting 海丨 jelly-fish			H
者^{3}	老 125	者 192	A "helping particle", added to verb forms noun 或丨 perhaps 再丨 again (in argument)			B
赭^{3}	赤 155	者 192	Ochre color, orange 丨色			K
襵^{3}	衣 145	聶 633	A tuck, fold 打丨·子 百丨裙 heavily plaited skirt			H
這^{4} 这^{4} 过^{4}	辵 162 減	言 740	This 丨·個. 丨件事 this affair 丨些 (個) these 丨·裏 here 丨兒 丨·麼 (着) thus 丨·們		chei^{4}	A
哲^{4}	口 30	折 210	Wise, discerning 丨學 philosophy 丨理			D
浙^{4}	水 85	折 210	A river 丨·江 Chekiang province			G
仄^{4}	人 9	人 429	Oblique tone	文	chai^{3} tse^{4}	G

Character	Radical	Phonetic	Meaning		Other reading	Class
輒⁴ 輙⁴	車 159	取 627	Abruptly, directly; unceremoniously ｜然 hastily, suddenly			I
柘⁴	木 75	石 722	Silk-worm oak			I
慴⁴	心 61	聶 633	Afraid, to subdue			K

Ch'e

Character	Radical	Phonetic	Meaning		Other reading	Class
車¹	車 159	車 836	A cart, carriage ｜廠 cart factory, livery｜行 小｜·子 wheel barrow	S. 俗		A
扯³ 撦³	手 64	止 126	To tear, pull apart, drag ｜拉 to pull, track			F
尺⁴	尸 44	尸 724	工｜字 Notes in music		ch'ih³	A
敀⁴	攴 66	敀 873	To penetrate			P
徹⁴	彳 60	敀 873	To penetrate; discerning, system 貫｜ penetrate, understand 通｜ 不透｜ superficial			G
撤⁴	手 64	敀 873	Carry off, remove ｜去 remove, put away			D
澈⁴	水 85	敀 873	Clear, pure, thoroughly; to search 澄｜ ｜底 thoroughly, from the bottom			G
轍⁴	車 159	敀 873	Rut, precedent	俗	che²	F
掣⁴	手 64	制 221	Obstruct, hinder ｜肘, draw ｜簽 to draw lots			E
屮⁴	屮 45	屮 659	Plants sprouting			K

Chei

Character	Radical	Phonetic	Meaning		Other reading	Class
這⁴	辵 162	言 740	This｜·個	俗	che⁴	A

Chen

眞[1] 真[1]	目 109	眞 843	Real, genuine; truly ｜正 real, bona fide ｜好 really good; fine! ｜相[4] real state of affairs ｜話 the truth ｜理		A
箴[1]	竹 118	咸 344	To probe; needle; to warn ｜言 maxims, proverbs		E
鍼[1] 針[1]	金 167	咸 344	A needle, pin; to prick; pine-needles ｜線活 needle work		B
珍[1] 珎[1]	玉 96	㐱 281	Precious, rare ｜珠 pearls.		C
診[13]	言 149	㐱 281	To examine a patient ｜視, ｜脈 ｜夢 interpret a dream		F
貞[1]	貝 154	貞 857	Chaste, virtuous ｜潔 undefiled, virgin ｜女 a virgin		E
偵[1]	人 9	貞 857	To spy, reconnoitre; a spy ｜探 ｜察 to inspect, investigate	cheng[1]	I
禎[1]	示 113	貞 857	Lucky, auspicious ｜祥 崇｜ last Ming Emperor	cheng[1]	K
斟[1]	斗 68	甚 104	To deliberate; pour out ｜酌 to consult, ponder		D
椹[1] 葚[1]	木 75	甚 104	Target; wood good for arrows	jen[4] shen[24]	K
榛[1]	木 75	秦 469	Hazel nut, filbert ｜·子		H
臻[1]	至 133	秦 469	Extremely, to reach		G
枕[3]	木 75	冘 176	A pillow, to pillow ｜·頭 ｜木 R.R. ties, sleepers ｜套 a pillow case		B

Character	Radical	Phonetic	Meaning	Other reading	Frequency
㐱^{3} 鬒^{3}	人 9	㐱 281	Bushy hair ｜髮 黑｜｜·的 glossy black		K
疹^{3} 胗^{3}	疒 104	㐱 281	Pustules, rash 出｜·子 to have measles 瘟｜ scarlet fever		F
鎭^{4}	金 167	眞 843	To repress; protect ｜店 market-town ｜市		D
娠^{4} 㛛^{4}	女 38	辰 355	Pregnant ｜婦 落｜ miscarriage	shen^{1}	K
振^{4}	手 64	辰 355	To shake, incite ｜·動 ｜興 cause to prosper		C
賑^{4}	貝 154	辰 355	Charitable; give in charity ｜災 relieve disaster 放｜ carry on relief work		D
震^{4}	雨 173	辰 355	To shock, shake, startle 地｜ earthquake		D
陣^{4} [illegible]^{4}	阜 170	車 836	Form in ranks, army; C. of gusts, blasts, a battle ｜｜·的 repeatedly ｜上 in battle ｜亡 killed in battle 上｜ to go to battle		D
酖^{4} 鴆^{4}	酉 164	冘 176	Poisonous, deadly ｜毒 ｜酒 poisoned wine		K
朕^{4}	月 74	天 462	I, we, (Imperial) ｜躬 We,—the Emperor		I

Ch'en

Character	Radical	Phonetic	Meaning	Other reading	Frequency
嗔^{1}	口 30	眞 843	To get angry; rail at, scold ｜怪 to rebuke sternly		G

Ch'en

<table>
<tr><td>瞋1</td><td>目
109</td><td>眞
843</td><td>To look angrily at | 怒</td><td></td><td></td><td>K</td></tr>
<tr><td>抻1
鍖1</td><td>手
64</td><td>曲
819</td><td>To stretch out, pull
| 麵 pull and work dough</td><td></td><td></td><td>I</td></tr>
<tr><td>辰2</td><td>辰
161</td><td>辰
355</td><td>Portion of time, hour,
7-9 a.m. | 時</td><td></td><td></td><td>E</td></tr>
<tr><td>晨2</td><td>日
72</td><td>辰
355</td><td>Morning, dawn 早 | ,淸 |
| 更 the morning watch</td><td></td><td></td><td>A</td></tr>
<tr><td>臣2</td><td>臣
131</td><td>臣
642</td><td>A statesman, minister 大·| ;
vassal, servant
| 宰 minister of state</td><td></td><td></td><td>B</td></tr>
<tr><td>忱2</td><td>心
61</td><td>冘
176</td><td>Sincere, trustworthy,
guileless 丹 |</td><td></td><td></td><td>G</td></tr>
<tr><td>沈2
沉2</td><td>水
85</td><td>冘
176</td><td>To sink, perish; deep, heavy
| 重 heavy, serious, weighty
| 淪 to perish</td><td></td><td>shen3</td><td>C</td></tr>
<tr><td>霃2</td><td>雨
173</td><td>冘
176</td><td>Dull, lowering skies 陰陰 | |</td><td></td><td></td><td>H</td></tr>
<tr><td>陳2</td><td>阜
170</td><td>東
504</td><td>To arrange; spread out, state;
old, stale
| 列品 Curios, exhibits | 設
| 明 state clearly
| 說 set forth</td><td>S.</td><td></td><td>D</td></tr>
<tr><td>蔯2</td><td>艸
140</td><td>東
504</td><td>Medicinal herb 茵 |</td><td></td><td></td><td>K</td></tr>
<tr><td>塵2</td><td>土
32</td><td>鹿
319</td><td>Dust, dirt; this world 紅 |
| 埃 dust | 土</td><td></td><td></td><td>E</td></tr>
<tr><td>橙2</td><td>木
75</td><td>登
733</td><td>Common orange |·子</td><td></td><td></td><td>F</td></tr>
<tr><td>岑2</td><td>山
46</td><td>今
434</td><td>Long peaks, lofty</td><td></td><td>ts'en2</td><td>K</td></tr>
<tr><td>磣3</td><td>石
112</td><td>參
282</td><td>Sand, grit
牙·| gritty</td><td></td><td></td><td>B</td></tr>
</table>

Character	Radical	Phonetic	Meaning	Variant	Grade
櫬^{4}	木 75	親 87	Coffin (inner) 棺｜		I
襯^{4} 儭^{4}	衣 145	親 87	Underclothing, shirt ｜衫 ｜袋 girdle-pouch 幫｜ to assist		B
趁^{4} 趂^{4}	走 156	㐱 281	To avail oneself of ｜·着 ｜早 "take time by the forelock" ｜機·會 seize an opportunity		C
稱^{4}	禾 115	冉 600	Suitable, appropriate, fitting 相^{1}｜	ch'eng^{1}	C

Cheng

Character	Radical	Phonetic	Meaning	Variant	Grade
正^{1}	止 77	正 127	｜·月 First moon, or month	cheng^{34}	A
征^{1}	彳 60	正 127	To attack, subjugate ｜戰 to levy taxes ｜取 capture ｜收 collect duties ｜討 to claim, demand		E
爭^{1}	爪 87	爭 413	To contest, wrangle ｜戰, ｜鬬 ｜先 strive for preeminence ｜論 to dispute		B
掙^{1}	手 64	爭 413	｜不開 Unable to wrench apart	cheng^{4}	B
睜^{1}	目 109	爭 413	To open the eyes wide ｜開眼 ｜眼 stare		B
箏^{1}	竹 118	爭 413	Kite 風·｜; musical instrument		F
諍^{1}	言 149	爭 413	To remonstrate, rebuke 諫｜		E
錚^{1}	金 167	爭 413	Clang of metal gong		I

Cheng

偵^{1}	人 9	貞 857	A spy, a scout; to spy ｜探 detective	chen^{1}	I
禎^{1}	示 113	貞 857	Lucky, auspicious ｜祥	chen^{1}	K
徵^{1}	彳 60	徵 550	To collect duty, evidence ｜求 beg for, enlist	chih^{3}	D
癥^{1}	疒 104	徵 550	Biliary calculus ｜結		K
蒸^{1} 烝^{1}	艸 140	丞 522	Steam; to steam, stew ｜熱 steaming hot ｜饅頭 to steam bread		F
傖^{1}	人 9	倉 679	A reckless fellow, outcast	ts'ang^{1}	H
整^{3}	攴 66	正 127	Whole, exact, without fractions, to adjust, reform ｜◦齊 "in ship-shape", to arrange ｜天家 the whole day long ｜·頓 to set in order, adjust	cheng^{14}	B
拯^{3} 抍^{3}	手 64	丞 522	To lift up, save ｜救 to rescue	ch'eng^{3}	C
正^{4}	止 77	正 127	Principal, orthodox, upright, exact, straight, right, just then ｜直 correct, straight ｜路 right road, straight ｜要 just about to, ｜想	cheng^{13}	A
政^{4}	攴 66	正 127	To rule; administration, law ｜界 government circles ｜◦治 government, politics ｜府 the government		A
症^{4}	疒 104	正 127	Disease 內外｜ ｜候 ailment 病｜		D
證^{4} 証^{4}	言 149	登 733	To testify, prove ｜·據 a proof ｜驗 見·｜ witness ｜見, ｜人		B

掙4	手 64	爭 413	Earn, nerve up |·起身來 pick self up, nerve up | 錢 earn money		cheng1	B
鄭4	邑 163	奠 782	A state under Chou	S.		F

Ch'eng

稱1 穪1	禾 115	冉 600	To style, call; a name, title |·呼 a title, to call |∘讚 to praise, extol | 頌		ch'en4	C
秤1	禾 115	平 36	To weigh | 鹽 buy salt at retail		ch'eng4	D
撐1 撑1	手 64	掌 587	To pole, punt, prop | 持 to assist | 船 pole a boat			E
橕1	木 75	掌 587	A rod; to prop window open | 開窗·戶			H
饓1	食 184	掌 587	To eat much, gormandize			H
成2	戈 62	成 347	To complete, accomplish perfect, become | 績 achievement, results | 家 to marry (man) | 親 | 就 complete, fulfil |∘全 | 事 complete an affair	S.		B
城2	土 32	成 347	A city, city-wall | 牆 city-wall | 門 city-gate			A
盛2	皿 108	成 347	To contain, fill | 滿 fill full		sheng4	D
誠2	言 149	成 347	Guileless; verily | 然 truly, indeed | 實 sincere, genuine | 心			B
呈2	口 30	呈 69	Plaint, accusation ; offer to superior | 稟 present petition			F

Character	Radical	Phonetic	Meaning		Other readings	Grade
程 2	禾 115	呈 69	A rule, pattern: journey; percentage ｜度 grade, qualifications, degree 路｜ a stage, itinerary ｜途	S		C
丞 2	一 1	丞 522	To aid, an assistant ｜相4 minister to the emperor			G
承 2	手 64	丞 522	To receive, contain; to undertake ｜認 acknowledge, confess ｜受 receive, inherit			C
乘 2	丿 4	乖 25	To ride, mount; to multiply ｜車 mount a carriage ｜法 multiplication		ch'eng4	D
懲 23 懲 23	心 61	徵 550	To chastise ｜治 to punish			F
澄 2	水 85	登 733	Clear, limpid		teng4	G
拯 3 抍 3	手 64	丞 522	To rescue, save ｜救	俗	cheng3	C
逞 3	辵 162	呈 69	Bold, forward, boastful, presumptuous ｜强 ｜兇 act outrageously			F
秤 4	禾 115	平 36	Steelyard, scale ｜・子 ｜砣 scale-weight		ch'eng1	C
乘 4	丿 4	乖 25	A team of four horses ; C. of vehicles ; records		ch'eng2 sheng4	D

Chi

Character	Radical	Phonetic	Meaning		Other readings	Grade
幾 1	幺 52	幾 346	Very nearly, just missed ｜乎		chi3	A
嘰 1	口 30	幾 346	嗶｜ A kind of cloth, longcloth			B

Chi

機^{1}	木 75	幾 346	A machine, or its power |·器 a machine |械 |∘會 opportunity |∘關 a spring; organ		B
磯^{1}	石 112	幾 346	Obstacle, to impede, steps | 頭 breakwater ; jetty		H
畿^{1}	田 102	幾 346	Imperial domains	ch'i^{2}	H
譏^{1}	言 149	幾 346	To slander, ridicule. satirize | 誚 ridicule | 刺		E
饑^{1} 飢^{1}	食 184	幾 346	Dearth, hunger |·荒 famine, trouble |饉 | 渴 hungry and thirsty | 餓 hungry		E
雞^{1} 鷄^{1} 鸡^{1}	隹 172 減	奚 881	Fowl, chicken 小| | 鳴 cock-crowing | 叫 | 子^{3} hen's egg | 蛋 公| cock, 母| hen		A
基^{1}	土 32	其 102	Foundation, property, patrimony |∘督 Christ |∘督教 Christian church | 業 family property, patrimony		B
期^{1}	月 74	其 102	何| what time? 文	ch'i^{12}	B
箕^{1}	竹 118	其 102	Winnowing basket 簸·| dust pan	ch'i^{2}	E
⿰口基^{1}	口 30	其 102	Sound for transliteration		F
擊^{1}	手 64	毄 405	To beat, strike | 打 攻| to attack		D
積^{14}	禾 115	責 83	To gather. store up | 極 positive, constructive | 攢 (or 儹) hoard up		D
績^{14}	糸 120	責 83	To spin, twist, merit affair | 成 to complete | 功 merit 勞|		I

Chi

敫[1]	攴 66	敫 551	To respect, beat		P
檄[1]	木 75	敫 551	A summons, urgent; despatch, to proclaim	hsi[2]	K
激[1]	水 85	敫 551	Overflowing, to rouse, stimulate ｜發 ｜勵 excite, spur ｜動		E
几[1]	几 16	儿 395	A table for k'ang[4] 茶｜ a stand, tea-poy		F
肌[1]	肉 130	几 396	The flesh under skin, muscle ｜·膚 body, skin		G
汲[1]	水 85	及 218	To draw well-water; imitate, eager, ｜水 draw water	chi[4]	G
芨[1]	艸 140	及 218	An orchid		K
唧[12]	口 30	即 364	Hum of insects; jabber, chatter, babble ｜｜咕咕 clamor, chatter		I
髻[14]	髟 190	吉 729	Chinese woman's hair-dress 梳｜ comb or do up hair		I
虀[1] 齏[1]	艸 140	齊 421	Leek; to mix, blend 和｜ to mix, as spices		K
躋[1] 隮[1]	足 157	齊 421	To ascend. climb; increase 攀｜ clamber up		I
觭[1] 犄[1]	角 148	奇 452	｜·角 entering corner	ch'i[2]	K
稽[1]	禾 115	旨 323	To investigate ｜察; delay 無｜之談 unfounded talk	chi[4] ch'i[3]	K
賫[1] 齎[1]	貝 154	貝 856	To give, offer, send ｜賜; prepare, supply 親｜ personally present		K
乩[1]	乙 5	占 720	To divine by planchette 扶｜ divine with stick in sand		K

Chi

羈[1]	网 122	馬 255	Halter, to seize 丨留 to detain 丨住		K
笄[1]	竹 118	开 34	To do up hair, marriageable 丨禮		K
急[2]	心 61	彐 667	Haste, impatience, anxious, urgent 丨着了 (caused) extreme impatience 丨忙 hasty, hurried 丨促 丨症 acute disease 丨性 impatient disposition		A
及[2]	又 29	及 218	Come up to, attain, and also 丨至 when, as soon as 累丨 to involve others	chi[4]	B
級[2] ⿰阝及[2]	糸 120	及 218	Series, rank, grade 階丨 caste, grade 等丨 a sort, class		A
亟[2]	二 7	亟 241	Haste, speed, urgent; a crisis 丨速 丨欲 to long for		K
極[2]	木 75	亟 241	Extreme limit; very 丨其 exceedingly 丨好 excellent 丨端 extremely; extremity, 丨點		B
集[2]	隹 172	隹 52	To assemble, collect, compile; a fair 聚丨 gather, assemble 丨聚 趕丨 attend a fair		B
藉[24]	艸 140	昔 799	To offer tribute, confused 丨恩 thanks to you 丨福	chieh[4]	C
籍[2]	竹 118	昔 799	A list, register 民丨 register of citizens	chi[4]	E
卽[2]	卩 26	卽 364	Instantly 丨時, 丨刻	chi[4]	C
疾[2]	疒 104	疾 476	Illness, disease 丨病; urgency; hastily 丨速		D
蒺[2]	艸 140	疾 476	Gorse, furze 丨藜 thorny calthrop		E

Chi

吉^{2}	口 30	吉 729	Auspicious, lucky, happy ｜兆 lucky omen ｜日 lucky day	S.		E
脊^{2}	肉 130	脊 618	The spine, back ｜·梁 ｜背 the back 梁｜ house-ridge			F
瘠^{2}	疒 104	脊 618	Lean, barren, ｜瘦 emaciated			G
幾^{3} 几^{3}	幺 52	幾 346	How much, or many ? Several, a few ｜個 ｜時 when? what date? ｜歲 how old ? (to child) ｜點鐘 what hour ?		chi^{1}	A
蟣^{3}	虫 142	幾 346	Nit ｜·子			I
己^{3}	己 49	己 311	Self ; selfish 自｜, ｜身 克｜ deny oneself 守｜ control self			A
紀^{3}	糸 120	己 311	Surname		chi^{4}	C
給^{3}	糸 120	合 708	Give, grant ｜與 供·｜ supply with food	文	kei^{3}	A
擠^{3}	手 64	齊 421	To crowd, press ｜奶 to milk 擁｜ press upon, crowd			D
濟^{3}	水 85	齊 421	Chinan, Shantung		chi^{4}	C
戟^{3}	戈 62	戈 331	Halberd, lance 持｜ grasp spear, take up arms			K
季^{4}	子 39	委 512	Quarter, season ; young 每｜ quarterly 四｜ four seasons	S.		A
既^{4}	无 71	既 366	Since. when, already ｜然 since it is so ｜·是			A
曁^{4}	日 72	既 366	To reach, up to, with, also ｜今 up to the present time	S.		H

Chi

Character	Radical	Phonetic	Meaning		Alt.	
忌^{4}	心 61	己 311	To dread, avoid; be jealous 丨恨 to hate 丨烟 give up opium			D
紀^{4}	糸 120	己 311	To arrange, record, narrate; annals 丨◦念 remember, keep in mind		chi^{3}	C
記^{4}	言 149	己 311	To remember, record 丨賬 put down in account 丨·號 a mark, sign 丨錄 minutes, record			A
及^{4}	又 29	及 218	To attain, reach to 不丨 not equal to, poor		chi^{2}	B
汲^{4}	水 85	及 218	To draw, imbibe 丨水, 丨井	S.	chi^{1}	G
祭^{4}	示 113	祭 515	To sacrifice, worship 丨神 丨司 a priest 丨祖 sacrifice to ancestors			C
際^{4}	阜 170	祭 515	A border, limit 交丨 intercourse of friends 時丨 a juncture, time			B
轂^{4}	殳 79	轂 405	To attack			P
繫^{4}	糸 120	轂 405	To tie, fasten 丨累 implicated 丨帶 tie, sash, belt		hsi^{4}	B
計^{4}	言 149	十 13	To plan, calculate 丨謀 scheme, plot 丨·畫 plan, policy	S		B
劑^{4}	刀 18	齊 421	To trim, cut even, adjust; a dose 藥丨 medicines, doses			H
濟^{4}	水 85	齊 421	To help; cross over 丨人 to rescue 丨貧 help the poor 賑丨		chi^{3}	C
霽^{4}	雨 173	齊 421	Sky clearing 晴丨			K

Chi

卽4	卩 26	卽 364	Now, then, forthwith, that is ; even if ｜或 even if ｜便 ｜是 that is, just so		chi2	C
鯽4	魚 195	卽 364	Carp, bream 金｜			K
蹟4 跡4 迹4	足 157 辵 162	責 83	Foot-prints, traces, clues 神｜ miracles 蹤｜ traces, remains ｜蹤			C
嫉4 ⿰女忌4	女 38	疾 476	Envy, jealousy ｜·妬, 妬·｜ ｜賢 envy the good			D
寄4	宀 40	奇 452	To lodge ; send ｜居 dwell temporarily ｜寓 ｜信 send a letter			D
棘4	木 75	朿 500	Thorny brambles 荆｜ 孔｜ earnest, urgent			D
籍4	竹 118	昔 799	書｜ Books, library	S	chi2	E
妓4	女 38	支 539	Singing-girl ｜女 a courtesan 娼｜			F
技4	手 64	支 539	Ability, talent ｜能 ｜巧 ingenious, clever			E
楫4	木 75	咠 631	Paddle, to row			K
輯4	車 159	咠 631	To collect, arrange 編·｜ compose, compile ｜編			E
𢇍4	幺 52	𢇍 882	To connect, continue			P
繼4	糸 120	𢇍 882	To connect, succeed 相｜ to adopt ; hereditary ｜續 succeed, continue ｜嗣 adopt a son ｜位 succeed to the throne 過·｜ give child for adoption			F

冀[4]	八 12	異 98	To hope, wish one 丨望 The province of Hopei	S.		G
薊[4]	艸 140		Thistle 丨縣 city in Hopei	S.		G
劇[42]	刀 18	豦 290	Distress, increase, to sport, comedy, very 丨烈 violent		chü[4]	I
寂[4]	宀 40	叔 123	Still, quiet, solitary 丨靜 perfect quiet			K
稽[4]	禾 115	旨 323	Surname	S	chi[1] ch'i[3]	K
覡[41]	見 147		Witch, necromancy 丨公 a wizard			K
彐[4] 彑[4]	彐 58	彐 667	Pig's snout, pig's head			K

Ch'i

七[1] 柒[1]	一 1	七 326	Seven (before 1,2,3) 丨情 joy, anger, sorrow, fear, love, hate, desire—7 emotions 丨°十 seventy 丨百 700 第丨 the seventh		ch'i[2]	A
沏[1]	水 85	七 326	To steep 丨茶 make tea			A
期[12]	月 74	其 102	A period, fixed time 日丨 星丨 a week 丨間 duration		chi[1]	B
欺[1]	欠 76	其 102	To cheat, deceive 丨哄, 丨騙 丨·負 humbug, 丨壓 oppress			C
妻[1]	女 38	妻 668	A wife 丨·子 取丨 to marry			C
淒[1] 凄[1]	水 85	妻 668	Very cold, freezing, afflicted; misery 丨凉 cold, lonely			H
悽[1]	心 61	妻 668	Grieved, suffering 丨慘 melancholy			G

Ch'i

Character	Radical	Phonetic	Meaning	Also read	
棲^{1} 栖^{1}	木 75	妻 668	To roost, rest, settle 鷄 | a roost	hsi^{1}	F
戚^{1}	戈 62	叔 123	Related to ; to pity 親·| relatives	ch'i^{24}	C
嘁^{1}	口 30	叔 123	Indistinct talking | | 喳喳		I
慼^{1} 慽^{1}	心 61	叔 123	Grief, sorrow, sad, mournful (used as 戚)		H
桼^{1}	木 75	桼 527	Varnish tree		P
漆^{1}	水 85	桼 527	Lacquer, varnish, sticky | 器 lacquer-ware | 樹 lacquer-tree	ch'ü^{1}	E
溪^{1}	水 85	奚 881	Mountain stream	hsi^{1}	F
攲^{1}	支 65	奇 452	Aslant, toppling	ch'ieh^{1}	I
咠^{1}	口 30	咠 631	Whisper, blame, slander		K
七^{2}	一 1	七 326	Seven (before 4th tone word)	ch'i^{1}	A
奇^{2} 竒^{2}	大 37	奇 452	Rare, wonderful 希 | | 計 remarkable stratagem | 怪 mysterious, strange | 事 a miracle		C
崎^{2}	山 46	奇 452	Steep, precipitous | 嶇		G
踦^{2}	足 157	奇 452	Crippled, lame | 足		K
觭^{2}	角 148	奇 452	Single, not matched | 角 uneven, irregular	chi^{1}	K
騎^{2}	馬 187	奇 452	To sit astride, ride | 馬 ride a horse | 兵 cavalry | 牲口 ride an animal		A

Ch'i

Character	Radical	Phonetic	Meaning		Other reading	
齊[2] 齐[2]	齊 210	齊 421	Even, equal, to arrange ｜整 orderly, even ｜全 complete ; prepared ｜備 ｜心 of one mind,	S.	chai[1]	C
臍[2]	肉 130	齊 421	The navel, peduncle 肚｜ ｜帶 umbilical cord			H
其[2]	八 12	其 102	He, she, it ; his ; this, that ｜寔 the fact is, ｜餘 the rest			B
旗[2]	方 70	其 102	Flag, banner, bannermen ｜人 Manchus			A
棋[2] 棊[2] 碁[2]	木 75 石 112	其 102	Chess ｜盤 chess board 下｜ to play chess 象｜ chess with 32 men 大｜ chess with 360 men 圍｜			G
箕[2]	竹 118	其 102	A winnowing basket ; dust-pan 簸｜ winnowing-pan		chi[1]	E
麒[2]	鹿 198	其 102	Unicorn ｜麟			G
戚[24]	戈 62	叔 123	A surname	S	ch'i[1]	C
祈[2]	示 113	示 514	To pray ｜求, ｜禱 ｜年 pray for good year			D
祇[2]	示 113	氏 348	Repose, great 地｜ earth deity			G
岐[2]	山 46	支 539	Double-peaked, ambiguity ; Shensi ｜峰 mountain peaks			G
歧[2]	止 77	支 539	Forked, divergent 兩｜ two meanings			H
耆[2]	老 125	老 189	Old (60), experienced ｜老 紳｜ gentry and elders			I
畿[2]	田 102	幾 346	Imperial domains; the court 皇｜		chi[1]	H
畦[2]	田 102	圭 48	Field of 50 mou 菜｜ small garden plot ｜子			I

Ch'i

<table>
<tr><td>起[3]</td><td>走
156</td><td>己
311</td><td>To rise, begin, raise
| 初 at first | 先
|·來 to rise, get up
| 色 gain, improvement
| 身 to start, move
| 首 the beginning | 頭, 原 |
| 點 starting point, origin | 原</td><td></td><td>A</td></tr>
<tr><td>豈[3]</td><td>豆
151</td><td>豈
732</td><td>How ? (implies negative)
| 敢 I am unworthy !
| 不知 how not know?</td><td></td><td>A</td></tr>
<tr><td>啓[3]</td><td>口
30</td><td>戶
728</td><td>To explain, open, begin
| 者 "to begin" (letter)
| 示 revelation</td><td></td><td>D</td></tr>
<tr><td>乞[3]</td><td>乙
5</td><td>乞
298</td><td>To beg alms, implore
| 丐 beggar</td><td></td><td>F</td></tr>
<tr><td>稽[3]</td><td>禾
115</td><td>旨
323</td><td>To prostrate oneself | 首</td><td>chi[14]</td><td>K</td></tr>
<tr><td>气[4]</td><td>气
84</td><td>乞
298</td><td>Breath ; vapor</td><td></td><td>K</td></tr>
<tr><td>汽[4]</td><td>水
85</td><td>乞
298</td><td>Steam (new character)
| 車 automobile
| 船 steamboat
| 水 aerated water</td><td></td><td>A</td></tr>
<tr><td>氣[4]</td><td>气
84</td><td>乞
298</td><td>Air, breath, steam; force; temper
| 質 temper, disposition | 志
| 象 appearance, weather
|∘候 climate, weather
| 人 enrage a person 惹人 |
|·力 strength 力·|
|∘味 flavor, taste</td><td></td><td>A</td></tr>
<tr><td>迄[4]</td><td>辵
162</td><td>乞
298</td><td>Reach to, as yet, | 今
| 竟 after all, finally</td><td></td><td>H</td></tr>
<tr><td>訖[4]</td><td>言
149</td><td>乞
298</td><td>To finish, reach to, up till 已 |
| 淸 settled up,—accounts</td><td></td><td>I</td></tr>
<tr><td>器[4]
噐[4]</td><td>口
30</td><td>吠
457</td><td>A vessel, dish, utensil, tool
|·具 utensils, vessels | 皿
兵∘| weapons | 械, 軍 |</td><td></td><td>B</td></tr>
</table>

棄[4]	木 75	枼 110	To abandon, reject |廢, 廢| |絕 cast off, renounce |嫌 reject disdainfully		D
泣[4]	水 85	立 84	To weep, lament 哭|		D
㓞[4]	刀 18	㓞 147	A notch, to cut a notch		P
契[4]	大 37	㓞 147	A covenant, bond, deed ; intimate |交 intimate fellowship |友 |券 deed, bond, evidence |約 a contract		E
緝[4]	糸 120	咠 631	To pursue; seize |拏; twist; join, continue 巡| get on trail of		I
葺[4]	艸 140	咠 631	To repair, build, |補; thatch, cover		K
砌[4]	石 112	七 326	To lay in mortar |牆 build a wall		E
企[43]	人 9	止 126	To stand expectant |望 |仰 anxiously look to for help		G
偈[4]	人 9	曷 239	To rest, take breath, enigma, sign	chieh[42]	K
憩[4]	心 61	甘 101	To rest, take breath |息 遊| rest after stroll		K

Chia

家[1]	宀 40	家 286	Family, relatives, home ; people ; class, |庭 S |產 family property |業 |·眷 wife and children |·裏 at home ; wife |務 home affairs 人·| other people		A
傢[1]	人 9	家 286	Tools, utensils, |·具 |·伙 tools, furniture |什		A

Chia

Character	Radical	Phonetic	Meaning	Other readings	
稼[14]	禾 115	家 286	To sow grain ; farm ｜穡 grain, crops 莊｜		B
夾[12]	大 37	夾 455	To press, squeeze, secrete ; lined; pick up with pincers ｜襖 a lined coat ｜道 ravine, passage		B
挾[1]	手 64	夾 455	To clasp under arm, pinch ; cherish, dislike ｜帶 carry under arm	chia[2] hsieh[2]	D
鋏[1]	金 167	夾 455	Pincers, tongs 火｜		I
頰[14]	頁 181	夾 455	The jaws, cheeks 腮｜	hsia[4]	G
加[1]	力 19	加 716	To add to, confer on; inflict ｜車 special train ｜一倍 double the number ｜倍 ｜添 to add, increase ｜增		C
伽[1]	人 9	加 716	A Buddhist word ka or ga	ch'ieh[2]	H
枷[1]	木 75	加 716	A cangue 擔｜, 扛｜ ｜打 to bamboo, and cangue		G
迦[1]	辵 162	加 716	Of Sakhyamuni, = ka sound in proper names		F
嘉[1]	口 30	加 716	Admirable, excellent ｜意 excellent idea		E
佳[1]	人 9	佳 51	Good, beautiful ｜美 ｜妙 excellent, admirable		D
戛[14]	戈 62	戈 331	Lance, long spear	ka[1]	H
嘎[1]	口 30	戈 331	Cackle, loud laugh	ka[1234]	G
葭[1]	艸 140	叚 639	Bulrush, reeds, ｜葦; flute ｜笛 reed pipe or flute		K
挾[2]	手 64	夾 455	｜棍 Pinching-stick	chia[1] hsieh[2]	D

Character	Radical	Phonetic	Meaning	Other reading	Freq.
袷[2] 裌[2]	衣 145	合 708	Lined garment ｜衣服 ｜被 lined quilt		F
假[3]	人 9	叚 639	False ; to pretend; to borrow; supposing ｜粧 to feign, pretend ｜充, ｜託 ｜若 if, supposing ｜如 ｜冒爲善 hypocrisy	chia[4]	A
甲[34]	田 102	甲 825	First "stem" ; scales, armor 指｜ finger nails		E
賈[3]	貝 154	貝 856	A surname S	ku[3]	G
架[4]	木 75	加 716	Frame, rack, staging ｜·子 ｜不住 cannot support		B
駕[4]	馬 187	加 716	To ride in or on, ｜車 勞｜ I trouble you, 尊｜ your honor		A
假[4]	人 9	叚 639	Leave of absence, vacation 放｜ grant leave, give holiday 告｜ request leave	chia[3]	A
價[4]	人 9	貝 856	Value, price ｜∘值 ｜·錢 price, cost ｜銀 有｜·值 valuable 無｜·值 worthless		B
嫁[4]	女 38	家 286	To marry a husband ｜娶 marriage ｜女 give girl in marriage		B
莢[2]	艸 140	夾 455	Pods ; seeds 豆｜ bean pods 豆角		F

Ch'ia

Character	Radical	Phonetic	Meaning	Other reading	Freq.
掐[1] 㓣[1]	手 64	臽 683	To claw, pinch with fingers twist, pluck, ｜住 seize firmly ｜花兒 pluck, flowers		D
卡[1]	卜 25	卜 119	｜庫倫 A place in Mongolia	ch'ia[23]	G

Character	Radical	Phonetic	Meaning		Other reading	
卡²	卜 25	卜 119	|·住·了 Held close between two things		ch'ia¹³	G
卡³	卜 25	卜 119	A guard-house, barrier ; to stick |路 guard station at a pass |口		ch'ia¹² k'a³	G
恰⁴	心 61	合 708	Fitting, opportune |巧 in the nick of time |當 the very thing |好			E
洽⁴	水 85	合 708	Harmonious, fitting, exactly 接| to deal with, manage		hsia⁴	F

Chiang

Character	Radical	Phonetic	Meaning		Other reading	
江¹	水 85	工 8	A large river |河 rivers in general |·西 province of Kiangsi |米 glutinous rice |·蘇 province of Kiangsu	S.		B
豇¹ 䜶¹	豆 151	工 8	Small kidney bean |豆			G
將¹ [illegible]¹ 将¹	寸 41 减	將 21	To take in the hand, hold, (more elegant than 把); to consider; just about to |近 near, approaching |·就 make best of, put up with |來 in future, hereafter |要去 about to go		chiang⁴	B
漿¹ [illegible]¹	水 85	將 21	Syrupy liquid ; broth, starch, pus |洗 wash and starch			E
僵¹	人 9	畺 812	Prostrate ; stiff |人 a corpse |屍			I
疆¹ 畺¹	田 102	畺 812	Boundary, frontier |界 frontier |宇 新| Turkestan 無| boundless			E

Chiang

薑^{1} 葁^{1}	艸 140	畺 812	Ginger 黃 | 粉 curry powder 咖喱粉 糖 | ginger preserved in sugar		E
韁^{1} 繮^{1}	革 177	畺 812	Bridle, halter, reins |·繩 reins, halter-strap	kang^{1}	G
姜^{1}	女 38	羊 151	A surname		H
講^{3}	言 149	冓 601	To talk, explain, discourse, analyze | 價 settle a price | 解 explain, interpret | 理 discuss reasonably | 論 talk of, a discourse | 說 | 演 to lecture 演 |		B
奬^{3}	大 37	將 21	To encourage, praise 誇·| | 賞 reward		C
槳^{3}	木 75	將 21	An oar ; centre board 搖 | to row, scull		G
蔣^{3}	艸 140	將 21	An aquatic grass S. | 茅 stubble		H
港^{3}	水 85	巷 96	Port, harbour | 口, 船 | 香 | Hongkong a.p. hsiang^{1}-kang^{3}		G
襁^{3} 繈^{3}	衣 145	虫 785	Swathing-cloth | 褓 | 負 "pick-a-pack"	ch'iang^{3}	K
將^{4}	寸 41	將 21	A general |^{1}·軍 | 帥 generalissimo 老 | the king in chess	chiang^{1}	B
醬^{4}	酉 164	將 21	Soy-bean sauce, condiment 乾 | | 油 bean oil		A
匠^{4}	匚 22	斤 209	A workman, mechanic | 人, 工 | 木·| a carpenter, 瓦·| etc.		C
佭^{4}	人 9	夂 540	Unsubmissive | 孩子 obstreperous child		I

絳^{4}	糸 120	夂 540	A purple-red ｜·色			H
降^{4} 夅^{4}	阜 170	夂 540	To descend; send down, to be degraded ｜禍 send calamity ｜災 ｜臨 condescending visit ｜生 incarnation ｜世, ｜凡 ｜雨 to rain		hsiang^{2}	E
虹^{4}	虫 142	工 8	Rainbow	俗	hung^{2} kang^{4}	E
糨^{4}	米 119	竟 94	Starch, paste, to starch 打｜·子 make paste			E

Ch'iang

搶^{1}	手 64	倉 679	｜風 Head wind	ch'iang^{3}	D
槍^{1}	木 75	倉 679	A spear, a lance of wood ｜桿 handle of spear		F
蹌^{1} 牄^{1}	足 157	倉 679	To walk rapidly, bustle about, 奔走趨｜		G
鎗^{1}	金 167	倉 679	A gun, pistol, opium-pipe ｜子兒 shot, bullets		D
啌^{1}	口 30	空 10	Sound of coughing ｜出血來 cough up blood		H
腔^{1}	肉 130	空 10	A singing tone of voice; brogue ｜·調 a tune; a singing tone 裝｜ pretentious 京｜ Peking accent		G
戕^{1}	戈 62	爿 162	Lance; to wound, ｜傷 kill, assault ｜暴 cruel, ruthless		K
羌^{1} 羗^{1}	羊 123	羊 151	A western tribe, ｜戎, ｜人		K

牆^2 墻^2	爿 90	嗇 770	A wall, built of earth, brick or stone, | 垣 | 堞子 buttress 砌 | build a wall 山 | end wall of house			B
檣^2 艢^2	木 75	嗇 770	A mast, spar, boom 帆 | sail and mast			K
薔^2	艸 140	嗇 770	A red rose | 薇水 attar of roses			K
強^2 强^2 彊^2	弓 57	虫 785	Strong, excellent, violent |·壯 strong and healthy | 如 better than, | 似 自 | exert self, persevere	S	ch'iang^3	B
強^3 强^3	弓 57	虫 785	To force, compel | 逼 | 留 detain by force 勉 | to urge; under compulsion		ch'iang^2	B
搶^3	手 64	倉 679	To take by force, rob, struggle for | 去 snatch away | 盜 robbery, brigandage		ch'iang^1	D
嗆^4	口 30	倉 679	To peck, hacking cough 喝 | choke			I

Chiao

交^1	亠 8	交 531	To join, unite; deliver | 際 social relations |·情 intercourse | 付 transfer, hand to | 給 |·涉 mutual relations; negotiate |∘代 hand over to successor | 託 entrust to | 通 communication, intercourse | 往 fellowship | 接			B

Chiao

<table>
<tr><td>蛟^{1}</td><td>虫
142</td><td>交
531</td><td>A dragon with scales
螞蟻 | ant-lion</td><td></td><td>K</td></tr>
<tr><td>跤^{1}</td><td>足
157</td><td>交
531</td><td>To wrestle 摔 |</td><td></td><td>H</td></tr>
<tr><td>郊^{1}</td><td>邑
163</td><td>交
531</td><td>Waste land, open country, frontier; common
| 天 sacrifice to Heaven
| 野 the country | 外</td><td></td><td>F</td></tr>
<tr><td>鉸^{1}</td><td>金
167</td><td>交
531</td><td>A pivot hinge
| 釘 the pin of a hinge</td><td>chiao^{3}</td><td>H</td></tr>
<tr><td>教^{1}</td><td>攴
66</td><td>孝
191</td><td>To teach
| 學 teach, instruction | 書
| 給 to teach | 授
| 導 educate; guide</td><td>chiao^{4}</td><td>B</td></tr>
<tr><td>椒^{1}</td><td>木
75</td><td>叔
123</td><td>Pepper, peppery, | 樹
胡 | black pepper 胡 | 麪</td><td></td><td>B</td></tr>
<tr><td>膠^{1}</td><td>肉
130</td><td>翏
283</td><td>Glue, gum; sticky, to adhere to 水 |
| 粘 to glue
| 水 mucilage</td><td></td><td>B</td></tr>
<tr><td>轇^{1}</td><td>車
159</td><td>翏
283</td><td>Indistinct, confused | 轕不清</td><td>chiu^{1}</td><td>K</td></tr>
<tr><td>澆^{1}</td><td>水
85</td><td>堯
391</td><td>To sprinkle, water
| 灌 to water, irrigate | 水</td><td></td><td>C</td></tr>
<tr><td>角^{1}</td><td>角
148</td><td>角
602</td><td>犄 | Animal's horn</td><td>chiao^{3}
chüeh^{2}</td><td>C</td></tr>
<tr><td>嬌^{1}</td><td>女
38</td><td>喬
583</td><td>Graceful, delicate | 美
| 妻 my dear wife
| 羞 bashful, modest
| 養 to pet, spoil</td><td></td><td>G</td></tr>
<tr><td>驕^{1}</td><td>馬
187</td><td>喬
583</td><td>Proud, boastful | 誇
| 傲 arrogant, haughty, | 矜
| 縱 overbearing, regardless</td><td></td><td>D</td></tr>
<tr><td>焦^{1}</td><td>火
86</td><td>焦
56</td><td>Scorched, dried; anxious, | 黑 S
| 悶 sad at heart, melancholy 心 |</td><td></td><td>E</td></tr>
<tr><td>噍^{14}</td><td>口
30</td><td>焦
56</td><td>To eat, bite, chew</td><td></td><td>I</td></tr>
</table>

Chiao

燋^{1}	火 86	焦 56	To char, scorch, |木 |心 sad at heart		H
礁^{1}	石 112	焦 56	Shoal rocks. |石		H
蕉^{1}	艸 140	焦 56	The plantain, banana |扇 palm-leaf fan		F
醮^{14}	酉 164	焦 56	A festival, sacrifice 打| |席 a wedding feast		K
嚼^{2}	口 30	爵 851	To chew, masticate |用 living, expenditure 倒| chew the cud	chiao^{4} chüeh^{2}	D
脚^{3} 腳^{3}	肉 130	去 44	Foot, base, bottom 俗 |掌 sole of foot |·錢 coolie-hire, freight |價, |費 |指頭 toes |·夫 a coolie, porter 失| to slip, lose footing	chüeh^{24}	A
覺^{3}	見 147	𦥯 692	To perceive, feel	chiao^{4} chüeh^{2}	A
攪^{3}	手 64	𦥯 692	To stir up, excite, mix |擾 make trouble for |亂, |動		D
角^{3}	角 148	角 602	Horn; angle; pod 牛| 三| triangular 直| right angle	chiao^{1} chüeh^{23}	C
狡^{3}	犬 94	交 531	Crafty, clever, wily |猾 |計 a crafty trick		E
皎^{3} 皦^{3} 皛^{3}	白 106	交 531	Effulgent, splendid; pure, bright |潔 pure, unsullied |日 bright daylight		G
絞^{3}	糸 120	交 531	To bind; twist rope |纜 |罪 strangulation |死		G
較^{3}	車 159	交 531	|比 to compare 比|	chiao^{4}	C
鉸^{3}	金 167	交 531	Door-pivot, to shear, cut |紙花 cut out paper flowers	chiao^{1}	H

Chiao

Character	Radical	Phonetic	Meaning	Other readings	
餃³	食 184	交 531	Meat dumplings |·子		E
剿³ 勦³	刀 18	巢 508	To attack, destroy; fatigue | 滅 exterminate | 絕		F
勦³	力 19	巢 508	To trouble, annoy, | 勞 nimble		I
僥³	人 9	堯 391	Fortunate, lucky | 償 try to evade payment		G
儌³	人 9	敫 551	To do, act, lucky | 倖 luckily, happily		G
繳³	糸 120	敫 551	To hand in, pay; wind round, | 線 | 還 pay back, return, | 納		G
鐵³	金 167	敫 551	To cut with shears | 開 cut in two		F
矯³	矢 111	喬 583	To feign; to force | 情 usurp; martial, strong | 强 force, exorbitant		I
叫⁴ 呌⁴	口 30	斗 23	To call, command, cause, let | 醒 awaken, arouse |·喚 call out, cry of animals | 呼 | 甚麼 what is it called? | 我 call me; cause me to; by me		A
覺⁴	見 147	𦥯 692	睡 | to sleep 睡不着 | cannot sleep	chiao³ chüeh²	A
校⁴	木 75	交 531	To compare; revise, | 訂 | 對 to correct proof, etc. | 正	hsiao⁴	A
較⁴	車 159	交 531	To compare, test | 量 comparatively | 準 adjust to standard | 多 comparatively more, | 量 etc.	chiao³	C
教⁴	攴 66	孝 191	Doctrines; sect |·訓 instruction, teachings | 化 conversion, civilization | 會 church | 門 a sect | 派	chiao¹	B

<table>
<tr><td>教[4]</td><td></td><td></td><td>| 師 school teacher
| 徒 church member | 友
|•育 education | 授 professor</td><td></td><td></td></tr>
<tr><td>酵[4]</td><td>酉
164</td><td>孝
191</td><td>Yeast, leaven 麵 |
無 | unleavened
有 | leavened</td><td>hsiao[4]</td><td>D</td></tr>
<tr><td>轎[4]</td><td>車
159</td><td>喬
583</td><td>Sedan chair |·子
| 杆 chair-poles
騾馱 | mule-litter</td><td></td><td>B</td></tr>
<tr><td>嚼[4]</td><td>口
30</td><td>爵
851</td><td>To chew, bite
倒 | chew cud</td><td>chiao[2]
chüeh[2]</td><td>D</td></tr>
<tr><td>窖[4]</td><td>穴
116</td><td>告
717</td><td>A cellar, store-pit 地 |
| 冰 to store ice
冰 | ice-house, or pit</td><td></td><td>E</td></tr>
</table>

Ch'iao

<table>
<tr><td>敲[1]</td><td>支
66</td><td>高
582</td><td>To pound, tap, rap
| 門 knock at door
| 打 knock, beat</td><td></td><td>E</td></tr>
<tr><td>幧[1]</td><td>巾
50</td><td>秋
450</td><td>To hem; a turban
| 邊 to hem the edge</td><td></td><td>F</td></tr>
<tr><td>鍫[1]
鍬[1]</td><td>金
167</td><td>秋
450</td><td>A shovel, spade 鐵 |
| 泥 to spade the ground</td><td></td><td>E</td></tr>
<tr><td>黲[1]</td><td>黑
203</td><td>喿
697</td><td>Spots on face 黑 |·子</td><td></td><td>I</td></tr>
<tr><td>蹻[1]
蹺[1]</td><td>足
157</td><td>喬
583</td><td>On tip-toe | 起脚兒來
| 脚 to cross legs; the stroke ㇂</td><td></td><td>I</td></tr>
<tr><td>鞽[1]
橇[1]</td><td>革
177</td><td>喬
583</td><td>Mud shoe, sledge for the feet</td><td></td><td>K</td></tr>
<tr><td>憔[2]</td><td>心
61</td><td>焦
56</td><td>Distressed, pining | 悴</td><td></td><td>H</td></tr>
</table>

Ch'iao

樵^2	木 75	焦 56	Fuel, to gather fuel ｜薪 ｜夫 woodcutter		G
瞧^2	目 109	焦 56	To glance at, see, look ｜·見 ｜·着作 act according to conditions ｜病 treat diseases; be treated ｜不見 can't see, ｜得見 can see ｜不起 despise, esteem lightly		B
喬^2 乔^2	口 30	喬 583	High, lofty, proud ｜志 S. ｜白 very white ｜答摩 Gautama-Buddha		H
僑^2	人 9	喬 583	Inn, to lodge ｜居 外｜ foreigners 華｜ oversea Chinese		G
橋^2	木 75	喬 583	A bridge; to bridge ｜空 arches of bridge ｜洞 浮｜ bridge of boats		B
蕎^2	艸 140	喬 583	Buck wheat ｜·麥 ｜麥麵 buck wheat flour		G
翹^2	羽 124	堯 391	To raise, stimulate tail feathers ｜發 to elevate ｜首 to raise the head 高｜ stilts		K
雀^3	隹 172	隹 52	Small birds; sparrow ｜鳥 麻｜ least bunting	ch'üeh^4	D
丂^3	一 1	丂 240	Air striving to free itself		P
巧^3	工 48	丂 240	Clever, skilful; lucky ｜計 clever scheme ｜·了 luckily, perchance ｜妙 ingenious 技｜,靈｜		D
鵲^3	鳥 196	昔 799	Jackdaw, jay, magpie 喜｜,鴉｜ 山喜｜ the blue magpie	ch'üeh^4	G
悄^{34}	心 61	肖 124	Sad; quiet, still ｜｜兒的 be quiet ｜沒聲兒的 in a whisper		H
煍^3	火 86	秋 450	To blacken by smoke ｜黑 烟｜之 cure by smoke		K

俏⁴	人 9	肖 124	Like; attractive, beautiful ｜生 lifelike ｜·皮 tasty, witty		G
誚⁴ 譙⁴	言 149	肖 124	To blame, scold, ｜讓 譏｜ to ridicule, satirize		E
鞘⁴ 鞩⁴	革 177	肖 124	A sheath, scabbard 劍｜·子 入｜ sheathe sword		E
竅⁴	穴 116	敫 551	Aperture, opening, pore, mind, ｜眼 心｜ the intelligence		E
撬⁴	手 64	毛 375	To pry, prise open ｜開 force up with lever ｜棍 a crowbar		G

Chieh

街¹	行 144	圭 48	A street, thoroughfare ｜·坊 neighbors; neighborhood ｜門 a street door ｜市 market, street 上｜ go to market		A
接¹	手 64	妾 85	To receive; succeed; splice, graft ｜洽 to deal or consult with ｜近 contiguous ｜·着 connectedly; to succeed to ｜觸 to come in contact ｜力賽跑 a relay race ｜連 connect in order ｜續 ｜受 to accept, receive ｜待 receive, entertain		A
結¹	糸 120	吉 729	To produce (fruit) ｜果 outcome, result ｜局 ｜菓子 bear fruit ｜·實 firm, strong ｜·巴 stutter	chieh²³	B
揭¹	手 64	曷 239	Lift off, raise, publish ｜·起來 raise up, ｜曉 publish		D

Chieh

揭[1]			|·開 open, lift a cover |短 show up shortcomings		C
皆[1]	白 106	皆 318	All, every, the whole |都 |然 all the same |同		D
偕[1]	人 9	皆 318	Together with |同 |行 go along with, walk with	hsieh[2]	D
階[1] 堦[1]	阜 170	皆 318	Steps; degrees |·級 official grades, castes (etc.) 台| a flight of steps		E
稭[1] 秸[1]	禾 115	皆 318	Stalks (of corn, hemp etc.) 花| wheat straw 麥|		G
癤[1]	疒 104	卽 364	Small sore, boil 瘡| 火|·子 a rash, prickly-heat		K
嗟[1]	口 30	差 178	To sigh, alas! |嘆 |乎 alas!	chüeh[2]	B
節[2] 卩[2]	竹 118	卽 364	Joint, verse; festival |·氣 24 solar terms |儉 frugal, within limits |制 temperance, control |度 過| keep the festival	chieh[3]	B
結[2]	糸 120	吉 729	Make contract; finish |交 become intimate |親 become related |婚 marriage |黨 form party, faction	chieh[13]	D
隔[24]	阜 170	鬲 589	Partition, to separate 俗 |開 separate, put apart	ke[24]	K
碣[2]	石 112	曷 239	Stone pillar, tablet |牌		C
竭[2]	立 117	曷 239	To exhaust, utmost, |盡 |力 utmost exertion		C
潔[2]	水 85	刧 147	Clean, pure, neat, tidy |凈 pure, clean, 清| |白 pure white		

Chieh

桀[2]	木 75	舛 273	Tyrant Chieh, B.C. 1818. cruel, courageous		K
傑[2]	人 9	舛 273	Hero, brave, eminent 豪｜ hero		F
截[2]	戈 62	𢦏 334	To cut off, intercept, divide ｜開 cut off, separate ｜路 cut off communications		F
捷[2]	手 64	徙 136	A victory, alert, active, quick ｜綱 rapid outline ｜目		G
刦[2] 劫[2] 刼[2]	刀 18	去 44	To rob forcibly, plunder; an era (kalpa) ｜盜 banditti, robbers ｜奪 rob, plunder 打｜		G
訐[2]	言 149	干 32	To accuse, denounce, 告｜ 面｜ accuse to one's face		K
卪[2] 卩[2]	冂 26	巳 306	Ancient seal (in halves), tally, 信｜		K
姐[3]	女 38	且 623	Elder sister, ｜｜ ｜∘妹 sisters 大｜ eldest sister 小｜ young lady; Miss		A
解[3] 觧[3]	角 148	解 603	To loosen, explain ｜勸 explain and admonish ｜決 solve, decide by vote ｜開 untie, explain ｜鈕·子 unbutton ｜釋 explain, definition ｜·說 ｜手 ease oneself, urinate 小｜	chieh[4] hsieh[4]	B
節[3]	竹 118	即 364	｜·子 Knot in wood	chieh[2]	B
結[3]	糸 120	吉 729	｜·子 A knot in cord	chieh[1,2]	B
借[4]	人 9	昔 799	To lend, borrow, suppose ｜·給 to lend, ｜·去 ｜光 please! allow me!		A

Chieh

借4			｜·來 borrow, ｜貸 ｜用 borrow for use		
藉4	艸 140	昔 799	To borrow, avail of, rely on ｜·着 through, by means of	chi24	C
解4	角 148	解 603	To deliver over ｜送 send under guard	chieh3 hsieh4	B
介4	人 9	介 433	Scales, armor; resolute, important, great; guest 不足｜意 unworthy of attention		G
价4	人 9	介 433	Servant. waiter, good 貴｜ your servant		K
疥4	疒 104	介 433	The itch, ｜瘡 ｜毒 itch infection		F
芥4	艸 140	介 433	Mustard ｜菜 ｜粉 ground mustard ｜麵		B
界4	田 102	介 433	A boundary; "world", "kingdom" ｜◦限 limit ｜石 boundary stone 商｜ the business world 世｜ the world; the times		B
戒4	戈 62	戒 337	To guard against, warn, abstain 切｜ ｜◦指 finger-ring ｜酒 break off drinking, so ｜烟		C
誡4	言 149	戒 337	Commandment ｜命 ｜勸 advice, admonition 禁｜ prohibition 規｜ rules of conduct 十｜ Ten Commandments		D
褯4	衣 145	席 559	Baby-napkin, diaper ｜·子		E
屆4 届4	尸 44	尸 724	To reach, limit; arrive in time ｜期 at appointed time ｜時 天｜ the horizon		F
詰4	言 149	吉 729	To examine, punish, ｜罪 restrain ｜問 to examine, question ｜訊		G

睫24 睞4	目 109	徒 136	Eye-lashes 眼 | 毛 眉 | 間 very near to		K
偈24	人 9	曷 239	Martial; diligent | | 爲義 earnest in duty	ch'i4	K

Ch'ieh

切1	刀 18	七 326	To cut, carve, mince | 肉 to slice meat, minced meat | 開 cut in pieces, mince | 碎 | 麪 flour strings	ch'ieh4	B
攲1	支 65	奇 452	Aslant, toppling	ch'i1	I
揩1	手 64	皆 318	To wipe off | 面, to dust | 磨 to rub clean	k'ai1	K
伽2	人 9	加 716	A Buddhist word	chia1	H
茄2	艸 140	加 716	Egg plant |·子, 牛 心 | 番 | the tomato		E
且3	一 1	且 623	Moreover, and; imperative | 住 stop a bit! stay! | 慢 | 說 to resume 暫 | temporarily		B
切4	刀 18	七 326	In earnest, important | 實 utmost truth and sincerity | 要 extremely important 一 | all, every 懇 | earnest	ch'ieh1	B
怯4	心 61	去 44	Timorous, cowardly 胆 | timid, fearful		D
竊4 窃4	穴 116	穴 394	To pilfer, usurp, steal; "my humble self" | 盜 to steal, petty thief 偷 | to steal		E
妾4	女 38	妾 85	Concubine 妻 | wives and concubines		G

唼⁴	口 30	妾 85	To talk sharply ｜喋 noise of geese feeding		H
趄⁴ 跙⁴	走 156	且 623	To trip and fall 打趔｜		H
挈⁴	手 64	㓞 147	To raise; help 提｜carry; recommend	hsieh²	I
愜⁴	心 61	夾 455	Pleased, satisfactory; to agree with｜意 爽｜joyful, in good spirits		K
篋⁴ 匧⁴	竹 118	夾 455	Box, satchel, book-chest 箱｜ 行｜traveling trunk		K

Chien

尖¹	小 42	小 121	Acute, point, sharp｜頭 ｜利 sharp point, clever｜刀 打｜ take refreshment		B
肩¹	肉 130	戶 728	Shoulder, to sustain ｜巾 shawl ｜膀 shoulder｜頭 ｜挑 carry on shoulder-pole		B
間¹	門 169	閒 636	Between, among, 中｜ 一｜房 one room house	chien⁴	B
漸¹	水 85	斬 212	To tinge, moisten｜染	chien⁴	B
臤¹	臣 131	臤 643	Firm, strong		P
堅¹	土 32	臤 643	Firm, hard, strong ｜振 confirmation (church)｜信 ｜壯 strong, robust, hearty ｜固 strong, firm, durably ｜守 guard safely		C
艱¹	艮 138	堇 107	Difficult, hard, calamity ｜險 difficult and dangerous｜危 ｜難 difficulty		C

Chien

Character	Radical	Phonetic	Meaning	Alt.	Grade
監1	皿 108	監 608	Survey, superintend, jail ｜禁 imprison ｜牢 a prison｜牢獄, ｜獄 ｜·督 superintend, bishop｜理	chien4	D
煎1	火 86	前 620	To fry in oil, decoct, harass ｜炒 to fry｜炸		E
姦1	女 38	女 552	Adultery, licentiousness ｜夫 adulterer,｜婦 adulteress ｜淫 adultery, fornication｜情		E
奸1	女 38	干 32	Crafty, wicked; inordinate｜邪 ｜詐 false, deceitful ｜惡 villainous		F
兼1	八 12	兼 671	Both, also, unite, equally, joint ｜愛 universal love ｜全 both complete ｜合 mix, blend ｜管 hold two offices at once｜任		F
戔1	戈 62	戔 332	Small, narrow, straitened｜狹		K
箋1 牋1	竹 118	戔 332	Note-paper, memo tablet｜紙 ｜札 a note, letter		G
緘1	糸 120	咸 344	Cords, to seal｜封; tie up ｜默 to keep silence		G
鐫1 鋑1	金 167	隹 52	To engrave, carve｜刻 ｜級 degrade from honors	chüan1	G
韉1	革 177	鹿 319	Saddle-cloth｜屜		I
犍1	牛 93	建 670	Ox; fabulous monster		K
剪3	刀 18	前 620	Cut off, shear, shears,｜鉸 ｜髮 cut hair｜頭·髮 ｜羊毛 to shear wool		B
儉3	人 9	僉 440	Frugal, economical｜節 ｜省 saving, thrifty｜少, ｜用		E

Chien

檢[3]	木 75	僉 440	To label; examine; pick up (used as 撿) 丨察 to inspect; search 丨柴 gather firewood 丨·起·來 to pick up		B
撿[3]	手 64	僉 440	To restrain, revise; pick up, (used as 檢) 丨點 look over, take account of 丨校 revise, collate		I
鹼[3] 鹻[3] 堿[3]	鹵 197 土 32	僉 440	Impure carbonate of soda 鹵丨 丨水 lye 丨地 salt soil 丨土		F
柬[3]	木 75	柬 505	Card, slip; memo; to select 丨帖 visiting-card		K
揀[3]	手 64	柬 505	To select, choose 丨·出·來 丨選 to choose, select 丨擇		B
簡[3]	竹 118	間 636	Bamboo slip; memo; to abridge, terse; to appoint; examine 丨章 prospectus, regulations 丨·便 more convenient, short-cut 丨·單 simple, in brief 丨截	S.	D
減[3] 减[3]	水 85	咸 344	To diminish, reduce, retrench; lighten 丨價 reduce price, bargain 丨去一半 diminish one-half 丨半 丨法 subtraction 丨色 lose color; deteriorate 丨少 lessen, diminish		D
繭[3]	糸 120	冂 556	Cocoon, pupae, 蠶丨 丨綢 coarse silk serge		F
蹇[3]	足 157	寒 100	Halt, lame 跛丨; proud		K
[illegible][3] [illegible][3]	干 51	束 501	A bunch, handful		K

Chien

見^{4}	見 147	見 865	To see, observe, 看·｜ ｜長^{3} make progress ｜·證 witness, testimony ｜解 view, opinion ｜輕 (in sickness) to be or seem ｜好 better, ｜功, ｜效 ｜笑 laughable; laugh at ｜面 have an interview, ｜｜ ｜·識 knowledge, observation ｜聞 ｜地 experience, insight ｜天 every day		A
件^{4}	人 9	牛 38	Item, thing 一｜事 C. of clothes etc. 點｜ count your goods		A
間^{4}	門 169	閒 636	Space between, to separate ｜接 indirect ｜壁 a partition wall	chien^{1}	B
澗^{4}	水 85	閒 636	Rivulet between hills 山｜		I
漸^{4}	水 85	斬 212	Gradually, by degrees, ｜次 ｜｜ gradually ｜進 gradual progress	chien^{1}	B
建^{4}	廴 54	建 670	To found, build, ｜立 ｜設 build up, construct ｜造 build, found, invent		C
健^{4} 徤^{4}	人 9	建 670	Strong, robust, to strengthen ｜壯 strong, robust ｜全 ｜康 well, hearty, 康｜		D
毽^{4}	毛 82	建 670	Shuttlecock ｜·子 踢｜ kick the shuttlecock		I
鍵^{4}	金 167	建 670	Spring, or bolt of lock 管｜ ｜閉 to lock up		G
踐^{4}	足 157	戔 332	To trample; tread, fulfil ｜壞 destroy, corrupt 作｜ ｜踏 to trample, spoil ｜殘 ｜言 fulfil one's promise		D

Chien

賤4	貝 154	戔 332	Mean, cheap; depreciate ｜價 cheap ｜姓 my humble name ｜名 ｜貨 cheap goods		A
濺4	水 85	戔 332	To spatter, dash up ｜水（泥）		H
餞4	食 184	戔 332	Farewell banquet ｜行, ｜別 ｜菓 preserved fruit		I
監4	皿 108	監 608	To examine, revise; eunuch 國子[3]｜ Hall of C'assics	chien[1]	D
檻4	木 75	監 608	Pen, railing, a cage for prisoners	hsien[4] k'an[3]	G
艦4	舟 137	監 608	War vessel 軍｜, 戰 鬭 ｜ battleship 巡 洋 ｜ cruiser 驅 逐 ｜ destroyer		E
鑑4 鑒4	金 167	監 608	Metal mirror; to examine, audit, survey; revise 航空母｜ aircraft carrier ｜察 reflect, consider, examine ｜書 historical book 通｜		F
劍4 劒4	刀 18	僉 440	Two-edged sword, rapier, 刀｜ straight sword ｜術 art of fencing 舞｜ 寶｜ trusty blade		D
箭4	竹 118	前 620	Arrow, dart; archer ｜直 directly, straight ahead 弓｜ bow and arrow, archery 射｜ to shoot an arrow		D
薦4 荐4	艸 140	鹿 319	To introduce, recommend ｜舉, 舉｜ ｜信 letter of recom. ｜書 ｜牲 sacrifice		E
諫4	言 149	柬 505	To admonish, reprove ｜規 ｜諍 rebuke, remonstrate ｜說		E
僭4	人 9	朁 801	To usurp, to arrogate to oneself ｜分 ｜妄 presumption, blasphemy ｜位 usurp a throne		F

Ch'ien

千[1]	十 24	千 24	Thousand, very many ｜金 another's daughter ｜里鏡 telescope ｜里眼 ｜萬 10 million; by all means	A
仟[1] 阡[1]	人 9	千 24	Chiliarch, thousand 阡陌 public roads in four directions, paths between fields	K
鉛[1]	金 167	㕣 719	Lead ore, lead ｜粉 white lead ｜油 ｜板 lead type, stereotype ｜字 ｜筆 lead pencil 白｜ pewter	A
遷[1] 迁[1]	辵 162	䙴 779	To move, remove ｜移, ｜居 ｜就 accommodate 押｜ evict, turn out	B
韆[1]	革 177	䙴 779	A swing 鞦·｜ 打鞦·｜ to swing	G
僉[1]	人 9	僉 440	All, unanimous ｜言如一 ｜稟 joint petition	G
簽[1]	竹 118	僉 440	Slips, lots ｜·子; subscribe ｜名 sign name ｜字 掣｜ draw lots 抽｜	B
謙[1]	言 140	兼 671	Humble, modest ｜遜 ｜讓 to yield, give way to others ｜卑 humility 太｜ over-modest 過｜	C
牽[1]	牛 93	牽 878	To pull, haul ｜◦連 connect, involve ｜牛 lead an ox ｜◦涉 implicate, ｜累	D
愆[1]	心 61	行 5	Fault, error, sin ｜尤 罪｜ crime, guilt	D
韱[1]	韭 179	韱 420	Wild garlic or onion	K

Character	Radical	Phonetic	Meaning		
籤[1]	竹 118	籤 420	Bamboo slip, tally; lot; warrant (see 簽) |·子 |筒 tube for lots 掣| drawlots, 抽|		F
鈐[1]	金 167	今 434	A seal |記, a latch |鎖 a door lock		I
黔[12]	黑 203	今 434	Black; province of Kweichow |黎 black-haired people—Chinese		G
鋟[1]	金 167	㑴 675	To engrave |刻		G
幵[1] 开[1]	干 51	幵 34	Even, level		K
錢[2] 不[2]	金 167	戔 332	Coin, cash, money S. |串 cash-strings |局 mint, bank |局·子 |·糧 taxes, revenue, military stipends |票 cash notes |鈔 |舖 a bank, cash-shop |店 |財 money, wealth		A
前[2]	刀 18	前 620	Before, front |朝 last dynasty, Ching |清 |進 progress, advance |去 go before, or forward |門 south central gate of Peking |·年 year before last, so |月 |半天 forenoon, 午| |提 premises in logic |·天 day before yesterday |日, |兒 (個)		A
乾[2]	乙 5	倝 17	Heaven; male; father |父坤母 heaven is father, earth is mother |坤 male and female |隆 Emperor Chien Lung	kan[1]	A

Character	Radical	Phonetic	Meaning	Alt.	Group
虔[2]	虍 141	文 546	Pious, devout, sincere 丨誠 reverent, devout, 丨心		D
拑[2]	手 64	甘 101	To nip, seize, 丨·住 丨釘·子 pull out a nail		K
鉗[2]	金 167	甘 101	Pincers, tongs, nippers, 丨·子		E
潛[2] 潜[2]	水 85	朁 801	To lie hid, hide, secret, careful; to abscond 丨伏 latent 丨水艇 submarine		I
淺[3]	水 85	戔 332	Shallow, easy, simple 丨見 slight experience 丨°近 plain and easy 丨深 depth, profundity, 深丨		B
遣[3]	辵 162	㠯 750	To depute, send, 丨差, 差丨 丨散 discharge, dismiss		B
欠[4]	欠 76	欠 441	To owe, debt, deficient, 缺丨 丨債 owe a debt, be in debt 丨賬 丨項 a debt 丨欵 丨單 bill, promissory note 丨帖 虧丨 be in debt, deficient in		C
縴[4]	糸 120	牽 878	Tow-rope, to haul, track 丨手 a mediator 拉丨 to track; negotiate sale		E
嵌[4]	山 46	甘 101	To inlay, inchase,鑲丨 丨銀匠 inlayer of silver		F
歉[4]	欠 76	兼 671	Inadequate: dissatisfied 丨事 an awkward business 丨收 bad harvest 丨薄		H

Chih

Character	Radical	Phonetic	Meaning	Alt.	Group
知[1]	矢 111	知 475	To know, perceive 丨己 intimate friend, 丨心 丨覺 to perceive, observe 丨·會 despatch, to inform	chih[4]	A

Chih

Character	Radical	Phonetic	Meaning	Other reading	
知[1]			丨不道 don't know 不丨·道 丨·識 knowledge 丨·道 to know 丨足 to be content, satisfied		
蜘[1]	虫 142	知 475	Spider 丨蛛		G
隻[1]	隹 172	隹 52	Classifier of birds, ships etc. 船丨 ships, shipping		A
指[1]	手 64	旨 323	丨·甲 Finger or toe nails 丨·甲套 finger-nail cases	chih[23]	B
脂[1]	肉 130	旨 323	Fat, gum; wealth 丨粉 cosmetics 丨油 lard, pork-fat		E
之[1]	丿 4	之 299	Sign of genitive; he, she, it, possessive; to go; this, that 丨乎者也 empty words, pedantry		C
芝[1]	艸 140	之 299	A kind of grass 丨草 Long-life plant; felicitous 丨·麻 sesamum		E
汁[1]	水 85	十 13	Juice, sap, 丨水 丨漿 meat or fruit juice		E
支[1]	支 65	支 539	Branch; put off; pay, advance S. 丨撐 prop up 丨會 branch church or society 丨·給 give or pay to 丨派 branch of family, tribe 丨配 to control, to allot		D
吱[1]	口 30	支 539	Hum, buzz	tzu[1]	K
枝[1]	木 75	支 539	Branch of tree, 樹丨·子 C. of slender things 丨梢 twigs, tips of branches		D
肢[1]	肉 130	支 539	The limbs 丨體 四丨百體 members of human body		C
戠[1]	戈 62	戠 93	A sword; to gather		P

Chih

織[1]	糸 120	戠 93	To weave |機 loom |布 weave cloth, so |蓆 etc.		C
擲[14]	手 64	啇 782	To throw, reject, |去 |下 throw down; give to		E
搘[1]	手 64	老 189	To prop up, shore up |·起·來 |窗·戶 prop a window		F
梔[1]	木 75	巴 312	Becho, yellow dye |·子 gardenia		K
騭[1] 隲[1]	馬 187	步 131	Stallion; to promote; determine 陰| secretly settled		K
直[2] 直[2]	目 109	直 842	Straight, straight on |接 direct, own initiative |隷 Chihli province , now 河北 |言 straight talk |話 一|·的 straight ahead		A
値[2]	人 9	直 842	Price, cost, value 價| |錢 worth money, of value |不| is it worth it?	chih[4]	B
植[2]	木 75	直 842	To plant 栽|, set up; vegetable |◦物 vegetable kingdom		E
殖[2]	歹 78	直 842	To get rich, abound 豐|; to plant |民 emigrants, |民地 colony		I
指[2]	手 64	旨 323	Finger or toe, |·頭 |·頭尖 tip of finger	chih[13]	B
職[2]	耳 128	戠 93	Official duty |任, |事 |分 duties, functions, |◦務 |員 officer		B
執[2] 执[2]	土 32	執 304	To hold, manage, seize, |持 |照 passport , license |行委辦 executive committee |拗 self-willed, obstinate |·事 manage, deacon |守 guard, maintain		C

Chih

姪^{2}	女 38	至 883	Nephew ｜兒, ｜·子 ｜·女 niece		D
紙^{3} 帋^{3}	糸 120	氏 348	Paper, document, ｜褙·子 pasteboard ｜烟 cigarette 打｜牌 to play cards		A
只^{3}	口 30	只 757	But, only ｜知 I only know ｜管 simply, just try ｜怕 but, but lest, only｜恐 ｜·是 just is, it is only ｜∘有 ｜願 only hope, would that !		A
咫^{3}	口 30	只 757	Ancient foot-measurs, 8 in. ｜尺之間 almost, very close		K
枳^{3}	木 75	只 757	Shrub thorns｜棘		F
旨^{3}	日 72	旨 323	Decree, meaning; excellent ｜意 will, import, 意｜ 宗｜scope, purpose		B
指^{3}	手 64	旨 323	Finger; to point ｜·着 pointing, referring to ｜∘揮 ｜教 point out, teach, ⌊to direct correct｜斥, ｜示 ｜∘出 point out, indicate｜明, ｜定 ｜南針 compass ｜∘望 hope, expect, desire	chih^{12}	B
止^{3}	止 77	止 126	To halt, cease; only｜住 ｜息 stop, discontinue 停｜ ｜留 detain		C
址^{3}	土 32	止 126	Foundation, boundaries 基｜foundation		E
祉^{3}	示 113	止 126	Blessedness 福｜		G
趾^{3}	足 157	止 126	Hoof, toes, foot 高｜pompous walk		G

Chih

Character	Radical	Phonetic	Meaning	Other reading	Grade
砥3	石 112	氐 349	Whetstone; to polish |·子 stone weights for exercise	ti3	K
祗3	示 113	氐 349	Only, yet; reverent | 可 the only recourse | 此 only this, nothing further		G
黹3	黹 204		To embroider, fancy-work 鍼 |		I
徵3	彳 60	徵 550	One of the five musical notes	cheng1	D
知4	矢 111	知 475	Wisdom 文	chih1	A
智4	日 72	知 475	Wisdom, knowledge, prudence |·慧, | 明 | 能 intelligence | 育 intellectual culture		C
治4	水 85	台 718	To govern, rule, heal | 掌 govern, keep in order | 理 | 好 cure 醫 | | 病 cure disease | 療		A
幟4 [illegible]4	巾 50	戠 93	A pennon, a flag, 旗 |		I
熾4	火 86	戠 93	A blaze, to burn; splendor 炎 | in a blaze		G
識4	言 149	戠 93	To keep in mind	shih24	A
至4	至 133	至 883	To arrive, to; utmost, very | 親 nearly related | 終 at last, to the end | 好 the best | 少 at the least | 多 etc. ∘ |·於 as to 甚·|·於 insomuch that		B
致4	至 133	至 883	To cause; reach; transmit; aim; extreme | 謝 convey thanks		D

Chih

致[4]			| 意 inform | 命 devote life, fatal | 身 以 | so as to cause, in order to		
窒[4]	穴 116	至 883	To stop up, block | 礙 obstacle		G
緻[4]	糸 120	至 883	Fine, close, delicate | 密 secret, close		H
值[4]	人 9	直 842	Happen, one's tnrn in course 相 | to meet 適 | just happen	chih[2]	B
置[4] 寘[4]	网 122	直 842	To set up; place, arrange; judge; buy | 買 purchase | 辦 安 | place, arrange		D
志[4]	心 61	士 65	The will, purpose | 意, 心 | |·氣 resolution, courage 氣 | |·向 resolution, purpose 定 | |·願 ideals, ambitions, volunteer		C
痣[4]	疒 104	士 65	A black spot, mole, 面 |		G
誌[4]	言 149	士 65	To remember; records, annals, | 文 | 念 keep in mind 雜 | a magazine		D
制[4]	刀 18	制 221	To regulate, restrain, govern; cut | 服 subdue, control, | 伏 |·度 rules, laws, polity | 法		D
製[4]	衣 145	制 221	Cut out; make |◦造, form | 品 manufactured goods | 藥 compound medicines		D
質[42]	貝 154	貝 856	Matter, substance; habit; plain, sincere; to confront | 點 atom | 問 inquire, investigate 原 | protoplasm 性 | characteristics		D
帙[4]	巾 50	失 481	Book-wrapper, portfolio 書 |		K

<table>
<tr><td>秩4</td><td>禾
115</td><td>失
481</td><td>Order, rank, method
| 序 order, program</td><td>D</td></tr>
<tr><td>稚4
穉4</td><td>禾
115</td><td>隹
52</td><td>Young, tender, small
| 子3 a young lad 童 |
幼 | 園 kindergarten</td><td>E</td></tr>
<tr><td>雉4</td><td>隹
172</td><td>隹
52</td><td>Pheasant, | 雞</td><td>G</td></tr>
<tr><td>痔4</td><td>疒
104</td><td>寺
46</td><td>Hemorrhoids, piles | 瘡</td><td>G</td></tr>
<tr><td>陟4</td><td>阜
170</td><td>步
131</td><td>To ascend, promotion
| 臨 go up and look down upon</td><td>G</td></tr>
<tr><td>贄4</td><td>貝
154</td><td>執
304</td><td>Make a present, homage
| 見 禮 present to teacher</td><td>G</td></tr>
<tr><td>鷙4</td><td>鳥
196</td><td>執
304</td><td>A hawk, birds of prey, | 鳥
猛 | ardent, ruthless</td><td>I</td></tr>
<tr><td>滯4</td><td>水
85</td><td>帶
560</td><td>To obstruct, hinder stoppage | 住
固 | obstinate</td><td>H</td></tr>
<tr><td>炙4</td><td>火
86</td><td>火
446</td><td>To broil, burn; dry; intimate
| 法 cautery
| 火 warm at a fire</td><td>H</td></tr>
<tr><td>胑4</td><td>肉
130</td><td>只
757</td><td>Upper arm; also for 肢</td><td>H</td></tr>
<tr><td>夂4</td><td>夂
34</td><td>夂
540</td><td>To step forward; follow</td><td>K</td></tr>
</table>

Ch'ih

<table>
<tr><td>吃1
喫1</td><td>口
30</td><td>乞
298</td><td>To eat; stammer; suffer
| 緊 urgent
| 飯 eat rice, take food
| 喝 eat and drink
| 苦 be in distress
| 虧 suffer loss
| 飽·了 eaten to the full
| 不 服 it does not agree with me
| 不 了3 cannot eat so much
|·不·得 not fit to eat
| 藥 take medicine</td><td>A</td></tr>
</table>

Ch'ih

侈[13]	人 9	多 269	Profuse, prodigal, | 費, 奢 |		F
眵[1]	目 109	多 269	Eyes blurred and sore, | 瞖 糊		I
癡[12] 痴[12]	疒 104	疑 479	Daft, silly; doting after | 情 infatuation | 獃 stupid, idiot, | 儍 |·子 idiot, simpleton		F
蚩[1]	虫 142	蚩 664	Ignorant, rustic; to despise | 民 common people, ''the masses''		K
嗤[1]	口 30	蚩 664	To laugh | 笑 laugh at		G
鴟[1]	鳥 169	氏 348	An owl | 鴞		H
笞[12]	竹 118	台 718	To bamboo, beat, flog, | 責		K
褫[14]	衣 145	虒 204	To disrobe, strip off | 脫		K
魑[1]	鬼 194	离 547	Elf, brownie | 魅		K
匙[2]	匕 21	是 139	Spoon, key	shih[2]	A
持[2]	手 64	寺 46	To grasp 執 | ,control, hold, restrain, firm | 住 hold fast, 堅 | to insist | 守 hold fast, maintain		C
池[2]	水 85	也 301	Pool, pond, tank, 水 | |·子 pool, moat, 城 | 魚 | fish-pond	S.	C
馳[2]	馬 187	也 301	To ride fast, pass quickly; | 行 | 馬 running horse		F
遲[2]	辵 162	犀 726	Slow, late, tardy; steady | 慢dilatory | 鈍 slow in thought | 延 defer, delay, | 留		D

Character	Radical	Phonetic	Meaning		
尺^{3}	尸 44	尸 724	Chinese foot-measure, a foot |^{2}·寸 length, measure, | 丈 | 度 degree, measurement	ch'e^{4}	A
恥^{3}	心 61	耳 626	Shame, ashamed, 羞 | , | 辱 | 笑 put to shame		C
齒^{3}	齒 211	止 126	Teeth | 牙, 牙 | ; age; serrated		E
斥^{4}	斤 69	斥 214	To dismiss, expel, | 逐 | 罵 to scold, abuse | 責 to reprove, blame		D
赤^{4} 烾^{4}	赤 155	赤 423	Flesh-color, red-hot | 心 sincere | 誠 | 化 Sovietized | 身 bare, naked, | 體 | 道 Equator | 子^{3} an infant		E
翅^{4} ⿰犭支^{4}	羽 124	支 539	Wing, fin, | 膀, |·子 展 | to spread the wing 魚 | shark's fins		E
飭^{4}	食 184	食 363	To order, direct, make ready | 令 a command | 行 | 催 to urge		G
勅^{4} 勑^{4} 敕^{4}	力 19 支 66	束 501	To order, permit, | 旨 | 封 imperially appointed | 令 imperial order, charter, | 命 | 賜 imperially bestowed		G
叱^{4}	口 30	匕 317	To hoot out, scold | 罵		K
彳^{4}	彳 60		To step with left foot		K

Chin

Character	Radical	Phonetic	Meaning		
斤^{1} 觔^{1}	斤 69	斤 209	Adze, hatchet; catty (1 $1/3$ lbs.) |·兩 weight | 重 斧 | axes and adzes		A

金1	金 167	金 79	Gold, metal, precious S. ｜安 welfare, health ｜雞 納 quinine, cinchona ｜融 currency; money market ｜剛 石 diamond ｜礦 gold mine ｜葉 gold leaf ｜銀 gold and silver, money ｜魚 gold fish		A
今1	人 9	今 434	Now, 現｜, 如｜, ｜時 ｜·年 this year ｜世 the present age ｜·天 to-day｜日, ｜兒 (個)		A
衿1 紟1	衣 145	今 434	A sash, string, elders ｜者 gentry		G
津1	水 85	聿 669	Ford, mart, sap	ching1	A
巾1	巾 50	巾 557	Napkin, towel, 手·｜ ｜帕 kerchief, turban, 頭｜		A
禁1	示 113	林 492	To bear, endure. ｜使 ｜穿 stand wear ｜不住 cannot bear	chin4	C
襟1	衣 145	林 492	A garment, lapel, literati ｜章 a medal ｜兄 弟 brother-in-law ｜懷 the feelings		D
筋1	竹 118	力 223	Sinews, tendons, muscle ｜骨 痛 rheumatism 腦｜brain, nerves		D
浸14	水 85	㑴 675	To soak, immerse ｜禮 會 Baptists. ｜信 會 ｜濕 wet, soaked, ｜透	ch'in4	E
緊3	糸 120	臤 643	Tight, urgent, important ｜挨 着 close to ｜急 urgent, pressing		A

Chin

緊 3
| 要 important 要 |
手 | hard up
嚴 | closely, strictly

堇 3 — 土 32 — 堇 106 — Loess, clay, 赤 | — K

僅 3 — 人 9 — 堇 106 — Barely, only, just | | — D
| 夠 just enough | 足

瑾 3 — 玉 96 — 堇 106 — Brilliant, luster — I
| 瑜 brilliant gem

覲 3 — 見 147 — 堇 106 — Audience with Emperor, 朝 | , | 見 — K

謹 3 — 言 149 — 堇 106 — Cautious, respectful, watchful — F
| 防 carefully guard
|∘愼 careful, cautious
| 守 guard carefully

饉 3 — 食 184 — 堇 106 — Dearth, famine 饑 | — H

儘 3 — 人 9 — 盡 607 — Utmost, extreme, barely — H
| 先 the very first, so | 末 後

錦 3 — 金 167 — 帛 806 — Brocade, embroider, elegant | 繡 — F
| 言 complimentary language

巹 3 — 卩 26 — 丞 522 — Nuptial, wine-cup — K
合 | to drink the nuptial cup

進 4 — 辵 162 — 隹 52 — To enter, advance; offer — A
|·去 enter | 入
|∘項 income | 欵
| 化 civilization, evolution
| 口 貨 imported goods
| 貢 present tribute
|∘步 progress | 行, | 益

劤 4 — 力 19 — 斤 209 — Strong, brawny — H
| 頭 strength | 兒
不 吃 | unavailing, ineffective
使 | make vigorous effort

近 4 — 辵 162 — 斤 209 — Near, draw near, recently 相 | — A
| 些 a little nearer

Chin

Character	Radical	Phonetic	Meaning		
近[4]			丨來 recently 丨日, 丨時 丨事 latest news 丨聞 丨東 Near East		
盡[4] 尽[4]	皿 108	盡 607	To exhaust, all, the uttermost 丨皆 all, every-one 丨忠 absolutely loyal 丨心 with whole heart 丨義務 do volunteer service 丨本分 perform one's duty 丨責 to do one's whole duty		C
燼[4]	火 86	盡 607	Ashes, embers, remnant 丨餘		H
禁[4]	示 113	林 492	To forbid, prohibit 丨城 forbidden city 丨止 forbid, prohibit, 丨戒 丨食 to fast 丨卒 jailer, turnkey	chin[1]	C
凚[4]	冫 15	林 492	Cold, chilled 打冷丨 a cold shiver		H
噤[4]	口 30	林 492	Unable to speak 丨口痢 tetanus, lock-jaw		K
勁[4]	力 19	巠 427	Muscular, strong, force 丨力 or 丨頭 strength 對丨 matched, congenial	ching[4]	G
晉[4] 晋[4]	日 72	㚘 35	To advance 丨朝 Chin dynasty 265-317 A.D. 丨封 posthumous honours 丨國 state in Shansi 737-420 B.C. 丨謁 to have a personal interview		G
縉[4]	糸 120	㚘 35	Carnation silk 丨紳 gentry		K
妗[4]	女 38	今 434	Wife's sisters, 丨娘		K
㪲[4]	又 29	㪲 675	To invade		P

Ch'in

親^{1}	見 147	親 87	To love, approach, self, relative ｜愛 love dearly ｜·戚 relatives ｜屬, ｜族 ｜·近 intimate, closely related ｜朋 relatives and friends ｜友 ｜身 one self ｜自 ｜手 personally, by own hand ｜嘴 a kiss, to kiss	ch'ing^{4}	A
侵^{1}	人 9	𠬶 675	To invade, appropriate, usurp ｜佔 encroach, usurp ｜犯		D
欽^{1}	欠 76	金 79	Imperial, to respect ｜差 envoy, minister		F
琴^{2}	玉 96	玨 77	Harp, lute, organ, etc. ｜瑟 harps and lutes, harmony ｜韻 music of the harp, etc. 彈｜ play instrument		B
勤^{2}	力 19	堇 106	Laborious, diligent ｜謹 diligently attentive ｜勞 laborious, painstaking ｜力		B
懃^{2}	心 61	堇 106	Zealous, earnest 慇·｜ careful, attentive		G
禽^{2}	内 114	离 547	Birds in general 飛｜ ｜獸 animals		D
噙^{2}	口 30	离 547	To hold in mouth ｜在口裏		K
擒^{2} 捦^{2}	手 64	离 547	To seize, arrest, clutch, grasp ｜獲 apprehend, arrest ｜捉 ｜拿 seize, take ｜住		F
芹^{2}	艸 140	斤 209	Celery, parsley ｜菜, ｜酌 feast to hsiu-ts'ai		F
秦^{2}	禾 115	𡗗 469	A dynasty ｜°朝; Shensi ｜椒 a kind of pepper ｜國 state in Shensi 897-221 B.C. 大｜ Syria	S.	G

Char.	Radical	Phonetic	Meaning		
衾[2]	衣 145	今 434	Quilt, coverlet, shroud ｜被 bedding, ｜枕		G
芩[2]	艸 140	今 434	Salt-marsh plant 黃｜		K
寢[3]	宀 40	㝲 675	To sleep, rest ｜寐, ｜息 ｜車 sleeping-car ｜室 bed-room, dormitory		F
浸[4]	水 85	㝲 675	To steep, immerse, baptize	chin[14]	E
吣[4] 唚[4]	口 30	心 377	To belch out, vomit 狗｜ 胡｜ to rail, abuse		H
沁[4]	水 85	心 377	To sound, fathom, soak ｜入		K

Ching

Char.	Radical	Phonetic	Meaning		
巠[1]	巛 47	巠 427	Streams (underground)		K
涇[1]	水 85	巠 427	A river, to flow through ｜涎		K
經[1] 経[1]	糸 120	巠 427	Past, a classic, ｜書 ｜濟 finances, economics ｜°費 expenditure, outlay ｜線 parallel of longitude ｜管 (my business) to look after ｜°過 pass by, have experienced ｜°歷 secretary; experience ｜°驗 ｜營 to transact, carry on 聖｜ Scripture, Bible	S.	A
莖[1]	艸 140	巠 427	Culm of grass, stalk 蓮｜ lotus stalk		H
睛[1]	目 109	青 82	Iris, eye-ball, pupil 眼·｜ the eyes		A
菁[1]	艸 140	青 82	Leafy, luxuriant, ｜華 韭｜ flower of the leek		I

Ching

精^1 米 119 青 82 Unmixed, fine, essence; semen, vigor; smart, versed in — B
| 金 pure gold
| 細 fine, subtle | 密
|·明 clear, intelligent
| 兵 picked troops
|·神 mind, soul, spirit, energy, animating purpose
| 微 minute, abstruse

蜻^1 虫 142 青 82 Dragon-fly |∘蜓 — ch'ing^1 — H

京^1 亠 8 京 747 Metropolis, capital | 都, | 城 — A
南∘| Nanking, 北 | Peking

鯨^1 魚 195 京 747 Whale | 魚 — 俗 — ch'ing^2 — G

更^1 曰 73 更 834 Night watch ,五 | 天 — 俗 — keng^{14} — A
| 夫 watchman 打 | 的
五 | 天 fifth watch, 3 A. M.

粳^1 粇^1 米 119 更 834; 秔^1 禾 115 Long white rice — keng^1 — H
| 米 dry soil rice 旱 稻 | 米

津^1 水 85 聿 669 Ford, mart, sap, | 口 — chin^1 — A
天·| Tientsin

耕^1 耒 127 井 415 To plough, | 地 — 俗 — keng^1 — D
| 種 plowing and sowing

驚^1 馬 187 敬 228 To alarm, startle, terrify — D
| 嚇 frighten | 動 startle, trouble
| 慌 affright, dismay

荊^1 艸 140 刑 34a Thorns, thorny, | 樹 — S. — D
| 棘 thorns, brambles. | 榛

兢^1 儿 10 克 704 To fear, cautious — E
| 懼 trembling, anxious 戰 |

矜^1 矛 110 今 434 To pity, boast, attend to — E
| 張 to boast | 誇

Ching

Character	Radical	Phonetic	Meaning		Alt.	
晶1	日 72	日 792	Crystal, quartz, luster, 水 丨			F
旌1	方 70	㫃 265	A banner 丨 旗, insignia, to mark			H
井3	二 7	井 415	Well, deep pit, 水 丨 丨 口 well-mouth	S.		B
穽3 陫3	穴 116	井 415	Hole, pitfall, snare 陷 丨 tumble into pit			H
景3	日 72	景 748	A view, appearance 丨·緻 view, scenery 丨 感 environment, atmosphere 丨∘況 circumstances 丨 象, 光 丨	S.		C
警3 儆3	言 149	敬 228	To warn, caution, alarm 丨 察廳 (or 局) police station 丨 戒 caution, warn 丨 教 丨 省 awake, watchful 丨 告 warn, give alarm 丨 備 prepared for emergencies			C
頸3	頁 181	巠 427	The neck, throat, 丨·子, 丨 項 丨 帶 a necktie 丨 巾		keng3	D
勁4	力 19	巠 427	Strong, muscular		chin4	G
徑4 俓4	彳 60	巠 427	A short-cut, diameter, direct 路 丨 road, cross-road 旁 丨 by-path, foot-path			F
脛4	肉 130	巠 427	The shin-bone, shank 丨 骨		hsing4	G
逕4	辵 162	巠 427	To pass, approach, direct 丨 啓 者 I beg to inform you 丨 情 straightforward disposition			I
淨4 凈4	水 85	爭 413	Pure, limpid, spotless; net 丨 口 to rinse the mouth 丨 利 the net profit 潔 丨 clean, cleanse, 乾·丨			A

靜^4	青 174	爭 413	Silence, calm, quiet 安·｜ ｜思 think quietly ｜聽 listen closely		C
竟^4	立 117	竟 94	End, finally, only, to utmost ｜然 ｜敢 do you dare? 究｜ after all, at last 畢｜, ｜自		B
境^4	土 32	竟 94	Region, place, circumstances, ｜地 ｜界 boundary, frontier ｜·遇 environment, circumstances ｜內 in the region		C
鏡^4	金 167	竟 94	Mirror ｜·子 千里｜ telescope 望遠｜ 顯微｜ microscope 眼｜ glasses, spectacles		B
敬^4	攴 66	敬 228	To revere, sedate, respectful ｜愛 venerate, ｜畏 ｜啓者 form for opening letter ｜奉 worship ｜神, ｜拜		C
競^4 誩^4	立 117	兄 755	To strive, emulate, dispute ｜存 struggle for existence 爭｜ to wrangle ｜爭 compete		D
靖^4	立 117	青 82	To quiet, pacify; plan 安｜ peace and quiet		E
甑^4	瓦 98	曾 832	A steamer, to steam 俗	tseng^4	H

Ch'ing

輕^1	車 159	巠 427	Light, to esteem lightly ｜｜·的 lightly, ｜易 ｜重 weight, estimation ｜易不 rarely does ｜看 despise ｜視 ｜省 light, easy, unburdened		A

Ch'ing

靑[1]	靑 174	靑 82	Colour of nature, green, blue, black ｜年 youth; young ｜年會 Y.M.C.A. ｜草 green grass 女｜年會 Y.W.C.A.		B
淸[1]	水 85	靑 82	Pure, clear, ringing ｜賬 settled account ｜◦朝 the Manchu dynasty 大｜ ｜眞教 Mohammedanism ｜潔 pure, clean ｜淨 ｜·楚 clear, settled ｜｜楚楚 ｜心 pure heart ｜◦明 feast of the tombs ｜單 invoice, memo		B
傾[12]	人 9	頃 867	To upset, overturn, pour out; melt ｜家 ruin family ｜向 tendency ｜國 subvert country		E
卿[1]	卩 26	卽 364	High minister, noble, ｜相		G
情[2]	心 61	靑 82	Feelings, emotions, affections; facts ｜·形 condition, aspect ｜狀 ｜緒 sensibilites , emotions ｜理 reason, in acc. with facts ｜慾 desire, lust ｜◦願（意）to wish, be willing. ｜甘 人｜ human feelings, social duties 事·｜ an affair, matter		A
晴[2]	日 72	靑 82	Clear, blue sky. ｜日，｜天 天｜·了 cleared off. 雨｜		A
頃[2]	頁 181	頃 867	A moment, just now ｜刻	ch'ing[3]	E
鯨[2]	魚 195	京 747	Whale ｜魚	ching[1]	G

Character	Radical	Phonetic	Meaning		Other reading	
擎^{2}	手 64	敬 228	To raise up, lift up ｜受 receive respectfully			H
請^{3}	言 149	靑 82	To request, invite; please ｜安 to salute, greet ｜假 ask leave of absence ｜吃 飯 invite for feast ｜求 to petition; to request ｜先·生 engage a teacher ｜客 give a feast ｜大·夫 call a doctor ｜坐 please be seated			A
頃^{3}	頁 181	頃 867	100 mu of land ｜畝 acreage		ch'ing^{2}	E
檾^{3} 䔛^{3}	木 75	𤇾 448	Tall hemp used for rope ｜蔴 hemp, jute			K
親^{4}	見 147	親 87	｜·家 Relatives	俗	ch'in^{1}	A
慶^{4}	心 61	心 377	To congratulate, ｜賀, ｜祝 ｜祝 會 a celebration ｜賀會 ｜新 年 New Year greetings			C
殸^{4}	殳 79	殸 404	Stone chimes			P
磬^{4}	石 112	殸 404	Stone chimes, inverted bell ｜音 the sound of the ch'ing			G
罄^{4}	缶 121	殸 404	Empty, exhausted, stern, strict ｜盡 completely exhausted			G

Chiu

Character	Radical	Phonetic	Meaning		Other reading	
究^{14}	穴 116	九 302	To investigate; after all ｜察 examine, investigate 追｜ ｜竟 at last, after all ｜之			C
鳩^{1}	鳥 196	九 302	Turtle-dove, pigeon 斑｜ partridge, pigeon			E

Chiu

揪[1]	手 64	秋 450	To clutch, pinch, pull 丨·着 丨·住 grasp tightly		C
鬮[1] 䦰[1]	鬥 191	龜 316	A lot, ballot, top 拈丨 to draw lots 抓丨		F
柩[14]	木 75	久 430	Coffin with corpse 丨車 a hearse		G
丩[1]	丨 2	丩 161	To join, twine		K
糾[13] 糺[13]	糸 120	丩 161	To collect, league, thin, to twist, examine, announce 丨合 bring people together 丨衆		I
酋[1]	酉 164	酋 782	Fermented liquor, to end 丨長 a chief	ch'iu²	K
九[3] 玖[3]	乙 5	九 302	Nine 丨·個; highest, deep 丨江 Kiukiang 丨丨arithmetic; 81 days winter 丨月丨 ch'ung yang festival		A
酒[3]	酉 164	酉 781	Liquor, wine, alcohol 丨政 cupbearer 丨·錢 bonus, cumshaw 丨精 alcohol 丨盅 small wine-cup 丨杯 丨館 wine shop 丨舖, 丨店 丨醉 drunken		A
久[3]	丿 4	久 430	For a long time, long since 丨已 丨交 long intercourse 丨違 long separated or disregarded 丨仰 long desired to meet 長丨 long time, in perpetuity 丨遠 日丨 many days, long time 許丨		B
灸[3]	火 86	久 430	To cauterize, blister 丨瘡		K
韭[3] 韮[3]	韭 179	韭 419	Scallions, leeks, 丨·菜		F

Chiu

臼[4]	臼 134	臼 680	A mortar |·子 門 | socket for door-pivot	K
舊[4] 旧[4]	臼 134	臼 680	Old, worn out, formerly | 金 山 California | 日 former times, | 時 | 年 last year | 約 Old Testament 原 | the same, as before	A
舅[4]	臼 134	臼 680	Maternal uncle. |·|, |°父 大 |·子, 小 |·子 wife's brothers	E
就[4]	尢 43	尢 175	Towards; then, at once, thereupon, avail of; complete |·着 avail of | 來 will come at once 這 | 來 |·是 it is just, even if |·是·了 that is all | 手 along with, incidentally | 他 來 come to him | 得·了 will do very well 成 | to accomplish, perfect 造·| to build up, edify	A
救[4]	支 66	求 524	To save, help 拯 | | 急 relieve anxiety |·濟 relieve, succor | 苦 | 主 Savior | 世 主 Jesus | 命 save life, murder! | 拔 save, rescue | 護, | 援 | 世 軍 The Salvation Army	B
咎[4]	口 30	咎 714	Fault, crime, blame, | 罪 引 | take blame on self	G
疚[4]	疒 104	久 430	Chronic disease; incorrigible | 惡 災 | an epidemic	K

Ch'iu

Character	Radical	Phonetic	Meaning			
秋[1] 穐[1]	禾 115	秋 450	Autumn, harvest, cool 丨季 autumn season 丨·天 丨分 autumnal equinox 丨後 in the autumn	S.		A
楸[1]	木 75	秋 450	A species of catalpa 丨樹			H
鞦[1]	革 177	秋 450	Traces, crupper 丨·韆 a swing		yu[1]	H
鰍[1]	魚 195	秋 450	Eel, lizard, 泥·丨			K
丘[1]	一 1	丘 213	A mound, Confucius' name (read mou[3]某); C. of mounds 丨陵 a mound, 丨·子 brick grave above ground			G
蚯[1]	虫 142	丘 213	Earth-worm 丨·蚓			K
邱[1]	邑 163	丘 213	A mound 丨園 one's home	S.		G
求[2]	水 85	求 524	To entreat, seek, aim at 丨情 ask a favor 丨恩 丨福 pray for happiness 丨告 to pray 祈丨, 懇丨 丨雨 pray for rain 有丨必應 "ask and receive"			A
俅[2]	人 9	求 524	To wear a cap, 丨冠			K
毬[2] 毯[2]	毛 82	求 524	A ball, knob, balloon, (used as 球) 氣丨 a balloon			F
球[2]	玉 96	求 524	Round gem, sphere 筐丨 basket-ball, 籃丨 踢丨 to kick the ball 網丨 tennis; 足丨 foot ball			B

Character	Radical	Phonetic	Meaning		Other reading	Grade
裘²	衣 145	求 524	Furs 丨裳 fur clothes	S.		H
仇²	人 9	九 302	Surname	S.	ch'ou²	C
囚²	口 31	人 429	Prison, to imprison, prisoner 丨禁 confine in cage or prison 丨犯 criminal, prisoner			D
泅²	水 85	人 429	To swim, float			H
糗³	米 119	自 852	Parched rice, etc. 丨糧 cured dry grain			G
𩞄³	食 184	自 852	Food spoiled or broken			H

Chiung

Character	Radical	Phonetic	Meaning		Other reading	Grade
窘³	穴 116	君 678	Distressed, in straits, to persecute 丨迫 straitened, pressed 丨急			F
冂³	冂 13	冂 556	Border, waste land			K
冋³ 埛³	冂 13	冋 578	Desert, border waste 畝丨 a desert, prairie, wild			K
逈³	辵 162	冋 578	Far apart, different, 丨別 丨不相同 not at all alike			G

Ch'iung

Character	Radical	Phonetic	Meaning		Other reading	Grade
穹²	穴 116	弓 244	Lofty, vast 丨蒼 the heavens			F
窮² 竆²	穴 116	弓 244	Poor, exhaust, thoroughly, the end 丨究 thoroughly investigate 丨乏 poor, in poverty, 貧丨 丨日·子 poor living 丨苦 wretched, miserable 丨困 無丨盡 inexhaustible, infinite			A

Character	Radical	Phonetic	Meaning	Other readings	
睘[2]	目 109	睘 371	Alone, alarmed, desolate		P

Cho

Character	Radical	Phonetic	Meaning	Other readings	
卓[14]	十 24	卓 15	Surpassing, lofty, deep, 超丨 S. 丨著 eminent; established		K
棹[1] 桌[1]	木 75	卓 15	Table, stand 丨·子 丨單 table-cover 八仙丨 square table for eight 擺丨 set the table	chao[4]	A
拙[12]	手 64	出 665	Stupid, clumsy 丨性 丨計 stupid plan 丨笨 clumsy, stupid 愚丨 dull, simple, rustic		C
捉[1]	手 64	足 133	Seize, arrest, catch 丨住 丨拿 arrest, seize 丨獲		C
涿[1]	水 85	豕 292	To drop, trickle 丨濕 丨縣 Cho Hsien in Hopei		H
着[2]	目 109	目 841	Right, to just hit	chao[12] che[2]	A
著[2]	艸 140	者 192	To attain, present part 丨緊 diligent, energetic 丨意 intentionally 丨落 resting place, home 丨手 to turn hand to a work	chao[2] che[2] chu[4]	C
酌[2]	酉 164	勺 231	To deliberate, consult 丨量, 丨議 丨酒 pour out wine 丨定 decide after consideration 斟·丨 think over	chao[14]	D
濁[2]	水 85	蜀 788	Muddy, turbid, stupid 丨意 muddy ideas		F
鐲[2]	金 167	蜀 788	Cymbal, bracelet 丨·子, 手丨		F
擢[2]	手 64	翟 57	To select, promote, employ 丨取 select for employment, 丨用		G

Character	Radical	Phonetic	Meaning	Other reading	Code
濯²	水 85	翟 57	To rinse, purify, wash, 洗｜ ｜手 wash hands, ｜足 wash feet		F
琢²	玉 96	豖 292	To cut (gems) 彫｜ ｜工 a lapidary ｜磨 to rub, polish		G
叕⁴	又 29	叕 534	To connect		P
啜⁴ 𣢕⁴ 歠⁴	口 30 欠 76	叕 534	To drink noisily, suck, sip ｜泣 to sob and weep ｜面 to kiss	ch'o⁴	K
啄⁴	口 30	豖 292	To peck up food, ｜食 ｜毛 plume the feathers		K
妁⁴	女 38	勺 231	A go-between	shuo²⁴	K
辵⁴ 辶⁴	辵 162		To run fast and stop	ch'o⁴	K

Ch'o

Character	Radical	Phonetic	Meaning	Other reading	Code
綽¹⁴	糸 120	卓 15	Spacious, liberal, generous, 寬·｜ ｜號 nickname, fancy name ｜態 gentle, loving ｜約	ch'ao¹⁴	G
擉¹	手 64	蜀 788	To spear, pinch, ｜刺 ｜碰 run against, collide		I
戳¹	戈 62	翟 57	A stamp, to stab, ｜·子 ｜印 a seal		F
觸⁴	角 148	蜀 788	To butt, move, offend, stir ｜犯 purposely offend ｜動 stir up, provoke ｜怒	ch'u⁴	E
黜⁴	黑 203	出 665	To dismiss, degrade	ch'u⁴	G

Chou

Character	Radical	Phonetic	Meaning	Other reading	Code
州¹	川 47	州 426	District, city, department ｜里 a neighborhood		C

Chou

洲^{1}	水 85	州 426	Island 大｜ continent 亞｜ Asia		B
周^{1}	口 30	周 730	On all sides, complete S. ｜∘朝 a dynasty, B.C. 1122-255 ｜全 complete ｜流 to wander, rove ｜備 fully prepared ｜全 ｜∘到 considerate, adequate ｜圍 all around, surround ｜遍		C
賙^{1}	貝 154	周 730	To bestow alms ｜給 ｜濟 to assist, relieve		D
週^{1}	辵 162	周 730	To revolve, year, week ｜刊 weekly paper 一｜ one turn, revolution, one week		E
粥^{1}	米 119	米 517	Congee, gruel, mush ｜廠 soup kitchen for poor 喝｜ eat porridge or cereal		C
舟^{1}	舟 137	舟 568	A boat, ship, saucer ｜人 boatman 方｜ the Ark		E
謅^{1}	言 149	芻 663	To jest, rail ｜謊 exaggerations and lies	tsou^{1}	G
妯^{2}	女 38	由 818	Sisters-in-law ｜·娌	chu^{2}	G
軸^{2}	車 159	由 818	Axle-tree, pivot 車｜ C. of scrolls, etc. ｜·子 roller for scrolls	chu^{2}	E
帚^{3} 箒^{3}	巾 50	帚 674	A broom, besom ｜星 a broom-star—comet 笤·｜ a broom 掃·｜	ch'u^{4}	E
肘^{3}	肉 130	寸 18	Elbow, forearm, a cubit ｜腋 under armpit, side 胳臂｜ elbow		F
呪^{4} 詋^{4}	口 30	兄 755	To curse, imprecate, ｜詛 ｜罵 abuse, revile ｜語 curses, spells 念｜ recite incantations 誦｜		C

Character	Radical	Phonetic	Meaning	
晝4	日 72	聿 669	Daylight, day time, 白 | | 寢 sleep in daytime | 夜 day and night	D
宙4	宀 40	由 818	The universe, infinite time 宇 | universe, all things	D
胄4 伷4	肉 130	由 818	Descendants, posterity | 子3 eldest son 世 | a nobleman	F
冑4	冂 13		A helmet 甲 | armour and helmets	
皺4	皮 107	芻 663	Wrinkled, creased | 眉 frown | 紋 wrinkles in face	G
縐4	糸 120	芻 663	Crape, wrinkles, to shrink | 紗 crape | 紬 | 紋 wrinkles in cloth	F
紂4	糸 120	寸 18	An infamous king	I

Ch'ou

Character	Radical	Phonetic	Meaning	
抽1 ⿰扌秀1	手 64	由 818	To draw out, levy, shrink, strike | 籤 draw lots | 瘋 have a fit | 象 abstract | 一 下·子 give a blow with whip | 冷·子 suddenly |·屜 drawer	A
搊1	手 64	芻 663	To grasp, crumple up |·起·來	H
酬2 酧2 醻2	酉 164	州 426	To pledge, thank | 謝, | 恩 | 報 requite | 答 | 應 to recompense 應·| to entertain	B

Ch'ou

仇² 讐² 讎²	人 9 言 149	九 302	To hate, revenge, enemy | 恨 hatred, animosity | 人 enemy, | 敵 | 視 to be hostile to 報 | take revenge		C
愁²	心 61	秋 450	Sad, anxious, to grieve 發 | | 煩 apprehensive, anxious | 人 vexatious | 容 sorrowful looks		C
稠²	禾 115	周 730	Crowded, dense, thick | 密 | 粥 thick porridge | 人 a crowd of people		D
綢² 紬²	糸 120	周 730	Silk goods, fine texture |·子 | 緞 silks and satins		D
儔²	人 9	壽 66	A company of four, partner. friend, who? | 伴 companions		I
疇²	田 102	壽 66	Cultivated field 田 | ; who? 古 | formerly | 日, | 昔		K
籌²	竹 118	壽 66	To calculate, a plan; tally | 計 calculate | 畫 consider, plan for | 備 prepare for action, supply | 算 reckon, count		D
瞅³ 矁³ [illegible]³	目 109	秋 450	To look at, gaze at | 準·了 saw with certainty | 睖·了 stare vacantly | 不 見 can not see it 你 |·| take a look at it		E
醜³	酉 164	鬼 808	Ugly, shameful, deformed | 陋 | 事 disgraceful affair		E
丑³	一 1	丑 676	Second horary, fourth watch | 兒 a comedian, 小 | | 時 fourth watch, 1-3 A.M.		G

臭[4]	自 132	自 852	To stink, smell ｜氣 bad smell, stench, ｜味 ｜名 bad reputation	hsiu[4]	E

Chu

猪[1] 豬[1]	犬 94	者 192	Pig, swine ｜圈 pig-pen, pig-sty ｜窩 ｜肉 pork ｜毛 bristles ｜油 lard		A
諸[1]	言 149	者 192	All, every ｜凡; final of doubt; S. at, on ｜人 all persons ｜葛 double surname S. ｜國 all nations ｜般 every kind or sort ｜品 ｜位 all of you ｜公 Gentlemen! 不識有｜not know if so or not 視｜斯 look at this		C
朱[1]	木 75	朱 499	Vermilion, red, ｜色, ｜紅色 S. ｜熹 Chu Hsi (commentator)		E
株[1]	木 75	朱 499	Tree-trunk ｜幹 C. of trees, posts, etc. ｜守 to adhere to		I
珠[1]	玉 96	朱 499	Pearl, bead, fine ｜寶 pearls and precious stones 珍｜pearls, jewels 串｜string of pearls, references		D
硃[1]	石 112	朱 499	Vermillion, Imperial ｜筆 Imperial pen 銀｜vermillion powder		F
蛛[1]	虫 142	朱 499	Spider ｜｜ ｜｜網 spider's web		E
誅[1]	言 149	朱 499	To punish, destroy, kill ｜殺 ｜滅 exterminate		G

Chu

主^{2}	丶 3	主 81	丨·意 A firm decision, plan	chu^{3}	B
竹^{2}	竹 118	竹 7	Bamboo 丨器 bamboo ware 丨竿 bamboo pole, rod 丨杆 丨林 bamboo grove 丨笋 bamboo shoots		D
築^{24}	竹 118	竹 7	To ram, build, make mud wall 丨城 build city wall		D
逐^{24}	辵 162	豕 285	To expel, drive out, 丨出, 趕丨 丨— one after another, seriatim 丨個 丨日 day by day 丨字 word by word, verbatim		D
燭^{2} 烛^{2}	火 86	蜀 788	Torch, candle, to illumine 丨剪 snuffers 丨力 candle-power 幾丨 丨焰 candle-flame 蠟丨 a candle		E
朮^{2}	木 75	朮 491	Medicine, plant 蒼丨	shu^{2}	K
豖^{2}	豕 152	豖 292	A shackled pig		P
丶^{3}	丶 3		A point, as of a flame		K
主^{3}	丶 3	主 81	Lord, master, host 丨·張 advocate, manage; opinion 丨前 B.C. 丨後 A.D. 丨席 chairman, leader, toastmaster 丨義 doctrine, policy, spirit, -ism 丨·人 host, master 丨日 Christian Sabbath 丨日學 Sunday school 丨筆 an editor 丨宰 to rule, supreme ruler	chu^{2}	B

Chu

Character	Radical	Phonetic	Meaning	Grade
主^3			｜動（力）motive power, chief mover 救｜Savior 作｜be master, decide	
拄^3	手 64	主 81	To shore-up, a crutch ｜拐 walk with stick ｜杖, ｜棍	I
麈^3	鹿 198	主 81	Chinese elk, yak ｜尾 yak's tail, fly brush	K
煮^3 煑^3	火 86	者 192	To boil, cook, decoct ｜爛·了 boiled soft, or too much ｜餑餑 meat dumplings	C
囑^3 嘱^3	口 30	蜀 788	To bid, order, direct ｜·咐 enjoin upon ｜託 request to do	D
住^4	人 9	主 81	To live, dwell, cease, firm, auxiliary verb of firmness ｜宅 residence ｜家 private house, live at home ｜·下 reside, stop ｜∘宿 spend a night ｜店 stay at an inn	A
'柱^4	木 75	主 81	Pillar, post ｜·子 ｜脚 foot of pillar ｜墩 ｜頂石 stone pillar-capital	C
注^4	水 85	主 81	To fix eyes or mind on, take notice, emphasize; to flow out ｜·重 emphasize ｜意 take notice ｜目 ｜射 to inject ｜音 indicate pronunciation	C
炷^4	火 86	主 81	Wick, to light, 燈｜ C. of incense sticks ｜香 burn incense	I
蛀^4	虫 142	主 81	Moth, book-worm ｜虫 to moth-eat ｜木虫 wood-eating insect	D

Chu

Character	Radical	Phonetic	Meaning		Other readings	
註^{4}	言 149	主 81	Note, comment, to define, ｜詮 ｜解 commentary ｜釋, ｜·子 ｜明 make clear			D
駐^{4}	馬 187	主 81	To lodge, reside, colonize ｜劄 stationed at ｜紮			F
助^{4}	力 19	助 624	To assist, help 帮｜, secondary ｜錢 assist with money ｜銀 協｜ to co-ōperate			A
祝^{4}	示 113	兄 755	Praise, thanks, to pray ｜禱 to pray ｜告 ｜福 invoke blessing ｜謝 thank God	S.		B
著^{4}	艸 140	者 192	Clear, to display 昭｜, 顯｜ ｜名 famous, notorious ｜書 make a book ｜·作 ｜作家 an author		chao^{2} che^{2} cho^{2}	C
箸^{4} 筯^{4}	竹 118	者 192	Chopsticks, take up food 火｜兒 a poker			G
鑄^{4}	金 167	壽 66	To fuse, cast metal, coin ｜鐘 cast a bell ｜幣廠 a mint			D
竺^{42}	竹 118	竹 7	A bamboo 天｜國 India	S.		G
宁^{4}	宀 40	宁 4	Space behind throne 朝｜			K
佇^{4} 竚^{4}	人 9	宁 4	To await, expect 望｜ hopefully expect ｜望			I
苧^{4}	艸 140	宁 4	China grass, hemp ｜麻 ｜店 grass-cloth shop			K
貯^{4}	貝 154	宁 4	To store, store-house ｜棧 ｜收 store up ｜存			I
杼^{4}	木 75	予 114	The shuttle with web, long			K

Ch'u

出[1] 凵 17 出 665 A

Out, to spring, from
| 產 natural products | 品
| 氣 aspirated
| 主[2]·意 offer plan, resolve
|·去 to go out, so |·來
| 汗 to perspire
| 學 leave school
| 閣 a woman marries | 門·子
| 口 export, | 口 稅 export duty
| 門 go out, to go abroad
| 版 to publish, an edition
| 殯 a funeral
| 頭 take the lead
| 外 go abroad | 遠 門
| 於 to proceed from | 乎

初[1] 刀 18 刀 219 A

At first, the first, to begin
| 起 the beginning 起 |
| 一 first of month, so | 二 etc.
| 生 first born
| 等 (or 級) 小 學 primary school
| 次 first time

齣[1] 齒 211 句 227 H

Stanza, couplet, play
一 | 戲 play-act, short play

廚[2] 厨[2] 广 53 尌 738 A

Kitchen, cook house | 房
|·子 cook |·師·傅

躕[2] 足 157 尌 738 K

Puzzled, undecided
躊·| irresolute, to hesitate

除[2] 阜 170 余 31 B

To exclude, subtract, division
|∘去 annul, remove, except
| 法 arithmetical division
|∘非 except, only if
|·了 aside from, not counting

Ch'u

除²			|滅 utterly destroy |皮 net weight |·掉 dispense with, remove		
芻² 蒭²	艸 140	芻 663	Hay, straw; to cut |草 grass, weeds |言 simple words		K
雛² 鶵²	隹 172	芻 663	Chick, fledgling, young; to rear, brood |雞 young chicken |鴿 young pigeon		E
鋤² 鉏²	金 167	助 624	A hoe |·頭, to hoe; mattock |板 head of hoe |地 hoe ground		F
儲²	人 9	者 192	To collect, store |收 S. |君 heir-apparent |蓄銀行 savings bank		G
躇²	足 157	者 192	Undecided 躊·|		K
楚³	木 75	林 492	Painful; orderly, clear |國 ancient state B. C. 740-330 清·| clear, distinct, settled 苦| distressful, grievous		B
礎³	石 112	林 492	Pedestal, foundation 基|		H
處³ 䖏³ 処³	虍 141 減	几 396	To dwell; judge, punish |治 regulate, punish |制 |女 a virgin, maiden 一塊兒|事 work together 同| live together	ch'u⁴	B
杵³	木 75	午 37	A pestle, to pound |碎 to pound small 砧| washerman's pounder		G
楮³	木 75	者 192	Mulberry tree |桑 |紙 mulberry paper		I

處^{4}	虍 141	几 396	Place, condition ; stop, rest | 所 a place, occasion 好·| a good advantage, 長·| 各 | everywhere 短·| disadvantage, shortcoming	ch'u^{3}	B
畜^{4}	田 102	畜 879	Cattle, domestic animals | 類 domestic animals |·牲, 牲 |	hsü^{4}	E
·箒^{4}	竹 118	帚 674	A broom, besom 笤·| 俗	chou^{3}	E
觸^{4}	角 148	蜀 788	To butt; move, offend, stir	ch'o^{4}	E
黜^{4}	黑 203	出 665	To dismiss, degrade	ch'o^{4}	G
怵^{4}	心 61	朮 491	Timorous, enticed | 事 apprehensive | 惕		I
儊^{4}	人 9	林 492	Rough, rugged		I

Chua

抓^{1}	手 64	爪 406	To scratch; grab, seize; tear | 車 impress carts | 鬮 draw lots | 人 arrest a man, so | 賊 | 破 scratch, tear open		C
髽^{1}	髟 190	坐 432	Dressing of hair | 髻		I
爪^{3}	爪 87	爪 406	Claws, talons	chao^{3}	E

Ch'ua

欻^{1}	欠 76	炎 447	Gust of wind, sudden | 吸 to sniff	hu^{1}	H

Chuai

Character	Radical	Phonetic	Meaning	Other readings	Grade
拽[1]	手 64	曳 835	To throw, fling 丨泥 fling mud at	chuai[4]	E
跩[3]	足 157	曳 835	To waddle limp 丨·起來 to walk with a swagger		G
⿰車曳[3]	車 159	曳 835	Pits in road 丨窩		G
曳[4] 拽[4]	曰 73	曳 835	To trail, drag, pull 丨拉 to pull, drag along 拉丨	chuai[1] i[4] yeh[4]	E

Ch'uai

Character	Radical	Phonetic	Meaning	Other readings	Grade
搋[1]	手 64	虒 204	To put in bosom, thump 丨·着手 put hands in sleeves 丨懷·裏 put in bosom		G
揣[3]	手 64	耑 614	To estimate, measure, think over; feel for, examine 丨摩 feel for, consider 丨摸 丨度 to estimate		E
踹[4]	足 157	耑 614	To stamp, trample 丨脚 stamp the foot 丨·死 stamp to death		F
嘬[4]	口 30	最 628	To lap, suck, eat 丨血 to suck blood	tso[1]	I

Chuan

Character	Radical	Phonetic	Meaning	Other readings	Grade
專[1]	寸 41	專 839	Singly, engrossed with, solely 丨車 special car 丨志 full determination 丨制 absolute monarchy 丨心 with whole heart 丨門 specialist, professional		B

甎[1] 磚[1]	瓦 98	專 839	A brick 方｜squarebrick ｜地 brick floor ｜·頭 bricks (esp'ly broken) ｜窰 brick-kiln		C
耑[1]	而 126	耑 614	Special, singly, only; used as 專	tuan[1]	H
轉[3]	車 159	專 839	To revolve, turn over｜動, change mind ｜機(之際) critical juncture ｜向 lose bearings, turn to ｜回 turn back｜·過來 ｜臉 escape without loss of face ｜身 turn self about	chuan[4]	C
賺[4] 賺[4] 賺[4]	貝 154	兼 671	To earn, gain, sell at profit｜利 ｜錢 make money. "squeeze" ｜·頭 profit 沒有｜兒 no profit in it	tsuan[4]	B
傳[4]	人 9	專 839	Annals, narrative 列｜biographies 作｜ 自｜autobiography	ch'uan[2]	C
轉[4]	車 159	專 839	To turn, roll, a revolution 輪｜	chuan[3]	C
撰[4]	手 64	巽 97	To compose, write books, edit ｜制 prepare a book｜文		G
饌[4]	食 184	巽 97	Viands, dainties, a meal 用｜to take a meal		I
篆[4]	竹 118	彖 287	"Seal" characters｜字 ｜書 seal character books		H

Ch'uan

穿[1]	穴 116	牙 165	To put on, put or go through ｜針 thread a needle		A

Ch'uan

穿[1]			丨孝 wear mourning 丨鞋 put on shoes 丨衣·服 (·裳) put on clothes 丨·上 to put on, so 丨不上 丨堂 open hall		
川[1] 巛[1]	川 47	川 425	Stream, river 丨連紙 note paper 四丨 Szechuan		E
船[2] 舡[2]	舟 137	㕣 719	Ship, boat 丨家 crew 丨隻 shipping 丨主 captain or owner 丨長[3] 丨行 a shipping-office -hang[2] 丨頭 the bow 丨首 丨艙 hold, cabin 丨桅 the mast 丨尾 the stern 上丨 embark 下丨 disembark		A
傳[2]	人 9	專 839	To transmit, promulgate; summon; preach, interpret, announce 丨敎 propagate religion 丨道 丨福音 preach the Gospel 丨·下 hand down 丨信 proclaim news 丨報 丨。染 contagious, infectious 丨人 summon a person 丨知, 丨証 丨開 spread fame 丨名 丨說 transmit by tradition 丨單 circular notice, hand bill 丨揚 spread abroad 丨言 hearsay, tradition 遺丨 heredity	chuan[4]	C
椽[2]	木 75	彖 287	Rafters, (small) 丨·子		F
喘[3]	口 30	耑 614	To pant, asthma 丨氣, 丨丨 丨·的·慌 breathless 丨不上氣		E

舛3	舛 136	舛 273	Perverse, contrary ｜忤 ｜錯 erroneous		H
串4	｜ 2	串 789	To string together; string; league; C. of strings ｜錢 to string cash ｜珠 cross references, ref. bible ｜門·子 to visit, gadabout ｜砲 string of fire-crackers		E
釧4	金 167	川 425	A bracelet ｜簪 ornaments ｜釵		G

Chuang

裝1	衣 145	壯 163	To dress, feign; load, pack ｜車 load a cart ｜槍 load a gun ｜藥 ｜箱 pack a box ｜載 contain, load, cargo		B
莊1	艸 140	壯 163	Sedate, serious, stern; a farm. S. (see 庄) ｜敬 serious, respectful ｜·重 端｜ modest, decorous		B
庄1	广 53	庄 199	A farm, shop, village ｜·稼 crops ｜戶 a farmer ｜丁 ｜村 a village		C
粧1 妝1	米 119	庄 199	To adorn, paint; pretend,假｜,｜假 disguise, gloss ｜糊·塗 pretend stupidity ｜傻 ｜·飾 ornament ｜·扮		E
舂1	臼 134	舂 473	To pound in a mortar	ch'ung1	G
樁1	木 75	舂 473	A post, stake, hitching post; C. of affairs ｜·子 a post		G

<table>
<tr><td>奘[3]</td><td>大
37</td><td>壯
163</td><td>Large, big, large around
| 細 thick and thin</td><td></td><td>E</td></tr>
<tr><td>狀[4]</td><td>犬
94</td><td>爿
162</td><td>Appearance, form; accuse, go to law
|∘況 look or state of affairs
| 態 air, appearance, status
|·子 accusation, petition | 詞
告 | indictment</td><td></td><td>C</td></tr>
<tr><td>壯[4]</td><td>士
33</td><td>壯
163</td><td>Strong, robust | 大
| 健 stout, robust 健 |, 强 |
| 年 20-30 years of age
| 士 able-bodied man | 丁</td><td></td><td>D</td></tr>
<tr><td>撞[4]</td><td>手
64</td><td>童
829</td><td>To strike against, meet
|·見 rush into presence
|·着 dash against | 碰
| 騙 swindle</td><td></td><td>D</td></tr>
</table>

Ch'uang

<table>
<tr><td>窗[1]
窓[1]
窻[1]
牕[1]</td><td>穴
116

片
91</td><td>囪
394</td><td>Window |·戶
| 帳·子 window curtain
| 紙 window-paper
| 框 window-frame
| 簾 window-screen, curtain
| 臺 window-sill
同 | classmates</td><td></td><td>A</td></tr>
<tr><td>創[1]</td><td>刀
18</td><td>倉
679</td><td>Cut, wound</td><td>ch'uang[34]</td><td>C</td></tr>
<tr><td>瘡[1]</td><td>疒
104</td><td>倉
679</td><td>A sore, ulcer, boil, abscess
| 疤 scar or scab | 瘢</td><td></td><td>C</td></tr>
<tr><td>床[2]
牀[2]</td><td>广
53</td><td>广
198</td><td>A bed, couch
| 氈 blanket
| 帳·子 bed-curtains | 幃
| 席 bed-mat
| 鋪 bed and bedding</td><td></td><td>C</td></tr>
</table>

Character	Radical	Phonetic	Meaning		
爿 2	爿 90	爿 162	A frame, couch		K
創 34 刱 34	刀 18	倉 679	To create, found 丨立, 丨建 丨辦 found, establish 丨設 丨始 commence 開丨 丨世記 Genesis 丨造 create, invent 丨作	ch'uang1	C
闖 34	門 169	馬 255	To rush in, dash ahead, suddenly 丨進 intrude, rush in 丨入 丨門 burst in at a gate		D

Chui

Character	Radical	Phonetic	Meaning		
追 1	辵 162	追 754	Pursue; recover; reflect 丨究 search out, investigate 丨°求 丨想 reflect upon 丨念 丨回 run after, recall 丨趕 pursue 丨問 question closely, examine		C
隹 1	隹 172	隹 52	Short-tailed birds		K
錐 1	金 167	隹 52	An awl, tip; to pierce, 丨·子 a trifle 丨眼 to bore holes		F
墜 4	土 32	彖 288	To fall, sink, descend 丨落, 丨·下 丨馬 fall from horse 丨·子 ear-drops		F
縋 4	糸 120	追 754	A cord, to suspend 丨繩 let down by a cord 丨·下·去 let it down		F
贅 4	貝 154	敖 264	To keep on and on, repetition, verbose 累·丨 embarrass, encumber 丨累		F
硾 4	石 112	垂 26	To press down, a weight, 丨·子		H

綴^{4}	糸 120	叕 534	To connect; mend; baste	G

Ch'ui

吹^{1} 歈^{1}	口 30	欠 441	To blow; puff; praise 丨氣 breathe, play wind instrument 丨號 give signal, blow trumpet 丨(鼓)手 musicians 丨滅 blow out 丨息 不丨響 can't bring out sound 丨哨 whistle 丨打 music 丨笛 play flute	C
炊^{1}	火 86	欠 441	To steam, cook, dress food 丨箒 whisk for dishes 丨餅 cook cakes	G
搥^{2}	手 64	追 754	To beat; shampoo 丨胸 beat the breast 丨鼓 beat the drum	G
槌^{2}	木 75	追 754	Mallet, to reject 丨衣·裳 mangle clothing	H
鎚^{2}	金 167	追 754	Mallet, hammer 丨·子 hammer	D
垂^{2}	士 32	垂 26	To drop, let fall; condescend 丨顧 regard condescendingly 丨憐 condescending pity 丨柳 weeping willow 丨念 think kindly of 丨聽 condescendingly listen	E
捶^{2}	手 64	垂 26	To beat, cudgel 丨布石 stone for beating clothes	F
錘^{2}	金 167	垂 26	Steelyard weight 秤丨; to hammer	F

Chun

Character	Radical	Phonetic	Meaning	Variant	Group
屯[1]	屮 45	屯 376	Avaricious, difficult	t'un[2]	F
諄[1]	言 149	享 743	To impress upon, earnestly ︱︱ ︱切 emphatically		F
準[3]	水 85	隼 54	Exact, a rule, to permit ︱成 accurate, certain ︱秤 adjusted scale︱斤兩 ︱信 reliable news ︱來 sure to come ︱∘備 to prepare, get ready ︱繩 marking line ︱當 certain, sure ︱·頭 accuracy. definite object ︱則 rule, standard		C
准[3]	冫 15	隹 51	To permit, grant; exactly ︱許 to permit, approve 允︱consent, grant, sanction		D

Ch'un

Character	Radical	Phonetic	Meaning	Variant	Group
春[1]	日 72	春 472	Spring, ︱季, ︱·天; prosperity; to rejuvenate ︱假[4] spring vacation ︱秋 spring and autumn ; age ︱分 spring equinox ︱雨 spring rains		A
椿[1]	木 75	春 472	A long-lived tree︱樹		K
唇[2] 脣[2]	口 30	辰 355	The lips, mouth 嘴︱ ︱笑 to smile ︱舌 plausible, eloquent 豁︱·子 hare-lip		C

純[2]	糸 120	屯 376	One-coloured, pure, sincere, simple. ｜厚 morally sound, honest ｜心 assiduously ｜一不雜 pure, unmixed ｜一無僞 pure, sincere ｜粹 pure, genuine, beautiful		D
淳[2] 湻[2]	水 85	享 743	Pure, unmixed, genuine ｜淸 pure and limpid ｜于 double surname 貞｜ pure and chaste	 S	G
醇[2] 醕[2]	酉 164	享 743	Rich, thick, pure ｜酒 good wine ｜厚 pure and honest		G
鶉[2]	鳥 196	享 743	Quail 鵪·｜		F
蠢[3]	虫 142	春 472	Stupid, foolish ｜拙 stupid, clumsy ｜笨 ｜子[3] a simpleton, ｜才		E

Chung

中[1]	｜ 2	中 784	Center, inside, in ｜正 upright ｜間 in middle, between, with ｜｜·的 middling, passable ｜西 Chinese and foreign ｜外 ｜心點 center, middle ｜央點 ｜學 middle school ｜華 China ｜·國, ｜華民國 ｜∘人 middle-man, go-between ｜立 neutral ｜保 mediator, surety ｜等 middle class, fair ｜庸 due medium, one of "Four Books" ｜用 capable, efficient	chung[4]	A

Chung

Character	Radical	Phonetic	Meaning	Also read	Frequency
忠^{1}	心 61	中 784	Loyal, upright, faithful ｜臣 faithful minister ｜心 loyalty, ｜信 faithfulness ｜·厚 upright, guileless, loyal		C
盅^{1}	皿 108	中 784	Covered cup 酒｜ wine-cup		F
衷^{1}	衣 145	中 784	Inner man, heart, feelings; goodness ｜腸 heart, conscience ｜正 just, right, correct		F
鐘^{1}	金 167	童 829	Bell, clock ｜樓 bell-tower ｜表 clocks and watches		A
終^{1}	糸 120	冬 541	End, all, finis　S. ｜久 a long time, always ｜日 whole day, every day, so ｜夜 ｜歸 ending in ｜身 whole life		C
鍾^{1}	金 167	重 27	A cup, to love　S. ｜離 double surname　S.		I
種^{3}	禾 115	重 27	Seed; kind, species ｜類, ｜樣 ｜族 race 人｜ ｜·子 a seed, sort ｜兒	chung^{4}	B
腫^{3}	肉 130	重 27	To swell, ｜脹, ｜·起·來 ｜鼓病 dropsy		E
踵^{3} 歱^{3}	足 157	重 27	To visit; imitate; precedent ｜骨 os calcis ｜跡 follow an example		I
冢^{3}	冖 14	豖 292	Mound, peak, eminent, ｜君 sovereign ｜子^{3} heir-apparent		I
塚^{3}	土 32	豖 292	Tomb, cemetery, tumulus ｜墳, ｜墓		G
中^{4}	｜ 2	中 784	To hit a mark, gain an end ｜意 hit one's wish, to like ｜·了 succeeded ｜的^{4} hit the mark	chung^{1}	A

Character	Radical	Phonetic	Meaning		Other reading	
仲4	人 9	中 784	Second in order of birth, younger	S.		G
			｜尼 the style of Confucius			
			｜孫 double surname	S.		
重4	里 166	重 27	Heavy, precious, grave		ch'ung2	A
			｜價 high price, great cost			
			｜心 center of gravity			
			｜任 onerous post			
			｜看 regard highly			
			｜傷 severe wound ｜病			
			｜擔 heavy load			
			｜要 important, ｜大			
種4	禾 115	重 27	To plant, sow, ｜植, ｜地		chung3	B
			｜庄稼 cultivate crops			
			｜4種3兒 (or·子) sow seed			
			｜牛痘 vaccinate			
眾4 衆4 乑4	目 109 俗	衆 850	Company of three or more, many, all; the people			C
			｜議 public opinion ｜論			
			｜議院 House of Representatives			
			｜人 every one 大｜			
			｜民 mankind			
			｜生 all living creatures			
			｜位 all of you present			

Ch'ung

Character	Radical	Phonetic	Meaning		Other reading	
充1	儿 10	充 870	To fill; act as; satiate	S.		C
			｜饑 satisfy hunger			
			｜軍 banish, exile ｜徒			
			｜滿 fill, full ｜塞, ｜盈			
			｜足 sufficient, ample			
			擴｜ expand, carry out			

Ch'ung

冲^{1} 沖^{1}	冫 15	中 784	To dash against, rush at; infuse | 撞 run against, offend |∘開 to sluice out or open | 破 burst through, defeat | 散 disturb a company | 動 shake, move		D
衝^{1} 衝^{1}	行 144	重 27	To rush against, collide | 撞 butt against, treat rudely | 衢 thoroughfare | 塗 |·突 opposition, variance | 動 impulse		F
舂^{1}	臼 134	舂 473	To pound, ram; hull | 米 hull rice	chuang^{1}	G
重^{2}	里 166	重 27	To repeat, double |·復 repetitious | 新 renewed, made over | 修 repair, revise, rebuild | 生 regenerate | 組 reorganize	chung^{4}	A
崇^{2}	山 46	宗 516	To reverence, lofty. | 拜 venerate, worship | 寔 reverence for truth		C •
蟲^{2} 虫^{2}	虫 142	虫 785	Insects, reptiles, worms |·子 | 類 論 entomology 昆 | 學 長·| serpent		D
寵^{3} 寵^{3}	宀 40	龍 815	Kindness, grace, esteem, to favor |愛 ardent affection | 臣 favorite minister		E
銃^{4}	金 167	充 870	Fire-arms, mortar gun, pistol, gingal | 炮 artillery		G
揰^{1}	手 64	重 27	To push, poke at, stir up | 通 clear out drain, etc.		H
聚^{4}	攴 66	取 627	To enter abruptly, nod, drop in at a meal |·着 sleepy, nodding		I

Chü

Character	Radical	Phonetic	Meaning		
居[1] 㞐[1]	尸 44	居 706	To dwell; be; remain; fill office S. 丨住 dwell, reside 丨留 丨心 bent upon, concentrate 丨官 fill office, hold office 丨民 resident population 丨喪 in mourning		D
拘[1]	手 64	句 227	To seize, arrest, restrain 丨執 to grasp, obstinate 丨板 丨管 check, control 丨緊 丨留 intern, detain 丨拿 seize, apprehend 丨泥 bigoted, obstinate 不丨 no matter		D
駒[1]	馬 187	句 227	A young horse, donkey or mule; spirited 驢丨·子 young donkey		E
俱[1]	人 9	具 625	All, every, altogether, all right 丨全 complete, the whole 丨各 all, every one, 丨都 丨樂部 club, guild 丨收 all received		E
局[2]	尸 44	局 724	A game; all; store, shop, office; to stoop 丨部 local 丨勢 situation, outlook 丨外 onlooker, neutral 大丨 public weal or situation 郵政丨 Post Office		A
橘[2]	木 75	矞 118	Bitter orange 丨·子 丨核 orange pips, seeds		E
掬[2] 匊[2]	手 64	匊 229	To hold in both hands; swollen 一丨 a handful		K

Chü

菊[2]	艸 140	匊 229	Chrysanthemum, china-aster ｜花 chrysanthemum 月｜花		F
諊[2] 鞫[2]	言 149	匊 229	To investigate judicially, reduced to extremity ｜審 to hear a case 訊｜		G
鞠[2]	革 177	匊 229	To bend over; nourish; ball ｜躬 salute, personal or in letter	chü[4]	B
矩[3]	矢 111	巨 641	Rule, pattern 規·｜ custom, usage		A
舉[3] 舁[3]	臼 134	與 691	To raise, appoint; introduce; old M.A.; whole ｜哀 cry out, weep ｜·起 raise, lift up ｜薦 introduce, recommend ｜止 behavior, conduct｜動 ｜意 make a motion｜端 ｜·人 provincial graduate (old) ｜目 raise the eyes ｜手 raise the hand, salute		C
齟[3]	齒 211	且 623	Irregular, cross-purposes		K
句[4]	口 30	句 227	A sentence, an hour; C. of speech or writing ｜鐘 an hour, o'clock ｜｜ every sentence 一｜話 a sentence		A
豦[4]	豕 152	豦 290	A wild boar, wrestling		K
劇[4]	刀 18	豦 290	Annoying; play 戲｜ theatrical plays	chi[42]	I
據[4]	手 64	豦 290	According to, evidence ｜你 說 according to you ｜守 guard, maintain ｜此 看·來 on these grounds		C
遽[4]	辵 162	豦 290	Agitated, suddenly ｜然 hurriedly		G

Chü

聚[4]	耳 128	取 627	To gather, assemble, meeting ｜集collect, gather, 湊｜,｜合 ｜齊 all assembled ｜會 assemble ｜歛 collect together, gather			B
鞠[4]	革 177	匊 229	Surname	S	chü[2]	B
瞿[4]	目 109	瞿 61	To fear, timid, in awe		ch'ü[2]	K
懼[4] 惧[4]	心 61	瞿 61	To fear, stand in awe of ｜怕 fear, afraid 恐｜ fear, apprehension			C
具[4]	八 12	具 625	To prepare; present, file; implements; all ｜稟 petition, hand in report ｜體 concrete 器·｜ utensils			D
倨[4]	人 9	居 706	Bold. haughty, strong			I
踞[4]	足 157	居 706	To squat, sit impolitely; occupy			K
鋸[4]	金 167	居 706	A saw, to saw; rivet ｜·匠 a sawyer ｜齒 teeth of saw｜牙 ｜◦開 saw in two｜斷 ｜末·子 saw dust ｜條 blade of saw			D F
巨[4]	工 48	巨 641	Great, very ｜口 to boast ｜萬 myriads, infinite			F F
拒[4]	手 64	巨 641	To resist, ward off, reject ｜絕 refuse, reject 抗｜ resist, disobey			
詎[4]	言 149	巨 641	How could it be? ｜知 who knows?			G

距[4]	足 157	巨 641	To go over, distant 丨離 distance 超丨 leap over			H

Ch'ü

區[1]	匸 23	區 696	Place, region; to discriminate 丨處 petty 丨°別 to separate, distinguish 丨域 circuit, district			D
嶇[1]	山 46	區 696	Rugged, mountainous			H
軀[1]	身 158	區 696	Body, self, person 丨體 physical body 捐丨 sacrifice life			D
驅[1] 敺[1]	馬 187	區 696	To expel, urge 丨逐 drive out 丨除 丨馬 gallop a horse			F
曲[1]	曰 73	曲 819	Crooked, perverse 丨斜 obliquely 丨心 deceitful 彎丨 winding, crooked 丨彎		ch'ü[3]	E
蛐[1]	虫 142	曲 819	Common earth-worm 丨蟮			G
麯[1] 麴[1]	麥 199	曲 819	Leaven, yeast, mother-of-vinegar 丨生 spirits, wine 丨·子 ferment for spirits	S.		I
屈[1]	尸 44	屈 666	To bend, wrong, oppression, grievance 丨膝 bend the knee 丨身 bend the body 丨背 丨他 wrong a man 委·丨 injustice, wrong	S.		D

Ch'ü

<table>
<tr><td>漆[1]</td><td>水
85</td><td>桼
527</td><td>| 黑 Pitch dark</td><td></td><td>ch'i[1]</td><td>E</td></tr>
<tr><td>趨[1]
趋[1]</td><td>走
156</td><td>芻
663</td><td>To hasten, hurry, run to
| 向 tendency
| 行 go ahead | 走
| 時 keep up with times</td><td></td><td></td><td>F</td></tr>
<tr><td>劬[12]</td><td>力
19</td><td>句
227</td><td>Toil, solicitude
| 勞 grievous toil</td><td></td><td></td><td>I</td></tr>
<tr><td>蛆[1]</td><td>虫
142</td><td>且
623</td><td>Maggots in putrid flesh
發 | breed maggots</td><td></td><td></td><td>H</td></tr>
<tr><td>瞿[2]</td><td>目
109</td><td>瞿
61</td><td>Surname</td><td>S</td><td>chü[4]</td><td>K</td></tr>
<tr><td>衢[21]</td><td>行
144</td><td>瞿
61</td><td>Thoroughfare, highway 街 |</td><td></td><td></td><td>I</td></tr>
<tr><td>渠[2]</td><td>水
85</td><td>巨
641</td><td>A drain, gutter | 溝; spacious, chief</td><td></td><td></td><td>I</td></tr>
<tr><td>取[3]</td><td>又
29</td><td>取
627</td><td>To take, bring; demand
| 其 take for, consider as
| 錢 draw money from bank, etc.
|·出 take out, withdraw
| 去 take away
| 消 withdraw motion, cancel
|·來 bring, fetch |·過·來
| 贖 take out of pawn
| 燈 match, light lamp | 火</td><td></td><td></td><td>B</td></tr>
<tr><td>娶[3]</td><td>女
38</td><td>取
627</td><td>To take a wife, marry
| 妻 to marry a wife, | 親
| 妾 take a concubine</td><td></td><td></td><td>B</td></tr>
<tr><td>曲[3]</td><td>曰
73</td><td>曲
819</td><td>Songs ballads | 兒, |·子, | 詞
| 調 song tunes</td><td></td><td>ch'ü[1]</td><td>E</td></tr>
<tr><td>趣[4]</td><td>走
156</td><td>取
627</td><td>Amusing, agreeable
| 處 enjoyment
| 話 a jest
|·味 agreeable, flavor</td><td></td><td></td><td>B</td></tr>
</table>

Character	Radical	Phonetic	Meaning	Variant	Class
去4	厶 28	去 44	To leave, go; dismiss ｜處 place to go to; occasion ｜·過 have been there, gone ｜路 a way of escape ｜·年 last year ｜歲 ｜·罷 begone! go! let's go! ｜聲 sinking tone, "fourth tone" ｜世 to die ｜·掉 get rid of ｜·頭 worth going, object		C
覷4	見 147	虍 206	To watch for, spy out ｜機·會 watch opportunity		K̄

Chüan

Character	Radical	Phonetic	Meaning	Variant	Class
捐1	手 64	肙 759	To contribute, give up; buy title, "give" tax ｜錢 subscribe money ｜輸 ｜軀 sacrifice life ｜命 ｜項 subscription ｜貲		C
卷3	卩 26	卷 467	To roll up	chüan4	D
捲3	手 64	卷 467	To roll up ｜·起來, ｜·上 ｜袖 roll up sleeve ｜簾·子 roll up screen 烟｜ cigar, cigarette		C
餋3	食 184	卷 467	Wafer rolls		H
卷4	卩 26	卷 467	Scroll, book, section; C. of books ｜紙 essay paper ｜·子 examination papers 書｜ books	chüan3	D
倦4	人 9	卷 467	Fatigued, weary ｜怠 乏｜ fatigued ｜惰		D

圈^{41}	口 31	卷 467	Coop, pen; to pen, shut up 猪 | pig-sty 馬 | stable 牛 | 羊 | sheep fold	ch'üan^{1}	C
眷^{4}	目 109	𠔉 466	To care for, love; wife, relatives, family | 顧 regard kindly, care for | 戀, | 念 家·| wife, family | 屬		C
絹^{4}	糸 120	肙 759	Thin silk, lustring | 紬 |·子 a napkin 手 | 兒 handkerchief		G

Ch'üan

圈^{1}	口 31	卷 467	To encircle, circle, ring | 限 sphere of influence | 套 a snare | 點 punctuation |·子 a trap	chüan^{4}	C
全^{2} 仝^{2}	入 11	全 78	All, whole, perfect 完 | S | 家 whole family | 球 the whole world | 權 full authority | 副 complete set, outfit, suit | 然 altogether | 能 almighty | 備 all ready, perfect | 體 all, the whole, unanimous | 在 all included, all depends		B
痊^{2}	疒 104	全 78	Cured, recovered, | 愈		C
詮^{2}	言 149	全 78	To explain, expound, comment on 註 | commentary | 註		G
銓^{2}	金 167	全 78	To estimate, select, weigh		I

Ch'üan

Character	Radical	Phonetic	Meaning			Class
權[2]	木 75	雚 60	Weight, power, authority | 限 limits of authority |·利 privilege, rights 特|, 利| |∘柄 authority | 能 | 勢 power, influence | 衡	S.		C
顴[2]	頁 181	雚 60	Cheek-bones | 骨			G
泉[2] 洤[2]	水 85	泉 528	Fountain, spring; money | 水 spring water | 頭 fountain head | 眼 spring | 源, 水 |			C
𠔉[2]		𠔉 466	A roll			P
拳[2]	手 64	𠔉 466	The fist, |·頭 | 法 art of boxing 空 | empty handed			C
踡[2]	足 157	卷 467	To contract legs | 腿			I
犬[3]	犬 94	犬 456	A dog, villainous | 子[3] a whelp, puppy, my son			F
勸[4] 劝[4]	力 19	雚 60	To exhort, advise | 教 advise, instruct | 解 to mediate | 和 | 戒 warn, caution | 捐 call for subscriptions | 化 convert | 勉 urge, stimulate | 善 preach morality | 世 文 tracts | 慰 soothe, console			B
券[4]	刀 18	𠔉 466	Bond, deed, document, contract, ticket | 契 bond, deed, | 約 入 場 | admission ticket			D

Chüeh

欮^{1}	欠 76	欮 662	To hiccough		P
噘^{1}	口 30	欮 662	|·着 嘴 To pout | 嘴		H
撅^{1}	手 64	欮 662	To throw down, strike; snap off | 折 break off -she^{2}		H
玨^{1}	玉 96	玨 77	Two kings, or two gems; used in names		P
覺^{2} 覚^{2}	見 147	𦥯 692	To perceive, feel, sensible of | 知 to perceive, know 知 | |·着 to feel, be conscious |·得, | 疼 feel pain | 悟 roused to a sense of	chiao^{34}	A
腳^{24} 脚^{24}	肉 130	去 44	Foot, base 文	chiao^{3}	A
絕^{2}	糸 120	色 313	To cut off, end, destroy; decidedly, very | 交 break friendship | 情 | 種 the race extinct | 對 absolute | 望 hopeless in despair		C
角^{2}	角 148	角 602	Horn 文	chiao^{13}	C
夬^{2}	大 37	夬 482	To fork, past, settled, differing	kuai^{3}	K
決^{2} 决^{2}	水 85	夬 482	To decide, decidedly, differing | 意 determined | 心, | 然 | 不 determined not to | 不 能 cannot possibly | 定 certain, positively | 斷 settle, decide | 無 surely none		C

Chüeh

訣²	言 149	夬 482	A farewell, mystery 密 | secret		F
爵²	爪 87	爵 851	Nobility, rank |。位 official rank, office		F
嚼²	口 30	爵 851	To chew 文	chiao²⁴	D
倔²	人 9	屈 666	Sulky; obstinate | 强 | 喪 churlish, boorish		H
掘²	手 64	屈 666	To dig, excavate | 井 dig a well |。開 dig open | 地 道 to sap or mine		E
厥²	厂 27	欮 662	He, she, this, that, his, its, etc.		G
橛² 橜²	木 75	欮 662	Post, joist, stake, axle, lever |·子 wooden peg		F
蹷²⁴ 蹶²⁴	足 157	欮 662	To stumble, slip, fall 崩 | crash down	chüeh³	H
钁²	金 167	欮 662	Pick-ax, | 頭; to pick		H
嗟¹²	口 30	差 178	To sigh, alas! | 嘆	chieh¹	K
譎² 憰²	言 149	矞 118	To feign; hypocritical; wily 欺 | to delude, gull		K
亅²	亅 6	亅 111	Hook, down-stroke; to mark off		K
蹷³	足 157	欮 662	To kick back	chüeh²	H

Ch'üeh

Character	Radical	Phonetic	Meaning		Alt.	Grade
缺¹	缶 121	夬 482	Broken, deficient; a vacancy, post ｜欠 shortcoming ｜點 ｜乏 short, lacking ｜短 ｜少 few, deficient ｜雨 drought ｜水			B
瘸²	疒 104	加 716	Lame, paralyzed, to limp ｜·了 ｜腿 lame leg, lame ｜·子 cripple			D
鵲⁴	鳥 196	昔 799	Magpie	文	ch'iao³	G
却⁴ 卻⁴	卩 26	去 44	To refuse; but; truly ｜是 nevertheless ｜有一件 but there is one thing			B
確⁴	石 112	隹 52	Solid; reliable, surely, verily 眞｜ ｜情 true circumstances ｜據 positive proof ｜信 reliable, assurance ｜實 true, trustworthy ｜定 definitely decided			D
雀⁴	隹 172	隹 52	A bird, sparrow	文	ch'iao³	D
殼⁴ 売⁴	殳 79	㱿 400	Shell, husk 地｜shell of the earth		k'o²	G
恪⁴	心 61	各 712	Respectful; reverent; faithful ｜遵 respectfully obey		k'o⁴	G
闕⁴	門 169	欮 662	Deficiency, waning Imperial (reserved) city ｜疑 omit the doubtful	S.		I

Chün

Character	Radical	Phonetic	Meaning		Alt.	Grade
均¹	土 32	匀 232	Equal, in balance, all ｜齊 even and regular			B

Chün

均[1]			丨分 divide evenly, impartial 丨可 all will do 丨·匀 equal, impartial 丨平 平丨 average 丨數		
鈞[1] 銁[1]	金 167	勻 232	To equalize, equitable; large; your; 30 catties 丨安 wish happiness		F
君[1]	口 30	君 678	King, prince, gentleman; my husband, my wife, Mr. (polite) 丨主 sovereign, monarchy 丨王 sovereign, 丨上 丨子[3]人 a royal man; gentleman 諸丨 my hearers; Gentlemen!		C
軍[1]	車 159	軍 838	Army, military, legion, general 丨器 implements of war 丨械 丨家 soldiers, the military 丨界 丨裝 armor 丨隊 troops 丨法 military law 丨需 munitions, equipments 丨用品 same 丨務 military affairs 丨營 encampment		C
夋[1]	夊 35	夋 542	To dawdle, Yao's father	tsun[1]	K
俊[4]	人 9	夋 542	Distinguished, refined 丨傑 person of talent 丨秀 丨美 beautiful 丨雅 graceful, elegant	tsun[4]	D
峻[4]	山 46	夋 542	Steep, lofty, stern 險丨 precipitous, dangerous		G
竣[4]	立 117	夋 542	To complete, finish 完丨 告丨 report completion	tsun[4]	G
駿[4]	馬 187	夋 542	Fine horse, swift, exalted 丨馬 丨速 very fleet		H
郡[4]	邑 163	君 678	Prefecture, political division 丨王 a prince (2nd class)		G

Ch'ün

Character	Radical	Phonetic	Meaning		
裙^{2} 裠^{2}	衣 145	君 678	Short skirt		B
			圍｜apron		
			｜帶 skirt-sash		
羣^{2} 群^{2}	羊 123	君 678	Flock, company, multitude, all		C
			｜學 sociology 社會學		
			｜化 social reform		
			｜神教 polytheism		
			｜生 mankind		
			｜羊 flock of sheep		

E see O

En

Character	Radical	Phonetic	Meaning		
恩^{1}	心 61	因 771	Grace, favor, show favor		B
			｜愛 affection, love		
			｜·典 favor, kindness, ｜惠, ｜慈		
			｜情 kindness, ｜澤		
			｜主 benefactor ｜人		
			｜寵 gracious favor		
			｜赦 gracious pardon		
按^{4} 搵^{4}	手 64	安 555	Lay hand on, press 俗	an^{4}	B
			｜着 pressing down		
			｜住 hold down		

Eng

Character	Radical	Phonetic	Meaning		
哼^{1}	口 30	亨 742	Exclam. of pain or displeasure	heng^{1}	G

Erh

Character	Radical	Phonetic	Meaning		
兒^{2}	儿 10	兒 684	Infant, boy, son; diminutive ending (see p. XXIV)		A
			｜媳婦 daughter-in-law		
			｜女 children		
			｜孫 sons and grandsons, posterity 子孫		
			｜童 a boy ｜·子 a son		

Character	Radical	Phonetic	Meaning		
而^{2}	而 126	而 612	And yet, still ｜且 also, moreover ｜今 now, at present ｜後 henceforth ｜已 that and no more		B
耳^{3}	耳 128	耳 626	Ear｜朵; handle; side ｜房 side-room (facing same way) ｜環 ear-ring ｜軟 credulous ｜聾 deaf ｜巴·子 cheek-bones, side face ｜聽 to hear, hearsay｜聞 ｜挖·子 an ear-pick		A
珥^{3}	玉 96	耳 626	Ear-ornament, sun-dog		G
爾^{3} 尔^{3}	爻 89	爾 564	You;｜｜ just so ｜撒 Jesus (Moslem) ｜等 you (plural) 偶｜ once in a while, suddenly		F
邇^{3}	辵 162	爾 564	Near, proximate ｜來 recently		G
二^{4} 貳^{4} 弍^{4}	二 7 减	一 1	Two, 第｜the second ｜價 two prices ｜親 parents ｜心 double-minded ｜忽 hesitating, confused ｜來 in the second place,｜則 ｜套車 two-horse cart ｜位 both of you		A

Fa

Character	Radical	Phonetic	Meaning		
發^{1}	癶 105	發 246	To put forth, rise, start, grow; become ｜展 open out, develop ｜脹 distended, sense of fulness		A

Character	Radical	Phonetic	Meaning		
發^{1}			丨潮 damp and mouldy		
			丨起 raise, start, promote		
			丨愁 become sad, find difficulty		
			丨·出 send forth		
			丨·去 send away		
			丨奮 show ardor 丨憤		
			丨福 (polite) you have put on flesh		
			丨現 become manifest, discover		
			丨行 to issue; publication		
			丨昏 faint, grow faint		
			丨熱 feverish 丨燒		
			丨乾 be or feel dry		
			丨懶 grow lazy, languid		
			丨冷 grow cold, ague		
			丨亂 grow confused		
			丨痲 grow numb		
			丨賣 for sale, to sell		
			丨悶 depressed, gloomy		
			丨明 invent, discover		
			丨怒 be angry		
			丨板 feel stiff, stereotyped		
			丨笨 grow clumsy		
			丨表 make known, set forth		
			丨喪^{1} to bury		
			丨達 rise in life, develop, succeed		
			丨獃 stupid, stare stupidly		
			丨條 a spring (in machine)		
			丨抖 to tremble		
			丨財 become rich		
			丨芽 put forth shoots		
			丨瘧·子 have fever and ague -yao^{4}-		
			丨暈 be or feel dizzy		
法^{1}	水 85	去 44	Plan, way 沒丨兒 no help for it.	fa^{234}	A
伐^{1}	人 9	伐 335	To cut down; chastise; destroy; act as a go-between 作丨 丨木 cut down timber 丨樹, 砍丨		F

Character	Radical	Phonetic	Meaning		
乏[2]	丿 4	乏 300	In want, poor, weary ｜地 exhausted soil 窮｜impoverished 困｜wearied, ｜困, ｜倦		A
法[2]	水 85	去 44	Standard weights ｜碼 ｜·子 method, plan	fa[134]	A
罰[2]	网 122	刀 219	To punish, punishments 刑｜ ｜錢 fine, ｜銀 ｜罪 punish offence		C
筏[2]	竹 118	伐 335	Raft, pontoon ｜渡 raft-ferry		K
閥[2]	門 169	伐 335	Left entrance of triple gate, rank		K
法[3]	水 85	去 44	Law, rule; means ｜治 jurisdiction ｜理 legality ｜輪 wheel of law (Buddhist) ｜律 laws, statutes 律｜, ｜度 ｜典 code of laws ｜庭 court of justice ｜則 regulations, method	fa[124]	A
髮[3]	髟 190	犮 188	Hair on head 頭·｜ 剪｜cut the hair		B
法[4]	水 85	去 44	Law ｜·國 France 文 ｜藍 cloisonné ｜門 Buddhists ｜文 French text or language	fa[123]	A

Fan

Character	Radical	Phonetic	Meaning		
番[1]	田 102	番 811	A time, turn; barbarians, foreign; C. of times ｜茄 the tomato 西紅柿		D
旛[1] 幡[1]	方 70	番 811	A banner, flutter, wave 旗｜streamer, ｜旗		H

Fan

Character	Radical	Phonetic	Meaning	Variant readings	Grade
繙[1]	糸 120	番 811	To interpret, translate ｜·譯 same, ·出·來		B
翻[1]	羽 124	番 811	To turn over; change, ｜·過·來 ｜開書 open book and turn pages ｜來覆去 tossing about, restless ｜臉 change countenance ｜·騰 topsy-turvy, fly about ｜滾 ｜印 infringe copyright		B
拚[1]	手 64	厶 868	To fly	p'an[4] pien[4] p'in[1]	F
帆[12] 杋[12]	巾 50	凡 397	A sail, canvas ｜船 sailing-vessel		G
煩[2]	火 86	頁 866	To annoy, trouble; ask ｜絮 repetitious ｜擾 vex, annoy, ｜勞 ｜悶 vexed, sorry ｜惱 annoyed, distressed ｜瑣 troublesome		A
凡[2] 几[2]	几 16	凡 397	All, human, usual, the world, generally ｜常 common, ordinary ｜間 the world, earthly ｜人 all men, mortals ｜論 in general terms ｜事 everything, ｜物 ｜有 every body, wherever 非｜ uncommon, extraordinary		B
繁[2]	糸 120	敏 573	Many; troublesome ｜難 ｜華 gaiety, show, pomp ｜盛 abundant, ｜多 ｜雜 multifarious		E
燔[2]	火 86	番 811	To roast for sacrifice ｜祭 burnt offering, 火｜祭 ｜葬 cremation		F
蕃[2]	艸 140	番 811	Flourishing ｜生 to generate		G

Fan

Character	Radical	Phonetic	Meaning		Grade
藩²	艸 140	番 811	Fence, frontier | 域		G
樊²	木 75	樊 493	Fence, cage, hedge | 籠 a cage	S.	G
礬²	石 112	樊 493	Alum, sulphates, | 石 飛 | burnt alum 白 | alum		G
反³	又 29	反 215	But, on the contrary; to turn back, rebel | 照 to reflect light |∘正 neg. and pos.; after all | 教 apostasy | 攻 counter-attack |·着 說 on the contrary |·復 again and again | 覆 | 回 turn back | 來 覆 去 coming and going | 亂 rebellion, anarchy | 叛 | 面 wrong side, turn against | 表 决 negative vote | 病 have a relapse | 身 turn around | 倒 upset, on the contrary | 對 oppose, vote against | 應 reaction | 動 reactionary		B
返³	辵 162	反 215	To return, revert to | 回 往 | round trip		D
⿸疒反⁴	疒 104	反 215	To vomit; faint		K
販⁴ ⿰買反⁴	貝 154	反 215	To deal in, peddle, traffic | 賣 | 貨 traffic in goods | 運 transport, convey		F
飯⁴	食 184	反 215	Cooked rice; food; a meal | 館 eating house, restaurant, | 庄, | 舖 same | 鍋 cooking-pot |·量 appetite, capacity for food		A

飯 4	食 184	反 215	｜食 food ｜盌 rice-bowl, living 乾｜ rice cooked dry	
犯 4	犬 94	巳 306	To transgress; a criminal ｜禁 violate prohibitions ｜境 break bounds, trespass ｜地 ｜法 violate law ｜例, ｜律 ｜·人 a criminal ｜病 suffer relapse ｜聖 sacrilege ｜罪 commit sin or crime 囚｜ a prisoner	B
氾 4	水 85	巳 306	Inundate, flood, Shantung river ｜濫 inundate	K
範 4	竹 118	車 836	Pattern, rule, mould 模｜ ｜常 constant usage ｜圍 bounds, sphere, jurisdiction	C
泛 4 汎 4	水 85	乏 300	To float; vague; overflowing, reckless ｜言 vague expressions	F
梵 4	木 75	林 492	Stillness; Brahma ｜王 ｜語 Sanskrit or Pali	I

Fang

方 1	方 70	方 261	Square; region; means S. ｜針 direction, policy ｜桌 square table; so ｜甎 ｜舟 Noah's ark ｜法 means, method ｜·向 direction, bearings ｜可 then it will do ｜面 side, aspect, phase, district ｜。便 advantage, convenient ｜纔 (才) just now	A

Fang

方[1]			丨寸 square inch; heart		
			丨·子 doctor's prescription		
			丨言 local dialect		
坊[1]	土 32	方 261	Locality, neighbourhood; hamlet		F
			丨表 good example		
			作丨 shop, factory		
妨[12]	女 38	方 261	To hinder, obstacle 丨事		D
			丨碍 objection, obstacle		
			丨害 detriment		
芳[1]	艸 140	方 261	Fragrant; excellent; virtuous		E
			丨美 delicate, beautiful		
			丨名 good reputation		
匚[1]	匚 22	匚 640	Open basket, peck		K
房[2]	戶 63	方 261	House, dwelling, room 丨·子	S.	B
			丨產 household property		
			丨間 a room, rooms 丨屋		
			丨·錢 house or room rent		
			丨主 landlord 丨東		
			丨客 tenant		
			丨頂 roof of a house		
防[2]	阜 170	方 261	To guard against, beware 丨守		C
			丨禁 forbid, prohibit		
			丨護 guard against 丨·備		
			丨身 self-defence		
倣[3] 仿[3]	人 9	方 261	Imitate, copy; like; a model		E
			丨紙 copying paper		
			丨圈 circular paper-weight		
			丨效 in imitation of 丨照		
			丨格 copy slips 丨影		
彷[3]	彳 60	方 261	Resembling; undecided; seeming		C
			丨·彿 like, as it were		
紡[3]	糸 120	方 261	To spin, reel, twist		C
			丨車·子 spinning-wheel		
			丨線 spin thread		
			丨棉·花 spin cotton 丨花		

Character	Radical	Phonetic	Meaning		
訪[3]	言 149	方 261	To search out; visit; inquire into ｜查 inquire into ｜問 ｜知 ascertain		D
放[4]	支 66	方 261	To let go, set free; lay down ｜債 lend money ｜賬 ｜賑 distribute relief ｜假[4] grant leave, vacation ｜鎗 fire a gun, ｜砲 ｜·出 let out ｜風·箏 fly a kite ｜·下 lay down, let down ｜心 make mind easy ｜學 dismiss school ｜火 set on fire ｜手 let go hold ｜鬆 ｜膽 pluck up courage ｜蕩 profligate, loose ｜肆 ｜縱 give liberty, license ｜羊 tend sheep, ｜牛 etc.		A

Fei

Character	Radical	Phonetic	Meaning		
非[1]	非 175	非 418	Not! not right, false ｜常 uncommon, infrequent ｜凡 ｜正·式 informal ｜禮 indecent, impudent ｜生物 inorganic matter ｜得 must of necessity -otei 除◦｜ except, only if 是｜ right and wrong; scandal 無◦｜ merely, truly		A
啡[1]	口 30	非 418	Sound for transliteration 咖｜ coffee		G
扉[1]	戶 63	非 418	Door, rustic house 柴｜ movable fence-bars		I
緋[1]	糸 120	非 418	Dark red ｜紅 兩頰｜紅 to blush for shame		K

Fei

菲[1]	艸 140	非 418	Fragrant, a radish 芳 ｜ fragrant	fei[3]	I
飛[1]	飛 183	升 414	Sudden, to fly; go quickly ｜ 機 airplane ｜ 禽 birds generally ｜ 鳥 ｜ 星 shooting star ｜ 行 家 aviator ｜ 快 very fast ｜ 跑 run swiftly		C
妃[1]	女 38	己 311	Wife, imperial concubine ｜ 嬪 royal concubine		H
肥[2]	肉 130	巴 312	Fat, fleshy; fertile; loose fit ｜ 胖 large, fleshy ｜ 壯 ｜ 皂 native soap ｜ 澤 fat and glossy, sleek ｜ 土 rich soil ｜ 美 之 地		B
腓[2]	肉 130	非 418	Calf of leg ｜ 腸; to protect, decay		H
匪[3]	匚 22	非 418	Banditti, rebels; seditious; not ｜ 類 bandits, vagabonds ｜ 人, ｜ 徒		E
斐[3]	文 67	非 418	Veins; polished, elegant ｜ 美		I
榧[3] 棐[3]	木 75	非 418	Hazel-shaped nuts ｜·子		G
翡[3]	羽 124	非 418	Variegated; kingfisher ｜ 翠 chrysoprase, emerald		G
菲[3]	艸 140	非 418	Frugal, poor, mean ｜ 薄 trifling, mean	fei[1]	I
沸[4] 濷[4]	水 85	弗 252	Bubble up, boil, stream in Shantung ｜ 水 boiling water ｜ 點 boiling point		H
疿[4]	疒 104	弗 252	Prickly heat, pimples ｜·子 prickly heat		H

費[4]	貝 154	弗 252	To spend, use; lavish; waste	S		A
			｜錢 expensive, wasteful			
			｜勁 expensive of energy ｜力			
			｜心 give trouble, thank you!			
			｜工 laborious			
			｜事 laborious, troublesome			
			｜手續 same			
			｜眼 hard on eyes			
			｜用 expenditure ｜項			
			耗｜ waste 靡｜			
			浪｜ extravagance, dissipation			
			盤｜ traveling expenses 路｜			
廢[4]	广 53	發 246	To cast aside, waste, cancel, void 作｜			C
			｜棄 abandon, cast out			
			｜紙 waste paper			
			｜·去 abolish, annul ｜掉			
			｜壞 spoil, ruin			
			｜·物 worthless thing			
			｜約 denounce a treaty			
癈[4]	疒 104	發 246	Chronic, incurable			E
			｜人 an incurable			
			殘｜ maimed, crippled			
肺[4]	肉 130	市 558	Lungs, pulmonary			E
			｜疫 pneumonic plague			
			｜病 lung disease			
			｜炎 pneumonia			
吠[4]	口 30	吠 457	To bark, yelp 狗｜			G
			｜噬 to bark and bite			

Fen

分[1]	刀 18	分 395	To divide, distinguish ｜∘開		fen[4]	A
			｜爭 dispute, contest			
			｜家 separation of family			
			｜輕重 judge relative values			

Fen

Character	Radical	Phonetic	Meaning	
分[1]			｜居 live separately ｜局 branch office ｜行 ·｜ divide up, share ｜·—·｜ ｜好歹 judge good & bad ｜高低 ｜心 divided mind, give a thought to ｜給 disburse ｜類 to classify ｜離 separate, leave ｜裂 divide, tear apart ｜路 go different roads ｜門 form parties, sects ｜明 distinguish, evidently ｜派 appoint, assign ｜·別 distinguish, difference ｜°辨 discriminate ｜不出 unable to distinguish ｜不清 same ｜散 disperse, distribute ｜身 in two places at once to get away ｜手 to part from a companion ｜·數 grade in studies ｜訴 explain grievance ｜子[3] molecule ｜銀·子 a candareen	
吩[1]	口 30	分 395	To order, command ｜·咐 command, charge	C
紛[1]	糸 120	分 395	Numerous, confused, ill-assorted ｜｜ abundant, confused ｜亂	E
芬[1]	艸 140	分 395	Fragrant, perfume ｜芳 fragrance	F
墳[2] 坆[2]	土 32	賁 417	Grave, tomb ｜地 cemetery ｜墓 grave, mound ｜塋 grave, tomb	D
焚[2]	火 86	林 492	To burn, consume by fire ｜燒 ｜紙 burn paper money ｜香 burn incense	D

粉^3 米 119 分 395 Rice-flour, pigment, powder B
  | 牆 whitewash a wall
  | 紅 flesh or salmon color
  | 飾 decorate, ornament
  | 碎 all to pieces, powdered
  | 條 vermicelli | 絲

分^4 份^4 刀 18 分 395 Duty, office, part, share fen^1 A
  | 兒 pitch, degree; share
  |·量 weight, heft
  | 內 within one's duty
  | 所當然 fitting, proper, duty
  | 子^3 fraction, section
  | 外 extra, extraordinary
  名 | station, rank, obligations
  本 | duty

忿^4 心 61 分 395 Anger, indignation | 怒 C
  | 恨 resentment

噴^4 口 30 賁 417 To sneeze 嚏·| p'en^{14} E

憤^4 心 61 賁 417 Ardour, zeal | 志 D
  | 恨 anger, resentment | 怒

奮^4 大 37 田 809 To rouse, exert, spirited action E
  | 興會 revival meetings
  | 力 exert one's strength
  | 勉 arouse energy, vigor | 勇

糞^4 米 119 異 98 Manure, dung, worthless | 土 E
  | 筐 manure basket

Feng

風^1 凨^1 風 182 風 786 Wind, breath; fashion, usage, custom; fame A
  |◦潮 disturbance, trouble
  | 車 windmill, whirligig
  |·箏 kite
  |◦氣 custom, fashion

Feng

Character	Radical	Phonetic	Meaning		
風[1]			｜琴 organ, accordeon ｜景 view, prospect, landscape ｜箱 bellows, ｜匣 ｜帽 wind-cap ｜領 ｜門 shutters, outer door ｜波 opposition ｜·水 geomancy, position ｜·俗 custom, usage, manners ｜聞 hearsay, rumor ｜聲 ｜雨表 barometer		
瘋[1]	疒 104	風 786	Paralysis, leprosy; mad, insane ｜話 ravings, gibberish ｜狗 mad dog ｜(癱) 病 paralysis ｜·子 madman, maniac		D
封[1]	寸 41	圭 48	To seal, stamp; to fence; C. of letters ｜禁 seal up ｜上, ｜口 ｜河 close river (frost) ｜門 seal a door ｜鎖 lock and seal 信｜ envelope	S.	A
豐[1]	豆 151	豐 736	Abundant, prolific ｜·富 ｜滿 abundant, plentiful ｜亨 ｜年 good harvest, year of plenty ｜盛 full, plentiful ｜足, ｜盈	S.	D
酆[1]	邑 163	豐 736	District in Szechuan,	S.	K
丰[1]	｜ 2	丰 145	Graceful, refined, fine ｜儀 easy, fine manner		K
夆[1]	夊 34	夆 148	To butt, oppose, push, clash		K
峯[1] 峰[1]	山 46	夆 148	Peak of a hill; hump of a camel ｜嶺 mountains		F
烽[1]	火 86	夆 148	Beacon ｜火臺		I

Feng

蜂[1]	虫 142	夆 148	A bee, wasp; to swarm, multiply ｜螫 sting of bee ｜房 bee-hive, comb ｜窩 ｜蠟 bee's wax ｜蜜 honey ｜王 bee king (queen) ｜擁 to swarm forward			E
鋒[1]	金 167	夆 148	Point of spear, lance ｜刃 point and edge ｜鋩 point of weapon			F
逢[2]	辵 162	逢 149	Meet, happen, occur, each time ｜集 on market day ｜雙 (markets) on even days ｜單 (markets) on odd days 每｜ each time, every			C
縫[2]	糸 120	逢 149	To seam, sew ｜線 sewing thread ｜衣機器 sewing machine ｜補 mend and patch 裁｜ tailor,		feng[4]	B
馮[2]	馬 187	馬 255	Horse running	S	p'ing[2]	H
諷[34]	言 149	風 786	Intone, chant; rehearse; ridicule ｜畫 caricatures ｜誦 chant, recite ｜詩 ｜刺 ridicule, satirize			I
縫[4]	糸 120	逢 149	A seam, crack, chance ｜兒		feng[2]	B
奉[4]	大 37	奉 470	Honoured, respectfully; receive ｜·承 flatter ｜教 instructed, join Church ｜求 request, entreat ｜獻 offer up, present ｜送 escort, present ｜天 Manchuria, Mukden, now 遼寧 ｜養 support parents 事。｜ serve superior ｜事			B

俸[4]	人 9	奉 470	Salary, emolument ｜祿 official salary ｜銀 ｜米 official rice		E
鳳[4]	鳥 196	鳥 253	Male phoenix S. ｜凰 phoenix, good omen		G

Fo

佛[2] 僊[2]	人 9	弗 252	Buddha, ｜爺, ｜祖 ｜教 Buddhism ｜門, ｜道 ｜心 pitiful, a pure heart ｜龕 small shrine ｜手 a kind of citron		D

Fou

浮[2]	水 85	孚 408	To float, drift; uncertain; 俗 volatile, ｜躁 ｜塵 dust ｜橋 floating bridge ｜梁 ｜華 superficial show ｜言 rumor, hearsay	fu[2]	E
否[3]	口 30	不 120	Not? if not, or not ｜決 decide against ｜定 negative ｜認 deny 是｜ is it, or is it not?	p'i[3]	F
缶[3] 缻[3]	缶 121	缶 657	Earthenware 瓦｜ earthenware vessels		K
阜[3] 阝[3]	阜 170	阜 752	A mound, fertile, abundant 豐｜ abundant 盛｜	fu[4]	G

Fu

夫[1]	大 37	夫 465	Husband, man, noble lady ｜妻 husband and wife ｜婦 ｜人 wife, lady ｜子 teacher, sage; you	fu[2]	A

Fu

麩^{1}	麥 199	夫 465	Wheat-bran |·子		G
敷^{1}	支 66	甫 597	To make known, proclaim; surplus |藥 apply medicine |油		A
膚^{1}	肉 130	胃 617	The skin, admirable, superficial |皮 the skin 皮·|, 肌|		E
尃^{1}	寸 41	尃 598	To diffuse		P
夫^{2}	大 37	夫 465	Adv., initial particle, now, then, so, as to; final particle |道者 now as to the way	fu^{1}	A
扶^{2}	手 64	夫 465	To uphold, support, help S. |·起 raise or help up |持 hold up, support, |·住, |助 |·手 support with hand		C
芙^{2}	艸 140	夫 465	Mimosa |蓉		K
服^{2}	月 74	月 621	To yield, assent, serve, dress, clothes, 衣·|; used to |·侍 serve, wait upon |·事 |水·土 acclimated |從 submit, comply |務社會 social service 順| obey, submit to		B
畐^{2}	田 102	畐 816	To fill, roll of cloth		P
幅^{24}	巾 50	畐 816	Scroll; hem, border; area; C. of sets 邊| border, frontier; externals		F
福^{2}	示 113	畐 816	Happiness, felicity |·氣 |安 peace and happiness |∘建 Fukien province |分 prosperous, share of joy |祿 prosperity, official favors |地 prosperous place, Heaven |音 the Gospel		B

Fu

蝠²	虫 142	畐 816	The bat, flying squirrel 蝙 | the bat | 鼠		F
輻²	車 159	畐 816	Spokes of wheel | 條		I
伏²	人 9	犬 456	To fall down; humble; suffer; ambush; dog-days, S. | 祈 humbly pray | 兵 ambuscade 埋·| | 地 prostrate self, ambush | 天 hot season, July 19-Aug 18 | 窩 sit on eggs | 卵		C
袱²	衣 145	犬 456	Square cloth, wrapper, 包·| cloth for wrapping bundle		E
弗²	弓 57	弗 252	Not, do not | 成 not complete | 能 unable		D
彿²⁴	彳 60	弗 252	Like, as if, indistinct 彷 | like, as it were, as if		E
孚²	子 39	孚 408	Confidence, to trust in | 信 交 | mutual confidence		K
俘²	人 9	孚 408	Prisoner, captive, to capture | 虜		H
浮²	水 85	孚 408	To float, drift; uncertain; volatile 文 | 塵 dust |⁴水 to swim | 水 雷 floating mines	fou²	E
符²	竹 118	付 19	Tally; charms; verify, match; credentials; fulfill S. | 前 言 fulfill a promise | 咒 spells, charms, incantations | 合 tally, to reconcile | 印 seal of office, credentials		E
覆²⁴	襾 146	復 545	To and fro; to overthrow; reply; further | 査 re-examine | 審 | 回 to reply 回 | | 議 to reconsider | 上 cover over, e.g., gilding	fu⁴	E

Fu

縛[2]	糸 120	尃 598	To tie, bind ｜綁 tie, bind fast｜住		F
复[24]		复 544	To go back		P
蝮[24]	虫 142	复 544	Adder, viper; deadly｜蛇 ｜虺 python		K
府[3]	广 53	府 20	Palace, prefecture; residence ｜庫 treasury, depot ｜·上 residence; family		A
俯[3]	人 9	府 20	To bow down, stoop; condescend ｜察 deign to examine ｜就 condescend, adapt ｜伏 prostrate, crouch		C
腑[3]	肉 130	府 20	Bowels, viscera｜臟, 臟｜		G
腐[3]	肉 130	府 20	Curd, putrid, rotten ｜朽 rotten｜爛 ｜乳 beanmilk, ｜敗 corrupt; old; worn out 豆｜beancurd, effete		F
斧[3]	斤 69	父 530	An axe, hatchet｜斤,｜·子		C
釜[3]	金 167	父 530	Caldron, 1½ bu. measure		H
撫[3] 捬[3]	手 64	無 259	To soothe, pacify, cherish; governor,｜養 to rear ｜育 foster, cherish ｜慰 soothe, pacify		D
甫[3]	用 101	甫 597	Begin; just; one's "style" ｜到 just arrived		G
哺[3]	口 30	甫 597	To feed by hand, suckle ｜乳 to suckle｜養	pu3'4	I
脯[3]	肉 130	甫 597	Dried meat, salary｜肉		H
輔[3]	車 159	甫 597	To support, aid, help, second ｜助 help, assist｜佐 ｜保 mutual guarantee; to protect		E

Fu

腹[34]	肉 130	复 544	The stomach; abdomen, middle 丨中 in belly or heart 丨悶 sad; uncomfortable 丨疼 pain in stomach	E
拊[3]	手 64	付 19	To tap, lay hand on 丨心 lay hand on heart	K
父[4]	父 88	父 530	Father, fatherly 丨·親 丨老 elders 丨母 father and mother, parents 丨子[3] father and son	A
婦[4] 媍[4]	女 38	帚 674	Woman, wife 丨人 丨孺 women and children 丨嬰 丨女 women, womankind 丨道 新丨 bride	A
副[4]	刀 18	畐 816	Assistant, deputy, second; C. of pairs, sets 丨會長[3] vice-president of society 丨°手 assistant 丨總統 vice-president 丨業 side business	B
匐[4]	勹 20	畐 816	To crawl, creep 匍丨	H
富[4]	宀 40	畐 816	Wealthy, rich, abundant S. 丨戶 wealthy man or family 丨貴 riches and honor, wealthy 丨厚 same 丨足 ample wealth 丨有 丨·裕 surplus of anything	C
付[4]	人 9	付 19	To deliver; pay; send 丨交 to deliver to 交丨 丨錢 hand money to, pay 丨給 to give to 丨與 丨托(託) to entrust, to commission, 托(託)丨	C
咐[4]	口 30	付 19	To order, command 吩丨	C

Fu

附^{4}	阜 170	付 19	To follow, adjoin, lean on, possessed ｜近 near, neighboring ｜和 to follow slavishly ｜鬼 possest by demon 被鬼｜ ｜編 supplement, appendix; to append ｜張, ｜錄 ｜身 possest by ｜手 join hands ｜隨 incidental, subordinate ｜屬 ｜則 by-laws ｜例 ｜從 follow, submit to		D
仆^{4}	人 9	卜 119	To fall prostrate ｜倒在地 fall to the ground	p'u^{1}	D
訃^{4}	言 149	卜 119	Announce parent's death ｜文 death notice		H
赴^{4}	走 156	卜 119	To go to, attend; reach ｜席 attend a banquet ｜宴 ｜會 attend a meeting ｜任 go to one's post		C
負^{4}	貝 154	貝 856	To bear on back; turn back on; ungrateful ｜債 be in debt ｜欠 ｜情 ungrateful ｜恩, ｜心 ｜苦 endure hardships ｜敗 loss, defeat 背｜ carry on back, bear ｜背		C
復^{4}	彳 60	復 545	To repeat, again ｜舊 as of old ｜新 to renew ｜興 revive, recover prosperity ｜活 return to life ｜生 ｜元 return to health ｜原		C
覆^{4}	襾 146	復 545	To cover, brood (as birds) ｜蓋 cover over	fu^{2}	E

Character	Radical	Phonetic	Meaning	Other readings	Grade
傅^{4}	人 9	尃 598	Teacher, tutor; to superintend; S. lay on colors ｜油 apply oil, anoint 師·｜ teacher, master		D
洑^{4}	水 85	犬 456	To swim, ｜水		E
複^{4}	衣 145	复 544	Double; double garment; again ｜姓 double surname ｜雜 miscellaneous, complicated		E
賦^{4}	貝 154	武 330	To spread; pay levy; bestow; poetry; idyll ｜性 natural disposition 稟｜ ｜予 implant, give		F
拂^{4}	手 64	弗 252	To brush away, dust off; oppose ｜淚 wipe away tears ｜拭		I

Ha

Character	Radical	Phonetic	Meaning	Other readings	Grade
哈^{1}	口 30	合 708	To expel breath; yawn ｜ ｜ hearty laughter ｜·息 gape, yawn 打｜·息 ｜·喇 spoiled by keeping, soured	ha^{3} k'a^{1}	F
蛤^{2}	虫 142	合 708	Frog ｜蟆 frog, toad 田｜ edible frog	ko^{2}	G
蝦^{2}	虫 142	叚 639	A frog, toad ｜·蟆	ho^{2} hsia^{1}	F
哈^{3}	口 30	合 708	｜一聲 Derisive sound ｜·達門 a Peking gate ｜·吧狗 Peking pug	ha^{1} k'a^{1}	F

Hai

Character	Radical	Phonetic	Meaning	Other readings	Grade
咳^{14}	口 30	亥 874	Exclamation of surprise	k'o^{2}	D
孩^{2}	子 39	亥 874	Child, youth ｜兒, ｜·子, ｜童 ｜·氣 childish, inexperienced ｜提 children 嬰｜		A

Hai

Character	Radical	Phonetic	Meaning		Romanization	
頦²	頁 181	亥 874	The chin		k'o¹	H
骸²	骨 188	亥 874	Human bones, ｜骨		hsieh²	F
還² 还²	辵 162	睘 371	Still more, again, yet ｜沒來 not yet come ｜不知足 still unsatisfied ｜不彀 not yet enough ｜得 also necessary ｜有 there is still, still have 沒哪｜ not yet (in reply) ｜沒哪	俗	huan²	A
海³	水 85	每 572	Sea, lake, oceanic; vast ｜潮 the tide ｜權 sea power ｜軍 the navy ｜狗 sea-dog, seal ｜口 sea-port ｜寇 pirates ｜賊, ｜盜 ｜股 gulf ｜關 the Customs ｜綿 a sponge ｜絨 ｜邊 sea-coast, shore ｜岸, ｜濱, ｜沿 ｜參 sea-slugs ｜市 mirage, groundless ｜帶 sea-weed ｜菜 ｜°棠 small apple ｜島 an island ｜隄 breakwater ｜底電線 submarine cable ｜灣 a bay ｜味 sea delicacy ｜腰 a strait			A
和⁴	口 30	禾 510	With	俗	ho²⁴ han⁴	A
害⁴	宀 40	害 146	To injure; suffer from; very ｜己 hurt self, suicide ｜·處 injuries			A

害[4]			｜性命 to kill ｜命, ｜死 ｜羞 shame, ashamed ｜臊 ｜人利己 selfishly injure others ｜怕 fear, feel afraid ｜病 become sick		
嗐[4]	口 30	害 146	Alack! haiya! ｜呀		H
亥[4]	亠 8	亥 874	9-11 p.m., 10th moon, 12th year ｜月 the tenth moon		H
駭[4]	馬 187	亥 874	Startled, alarmed	hsieh[4]	F

Han

憨[1]	心 61	敢 629	Silly, idiotic ｜包, ｜生 ｜厚 simple, honest		I
頇[1]	頁 181	干 32	Tediously slow ｜慢 tardy, dawdling 慢｜		I
鼾[1]	鼻 209	干 32	To snore 鼻｜		H
酣[1]	酉 164	甘 101	Merry, tipsy, half-drunk ｜醉		K
寒[2]	宀 40	寒 100	Cold; poor; my, mine ｜顫 tremble with cold ｜苦 poor, poverty 貧｜ ｜冷 cold, winter ｜天 ｜舍, ｜門 my house, my family ｜暑表 thermometer ｜帶 Arctic circle, zone 小｜, 大｜ divisions of winter		A
含[2]	口 32	含 437	To hold, contain; cherish; restrain ｜磣 disgraceful, looks bad ｜恨 cherish resentment, ｜怒 ｜糊 mutter, reticent; indefinite ｜忍 bear, put up with ｜容	hen[2]	D

Han

Character	Radical	Phonetic	Meaning	Other readings	Code
函^{2} 凾^{2} 圅^{2}	凵 17	函 652	To enfold; letter; contain ｜信 a letter 信｜,｜件 ｜授學校 correspondence school ｜託 request by letter		F
涵^{2}	水 85	函 652	To swamp, soak, bear, magnan-imous ｜量 treat leniently｜容, 包｜		H
喊^{3}	口 30	咸 344	To call, cry aloud, call after ｜叫 vociferate, call loudly, 呼｜ ｜醒 awake by calling ｜冤 cry for justice		C
罕^{3}	网 122	干 32	Rare, few, seldom; a net ｜見 rarely seen ｜聞 rarely heard ｜有 very seldom, rare thing 稀·｜ rare, remarkable		C
頷^{34}	頁 181	含 437	The chin, jaws,		K
和^{4}	口 30	禾 510	With,｜別·人 俗	hai^{2} ho^{24}	A
嘆^{4}		茣 107	Chinese		P
漢^{4}	水 85	茣 107	Han dynasty, B.C. 206—A.D. 220 Chinese ｜◦朝 the Han dynasty,｜室 ｜◦人 the Chinese race,｜種,｜族 ｜口 Hankow ｜文 Chinese literature, language		B
汗^{4}	水 85	干 32	Sweat, perspiration; vast ｜毛 short hair on cuticle ｜衫 sweat-shirt｜溻兒 ｜溻了 soakt with sweat		B
矸^{4}	石 112	干 32	Marble; a cliff ｜白玉 white marble 丹｜ cinnabar		H

Character	Radical	Phonetic	Meaning	Alternate	
旱[4]	日 72	旱 33	Dry, drought, ｜天 ｜路 road, land route ｜傘 sun umbrella ｜災 a great drought		B
悍[4]	心 61	旱 33	Overbearing, fierce, cruel ｜婦 a virago		H
捍[4] 扞[4]	手 64	旱 33	To ward off, defend ｜禦 ｜患 ward off calamity		K
銲[4] 釬[4]	金 167	旱 33	Solder, to solder metals ｜錫 solder ｜·上 solder on		E
翰[4]	羽 124	倝 17	Pencil, letter; literary ｜·林 Han-lin graduate		C
憾[4]	心 61	感 345	Regret, resentment, vexed at ｜恨 resentful hate		G
撼[4]	手 64	感 345	To move, shake ｜動 brandish, shake ｜搖 move, shake, excite, 搖｜		H
厂[34]	厂 27	厂 193	A cliff		K

Hang

Character	Radical	Phonetic	Meaning	Alternate	
碚[1] 夯[1]	石 112	夊 540	A piledriver, earth-pounder ｜號 the rammers' song ｜歌 打｜ pound earth solid		K
航[2]	舟 137	亢 398	Ship, barge; to sail ｜海 sail the sea, navigation ｜空 sail the air, aviation		E
行[2]	行 144	行 5	Trade, store, row, series, kind ｜幾 which brother are you? ｜◦家 class, men of trade ｜情 trade-custom; state of market ｜·市 market price 在｜ in the particular trade 外｜ amateurish, layman	hsing[24]	A

Hao

蒿^1	艸 140	高 582	A strong tall weed |·子 artemisia, sage-brush		F
薅^1	艸 140	辱 356	To weed, pull out | 草 | 頭·髮 pull out hair		F
號^2	虍 141	虍 203	To cry out, scream | 泣 to weep aloud | 咷 大 哭 loud lamentations | 天 call to heaven for aid	hao^4	A
毫^2	毛 82	毛 375	Downy; minute, atom; one ten-thousandth of a tael | 厘 a small degree the least | 無 相 干 no connection with | 無 干 涉 | 無 可 取 no single good point		D
鶴^2	鳥 196	鳥 **253**	The crane 仙 | ; longevity, 俗	ho^4	F
豪^2	豕 152	豕 285	Heroic, brave; overbearing | 氣 a brave disposition | 傑 a hero		F
嚎^2 嘷^2	口 30	豕 285	Roar of beasts, to howl, wail | | 聲 a roaring, howling		G
壕^2	土 32	豕 285	City moat | 坑 | 溝 trench, moat		H
濠^2	水 85	豕 285	City moat, ditch | 溝 ditch, drain		I
好^3	女 38	女 552	Good, well, friendly; very | 極·了 exceedingly good | 幾 次 a good many times | 久 a long while |·處 advantage, benefit	hao^4	A

Hao

好3			| 漢·子 a fine fellow, a stout Chinese | |1·的 quietly, peacefully | 像 just like, as if, | 似 | 學 easy to learn | 些1(個) a good many |·些 a little better | 意(思) good or kind intention | 熱 very hot, so | 冷, | 大, etc. | 日·子 birthday; lucky day | 容·易 "precious easy"=hard | 看 good looking | 過 easy to pass |·了 finished, ready, recovered | 能 so that... |∘比 for instance | 脾 氣 good tempered | 不 | is it good? will it do? | 使 usable, handy for use, | 用 |·是 | ......it is all right but...... | 說 thank you for compliment |·得 很 exceedingly good |∘在 luckily... | 造·化 good fortune |·哇 how do you do? |·阿			
郝3	邑 163	赤 432	Surname	S	ho4	H
好4	女 38	女 552	To love, be fond of | 酒 色 addicted to profligacy | 學 devoted to learning | 利 covetous, selfish | 事 fond of affairs | 說 話 fond of talking 嗜∘| appetites, tastes		hao3	A
號4 号4	虍 141	虍 203	Appellation, "style"; sign, number, label; to mark, register |·令 order, word of command		hao2	A

號4			| 脈 to feel the pulse | 頭 number or mark; carter | 筒 a trumpet, 掛 | register, check (as baggage)		
耗4	耒 127	毛 375	To waste; depreciate, |°費 | 減 to diminish |·子 a rat		E
浩4	水 85	告 717	Vast, great; liberal mind | 大 great, broad, extensive | 蕩		F
皓4	白 106	告 717	Luminous, white | 白 | 月 bright moonlight		K
涸4	水 85	固 703	To dry up, exhausted | 乾·了	ho4	H
昊4	日 72	天 462	Luminous, grand, vast | 天 Great Heaven, God		I

He, see Ho

Hei

黑1	黑 203	黑 831	Black, dark | 暗 俗 |·下 night time | 夜 | 心 black at heart, evil | 龍江 the Amoor | 麵 dark flour | 白 black & white; good & bad | 牲·口 euphemism for pig | 糖 dark sugar | 豆 black beans	ho4	A

Hen

含2	口 32	含 437	To hold in mouth | 在嘴·裏 文	han2	D
痕2	疒 104	艮 359	Scar, cicatrix, stain, flaw | 跡 scars of wounds, traces		E

Character	Radical	Phonetic	Meaning		
很³	彳 40	艮 359	Very, extremely ｜好 very good 好·得｜ ｜難 very difficult, so too｜少 etc. ｜是 it is very true		A
狠³	犬 96	艮 359	Rankling hate, very ｜心 harsh, mind fixed ｜毒 cruel, savage		C
恨⁴	心 61	艮 359	To hate, hatred,｜惡 ｜怒 angry, animosity ｜·不能 (or·得) vexed at inability, would that! ｜怨 animosity, grudge		A

Heng

Character	Radical	Phonetic	Meaning		
哼¹	口 30	亨 742	Exclam. of pain, displeasure ｜哈 to hem and haw ｜·｜ to moan, groan; grunt	eng¹	G
橫²	木 75	黃 822	Crosswise, horizontal ｜桌 a long side table ｜斜 criss-cross ｜梁 crossbeams ｜·豎 horizontal and perpendicular; on no account ｜·是	heng⁴	B
恒² 恆²	心 61	亘 795	Constant, persevering, permanent ｜產 patrimony, property ｜勁 perseverance ｜情 general disposition ｜心 perseverance, constancy		C
衡² 衝²	行 144	行 5	Balance, to weigh; crosswise S. ｜量 to measure, estimate ｜平 pair of scales 權｜ authority		E
亨¹²	亠 8	亨 742	To pervade; prosperous ｜通 persevering, successful		E
橫⁴	木 75	黃 822	Perverse, mulish.｜逆, 發｜ ｜行 wicked conduct ｜事 misfortune	heng²	B

誶[4]	言 149	幸 159	Angry words, to berate 發 | to scold		I

Ho

喝[1]	口 30	曷 239	To drink, cry out | 茶 drink tea | 酒, | 水, etc. | 足·了 have drunk enough | 醉·了 to get drunk 吃 | eat and drink	ho4	A
呵[1]	口 30	可 699	To gape, scold | 欠 a gape, a yawn		I
苛[1]	艸 140	可 699	Vexatious, harsh; to annoy	k'o1	K
禾[2]	禾 115	禾 510	Growing grain, crops, | 稼 | 苗 young blades of grain | 穗 an ear of grain | 田 grain field		E
和[2] 龢[2]	口 30	禾 510	To unite; filling; harmony with, S. |·氣 friendly feeling, good will | 好 reconcile, agree, | 息 | 合 agree, harmonious union | 美 peaceable, harmonious | 睦 | 泥 mix earth with water huo4- | 煖 warm 煖·| --huo | 平 peace; peaceful, temperate | 平解决 settle amicably | 解 |·尙 a Buddhist priest | 順 agreeable, complaisant | 他 with him | 約 a treaty	hai4 han4 ho4	A
合[24]	口 30	合 708	In accord with; to shut; join, add | 其中 average, proper, medium | 羣 social, gregarious, union | 而爲一 bring into one, unite | 法 according to law, legal		B

Ho

<table>
<tr><td>合[24]</td><td></td><td></td><td>| 乎理 right, reasonable, | 理
| 宜 fit, proper, suitable, | 式
| 意 suit one's views
| 格(的) having the qualifications
| 規·矩 according to custom
| 算 add up, reckon
|°在一塊 join together
| 同 a contract, agreement
| 頁 hinges
| 用 answer the purpose</td><td></td><td></td><td></td></tr>
<tr><td>盒[2]</td><td>皿
108</td><td>合
708</td><td>Box, casket |·子
| 蓋 lid of box
| 子鎗 quick-firing gun</td><td></td><td></td><td>B</td></tr>
<tr><td>閤[2]</td><td>門
169</td><td>合
708</td><td>A small side door
(used as 閣)</td><td></td><td>ko[2]</td><td>F</td></tr>
<tr><td>河[2]</td><td>水
85</td><td>可
699</td><td>A river, canal
| 岸 river-bank | 邊, | 沿兒[4]
| 溝 dry bed of torrent
| 口 mouth of river
| 流 current of river
| 路 river travel | 道
| 南 province of Honan; so | 北
| 堤 dyke on river bank</td><td></td><td></td><td>B</td></tr>
<tr><td>何[2]</td><td>人
9</td><td>何
700</td><td>Who? what? how?
| 妨 what objection?
| 如 how? in what manner?
| 干 what concern?
| 故 why? on what account?
| 必 what need? why must?
| 不 to be sure; why shouldn't?
| 時 at what time?
| 事 what affair?
| 等 what sort? how great!</td><td>S.</td><td></td><td>C</td></tr>
<tr><td>荷[2]</td><td>艸
140</td><td>何
700</td><td>Lotus; Holland; to sustain
| 花 lotus blossom
| 蘭國 Holland
| 蘭水 soda water</td><td></td><td></td><td>G</td></tr>
</table>

Ho

劾$^{2, 4}$	力 19	亥 874	To investigate; impeach, accuse | 究 investigate | 問, 考 | 彈 | impeach | 參		K
核^{2}	木 75	亥 874	Kernel, stone, gist; examine | 疫 bubonic plague |·子 病 | 仁 kernel of nuts | 算 to calculate |·桃 the walnut	hu^{2}	E
盍^{2} 盇^{2}	皿 108	盍 45	Why not? | 反 其 本 矣 why not go back to the root?		G
闔^{2}	門 169	盍 45	Door, to close; whole, all | 家 the whole family | 宅, | 府 | 城 the whole town | 門 close a door		F
蝦^{2}	虫 142	叚 639	| 蟆 Frog 文	ha^{2} hsia^{1}	F
曷^{2}	曰 73	曷 239	How? what? why not? | 故 | 可 how was it possible?		G
喝^{4}	口 30	曷 239	吆 | Cry out 俗	ho^{1}	A
黑^{4}	黑 203	黑 831	Black, | 龍 江 Amoor river, 文	hei^{1}	A
赫^{4}	赤 155	赫 424	Bright, fiery; awe-inspiring S. | | (有 名) great reputation | 連 double surname S.		G
嚇^{4}	口 30	赫 424	To anger, frighten 文 | 詐 extort	hsia^{4}	A
和^{4}	口 30	禾 510	With; to respond to in singing	hai^{4} hau^{4} ho^{2}	A
賀^{4}	貝 154	加 716	To congratulate 慶 | , | 喜 S. | 新 年 New Year's congratulation | 新 禧 | 壽 birthday congratulations		D
鶴^{4}	鳥 196	鳥 253	The crane; longevity 文	hao^{2}	F

郝^{4}	邑 163	赤 423	Ancient place in Shantung		hao^{3}	H
壑^{4}	土 32	谷 700	Gully, ditch, pool | 溝			K
涸^{4}	水 85	固 703	To dry up		hao^{4}	I

Hou

齁^{1} 齁^{1}	鼻 209	勾 225	To snore, | 鼾; very | 臭 stinking | 腥 | 鹹 extremely salt, briny salt | 苦 dreadfully bitter ; so too | 臊, | 酸			I
侯^{2}	人 9	侯 478	Marquis, noble | 爵, | 爺 諸 | feudal lords	S.		F
喉^{2}	口 30	侯 478	Throat, gullet, guttural | 腫 症 goitre |·嚨 throat			D
睺^{2}	日 72	侯 478	A constellation 羅 |			K
猴^{2}	犬 94	侯 478	Monkey | 兒 | 精 clever, sharp, shrewd			E
瘊^{2}	疒 104	侯 478	Mole, wart, pimple			H
吼^{3}	口 30	乙 297	Cry of beasts | 叫 to bawl out			G
候^{4}	人 9	侯 478	To wait, wait for ; time |·著 waiting | 缺 wait for a vacancy | 補 時·| time, occasion			A
後^{4}	彳 40	幺 876	After, then ; heir | 街 street on north side | 兒 (·個) day after to-morrow | 日, |·天 same | 悔 regret, repent | 裔 posterity | 人 |·來 afterwards, hereafter | 手	S.		A

後[4]			｜媽 step-mother, ｜母	
			｜門 back door	
			｜。面 behind ｜·邊, ｜·頭	
			｜·半·天 afternoon ｜晌	
			｜·輩 after generations ｜代	
			｜世 after-life, later ages	
			｜嗣 an heir	
			｜隊 rear-guard ｜防	
厚[4]	厂 27	厂 193	Thick, generous; reliable	B
			｜恩 great kindness	
			｜臉 brazen-faced	
			｜薄 thickness, liberal and stingy	
			｜待 treat liberally	
			｜·道 liberal, considerate	
后[4]	口 30	后 721	Sovereign, empress, queen	F
			皇｜the Empress	
			皇太｜Empress Dowager	

Hsi

西[1]	西 146	西 775	West, foreign, ｜方	A
			｜裝 foreign dress	
			｜法 European method	
			｜紅柿(子) the tomato	
			｜·瓜 water-melon	
			｜國 western countries, Europe ｜洋	
			｜曆 foreign calendar	
			｜陵 western imperial tombs	
			｜南 south-west ｜北 north-west	
			｜·邊 on the west side	
			｜藏 Tibet	
惜[1]	心 61	昔 799	A sigh of pity, regret	B
			｜愛 to pity 愛｜sparing	
			｜錢 use money sparingly	
			｜身 take care of oneself	
			｜字紙 respect written paper	
			可｜how sad! I am sorry	

Hsi

希[1]	巾 50	希 172	Rare; seldom; to hope; very ｜·奇 wonderful ｜·罕 rare ｜少 few ｜軟 very soft, limber ｜臘 Greece, ｜臘國 ｜臘教 Greek church ｜臘·的 Grecian ｜伯來 Hebrew ｜碎 in bits, all to flinders ｜望 hope, to hope for			C
稀[1]	禾 115	希 172	Open, thin, ｜薄; apart ｜稠 thickness, viscidity ｜飯 congee-porridge ｜粥 ｜爛 cooked very soft ｜密 density, openness			E
吸[1] 噏[1]	口 30	及 218	To inhale, suck up; attract ｜氣 draw in the breath ｜氣筒 air-pump ｜力 attraction, gravitation ｜鐵石 lode-stone ｜烟 smoke tobacco or opium ｜引 to draw, attract			E
羲[1]	羊 123	秀 217	Breath, vapour 伏｜ Emperor Fu Hsi			H
犧[1]	牛 93	秀 217	Victims for sacrifice, ｜牲 ｜牲性命 give life to a cause			E
棲[1] 栖[1]	木 75	妻 668	To roost, rest, settle ｜止 to stop, cease 鷄｜ chicken-roost		ch'i[1]	F
奚[1]	大 37	奚 881	Why? how? what? ｜堪 how endure it?	S		G
溪[1]	水 85	奚 881	Mountain-stream, rivulet ｜水 淸｜ clear water stream		ch'i[1]	F
熙[1]	火 86	己 311	Splendid, glorious, crowds ｜和 flourishing, prosperous 康｜ Emperor K'ang-Hsi			G

Hsi

<table>
<tr><td>兮[1]
兮[1]</td><td>八
12</td><td>丂
240</td><td>Interjection of inquiry, doubt, admiration</td><td></td><td>G</td></tr>
<tr><td>攜[1]
携[1]</td><td>手
64</td><td>隹
52</td><td>To lead by hand, take with, carry 俗
| 眷 bring one's family
| 同 accompanied by</td><td>hsieh²</td><td>G</td></tr>
<tr><td>嬉[1]</td><td>女
38</td><td>喜
739</td><td>Pretty, play, pleasure; ramble
| 笑 to make fun</td><td></td><td>H</td></tr>
<tr><td>悉[14]</td><td>心
61</td><td>心
377</td><td>All, altogether, | 皆
| 知 know fully, "take notice"</td><td></td><td>E</td></tr>
<tr><td>膝[1]</td><td>肉
130</td><td>桼
527</td><td>Knee, lap; to kneel
| 下 the children
屈 | to bend the knee</td><td></td><td>E</td></tr>
<tr><td>析[1]</td><td>木
75</td><td>析
211</td><td>To split wood, divide, 分·|
| 義 explain</td><td></td><td>H</td></tr>
<tr><td>晰[1]
晳[1]</td><td>日
72</td><td>析
211</td><td>Clear, bright, detail; to discriminate
明 | clear, perspicuous</td><td></td><td>I</td></tr>
<tr><td>犀[1]</td><td>牛
93</td><td>犀
726</td><td>Rhinoceros, | 牛; sharp
| 角 rhinoceros horn</td><td></td><td>K</td></tr>
<tr><td>息[21]</td><td>心
61</td><td>息
853</td><td>Breath, 氣·|; sigh, 嘆 |
stop, rest, interest
| 戰 to stop war
| 止 to stop, cease 止 |
| 利 interest 利 |
| 怒 appease anger
安 | rest, quiet</td><td></td><td>B</td></tr>
<tr><td>媳[2]</td><td>女
38</td><td>息
853</td><td>Bride, wife, daughter-in-law |·婦</td><td></td><td>A</td></tr>
<tr><td>熄[2]</td><td>火
86</td><td>息
853</td><td>To extinguish, put out
| 滅 extinguish fire</td><td></td><td>F</td></tr>
<tr><td>習[2]</td><td>羽
124</td><td>習
294</td><td>To practice, habit
|·氣 habit |∘慣
| 學 to learn, to practice
| 慣 accustomed to, versed in
| 熟 perfect, versed in, 熟 |</td><td>S.</td><td>B</td></tr>
</table>

Hsi

Character	Radical	Phonetic	Meaning	Grade
習²			丨業 practising a profession 丨練 to train, practice, 練·丨 溫丨 rehearse, review	
席²	巾 50	席 559	A mat, a feast; place to sit S. 酒丨 a dinner, a banquet 主丨 chairman, toastmaster 退丨 withdraw from meeting	C
蓆²	艸 140	席 559	A mat, matting 丨棚 mat awning 炕丨 mat on stove-bed 涼丨 mat for warm weather	G
錫²	金 167	易 235	Pewter, tin; to bestow, give; abbot 丨器 tinware 丨·匠 a tinker 丨恩 to bestow grace 丨壺 pewter pot	E
昔²	日 72	昔 799	Ancient, formerly, 丨年 丨日 on a former day	E
襲²	衣 145	衣 367	Lining, double; to raid, surprise; inherit 丨爵 hereditary rank	K
洗³	水 85	先 39	To wash, cleanse; baptize; reform 丨心 cleanse the heart 丨衣·裳 wash clothes 丨禮 rite of baptism, 領丨 丨臉盆 a wash-basin 丨·不掉 can't wash out 丨三 washing baby on 3rd day 丨澡 take a bath	A
喜³	口 30	喜 739	Joy, to rejoice, delight 丨樂 丨愛 to delight in 丨好⁴ 丨轎 bridal chair 丨·鵲 the magpie 丨笑 smile with pleasure 丨信 joyful news 丨·歡 feel pleasure, delight 歡·丨 丨容 a pleased countenance	B

喜^{3}			丨色 a joyful face 丨◦事 a joyful event, wedding 丨悅 gratified, pleased		
禧^{3}	示 113	喜 739	God-given joy, good luck 丨慶 felicitous 丨年 New Year's joy		E
璽^{3}	玉 96	爾 564	Imperial seal, 國丨, 玉丨 丨書 Imperial letter		G
徙^{3}	彳 40	徙 136	To remove, shift 丨移 to remove 遷丨		K
屣^{3} 蹝^{3}	尸 44	徙 136	Straw sandals, slippers 脫丨 take off slipper		K
匸^{3}	匸 23	匸 645	A box, coffer, chest		K
細^{4}	糸 120	糸 886	Fine, carefully, delicate 丨察 examine minutely 丨看 丨講 go into details, 丨說 丨究 carefully investigate 丨丨^{1} carefully, minutely 丨小 petty, trifling 丨心 attentive 丨軟 fine and soft 丨密 small, delicate 丨微 丨胞 physical cells 丨作 a spy 奸·丨 丨粗 fine and coarse 粗丨 底·丨 bottom facts 仔·丨		B
繫^{4}	糸 120	毄 405	To let down, draw 丨念 longing thoughts 丨·下·來 let down 丨·上◦去 draw up	chi^{4}	B
戲^{4}	戈 62	戈 331	Theatricals; play, joke; mock 丨場 a theatre 丨園 丨劇 theatricals		D

戲[4]			｜法 sleight-of-hand, juggling 變｜法 ｜弄 to mock, trifle ｜耍 ｜臺 theatrical stage ｜談 to jest, to joke ｜言 ｜°子 an actor	
系[4]	糸 120	系 887	Succession, genealogy, clue, link ｜統 synthesis; a system	G
係[4]	人 9	系 887	Connected with, is ｜親 related to, connected, ｜屬 ｜友 friendly relations	F
隙[4]	阜 170	小 121	A crack, fissure; pretext; quarrel 開｜ begin quarrel 尋｜ seek quarrel	G
夕[41]	夕 36	夕 267	Evening, late 旦｜ morning and evening 朝｜ 除｜ New Year's eve	G
汐[4]	水 85	夕 267	Night tide 潮｜ morning and night tides	I
盻[4]	目 109	丂 240	Look at angrily; perplexed ｜視 glare at	I
翕[4]	羽 124	合 708	In harmony, united; all 和｜ at peace	K
鬩[4]	門 191	兒 684	Resentment, quarrel ｜牆 civil strife	K
舄[4]	臼 134	舄 688	Large, splendid; slipper, clog 金｜ gold-embroidered slippers	K

Hsia

瞎[1]	目 109	害 146	Blind, ignorant; heedless ｜闖 blindly run against ｜話 lies, falsehood, nonsense ｜·子 a blind person ｜眼 blind 眼｜	C

Hsia

Character	Radical	Phonetic	Meaning			
蝦^{1} 鰕^{1}	虫 142	叚 639	A shrimp, a prawn |米 dried prawns or shrimps		ha^{2} ho^{2}	F
匣^{2}	匚 22	甲 825	Case, small box, casket |·子 話|·子 phonograph			B
狎^{2}	犬 94	甲 825	Familiar, intimate |習; caress |愛 fond of, love.			I
斜^{2}	斗 68	余 31	Oblique, slanting |坡 sloping bank	文	hsieh^{2}	D
轄^{2}	車 159	害 146	To control, govern |管, 管| |制 to rule over, control			D
狹^{2} 陜^{2}	犬 94	夾 455	Narrow; narrow-minded |窄 petty, narrow |小 |道 a narrow road			E
俠^{2}	人 9	夾 455	Magnanimous, valiant, a hero |氣 magnanimity, courage			G
叚^{2}	又 29	叚 639	False	S		K
暇^{2}	日 72	叚 639	Leisure, relaxation |時 |日 a day of leisure			F
瑕^{2}	玉 96	叚 639	Flaw, blemish |疵 a weak point, flaw			E
遐^{2}	辵 162	叚 639	Distant, far; enduring |邇 far and near			G
霞^{2}	雨 173	叚 639	Red clouds, glow, lowering 晚| glow of sunset			H
𡨄^{3}	宀 40	𡨄 100	To stop up			P
下^{4}	一 1	卜 119	Below, down, next |車 leave carriage, so |船, |馬, etc. |棋 to play chess |降 to descend 降| |賤 mean, vile |·去·罷 go down! get down! |牀 leave one's bed			A

Character	Radical	Phonetic	Meaning	Other reading	Grade
下^{4}			｜凡 Incarnation of deity ｜鄉 go into the country ｜學 quit school ｜雪 to snow, so ｜霜, ｜雨, etc. ｜∘回 the next time ｜遍, ｜次 ｜議院 Lower House ｜·人 servants ｜·來 to come down ｜流 down river; depraved ｜∘落 residence, lodging ｜樓 come down stairs, so ｜山 etc. ｜錨 to drop anchor ｜·巴 (頦兒) the chin ｜·半·天 the afternoon ｜午 ｜·邊 below, the bottom ｜平 lower even tone (2nd) ｜·不去 can't go down, will not do ｜·不來 can't come down ｜身 lower parts of body ｜手 put one's hand to ｜水 go into the water ｜蛋 to lay an egg ｜地獄 to go to hell ｜月 next month		
夏^{4}	夊 35	夏 854	Summer, ｜·天, ｜季 S. ｜∘朝 Hsia dynasty B.C. 2205-1766 ｜至 summer solstice ｜侯 double surname S. ｜令會 summer conference ｜令學校 summer-school ｜布 grass-cloth		A
廈^{4} 厦^{4}	广 53	夏 854	Mansion, front room	sha^{4}	G
嚇^{4}	口 30	赫 424	To frighten, terrify ｜·呼 ｜跑·了 frightened into flight	ho^{4}	A

嚇^{4}			|·死人 to scare to death |我一跳 made me jump with fright			
洽^{24}	水 85	合 708	To blend, harmonize |于	文	ch'ia^{4}	F
頰^{4}	頁 181	夾 455	The chin	文	chia^{14}	G
罅^{4} [illegible]^{4}	缶 121	乎 29	Crack, fissure; grudge; pretext |隙 crack, split, grudge 裂| a rent, crack			K
襾^{4}	襾 146	襾 775	A cover			K

Hsiang

香^{1}	香 186	禾 510	Fragrant, incense |氣 aromatic, fragrance |味 |港 Hongkong |蕉 banana |·椿 sweet-smelling ailanthus |·瓜 various melons |料 perfumery, spices |爐 an incense pot or vase |柏 the cypress tree |水 liquid scents, flavors |桃 the lemon 檸檬 |烟 cigarettes |油 sesame oil 燒| burn incense			B
鄉^{1}	邑 163	鄉 365	Country, village, rustic |長^{3} village elder |親 country neighbors |·下 country |間 |里 a village |村 |民 villagers |紳 village gentleman			B

Hsiang

Character	Radical	Phonetic	Meaning	Other reading	
鄉^{1}			｜談 local dialect ｜黨 village clan ｜勇 village braves		
相^{1}	目 109	相 847	Reciprocal, mutual ｜愛 love one another [-ch'en^{4} ｜稱 in harmony with one another ｜爭 to compete, fight ｜交 to associate ｜較 to compare ｜見 an interview, meeting ｜近 near together ｜助 to help｜幫 ｜傳 to transmit, hand down ｜反 contrary, opposite ｜倣 alike｜倣·彿 ｜符 to correspond｜應^{4} ｜好 an acquaintance ｜合 join together, harmonize ｜信 to believe ｜會 to meet｜遇 ｜宜 befitting, right,｜當 ｜干 involved in, concerned ｜隔 separated ｜關 mutual connection ｜連 to join, connected ｜識 mutually acquainted ｜似 similar, like｜同 ｜投 pleased with each other ｜對 opposite, agreeing, relative	hsiang^{4}	C
廂^{1}	广 53	相 847	Side apartment; suburbs ｜房 side room or house (facing at right angles to main house). 城內｜外 city and suburbs		F
箱^{1}	竹 118	相 847	A box or trunk｜·子 ｜蓋 a box lid		C

Hsiang

襄¹	衣 145	襄 369	To move; do; praise ｜同 take part, assist｜助 贊｜praise, eulogize		G
鑲¹	金 167	襄 369	To inlay, set in, border｜嵌 ｜牙 to fill teeth		G
庠²	广 53	羊 151	Asylum; college; B. A. 入｜matriculate		I
祥²	示 113	羊 151	Felicitous, good luck ｜瑞 prosperous condition		D
翔²	羽 124	羊 151	To soar, roam 高｜ 回｜wheel around, as a kite		G
詳²	言 149	羊 151	Detail, report, particular｜·細 ｜察 to examine minutely｜問 ｜明 clear, to explain		B
降²	阜 170	夂 540	To surrender, 投｜, 歸｜ ｜服 to cause to submit	chiang⁴	E
想³	心 61	相 847	To think, meditate 思｜; probably ｜·起·來 to call to mind, advert to ｜家 home-sick ｜·出 think out a case ｜法·子 devise a plan ｜像 an idea, imagination ｜許 I presume; it may be ｜一｜consider, think over｜念 ｜必 I suppose, I presume ｜·不 起 來 unable to call to mind ｜·不 到 unanticipated ｜°到 to think of, anticipate ｜望 to expect		A
享³	亠 8	享 743	To enjoy, receive｜受 ｜福 enjoy happiness ｜壽 enjoy old age, longevity		B
響³ 响³	音 180	鄉 365	Sound, noise, echo, effect ｜鐘 alarm clock ｜音 noise, sound ｜應⁴ to be influenced by		C

Hsiang

饗 3	食 184	鄉 365	To sacrifice, offer up; entertain │飯 sacrificial rice		K
餉 3	食 184	向 579	Rations; revenue, taxes │項 soldier's pay │銀		E
鯗 3	魚 195	羊 151	Dried salt fish of various kinds		K
象 4	豕 152	象 291	Elephant; form, image; star │棋 chess with 32 pieces │皮 rubber │牙 elephant's tusks, ivory		C
像 4	人 9	象 291	Like, │似, image, idol │·貌 likeness in general │·不·│ is it like? │·是 it seems │樣 like the pattern, good 形│ form, figure		B
橡 4	木 75	象 291	Chestnut oak		K
巷 4	己 49	巷 96	A lane, alley │口 the entrance to a lane 交民│ Legation Street, Peking		B
向 4	口 30	向 579	Towards; in favor of; hitherto S. │前 to advance, forward │·着 facing │南 etc. │後 in future, to retreat │來 heretofore, a while past │年 │他 partial to him │他說 said to him 方│ direction		B
嚮 4	口 30	向 579	Toward, facing, incline; guide │先 towards the front │背 towards the back		G
相 4	目 109	相 847	To help, lead; a minister. S. │·貌 likeness, physiognomy 宰│ prime minister	hsiang1	C

項[4]	頁 181	工 8	Neck; item, sort, funds, C. of items S. ｜巾 tippet, scarf ｜頸 the neck 頸｜ 欵｜items, funds		E

Hsiao

削[1]	刀 18	肖 124	To cut, slice off, deduct｜去 ｜職 degrade in rank ｜筆 sharpen a pencil ｜薄 thin	hsüeh[14]	B
宵[1]	宀 40	肖 124	Night, dark 深｜dead of night		H
消[1]	水 85	肖 124	To melt, disperse, digest; lessen. cancel｜減 ｜極 negative, minimum ｜氣 abate anger｜恨,｜悶, etc. ｜°遣 diversion, to pass the time ｜除 to abolish, delete ｜息 news, tidings ｜·化 to dissolve, digest ｜°滅 to extinguish ｜散 disperse by medicine ｜毒藥 disinfectant		C
硝[1]	石 112	肖 124	Nitre, saltpetre; to tan ｜礮水 nitric acid ｜皮 to tan hides ｜鹽 carbonate of soda		F
逍[1]	辵 162	肖 124	To roam, saunter｜遣,｜遙		K
銷[1]	金 167	肖 124	To melt, cancel, finish, dissolve ｜·路 market for goods, demand ｜售 place on sale		E
霄[1]	雨 173	肖 124	Mist, the sky ｜漢 milky way		H

Hsiao

簫[1]	竹 118	肅 164a	Flute, flagiolet 吹 | play the flute 排 | Chinese pan-pipes		G
蕭[1]	艸 140	肅 164a	An artemisia; annoying S. mournful |∘條 lonely and desolate		I
梟[1] 鴞[1]	木 75	鳥 253	Owl, | 鳥; wicked 私 | a smuggler		G
枵[1]	木 75		Hollow, empty | 耗 to waste, squander		I
囂[1]	口 30	口 694	Clamor; contemn, contemptuous | 塵 the world		K
唬[1]	口 30	虍 203	Growl of tiger, roar | 怒 roar with anger	hu[1]	H
哮[1]	口 30	孝 191	Howl, roar, 咆 |; bluster | 赫 terrify by howling		K
學[2] 斈[2]	子 39	𦥯 692	To learn, imitate, (local reading)	hsüeh[2]	A
小[3]	小 42	小 121	Small, petty | |[1]·的 |·車·子 a wheel-barrow | 雞·子 (or 兒) a chicken | 器 narrow-minded | 性兒, |∘人 |·氣 mean-spirited | 脚 bound feet of woman |[2]·姐 Miss, a young girl | 錢 illicit cash, small cash | 處 smallness, inferiority | 孩·子 a child | 子 |·心 take care! mean-spirited | 看 人 to despise another | 工 unskilled laborer | 過 small fault | 爐 匠 a travelling tinker | 米·子 millet. | 米 兒		A

Character	Radical	Phonetic	Meaning		Frequency
小³			｜民 the common people ｜名 name given child a month old ｜便 urine, urinate ｜聲兒 low tones, whispers ｜時 an hour ｜說 small talk, novels ｜·的 a servant, a little one ｜腿 lower part of the leg		
曉³	日 72	堯 391	To know, dawn, perspicuous ｜明 understand, day break 明｜ ｜·得 comprehend, understand ｜諭 clear proclamation		C
笑⁴ 咲⁴	竹 118	夭 463	To laugh, smile, glad ｜哈哈 laugh heartily ｜·話 ridicule, jests ｜容 laughing countenance｜臉 ｜林 funny column of paper ｜罵派 adverse critics, satirists ｜談 laughing and chatting 可｜laughable		A
效⁴	攴 66	交 531	To follow, imitate, efficacious ｜法 imitate a pattern ｜果 results, effects｜驗 ｜·力 to take effect, results		C
傚⁴	人 9	交 531	To imitate, pattern after (used for last) 傚｜		H
効⁴	力 19	交 531	To toil, exert, serve ; imitate ｜功 meritorious results, 功｜ ｜力 to exert ones strength		C
校⁴	木 75	交 531	School house, school ｜長³ rector, president, principal ｜外科 correspondence course	chiao⁴	A
孝⁴	子 39	孝 191	Filial piety, to obey parents and superiors｜悌 ｜親 obedience to parents ｜經 Book of Filial Piety ｜敬 dutiful and respectful｜·順		C

<table>
<tr><td>孝^{4}</td><td></td><td></td><td>| 服 mourning clothes | 衣
| 心 dutiful mind
| 道 path of filial duty
| 子^{3} a filial son</td><td></td><td></td></tr>
<tr><td>肖^{4}</td><td>肉
130</td><td>肖
124</td><td>Like, resembling, likeness | 像</td><td></td><td>F</td></tr>
<tr><td>斅^{4}</td><td>攴
66</td><td>𦥯
692</td><td>To arouse, teach, imitate
| 悟 to arouse.</td><td></td><td>K</td></tr>
</table>

Hsieh

<table>
<tr><td>些^{1}</td><td>二
7</td><td>此
129</td><td>A little, a few 一 |
| 事 a little business
| 微 a trifle, slightly
好 | a good many, a little better</td><td>hsieh^{3}
hsüeh^{1}</td><td>A</td></tr>
<tr><td>歇^{1}</td><td>欠
76</td><td>曷
239</td><td>To rest; desist, halt | 住
| 止 rest, leave off | 息
| 伏 rest during hot season
| 宿 stop and rest for night
|·一·| rest a while, stop a bit
| 工 stop work
| 手 desist from undertaking</td><td></td><td>A</td></tr>
<tr><td>蠍^{1}</td><td>虫
142</td><td>曷
239</td><td>Scorpion, |·子 ; lizard
| 螫 sting from scorpion
| 虎·子 house lizard
| 毒 venom of scorpion
| (·子) 勾子 a scorpion's sting</td><td></td><td>F</td></tr>
<tr><td>鞋^{2}
鞵^{2}</td><td>革
177</td><td>圭
48</td><td>Shoe, slippers
| 後根 heel of shoe
| 底 sole of shoe
| 襪·子 shoes and stockings
| 拔·子 shoe-loop, for pulling on
| 油 shoe-blacking</td><td></td><td>A</td></tr>
<tr><td>邪^{2}</td><td>邑
163</td><td>牙
165</td><td>Depraved ; heterodox; erroneous
| 正 false and true, good and bad 正 |</td><td></td><td>C</td></tr>
</table>

Hsieh

<table>
<tr><td>邪^2</td><td></td><td></td><td>| 教 heretical teaching | 道
| 法 conjuring tricks. sorcery | 術
| 心 a depraved mind | 念
|·了 haunted
| 僻 lewd, licentious | 淫
| 神 false gods
| 事 vices, depraved deeds
| 說 corrupt speaking</td><td></td><td></td></tr>
<tr><td>協^2
勰^2</td><td>十
24</td><td>力
223</td><td>In harmony, aid, union ; colonel
| 助 united action, coöperation | 力
| 和 harmonious, to unite | 同
| 辦 assistant, to coöperate
| 商 國 allied powers
| 約 alliance; international agreement</td><td></td><td>C</td></tr>
<tr><td>脅^2
脇^2</td><td>肉
130</td><td>力
223</td><td>Part of body under arms, ribs; to coërce
| 骨 ribs</td><td></td><td>I</td></tr>
<tr><td>斜^2</td><td>斗
68</td><td>余
31</td><td>Oblique, slanting | 歪
| 街 a slanting street
| 風 a side wind
| 對 not quite opposite</td><td>hsia^2</td><td>D</td></tr>
<tr><td>挾^2</td><td>手
64</td><td>夾
455</td><td>To clasp under arm, pinch. squeeze, cherish; presume on
| 制 to oppress
| 告 to accuse at law</td><td>chia^{12}</td><td>D</td></tr>
<tr><td>偕^2</td><td>人
9</td><td>皆
318</td><td>Accompany, together | 同
| 行 go along with, walk with</td><td>chieh^1</td><td>D</td></tr>
<tr><td>諧^2</td><td>言
149</td><td>皆
318</td><td>Harmonize, accord with, laugh at
| 笑 to laugh at
和 | in accord, harmony</td><td></td><td>F</td></tr>
<tr><td>攜^2
携^2</td><td>手
64</td><td>隹
52</td><td>To lead by hand, take with ; carry
| 眷 bring one's family along
| 手 lead by the hand, | 領
| 帶 bring along with one</td><td>hsi^1</td><td>G</td></tr>
<tr><td>骸^2</td><td>骨
188</td><td>亥
874</td><td>Human bones | 骨</td><td>hai^2</td><td>F</td></tr>
</table>

Hsieh

Character	Radical	Phonetic	Meaning	Other readings	Freq.
叶[2]	口 30	十 13	To harmonize, rhyme; a sound (like 協) ｜韻 pronunciation for rhyme ｜音		I
寫[3] 冩[3]	宀 40	舄 688	To write, sketch; photograph; tranquillize ｜賬 keep accounts ｜眞 paint likeness, photograph ｜法 penmanship ｜信 write a letter ｜書 ｜字 write words		A
些[3]	二 7	此 129	好｜個 Many	hsieh[1] hsüeh[1]	A
血[3]	血 143	血 611	Blood; consanguinity 俗 ｜戰 bloody battle ｜·氣 the constitution, animal passions ｜心 affection, sympathy ｜肉 flesh and blood, man ｜管 blood vessel ｜漏 an issue of blood ｜脈 the arteries, consanguinity 吐｜ to spit blood	hsüeh[4]	C
榭[4]	木 75	身 634	Arbor among trees 臺｜ raised kiosk		I
謝[4]	言 149	身 634	To thank; decline; die S. ｜恩 thankful for favors 道｜ ｜·｜ thanks, thank you ｜賞 thank one for gift ｜神 to thank the gods ｜帖 card of thanks, reward 凋｜ leaves die and fall		A
解[4]	角 148	解 603	Unloose, fall off S. ｜·不開 cannot explain it	chieh[34]	B
懈[4]	心 61	解 603	Lazy, lax, remiss ｜鬆 loose, lax		E
澥[4]	水 85	解 603	Thin consistency; a creek 糨·子·｜·了 paste grown watery		G

蟹[4] 蠏[4]	虫 142	解 603	The crab, 螃| |黃 spawn of crabs |肉 flesh of crabs		F
卸[4]	卩 26	卸 307	To unload ; resign, lay aside |貨 discharge cargo |任 give up office |擔 lay down a burden		D
褻[4]	衣 145	埶 305	Ragged, vile; to revile, treat irreverently |服 ragged, dirty clothes |慢 treat with contumely |瀆 to blaspheme		E
械[4]	木 75	戒 337	Manacles ; weapons ; mechanical contrivance |鬪 fight with weapons 兵| weapons of war		F
洩[4] 泄[4] 渫[4]	水 85	曳 835	To leak, divulge ; diminish |忿 gratify hate |漏 to disclose, ooze out		F
絏[4]	糸 120	曳 835	To fetter ; rope 縲| fetters, bonds		H
駭[4]	馬 187	亥 874	Startled, alarmed 驚|	hai[4]	F
瀉[4]	水 85	舄 688	To purge, drain ; dysentery |肚 dysentery, purgative |藥 a purgative		G
屑[4]	尸 44	肖 124	Trifling, lightly 輕| to depreciate		I
挈[4,2]	手 64	㓞 147	To help	ch'ieh[4]	I

Hsien

先[1]	儿 10	先 39	First, before, ancient |見 prognostic, sign, to foresee	hsien[4]	A

Hsien

Character	Radical	Phonetic	Meaning	Other reading	Class
先[1]			｜前 formerly ｜頭(·裏) ｜知 foreknowledge, a prophet ｜鋒 vanguard, forerunner ｜導 ｜父 my deceased father ｜後 before and after, about ｜擱·着·罷 let it be for a bit! ｜年 in previous year ｜農壇 Temple of Agriculture ｜·生 first born, teacher; Sir. Mr. ｜世 the former life, or times ｜祖 ancestors ｜要 the first thing required		
鮮[1]	魚 195	鮮 153	Fresh, new, just slaughtered 新·｜ ｜花 fresh flowers, so ｜菓·子 ｜肉 fresh meat, so ｜菜, ｜魚 ｜明 bright, clear, fresh	hsien[3]	B
掀[1]	手 64	折 210	To lift up, open, raise ｜·起·來 ｜·開 to raise up, to pull open		D
仙[1] 僊[1]	人 9	山 655	Genii, immortals, fairies ｜人 ｜家 genii, of Taoism and Budd. ｜景 a beautiful prospèct ｜法 conjuring tricks		E
秈[1] 籼[1]	禾 115	山 655	Common rice growing, ｜米 upland rice		H
杴[1]	木 75	欠 441	Trough, flume; shovel 木｜ wooden shovel, so 鉄｜		I
暹[1]	辵 162	隹 52	Siam ｜邏		I
纖[1]	糸 120	韱 420	Fine, small, slender, ｜小, ｜細 ｜毫 an atom		I
䙴[1]	西 146	䙴 779	To rise high		P
閑[2]	門 169	閑 637	Leisure, idle, empty ｜錢 spare cash ｜住 retired, disengaged ｜居 ｜暇 leisure ｜空, ｜時		B

Hsien

閒²

| 話 complain; leisure talk | 言 | 語
| 人 disengaged person; so | 民
| 逛 to stroll about | 游
| 散 to relax, sinecures
| 事 anything extraneous to duty
| 談 to chat, gossip
| 在 at leisure

嫺² 女 38 閒 637 — I
Accomplished, refined
| 熟 perfect in, accustomed to

癇² 疒 104 閒 637 — G
Convulsions, fits, epilepsy
風 | convulsions, (in children)
癲 | epileptic fits

咸² 口 30 咸 344 — F
All, entirely, | 共. S.
| 見 seen by all
| 豐 Emperor Hsien Feng

鹹² 鹵 197 咸 344 — B
Salty, salted, brackish
| 肉 salted meat | 魚
| 苦 acrid, bitter, briny
| 水 salt or brackish water
| 淡 salt and fresh
| 菜 salted vegetables

賢² 贒² 貝 154 臤 643 — C
Worthy, virtuous | 良
| 妻 my virtuous wife
| 慧 virtuous, discreet
| 人 a sage, worthies
| 士 a virtuous scholar

嫌² 女 38 兼 671 — D
To dislike, object to; aversion
| 棄 throw away in disdain
|∘疑 dislike and suspicion
| 少 think insufficient
| 惡 dislike and hate -u⁴

弦² 絃² 弓 57 玄 877 — E
Lute cord; string
| 機 a spring, springs
|·子 a lute

Hsien

Character	Radical	Phonetic	Meaning	Other reading	Grade
啣² 嘀²	口 30	卸 307	To take in bill or mouth ｜草 carry grass for nest		F
銜²	金 167	行 5	Horse's bit 馬｜; control, 官｜full official title		G
涎²	水 85	延 128	Saliva 垂｜ desire for	yen²	F
閑²	門 169	門 635	Barrier, train, leisure ｜習 trained, broken in 防｜to guard against		I
鷳²	鳥 196	門 635	Silver pheasant 白｜		K
㬎³	日 72	㬎 802	Volatile; infinitesimal; fibrous		K
顯³ 顕³	頁 181	㬎 802	Manifest, display; make plain｜現 ｜而易見 obvious, evident｜然 ｜亮 clear, manifest, bright ｜明 ｜露 come out, as the truth ｜微鏡 the microscope		B
險³	阜 170	僉 440	Dangerous, hazardous 危｜ ｜詐 to backbite ｜處 a dangerous place｜地 ｜象 crisis, important position｜要 ｜事 a dangerous affair		C
鮮³	魚 195	鮮 153	Rare, few, seldom ｜少 few, rare	hsien¹	B
癬³	疒 104	鮮 153	Ringworm, skin disease 環｜	hsüan³	G
現⁴	玉 96	見 865	To manifest, make plain; now ｜成·的 ready, ready made ｜錢 ready money ｜今 now, at present ｜時,｜在 ｜·出 to appear ｜狀 appearance, present emergency ｜象 phenomena, condition	hsüan⁴	A

Hsien

Character	Radical	Phonetic	Meaning	Other reading	Class
現4			|行 temporary |世 modern world |用|買 to buy as needed		
先4	儿 10	先 39	Take precedence 不如|之 better strike first blow	hsien1	A
線4 綫4	糸 120	泉 523	Thread, wire; spy |花 cotton for making thread 紡| to spin thread 絲| silk thread		B
臽4	臼 134	臽 683	Pitfall, pit		K
陷4	阜 170	臽 683	To fall into, sink into; involve; ruin, betray |害 |坑 a pitfall, fall into pit |阱 |溺 infatuated, fallen into |罪 sinned, involved in crime	hsüan4	C
餡4	食 184	臽 683	Stuffing for pastry etc. |兒餅 cake with stuffing |包·子 fruit or meat dumplings		G
縣4	糸 120	系 887	District; magistrate |城 chief town in district |知事 district magistrate |立學校 county school |衙·門 district magistrate's office		C
限4	阜 170	艮 359	Limit, to fix boundary |期 limited time, a given date |制 control, delimitation 界| |量 measure, limit, estimate |滿 time expired |內 within the limit; vs. outside it |外 |·他三天 limit him to 3 days 定| fix a limit		C
獻4 献4	犬 94	犬 456	To offer up, present |上,奉|,貢| |己 Consecrate oneself |祭 to sacrifice |禮 to make presents		D

羨[4] 羡[4]	羊 123	羊 151	To desire; long for admire ǀ 美 ǀ 慕 admire, fond of		D
憲[4]	心 61	㥶 381	High official ; constitutional law ǀ 禁 government prohibition ǀ 法 constitution ǀ 兵 military police		E
檻[4]	木 75	監 608	Railing, cage 圈 ǀ enclosure, pen	chien[4] k'an[3]	G
霰[4] 霓[4]	雨 173	散 800	Snow and sleet falling ǀ 霅 sleet		K

Hsin

心[1]	心 61	心 377	Heart, mind; center ǀ∘腸 the heart, affections ǀ 胸 ǀ 志 the will ǀ 竅 heart-orifices, intelligence ǀ 怯 timorous ǀ 中 in the heart, ǀ 內, ǀ·裏 ǀ 腹 intimate; the bosom ǀ 懷 ǀ∘想 to think, thought ǀ·思 ǀ 性 temper, disposition ǀ 意 thought, aspiration ǀ 軟 tender-hearted, lenient ǀ 口 the breast, pit of stomach ǀ 理 bent, inclination, ǀ 理學 psychology ǀ 靈 intellect, intellectual , mental ǀ 亂 the mind disturbed ǀ 滿意足 self-confident, content ǀ 不平 discontented, anxious ǀ 不在 inattentive ǀ 上人 sweetheart ǀ 神 the mind, the wits		A

心[1]
|∘事 affairs of the heart
|得 heart acquisition
|地 the heart, moral nature |田
|跳 palpitation of the heart
|眼 heart's core, intelligence
|願 to wish, desire

新[1] 斤 69 新 86 New, fresh ; recently |·鮮 — A
|奇 new and curious
|加 坡 Singapore
|∘疆 New Dominion, Sinkiang
|金 山 Australia
|近 recently
|舊 new & old, recent & former
|出 recently issued
|發 明 to invent, discover
|婦 a bride |娘·子, |媳·婦
|禧 New Year congratulations
|來·的 recently arrived
|郎 a bridegroom |姑 爺
|歷 new calendar (Gregorian)
|年 the new year
|聞 news, |聞 紙 newspaper
|約 New Testament,

薪[1] 艸 140 新 86 Fuel, firewood; salary — D
|金 teacher's salary |∘水

辛[1] 辛 160 辛 157 Bitter, toil, miserable |·苦 S. — C
|·苦 錢 cumshaw, wine-money
|苦 |苦 salutation between strangers

欣[1] **忻**[1] 欠 76 斤 209 Delight, joy 歡 | , | 歡 — D
|喜 rejoice, be delighted
|然 extremely pleased

馨[1] 香 186 殸 404 Fragrant |香 — hsing[1] — D

歆[1] 欠 76 音 90 To taste, pleased with sacrifices — K
|享 to enjoy, be pleased with

Hsin

尋[2]	寸 41	寸 18	Usual, to seek, search for ｜東·西 ask small gift	hsün[2]	C
伈[3]	人 9	心 377	Nervous, timorous, cowardly		I
信[4]	人 9	言 740	Faith; sincerity; to believe; a letter ; follow aimlessly ｜札 a letter 書｜ ｜敎自由 religious liberty｜仰自由 ｜經 (or 條) any creed, Apostles' Creed 使徒｜經 ｜主·的人 a Christian believer｜徒 ｜局 a post-office ｜封 an envelope｜皮 ｜服 to believe, trust 相｜,｜靠 ｜任 trust in, confidence ｜息 news,｜音 ｜箱 letter box, or pillar｜筒 ｜心 trustful, faith ｜口說 to talk at random ｜票 warrant, postage stamp ｜步行 aimless wandering ｜實 sincere, faithful, trusty｜·用 ｜道 believe a doctrine or sect ｜德 truth, faith, belief ｜託 confide in, entrust to ｜∘仰 religious belief, to trust ｜從 obedience of faith 口｜word of mouth 失｜to forfeit one's word		A
䜣[4]	石 112	言 740	Arsenic		I
汛[4]	水 85	卂 397a	Quick, station, guard house	hsün[4]	G
訊[4]	言 149	卂 397a	To try case, examine	hsün[4]	G
迅[4]	辵 162	卂 397a	Quick, to hurry｜速 俗	hsün[4]	F

Character	Radical	Phonetic	Meaning	Other reading	
顖4 囟4	頁 181	恖 380	Forehead, top of skull	hsing4	H
釁4 衅4	酉 164	同 580	To smear with blood, feud, offence 搆 | stir up trouble, embroil		K

Hsing

Character	Radical	Phonetic	Meaning	Other reading	
星1	日 72	星 42	Star, dot, least bit | 辰 stars, heavenly bodies | | | 期 a week | 期日 Sunday | 河 Milky Way | 雲 nebula | 宿 constellations | 座, | 象 占 | 家 astrologer 火 | a spark 雨 | tiny rain-drop		B
惺1 [illegible]1	心 61	星 42	Intelligent, tranquil | 悟 become aware, realize		I
腥1	肉 130	星 42	Rank, strong-smelling |·氣 | 穢 filthy | 味 unpleasant flavour		F
興1 㒷1	臼 134	同 580	To prosper, originate, begin | 起 to raise, to get up | 敗 prosperity and failure | 衰 |·不開 cannot make it prosper | 盛 flourish, become full | 旺, | 隆 | 時 fashionable 時 |	hsing4	B
馨1	香 186	殸 404	Fragrant | 香	hsin1	D
行2	行 144	行 5	To walk, act, motion, conduct | 常 usual, common ; ordinarily | 政 executive, administration | 止 conduct, behaviour | 裝 baggage | 李	hang2 hsing4	A

Hsing

Character	Radical	Phonetic	Meaning	Other reading	Grade
行^{2}			丨好 do good, charitable acts 丨善 丨星 the planets 丨許 possibly 丨醫 healing; to practice medicine 丨人 a passenger, a traveller 丨·了 that will do ; 不丨 will not do 丨禮 to make obeisance 丨路 go, travel, walk 丨走 丨囊 travelling bag, knapsack 丨·不·丨 will it do ? 丨事 to act, do work or service 丨道 to be righteous 丨動 conduct, movements 運丨 丨·為 conduct, practice 丨事為人		
形^{2}	彡 59	幵 34	Form, figure, to give form gesture 丨容 丨狀 appearance, form 丨像, 丨·式 丨學 geometry 幾何(學) 丨勢 aspect, outline, configuration 丨體 substance, the body		C
刑^{2}	刀 18	刑 34a	To punish, punishment 丨罰 丨具 implements of punishment 丨問 to examine by torture		C
型^{2}	土 32	刑 34a	A mould 模丨, to mould 典丨 a law, statute		F
醒^{31}	酉 164	星 42	To awake, rouse up, 睡丨 丨酒 recover from debauch 丨鐘 alarm clock 丨世之言 words to rouse the age 丨悟·過·來 come to self, realize error 振丨 to arouse, move		A
省^{3}	目 109	少 122	To waken, watchful 丨察 to enquire, to examine 丨悟 to understand, to perceive	sheng^{3}	A
擤^{3}	手 64	自 852	To blow nose 丨鼻·子		F

姓[4]	女 38	生 41	Surname, family name 貴 | what is your name, sir? 百家 | List of Common Surnames 百· | "hundred names," the people		A
性[4]	心 61	生 41	Nature, quality; disposition |·情, | 格; the two sexes 兩 | | 傲 arrogant, haughty | 急 hasty temper |·質 nature, characteristics | 學 metaphysics, psychology, | 理 |·命 life		C
行[4]	行 144	行 5	Virtue 德 |	hang[2] hsing[2]	A
興[4]	臼 134	同 580	Spirits, feelings |·趣 flavor, interest | 味 高 | glad	hsing[1]	B
杏[4]	木 75	木 484	Apricot or almond | 兒 | 花 apricot blossom | 仁 apricot kernels, almonds | 乾 (兒) dried apricots | 林 apricot orchard		C
幸[4] 倖[4]	干 51	幸 159	Lucky, fortunate, happy | 福 S, |·而 fortunately |·虧, | 喜 | 福主義 hedonism | 得 obtain by improper means		D
顖[4] 囟[4]	頁 181	囟 380	Forehead, top of skull | 帽 common skull cap	hsin[4]	H
脛[4]	肉 130	巠 427	The shin-bone, shank | 骨	ching[4]	G

Hsiu

修[1]	人 9	攸 549	To adorn, repair; practise | 眞 cultivate the divine element with in | 整 repair, put in order |·理, | 補		A

Hsiu

<table>
<tr><td>修[1]</td><td></td><td></td><td>| 正 案 amendment
| 城 repair or build city-wall
| 橋 補 路 public benefits, "merit"
| 築 build, repair, rebuild | 蓋, | 造
| 好 cultivate good deeds | 善
|·行 devote oneself to religion
| 改 revise, amend
| 身 improve moral nature | 德
|∘飾 to adorn, make, cultivate
| 辭 rhetoric
| 養 to care for self after illness; to train body or mind.
| 業 study in institution</td><td></td><td></td></tr>
<tr><td>脩[1]</td><td>肉
130</td><td>攸
549</td><td>Dried meat; living
| 金 teacher's salary 束 |</td><td></td><td>F</td></tr>
<tr><td>休[1]</td><td>人
9</td><td>休
486</td><td>To rest, desist, give up, resign; divorce; good fortune
| 妻 divorce wife, | 書 a divorce
| 棄 abandon, repudiate
|·息 rest, as from toil
| 怪 don't think it strange
| 說 don't speak!
| 業 holidays</td><td></td><td>B</td></tr>
<tr><td>羞[1]</td><td>羊
123</td><td>丑
676</td><td>To blush, shame, ashamed
| 恥 shame, ashamed 害 |
| 人 to abash or shame one
| 辱 to abuse, revile; shame
| 愧 to feel ashamed | 慚</td><td></td><td>C</td></tr>
<tr><td>饈[1]
䐪[1]</td><td>食
184</td><td>丑
676</td><td>Viands, delicacies
珍 | 美 味 dainties</td><td></td><td>G</td></tr>
<tr><td>宿[1]</td><td>宀
40</td><td>百
805</td><td>A night, lodging
尋 | 兒 seek for lodging</td><td>hsiu[3]
hsü[1]
su[4]</td><td>D</td></tr>
<tr><td>朽[3]</td><td>木
75</td><td>丂
240</td><td>Rotten, used up, worn out
| 壞 decayed, spoilt | 爛
| 木 rotten wood</td><td></td><td>C</td></tr>
</table>

宿[3]	宀 40	百 805	A night, to rest 住一| |一| to rest a night (su i hsiu)	hsiu[1] hsü[1] su[4]	D
袖[4]	衣 145	由 818	Sleeve, to sleeve; leader |章 rank-stripes on sleeve |口 mouth of sleeve, |手 put hands into sleeves 領| a leader, manager		A
繡[4] 綉[4]	糸 120	肅 164a	To embroider, embroidery |鞋 embroidered shoes |花 embroider flowers |貨 embroidered goods		D
秀[4]	禾 115	秀 217	Maturing, accomplished, elegant |·氣 talent, elegant manners |美 beautiful, handsome |穗 the ears of corn |·才 talents, B. A. (Old)		F
銹[4] 鏽[4]	金 167	秀 217	Rust of metal 長[3]| to rust 銅| verdigris		E
臭[4]	自 132	自 852	To stink, stench 文	ch'ou[4]	E
嗅[4]	口 30	自 852	To smell, scent | 花		G

Hsiung

兄[1]	儿 10	兄 755	Elder brother | 長, senior; sir |台 "eminent brother," term of respect |·弟 a younger brother 弟·| older and younger brothers; soldiers		A
凶[1]	凵 17	凶 651	Unlucky, malignant, calamity |兆 bad omen or sign |服 mourning clothes |信 bad news |荒 famine		E

凶[1]			丨命 unhappy fate 丨年 bad year, famine, war, etc.	
兇[1]	儿 10	凶 651	Dreadful, violent, malevolent 丨犯 a murderer 丨險 dangerous, malignant 丨心 malevolent heart 丨猛 fierce, cruel 丨惡, 丨暴 丨殺 murder; 丨·手 murderer 丨徒	D
胸[1] 胷[1] 匈[1]	肉 130	凶 651	Thorax, breast; feelings, affections; Huns 匈奴 丨前 the breast, 丨膛, 丨脯·子 丨中 in the mind or breast 捶丨 beat upon the breast	D
訩[1] 詾[1]	言 149	凶 651	To brawl, scold, threaten; litigate; full, as of trouble 天下丨丨 whole empire murmuring	I
雄[2]	隹 172	厷 167	Cock-bird, brave, martial 英。丨 丨雞 the cock 丨壯 brave, strong 丨心 heroic, noble-minded	D
熊[2]	火 86	能 324	A bear; brown bear 人丨, 丨人 S. 丨掌 bear's paws 狗丨 small performing bear	D

Hsü

虛[1]	虍 141	虛 206	Empty, unreal, untrue; humble; pure 丨假 false, fictitious 丨僞 丨傳 a legend 丨浮 vague, unsubstantial 丨心 humble-minded; false-hearted 丨空 empty, hollow, meaningless 空丨	B

Hsü

Character	Radical	Phonetic	Meaning		Other readings	
虛^{1}			｜名 spurious reputation ｜套 empty compliments ｜度 to no purpose; waste time ｜文 formal writing ｜無主義 Nihilism ｜無黨 ｜言 empty words			
嘘^{1}	口 30	虛 206	To blow, breathe softly, puff ｜手 blow on one's hands			I
須^{1} 湏^{1}	頁 181	彡 280	Ought, necessary, must, ｜是 it must be ｜當 must ｜得, 必｜ ｜要 must, necessary ｜用	S.		C
鬚^{1}	髟 190	彡 280	Moustache 鬍｜ whiskers and moustache			D
需^{1}	雨 173	需 613	To need; bent on doing ｜用 necessary things			D
宿^{1}	宀 40	百 805	｜A night		hsiu^{13} su^{4}	D
戌^{1}	戈 62	戌 342	7-9 P. M., the eleventh of the twelve "branches"			H
胥^{1}	肉 130	胥 140	Together, all; clerk; to help ｜吏 police runners	S.		H
吁^{1}	口 30	于 30	Ugh! alas! to sigh 長｜短歎 sighing and moaning			K
俗^{2}	人 9	谷 710	還｜To leave the priest-hood and return to common life		su^{2}	A
徐^{2}	彳 60	余 31	Sedate, placid, slow, ｜圖 to deliberate, to devise	S.		G
許^{3}	言 149	午 37	To permit; promise; probably ｜嫁 to betroth ｜婚, ｜聘, ｜配 ｜久 a very long time ｜可 to allow 准｜, 允｜ ｜多 a great many ｜願 to vow, make oath 也｜ perhaps 應｜ to promise	S.		B

Hsü

旭^{34} 日 72 九 302
Dawn, rising sun | 日
I

詡^{3} 言 149 羽 293
To boast, exaggerate 誇 |
遍 | extend everywhere
K

序^{4} 广 53 予 114
Preface; seriatim, series 次 |
| 文 preface
秩 | order, program
C

恤^{4} 卹^{4} 心 61 血 611
To pity, sympathize, compassionate
| 老 pity the aged
| 憐 to compassionate 憐 |, 體 |
C

續^{4} 糸 120 賣 864
To join on, continue, succeed to
| 娶 widower remarries | 絃
| 登 continued from last issue
接 | connect, supplement
D

壻^{4} 婿^{4} 士 33 胥 140
Son-in-law 女 |
| 家 son-in-law's family
E

畜^{4} 田 102 畜 879
To rear, cultivate, store up
| 牧 時 代 pastoral stage
| 養 to rear; feed
ch'u^{4}
E

蓄^{4} 艸 140 畜 879
To store up; rear 積 |
| 糧 store up grain
E

敍^{4} 敘^{4} 攴 66 余 31
To discuss, converse; series; rank,
|·| 家 常 chat, gossip, | 談, | 話
| 論 discuss in detail
| 述 narrate in order
G

絮^{4} 糸 120 如 554
Cotton wool; refuse; talkative
| 繁 repetitious, weariness 繁 |
| 被 a quilted coverlet
G

緒^{4} 糸 120 者 192
Clue; to continue | 接
情 | sensibilities, emotions
光 | Emperor Kwang Hsü
頭 | clue, way, opening
G

蓿^{4} 艸 140 百 805
Clover 苜 |
su^{4}
G

Hsüan

亘[1] 二 7 亘 795 To revolve in an orbit — K

宣[1] 宀 40 亘 795 To proclaim, publish, | 傳, | 佈 — S — C
| 戰 to declare war
| 教 proclaim the Gospel
| 講福音 preach the Gospel
| 告 to publish | 開, | 示
| 徧 to publish everywhere | 揚
| 讀 to read aloud
| 言 a message to be proclaimed

喧[1] 諠[1] 口 30 亘 795 Clamor, hubbub | 譁 — E
| 嚷 clamor of many voices
| 鬧 high words, noise, uproar

軒[1] 車 159 干 32 Side-house, porch, shop, saloon — H
|·子 a comfortable room
| 轅 double surname — S

諼[1] 言 149 爰 187 Deceitful, impose on; forget — I
| 詐 crafty tricks, stratagems

懸[2] 心 61 系 887 To suspend, hang, anxious — D
|·起·來 to hang up | 掛, | 上
| 橋 suspension bridge
| 心 be in suspense | 想, | 念

旋[2] 方 70 㫃 265 To turn, revolve; thereupon, in turn — hsüan[4] — F
| 轉 to revolve, return
| 窩 a whirlpool

漩[2] 水 85 㫃 265 Circling, eddy | 兒 — G
流 | a water "race"

玄[2] 玄 95 玄 877 Dark, mystic, abstruse | 妙 — G
| 學 metaphysics
| 門 Taoism
| 默 still and meditative

Character	Radical	Phonetic	Definition		Alt.	
眩²	目 109	玄 877	Dizzy, dazed, to deceive ｜暈 ｜目 eyes dazzled; near-sighted			I
選³	辵 162	巽 97	To choose, select, elect, ｜舉 to elect by ballot ｜定 ｜舉權 right to vote ｜科 elective course ｜民 chosen people, e.g., the Jews ｜派 elect and commission ｜擇 to choose, select 揀｜,挑｜			B
癬³	疒 104	鮮 153	Ringworm, skin disease ｜瘡	文	hsien³	G
現⁴	玉 96	見 865	At present, now ｜用｜買 to buy as needed	俗	hsien⁴	A
楦⁴ 楥⁴	木 75	亘 795	A shoe last; arch; to mould; turn in a lathe ｜·頭 a last, boot-tree ｜鞋 fit shoe to last			B
陷⁴	阜 170	臽 683	天塌地｜ All falling into ruin		hsien⁴	C
旋⁴	方 70	㫃 265	Whirlwind ｜·風; dizzy ｜暈 dizzy, giddy		hsüan²	F
鏇⁴	金 167	㫃 265	To turn in lathe ｜床 the bed of a lathe ｜圓 turn it round on lathe			F
炫⁴	火 86	玄 877	Brilliant, dazzling ｜光 ｜人耳目 confuse senses, dazzle			I
衒⁴	行 144	玄 877	To brag, display 自｜ ｜天｜地 exaggerated, bombastic			K

Hsüeh

Character	Radical	Phonetic	Definition		Alt.	
些¹	二 7	此 129	｜微 Very little	俗	hsieh¹³	A
削¹⁴	刀 18	肖 124	To cut or pare off	文	hsiao¹	B

Hsüeh

鞾[1] 韡[1]	革 177	化 327	Boots |·子			D
薛[1]	艸 140	辛 157	Marsh grass,	S.		G
斆[2]		斆 692	To learn			P
學[2] 斈[2]	子 39	斆 692	To learn, practice, education |者 a high or noted scholar |期 school term |界 educational circles |·着 learning by doing |費 tuition fees |好 to learn to do well |∘習 to learn and practice |校 a school |堂 |壞 to learn evil |科 department, course |力 education, knowledge, scholarship |名 name while in school |年 (齡) school age |派 school of thought |門 |不會 cannot learn |·生 a student |員 |徒 an apprentice, to learn |文 learning |問 |位 academic degree		hsiao[2]	A
眣[2]	目 109	穴 394	To look sharply, spy about |一|			I
雪[34]	雨 173	彐 667	Snow,[3] white;[3] to avenge[4] |[3]景 snow-covered landscape |[4]恨 to have revenge |[4]寃 |[3]花 flakes of snow |[3]片 |[4]白的 white as snow			A

血4	血 143	血 611	Blood, | 輪 corpuscles | 球 文 | 清 serum, anti-toxin	hsieh3	C
穴4	穴 116	穴 394	Cave, hole, den, cavern 孔 | | 居 to live in caves | 道 grave; subterranean passage 窟 | to dig a hole		F

Hsün

熏1 燻1	火 86	熏 28	To smoke, kipper, dry, scent, heat | 蒸 steamy vapor after rain | 黑 blacken with smoke | 香 disinfect by burning herbs | 肉 to smoke meat | 蚊·子 smoke out mosquitoes | 藥 chloroform, or ether		E
勳1 勛1	力 19	熏 28	Merit, loyal | 功 | 章 a decoration | 位 honors, orders of merit		G
薰1	艸 140	熏 28	Fragrant, to perfume | 草 fragrant herbs or plants		H
醺1	酉 164	熏 28	Intoxicated, very drunk 醉 | |		H
尋2	寸 41	寸 18	Usual; to seek, search for | 常 commonly, ordinary | 找 to seek for | 訪 to inquire into or for | 思 to study, to consider	hsin2	C
巡2 廵2	巛 47	川 425	Patrol, inspect; go on circuit | 察 go rounds as watchmen | 警 police, constable | 捕 | 船 a cruiser | 洋 艦 | 哨 patrol, military watch		C
馴24	馬 187	川 425	Tame, well-bred, docile | 良 | 畜 tame, trained animals		E

Hsün

<table>
<tr><td>循[2]</td><td>彳
60</td><td>盾
844</td><td>To revolve, accord with
| 序 normal
| 規蹈矩 follow regulations
| 理 agreeably to reason
| 良 docile</td><td></td><td>E</td></tr>
<tr><td>旬[2]</td><td>日
72</td><td>旬
230</td><td>Ten days, decade, all; seven days of mourning
| 內 within ten days</td><td></td><td>F</td></tr>
<tr><td>徇[2]</td><td>彳
60</td><td>旬
230</td><td>To follow; quickly; cause
| 情 influenced by feelings</td><td></td><td>F</td></tr>
<tr><td>詢[24]</td><td>言
149</td><td>旬
230</td><td>To consult, inquire about | 問
| 事 to deliberate on affairs</td><td></td><td>G</td></tr>
<tr><td>郇[2]</td><td>邑
163</td><td>旬
230</td><td>A small feudal state</td><td></td><td>K</td></tr>
<tr><td>訓[4]</td><td>言
149</td><td>川
425</td><td>To teach, instruct; teachings
| 敎 to instruct 敎·|, | 誡, | 誨
|·練 to drill. to practice
| 蒙 to instruct the young
| 詞 moral teaching</td><td></td><td>B</td></tr>
<tr><td>遜[4]
愻[4]</td><td>辵
162</td><td>系
887</td><td>To yield, accord; humble, modest
| 順 respectful, yielding | 讓
| 位 to abdicate
謙 | humble, yielding, meek</td><td></td><td>E</td></tr>
<tr><td>卂[4]</td><td>丶
3</td><td>卂
397a</td><td>Quick</td><td></td><td>P</td></tr>
<tr><td>汛[4]</td><td>水
85</td><td>卂
397a</td><td>Quick; station, guard house
| 所 military post, guardhouse | 地</td><td>hsin[4]</td><td>G</td></tr>
<tr><td>訊[4]</td><td>言
149</td><td>卂
397a</td><td>To try case, examine, admonish | 案
| 訪 to investigate, inquire | 問</td><td>hsin[4]</td><td>G</td></tr>
<tr><td>迅[4]</td><td>辵
162</td><td>卂
397a</td><td>Quick, hasty | 疾
| 速 prompt, speedy</td><td>hsin[4]</td><td>F</td></tr>
<tr><td>殉[4]
狥[4]
侚[4]</td><td>歹
78</td><td>旬
230</td><td>Bent on, to follow after, bury alive; die for
| 情 obsequiousness
| 利 to follow after gain
| 難 to die for duty</td><td></td><td>F</td></tr>
</table>

巽[4]	己 49	巽 97	A diagram, mild, gentle	sun[4]	K

Hu

囫[1]	口 31	勿 233	Whole, complete; rough | 圇 | 圇 睡 sleep in one's clothes | 圇 吞 swallow whole		H
忽[1]	心 61	勿 233	Suddenly; to disregard | | 悠 whirligig, merry-go-round | 然 (間) unexpectedly, suddenly | 略 carelessness, to despise		C
惚[1]	心 61	勿 233	Confused, obscured, vague 慌 |		H
曶[1]	目 109	勿 233	To see obscurely 瞖 |		I
颮[1]	風 182	勿 233	Sound of wind		K
乎[1]	丿 4	乎 29	Interrogative adverb; exclamation 幾 | almost, nearly 合。| agreeing with 可 | can it be so? 在。| consists in, depends on; care for		D
呼[1]	口 30	乎 29	Breathe out, call | 喊 call out loudly | 叫 |·吸 exhale and inhale | 喚 call to or for, 招·| | 冤 proclaim a grievance		D
欻[1]	欠 76	炎 447	Suddenly 奄 | ; flitting, undecided; whirring sound | | 聲,	ch'ua[1]	H
唬[1]	口 30	虍 203	A rude call 嚇·| 人 to scare people	hsiao[1]	H
壺[2]	士 33	亞 247	Jug, pot, tankard, kettle | 提 梁 handle of kettle | 嘴 spout of kettle 茶 | tea-pot | 蓋 pot-lid		A

Hu

胡^2 肉 130 胡 705 — A

Why, what, how? lane, street S
(used for 衚 also for 糊)
| 椒 pepper | 椒麵
|·琴 a sort of fiddle
| 行 careless, reckless | 說 etc.
| 鬧 unreasonable outbreak, bosh
|·弄 to deceive, to cheat
| 說霸道 talk outrageously
| 思亂想 random, disorderly thoughts
| 同 for 衚 衕, street, lane
| 言 | 語 talk nonsense | 言亂語

湖^2 水 85 胡 705 — B

Lake, large pool; Hunan
|∘南 Hunan | 北 Hupeh
| 邊 margin of a lake | 廣
兩 | Hunan and Hupeh

煳^2 火 86 胡 705 — F

To scorch, blacken 俗
燒 |·了 to scorch

瑚^2 玉 96 胡 705 — G

Coral 珊 |

糊^2 米 119 胡 705 — B

To paste; foolish, (also 胡)
| 牆 paper a wall so | 窗, | 縫
|·裏 | 塗 very stupid, foolish
| 裱匠 paper hanger 裱·| 匠
|·塗 dull, stupid

葫^2 艸 140 胡 705 — F

Gourd, calabash, |·蘆

蝴^2 虫 142 胡 705 — D

Butterfly | 蝶

衚^2 行 144 胡 705 — A

Street, lane | 衕 See 胡

餬^2 食 184 胡 705 — F

Food, gruel
| 口 fill mouth, make living

鬍^2 髟 190 胡 705 — B

Beard |·子
| 鬚 whiskers and moustache

Hu

鶘^{2}	鳥 196	胡 705	Pelican 鵜｜		G
狐^{2}	犬 94	瓜 407	Fox; suspicious ｜·狸 the fox		D
核^{2}	木 75	亥 874	Kernel, stone of fruit 俗	ho^{2}	E
瓠^{2}	瓜 97	夸 242	Gourd, calabash ｜·蘆 see 葫		F
斛^{2}	斗 68	角 602	Bushel of about five 斗		G
虍^{3}	虍 141	虍 203	Tiger		K
虎^{3}	虍 141	虍 203	Tiger 老｜; fierce, cruel ｜爪 tiger's claws ｜嘯 the roar of a tiger ｜視 to glare fiercely, to covet		C
琥^{3}	玉 96	虍 203	A goblet, signet of veined stone, amber, ｜·珀 amber, ｜珀珠 amber beads		I
護^{4}	言 149	蒦 58	To protect, defend 保·｜, ｜庇, ｜佑 ｜照 a passport ｜城河 a city moat ｜敎派 apologists ｜持 to support, to assist ｜心鏡 a breastplate ｜送 to escort, to convoy		C
戶^{4}	戶 63	戶 728	Door, family 門｜ ｜口 family, population ｜冊 a register of population		D
滬^{4}	水 85	戶 728	Name for Shanghai ｜關 Shanghai Customs		H
互^{4}	二 7	吾 763	Mutually, reciprocal 交｜, ｜相 ｜換 to exchange		E
怙^{4}	心 61	古 702	To rely on, presume on 失｜恃 lose father and mother		G
祜^{4}	示 113	古 702	Protection of heaven ｜佑 prosperous, protection		H

Hua

Character	Radical	Phonetic	Meaning		
花[1]	艸 140	化 327	Flower, ornament; vice; to spend; smallpox ｜車 palace car, gala carriage ｜旗 the American flag ｜甲 cycle of sixty years ｜錢 to spend money ｜用 ｜兒 市 flower-market ｜費 expenditure ｜消 expense, outlay, "tip" ｜衣 flowered clothes ｜盆 a flower-pot ｜邊 lace ｜片 a petal ｜瓶 a flower-vase ｜生 pea-nuts, ground nuts ｜洞·子 flower vault, green house ｜·子 a beggar ｜洋 布 chintz, printed cottons ｜園·子 a flower garden		A
華[1]	艸 140	華 64	唐 棣 之 ｜ Aspen plum blossoms	hua[24]	A
㸸[1]	巾 50	聿 669	Ripping, roaring sound ｜拉 一 聲 ripping sound		H
華[2] 蕐[2]	艸 140	華 64	Splendor, glory; China ｜僑 Chinese emigrants abroad ｜工 Chinese workmen abroad ｜國 China 中｜ ｜麗 beautiful, elegant ｜美 ｜商 Chinese merchants	hua[14]	A
譁[2] 嘩[2]	言 149	華 64	Noise, hurrah, clamor, hubbub 喧｜ clamor, noise		G
鏵[2]	金 167	華 64	Spade, plough share 犁｜		F

Hua

劃^{2} 划^{2}	刀 18	聿 669	A scow, open boat 划·子; to split, scratch 丨取燈 to scratch match	hua^{4}	A
滑^{2}	水 85	骨 616	Slippery; artful, 丨車·子 a pulley, a block 丨∘稽 satire, comic 丨石 soap-stone 丨倒 to slip down 丨·子 a wooden catch or latch	hua^{4}	D
猾^{2}	犬 94	骨 616	Treachérous, cunning 狡丨 丨弄 to deceive, to misguide		E
話^{4}	言 149	舌 707	Language, speech, words 丨匣·子 a chatterbox, phonograph 丨片 phonograph record 丨柄 a subject; accusation 丨說 the story goes; it is said 丨條·子 phrases reading slips 丨語 conversation, to utter		A
華^{4}	艸 140	華 64	Surname S	hua$^{1\&2}$	A
樺^{4}	木 75	華 64	Manchurian birch 丨皮 birch-bark		K
畫^{4} 画^{4}	田 102	聿 669	To draw; picture; mark; map 丨匠 a painter, artist 丨像 to paint a portrait 丨丨 to paint or draw picture 丨圖 丨工 an artist; painting 丨堂 drawing room; picture gallery 丨室 丨店 a picture-shop 丨舖		B
劃^{4}	刀 18	聿 669	To mark off, set apart 丨一 uniformity, unity	hua^{2}	A
化^{4}	匕 21	化 327	To change, transform, melt, digest, a suffix for — ized, etc. 丨消 to melt, consume; digest 消丨 丨學 chemistry, 丨學品 chemicals		C

化⁴			丨外 outside pale of civilization 丨驗 to analyze 歐丨 Europeanized		
滑⁴	水 85	骨 616	Surname S	hua²	D

Huai

褱²	衣 145	褱 368	To hide in bosom, hide		K
懷² 怀²	心 61	褱 368	Bosom; carry in bosom; cherish; the affection 心丨 S 丨仇 to cherish hatred 丨恨 丨揣 to guess; to thrust in breast 丨中 in the bosom 丨·裏 丨想 think, cherish a thought 丨念 丨疑 a doubt 丨疑派 skeptics 丨·裏 (or 兒) 來 go to the left 丨抱 to carry in the bosom 丨胎 to be pregnant 丨孕 丨慚 to blush, be ashamed		D
踝²	足 157	果 507	Ankle 丨·子骨 the ankle-bone		F
槐²	木 75	鬼 808	A locust tree; the pagoda tree		K
壞⁴	土 32	褱 368	To spoil, ruined; morally bad 丨·處 bad points 丨船 a shipwreck 丨意 evil thought 丨人 a bad person, to ruin person 丨名 bad reputation 丨事 ruin an affair, wickedness 丨透·了 thoroughly bad		A

Huan

Character	Radical	Phonetic	Meaning	Other reading	Grade
歡^{1} 懽^{1} 欢^{1}	欠 76 減	雚 60	To rejoice, happy ｜·喜 ｜呼 to cheer, hurrah ｜樂 to make merry, delight ｜送會 farewell meeting ｜迎 to welcome, so ｜迎會 ｜悅 pleased, delighted		B
獾^{1} 貛^{1}	犬 94	雚 60	Badger 狗｜, 猪｜ 海｜ beaver		H
驩^{1}	馬 187	雚 60	Happy, peaceable; gentle horse 撒｜ to frisk, as a horse		K
寰^{2}	宀 40	睘 371	Emperor's domain		H
環^{2}	玉 96	睘 371	A ring, to encircle, world ｜球 ｜境 environment ｜球旅行 tour of the world ｜繞 to go round about ｜繩 a skipping-rope 耳｜ ear-ring		E
還^{2} 还^{2}	辵 162	睘 371	To repay, still more, yet; or ｜債 to pay a debt ｜賬, ｜錢 ｜價 beat down price; make offer ｜淸 to pay off, to pay in full ｜口 to talk back; so ｜手 ｜禮 to return the compliment ｜拜 to return a visit ｜在 still living ｜願 to pay one's vow	hai^{2}	A
鐶^{2}	金 167	睘 371	Metal ring, bracelet, weight; used as 環 門｜ ring on door		F
鬟^{2}	髟 190	睘 371	Top-knot; maid-servant 丫｜ a slave girl		H

Huan

桓^{2}	木 75	亘 795	Tablets; martial S. ｜表 tablets at grave		I
緩^{3}	糸 120	爰 187	Remiss, slow, gradual; to neglect, ｜限 to extend a limit of time ｜慢 slow		F
浣^{3} 澣^{3}	水 85	完 389	To wash, bathe ｜沐; ten days, ｜濯 to wash, cleanse 中｜ middle ten days of month	wan^{3}	H
皖^{3}	白 106	完 389	Bright, luminous, Anhui	wan^{3}	G
奐^{4}	大 37	奐 774	Excellent, gay, beautiful 明｜ gay, brilliant		K
喚^{4}	口 30	奐 774	To call, summon, name ｜人 call to a person to come ｜狗 to call a dog		C
換^{4}	手 64	奐 774	To exchange, barter; alter ｜肩 change shoulders ｜錢 change money ｜轉 transpose ｜新 change new for old ｜衣·裳 change the clothes ｜衣·服 ｜班 relieve guard ｜帖 exchange cards, sworn brothers ｜言之 in other words		A
煥^{4}	火 86	奐 774	Bright, lustrous 明｜ ｜然一新 brand-new		I
瘓^{4}	疒 104	奐 774	Sick, ailing ｜病 palsy, paralysis		E
患^{4}	心 61	串 789	Misfortune; to suffer; distress ｜病 afflicted with disease 禍｜ misfortune, ｜難^{4}		B
幻^{4}	幺 52	幺 876	Magical; illusion, unreal, dream ｜想 imagination, fancy, ｜術 magical arts, ｜影 shadowy		F

宦[4]	宀 40	臣 642	Officials S. 丨家 an official family 丨官 government officer, eunuch 丨途 official career	G

Huang

荒[1]	艸 140	巟 649	Wild; famine; barren; reckless 丨塲 a deserted open space 丨郊 a wilderness 丨空 empty, waste 丨年 a year of dearth 丨唐 to exaggerate; lies 丨地（田）barren ground	D
慌[1]	心 61	巟 649	Agitated, hurried; frightfully 丨·張 confused, hurried, unsettled 丨惚 vague, fluttered, confused 丨亂 agitated, confused 丨速 hasty, hurried	B
肓[1]	肉 130	亡 646	Vitals, aorta	K
黃[2]	黃 201	黃 822	Yellow, imperial S. 丨金 gold 丨種 the yellow race 丨風 yellow wind, dust-storm 丨蜂 the wasp 丨河 the Yellow River 丨昏 twilight 丨·瓜 the cucumber 丨道 zodiac, ecliptic 丨土 yellow earth, loess, clay 丨油 butter	A
癀[2]	疒 104	黃 822	Jaundice 丨病	H
磺[2]	石 112	黃 822	Sulphur, brimstone 硫。丨 丨坑 sulphur springs 丨孔	F

Huang

Character	Radical	Phonetic	Meaning		
簧²	竹 118	黃 822	Organ-reed; spring, catch, 鎖 | catch in Chinese padlock		H
[illegible]²	黃 201	黃 822	Egg-yolk | 兒, also 黃		K
皇²	白 106	皇 74	Emperor, imperial | 城 the imperial city | 甫 double surname | 后 the empress | 宮 the imperial palace | 曆 almanac |∘上 the emperor of China |∘帝 | 太 后 the empress dowager	S.	D
凰²	几 16	皇 74	Female phoenix 鳳∘| phoenix; good omen		H
徨²	彳 60	皇 74	Doubtful, irresolute 徊 | back and forth, irresolute		I
惶²	心 61	皇 74	Afraid, alarmed, perturbed | 恐 fear, terror | 愧		D
煌²	火 86	皇 74	Brilliant, luminous 輝 | blaze, bright		G
蝗²	虫 142	皇 74	Locust |∘蟲 蚱 | migratory locust		E
遑²	辵 162	皇 74	Leisure; careless; to hasten 怠 | indolent		I
隍² 堭²	阜 170	皇 74	City moat, dry ditch 城∘| tutelary god of a city		I
鰉² 鱑²	魚 195	皇 74	Sturgeon | 魚		K
謊³ 詤³	言 149	荒 649	Lie, 說 | , 撒 | , false | 詐 false, double tongued | 話 falsehood; to tell lie | 言, | 誕 | 騙 to deceive by falsehood,		B

Character	Radical	Phonetic	Meaning		
恍[3] 怳[3]	心 61	光 390	Wild, confused, delirium ｜耀 confused, blurred		E
晃[3]	日 72	光 390	Bright, dazzling ｜耀 ｜眼 dazzle the eyes		E
幌[3]	巾 50	光 390	A curtain, screen, sign ｜·子 shop sign		F
愰[3]	心 61	光 390	Unsettled ｜｜兒 at times, occasionally		F
貺[4]	貝 154	兄 755	To bestow, grant ｜施 ｜儀 a present	k'uang[4]	I

Hui

Character	Radical	Phonetic	Meaning		
灰[1] 灰[1]	火 86	灰 173	Ashes, lime ｜◦塵 ashes and dust, ｜土 ｜線 a marking line ｜心 to despair, discouraged ｜·色 ash color, drab ｜兜 a bricklayer's hod		B
恢[1]	心 61	灰 173	Magnanimous, great ｜◦復 to revert to the type		I
詼[1]	言 149	灰 173	To play with ｜笑 make sport of		I
揮[1]	手 64	軍 838	To shake, wave, scatter; direct ｜棄 to throw away ｜散 to scatter, to dismiss ｜手 to wave the hand, to direct		F
輝[1] 煇[1]	車 159	軍 838	Bright, glorious ｜煌 bright, dazzling 光｜ brilliant, bright		E
徽[1]	彳 60	徵 550	Honorable, excellent; urgent ｜章 cloth badge on coat 安◦｜ Anhui		H

Hui

Character	Radical	Phonetic	Meaning	Other readings	
麾1	麻 200	麻 494	Signal flag 旗 | 指 | direct with a flag		H
回2 囘2 囬2	囗 31 俗	口 765	To turn back; a time, occasion | 家 to return home |·去 to go back, return | 轉 | 復 to return; reply to | 想 to reflect, recollect | 思 | 信 reply to a letter | 話 (音) an answer, reply | 答 ·| 教 the Mohammedan faith | 國 return to one's country |·來 to return, by and by | 拜 to return a visit | 報 a reply, report | 片·子 a card to acknowledge		A
徊2	彳 60	口 765	To and fro, irresolute 徘 | back and forth		H
蛔2	虫 142	口 765	Tape-worm; common intestinal worms, or lumbricoids | 虫 body-worms		K
茴2	艸 140	口 765	Fennel, anise-seed, | 香 小 | 香 fragrant dill seed		G
迴2 廻2	辵 162	口 765	To return, revolve | 血 管 veins | 流 水 an eddy | 避 to retire, withdraw, avoid		F
虺21	虫 142	兀 387	Venomous serpent | 蛇 蝮 | a viper		E
會3	曰 73	會 833	In a few moments—| 兒, a while	hui4 k'uai4	A
悔3	心 61	每 572	To repent, regret; contrition | 恨 repent, be vexed with self | 改 to repent, reform | 罪 to repent of sin		C
誨3	言 149	每 572	To instruct, teach, counsel 訓 | to instruct		D

Hui

毀[3]	殳 79	毀 687	To destroy, slander, ruin |∘壞 | 滅 to exterminate utterly		C
燬[3]	火 86	毀 687	To blaze; burn down 燒 | consume by fire		F
譭[3] 諱[3]	言 149	毀 687	To slander, defame | 謗 defame, vilify | 罵 slander, backbite		D
會[4] 会[4]	曰 73	會 833	To assemble; a sect, society; acquired ability | 長[3] head of society; priest | 正 president or chairman | 集 to assemble, | 齊, | 合 | 期 time of meeting | 議 to meet, discuss at meeting | 意 to understand | 館 club-house, club, guild |·過 seen, met, before | 過 日·子 able to economise | 面 to visit, to meet |·不·| can you? have you learned? | 水 to know how to swim | 說 able to speak, eloquent | 堂 a meeting-house, church | 做 able to do or make | 同 conjointly | 友 member of a society | 員	hui[3] k'uai[4]	A
繪[4]	糸 120	會 833	To draw, sketch; embroider | 畫 to paint or draw a picture		F
彗[4]	彐 58	彗 673	A broom, | 星 a comet	sao[4]	H
慧[4]	心 61	彗 673	Wisdom, sagacity 智∘| practical wisdom | 明		C
噦[4]	口 30	歲 132	Rumbling hum; spacious	yüeh[1]	I
穢[4]	禾 115	歲 132	Filthy, foul; to defile 汚 | | 物 a filthy thing	wei[4]	C

Hui

Character	Radical	Phonetic	Meaning	Other reading	
惠⁴	心 61	惠 840	Kindness, grace, kind 恩｜ S ｜愛 affectionate, loving ｜順 accord with, treat kindly		D
蕙⁴	艸 140	惠 840	A fragrant orchid 雪｜Yünnan snow-orchid		I
匯⁴ 滙⁴	匚 22	隹 52	To converge, eddy; bankdraft, letter of credit; to remit money ｜∘豐銀行 Hongkong & Shanghai bank ｜付 pay to, remit to ｜欵 remittances, drafts ｜票 bill of exchange｜單 ｜∘水 commission on draft ｜兌局 an exchange office		E
賄⁴	貝 154	有 184	Bribe, hush-money｜賂 ｜買 to suborn		E
彙⁴	彐 58	果 507	A collection, class; to classify ｜集 a collection of books ｜編 concordance 字｜dictionary, vocabulary		E
晦⁴	日 72	每 572	Obscure,｜冥; stupid, unlucky 月｜last day of moon		G
諱⁴	言 149	韋 764	To conceal｜隱; forbidden, taboo 避｜avoiduse of (a name)		G
卉⁴ 芔⁴	十 24	卉 416	Plants, herbs ｜草 general term for grass, herbs		G
潰⁴	水 85	貴 862	Overflowing stream; rush; destroy; flee ｜敗 destroyed, spoilt	k'uei⁴	H
殨⁴	歹 78	貴 862	Running ulcer 瘡｜ ｜爛 broken out with sores	k'uei⁴	K
瞶⁴	目 109	貴 862	Blurred, vision, dim sight 昏｜dim-sighted	k'uei⁴	K
喙⁴	口 30	彖 287	Mouth; to pant; a hook, beak ｜息 to pant		K

Hun

葷[1]	艸 140	軍 838	Meat, onions, etc. forbidden to fasters 丨素 meat diet and vegetable diet 丨菜 meat dishes		A
昏[1]	日 72	昏 351	Dusk, dull 丨暗; confused 丨花 specks flitting before the eyes 丨·過·去 to faint 丨暈 丨亂 confused, stupid 丨迷 in a fit; infatuated		D
婚[1]	女 38	昏 351	To marry; the bridegroom 丨證 marriage certificate 丨家 bridegroom's family 丨娶 to marry a woman 丨配 丨禮 marriage ceremonies 丨姻之禮 丨書 a marriage contract 丨姻 marriage, nuptial		C
惛[1] 惽[1]	心 61	昏 351	Confused, stupid; forgetful 丨迷 confused ideas, forgetfulness		E
殙[1]	歹 78	昏 351	Stupid, dim, fameless death		K
睧[1]	目 109	昏 351	Dull vision, 漠丨		G
閽[1]	門 169	昏 351	A gate; door-keeper 丨人 叩丨 knock at a gate		K
魂[2]	鬼 194	云 875	Soul, mind, faculties 丨•靈 soul or spirit 靈丨 三丨 Taoist three souls 失丨 lose one's wits		C
渾[2]	水 85	軍 838	Entire; turbid 丨濁 muddy, polluted 丨身 the whole body 丨雜 mixed up or together 丨沌 (or 淪) chaos, chaotic	hun[4]	D

餛^2 餫^2	食 184	昆 798	A fritter-cake; provisions |·飩 pork dumplings in soup		K
渾^4	水 85	軍 838	Confused, chaotic | 河 Yung-ting River	hun^2	D
混^4	水 85	昆 798	Disorderly, confused, chaos, turbid | 和 to jumble together | 亂 in great confusion | 鬧 clamor, confused, uproar | 雜 mixed, blended		E
溷^4	水 85	豕 285	Turbid, dirty 攪 | to disturb, make muddy		I

Hung

哄^1	口 30	共 95	To rouse up |·起·來	hung^3	D
烘^1 灴^1	火 86	共 95	To dry, toast; to warm | 烤 to roast, to warm | 屋·子 to warm the room		G
轟^1	車 159	車 836	To rumble, roar; explode | 擊 to peal, to bombard | 炸 | 擊 物 explosives |·出·去 to drive out		E
訇^1	言 149	言 740	Crashing noise 匉 |		G
紅^2	糸 120	工 8	Red | 色, ruddy; lucky S | 茶 black tea | 塵 the world | 契 stamped deed | 轎 bridal chair | 海 Red Sea |·了 臉 blushing | 寶·石(or 玉) the ruby or carbuncle | 十 字 會 Red Cross Society |∘事 a wedding		A

虹[2] 虫 142 工 8 Rainbow 天 | , | 橋 — chiang[4] kang[4] — E

鴻[2] 鳥 196 工 8 Swan, wild goose | 雁; vast — E
| 恩 great favor, mercy
| 禧 may you have great joy

洪[2] 水 85 共 95 Flood; vast; very S. — D
| 恩 great favor, mercy
| 福 great happiness
| 水 The Flood, a flood

宏[2] 宀 40 厷 167 Vast, spacious, large, ample — E
| 恩 great kindness or favor
| 遠 widely extended

肱[2] 厷[2] 肉 130 厷 167 Humerus, the arm — kung[1] — K

弘[2] 弓 57 弓 244 Vast, liberal, great S. — F
| 大 very great

黌[2] 黃 201 䶡 692 College; to learn — I
| 宮 College, Confucian temple

哄[3] 口 30 共 95 To deceive; amuse; din — hung[1] — D
|·出·去 to coax out
| 孩·子 to coax a child
| 騙 to cheat, to beguile

鬨[4] 鬥 191 共 95 Noise of battle, to fight, clamor — H
| 嚷 uproar, clamor

Huo

豁[1] 谷 150 害 146 Clear, intelligent; to remit; open out; penetrate — B
| 免 to generously pardon
|·子 gate cut for convenience

劐[1] 刀 18 蒦 58 To rip open; plough | 地 — H
| 嘴 a hare-lip
|·子 a plough; man with hare-lip

Huo

活[2] 水 85 舌 707 — A

Alive, active; to live; motion, movable; work

| 佛 a living Buddha
| 話 indefinite words
| 人 a living person
| 命 life; to give life
| 拿 to take prisoner alive
| 板 movable types
|·潑 living; active; quick
| 不 了[3] it will not live
| 水 running water
| 說·着 speak indefinitely
|∘動 alive, movable, exercise
| 動 影 戲 cinema
| 字 movable types; a substantive

火[3] 火 86 火 446 — A

Fire, fever, to burn

| 車 steam-engine
| 車 站 railway station
| 車 頭 locomotive
| 蟲 兒 glow-worms, fire-flies
| 星 a spark; the planet Mars
| 爐 a fire-place, a furnace
| 輪 船 steamer
|∘把 a torch
| 山 a volcano
| 燒 to burn; a kind of bun
| 神 god of fire
| 石 flint
| 災 the calamity of fire
| 腿 ham
| 曜 日 Tuesday
|·藥 gunpowder
| 焰 flame of fire

伙[3] 人 9 火 446 — A

Tools, goods

傢·| tools, furniture

Huo

夥[3]	夕 36	果 507	Company, partner; C. of companies |·計 partner, assistant, comrade |居 live together, as a mess |伴 a partner, companion		B
貨[4]	貝 154	化 327	Goods, wares |物, |品 |車 goods train, freight car |眞價實 goods genuine and price fair |單 an invoice, a bill of sale |財 goods and chattels		B
或[4]	戈 62	或 333	Perchance, if, may, or, some one |者 perhaps, probably |是 好|歹 whether good or bad |謂 somebody said, some say |曰		B
惑[4]	心 61	或 333	To doubt, mislead, |心 疑◦| to doubt, suspect 迷◦| to be fooled; lead astray 誘| to tempt, beguile		D
禍[4]	示 113	咼 581	Calamity, evil, adversity 福| misery and happiness 患| calamity, misfortune |災		D
蒦[4]	艸 140	蒦 58	A measure; to measure		K
獲[4]	犬 94	蒦 58	To catch, seize, get, obtain |住 |恩 to obtain favor |利 to get profit |勝 to gain the victory |得 to obtain |罪 to commit a crime		D
鑊[4]	金 167	蒦 58	Rice pan, a boiler 鐵| 鼎| a caldron, boiler		K
攉[4]	手 64	隹 52	To knead, mix up |麵 to make dough		G
癨[4]	疒 104	隹 52	Cholera |◦亂病		F

I, Yi

一^{1} 壹^{1} 弌^{1}	一 1 減	一 1	One, a; the first; all; uniform (generally before second tone)	i^{24}	A
			｜齊 all at once, all together	i^{4}	
			｜直 straight, directly ｜直·的	i^{4}	
			｜羣 a flock, herd, some group	i^{4}	
			｜二 one or two		
			｜回 once, a chapter in book	i^{4}	
			｜｜·的 one by one ｜個 ｜個·的	i^{2} ko^{4} ...	
			｜來 in the first place ｜則	i^{4}	
			｜連 in close succession	i^{4}	
			｜神敎 monothism		
			｜十 ten		
衣^{1} 衤^{1}	衣 145	衣 367	Clothes, covering; husk ｜·服, ｜·裳	i^{4}	A
			｜架 a clothes rack or horse		
			｜箱 a clothes-chest ｜櫃		
			｜舖 a clothier's shop		
			｜食 food and clothes, a livelihood		
			｜食住 necessities of life		
依^{1}	人 9	衣 367	To rely on, depend on; assent; according to		B
			｜舊 as before ｜然		
			｜·着 relying on, leaning against,		
			｜賴 to depend on		
			｜律 according to law		
			｜實 I acquiesce (polite); lit. yield to reality		
			｜從 to comply, obey		
裔^{14}	衣 145	衣 367	Skirt, border; posterity		E
			後｜ descendants 苗｜		
殹^{1}	殳 79	殹 403	An echo		P
翳^{14}	羽 124	殹 403	To screen, vanish; film		I
			｜毛 eyelashes		

I, Yi

Character	Radical	Phonetic	Meaning		
醫[1] 医[1]	酉 164	殹 403	To heal; medical; physician ｜家 medical practitioners ｜治 to heal, to cure ｜金 doctor's fees ｜學 Medicine, medical science ｜學校 a medical school ｜學士 M. D., Doctor of Medicine ｜科 medical course ｜·生 a doctor ｜道 practice of medicine ｜院 a hospital		B
揖[1]	手 64	咠 631	To bow, salute, 作[1]｜ bow with folded hands		E
乙[1]	乙 5	乙 297	One	i43	E
伊[1]	人 9	尹 677	He, she, it, this S. ｜犁 I-li, Chinese Turkestan ｜等 they, them, those		F
噫[1]	口 30	意 91	To sigh; alas! groaning, moaning ｜嘻 dear me! alack!		G
一[2] 壹[2] 弌[2]	一 1 减	一 1	One, (before fourth tone) ｜個 ｜兆 a million ｜切 all, the whole of ｜概 ｜致 uniformity, of one kind ｜項 one sort, kind, item ｜刻 a quarter of an hour ｜塊兒 together with ｜共 all, the whole of, sum total ｜類 the same class or sort ｜律 the same principle, unity ｜面 on the one hand ｜輩·子 a whole life-time ｜遍 once, a time ｜次, ｜邊 ｜並 the whole, together, all ｜步 a step ｜部·分 integral part, fraction ｜帶 all along, neighborhood, region	i14	A

I, Yi

一[2]			｜套 a set, ｜對 a pair ｜定 positively certain ｜樣 the same, like		
益[24]	皿 108	益 610	Benefit; increase; advantage S. ｜加 to increase ｜進 to advance ｜·處 benefit, advantage ｜發 all the more		B
宜[2]	宀 40	宜 624a	Proper, fit; right, ought 合｜fitting, right 相｜	i[4]	B
誼[2]	言 149	宜 624a	Related, intimate; suitable, fit 友｜friendship		H
夷[2]	大 37	夷 251	Barbarians; to squat; destroy ｜狄 foreigners, barbarians ｜人		F
姨[2]	女 38	夷 251	Mother's sister, wife's sister ｜母 mother's sister, aunt ｜娘 ｜·子 wife's sister		F
痍[2]	疒 104	夷 251	Ulcer, sore 瘡｜		K
胰[2]	肉 130	夷 251	Caul; soap ｜·子, ｜皂 ｜·子 末 兒 lather of soap		B
疑[2]	疋 103	疑 479	To doubt, suspect ｜·心, ｜·惑 ｜懼 doubts and fears ｜難 a suspicious and hard matter 懷｜cherish suspicions		C
移[2] 迻[2]	禾 115	多 269	Transplant; change residence, migrate ｜遷 to remove 遷｜ ｜居 remove place of residence ｜民 開 墾 colonization		C
儀[2]	人 9	義 339	Etiquette, ceremony, rites ｜器 scientific apparatus ｜禮 rites, observances 禮｜ ｜式 ceremony, ritual, form ｜文 deportment. ceremony		D

I, Yi

<table>
<tr><td>遺²</td><td>辵
162</td><td>貴
862</td><td>To leave, bequeath; lose
| 傳 tradition, heredity
|·下 bequeath, hand down | 留
| 漏 to leave out
| 命 dying command, a will | 書
| 失 to lose, to mislay</td><td>wei⁴</td><td>E</td></tr>
<tr><td>怡²</td><td>心
61</td><td>台
718</td><td>Gratified, concord, joyful
| 悅 delighted</td><td></td><td>H</td></tr>
<tr><td>貽²</td><td>貝
154</td><td>台
718</td><td>To hand down, leave, bequeath | 遺</td><td></td><td>G</td></tr>
<tr><td>頤²</td><td>頁
181</td><td>𦣞
642</td><td>Chin, jaws, chops
解 | 語 a joke</td><td></td><td>H</td></tr>
<tr><td>倪²</td><td>人
9</td><td>兒
684</td><td>Beginning; young; to glance at
端 | clue, trace</td><td>ni²</td><td>G</td></tr>
<tr><td>沂²</td><td>水
85</td><td>斤
209</td><td>River in Shantung
| 州 府 Ichowfu in Shantung</td><td></td><td>H</td></tr>
<tr><td>以³
㠯³</td><td>人
9</td><td>以
431
㠯
750</td><td>According to; to use; with, for
| 及 together with, and also
| 前 before, in front of | 先
| 致 and cause, so that, etc.
| 後 after, behind
| 內 inside of, within
| 上 above, on the top
| 外 to except; beyond
| 爲 in order that; to esteem as
所·| therefore, 所 | 然 reason</td><td></td><td>A
K</td></tr>
<tr><td>苡³
苢³</td><td>艸
140</td><td>以
431</td><td>A plant, pearl barley | 米
芣 | the plantago, plantain (weed)</td><td></td><td>K</td></tr>
<tr><td>已³</td><td>己
49</td><td>己
311</td><td>Already, finished, final particle
| 成 already completed | 畢
|·經 already | 然
| 久 for a long time
| 過·了 already past | 往
| 滿 already full, expired
| 定 already, decided
而 | merely, simply, only</td><td></td><td>A</td></tr>
</table>

I, Yi

<table>
<tr><td>倚^3</td><td>人
9</td><td>奇
452</td><td>To lean against; depend upon
| 仗 depend upon | 靠, | 賴, | 恃
| 勢 depend on power or influence</td><td></td><td>C</td></tr>
<tr><td>椅^3</td><td>木
75</td><td>奇
452</td><td>Chair, seat, |·子
| 墊·子 a chair cushion
|·子 檔 rung of chair</td><td></td><td>A</td></tr>
<tr><td>尾^3</td><td>尸
44</td><td>毛
375</td><td>Tail |·巴, | 兒, 俗</td><td>wei^3</td><td>C</td></tr>
<tr><td>矣^3</td><td>矢
111</td><td>矣
477</td><td>Final particle, completing sense
而 已 | and there's an end of it</td><td></td><td>E</td></tr>
<tr><td>蟻^3</td><td>虫
142</td><td>義
339</td><td>The ant 螞 |
螞 | 窩 an ant-hill | 丘,</td><td></td><td>F</td></tr>
<tr><td>一^4
壹^4
弌^4</td><td>一
1

減</td><td>一
1</td><td>One (before first and third tones)
| 眨 眼 in a twinkling | 展 眼,
| 千 a thousand, | 百 a hundred
| 週 once round; a year, century
| 角 10 cents
| 種 a kind, same kind, | 流
| 番 once
| 方 a whole neighborhood
| 些 a little of
| 心 the whole heart
| 里 路 one li distance | 里 地
| 兩 a tael, an ounce
| 把 a handful
| 般 alike, of the same sort, etc.
| 邊 on one side
| 生 all one's life |^{4}生 |^{2}世</td><td>i12</td><td>A</td></tr>
<tr><td>意^4</td><td>心
61</td><td>意
91</td><td>Thought, will, intention
|·氣 spirit; stubborn feelings.
|·見 an idea, an opinion
| 志 the will, volition
| 想 to think, thought
| 向 intention, end in view
| 會 to conceive mentally
| 義 meaning, signification
|·識 consciousness; discernment</td><td></td><td>A</td></tr>
</table>

I, Yi

<table>
<tr><td>意^4</td><td></td><td></td><td>|·思 thought, intention, meaning
| 外 beyond one's thought
|·味 interest; beauty (in art etc.)
| 願 a wish 願·| willing</td><td></td><td></td></tr>
<tr><td>億^4</td><td>人
9</td><td>意
91</td><td>Hundred thousand; calculate; quiet
| 兆 100,000,000,000; the people</td><td></td><td>G</td></tr>
<tr><td>憶^4</td><td>心
61</td><td>意
91</td><td>To reflect on, recall, | 記
| 念 to bear in mind</td><td></td><td>D</td></tr>
<tr><td>臆^4</td><td>肉
130</td><td>意
91</td><td>Bosom, feelings; full; subjective
| 論 theory, hypothesis | 說</td><td></td><td>G</td></tr>
<tr><td>易^4</td><td>日
72</td><td>易
235</td><td>To change; easy, 容·| S.
| 經 Book of Changes
| 覺 sensitive, easily moved
| 信 easy of belief, credulous</td><td></td><td>A</td></tr>
<tr><td>衣^4</td><td>衣
145</td><td>衣
397</td><td>To dress, wear 文</td><td>i^1</td><td>A</td></tr>
<tr><td>語^4</td><td>言
149</td><td>吾
763</td><td>To speak 言 | yuan^2·i 俗</td><td>yü^{34}</td><td>A</td></tr>
<tr><td>宜^4</td><td>宀
40</td><td>宜
624 a</td><td>Advantage 便 | p'ien^2·i</td><td>i^2</td><td>B</td></tr>
<tr><td>睪^4</td><td>目
109</td><td>睪
160</td><td>To spy out, pleased</td><td></td><td>K</td></tr>
<tr><td>繹^4</td><td>糸
120</td><td>睪
160</td><td>To explain, unfold; long, unceasing
| 續 continuous, uninterrupted</td><td></td><td>D</td></tr>
<tr><td>譯^4</td><td>言
149</td><td>睪
160</td><td>To interpret, translate 繙 |
| 義 translate the meaning
| 音 to translate the sound</td><td></td><td>B</td></tr>
<tr><td>驛^4</td><td>馬
187</td><td>睪
160</td><td>Post, postal station; courier
| 站 post station
| 馬 post horses</td><td></td><td>I</td></tr>
<tr><td>義^4
乂^4</td><td>羊
123</td><td>義
339</td><td>Righteousness; public; adopted (child); meaning
|·氣 heroism, patriotism
| 兒^2 an adopted son | 子^3, | 女
| 父 an adopted father
|·和 拳 the "Boxers" |·和 團</td><td></td><td>B</td></tr>
</table>

I, Yi

義^{4}			| 學 a free or public school | 人 a righteous man | 士 a worthy knight | 地 a public cemetery |·務 duty, voluntary service | 勇 軍 volunteers, irregulars		
議^{4}	言 149	義 339	To deliberate, discuss, criticise, | 案 a motion, a bill | 端 | 長^{3} president of senate | 程 programme, agenda | 決 confirm by vote, decide | 會 local council ·| 論 to debate, to discuss | 定 deliberate and determine | 定 書 protocol | 員 member of Parliament | 院 Parliament		B
異^{4}	田 102	異 98	Different, strange; foreign; false | 教 heathenism, heresy | 端 | 種 an alien race | 象 a vision | 議 objection | 能 uncommon abilities | 邦 a foreign country | 點 point of difference | 字 同 義 synonym		C
翼^{4}	羽 124	異 98	Wings, to shelter; assist 扶 | to aid, support		F
埶^{4}	土 32	埶 305	Skill, craft, (same as next)		P
藝^{4} 蓺^{4}	艸 140	埶 305	Skill, craft, an art | 術 | 能 talent ability, skill, | 業 trade, profession 六 | six liberal arts 手◦| skill, handicraft		D
乙^{43}	乙 5	乙 297	Second of ten Stems; curved | 班 Junior Class	i1	E

I, Yi

役^4	彳 60	殳 399	To serve; employ as servant, | 使 | 夫 inferior employees 差 |		E
疫^4	疒 104	殳 399	Epidemic, pestilence | 症 瘟 | contagion, plague		D
毅^4	殳 79	殳 399	Bold, resolute, enduring | 然 resolutely; | 力 energy		I
亦^4	亠 8	亦 422	Also, moreover, then, even | 好 also good | 然 in like manner		E
奕^4 弈^4	大 37	亦 422	Great, grand; chess | 棋 博 | play chess		H
拽^4 曳^4	手 64	曳 835	To drag, saunter | 尾 trail the tail, or wag it | 踵 drag the heels, shuffle	chuai^4 yeh^4	E
邑^4	邑 163	邑 314	City 城 | ,hamlet; camp, a district city		F
逸^4	辵 162	兔 384	Indulgence, ease, quiet, retired 安 | peaceful leisure 一勞永 | once for all		F
詣^4	言 149	旨 323	To go to, reach; visit | 談 visit and talk over 親 | to go in person 造 | make progress (in studies etc.)		G
抑^4	手 64	卬 308	To curb, repress; or, else | 制 to repress | 或 or, whether, perhaps, if		G
懿^{42}	心 61	壹 734	Virtuous, admirable, accomplished | 德 admirable virtue		G
肄^4	聿 129	聿 669	To practise; acquire skill | 習 to render familiar | 業 to study a profession | 業生 undergraduates		G
溢^4	水 85	益 610	Overflow, surplus, full | 數 a surplus		H

Character	Radical	Phonetic	Meaning		
縊4	糸 120	益 610	To hang oneself 自丨, 丨死		H
乂4	丿 4	乂 528	To regulate; aid; able 保丨 preserve, protect		K
刈4	刀 18	乂 528	To reap, cut off; kill 丨穫 to cut down and reap		H
翌4	羽 124	立 84	Bright; tomorrow 丨日 丨朝 tomorrow morning		I
佚4	人 9	失 481	Ease; to err, fail; luxury 淫丨 vicious indulgence		I
弋4	弋 56	弋 328	Arrow; to shoot, aim at 丨取 to seize, take		K

Jan

Character	Radical	Phonetic	Meaning		
然2	火 86	然 459	Certainly, yes; but; right; however; adverbial suffix 丨而 but, nevertheless 丨否 whether or not, uncertain 丨後 then, afterwards 偶丨 suddenly, by chance 雖丨 although, even if		A
燃2	火 86	然 459	To light fire, burn 丨火		H
髯2	髟 190	冉 600	Whiskers, beard 丨鬚 beard and mustache		H
染3	木 75	九 302	To dye; infect, "catch" 丨坊 a dye-shop 丨布 to dye cloth 丨汚 to pollute; to infect 丨病, 傳丨		D
冉3	冂 13	冉 600	Tender, gradually, 丨丨 S. 丨子3 disciple of Confucius, 丨伯牛		H

Jang

Character	Radical	Phonetic	Meaning		
嚷1	口 30	口 369	To bawl, wrangle 丨·丨 俗	jang3	E

<table>
<tr><td>禳^{2}</td><td>示
113</td><td>襄
369</td><td>To pray to avert evil
| 禍 avert calamity by prayer | 災</td><td></td><td>K</td></tr>
<tr><td>攘^{2}</td><td>手
64</td><td>襄
369</td><td>To seize, plunder; reject
| 奪 carry off, rob 奪 |
| 羊 to steal sheep</td><td>jang^{3}</td><td>G</td></tr>
<tr><td>瓤^{2}</td><td>瓜
97</td><td>襄
369</td><td>Pulp, pith, kernel 瓜 |
核 桃 | walnut kernels</td><td></td><td>F</td></tr>
<tr><td>嚷^{3}</td><td>口
30</td><td>襄
369</td><td>Clamor, brawl, cry out, scold
| 鬧 to quarrel, to wrangle</td><td>jang^{1}</td><td>E</td></tr>
<tr><td>壤^{3}</td><td>土
32</td><td>襄
369</td><td>Soil, earth; fat; region
接 | neighboring</td><td></td><td>G</td></tr>
<tr><td>攘^{3}</td><td>手
64</td><td>襄
369</td><td>To cause confusion
天 下 攘 | the country was thrown into disorder</td><td>jang^{2}</td><td>G</td></tr>
<tr><td>讓^{4}</td><td>言
149</td><td>襄
369</td><td>To yield, resign, let, waive rights; be humble, 謙 |
|·一·步 stand aside! | 路 give way
| 人 politely invite; yield
| 人 打·了 was beaten
| 坐 press one to be seated
| 走 request one to go
| 位 yield a place or seat</td><td></td><td>C</td></tr>
</table>

Jao

<table>
<tr><td>饒^{2}</td><td>食
184</td><td>堯
391</td><td>Abundant; to pardon |·恕 S.
|·了·我·罷 forgive me!</td><td></td><td>C</td></tr>
<tr><td>擾^{3}</td><td>手
64</td><td>憂
412</td><td>To annoy, disturb 攪 |
| 害 disturb, cause confusion | 乱
騷 | harass, fidget</td><td></td><td>C</td></tr>
<tr><td>繞^{4}
遶^{4}</td><td>糸
120</td><td>堯
391</td><td>To wind around, bind; environ
|·着 走 taking roundabout course
| 彎 兒 to go round a corner
| 遠 a long way round</td><td></td><td>C</td></tr>
</table>

Jen

人² 人 9 人 429 Man, human, a person | 丁 — A

| ·家 families; the people; others
| 情 human feelings; kindness, a present
| 羣 society
| 種 human race, a race
| | all men, everybody
| 格 personality, manhood
| 口 persons; population ings
| 類 mankind
| 力 human strength or ability
| 力 車 jinricksha
| 倫 five relations of mankind
| 命 human life, a case of life and death
| 品 a person's conduct or manner
| 生 觀 view of life
| 壽 保 險 life-insurance
| 道 principles of humanity
| 道 主 義 humanitarianism
| 才 ability, talent, man-force
| 造 artificial | 爲·的
| 子³ a son of man; Christ
| 物 a man of mark
| 烟 population

仁² 人 9 人 429 Benevolence, humanity; a kernel — D

| 愛 humanity, benevolence | 心
| 政 humane government
| 兒 a seed, a kernel
| 義 benevolence and justice
| 德 benevolence, charity | 慈, | 恩

壬² 士 33 壬 67 Fully, great; 9th stem — F

Jen

任²	人 9	任 68	To bear, allow S ｜邱 district in Hopei	jen⁴	D
紉²	糸 120	刃 222	To twist thread, cord ｜絲	jen⁴	H
儿²	儿 10	儿 382	Legs of a man, a man		K
忍³	心 61	刃 222	To endure, bear; repress; harsh, severe ｜飢 to bear hunger ｜·着·能 be patient! ｜心 passionate, hard-hearted ｜性 a patient disposition ｜耐 to endure, patient ｜受		C
稔³˒⁴	禾 115	念 436	A year; ripe, harvest; store; familiar with ｜悉 thorough knowledge of ｜穀 grain in ear, good crops		I
飪⁴ 肛⁴	食 184	壬 67	To cook food, flavor ｜熟 well-cooked 烹｜班 cooking-class		K
刃⁴ 刄⁴	刀 18	刃 222	A blade, sword; edge; to kill, ｜兒 edge of knife 刀｜ 兵｜ weapons		E
仞⁴	人 9	刃 222	A fathom (10 Eng, feet) to fill,		I
紉⁴	糸 120	刃 222	To thread a needle; join ｜針 to thread a needle 縫｜ mend, sew together	jen²	H
認⁴	言 149	刃 222	To recognize, confess, know ｜眞 in good earnest, acknowledge ｜準 recognize certainly ｜明 ｜罰 admit one deserves a fine ｜可 to authorise, approve ｜·不 淸 can't make out for certain ｜不²是 acknowledge fault ｜錯		A

認[4]			｜生 regard as a stranger ｜·識 to recognize, know ｜得 ｜罪 confess one's guilt ｜·爲 deemed, considered as ｜字 to recognize characters		
軔[4]	車 159	刃 222	To block a wheel; hitch 發｜ release a block or catch; the beginnings of a thing		H
任[4]	人 9	任 68	Office; employ; responsibility; to allow, to tolerate ｜期 term of office ｜性 to do as one pleases ｜意 to indulge one's self ｜命 to appoint, ｜免 dismissal ｜憑 at liberty to; to allow ｜聽 ｜∘甚·麼 anything, no matter what ｜何 ｜誰 anyone, no matter who ｜務 public duty 擔｜ undertake, bear burden	jen[2]	D
鵀[4]	鳥 196	任 68	Feather, head-dress		K
葚[4] 椹[4]	艸 140	甚 104	Mulberry fruit, 桑｜兒 俗	chen[1] shen[4]	K

Jeng

扔[13]	手 64	乃 216	To throw away, throw ｜·開 ｜·出·去 thrown out ｜∘去 ｜孩·子 to lose a baby by death ｜·下 to throw down, leave behind ｜石·頭 to throw stones		C
仍[2]	人 9	乃 216	Yet, still, as before ｜然 ｜舊 as of old, as formerly, still ｜·是不聽 disobedient as ever		B

Jih

日[4]	日 72	日 792	Sun 日·頭, day, daily, time of ｜常 daily, ordinary, usual ｜記簿 log-book, diary ｜·期 a day, a date ｜起 sun-rise, ｜出 ｜見增長 to increase daily ｜久 many days, a long time ｜耳曼 Germany ｜後再說 we will speak of it later ｜｜every day, daily 每｜ ｜光 light of the sun, day-light ｜落 sun-set ｜沒, so ｜·頭平西 ｜報 daily paper ｜本 Japan ｜·子 a day ｜夜 day and night ｜曜｜Sabbath, Sunday ｜用 daily expenditure or use 今｜to-day, 不｜shortly	A

Jo, Je

惹[3]	心 61	若 182	To provoke, irritate ｜氣, ｜惱 ｜·出是·非 make a scandal ｜禍 invite calamities ｜·不起 cannot afford to irritate ｜·不·得 better not provoke him	D
熱[4] 熱[4]	火 86	埶 305	Hot, heat; to heat; feverish ｜誠 zealous, ardent zeal, ｜血 ｜氣 steam, hot vapour; so ｜水 ｜河 Jehol, Imperial Summer Palace ｜心 affectionate, zealous	A

熱^{4}			| 狂 fanatic, | 烈 fiery | 鬧 excitement, bustle, clamor | 帶 torrid zone, tropics | 度 temperature	
若^{4}	艸 140	若 182	If, like, as to, as; to follow | 許 so long, so many | 干 numerous, so much | 論 if it be argued, as regards | 不 if not, | 不 然 if not so | 是 if, if it is, 倘 | | 要 if you want; in case of | 有 if there are, if you have 倘 | supposing, 莫 | nothing like	B
箬^{4}	竹 118	若 182	Broad leaf bamboo	K
弱^{4}	弓 57	弱 245	Weak, pliable; weak of purpose | 冠 a young man up to twenty | 點 weak point 軟 | weak feeble 懦 |	C

Jou

柔^{2}	木 75	柔 117	Yielding, soft, tender, mild | 和 mild, forbearing, | 順 | 弱 pliable, soft, flexible | 軟 | 嫩 tender, delicate | 聲 passive voice; a soft voice | 術 art of wrestling | 道 温◦| gentle, meek	C
揉^{2}	手 64	柔 117	To twist, roll in hand; knead; bend; subdue | 球 roll balls in hand | 搓 to crush between hands; to bully | 眼·睛 rub the eyes	F
蹂^{2}	足 157	柔 117	To tread out, tread down | 踐 to trample on | 躪	K

禸^{23}	禸 114	禸 574	Footprint, step, track,		K
肉^{4}	肉 130	肉 615	Flesh, meat, fleshy; pulp 俗	ju^{4}	A
			| 案·子 butcher's block or table		
			| 包·子 meat dumplings		
			| 片 a slice of meat		
			| 舖 a butcher's shop		
			| 身 the human body		
			| 絲 shreds of lean meat		
			| 丸·子 meat balls		

Ju

如^{2}	女 38	如 554	As, like, for example, if, | 若		B
			| 今 now, at present		
			| 何 how? of what sort?		
			| 意 as one likes; a Budd. sceptre		
			∘| 果 if indeed, in case		
			| 來 佛 title of a Buddha		
			| 命 according to order		
			| 是 thus, so		
			| 同 like, as		
			| 此 thus, as this, in this manner		
茹^{2}	艸 140	如 554	To eat; receive, reckon S.	ju^{4}	I
			貪 | a great appetite		
儒^{2}	人 9	需 613	Literati, scholar, Confucian		D
			| 家 scholar, Confucianists		
			| 教 Confucianism		
			| 士 learned man		
孺^{24}	子 39	需 613	A suckling, dependent, | 子^{3}		G
濡^{2}	水 85	需 613	To immerse, moisten; imbued; patient		K
			| 染 to dye		
辱^{34}	辰 161	辱 356	Disgrace, insult; to reproach; defile		C
			| 國 disgrace one's country		
			| 罵 to insult and revile		

Character	Radical	Phonetic	Meaning		Alt.	
辱³⁴			丨身 disgrace oneself 羞丨 treat insultingly 凌丨			
汝³	水 85	女 552	You, your			F
乳³	乙 5	孚 408	Milk; teats, breasts; to suckle 丨哺 to give the breast, suckle 丨香 olibanum, frankincense 丨名 name given soon after birth 丨母 wet-nurse, foster-mother			F
肉⁴	肉 130	肉 615	Flesh, meat, fleshy	文	jou⁴	A
褥⁴	衣 145	辱 356	Mattress 丨·子, cushion 丨套 a bed-bag			B
入⁴	入 11	入 443	To enter, put into 丨場券 entrance ticket 丨籍 to acquire citizenship 丨教 to enter the church 丨學 go to school, 丨口貨 imports, 丨口稅 duty 丨欵 receipts 丨門 enter door; commence study 丨聲 the entering tone			C
廿⁴ 廾⁴	廾 55	十 13	Twenty, a score		nien⁴	G

Juan

Character	Radical	Phonetic	Meaning		Alt.	
軟³ 輭³	車 159	欠 441	Weak, soft, yielding; elastic 丨·和 soft, yielding, meek, 柔丨 丨弱 weak, feeble 丨硬 soft and hard, hardness 丨語 soft words, kind words			B
阮³	阜 170	元 388	Surname	S	yüan²³	K

Jui

Character	Radical	Phonetic	Meaning	Alt.	Grade
蕊[3] 蘂[3]	艸 140	心 377	Bud, stamen; wick, 發｜put forth buds 花｜center of flower, stamens and pistil.		G
瑞[4]	玉 96	耑 614	Lucky, auspicious; jade token ｜氣 an auspicious omen ｜日 auspicious day ｜國 Sweden｜典;｜士 Switzerland		E
銳[4]	金 167	兌 756	Pointed, acute, keen, valiant ｜敏 acute, vigorous, sharp 敏｜ 奮｜zealous, intense		F
睿[4] 叡[4]	目 109	目 841	Clever, profound, shrewd ｜智 intuitive wisdom		F

Jun

Character	Radical	Phonetic	Meaning	Alt.	Grade
允[3]	儿 10	允 869	To permit, assent｜許	yün³	D
閏[4]	門 169	閏 75	Intercalary, extra ｜日 intercalary day (Feb. 29) ｜月 intercalary month		D
潤[4]	水 85	閏 75	To soak, moisten; enrich, benefit; sleek ｜澤 moist, to moisten; agreeable		C

Jung

Character	Radical	Phonetic	Meaning	Alt.	Grade
容[2]	宀 40	容 711	To contain, endure; face, looks, air; forgive S. ｜止 carriage, address, behavior ｜像 a portrait ｜·易 easy, 好｜·易 difficult	yung²	A

Jung

容[2]			｜讓 polite, complaisant, yielding ｜忍 to endure, tolerate, 包｜ ｜留 to allow to remain ｜貌 figure, countenance ｜顏 ｜·不下 not large enough to hold	
榕[2]	木 75	容 711	The bastard banian ｜樹 ｜城 Foochow	K
蓉[2]	艸 140	容 711	African marigold 芙｜mimosa ｜花	K
鎔[2]	金 167	容 711	To melt; cast; a mold, die ｜化 to smelt metal 銷｜	E
榮[2] 栄[2]	木 75	𤇾 448	Glory, honour, splendid S. ｜幸 honor and happiness ｜華 splendid, glorious ｜光 ｜典 decoration bestowed ｜耀 brilliant, glory	B
縈[2]	糸 120	𤇾 448	Entwine, wind round ｜繞 ｜回 go round and round	K
戎[2]	戈 62	戎 336	Weapons; wary; wild tribes, S. ｜裝 military clothing, equipment	H
毧[2]	毛 82	戎 336	Felt, soft hair ｜毯·子 felt rugs; so ｜鞋, ｜帽	G
絨[2]	糸 120	戎 336	Floss, velvet, wool ｜毛; sponge 海｜ ｜線 woolen yarn ｜毯·子 woolen rugs	C
融[2]	虫 142	鬲 589	To blend, bright, harmonize S. ｜洽 blend, mutual consideration ｜和 mix together, blend ｜化 to melt, destroy	F
宂[3] 冗[3]	宀 40	几 382	Business, duty, extra; mixed, scattered ｜費 extra expenditure ｜食 sinecures ｜雜 confused, miscellaneous	I

Ka

Character	Radical	Phonetic	Meaning		
戛[1]	戈 62	戈 331	Lance; to tap; propriety ｜｜乎 hesitatingly ｜剌[2]兒 an inner corner 旮旯兒	chia14	H
嘎[1,2,3,4]	口 30	戈 331	Cackle, loud laugh ｜｜ ｜吱一聲 there was a crash ｜謬 eccentric, queer ｜｜雞 chukar partridge	chia1	G

K'a

Character	Radical	Phonetic	Meaning		
哈[1]	口 30	合 708	｜喇呢 "kara" — cloth, broad cloth	ha13	F

Kai

Character	Radical	Phonetic	Meaning		
該[1]	言 149	亥 874	Ought, to owe, include; the said ｜賬·的 a debtor; ｜錢 to owe ｜·著 ought, right, proper; owing ｜死 he deserves to die; so ｜打 ｜當 ought, should, it is my duty		B
賅[1] 侅[1]	貝 154	亥 874	To present, give; rare ｜備 to be provided for		I
改[3]	攴 66	己 311	To change, amend, correct ｜·變 ｜正 to reform, correct; alter ｜革 ｜期 to change the date ｜行 change one's occupation -hang[2] ｜建 to reconstruct ｜造 ｜換 to change, exchange ｜日 another day, some other time ｜過 to amend, to repent 悔｜ ｜·過來 to correct (a mistake) ｜良 to reform, ｜惡從善		B

蓋[4] 葢[4] 盖[4]	艸 140 皿 108	盍 45	To cover; screen; since, because S. ｜兒 a cover ｜房子 build a house ｜·上 to cover. ｜印 to affix a seal	A
[illegible][4]	頁 181	盍 45	Fontanelle, cranium 天靈｜ cranium, top of head	K
概[4] 槩[4]	木 75	既 366	A resumé; to level; all, general, probably 大｜ ｜觀 concept, idea ｜括 generalization ｜念 abstraction, concept 一｜ all, whole of	B
漑[4]	水 85	既 366	To flow, wash, flood 灌｜ to irrigate	H
丐[4]	一 1	丐 127	To beg, a beggar 乞｜; ｜·子 ｜頭 head of the beggars	E

K'ai

開[1]	門 169	門 635	To open, begin; boil ｜拆 to break open 拆·｜ ｜戰 to begin to fight ｜張 begin day's business ｜賬 open an account ｜講 explain, begin to expound ｜鎗 to fire, open fire on ｜船 to set sail ｜恩 be gracious, show favor ｜∘發 to disperse, distribute ｜飯 set forth or serve a meal ｜方子· to write prescription ｜放門戶 "open door" (policy) ｜花 an opening flower, blossom ｜荒 break new ground ｜墾 ｜會 open society or meeting	A

<table>
<tr><td>開[1]</td><td></td><td></td><td>| 口 open the mouth, commence
| 工錢 give out work money, pay off
| 門 open a door, open the door !
| 辦 start a new enterprise
| 不 | cannot open
| 步走 forward march!
| 市 to open a shop or market
| 手 to open the hand, begin | 頭
| 水 boil water, boiling water
| 鎖 to unlock, release
| 單 to make out a bill
| 導 explain clearly, instruct
| 天闢地 the creation
| 端 the first principles
|∘通 clear-headed, judicious
| 眼 open the eyes, gain experience</td><td></td><td></td></tr>
<tr><td>楷[3]</td><td>木
75</td><td>皆
318</td><td>Square character | 字
| 書 clerkly hand, every stroke correct</td><td></td><td>F</td></tr>
<tr><td>凱[3]</td><td>几
16</td><td>豈
732</td><td>A victory | 歌 song of victory</td><td></td><td>F</td></tr>
<tr><td>鎧[3]</td><td>金
167</td><td>豈
732</td><td>Armour, mail, | 甲</td><td></td><td>F</td></tr>
<tr><td>慨[34]</td><td>心
61</td><td>既
366</td><td>Magnanimous, loyal, to bewail
| 嘆 oh dear! what a pity!</td><td></td><td>G</td></tr>
</table>

Kan

<table>
<tr><td>乾[1]
乾[1]</td><td>乙
5</td><td>倝
17</td><td>Dry, clean; exhausted
|·淨 clean, tidy
| 兒子, | 媽, | 爹 etc., (all adopted relatives)
| 飯 dry food, rice without gravy
| 旱 drought, parched |∘燥
| 枯 withered 枯 |
| 菓子 dried fruits
|·糧 dry bread, traveler's lunch
| 草 hay, dried millet straw</td><td>ch'ien[2]</td><td>A</td></tr>
</table>

Kan

甘[1]	甘 99	甘 101	Sweet, 丨甜; willing, pleasant, S. 丨·蔗 sugar-cane 丨心 willingly, voluntarily 丨苦 sweet and bitter 丨·肅 the province of Kansu 丨雨 refreshing rain 丨霖	C
柑[1]	木 75	甘 101	Mandarin orange 丨·子	H
泔[1]	水 85	甘 101	To boil thick 淘米丨·水 water from washing rice 丨水 slops	K
疳[1]	疒 104	甘 101	Ulcers; children's disease 丨瘡 venereal sores, ulcers	H
干[1]	干 51	干 32	Shield; stem; offend; concern S. 丨犯 to trespass, offend 丨·係 consequences, implication 丨戈 shields and spears,-war 動丨戈 丨涉 implicate, interfere 丨預	D
杆[1]	木 75	干 32	Staff, pole, mast 桅·丨; C. of spears and guns 旗·丨 a flag staff	F
竿[1] ⿰木竿[1]	竹 118	干 32	Cane, rod, pole, staff 丨·子 竹丨 bamboo pole 釣丨 a fishing-rod	D
肝[1]	肉 130	干 32	The liver, feelings 心丨 disposition; intimate	E
桿[3]	木 75	旱 33	A pole, staff, handle; lever; C. of guns 丨棒 Indian clubs 秤丨 beam of steelyard	E
稈[3] 秆[3]	禾 115	旱 33	Straw, stalks of grain 禾丨 丨人 a straw man, effigy 丨頭 stubble	H
趕[3] 赶[3]	走 156	旱 33	To drive, hurry, strive for 丨車的 a carter; so 丨驢的, 丨脚的 丨集 attend a market	A

趕[3]			|∘緊 quickly, at once		
			| 逐 to drive out, to expel |·出去		
			|·回來 to hurry back, drive back		
			| 鬼 drive out devils		
			| 明天說 speak of it to-morrow		
			|∘到 overtake, by the time when		
			|·得上 able to overtake; so |·不上		
			| 早 very early on road; so | 晚		
敢[3]	攴 66	敢 629	To dare, bold, presumptuous		B
			|·情 sure enough, truly! |·是, | 自		
			| 保 willing to guarantee		
			| 當 I did it, I dare to do it, | 做		
			| 問 I venture to ask		
橄[3]	木 75	敢 629	The olive, |·欖		E
			|·欖山 Mount of Olives		
感[3]	心 61	感 345	To influence, move, affected by		C
			|·激 grateful |·激不盡		
			| 覺 feeling, sensation		
			|∘情 gratitude, the feelings		
			| 想 impressions (in the mind)		
			| 謝 to be grateful		
			| 化 to reform, regenerate		
			| 官 sense organs		
			| 動 move, influence the feelings		
擀[3]	手 64	倝 17	To roll out, open out		H
			|∘麵杖 a rolling-pin		
倝[4]	人 9	倝 17	Dawn		P
幹[4]	干 51	倝 17	To manage; business; ability, trunk of tree		C
			| 路 trunk-line of railway		
			| 辦 to transact, manage		
			| 甚麼 what are you doing? why?		
			| 營生 to work for a living		
			| 員 an able official		
贛[4]	貝 154	工 8	City in Kiangsi | 縣	kung[4]	G
			| 省 Province of Kiangsi		

K'an

看[1]	目 109	目 841	To watch, look after ｜家 guard the house ｜孩子 take care of a child ｜。護 a nurse ｜門的 a gate keeper, porter ｜。守 keep guard, look after ｜管	k'an[4]	A
刊[1]	刀 18	干 32	To cut, engrave; paper, magazine ｜發 print, publish ｜刻 to engrave, to cut ｜字 週｜ weekly paper		C
堪[1]	土 32	甚 104	Able, to bear, adequate, worthy ｜可 tolerable, adequate ｜當 worthy of; ought to be ｜用 useful, serviceable		D
龕[1]	龍 212	龍 315	Shrine box, niche for idol 佛｜ Buddha shrine 香｜ an incense box		F
坎[3] 埳[3]	土 32	欠 441	A pit; uneven; hazard; to strike ｜坑 a pit, den or cave 坑｜ ｜坷 uneven, irregular		B
扻[3]	手 64	欠 441	To strike, knock; throw at ｜狗 throw a stone at a dog		H
砍[3]	石 112	欠 441	To cut, chop 刀｜; to stone ｜肩兒 waistcoat without sleeves ｜樹木 cut down timber, ｜伐 ｜·下來 to cut down ｜·得動 able to cut, so ｜·不動		E
檻[3]	木 75	監 608	Door-sill 門｜兒 俗	chien[4] hsien[4]	G
侃[3]	人 9	口 694	Direct speech, boldness ｜｜ straightforward speech		K
矙[34] 瞰[34]	目 109	敢 629	To spy, watch; seek to find out 鳥｜ bird's-eye view 魚｜ open-eyed like a fish		K

<table>
<tr><td>凵^{3}</td><td>凵
17</td><td>凵
650</td><td>To contain, a vessel</td><td></td><td>K</td></tr>
<tr><td>看^{4}
看^{4}</td><td>目
109</td><td>目
841</td><td>To look at, examine, see; peruse
| 機會 seize an opportunity
|·見 to see, |·得見 can see
|·不見 unable to see
| 輕·了 to esteem lightly 輕 |·了
|·着辦 to act according to circumstances
| 準·了 to be correct in judging
| 中^{4} pleased with, prefer
| 風·水 exercise geomantic art
|·一·| take a look
| 熱鬧 to look at any bustle
| 顧 look after, take care of
| 明·白 to see clearly
| 脈 to feel the pulse
| 病 attend to case of illness
| 破 to see through an affair
|·不得 not fit to be seen
| 書 to read books
| 待 to treat another
|·頭 something worth seeing
| 透 to see through; so |·不透</td><td>k'an^{1}</td><td>A</td></tr>
<tr><td>勘^{4}</td><td>力
19</td><td>甚
104</td><td>To investigate, examine, 查 |
| 風·水 geomancy</td><td></td><td>I</td></tr>
<tr><td>墈^{4}
磡^{4}</td><td>土
32</td><td>甚
104</td><td>Precipitous ledge, cliff, bank 山 |
井 | brink of a well
石 |·子 stone door-sill</td><td></td><td>I</td></tr>
</table>

Kang

<table>
<tr><td>岡^{1}</td><td>山
46</td><td>岡
592</td><td>A ridge, hill, mound 山 |
高 | lofty ridge</td><td></td><td>E</td></tr>
<tr><td>剛^{1}</td><td>刀
18</td><td>岡
592</td><td>Hard, firm; just now, recently
| 強 violent, brutal, headstrong</td><td></td><td>A</td></tr>
</table>

剛[1]			｜柔 hard and soft, firm and yielding ｜｜just now, a moment ago ｜纔 ｜來 just come, arrived ｜到 ｜硬 headstrong, obstinate, hard		
綱[1]	糸 120	岡 592	Bond; law, principle ｜紀 ｜常 moral obligations ｜鑑 chronological annals ｜領 bond, connecting idea ｜目 general outline, head		D
鋼[1]	金 167	岡 592	Steel, hard; to sharpen ｜琴 piano ｜版 steel engraving ｜筆 steel pen		E
缸[1]	缶 121	工 8	A cistern; jar; vat 水｜ ｜蓋 a vat cover ｜瓦市 a mart for vats and tiles 金魚｜jar to hold gold-fish		B
韁[1] 繮[1]	革 177	畺 812	Bridle, halter, reins ｜·繩 俗	chiang[1]	G
肛[1]	肉 130	工 8	The large intestine; rectum ｜門		H
亢[1]	亠 8	亢 398	Neck, throat	k'ang[4]	K
槓[4] 杠[4]	木 75	工 8	Frame to bear coffin, catafalque ｜房 funeral paraphernalia shop 抬｜(2 men) carry on pole; dispute		E
虹[4]	虫 142	工 8	Rainbow 俗 出·了 ｜·了 there is a rainbow	chiang[4] hung[2]	E

K'ang

康[1]	广 53	隶 526	Ease; health; peace S. ｜强 stout, hearty ｜健 ｜熙 Emperor K'ang-Hsi ｜寧 repose, tranquillity		D

Character	Radical	Phonetic	Meaning		
慷[1]	心 61	隶 526	Firm; generous, noble ｜慨的很 very generous		H
糠[1] 穅[1]	米 119	隶 526	Chaff ｜秕, husks, poor, chaffy, 鋸｜sawdust 麥｜wheat chaff		F
躿[1]	身 158	隶 526	Very tall 躴｜		K
扛[2]	手 64	工 8	Carry on shoulders; lift ｜枷 to wear wooden collar ｜·不動 unable to carry it		B
亢[4]	亠 8	亢 398	Violent, overbearing ｜氣; very ｜旱 hot and dry weather	kang[1]	K
伉[4]	人 9	亢 398	Compare, match; a pair ｜儷		K
抗[4]	手 64	亢 398	To oppose, resist, rebel ｜拒 to disobey, to thwart ｜逆 to resist, disobey ｜敵 to oppose, to resist enemy 反｜oppose, prevent		E
炕[4]	火 86	亢 398	A brick bed; to dry ｜氈 a rug on a k'ang ｜棹 low table for k'ang ｜蓆 the mat on a stove bed ｜·一·｜ to dry or warm by a fire ｜爐子 a heating stove ｜面子 top of a stove-bed ｜布 the cloth on a bed ｜洞 the fire pit in a stove-bed ｜沿 the edge of a stove-bed		C

Kao

Character	Radical	Phonetic	Meaning		
高[1] 髙[1]	高 189	高 582	High, tall, eminent; noble; old, fine quality S. ｜矮 tall & short, height ｜低 ｜傲 haughty, ambitious		B

Kao

高^{1}			｜超 to exceed others		
			｜蹺 stilts		
			｜見 your opinion		
			｜興^{4} elated, pleased, high spirits		
			｜｜·的 lofty, very tall ｜大		
			｜◦貴 honorable		
			｜·麗 Korea ｜·麗紙 Korean paper		
			｜粱 sorghum		
			｜尚 superior, high grade ｜等		
			｜升 lofty promotion ｜位 station		
			｜聲 in a loud voice		
			｜壽 what is your age?		
			｜等小學 Intermediate school		
			｜跳 high jump		
			｜才 great ability		
篙^{1}	竹 118	高 582	Boat pole 船｜		F
			撐｜ to pole, punt		
膏^{1}	肉 130	高 582	Ointment ｜油; fat; rich	kao^{4}	B
			｜肥 fat, greasy		
			｜·藥 plaster for wound or sore		
羔^{1}	羊 123	羔 154	Lamb, kid ｜羊, 羊｜		C
			山羊｜ kid		
糕^{1} 餻^{1}	米 119	羔 154	Cakes, pastry; dumplings		D
			｜乾 a dry, sweetish rice-flour cake		
			雞蛋｜ sponge cake		
			槽｜ cake		
槁^{3}	木 75	高 582	Dry, withered, rotten ｜枯, 枯｜		F
稾^{3} 稿^{3}	禾 115	高 582	Straw draft; original copy; proof		F
			｜·子 draft of a letter etc. 草｜		
			打｜ make a rough draft		
告^{4}	口 30	告 717	Tell, to announce; accuse; request		A
			｜成 notice of completion		
			｜假^{4} ask leave of absence		
			｜知 to inform, tell ｜·訴		

告4			｜狀 a plaint, an indictment		
			｜發 to inform on another (legal.)		
			｜人 accuse, prosecute a person		
			｜白 a notice, advertisement		
			｜別 to take leave, retire ｜辭		
			｜·示 a proclamation		
			｜退 to retire from office		
膏4	肉 130	高 582	To anoint with oil	kao1	B
			｜車 oil cart wheels		
			｜油 oil a machine		
誥4	言 149	告 717	To enjoin upon; confer patent, or title ｜命; a decoration		G
			｜誡 to solemnly enjoin		

K'ao

尻1 髛1	尸 44	九 302	End of spine, rump ｜骨		K
			黑｜black rump,—the heron		
考3 攷3	老 125	考 190	To examine, question ｜。察, ｜驗		C
			｜場 the examination hall		
			｜·究 to examine, inquire into ｜問		
			｜中·了 passed examination successfully		
			｜試 examination		
拷3	手 64	考 190	To beat; examine by torture		G
			｜訊 to examine by torture ｜問		
烤3	火 86	考 190	To toast, roast, bake; dry, to warm		C
			｜焦 to scorch in baking		
			｜火 to warm by a fire ｜手		
			｜肉 to roast meat		
			｜麪包 to toast or bake bread		
⿱竹考34	竹 118	考 190	Basket with handle		I

<table>
<tr><td>靠⁴</td><td>非
175</td><td>告
717</td><td>To trust; lean on, near to |·着
|椅 a chair with a back
|賴 to rely on 倚|
|·得住 to be depended on, so
|·不住 undependable
|頭 a support, as chair-back</td><td></td><td>A</td></tr>
<tr><td>犒⁴</td><td>牛
93</td><td>高
582</td><td>To feast, reward, bounty |賞
|勞 a feast to workmen or soldiers</td><td></td><td>G</td></tr>
<tr><td>銬⁴</td><td>金
167</td><td>考
190</td><td>Hand-fetters, manacles</td><td></td><td>I</td></tr>
</table>

Ke, see Ko P. 249

K'e, see K'o P. 252

Kei

<table>
<tr><td>給³</td><td>糸
120</td><td>合
708</td><td>To give; for, to 俗
|·他 to give him, for him
∘|·我做罷 do it for me
∘|·我寫信 write a letter for me
寫信·|·我 write a letter to me</td><td>chi3</td><td>A</td></tr>
</table>

Ken

<table>
<tr><td>根¹</td><td>木
75</td><td>艮
359</td><td>Root, foundation, origin
|∘基 the foundation |脚
|·據地 military base, standpoint
|本 root, source or origin |∘底
|本要道 fundamental doctrines
|源 origin, source, cause |由</td><td></td><td>C</td></tr>
<tr><td>跟¹</td><td>足
157</td><td>艮
359</td><td>Heel; to follow, imitate; with
|∘前 in front of
|官的 followers of an official
|·你要 to require from you
|班的 a servant, a follower</td><td></td><td>A</td></tr>
</table>

<table>
<tr><td>跟1</td><td></td><td></td><td>|·不上 cannot keep up with
| 隨 accompany, follow | 從, |·着
|·我去 go with me
脚 | the heel</td><td></td><td></td></tr>
<tr><td>艮4</td><td>艮
138</td><td>艮
359</td><td>A limit; perverse, obstinate; 1 of 8 diagrams</td><td></td><td>K</td></tr>
</table>

K'en

<table>
<tr><td>豤23</td><td></td><td>豤
360</td><td>To root, gnaw</td><td></td><td>P</td></tr>
<tr><td>肯3</td><td>肉
130</td><td>肯
130</td><td>To consent, be willing
|·不·| are you willing?</td><td></td><td>C</td></tr>
<tr><td>掯3</td><td>手
64</td><td>肯
130</td><td>To oppress, extort
勒 | to extort money, to squeeze</td><td></td><td>K</td></tr>
<tr><td>墾3</td><td>土
32</td><td>豤
360</td><td>To break new soil, 開 | , | 荒</td><td></td><td>F</td></tr>
<tr><td>懇3</td><td>心
61</td><td>豤
360</td><td>To implore, beg; urgent
| 祈 to beg earnestly
| 切 earnest, urgently entreat
| 求（乞）to beseech
| 恩 to importune a favour</td><td></td><td>C</td></tr>
<tr><td>齦3
啃3</td><td>齒
211</td><td>艮
359</td><td>To gnaw, nibble, bite
| 骨 gnaw a bone
| 草 nibble the grass</td><td></td><td>E</td></tr>
<tr><td>裉4
褃4</td><td>衣
145</td><td>艮
359</td><td>Gusset under arm
小 | a small seam
繚 | sew a seam</td><td></td><td>H</td></tr>
</table>

Keng

<table>
<tr><td>更1</td><td>曰
73</td><td>更
834</td><td>To change; night watch
| 正 to reform, correct
| 夫 a watchman
| 新之時 a new era
| 換 to substitute, exchange
| 改 to change, to alter | 變</td><td>ching1
keng4</td><td>A</td></tr>
</table>

庚[1]	广 53	更 834	Age; to change; west; reward | 帖 paper with 8 natal characters | 子[3]年 Boxer Year, 1900 貴 | what is your age?		F
粳[1] 稉[1] 秔[1]	米 119 禾 115	更 834	Long white rice | 米 non-glutinous rice 旱稻 | 米 upland rice	ching[1]	H
耕[1] 畊[1]	耒 127	井 415	To plough, till 文 | 種 to plough and sow | 地 to plough land	ching[1]	D
羹[1]	羊 123	羔 154	Soup, broth | 湯 | 匙 a soup-ladle or spoon 調 |		F
頸[3]	頁 181	巠 427	The neck 脖 |·子	ching[3]	D
哽[3]	口 30	更 834	To stammer from feeling, sob | 咽 | 塞 speechless with choking		K
梗[3]	木 75	更 834	Plant-stem; stubborn, strong, blunt | 概 on the whole, in general |·子 stem of a plant, flower, etc.		F
耿[3]	耳 128	火 446	Bright, luminous; constant S. | 直 upright, honest		H
更[4]	曰 73	更 834	Still more, further, again | 强 better, stronger | 多 more, greater quantity	ching[1] keng[1]	A
亙[4]	二 7	亙 763	From, extreme, a limit | 古以來 from earliest antiquity		F

K'eng

坑[1]	土 32	亢 398	Pit, gully; to entrap, injure | 害 to hurt, injure, entrap | 人 to do people mischief | 坎 a pit, hole | 騙 to entrap, to cheat		C

Ko, Ke

哥[1]	口 30	可 699	Elder brother ｜｜		A
			｜兒倆 two brothers, both brothers		
			｜嫂 an elder brother's wife		
歌[1]	欠 76	可 699	To sing, chant; a song, ballad		C
謌[1]			｜唱 to sing hymns, etc. ｜詩		
			｜曲 to sing songs		
			｜本 a song book		
			｜誦 to chant		
			｜舞 to sing and dance		
鴚[1]	鳥 196	可 699	A parrot, 鸚｜		F
			八·｜ mina bird		
咯[1]	口 30	各 712	To creak, hum ｜吱	lo[4]	I
擱[1]	手 64	各 712	To lay, put, place; hinder		A
			｜正了 placed straight		
			｜淺 to run aground or ashore		
			｜·下 to put down; so ｜·不下		
			｜一邊 to lay aside		
			｜·開 to remove; to delay		
			｜板 a shelf		
			｜穩當 placed firmly		
胳[1]	肉 130	各 712	Arm, side		B
肐[1]			｜·肢窩 the armpit,		
			｜星兒 a defect, fault		
骼[1]	骨 188		｜·臂 the upper arm		
			｜·膊肘兒 elbow		
割[1]	刀 18	害 146	To cut, cut off; deduct		B
			｜肉 to cut meat, buy meat		
			｜·開 to cut open		
			｜禮 circumcision		
			｜麥子 to reap wheat		
			｜斷 to cut asunder		
			收｜ to harvest		

Ko, Ke

疙^{1}	疒 104	乞 298	A boil, sore, pimple |·瘩 長·^{3}了 |·瘩 to have a boil		F
紇^{1}	糸 120	乞 298	A knot, knob |·縫		I
趷^{1}	足 157	乞 298	Thumping, jolting |·蹬		B
鴿^{1}	鳥 196	合 708	Dove, pigeon |·子, 雛 | squab		C
戈^{1}	戈 62	戈 331	A spear, lance | 矛 S. 干 | shields and spears,—war		G
各^{2}	口 30	各 712	Oneself | 自 俗 | 自 | ^{3}兒 by oneself, of oneself	ko^{34}	B
格^{2}	木 75	各 712	Rule, pattern; to reach; wise; re-search, science | 致 scientific researches |◦式 a form, a pattern |·子 trellis, framework | 字紙 quadrille paper | 外 extraordinary, out of rule | 物 physics; to investigate nature of things | 言 motto, proverb, maxim 人 | personality, manhood		C
閣^{2}	門 169	各 712	Cabinet, council; women's rooms | 下 Sir, master, you 出 | to marry (the woman)		B
膈^{2}	肉 130	鬲 589	Breast; the diaphragm | 膜 misunderstanding, separation 打 | 兒 gulp up (after eating) 噎 | hiccough,		I
隔^{2}	阜 170	鬲 589	To separate, parted; partition | 肢·|·肢 to tickle, scratch | 河 separated by a river | 一道街 in the next street | 日 the day after	chieh^{24} ko^{4}.	D

隔²			｜開 separated or put apart ｜斷 ｜扇 screen, movable partition		
革²	革 177	革 105	Skin; cut off; to degrade, remove, change ｜職 to degrade an official ｜官 ｜除 to reject, deduct ｜新 innovation ｜命 revolution ｜命黨 revolutionary party ｜退 degrade and discharge, reject 改｜ to change, reform		D
蛤²	虫 142	合 708	Clams, oysters, mussels ｜蜊 species of clam ｜·子 ｜蚌 oyster	ha²	G
閤²	門 169	合 708	Side door, see 閣 P. 250.	ho²	F
葛²	艸 140	曷 239	Creeping bean; connection ｜布 a kind of grass cloth ｜藤 creepers; complications ｜草 grass-cloth plant—pooah (a nettle)	ko³⁴	G
各³	口 30	各 712	One's self 自｜兒 俗 each one ｜²自｜兒	ko²⁴	B
葛³⁴	艸 140	曷 239	Surname S.	ko²	G
箇⁴ 個⁴ 个⁴	竹 118 ｜ 2	固 703	A classifier or numerator of widest use; individual ｜換｜ change piece for piece ｜人 the individual ｜體 ｜人主義 individualism ｜｜ all, every one ｜半月 a month and half ｜·子大 of tall stature ｜兒大 一｜·一·｜·的 one by one		A
各⁴	口 30	各 712	Each, every, all ｜處 everywhere ｜種 various sorts	ko²³	B

各[4]			丨方面 from every point of view 丨人 each person, every one; so 丨國 丨丨every one, each singly 丨様 each or every sort		
隔[4]	阜 170	鬲 589	Feeling of strangeness 丨磨	chieh[24] ko[2]	D
蛇[4]	虫 142	乞 298	An insect, flea 丨·蚤		F
搕[4]	手 64	曷 239	Noise of scraping etc.		I
轕[42] 輵[42]	車 159	曷 239	Hubbub, confusion 轇丨不清 mixed up, confused		I
鉿[4]	金 167	合 708	Creaking sound		I

K'o, K'e

刻[1]	刀 18	亥 874	To carve, cut into 雕丨 俗 丨板 to cut type blocks 丨圖書 engrave a map or seal 丨字匠 a type cutter	k'o[4]	A
頦[1]	頁 181	亥 874	Chin 頦巴丨兒	hai[2]	H
科[1]	禾 115	禾 510	Class, series; science, 丨長[3] head of department 丨∘學 science 丨學家 scientists 丨∘目 studies of curriculum, 丨員 clerk of department		C
蝌[1]	虫 142	禾 510	Tadpole, toad 丨蚪虫		K
棵[1]	木 75	果 507	Classifier of trees, plants		F
窠[1]	穴 116	果 507	Hole, nest; to burrow 蜂丨wasp's nest	wo[1]	G

K'o, K'e

顆[1]	頁 181	果 507	Kernel, pearl; C. of pearls, beads etc.		E
磕[1]	石 112	盍 45	To knock, bump 丨碰 丨頭 Chinese highest reverence		F
瞌[12]	目 109	盍 45	Sleepy, eyes heavy 丨·睡		K
柯[1]	木 75	可 699	Axe handle; agent S.		G
苛[1]	艸 140	可 699	Vexatious, harsh, to annoy; reprove 丨刻 oppress, very severe	ho[1]	K
軻[1]	車 159	可 699	Wheels joined by axle 孟丨 name of Mencius		K
殼[1]	殳 79	㱿 400	Shell, husk		P
殼[2] 壳[2]	殳 79	㱿 400	Shell, husk 水丨 a water dipper 湯丨 a soup-ladle	ch'üeh[4]	G
咳[2] 欬[2]	口 30	亥 874	To cough, a cough 丨·嗽 丨痰 to cough up phlegm	hai[14]	D
可[3]	口 30	可 699	To permit, be able, may, can 丨愛 amiable, worthy to be loved; (many adjectives similarly formed) 丨巧 fortunately 丨見 able to see; visible, evident 丨·着 everywhere (Peking) 丨取 worthy, good qualities 丨用 丨否 whether possible or not 丨惜 alas! lamentable, pitiable 丨·以 may, can, it will do 丨靠 reliable 丨口 good to eat, palatable 丨累·了 I'm tired indeed! 丨憐 pitiable, take pity! 丨不是 to be sure, right, certainly		A

Character	Radical	Phonetic	Definition	Alternate	Grade
可³			◦丨·是 but, however 丨算 may be considered		
渴³	水 85	曷 239	To thirst 丨·了; long for 丨想 to anxiously expect 丨慕 long for, ardently desire 丨·死 die of thirst		A
客⁴	宀 40	各 712	Guest, passenger; traveler; merchant; objective 丨棧 a lodging-house 丨店 丨車 passenger car 丨·氣 formal, conventional 丨房 guest room 丨人 visitor, guest, traveler 丨旅 丨觀 objective 丨體 丨商 a traveling merchant 丨堂 guest hall, parlor 丨廳 丨套話 mere complimentary phrases		A
恪⁴	心 61	各 712	Respectful; reverent, faithful	ch'üeh⁴	G
課⁴	言 149	果 507	Lessons, task; C. of lessons 丨◦程 curriculum, schedule 丨表 丨本 text-books 丨堂 recitation room 丨室		A
錁⁴	金 167	果 507	Bullion, ingot 燒丨錠 burn paper ingots 銀一丨 small ingot of silver		G
騍⁴	馬 187	果 507	Mare 丨馬 丨騾 she-mule		H
刻⁴	刀 18	亥 874	Time; 15 minutes; to oppress 丨下 now 一丨鐘 a quarter hour 時丨 time, incessantly 時時丨丨	k'o¹	A
克⁴	儿 10	克 704	To be able, capable; overcome 丨己 to control one's self, cheap 丨當 adequate to, fit for 丨堪		E

剋[41] 尅[41]	刀 18	克 704	To subdue, repress, exercisec, ontrol ｜期 appointed time, appoint day ｜制 dominate, prevail against ｜扣 to deduct, "squeeze"		H
疴[41]	疒 104	可 699	Sickness, pain, diarrhoea ｜痢 口｜sores about the mouth	o1	K
⿰齒可[4]	齒 211	可 699	To crack with teeth		I

Kou

勾[1]	勹 20	勾 225a	To mark off; entice; hook　　S. ｜賬 to cancel an account ｜除 mark off for rejection ｜串 in collusion ｜消 to cancel ｜當 business, affair ｜引 to entice, inveigle 挑｜		D
抅[1]	手 64	勾 225a	To hook on, join ｜牽 to drag along ｜留 to detain, keep ｜抹牆縫 plaster cracks in wall		G
鈎[1] 鉤[1]	金 167	勾 225a	Hook ｜·子; to entice; search into ｜針 crochet needle ｜·起 hook up ｜·住 hook fast 釣魚｜fish hook		B
溝[1]	水 85	冓 601	Drain, ditch, moat 水｜, ｜池 ｜沿[4] banks of gutters		B
狗[3]	犬 94	句 227	Dog, brat; contemptible ｜叫 dog barks, ｜吠 ｜熊 the black Tibetan bear ｜獾 a badger ｜豆子 "dogbeans," ticks ｜咬 the bite of a dog, dog barks		A
苟[3]	艸 140	句 227	If; illicit, careless ｜且 ｜合 illicit intercourse		G

彀[4] 夠[4] 够[4]	弓 57 夕 36	彀 400	To stretch, reach, full, enough 丨吃的 enough to support me 丨用了 enough for use 不丨本 less than (in) cost price 足丨 quite sufficient	A
冓[4]	冂 13	冓 601	Inner chamber, ten billions	K
搆[4]	手 14	冓 601	To drag; incur, reach, 丨着了 able to reach; so 丨不着	E
構[4]	木 75	冓 601	To roof; finish; unite; mix 丨造 to build	H
覯[4]	見 147	冓 601	To meet with, unforeseen 丨見 丨成 see business finished	K
購[4]	貝 154	冓 601	To buy, hire 丨買 丨辦 to buy up at wholesale	F
垢[4]	土 32	后 721	A stain, dirt, foul 泥丨, immoral 刮丨 to scrape off the dirt	I

K'ou

剾[1]	刀 18	區 696	To pick out with knife, carve	I
摳[1]	手 64	區 696	To claw up, scrape; raise 丨起來 丨不動 cannot scratch	G
瞘[1]	目 109	區 696	Deep-set eyes 丨瞜眼 eyes sunken from sickness	I
口[3]	口 30	口 694	Mouth; hole; pass; harbor; C. of men, pigs, swords etc. 丨氣 speech, sentiments 丨話 丨吃 to stammer, stutter 丨齒 the teeth; speech, utterance 丨緊 reticent 丨輕的 young (as a horse); flat taste 丨臭 foul-mouthed 丨號 slogan, pass-word	A

K'ou

Character	Radical	Phonetic	Meaning	
口[3]			｜渴 thirsty	
			｜•供 evidence, confession	
			｜糧 food, provisions	
			｜北 beyond the frontiers ｜外	
			｜•舌 altercation	
			｜是心非 deceitful, doublefaced	
			｜述 oral method; to dictate	
			｜•袋 a bag or sack	
			｜頭 flavor, talk	
			｜頭的話 mere compliment, common talk	
			｜頭語兒 common saying, pet phrase	
			｜才 eloquence	
			｜•子 a port; a breach in river banks	
			｜味兒 taste, flavour	
			｜•音 pronunciation, dialect	
牭[3]	牛 93	口 694	Cattle, domestic animal 牲•｜	E
叩[4]	口 30	口 694	Knock, humbly, kotow	D
			｜謝 thank with much earnestness	
			｜門 to knock at a door	
			｜首 bump head in salutation ｜頭	
扣[4]	手 64	口 694	To knock, button, detain; discount	B
			｜車 official impressing of carts	
			｜針 safety pin	
			｜除 to deduct, subtract	
			｜工錢 to hold up or discount one's wages	
			｜留 to keep, confiscate	
			｜鈕 to button, clasp	
			｜•上 to cover over	
			｜水 discount, 八｜20% off	
			｜底子 deduct discounts 折｜	
			｜•頭 squeeze, peculation, discount	
釦[4]	金 167	口 694	A button, a clasp, ｜•子	E
			｜襻 a button loop	

寇4	宀 40	完 389	To rob, pillage; pirate S. │盜 banditti, rebels │賊		H
蔻4	艸 140	完 389	Seeds of cardamon, etc. 豆│nutmeg │仁		K

Ku

估1	人 9	古 702	To guess, estimate, reckon │計 to value, conjecture │量 │價 to estimate the price │値 │猜 to conjecture, to guess │摸 │堆買的 bought in the lump	ku4	E
咕1	口 30	古 702	To mutter, whisper │ │唧唧 │·嚷 to mutter, speak to oneself │·朵兒 bud of flower; pole-cap		I
姑1	女 38	古 702	Girl; paternal aunt; to tolerate │·│ father's sister i. e. aunt │奶奶 married daughter; great aunt │·娘 Miss, a girl, aunt │·子庵 Buddhist nunnery │爺 son-in-law, bridegroom		A
沽1	水 85	古 702	To buy; sell, trade │名 to get credit by deceit		F
菇1	艸 140	古 702	Tuber; fungus 蘑│mushrooms		I
蛄1 蛌1	虫 142	古 702	Mole cricket 螻│ 喇喇│molecricket		H
鴣1	鳥 196	古 702	Partridge 鷓│		H
辜1	辛 160	古 702	Fault, crime; ungrateful │∘負 to be ungrateful │∘負光陰 to waste time		E

Ku

Character	Radical	Phonetic	Meaning	Other reading	
轂[1] 軲[1]	車 159	㱿 400	To roll, wheel 丨·轆 丨輪 to roll	ku[3]	B
呱[1]	口 30	瓜 407	To sob, wail 丨 丨	wa[14]	I
孤[1]	子 39	瓜 407	Solitary; orphan, 丨兒[2], 丨女, 丨子[3] 丨·兒院 orphan asylum 丨苦人 one with no relatives 丨身 丨寡 orphan and widow 丨單 isolated, lonely, orphanlike 丨獨		D
觚[1]	角 148	瓜 407	Cornered goblet; corner; rule 丨法 method, tactics		K
箍[1] 箛[1]	竹 118	巾 557	Hoop, circlet, belt, fillet; C. of firewood 丨木桶 to hoop a barrel 花丨 wreath 打丨 to hoop, put on hoop		F
骨[2]	骨 188	骨 616	Bone 丨·頭 俗 丨力 firm, strong	ku[3]	C
古[3]	口 30	古 702	Ancient, antiquity, from of old S. 丨跡 traces of antiquity, ruins 丨錢 ancient cash 丨制 the old regime 丨今 ancient and modern 丨人 ancients, men of old time 丨·怪 strange, curious, odd 丨來 from of old 丨北口 a pass into Jehol 丨式 old fashioned 丨銅 a bronze antique 丨玩 curiosities, antiques 丨文 ancient literature 丨語 an old saying, a proverb		B
牯[3]	牛 93	古 702	Bull, male 丨嶺 Kuling (summer resort)		K

Ku

盬[3]	皿 108	古 702	Earthen utensil 沙丨·子		G
罟[3]	网 122	古 702	A net; to snare; implicate 一丨撓 at one haul of the net		I
穀[3] 榖[3]	禾 115	㱿 400	Grain, cereal; real 丨·子 spiked millet 丨雨 "corn rain", one of the solar periods 五丨 cereals in general		B
轂[3]	車 159	㱿 400	Nave, hub 輪丨	ku[1]	B
鼓[3] 鼔[3] 皷[3]	鼓 207 皮 107	鼓 737	Drum, drum shaped; to excite, arouse 丨掌 to clap the hands 丨°吹 to applaud, eulogize, advocate 丨勵 stimulate, excite 丨舞 丨樓 drum tower 丨手 drummer, 丨吏 打丨 to drum, 擂丨, 擊丨		C
瞽[3]	目 109	鼓 737	Blind 丨目; blind musicians 丨目院 asylum for blind		E
臌[3]	肉 130	鼓 737	Swollen, dropsical 丨脹 氣丨 flatulent		F
骨[3]	骨 188	骨 616	Bone, rib; seam; frame 丨節 joints, articulations 丨肉 blood relationship, relatives 丨髓 bones and marrow; marrow	ku[2]	C
榾[3]	木 75	骨 616	A kind of wood, kernel		I
股[3]	肉 130	殳 399	Leg, haunch; a share; group 丨分 share in business 丨利 dividend 丨票 certificate of stock 丨°東 shareholder		C
谷[3]	谷 150	谷 710	Valley 山丨, ravine; difficult, S. 丨水 mountain streams		D

Ku

凸3	凵 17	凵 650	Projecting, protruding, in relief	tieh4	G
賈3	貝 154	貝 856	Resident merchant; to traffic ｜買 to buy ｜售 to sell	chia3	G
汩3	水 85	日 792	Confused, to float ｜沒 floating and sinking		I
鵠3	鳥 196	告 717	Snow goose; hoary ｜立 stand on lookout, like goose		I
蠱3	虫 142	虫 785	Worms in belly; poison; insanity ｜惑 to excite doubts		I
雇4 僱4	隹 172	雇 55	To hire; borrow ｜車 to hire a cart; so ｜船, ｜工人 ｜脚 hire coolies or conveyances ｜妥·了 hired satisfactorily		B
顧4 頋4	頁 181	雇 55	To regard, care for, consider S ｜主 a customer ｜客 ｜惜 to shield, to pity ｜臉 to have regard to face ｜念 think of, care for ｜·不得 can't think of or attend to ｜·不得去 can't find time to go ｜問 advisor ｜問官 眷｜ regard, think of with affection		B
估4	人 9	古 702	Old, second-hand ｜衣舖 an old clothes shop	ku1	E
故4	攴 66	古 702	Cause; old; to die; therefore ｜犯 to purposely offend ｜鄉 one's native place ｜·意 to design, purposely ｜殺 malicious murder ｜·事 old affair, a story ｜∘典 historical allusion 典∘｜ ｜此 wherefore, therefore 緣·｜ cause, reason		C

固4	口 31	固 703	Firm, strong; assuredly; obstinate |·執 obstinate | 然 certainly, assuredly | 守 maintain, strengthen | 定 firm, fixed, natural		C
錮4	金 167	固 703	To restrain; mend cracked metal | 鏴鍋 to mend old kettles		I
搰4	手 64	骨 616	To mix, stir, twist, |·擁不動 can't wriggle or stir		I

K'u

哭1	口 30	吠 457	To weep, cry, lament | 泣, 哀 | | 喪 to wail for the dead | 甚麼 what are you crying for? | 也無益 no use to cry about it		A
枯1	木 75	古 702	Dry, decayed, withered | 乾 | 瘦 lean, shriveled		E
窟1	穴 116	屈 666	Cave, hole in the ground | 穴 |·窿 a small hole | 窿眼		F
髑1	骨 188	蜀 788	Skull, skeleton | 髏	tu2	G
苦3	艸 140	古 702	Bitter, hard; affliction | 楚, 困 | | 極·了 extremely distressing | 衷 bitterness of heart | 勸 to severely lecture, exhort | 功 strenuous effort | 工 hard labor | 命 a bitter fate | 難 misery, calamity | 惱 | 水 bitter water, alkaline | 待 to maltreat, treat harshly		B
庫4	广 53	車 836	Treasury, storehouse, | 房 | 倫 Urga | 平銀 silver by treasury scale		D

褲[4] 袴[4]	衣 145	車 936	Trousers, drawers, pantaloons 丨·子 丨帶子 trousers belt or string 丨腰帶 丨襠 trouser seat 丨腿 trouser legs		B
酷[4]	酉 164	告 717	Tyrannical, very, inhuman 丨熱 very hot		I

Kua

刮[1]	刀 18	舌 707	To scrape off, brush away; shave, (used for 颳) 丨垢 scrape off the dirt 丨臉 shave the face 丨木 to plane wood		B
聒[14]	耳 128	舌 707	Clamor, din, 丨丨, 丨擾 蛙丨 frogs croaking	kuo[14] k'uo[4]	I
颳[1]	風 182	舌 707	To blow, be blown 丨風 丨晴·了天 wind cleared the sky 丨開·了 blown open by the wind		A
鴰[1]	鳥 196	舌 707	Gray heron; the caw of a rook 老·丨 crow, rook		H
瓜[1]	瓜 97	瓜 407	Gourd, melon, cucumber 丨分 to partition 丨瓤 edible inside of melons 丨子[3] melon seed 丨子兒 西·丨 watermelon 木丨 quince		C
蝸[1]	虫 142	咼 581	Snail; poor hovel 丨牛 a snail		H
寡[3]	宀 40	頁 866	Few, alone, rare, 丨·居 live in widowhood, live alone 丨·婦 a widow 丨言 to speak little, reticent 丨慾 few desires		D
咼[3]	口 30	咼 581	Crooked mouth		K

Character	Radical	Phonetic	Meaning		
剮^{3}	刀 18	咼 581	To cut criminal to pieces ｜死 ｜罪 punish by hacking to death		K
卦^{4}	卜 25	卦 49	To divine, eight diagrams 算｜ to tell fortunes		E
掛^{4} 挂^{4}	手 64	卦 49	To hang, in suspense, think on ｜賬 run up a bill, buy on credit ｜帳·子 hang up curtain; so ｜旗, ｜畫 ｜車 a pulley, a block ｜·起來 to hang up, suspend ｜號 to register name, or mail ｜心 suspense, anxiety ｜意, ｜慮, ｜念 ｜∘麪 long strings of dough ｜匾 hang up a tablet in honor ｜彩 decorate for festal occasions		B
褂^{4}	衣 145	卦 49	Jacket, coat ｜·子 馬｜ short coat, riding-jacket		C
罣^{4}	网 122	圭 48	Obstacle; to think on ｜念 ｜碍 affect, concern, hinder		E

K'ua

Character	Radical	Phonetic	Meaning		
夸^{1}	大 37	夸 242	To brag, boast		K
誇^{1}	言 149	夸 242	To boast, brag, 自｜; laudatory ｜張 to praise, to boast ｜大 ｜奬 to praise, extol ｜讚 ｜口 to boast, to brag ｜海口, ｜嘴		C
咵^{3}	口 30	夸 242	To revile; a brogue ｜話		K
胯^{4}	肉 130	夸 242	Legs, hips, thighs ｜·子, ｜股 ｜下 between legs, underthighs		F
跨^{4}	足 157	夸 242	To bestride; excel, pass over ｜過去 ｜車沿 to sit on cart's shaft -yüar^{2} ｜馬 bestride a horse ｜所兒 side rooms ｜院		E

Kuai

乖[1]	丿 4	乖 25	Crafty, perverse; spoilt 丨·巧 clever, ingenious, tricky 丨異 strange, odd, eccentric 丨丨a kiss, 丨丨·的 keep quiet! 丨謬 perverse 丨僻		D
拐[3]	手 64	另 224	To kidnap, decoy; turn 丨·去 to kidnap, swindle 丨帶 丨·回來 to turn back 丨·過去 to go round 丨騙 to swindle, to defraud 丨·子 a kidnapper, a swindler 丨彎兒 corner, turn a corner		F
枴[3]	木 75	另 224	Staff, cane 丨·杖 a staff, a stick 丨棒, 丨棍		D
夬[4]	大 37	夬 482	To fork; settled; differing	chüeh[2]	K
怪[4] 恠[4]	心 61	土 43	Strange, weird; find fault with, exceedingly 丨好 very good; so 丨苦, 丨難, 丨可惜 丨性 a strange disposition 丨僻 丨·不得 no wonder that 丨事 a strange affair; so 丨物 奇丨 strange, marvelous 別丨·我 don't be offended at me		B

K'uai

擓[3]	手 64	隹 52	To scratch, rub; carry on arm 丨筐·子 to carry a basket on arm 丨破·了 wounded by scratching		K
快[4]	心 61	夬 482	Quick; happy; sharp; soon 丨暢 delightful, comfortable 暢·丨 丨車 a fast cart or train		A

快^{4}			| 鎗 quick-fire guns | 信 special delivery, express letter |·活 lively, cheerful 爽·| | |·的 make haste! be quick! | 來 come quickly; so | 去 |∘樂 pleased, happy | 慢 fast and slow, speed |·當 prompt, quick | 刀 sharp knife | 到·了 soon be there		
筷^{4}	竹 118	夬 482	Chop-sticks |·子		A
塊^{4}	土 32	鬼 808	Clod, lump, piece; doltish; C. of parts 一 | 錢 a dollar 在一 | 兒 together		A
會^{4}	日 73	會 833	To calculate |∘計 to calculate, accounting	hui^{34}	A
儈^{4}	人 9	會 833	A broker 市 |, agent; to hint |∘計 treasurer of a society		I

Kuan

關^{1} 關^{1} 関^{1}	門 169	門 635	To shut a door; frontier pass, guard house; crisis, results S. |·照 a passport; to look after |·鍵 pivot, crux, key to situation | 窗·戶 shut a window; so | 門 | 俸 to draw one's pay | 餉 |·係 concern, affect, result | 涉, 相 | | 口 a pass, Custom house | 帝 the god of war | 夫子^{3}, | 公, | 老爺 | 東 Manchuria |∘於 respecting, concerning |∘乎		A

Kuan

Character	Radical	Phonetic	Meaning	Alt.	
觀[1] 观[1]	見 147	雚 60	Look at, examine, inspect 丨察, 丨看 丨星台 observatory 丨象台 丨念 concept, idea 丨兵 to review troops 閱兵 丨∘望 merely look on 丨∘音 Goddess of Mercy (Buddhist)	kuan4	B
官[1]	宀 40	官 751	Officer, official, public, civil 丨差 official messengers, servants 丨長[3] the authorities 丨員 丨職 official appointment 丨制 official system 丨爵 official rank 丨話 the mandarin dialect 丨客 male guests 丨署 government office 丨·司 law-suit, to go to law 打丨·司 五丨(知覺) physical senses		C
棺[1]	木 75	官 751	Coffin 丨材 丨罩 a funeral pall 丨槨 a coffin and its outer case		D
冠[1]	冖 14	元 388	Cap, crest, crown 丨冕 丨戴 put on the cap, dress smartly	kuan4	E
鰥[1]	魚 195	眔 850	A huge fish; widower, lonely 丨居 to live alone; a widower 丨棍 a widower; a bachelor		I
管[3]	竹 118	官 751	A tube; to oversee, rule S. 丨賬的 accountant 丨家的 a majordomo, a steward 丨敎 keep in order, correct 丨船的 captain of a boat 丨飯 to provide food 丨轄 to regulate, govern 丨∘束 丨閒事 manage others' affairs 丨∘理 to manage, take care of 丨∘保 to guarantee 丨·不住 can't manage or control		B

Kuan

Character	Radical	Phonetic	Meaning	Alt. reading	Frequency
管³			｜事 to manage affairs ｜挑｜換 exchange if unsatisfactory		
館³ 舘³	食 184	官 751	Establishment; hotel, inn ｜·子 eating house, 飯｜(·子) 茶｜tea house, restaurant 會｜a guild house		B
雚⁴	艸 140	雚 60	A heron; a small cup		P
灌⁴	水 85	雚 60	To water, pour, irrigate 澆｜ ｜漿 pour mortar in cracks ｜水 water flowers, or meat by injection		A
罐⁴ 礶⁴	缶 121	雚 60	Pot, jar, jug, pitcher ｜·子 ｜∘頭 (食品) canned goods 茶｜tea-canister 水｜pitcher, jar for water		B
觀⁴	見 147	雚 60	Monastery, Taoist nunnery ｜寺 a Taoist temple, ｜宇	kuan¹	B
鑵⁴	金 167	雚 60	Water-bucket, used for 罐 柳｜willow basket-ware bucket		H
鸛⁴	鳥 196	雚 60	Heron, crane, stork ｜鵲 rooks, magpies		I
貫⁴	貝 154	貫 861	To go through, connect; a string (of cash etc.) ｜串 to string, connect ｜通 to pass through, pervading		E
慣⁴	心 61	貫 861	Accustomed to, experienced, habitual, habit 習｜ ｜壞·了 spoiled through indulgence ｜熟 fully acquainted with		B
冠⁴	冖 14	元 388	To cap; married; excel; promote ｜禮 the ceremony of capping	kuan¹	E
盥⁴	皿 108	皿 604	To wash, wash hands, ｜洗, ｜沐 ｜盤 a bath-tub		I

K'uan

寬[1]	宀 40	見 865	Broad, ample, indulgent, forbearing 丨窄 broad and narrow, breadth 丨期 extend a time limit, 丨限 丨·綽 comfortable, easy circumstances 丨宏 broad, extensive, liberal 丨饒 indulgent, forgiving 丨容 丨廣 extensive, broad 丨闊, 丨大 丨門 broad in theology, liberal 丨恕 to excuse, to forgive 丨免 丨待 to treat leniently	A
款[3] 欵[3]	欠 76	欵 480	A sort, item; detain; entertain; funds 丨項 丨留 to detain hospitably 丨式 a specimen, a pattern 丨∘待 to treat well, to entertain 來丨 income, grants	D

Kuang

光[1]	儿 10	光 390	Light, glory; naked; only; to adorn, illumine 丨照 to illumine, lighten 丨脚 bare foot; so 丨着脊梁, 丨身 丨線 ray of light 丨射 丨緒 Emperor Kwang Hsü 丨華 bright, splendid, gay 丨輝 丨滑 glossy, polished, smooth 丨∘棍 a local bully, idle rowdy 丨亮 bright, spotless 丨臨 visit of esteemed guest 丨明 bright. splendid; intelligent 丨彩 brilliant, splendid, glory 丨·陰 light and shade, Time 借丨 allow me; kindly inform me	A

洸[1]	水 85	光 390	River in Shantung; wide, cold ｜蕩 to wobble, to slop over	I
胱[1]	肉 130	光 390	The bladder 膀｜	K
廣[3]	广 53	廣 823	Broad, wide, enlarged ｜大 S. ｜交 extensive acquaintance ｜州 Canton ｜·西 Kwangsi ｜·東 Kwangtung ｜學會 Christian Literature Society ｜貨 Canton and Kwangsi goods ｜告 advertisement ｜闊 broad, extensive 寬｜	C
逛[4]	辵 162	狂 73	To stroll, ramble; sight-see ｜景 walk for pleasure, sight-see ·｜·去 to take a walk ｜廟 visit temple on fete day ｜山 stroll on mountain ｜燈 to view illuminations	A
絖[4] 纊[4]	糸 120	光 390	Fine floss; basket 絲｜ refuse silk after spooling	H

K'uang

匡[1]	匚 22	匡 72	To aid, correct, reform, S. ｜正 reform, put in order ｜救 to preserve, save	H
筐[1]	竹 118	匡 72	Open basket ｜·子 ｜球 basket ball 籃球	C
誆[1]	言 149	匡 72	To deceive, cheat ｜哄 ｜騙 to defraud by falsehood	H
誑[14]	言 149	狂 73	Lies, to deceive, cheat 欺｜ ｜話 deceitful language ｜言	F
狂[2]	犬 94	狂 73	Mad, wild, raging, tempest ｜傲 mad, proud, ambitious ｜風 furious gale, tempest	C

狂[2]
| 病 madness, frenzy
| 言 extravagant talk
癲 | insane, deranged

壙[4] 土 32 廣 823 A tomb, vault, desert | 野 — H
進 | put in tomb, inter

曠[4] 日 72 廣 823 Waste, wild, desert | 野 — B
| 費 waste, prodigality
| 課 be absent from class
| 功 neglect one's duty,

礦[4] **鑛**[4] 石 112 廣 823 Mine, ore 俗 — kung[3] — E

况[4] 二 7 兄 755 More, further, moreover | 且; outlook, condition — C
何 | how much more! a fortiori
景∘| condition, circumstances

貺[4] 貝 154 兄 755 To bestow, grant — huang[4] — I

框[4] 木 75 匡 72 Frame, door frame 門 | — F

眶[4] 目 109 匡 72 Eye socket 眼 | — G

Kuei

規[1] 見 147 夫 465 Compasses, rule, law, custom, usage, |·矩 — A
| 諫 to admonish; rules
|·|·矩矩 very careful of custom
| 模 a pattern, rule, law, scale
| 條 regulations |∘則
| 定 to enact, conventional

歸[1] **归**[1] 止 77 帚 674 To return, revert, end, yield — B
| 家 to return home
| 主 to return to God, die
| 服 to revert to, submit | 向主

Character	Radical	Phonetic	Meaning		
歸^1			│還 to send back, repay │納 inductive		
圭^1 珪^1	土 32	圭 48	Baton, sceptre; token │玉 a jade sceptre 執│grasp token, be in office		F
閨^1	門 169	圭 48	Virgin, women's room │房 ladies' apartments │·女 daughter		F
龜^1 亀^1	龜 213	黽 316	Tortoise, turtle │殼 tortoise-shell │卜 divination by tortoise 水│sea-turtle		G
皈^1	白 106	反 215	To return, revert, conform; a Buddhist word │正 return to the right way		K
鬼^3	鬼 194	鬼 808	Spirit, demon, devil; fine │附着 demon-possessed │魂 a ghost, spirit │怪 bogey, sprite │魔 evil spirits, devils 魔│		B
詭^3	言 149	危 197	Deceptive, crafty, treacherous │詐 │計多端 full of stratagems │辯 sophism		D
軌^3	車 159	九 302	A rut, rule, orbit, rails │道 不│irregular, eccentric		F
餜^3	食 184	果 507	Doughnuts 油炸│fried dough strips	kuo^3	G
癸^3	癶 105	癸 464	The 10th stem │水 the menses		H
晷^3	日 72	咎 714	Shadow, time, sun-dial 日│ 飛│time flies		H
貴^4	貝 154	貴 862	Expensive, honorable; valuable │甲子 how old are you? │庚 │賤 noble and base; dear and cheap		A

貴4

|·州 Kuei-chow province
|處 your residence |府
|·重 valuable, honorable 寶|
|縣 magistrate; your native city
|姓 what is your name?
|幹 what is your business?
|國 your country
|恙 your disease
|寓 where are your lodgings?

櫃4 匱4 — 木 75 — 貴 862 — Shop-counter, cupboard chest; treasury |·子 — B

|房 a counting house
|臺 counter of a shop

跪4 — 足 157 — 危 197 — To kneel |·下 — C

|香 kneel while incense burns
|拜 kneel in reverence

桂4 — 木 75 — 圭 48 — Cassia, cinnamon |肉, |枝 S. — F

|花油 cassia oil
|林 Kweilin, capital of Kwangsi
|皮 cassia-bark, cinnamon

瑰4 — 玉 96 — 鬼 808 — Pearl, jasper; extraordinary — G

玫|花 red rose

劊4 — 刀 18 — 會 833 — To cut, break asunder; executioner |·子手 — k'uai4 — H

檜4 — 木 75 — 會 833 — Cypress tree, Chinese juniper — k'uai4 — I

K'uei

虧1 — 虍 141 — 隹 52 — Deficiency, loss; luckily 幸| — C

|欠 in debt; deficiency |缺
|負 to fail, treat unfairly
|心事 unprincipled conduct
|·空 deficit, failure to pay
|良心 violate conscience

K'uei

虧[1]			丨·了你·了 thank you; troubled you, indebted to you 丨損 to injure, fail, loss 吃丨suffer loss 受丨		
盔[1]	皿 108	灰 173	Helmet, 頭丨; basin; block 丨·甲 helmet and mail 丨頭 a hat-block		E
窺[21]	穴 116	夫 465	To peep, spy, watch 丨探 丨覷 to peep, look furtively		D
揆[2]	手 64	癸 464	To calculate, consider 丨度 丨手 master-mind, best hand		G
暌[2]	日 72	癸 464	Separated; stars in opposition 丨隔 separated, isolation		K
葵[2]	艸 140	癸 464	Mallow, sunflower 向日丨 丨花 sunflower		G
魁[2]	鬼 194	鬼 808	First, chief, best, 丨首 a head, chief, foreman 丨偉 gigantic, stalwart,		H
奎[2]	大 37	圭 48	A man's stride 丨宿 constellation Andromeda 丨光 god of literature		K
傀[3]	人 9	鬼 808	Gigantic, monstrous 丨儡 puppet		H
愧[4] 媿[4]	心 61	鬼 808	Conscience-stricken, mortified 羞丨 feel ashamed 自丨 慚丨 mortification, remorse, 丨悔 問心無丨 no cause for shame		D
餽[4] 饋[4]	食 184	鬼 808	Sacrifice, presents, provisions 丨餞 parting presents of food 丨送 to make present 丨禮		F
潰[4]	水 85	貴 862	Overflowing stream, rush; destroy; flee	hui[4]	H
殨[1]	歹 78	貴 862	Running ulcer 瘡丨; break open	hui[4]	K
瞶[4]	目 109	貴 862	Blurred vision 昏丨	hui[4]	K

Kun

Character	Radical	Phonetic	Definition	
滾[3]	水 85	衣 367	To roll; bubble, boil; well up 丨熱 boiling hot; e.g. 丨水 丨∘開 to boil, bubble; be off with you!	E
輥[3]	車 159	昆 798	To roll, rotatory motion 丨動 丨·子 stone roller	F
丨[3]	丨 2	丨 111	Down stroke, perpendicular	K
棍[4]	木 75	昆 798	Stick, club, staff, 丨·子 丨棒 a club 丨打 to beat with a stick 光丨 rowdy, bully 丨匪 鐵丨 an iron bar	D

K'un

Character	Radical	Phonetic	Definition	
坤[1] 堃[1]	土 32	申 824	Subordinate; the earth; female 丨道 earth, female 丨門 乾丨 heaven and earth	F
昆[1]	日 72	昆 798	Together; elder brother 丨仲 brothers, 丨弟	F
崑[1]	山 46	昆 798	Kunlun mts. 丨崙山	I
琨[1]	玉 96	昆 798	Mother-of-pearl; fine kind of jade	K
悃[3]	心 61	困 772	Sincere, unadorned	I
捆[3]	手 64	困 772	To plait, tie, bind 丨綁 to tie, to bind 丨·上 丨·不住 cannot be bound together 丨·子 a bundle, e.g., of firewood	C

綑[3]	糸 120	困 772	To bind, weave, tie on | 綁, | 上 | 織 to weave	D
閫[3]	門 169	困 772	Gate to women's rooms; threshold | 內 within the threshold, so | 外	K
困[4] 睏[4]	口 33	困 772	Weary, sleepy; to surround | 城 besiege, blockade a city | 窮 exhausted, very poor, | 苦 |·住 to surround, restrain |∘倦 fatigued, wearied, | 乏 | 難 difficulties, hardships | 守 surrounded, besieged 圍 | 發 | sleepy	A

Kung

工[1]	工 48	工 8	Work, art; time; duty; workman | 廠 factory, workshop, | 房 |·程 (engineering) work | 程師 contractor, architect | 價 price of work, wages |·錢 | 匠 an artisan, mechanic | 人 | 界 labor world | 黨 labor union |·夫 work, labor; leisure | 作 work | 程學 engineering | 科 industrial, technical course | 業 industries, manufactures | 業學校 industrial school	A
功[1]	力 19	工 8	Merit, efficacy, service | 勞 |·夫 ability, learning work | 效 merit, result, 成 | |∘課 task, school-work, lesson |∘名 merit and fame; rank | 德 merit, virtuous deeds | 用 effect, use, function	D
攻[1]	攴 66	工 8	To attack, assault; work at | 城 assault a city	C

Character	Radical	Phonetic	Definition		Alt.	Class
攻[1]			|·擊 to attack, assault | 取 to capture, seize | 破 | 勝 to overthrow, conquer			
公[1]	八 12	八 392	Public, just; a duke; male, | 債 public debt; so also | 產 | 局, | 法, | 費, | 益, | 僕, | 事, | 敵, | 文, | 園 | 雞 a cock; so also | 貓 | 見 consensus, public opinion |∘主 a princess | 舉 public election | 選 | 心 public spirit | 議 a public meeting | 認 motion passed | 開 frank; open to the public |·| a woman's husband's father | 共 the general public | 理會 Congregational Church | 立 public; e.g. schools | 論 to discuss fairly | 母倆 husband and wife |·平 just, equitable | 正, |·道 | 使[3] an envoy, diplomat |·使館 legation | 署 public offices | 所 | 孫 double surname |∘司 a public company, offices | 羊 double surname | 冶 double surname	S. S. S. S.		B
蚣[1]	虫 142	八 392	Centipede 蜈 |			G
供[1]	人 9	共 95	To give; evidence 口 | |·給 supply, provide with | 詞 give evidence, depose |∘養 support, nourish parents		kung[4]	D

Kung

Character	Radical	Phonetic	Meaning		Other reading	Class
恭[1]	心 61	共 95	Respectful, polite |·敬 |賀 to congratulate |喜 出| go to stool			B
弓[1]	弓 57	弓 244	A bow; arched |箭 bow and arrows |矢 |箭手 archers |手 |上弦 string a bow; prepare 拉| draw a bow, 開|, 張|	S.		C
躬[1] 躳[1]	身 158	弓 244	Body, person, personally |親 |行 do a thing oneself |身 bend the body; politeness 鞠| make a bow 曲|			B
宮[1]	宀 40	呂 749	Palace; eunuch; mansion |殿 large hall in the palace |庭 the palace 皇|, 王|	S.		C
肱[1] 厷[1]	肉 130	厷 167	Humerus, the arm	文	hung[2]	K
共[3]	八 12	共 95	To give; bow 衆星|之 all stars bow to pole-star		kung[4]	B
拱[3]	手 64	共 95	To bow, salute, bowed, arched |立 stand with hands folded |手作揖 fold the hands and salute			H
礦[3] 鑛[3]	石 112	廣 823	A mine; ore of metals |井 shaft of mine |權 mining right |科 mining course |師 a mining engineer |鐵 iron ore |銅 copper ore |務 mining |·物學 mineralogy		k'uang[4]	E
鞏[3]	革 177	工 8	To strengthen, guard, guarded well |固	S.		G
廾[3]	廾 55	廾 414	Hands folded			K

共⁴	八 12	共 95	All together, whole of; to share ｜產主義 Communism ｜計 the sum total, ｜合 ｜和 unity, united ｜和政體 republican form of government ｜事 work together; have dealings ｜總 all together, collectively	kung³	B
供⁴	人 9	共 95	To offer, worship ｜奉 to present, to offer to ｜偶像 to worship idols ｜祖師 to worship ancestors	kung¹	D
貢⁴	貝 154	工 8	Tribute; to present; best S. ｜獻 to offer; gift; (to God, society, etc.) ｜品 articles of tribute ｜上 offer present to superior		E
贛⁴	貝 154	工 8	Tribute, presents	kan⁴	G

K'ung

空¹	穴 116	空 10	Empty, void; vanity ｜虛 ｜間 space ｜中 space, the air ｜想 fancy, vision ｜閒 unoccupied, at leisure ｜軍 air force ｜曠 waste, void ｜白 blank space ｜襲 air raid ｜地 vacant ground ｜言 empty talk	k'ung⁴	B
恐³	心 61	工 8	Alarmed, to doubt, fear ｜懼 ｜其 I fear, lest, probably ｜。怕 ｜嚇 to frighten, extort ｜口無憑 lest word of mouth be no proof		A

孔[3]	子 39	乙 297	A hole, great, very 丨教 Confucianism 丨道 丨·雀 the peacock 丨竅 opening, pore, duct 丨門 Confucianists, Confucius' family 丨道 thoroughfare 丨子[3] Confucius 丨夫子[3], 丨聖人	S.		D
空[4]	穴 116	空 10	Leisure, blank 丨兒 閒丨 empty, leisure	S.	k'ung[1]	B
控[4]	手 64	空 10	To accuse 丨告 丨詞 a plaint, charge 上丨 appeal to superior court			D

Kuo

鍋[1]	金 167	咼 581	A cauldron, boiler; kettle 丨蓋兒 lid of cooking pan 丨把[4]兒 handle of kettle or pot 丨台 brick work around boiler (火)丨·子 Chinese chafing-dish			C
郭[1]	邑 163	郭 745	Surname	S.	kuo[3]	G
蟈[1]	虫 142	或 333	A kind of fat, green, locust (N. China) 丨丨兒			H
聒[14]	耳 128	舌 707	Clamor, din		kua[14] k'uo[4]	I
國[2] 国[2]	口 31	或 333	Country, kingdom, nation 丨債 national debt 丨政 national government 丨度 丨際 international 丨際聯盟會 League of Nations 丨聯 丨計 national economy, politics 丨旗 national flag 丨家 the state, government	S.		A

Kuo

<table>
<tr><td>國[2]</td><td></td><td></td><td>| 教 state religion
| 志 national history | 史
| 權 national sovereignty
| 法 laws of the state
| 防 national defences
| 費 national expenditure
| 風 custom of a country
| 會 parliament, congress
| 魂 spirit of a people
| 貨 native goods
| 民 the people
| 民黨 Nationalist party
| 事 national affairs
| 術 Chinese boxing | 技
| 體 national prestige, form of state
| 子[3]監 Imperial Academy, Peking
| 文 national language or literature
| 務總理 the Premier
君主 | monarchy
開 | to found a state 立 |
民 | republic 共和 |</td><td></td><td></td></tr>
<tr><td>果[3]
菓[3]</td><td>木
75</td><td>果
507</td><td>Fruit |·子·; result, effect; truly
| 然 indeed, truly, really
| 木 fruit trees | 樹
| 品 fruits generally
| 實 fruit; result; a kernel
| 攤 a fruit-stall
| 園子 an orchard
如 | if indeed</td><td></td><td>A</td></tr>
<tr><td>裹[3]</td><td>衣
145</td><td>果
507</td><td>To bind, wrap
| 脚 to bind the feet</td><td></td><td>D</td></tr>
<tr><td>餜[3]</td><td>食
184</td><td>果
507</td><td>Wheat-flour cakes
喜 | post-betrothal cakes</td><td>kuei[3]</td><td>G</td></tr>
<tr><td>郭[3]</td><td>邑
163</td><td>郭
745</td><td>Outer wall, suburbs | 外
東 | eastern suburbs</td><td>kuo[1]</td><td>G</td></tr>
</table>

槨[3] 椁[3]	木 75	郭 745	Outer coffin 棺 ｜ coffin and its outer case 石 ｜ stone sarcophagus	I
過[4] 过[4]	辵 162	咼 581	To pass by, past; experience; transgression, fault ｜秤 to be weighed ｜磅 ｜∘繼 to be adopted ｜奬 excessive praise ｜橋 cross a bridge; so also ｜河 ｜節 keep festival, ill-mannered ｜去 to pass by, bygone ｜犯 a sin, a trangression ｜分[4] beyond duty, excessive ｜愈 ｜後 afterwards ｜日·子 to get along, live ｜客 a passing traveler ｜關 to pass Customs ｜·｜目 to glance over ｜·了期 past the time-limit ｜門 to be married—of girls ｜年 the new year, next year ｜·失 fault, an error ｜∘錯 ｜堂 be tried by magistrate ｜·得去 able to pass, or bear, ｜·不去 unable to pass ｜多 excessive number or quantity ｜渡 to cross a ferry, transition ｜∘於 to exceed, more than	A

K'uo

擴[4]	手 64	廣 823	To extend, enlarge ｜大, ｜張 ｜充 carry out, extend, fill	D
括[4]	手 64	舌 707	To enfold, include 包∘｜ ｜弧 parentheses, brackets, ｜號	E

聒[4]	耳 128	舌 707	Clamor, din	kua[14] kuo[14]	I
闊[4] 濶[4]	門 169	舌 707	Broad, separated, ample, liberal, rich | 家主 a well-to-do family 寬 | extensive, broad, liberal | 綽 luxurious		E

La

拉[1]	手 64	立 84	To draw, pull, lead, drag | 賬 run up an account | 車 draw a cart |°扯 pull, implicate, dealing | 飢荒 contract debts | 虧空 | 縴 track boat; go-between | 鋸 work two-handed saw | 胡琴 play the violin (Chinese) | 弓 draw the bow, shoot | 買·賣 drive cart for hire; take orders, advertise for sale | 磨 turn the millstone | 扇 pull a punkah | 屎 to go to stool (vulg.) | 手 hold or shake hands | 倒 no consequence; never mind |·得了[3] able to draw, so |·不了[3] |·得動 can pull it, so |·不動 cannot pull it—a heavy cart | 丁 Latin | 丁文		B
喇[1]	口 30	束 501	To talk, chatter; boast, | 嘴; a final indicating finished action | | loquacity	la[3]	D
瘌[1]	疒 104	束 501	Severe, grievous; bald 疤·| scar, cicatrix		I
揦 攋[1]	手 64	束 501	To turn over; pull about 撥·| |·子 opportunity, opening, slip		I

剌²	刀 18	束 501	To cut in two, cut, slash, mutilate ｜·下 cut off, to amputate ｜·去 ｜破·了 cut so blood flows ｜手 ｜斷·了 cut off, amputate		D
邋²	辵 162	巤 690	Slovenly, untidy, dirty ｜遢 ｜雜 mixed, in confusion	la⁴	H
喇³	口 30	束 501	｜·嘛 Lama priest ｜·叭 trumpet	la¹	D
辣⁴	辛 160	束 501	Acrid, pungent, hot; severe ｜椒 pepper, chili, capsicum ｜味兒 acrid flavor		B
落⁴	艸 140	各 712	To leave behind ｜·下 ｜兒 error, fault ｜·了 left behind, forgotten	lao⁴ le⁴ lo⁴	B
臘⁴ 腊⁴ 臈⁴	肉 130 ◆	巤 690	Winter sacrifice; 12th moon; dried meats ｜肉 dried and salted meats ｜八粥 congee for 8th of 12th moon ｜·月 12th month of the year		F
蠟⁴ 蜡⁴	虫 142	巤 690	Wax 蜜｜, candle; fossil copal ｜紙 wax paper, parafine paper ｜燭 a candle, a wax candle ｜燈 a candle; a candlestick ｜台	cha¹	E
邋⁴	辵 162	巤 690	To leave behind ｜·下	la²	H
鑞⁴	金 167	巤 690	Tin, copper, pewter, 錫｜ 白｜pewter		G

Lai

褦¹	衣 145	能 324	Stupid, raw; ignorant of life ｜·襶	nai⁴	I
來² 来²	人 9	木 484	To come, coming; pluperfect ｜函 the letter which has come ｜回的走 going back and forth ｜人 messenger, someone came		A

Lai

來[2]			丨稿 contributed articles (news paper) 丨客 a guest, visitor, 丨賓 丨丨help yourself, come on 丨丨往往 frequent intercourse 丨·歷 antecedents, circumstances 丨·了 come, came, has arrived 丨到 丨臨 to draw near 丨·路 the source 丨由, 丨原 丨年 next year 丨·罷 come! 丨·不及 not time-enough 丨·不了[3] unable to come 丨生 the life to come 丨世 丨時 the future 丨·得遲 come late 丨·得晚 丨此 come here! came here ·丨·着 forms pluperfect tense	
徠[24] 倈[24]	彳 60	木 484	To meet, encourage, induce 招丨百姓 encourage immigration 丨獃先生 a poor scholar	I
萊[2]	艸 140	木 484	Thistles, goosefoot 丨草 sow-thistle	I
賴[4] 頼[4]	貝 154	賴 503	Rely upon, throw burden on; repudiate S 丨債 repudiate a debt 丨別人 throw blame on another 倚丨 rely upon, depend 仰丨	C
癩[4]	疒 104	賴 503	Scab, itch, leprous, eruption 生丨 to get the itch 長丨(癘瘋)	F
籟[4]	竹 118	賴 503	Musical pipe; whizzing or creaking sound 竹丨 creak of bamboos in wind	I
賚[4]	貝 154	木 484	To confer, bestow on inferior 丨予 勞丨 reward for services	I

Lan

籃^{2} 竹 118 監 608 Basket with handle |·子 B
|球 basket ball

藍^{2} 艸 140 監 608 Blue, indigo |靛, |色 S. A
洋| foreign indigo, bluing
|寶石 the sapphire

襤^{2} 衣 145 監 608 Ragged, slovenly |褸 G

闌^{2} 門 169 闌 506 Screen; late, end; abruptly I
月| the waning moon

攔^{2} 手 64 闌 506 To obstruct, hinder |·住, |擋 C
|路 obstruct thoroughfare
|·不住 cannot be stopped
|阻 to prevent, hinder

欄^{2} 木 75 闌 506 Railing, pen, cage; den; depart ment in news paper E
|杆 railing

瀾^{2} 水 85 闌 506 Waves, billows, 波| G
|漫 heavy showers, flood

蘭^{2} 艸 140 闌 506 Orchid |花, |類 G
|兄, |姐 sworn brother, sister
|心 elegant, refined nature

婪^{2} 女 38 林 492 Covetous, greedy 貪| E
|索 squeeze money

懶^{3} 心 61 賴 503 Lazy, disinclined |◦惰, |人 A
|怠 negligent
|·得動 unwilling to move, lazy

覽^{3} 覧^{3} 見 147 覽 609 To look at; inspect, perceive I
|視 to observe, to inspect
一|盡知 understand at a glance

攬^{3} 手 64 覽 609 To seize; monopolize; armful G
|取 to grasp, to seize

欖^{3} 木 75 覽 609 The olive 橄·|樹 E
|仁 olive seeds

纜^{3}	糸 120	覽 609	A rope, cable, hawser | 索 | 船 to make a boat fast | 路 tow-path		F
漤^{3}	水 85	林 492	To pickle fruit in brine, or ripen by scalding		K
亂^{4} 乱^{4}	乙 5	𤔔 535	Confused 俗 |·子 disturbance	luan^{4}	B
爛^{4}	火 86	闌 506	Glittering; pulp, soft, rotten | 紙 waste paper | 肉 meat boiled to shreds | 泥 soft mud		D
濫^{4}	水 85	監 608	To overflow; random; profuse | 交 make friends at random | 支 expend too much | 取 take too much | 用 use profusely		F

Lang

踉^{1}	足 157	良 361	蹡 | Jump along	lang^{2} liang^{2}	H
狼^{2}	犬 94	良 361	Wolf; fierce, cruel; very | 心 wolf-hearted, merciless | 狽 inseparable; distress | 崽·子 a wolf-cub | 窩 the wolf's den		D
踉^{2}	足 157	良 361	Urgent; to go, jump | 蹡 hurriedly	lang^{1} liang^{2}	H
躴^{2}	身 158	良 361	Very tall | 躿		K
郎^{2}	邑 163	郎 362	Gentleman, son, bridegroom S. 新 | bridegroom 令 | your son		B

Character	Radical	Phonetic	Definition		
廊²	广 53	郎 362	Verandah, corridor, porch 丨·子 丨·子底·下 under the verandah 丨簷 the eaves of the verandah 遊丨 passages, corridors		D
榔²	木 75	郎 362	Betel palm 檳丨 betel nut		H
瑯² 琅²	玉 96	郎 362	Whitish stone, of jade or agate class 丨璫 pendants, tinkling jingles		K
螂² 蜋²	虫 142	郎 362	Praying mantis 屎·科丨 tumble-bug 螳丨擋車 an ineffectual effort		I
朗³	月 74	良 361	Clear, open; moonlight 光丨 丨照 solicit assistance 丨誦 read in clear voice		H
浪⁴	水 85	良 361	Waves, 波丨, 丨·頭 丨費 extravagant 丨用 丨蕩 profligate, dissipated 丨子³ 丨隄 break-water		C

Lao

Character	Radical	Phonetic	Definition		
撈¹²	手 64	勞 449	Fish up; drag out, drag for 丨本 get one's money back 丨·上來·了 pulled up from water 丨魚 scoop up fish with net		E
勞² 劳²	力 19	勞 449	To toil, trouble, labor 丨駕 give trouble, thank you 丨·動 丨金 wages, recompense 丨乏 trouble, labour; weary 丨碌 丨心 mental labour 丨苦 toilsome labour, misery 丨力 bodily labour	lao⁴	A
嘮²	口 30	勞 449	To gabble 丨叨 noisy, clamorous		H

Lao

嶗²	山 46	勞 449	Mountains in Shantung 丨山	K
癆²	疒 104	勞 449	Wasting, injurious 丨症 consumption 丨·病	D
牢²	牛 93	牛 38	Jail, fold; firm, secure 丨記 hold firm in memory 丨記不忘 丨·靠 firm, steady, trusty 丨固 丨籠 a cage, prison 丨獄 a prison 監丨	C
哰²	口 30	牛 38	To gabble, loquacious 丨叨 丨 丨twitter of birds	I
醪²	酉 164	翏 283	The lees of wine, wine 香丨 fragrant wine	K
老³	老 125	老 189	Venerable, old; skilled; very 丨·成 experienced, discreet 丨練 丨先生 venerable teacher, sir 丨·夫子³ 丨兄 you, sir 丨∘虎 the tiger; the stocks 丨人 elderly person, 丨年人, 丨頭子(兒) 丨姑娘 old maid, youngest girl 丨·鴰 crow or rook 丨媽(兒) female servant, nurse 丨沒見 not seen for long time 丨米 old rice 丨板 captain of a boat. actor 丨伴 wife, 丨半天 a long time 丨婆·子(兒) an old woman, wife 丨不 never 丨少 old and youny, all 丨幼 丨師 a teacher; Moslem priest 丨·實 honest, without vice 丨手 an expert 丨∘鼠 a rat, mouse 丨大 eldest brother	A

Character	Radical	Phonetic	Definition	Note	Other readings	Code
老^{3}			｜太太 an old lady ｜天爺 the Supreme Being ｜早 long since, very early ｜·子 father; Laotze ｜·爺 sir; maternal grandfather ｜爺兒 the sun ｜爺廟 Kuan Ti temple ｜遠 ever so far			
佬^{3}	人 9	老 189	A burly old man; great			I
姥^{3} 姆^{3}	女 38	老 189	Matron, dame; midwife; maternal grandmother ｜ ｜ (Used as 老)	俗	mu^{3}	G
潦^{3}	水 85	尞 454	Water left in pool 水｜	文	lao^{4} liao^{2}	I
勞^{4}	力 19	勞 449	To reward labor 賞｜, aid ｜兵 reward soldiers	S.	lao^{2}	A
澇^{4} 潦^{4}	水 85	勞 449	To overflow, wet, flood ｜壞·了 spoilt by flood ｜天 excessive rains		lao^{3} liao^{2}	H F
烙^{4}	火 86	各 712	To burn; brand, iron, fry ｜糊·了 burnt, dried up ｜焦·了 ｜衣裳 to iron clothes ｜餅 a sort of pancake ｜·鐵 a clothes-iron ｜·鐵印 a brand, ｜印			B
絡^{4}	糸 120	各 712	Netted case ｜·子 ｜網 net, network on sedan chair		lo^{4}	D
落^{4}	艸 140	各 712	To fall, drop, settle down ｜·下 ｜潮 low water, ebbtide ｜平 ｜空 come to naught ｜篷 lower the sail ｜·不下 unable to fall or settle ｜·不是 have fault found with ｜地 fall to earth, be born ｜定銀 pay earnest-money ｜坐 to sit down		la^{4} lo^{4} le^{4}	B

Le

勒[1]	力 19	革 105	Bridle; extort, force ｜索 extortion	le[24] lei[1]	D
嘞[1]	口 30	慮 208	Call for pigs ｜｜ 俗		K
勒[2]	力 19	革 105	Bridle, extort, force ｜令 force compliance	le[14] lei[1]	D
樂[4]	木 75	樂 490	Joy, to rejoice, laugh; dissipation ｜極·了 extremely delighted ｜◦處 cause for joy ｜境 ｜·意 pleased, glad to do it ｜觀（主義）optimism ｜善 delighting in good ｜天命 rejoicing in will of God ｜業 content with one's lot 喜｜be glad, pleasure, 懽｜	yao[4] yueh[4]	A
珞[4]	玉 96	各 712	Neck ornament 瓔｜		I
絡[4]	糸 120	各 712	Continous, to connect 連◦｜	lao[4]	D
落[4]	艸 140	各 712	To fall, drop 日｜sunset	la[4] lao[4] lo[4]	B
駱[4]	馬 187	各 712	Camel ｜·駝 俗	lo[4]	C
勒[4]	力 19	革 105	Bridle, extort, force ｜逼, ｜令	le[12] lei[1]	D
泐[4]	水 85	力 223	To split, to write; cleavage 石｜cleavage of rocks		K
·了	亅 6		perfective particle 好｜ all right now		

Lei

勒[1]	力 19	革 105	To rein in; strangle ｜·不住 cannot rein in ｜·死 to strangle	le[124]	D

Lei

累[2]	糸 120	累 815	Repetitious, tedious 丨·贅	lei[34]	A
雷[2]	雨 173	雷 813	Thunder, 打丨; torpedo S. 丨擊 struck by thunder 丨劈 丨神 the god of thunder 丨·公 丨同 one (essay) like another, copied 水丨 a submarine torpedo, so 地丨		D
擂[2]	手 64	雷 813	To drum, pound; triturate 丨鼓 to beat a drum		G
纍[2]	糸 120	畾 814	To creep; bind, string; cling to 丨垂 to hang down		I
羸[2]	羊 123	羊 151	Lean, cadaverous 丨瘦 emaciated		I
累[3]	糸 120	累 815	To connect, implicate; often 丨丨 repeatedly, often 丨次 連丨[4] involve, implicate 帶丨[4]	lei[24]	A
縲[3]	糸 120	累 815	To bind with ropes 丨絏 bonds, fetters		E
耒[3]	耒 127	耒 498	To plough, a plow		G
誄[3]	言 149	耒 498	Eulogy, obituary 丨文 丨述 write a biography		K
畾[3]	田 102	畾 814	Fields separated by dykes		K
儡[3]	人 9	畾 814	To injure, destroy; puppets 傀丨 敗丨 to be routed		I
壘[3]	土 32	畾 814	Rampart; a heap, to pile up, 丨石 丨牆 to build a wall 丨石山 artificial mountains		E
磊[3]	石 112	石 722	A heap of stones 丨落 uneven, superior		K
累[4]	糸 120	累 815	Weary 丨乏; a trouble 丨心 bothersome, requiring thought 丨·了 hard worked, fatigued 丨·得慌 very tired	lei[23]	A

淚⁴ 泪⁴	水 85	戾 458	Tears, drops like tears ｜珠 ｜下 to drop tears, to weep ｜汪汪的 to weep bitterly 流眼｜ to shed tears 流｜		C
類⁴ 類⁴	頁 181	頁 866	Class, species, to class with ｜·乎那個 like that, of that sort ｜此 ｜似 resembling, as if ｜推 to reason by analogy ｜同 resembling, as if, same as 同｜ of same sort, or class		C
肋⁴	肉 180	力 223	The ribs. ｜條, 脊｜, ｜骨 ｜傍 the side ｜門	le⁴	D

Leng

稜² 棱² 楞²	禾 115 木 75	夌 543	Edge, corner; C. of fields ｜角 edge and corner ｜縫 peccadilloes ｜｜ bumpy, lumpy ｜木 floor beams 地｜		F
踜²	足 157	夌 543	A slip, pitch of body		I
冷³	冫 15	令 438	Cool, chilly, cold, frigid S. ｜汗 a cold sweat ｜笑 a sneer, sardonic smile ｜心 cold-hearted ｜血 cold-blooded ｜熱 cold and hot, temperature ｜孤丁的 suddenly ｜·不防 ｜淡 cool, indifferent ｜天 a cold day, 天｜·了 ｜字 an unusual character		A
睖⁴	目 109	夌 543	To stare ｜·着, ｜｜瞪瞪 ｜眼 to stare; staring eyes		H

Li

璃[12] 瓈[12]	玉 96	离 547	Vitreous substance, glass 玻·丨 琉·丨 a glass-like substance, strass		A
哩[1]	口 30	里 827	Adverb; final particle; an English mile		F
麗[1]	鹿 198	麗 320	高·丨國 Korea	li4	F
离[2]	内 114	离 547	A bogey; bright, elegant		K
漓[2]	水 85	离 547	Water dripping 淋丨		I
篱[2]	竹 118	离 547	Skimmer 笊·丨		F
籬[2]	竹 118	离 547	Bamboo fence, hedge 丨·笆; to enclose 丨·笆頭 a greenhorn		E
離[2] 离[2]	隹 172	离 547	To part, separate, apart; distant 丨家 to leave home 丨間[4] to sow discord 丨去 to leave, separate 丨床 to get up; convalescent 丨婚 divorce sought by both 丨·開 to leave, separate 丨別 丨散 to be scattered 丨·得開 able to part with 丨·不開 unable to part		B
梨[2] 棃[2]	木 75	利 511	The pear 丨花 pear blossom 廣丨 rough-skin, juicy pear 白丨 small white pear of Peking		C
犁[2] 犂[2]	牛 93	利 511	A plough; dark; piebald 丨刀 a coulter 丨鏵 丨田 to plough the land		D

Li

Character	Radical	Phonetic	Meaning		
藜 2	艸 140	利 511	An herb, bramble; jade 丨杖 old man's staff		I
蜊 2	虫 142	利 511	Clam 蛤·丨		H
黎 2	黍 202	利 511	Black, black-haired S. 丨民 black-haired Chinese 丨明 day break, twilight		F
黧 2	黑 203	利 511	A dark dun, brindled 丨花 丨黃 the oriole 黃丨		I
狸 2 貍 2	犬 94	里 827	Wild cat 野丨, 丨猫, fox 狐丨 the fox, 香丨 the civet		E
𠩺 2	厂 27	𠩺 497	To split, rive, crack; chap		P
嫠 2	女 38	𠩺 497	A widow 丨婦		I
釐 2 厘 2 兀 2	里 166 減	𠩺 497	To regulate; give; thousandth part of a tael 丨制 regulate, arrange 丨定 丨金 likin i. e. inland custom tax 丨捐 丨分 minute, scanty, few		F
鸝 2	鳥 196	麗 320	The oriole or mango bird, 黃丨		H
里 3	里 166	里 827	Residence, country, Chinese mile (1/3 English mile) 丨長 a kind of village headman 鄰丨 a neighbourhood		B
俚 3	人 9	里 827	Coarse, vulgar, rustic 丨俗 丨言 vulgar expressions		I
娌 3	女 38	里 827	wives of brothers to each other 妯·丨		G
理 3	玉 96	里 827	To manage; notice; principles, reason, abstract right 丨髮 barber, to cut hair 丨想 ideals, theories	lii3	A

Character	Radical	Phonetic	Meaning		
理[3]			丨學 moral science		
			丨∘會 to observe, notice		
			丨科 scientific course		
			丨論 to reason, argument		
			丨偏 reasoning forced, one-sided		
			丨所當然 quite in accord with right		
			丨當		
			丨·他 to notice him		
			丨由 ground of right, reason		
裏[3] 裡[3]	衣 145	里 827	Inside, in, inner, lining		A
			丨衣 inner clothing		
			丨面 inside, within, essential, 丨·邊, 丨·頭		
			丨走 go to the left		
			丨·子 lining in the clothes		
			丨外 inside and outside		
鯉[3]	魚 195	里 827	The carp 丨魚		G
			金丨 the yellow carp		
豊[3]	豆 151	豊 735	Sacrificial vessel		P
禮[3] 礼[3]	示 113	豊 735	Ceremony, etiquette, worship; offerings, presents		A
			丨記 the Book of Rites		
			丨節 etiquette 丨法		
			丨服 full dress		
			丨儀 rites and observances		
			丨義 decorum		
			丨貌 politeness, manners		
			丨拜 worship; Sunday, a week		
			丨拜幾 what day of the week is it?		
			丨拜寺 Mohammedan mosque		
			丨拜堂 church		
			丨拜日 Sunday, the Sabbath		
			丨堂 ceremonial hall		
			丨物 presents, gifts		

Li

李³	木 75	木 484	Plum, prune, |·子		B
			|花 plum blossom		
			行| luggage, baggage		
履³	尸 44	復 545	Shoe; to walk	lü³	G
蠡³	虫 142	彖 287	A wood-borer		K
			|魚 the snake-fish		
利⁴	刀 18	利 511	Sharp, clever, gain, interest S.		A
			|己（主義）selfishness		
			|器 edged tools, "cat's paw"		
			|劍 sharp sword |刀		
			|權 vested rights		
			|·害 severe, extreme, dangerous		
			|·息 profit, interest |·錢		
			|·益 advantage, gain		
			|口 loquacious; quick repartee		
			|∘用 utility, to utilize		
俐⁴	人 9	利 511	Clever, sharp; quick 伶|		D
			|·羅 clean, smart, trim		
			|束 in order, satisfactory		
痢⁴	疒 104	利 511	A purging, dysentery |·疾		E
莉⁴	艸 140	利 511	White jasmine		H
力⁴	力 19	力 223	Strength, force, vigorously		B
			|·氣 strength, spirit |·量		
			|强 robust, strong		
			|行 practice sedulously |作		
			|辯 to argue strenuously		
			|不足 strength insufficient		
			極| earnestly, emphatically		
荔⁴ 栛⁴	艸 140	力 223	Lichee, custard-apple |∘枝		H
立⁴	立 117	立 84	To set up, stand; instantly		B
			|案 to put on record; register		

Character	Radical	Phonetic	Meaning		
立⁴			丨正 attention! halt! 丨家 to establish a family 丨志 to make a resolution 丨春, 夏, 秋, 冬 opening of spring, summer, autumn, winter 丨法 establish a law, legislate 丨合同 to make a contract 丨憲 to establish a political constitution 丨選 elect by rising vote 丨刻 directly, immediately 丨時 丨功 establish merit 丨國 found a country 丨名 establish a reputation 丨·不住 cannot stand firmly 丨嗣 to adopt an heir 丨文書 write deed or document 丨約 make a covenant		
笠⁴	竹 118	立 84	Sun hat; 一頂丨; hamper, crate 戴丨 to be a servant		I
粒⁴	米 119	立 84	A grain, kernel; C. of beads etc. 麥丨(兒) grain of wheat		D
蒞⁴ 莅⁴ 涖⁴	艸 140 水 85	立 84	Water-rushes; to manage, rule; officer's chair 丨治 to rule, govern 丨民 丨任 come into office		I
厲⁴ 历⁴	厂 27	厲 577	Severe, oppress; whetstone 丨色 to be stern 丨聲 speak sharply or sternly 嚴丨 severe, strict, rigorous	S.	F
勵⁴	力 19	厲 577	To encourage, urge 勉丨 arouse, encourage 鼓丨		C
礪⁴	石 112	厲 577	Whetstone, whet 磨丨 丨石 sandstone		I
蠣⁴	虫 142	厲 577	Rock oysters 牡·丨 丨殼 oyster-shells		I

Li

例⁴	人 9	列 279	Law; precedent; regulations ｜條 laws, bye-laws, code 律｜ 一｜one rule, all the same		C
吏⁴	口 30	吏 170	Government servant, official 稅｜publican, tax-collector		D
栗⁴	木 75	栗 778	Chestnut ｜·子, ｜菓 ｜色 chestnut color		D
慄⁴	心 61	栗 778	Terrified, afraid, pale 戰｜quaking with fear		G
歷⁴ 厯⁴	止 77	歷 513	To calculate; pass through, successive; calendar ｜日 a diary, journal ｜｜arranged in order, constantly ｜練 experienced ｜年 progressive years ｜代 ｜年賬 a ledger ｜史 history 陽｜solar calendar 陰｜lunar cal.		D
曆⁴	日 72	歷 513	Calendar, almanac 黃｜ ｜家 astronomers ｜數 astronomical calculations		H
瀝⁴	水 85	歷 513	A drop, drip; strain; gum ｜青 gum, resin ｜血 to shed, drip blood		K
癧⁴	疒 104	歷 513	Scrofulous, swellings 瘰｜swelling of the glands		I
靂⁴	雨 173	歷 513	Clap of thunder 霹｜rapid claps of thunder		I
隸⁴ 隷⁴	隶 171	隶 526	To belong to, control ｜卒 attendants, jailers 直｜Chihli province 僕｜retainers, servants		E
麗⁴	鹿 198	麗 320	Elegant, beautiful, 美｜; display ｜人 a beauty 華｜ornamental, elegant 秀｜	li¹	F
儷⁴	人 9	麗 320	A pair, mate. 伉｜ married couple 失｜to lose one's wife		H

戾^{4}	戶 63	戾 458	Calamity, offence 乖｜ perverse, violent		G
唳^{4}	口 30	戾 458	Cry of wild geese		K
詈^{4}	言 149	言 740	To revile, curse, scold ｜罵 ｜辱 revile, abuse, slander ｜謗		K
鬲^{4}	鬲 193	鬲 589	Large iron cauldron		K

Lia

倆^{3}	人 9	兩 562	Two. 偺·們｜ we two 俗 ｜人 two or both men ｜三 (sa^1) two or three 三 (sa^1)｜	liang^{3}	F

Liang

涼^{2} 凉^{2}	水 85	京 747	Cool, fresh, coldly ｜茶 cold tea; so ｜氣, ｜風, ｜水, ｜汗 ｜蓆 a mat for warm weather ｜血 cold hearted ｜·一·｜ to let a thing cool ｜開水 cold boiled water ｜·快 cool and pleasant ｜棚 an awning ｜傘 a sun shade, umbrella ｜亭 summer house ｜菜 a salad		A
梁^{2}	木 75	梁 489	Ridge pole, beam; bridge S. ｜木 timber, beam 脊·｜ the back, spine --niang		A
粱^{2}	米 119	梁 489	Tall millet, ｜稭 stalks of same ｜米 seed of same 高·｜ tall millet (like sorghum)		D

Liang

Character	Radical	Phonetic	Meaning	Ref.	Grade
量^{2}	里 166	量 828	To estimate, measure ｜·一·｜	liang^{4}	B
			｜米 to measure rice		
			｜地 to measure land		
糧^{2} 粮^{2}	米 119	量 828	Grain, food; rations; taxes in grain		C
			｜集 grain market, ｜市		
			｜行 wholesale grain firm		
			｜餉 rations for troops		
			｜·食 grain ｜·食店 grain shop		
			｜草 grain and straw, forage		
			錢·｜ taxes in money and grain		
良^{2}	艮 138	良 361	Good, virtuous, 善｜; very		C
			｜辰 fortunate day or hour		
			｜將^{4} a good general		
			｜知 know naturally, instinct		
			｜久 a long time		
			｜方 a good prescription		
			｜·心 a good heart; conscience		
			｜·心發現 conscience stirred		
			｜·心無愧 a clear conscience		
			｜醫 a first-rate physician		
			｜人 good man, my husband		
			｜能 natural ability, instinct		
			｜朋 a good friend ｜友		
			｜善 good, virtuous, naturally good		
			｜言 good advice		
踉^{2}	足 157	良 361	Urgent, to go; jump 跳｜	laug^{12}	H
兩^{3} 两^{3} 両^{3}	入 11 減	兩 562	Two, a pair ｜·個; ounce, tael		A
			｜江 Kiangsu, Kiangsi and Anhui		
			｜間房子 two rooms of house		
			｜親 parents		
			｜清 both sides square (accounts)		
			｜方面 both sides of matter		
			｜合式 agreeable to both sides		
			｜湖 Hupei and Hunan		
			｜下·裏 both parties; on both sides		
			｜可之間 two courses open		

兩^{3}			｜口子 husband and wife ｜廣 Kwangtung and Kwangsi ｜難之間 dilemma ｜便 each as convenient ｜步 a few steps, short distance ｜不找 to trade even, no boot ｜天 two days, a few days ｜頭忙 busy at both ends ｜造 plaintiff and defendant ｜位 two gentlemen ｜樣 two sorts, different, both ways		
倆^{3}	人 9	兩 562	Clever, skilled 伎｜	lia^{3}	F
魎^{3}	鬼 194	兩 562	A naiad, sprite 魍｜ river spirit, penumbra		I
亮^{4}	亠 8	儿 382	Bright, clear 明｜; sonorous 響｜ ｜堂堂的 very bright 天｜ dawn, daylight 月｜ moon, moonlight		A
輛^{4}	車 159	兩 562	Chariot, cart, carriage 車｜, C. of vehicles		A
量^{4}	里 166	量 828	A measure; capacity 器·｜ ｜窄 poor judgment, narrow｜小 ｜大 broad, magnanimous 器·｜ 限｜ limit set, period	liang^{2}	B
晾^{4}	日 72	京 747	To dry or air in the sun ｜一｜ ｜乾了 thoroughly dried in air		E
諒^{4}	言 149	京 747	To believe, trust; faithful; to consider, excuse ｜情 to consider circumstances ｜來 I feel sure that, probably｜必 原◦｜ allow for, excuse 體◦｜		E

Liao

撩[1]	手 64	尞 454	To lift up, raise, open 丨·起來 丨衣裳 to lift the skirts or long coat 丨水 splash up water by hand	liao24	H
僚[2]	人 9	尞 454	Companion, colleague; kind, class 丨屬 companion, colleague, 丨友 官丨 fellow officials, officialdom		I
寮[2]	宀 40	尞 454	Fellow-official, shanty 丨房 officers' tea-room in yamen		I
撩[2]	手 64	尞 454	To rouse, stir, 丨火, 丨撥 丨邊 to hem	liao14	H
潦[2]	水 85	尞 454	Slack, careless, 丨·草	lao34	F
燎[2]	火 86	尞 454	Torch, fagot 丨漿泡 blister raised by burn	liao34	G
療[2]	疒 104	尞 454	To cure, heal, 丨治, 丨病 丨愈 convalescent, cured		G
繚[2]	糸 120	尞 454	To wind, wind up 丨繞 丨鈕 to wind ball, make button		G
遼[2]	辵 162	尞 454	Distant, far, remote 丨遠 丨東 Manchuria, east of Liao R. 丨望 look far off		G
翏[2]	羽 124	翏 283	Sound of wind		P
寥[2]	宀 40	翏 283	Desolate, vast, vacant 丨落 丨丨無幾 very few		G
聊[2]	耳 128	卯 309	To depend on, purpose to 丨表寸心 a mere token of my gratitude 無丨 without resource, in despair		H
了[3]	亅 6	亅 111	Finished, past, over 完·丨 丨案 close a case at law 丨斷 丨結 to finish; to die	·le	A

Liao

Character	Radical	Phonetic	Meaning		
了[3]			| 解 comprehend fully | 局 to settle, finish up | 事 | 法 plan for settling case | 然 certainly, evidently |·| completely finished; clear |·不| irreparable, can't be done |·不得 this will never do! very | 手 bring work to an end		
燎[3]	火 86	尞 454	To blaze, burn; clear | 光 beacon light	liao[24]	G
瞭[3]	目 109	尞 454	Good eye-sight, far sighted | 見 | 亮 intelligent | 望 keep look-out, watchman 一目 | 然 take in at a glance		F
料[4]	斗 68	斗 23	Material; glass; grain; calculate | 器 glassware | 貨 | 想 to reflect, consider | 估 calculate, estimate | 算 |·理 to manage; a meal (Jap) 不 | unexpectedly 誰 | who would have thought? 材·| materials, stuff | 物		B
略[4] 畧[4]	田 102	各 712	In general, a little, a resumé | | a little, to reflect | 微 a very little 大 | in general, 要 | the gist	lüeh[4]	B
⿱罒⿱夂手[4] 撂[4]	手 64	各 712	To lay down, put down |·下 |·下來 let down (as curtain) | 香錢 leave present for priest		E
掠[4]	手 64	京 747	To plunder, rob 搶 |	lüeh[34]	E
尞[4]	小 42	尞 454	Sacrificial fuel		K
撩[4]	手 64	尞 454	To lay down | 跤 wrestle |·得下 postponable	liao[12]	H

Character	Radical	Phonetic	Meaning		
燎[4]	火 86	尞 454	To burn, illuminate 黑漆｜光 bright polish	liao[23]	G
鐐[4]	金 167	尞 454	Furnace; fetters 脚｜foot-irons, fetters, so 手｜		F

Lieh

Character	Radical	Phonetic	Meaning		
咧[1]	口 30	列 279	｜｜｜Sobbing of a child	lieh[234]	H
咧[2]	口 30	列 279	Talk full of lies, 瞎｜·｜	lieh[134]	H
咧[3]	口 30	列 279	Pout out the lips ｜·｜嘴	lieh[124]	H
列[4]	刀 18	列 279	To arrange in order, rank; enumerate, 排｜,｜成 ｜車 a train of cars ｜陣 draw up in array ｜强 the Great Powers ｜强均勢 balance of power ｜傳[4] biography ｜國 the various nations ｜·在後頭 enumerated below ｜位 you, gentlemen ｜公 ｜於左 as follows, ｜下,｜後		C
咧[4]	口 30	列 279	Trumpet 喇[3]｜	lieh[123]	H
烈[4]	火 86	列 279	Burning, fiery, ardent; virtuous, heroic ｜風 violent wind; so ｜火,｜日 ｜性 energetic, energy ｜女 a virgin, virtuous women ｜士 martyr, patriot, hero		C
裂[4]	衣 145	列 279	To crack, split ｜開; a flaw ｜紋 a crack, fissure 破｜broken, torn		D

趔[4]	走 156	列 279	To stumble 打丨趄		H
劣[4]	力 19	力 223	Inferior, vile, infirm, poor 丨跡 traces of faults 丨敗 decayed, the unfit fails 丨點 badness, depravity		F
鬣[4] 巤[4]	髟 190	巤 690	Bristles, mane 馬丨 長丨 a long beard 剛丨 stiff bristles		I
獵[4]	犬 94	巤 690	To hunt wild animals 打丨 丨戶 hunter, 丨狗 a hunting dog		F
躐[4]	足 157	巤 690	To stride over, step across; skip 丨等 to skip grades		I

Lien

連[2]	辵 162	連 837	To connect, also; consecutive; even; a company of soldiers S. 丨合 (同) united together 丨環 to link, several links 丨任 reelected to office 丨累 to implicate 丨丨(不斷) joined in succession 丨忙 instantly, hastily, at once 丨年不收 successive bad harvests 丨本帶利 principal and interest 丨屬 related to, connected 丨他 he also, even he 丨帶關係 direct connection 丨陰天 steady cloudy weather		A
嗹[2]	口 30	連 837	Stain on clothing 哦丨		H
漣[2]	水 85	連 837	Unceasing flow 丨丨 丨江 river in Hunan		K
璉[2]	玉 96	連 837	Vase for sacrifice 瑚丨		I

Lien

蓮[2]	艸 140	連 837	Lotus, waterlily ｜花 ｜粉 ground lotus root (like arrow-root) ｜花池 a lily-pond ｜·蓬 the lotus head ｜房 ｜子[3] lily seeds, lotus kernels ｜·蓬子兒[3]		E
褳[2]	衣 145	連 837	Pouch, purse 褡｜(袋)		G
鏈[2]	金 167	連 837	Lead or tin ore; chain ｜環 linked, a chain-link	lien[4]	D
憐[2]	心 61	粦 275	To pity, have mercy, sympathize ｜愛 to love; kind-hearted ｜惜 to sympathize ｜念 ｜恤 to compassionate, pity ｜憫		B
帘[2]	巾 50	巾 557	Flag, sign, screen 門｜ 酒｜ a tavern, grog-shop		B
聯[2]	耳 128	耳 626	Joint, united, associate; scrolls ｜軍 allied forces ｜羣 to flock together ｜合 to attach, join, unite ｜貫 strung together ｜絡 bind together, associate ｜盟 alliance, covenant ｜屬 related to, connected with ｜姻 a connection by marriage 對｜ antithetical couplets		C
廉[2]	广 53	廉 672	Incorrupt, scrupulous, frugal, modest; examine S. ｜節 moderate, sparing ｜恥 modest, sense of shame		F
簾[2] 幨[2]	竹 118	廉 672	Curtain, blinds, door or window screen ｜·子 竹｜ bamboo screen 布｜ a cloth screen		E
臁[2]	肉 130	廉 672	Calf of leg ｜肉		K

Lien

鐮² 鎌²	金 167	廉 672	A hook, sickle | 刀, 禾 | 鈎 | pruning-hook		F
奩² 匳²	大 37	區 696	Lady's dressing-case; trousseau | 儀 money given to a bride 粧 | a lady's toilet		I
臉³	肉 130	僉 440	Face, honor, "face" | 面 | 紅·了 the face red, blushing | 盆 a wash-basin 洗 | 盆 | 皮厚 shameless, not sensitive | 皮薄 bashful, sensitive | 酸 sour looking, crabbed | 對 | face to face		A
煉⁴	火 86	柬 505	To refine, | 猪油 to fry pork fat | 丹 prepare the magic drug | 糖 to refine sugar | 獄 purgatory		D
練⁴	糸 120	柬 505	To train, practise |·習, | 達; select | 把式 to practise gymnastics | 兵 to drill troops | 軍 |·的不到 not well enough drilled		B
鍊⁴	金 167	柬 505	To smelt, refine; expert; chain | 金 to melt or refine gold, so | 銀 | 熟 experienced |·子 a chain		C
鏈⁴	金 167	連 837	A chain |·子	lien²	D
戀⁴ 恋⁴	心 61	䜌 888	Warm affection, fond of | 愛 to love tenderly, long for | 家 to be a stay-at-home | | 不捨 hankering after | 色 lecherous	luan⁴ lüan⁴	E
斂⁴	攴 66	僉 440	To gather in, collect; withdraw 收 | | 錢 to collect money, hoard | 聚 to collect; to extort 聚 |		E

殮[4]	歹 78	僉 440	To dress a corpse 收｜ ｜具 things for coffining ｜埋 to bury, inter｜葬 入｜put body in coffin		G

Lin

臨[2]	臣 131	品 695	To draw near; just before; provisional; about to ｜期 near the time ｜近 to draw near, approach ｜終 about to die｜死,｜危 ｜凡 to come down to earth ｜行 about to start｜走 ｜時 near the time, provisional ｜時政府 provisional government ｜時會 extra or special session	lin4	B
林[2]	木 75	林 492	Forest, grove,｜木; collection S 士｜body of literary men 樹｜·子 forest, grove 紫竹｜Tientsin settlement		C
淋[2]	水 85	林 492	To moisten, soak ｜池 a pool, a pond ｜漓 thoroughly wet｜濕,｜透	lin4 lun2	D
琳[2]	玉 96	林 492	A jade, precious stone ｜國 a land near the Caspian which produced topazes		I
霖[2]	雨 173	林 492	Abundant genial rain ｜雨 delightful rain 甘｜		E
燐[2] 粦[2]	火 86	粦 275	Will-o'-the-wisp, flitting light, phosphorus 鬼火｜｜ghost-lights flit about		I
遴[24]	辵 162	粦 275	To select, choose｜選 ｜才 choose talented men		K

Character	Radical	Phonetic	Meaning	Alt.	Tone class
鄰2 隣2	邑 163	粦 275	Neighbor, neighbouring, near 丨近 丨居 a neighbour 丨舍, 丨人 丨國 neighbouring countries 丨里 neighbouring villages 鄉丨		C
鱗2	魚 195	粦 275	Fish-scales, scaly 丨類 scaly creatures, fish		E
麟2 麐2	鹿 198	粦 275	Female unicorn 麒丨 unicorns		H
稟3	禾 115	稟 769	Grain allowance to students 丨俸 stipend		G
凜3 懍3	冫 15	稟 769	Fear, awe-struck, shiver 丨遵 I tremblingly obey 慘丨 cool, cold as spring water		I
廩3	广 53	稟 769	Government granary, stipend 丨·生 a literary graduate		I
檁3	木 75	稟 769	Purlin, 丨·子 (cross beams under rafters)		E
臨4	臣 131	品 695	To weep, wail	lin2	B
賃4	貝 154	任 68	To rent, lease 丨傢伙 hire furniture, utensils 丨房·子 to rent a house (from another) 出丨 lease to, rent out		D
淋4	水 85	林 492	To drip, strain, filter 丨酒 丨灰 slake lime, leach ashes 丨醋 to make vinegar	lin2 lun2	D
吝4 悋4	口 30	文 546	Stingy, sparing, sordid 丨惜 mean, niggardly 丨嗇 丨步 chary of steps, rare visits		E

Ling

Character	Radical	Phonetic	Meaning	Alt.	Tone class
霝2	雨 173	霝 698	Raindrops; to fall in drops		P

Ling

靈^2 灵^2	雨 173	霝 698	Spirit, spiritual force; divine, efficacious 丨機 a clever contrivance 丨·巧 ingenious, clever 丨妙, 丨敏 丨界 spiritual realm, spiritual 丨柩 coffin with corpse in it 丨性 spiritual nature 丨慧 quick perception 丨魂 the soul 丨牌 tablet of deceased 丨位 丨·便 handy, clever 丨動 ingenious, active 丨藥 efficacious drug 丨驗 efficacious, a miracle 丨育 spiritual culture 百丨 Mongolian lark 聖丨 the Holy Spirit		C
伶^2	人 9	令 438	Clever, active; lonely, musician 丨·巧 clever, ingenious 丨·俐 丨界 actors, musicians 丨·便 handy, convenient		D
囹^2	口 31	令 438	A prison, jail 丨圄		K
羚^2	羊 123	令 438	Chamois-like antelope 丨羊 a goral		K
聆^2	耳 128	令 438	To hear, apprehend 丨教 耳丨心悅 ear hears, heart charmed		I
蛉^2	虫 142	令 438	Sand-fly 白丨·子 蜻丨 dragon-fly		E
翎^2	羽 124	令 438	Plume, wing feather 丨毛, 丨·子 丨扇 feather fan		F
鈴^2	金 167	令 438	A small bell 丨·鐺 馬丨 bells on horses		D
零^2	雨 173	令 438	Fragments, remains, fraction 丨錢 odd cash		D

Ling

零[2]			丨花費 sundry expense 丨賣 sell in small quantities 丨碎 odds and ends 丨物 丨餘 a surplus 一百丨五 one hundred and five		
鴒[2]	鳥 196	令 438	Wagtail, 角丨the crested lark		I
齡[2]	齒 211	令 438	Front teeth; age, 壽丨 年丨one's age 丨壽		H
夌[2]	夊 35	夌 543	A mound		P
凌[2]	冫 15	夌 543	Ice, chaste; oppress, insult, maltreat, 丨辱 to disgrace, insult 丨虐 to tyrannize over 丨逼	S	D
綾[2]	糸 120	夌 543	Thin silk, damask 花丨 丨絹 silk gauze 丨羅		H
菱[2]	艸 140	夌 543	Water chestnut 丨·角 丨粉 water-chestnut-root flour		K
陵[2]	阜 170	夌 543	Mound, tomb 丘丨; invade 侵丨 丨寢 imperial tombs 皇丨 金丨Nanking		E
領[3]	頁 181	令 438	Collar; to receive, lead 引丨 丨章 rank, marks on collar 丨賑 receive famine relief 丨教 may I ask? thank you 丨錢 receive money; so 丨命, 丨賞 丨情 to be indebted to, appreciate 丨洗 receive baptism 丨°袖 manager, a leader 丨頭兒 丨路 show the road 丨·事官 consul, 丨·事署 consulate 丨收 to receive, accept 丨受 丨帶 necktie; to lead, direct 帶丨 丨土 territory, 丨土權 sovereignty		A
嶺[3]	山 46	令 438	Mountain range 山丨 牯丨Kuling (summer resort)		B

命^{4} 令^{4}	人 9	令 438	Law; to cause; good; your, your honored ｜愛 your daughter ｜郎 your son ｜正 your wife ｜兄 your brother ｜弟 ｜狐 double surname S ｜人生氣 make people angry ｜妹 your sister ｜尊 your father; ｜堂 mother ｜慈 命·｜ command, order		B
另^{4}	口 30	另 224	Separate, besides, another ｜娶 take another wife ｜換 change for another ｜做 make another ｜∘外 besides, additionally ｜有 there is another		D

Liu

溜^{1}	水 85	留 310	To ramble; flow gently; slippery ｜滑 slippery, tricky 滑·｜ ｜冰 skate, ｜冰塲 rink ｜平 perfectly smooth	liu^{4}	B
遛^{1}	辵 162	留 310	To ramble, saunter ｜^{4}·打 ｜^{4}·打 take a walk, stroll	liu^{24}	D
㐬^{2}	亠 8	㐬 871	Fringed cap		P
流^{2}	水 85	㐬 871	To flow, spread, circulate; set, kind ｜出來 to flow out ｜傳 hand down, transmit ｜血 to bleed, blood-shed ｜·星 a meteor ｜行 to spread, as epidemic ｜淚 to shed tears ｜民 vagrants, tramps ｜氓 ｜聲器 phonograph 留聲機		C

Liu

流^{2}			丨水賬 day-book; current accounts 丨蕩 to wander, rove about 丨通 flow freely through		
琉^{2} 瑠^{2}	玉 96	㐬 871	Vitreous, glass, glazed 丨∘球 Loochoo Islands 丨·璃 glassy substance, strass 丨·璃廠 Peking's book street 丨·璃瓦 glazed tiles		B
硫^{2}	石 112	㐬 871	Sulphur, brimstone 丨∘黃 丨∘黃强水 sulphuric acid, vitriol 丨∘黃面子 flour of brimstone 丨∘黃末子		F
留^{2} 畄^{2} 畱^{2}	田 102	留 310	Keep, hand down; lay up, leave; detain 丨情 allow for social ties 丨·住 keep, detain, restrain 丨·不住 丨·下 take care of, keep, leave 丨學生 students abroad 丨心聽 carefully listen 丨宿 to keep for the night 丨意 to notice 丨客 to detain a guest 丨空⁺兒 to leave a space 丨辮子 to grow a queue 丨步丨步 do not come farther (said by departing visitor) 丨神 take care, bear in mind 丨地步 leave an opportunity 丨養 keep and rear		C
榴^{2}	木 75	留 310	Pomegranate 石·丨, 安石·丨 石·丨茶 the camellia		F
瘤^{2}	疒 104	留 310	Tumor, wen, swelling 丨∘子 肉丨 a fleshy tumor		F
遛^{2}	辵 162	留 310	To loiter, dawdle 逗丨	liu^{14}	D
飀^{2}	風 182	留 310	Sighing of wind		I

Character	Radical	Phonetic	Meaning		Alt.	
劉² 刘²	刀 18	丣 309	To slay, destroy	S		G
柳³	木 75	丣 309	Willow, slender; gaiety ｜絮 willow down ｜罐 willow bucket (basket-ware) ｜條 willow wand, switch, osier 垂｜ weeping willow	S		B
綹³	糸 120	咎 714	Skein of silk; C. of skeins 五｜長髯 (almost a) full beard 剪｜ pick-pocket			F
六⁴ 陸⁴	八 12	亠 80	Six ｜·個 ｜藝 six kinds of knowledge ｜穀 six kinds of grain ｜律 six upper musical accords ｜°十 sixty, ｜百 six hundred		lu⁴	A
溜⁴	水 85	留 310	A current 水｜ 一｜房子 a row of houses 一｜煙的跑 to hurriedly depart		liu¹	B
遛⁴	辵 162	留 310	Go slowly for gentle exercise ｜馬 lead a horse slowly, so ｜狗, ｜人		liu¹²	D
餾⁴	食 184	留 310	To steam rice or bread			I

Lo

Character	Radical	Phonetic	Meaning		Alt.	
擄¹	手 64	慮 208	To tuck up ｜·起袖子		lo³ lu³	D
囉¹	口 30	羅 63	A tone, note; prattle of child ｜·唆 troublesome, annoying			G
羅² 罗²	网 122	羅 63	Net, gauze; to spread out ｜·漢 Buddha's disciples ｜鍋 humpbacked ｜馬教 Roman Catholic Church ｜馬國 Roman Empire	S		B

Lo

羅^{2}			丨麪 sift or bolt flour 丨盤 a compass 丨經 丨網 bird or fish net		
籮^{2}	竹 118	羅 63	Bamboo basket or crate 丨筐 笸 丨 large shallow basket		F
蘿^{2}	艸 140	羅 63	Carrots, turnips; parasite 丨·蔔 the turnip 藤 丨 the wistaria		E
邏^{2}	辵 162	羅 63	To patrol 巡丨; spy; guide 偵丨 to watch, spy		I
鑼^{2}	金 167	羅 63	A gong 打丨 丨槌 a stick to beat gong 丨鼓 gongs and drums		E
螺^{2}	虫 142	累 815	Conch, snail, screw, spiral, 丨殼 丨·絲 a screw, 丨·絲釘 丨·絲錐 cork screw 丨·絲刀 screw-driver 趕錐		F
騾^{2}	馬 187	累 815	A mule, offspring of ass and mare 丨馬 mule and horse 丨馱 to⁴·子 a mule's load 丨馱 t'o² 轎 mule-litter		C
擄^{3} 虜^{3}	手 64	慮 208	To capture, plunder; prisoner 丨·去 sieze, to plunder 丨掠 丨刦 to rob, plunder 丨勒 to extort	lo¹ lu³	D
裸^{3} 躶^{3}	衣 145	果 507	Naked; to strip 丨體 stark naked, bare body 丨身 衣丨 to clothe the naked		H
瘰^{3}	疒 104	累 815	Scrofulous, king's evil 丨癧		I
咯^{4}	口 30	各 712	Final particle＝了, 是·丨	ko¹	I
落^{4}	艸 140	各 712	To fall, drop 丨戶 to take up residence 着·丨 丨花生 peanuts 丨紙 put down on paper	la⁴ lao⁴ le⁴	B

駱^4	馬 187	各 712	|·駝 a camel S. |·駝絨 camel's wool	le^4	C
摞^4	手 64	累 815	To pile up; a pile |·在一塊 pile together		H

Lou

摟^1	手 64	婁 790	To rake up | 柴火 rake fuel together | 糞 to collect manure | 頭一槓 a blow on the head	lou^3	E
婁^2	女 38	婁 790	To trail along; wear; annoying, S.		K
僂^2	人 9	婁 790	Hunchback, bent		I
樓^2	木 75	婁 790	Loft, story, tower | 房 house with upper story | 下 a ground floor |∘上 up stairs, in upper story | 梯 a staircase		A
螻^2	虫 142	婁 790	Mole cricket | 蛄		I
髏^2	骨 188	婁 790	Skull 髑 |		E
摟^3	手 64	婁 790	To embrace, enfold | 抱, |·住 | 在懷中 hold to one's bosom	lou^1	E
簍^3	竹 118	婁 790	Crate, osier-basket |·子 油 | lined basket for oil, so 酒 |		F
露^4	雨 173	路 713	To expose, transpire |·出來 俗 |·着肉 skin seen through clothes | 面 show or disclose face | 體 expose naked body	lu^4	C
漏^4	水 85	戸 724	To leak, | 水; divulge | 洩 let out a secret, 洩 | | 空 to reveal weakness		D

漏^{4}			丨勺 a colander, strainer 丨·子 a funnel 丨卮 a syphon		
陋^{4}	阜 170	丙 445	Low, mean, rustic, vulgar 丨劣 丨巷 a mean lane, alley 醜丨 ugly, ill-favored		E
鏤^{4}	金 167	婁 790	To carve out, engrave, 彫丨; 丨刻 丨花 elegance in style		I

Lu

嚕^{13}	口 30	魯 258	Pout out the lips 吐·丨·了嘴		H
盧^{2}	皿 108	盧 207	Fire-pan, rice vessel; black	S.	G
廬^{2}	广 53	盧 207	Hut, hovel 丨舍, 丨屋 田丨 a hut in the fields		I
爐^{2} 炉^{2}	火 86	盧 207	Stove, furnace, fireplace, grate 丨灰 ashes from a stove 丨條 the bars of a grate 丨灶 a kitchen stove 丨·子 行丨 stove carried by hawkers 火丨 fireplace, furnace		B
臚^{2}	肉 130	盧 207	Skin; spread out, state 丨脹 dropsical swelling 丨列 spread out, arrange 丨陳		K
蘆^{2} 芦^{2}	艸 140	盧 207	Reeds, rushes 丨葦 丨蓆 reed mats 丨花 the flower of reeds		F
轤^{2}	車 159	盧 207	Windlass, pulley 轆丨		G
鑪^{2}	金 167	盧 207	Stove, brazier, censer 香丨 incense pot or vase, censer		H
鱸^{2}	魚 195	盧 207	A perch 丨魚		G

Lu

鸕[2]	鳥 196	盧 207	Fishing cormorant 丨鷀		I
魯[3]	魚 195	魯 258	Stupid; State of Lu S. 丨國 Native State of Confucius 丨莽 stupid, blunt, careless 粗丨		E
櫓[3] 艪[3]	木 75	魯 258	Turret, tower; scull, sweep 丨船 boat with long sweep 搖丨 to scull a boat		B
虜[3] 擄[3]	虍 141	慮 208	To capture 丨掠; prisoner 丨禁 carry off and imprison	lo[13]	D
鹵[3]	鹵 197	鹵 654	Rock salt; rude, violent 丨莽 rough, careless, abrupt 粗丨 丨鹽 natural salt		K
滷[3]	水 85	鹵 654	To salt, pickle; salt land 丨水 lye (for bean-curd)		G
啛[3]	口 30	彔 525	Indistinct; nasal 嘵丨 to mutter, mumble; ravel		I
路[4]	足 157	路 713	Road, way, path, 丨途, 道丨 S 丨·程 route 丨·程單 road-guide 丨劫 highway-robbery 丨緊 the road is dangerous 丨徑 a road, cross-road, 小丨 丨費 travelling expenses 丨人 traveller, "man in the street" 丨口 head of a road 丨過 pass through a place 丨·上 on the road or journey 丨燈 lamps to show the road 旱丨 land-way 水丨 water-way		B
嚕[4]	口 30	路 713	Sound in transliteration		G
鏴[4]	金 167	路 713	To solder, stop up, plug 錮丨鍋 mend old kettles		K

Lu

露4	雨 173	路 713	Dew,·丨水 (珠) 丨天學校 open-air school 白丨the 15th solar term		lou4	C
鷺4	鳥 196	路 713	An egret heron, paddy-bird 丨·鷥			G
鹿4	鹿 198	鹿 319	Deer, stag, 梅花丨spotted deer 丨犄角 antlers of deer			B
簏4	竹 118	鹿 319	A basket 筐丨, dressing-box 書丨book-basket, bookworm			K
轆4	車 159	鹿 319	Wheel, pulley, windlass 丨轤 線丨spinning-wheel			B
彔4	彐 58	彔 525	To carve wood			K
碌4	石 112	彔 525	Green jasper; rough; laborious 勞∘丨toilworn, pains-taking 丨丨rough, irregular			I
祿4	示 113	彔 525	Happiness, official pay, salary 丨位 pay and rank 俸丨official salary	S.		D
綠4	糸 120	彔 525	Green	文	lü4	B
錄4	金 167	彔 525	To record, copy, make entry 丨籍 a record, register 抄丨to copy out 記·丨record, minutes, to record 目·丨an index, table of contents			C
坴4	土 32	坴 47	A clod of earth, land			P
陸4	阜 170	坴 47	Six; dry land 丨續 following in succession 丨軍 land force 丨道 a road by land	S.		D A
賂4	貝 154	各 712	Bribe, present 賄丨			E
戮4	戈 62	翏 283	To slay, exterminate 誅丨, 殺丨			G

Luan

Character	Radical	Phonetic	Meaning		Variant	
綠²	言 149	䜌 888	To bind, tie together			P
圝²	口 31	䜌 888	Spherical, globular 團 |			I
欒²	木 75	䜌 888	City and river in Hopei	S.		I
鑾²	金 167	䜌 888	Imperial chariot; bells; royal | 駕 the Imperial carriage | 鈴 carriage bells			K
鸞²	鳥 196	䜌 888	Phoenix (young?), small bells | 鷄 argus pheasant | 鳳 female and male			I
卵³	卩 26	卯 309	Egg, roe of fishes | 蛋 | 包子 scrotum, |子 testicles | 生 produced from an egg			I
𤔔⁴	爪 87	𤔔 535	To govern			P
亂⁴ 乱⁴	乙 5	𤔔 535	Confusion, rebellion, anarchy |七八糟 topsy-turvy | 民 rebels | 黨 | 跑 run wildly about | 頭緒 tangled; lose the clue		lan⁴	B
戀⁴	心 61	䜌 888	To long for, lust after	俗	lien⁴ lüan⁴	E
糷⁴	米 119	䜌 888	Thick congee		lüan⁴	K

Lun, lün

Character	Radical	Phonetic	Meaning		Variant	
掄¹	手 64	侖 439	To whirl, swing, brandish | 打 | 刀 brandishing sword | 拳 to flourish the fists		lun²	E
侖²	人 9	侖 439	To arrange, set in order			K

Lun

崙²			崑｜Kunlun Mountains (Koul Kun)		
倫²	人 9	侖 439	Natural relationships; degree ｜常 five human relations ｜理 proper, right, ethics ｜理學 ethics, moral philosophy ｜敦 London, ｜敦會 London Missionary Society ｜次 order, in order		C
圇²	口 31	侖 439	To gulp down whole 囫｜	lun³	H
掄²	手 64	侖 439	To select ｜選, ｜擇; by turns ｜才 choose men of ability	lun¹	E
淪²	水 85	侖 439	Eddy, swirling; engulfed 沉｜lost, perish ｜沒		K
綸²	糸 120	侖 439	Silk threads; to compare, classify, adjust ｜絮 a thread, clue		H
論²	言 149	侖 439	｜語 Analects of Confucius	lun⁴	B
輪²	車 159	侖 439	Wheel ｜·子; to revolve, a turn ｜轉 to go through a series ｜船 a steamer 火｜船 ｜換 alternate, serve in turn ｜班 ｜迴 transmigration ｜流 in rotation		A
淋²	水 85	林 492	Soak, drench ｜濕, ｜透 ｜·了一宿³ was rained on for a night	lin²⁴	D
圇³	口 31	侖 439	Chaotic, in a mass 囫｜·着	lun²	H
論⁴	言 149	侖 439	To discuss, reason, discourse, essay ｜·起這個 with reference to this ｜·到 ｜斤 by the pound ｜理 to reason, ｜理學 logic ｜說 leading article in paper ｜道 discourse on right principles ｜斷 to settle, criticize	lun²	B

Lung

Character	Radical	Phonetic	Meaning			
龍²	龍 212	龍 315	Dragon, Imperial ｜爪 dragon's claws ｜鱗 scales ｜船 dragon boat in 5th of 5th moon ｜頭 a water tap, hydrant ｜·王 dragon king, god of rain 水｜pump, fire-engine	S.		D
嚨²	口 30	龍 315	The throat 喉·｜			D
爖²	火 86	龍 315	To kindle fire ｜火 ｜爐子 to light the stove			B
籠²	竹 118	龍 315	Cage 雀｜; crate; to ensnare ｜絡 to entice, tempt ｜屜 bamboo steaming tray 燈·｜ a lantern			B
聾²	耳 128	龍 315	Deaf, hard of hearing 耳｜ ｜·子 a deaf person ｜人			C
朧²	月 74	龍 315	Rising moon; obscure 朦｜; fat			I
蹱²	足 157	龍 315	To walk unsteadily ｜踵 heels over head, toddling			I
韁²	革 177	龍 315	Halter ｜頭			F
隆²	阜 170	生 41	Eminent, abundant, glorious ｜厚 rich, generous ｜盛 full, abundant ｜多	S		D
窿²	穴 116	生 41	Hole, cavity 窟·｜			F
攏³	手 64	龍 315	To seize, drag, collect ｜·住口 muzzled ｜·｜頭 to comb the head ｜總 total, altogether			D
弄⁴	廾 55	王 71	Toy with 擺｜, do	俗	neng⁴ nung⁴	C

Lü

驢[2] 馿[2]	馬 187	盧 207	Donkey, | 駒子 donkey foal | 呌 the bray of a donkey 呌 | a jack, 騍 | a jenny		B
閭[2]	門 169	呂 749	Village gate, village | 里 rural population		I
理[3]	玉 96	里 827	To notice |。會 俗	li[3]	A
旅[3]	方 70	㫃 265	Regiment, troops; to lodge; traveler | 行 travel, excursion to country | 客 a visitor, a trader 客 | | 館 an inn, hotel | 店 | 順口 Port Arthur		D
膂[3]	肉 130	㫃 265	Backbone, strength | 力 main strength		H
屢[3]	尸 44	婁 790	Repeatedly, often | |, | 次 | 年 for many years		D
縷[3]	糸 120	婁 790	A thread, detail, hank, knot | 麻 silk and flax thread		H
履[3]	尸 44	復 545	A shoe; to tread, act | 行 to carry out (a plan, contract) |·歷 ancestry, antecedents	li[3]	G
呂[3]	口 30	呂 749	Musical pipe; vertebrae, S. | 宋 Luzon; Manila		I
侶[3]	人 9	呂 749	Companion, mate | 伴, 行 | | 行 go in company with		G
律[4]	彳 60	聿 669	Law, statute 法 |; principle | 法 laws | 例, | 條 | 師 lawyer		C
慮[4]	心 61	慮 208	To care for, plan, anxious | 念 anxious thoughts 思 |, | 想 掛 | anxiety, suspense		C

濾[4]	水 85	慮 208	To strain, filter |·去渣 |水羅 filter, straining-cloth |布		E
綠[4]	糸 120	彔 525	Green. 靑| grass-green |茶 green tea |豆 green beans	lu[4]	B
率[4]	玄 95	十 13	Standard, rate 稅| rate of duty 速| rate of speed	shuai[4]	D

Lüan

攣[2]	手 64	䜌 888	To tie, bind; bend, crooked |曲 |腰 bent back, hunchbacked 拘| bent, numbed, cramped		K
孌[34]	女 38	䜌 888	Beautiful, admirable |童 a catamite; effeminate		H
臠[3]	肉 130	䜌 888	A slice, flesh minced—|肉 |魚 dried fish		K
戀[4]	心 61	䜌 888	To be fond of, hanker, long for |愛 think fondly upon |慕	lien[4] luan[4]	E
⿰米䜌[4]	米 119	䜌 888	Thick congee or paste	luan[4]	K

Lüeh

掠[34]	手 64	京 747	To plunder, seize, carry off |取 plunder, burglary 搶|	liao[4]	E
略[4] 畧[4]	田 102	各 712	A little, in general, a resumé ||·的 in general, in brief 簡| abridgement, resumé	liao[4]	B

Ma

麼[1] 庅[1]	麻 200	麻 494	Interrogative, auxiliary particle 甚·| what? 什庅 這·|·着 thus; this being so	·me	A

Ma

嗎[13]	口 30	馬 255	Interrogative particle | 啡 morphia		C
媽[1]	女 38	馬 255	Nurse, mother, mama | | 老 | 兒 a female servant, nurse		E
摸[1]	手 64	莫 453	To rub, stroke |·撒	mao[1] mo[1]	C
蟆[1]	虫 142	莫 453	Frog 蛤·|	mo[14]	F
痲[2] 蔴[2]	痲 200	痲 494	Hemp, sesamum; numbness | 木 S. | 雀兒 sparrow, least bunting |·繁 troublesome, complicated | 線 hemp thread, cord | 繩 |·俐 ready. quick, clever |·了 numb, asleep | 包 a sack, hemp bag | 袋 | 布 sacking, burlap |·刀 chopped rope for mortar |·子 hemp seed, pock-mark |·子油 hemp seed oil | 藥 anaesthetic		D
嘛[2]	口 30	痲 494	Colloquial for 甚麼 幹 | what for? what are you up to?		I
痲[2]	疒 104	痲 494	Numb, paralysed; leprosy | 瘋 leprosy 大 | 瘋 |∘木 numbness		E
馬[3]	馬 187	馬 255	Horse; knight (in chess) S. | 鞍子 a saddle | 鞘 horse-shoe | 車 horse-cart; carriage | 韁繩 horse bridle, reins |·錢 doctor's fee | 樁子 a hitching post | 圈 a horse-yard | 號 | 蜂 horse-fly, hornet, wasp· |·夫 a groom | 戲 circus		A

Character	Radical	Phonetic	Meaning	Other reading	Frequency
馬^{3}			丨尾羅兒 a horse-hair sieve 丨褂 short coat, riding jacket 丨力 horse power 丨路 high road, paved road 丨棚 horse shed 丨槽 manger 丨匹 a horse, horses 丨∘上 quickly, just now 丨蹄 horse hoof; water-chestnut 丨隊 cavalry		
瑪^{3}	玉 96	馬 255	Agate, carnelian, veined stones, manna 丨∘瑙 the carnelian		F
碼^{3}	石 112	馬 255	Weights; figures; a jetty 丨∘頭 jetty, mart on river 丨·子 weights 法丨 丨字 business numerals		B
螞^{3}	虫 142	馬 255	Leech; locust; ant 丨蟻 ant 丨∘蜂 hornet	ma^{4}	F
䁶^{3}	目 109	麻 494	Blurred eyes 丨眢 to see dimly; careless		I
罵^{4}	网 122	馬 255	To curse, scold, rail 丨名 an execrated name 丨·他一頓 give him a scolding 辱丨 revile and insult		D
螞^{4}	虫 142	馬 255	丨·蚻 (or·蚱) the grasshopper	ma^{3}	F

Mai

Character	Radical	Phonetic	Meaning	Other reading	Frequency
埋^{2}	土 32	里 827	To bury, conceal 丨∘伏 an ambush 丨人 to bury a person 丨葬	man^{2}	C
買^{3}	貝 154	買 863	To buy, purchase 丨主 the purchaser, customer 丨·來·了 to have purchased 丨·賣 to buy and sell, trade 丨·辦 a compradore		A

買[3]			丨·不起 unable to afford it 丨·不來 can't be had for money 丨·不了[3] unable to buy 丨·的便宜 bought cheap 丨停當·了 bought and settled		
賣[4]	貝 154	賣 864	To sell, betray 丨主 the seller, dealer 丨國 sell one's country; 丨國奴 丨力氣 work hard, coolie labor 丨·不出去 can't sell, no buyers 丨·不了[3] unable to sell 丨·不動 can't get rid of goods 丨·得貴 sold at high price		A
麥[4]	麥 199	人 429	Wheat. 丨苗 young wheat 丨稭 wheat-straw 丨秋 wheat harvest 丨莖 stalk of wheat 丨穗子 ear or head of wheat		B
脈[4] 脉[4]	肉 130	𠂢 350	The pulse 俗 診丨 or 看丨 feel the pulse	mo[4]	D
邁[4]	辵 162	萬 576	To go, pass, step, old; to make an effort 丨·過去·了 to pass beyond 丨步 to go a step 丨大步 丨·不開步 unable to take a full step 老丨 old, aged		E

Man

顢[1]	頁 181	㒼 563	Full round face 丨頇 dilatory, apathetic		I
㒼[2]	艸 140	㒼 563	Equal		P

<table>
<tr><td>瞞^2</td><td>目
109</td><td>㒼
563</td><td>To deceive, blind, conceal, |·着
|哄 to blind, to deceive |昧
|人 hide from a person
|·不過 unable to deceive</td><td></td><td></td><td>C</td></tr>
<tr><td>曼^2</td><td>曰
73</td><td>曼
849</td><td>Wide, long
日耳| Germany</td><td></td><td></td><td>K</td></tr>
<tr><td>蔓^2</td><td>艸
140</td><td>曼
849</td><td>Turnip, beet
|菁 a sort of turnip, beet</td><td></td><td>wan^4</td><td>G</td></tr>
<tr><td>謾^2</td><td>言
149</td><td>曼
849</td><td>To deceive; exaggerate; insult
|言 exaggeration
詐| impose upon</td><td></td><td></td><td>H</td></tr>
<tr><td>鏝^2</td><td>金
167</td><td>曼
849</td><td>Mason's tool to trim brick and spread mortar, trowel |刀</td><td></td><td>man^4</td><td>K</td></tr>
<tr><td>饅^2</td><td>食
184</td><td>曼
849</td><td>Cakes, bread
|·頭 steamed dumplings, bread</td><td></td><td></td><td>C</td></tr>
<tr><td>埋^2</td><td>土
32</td><td>里
827</td><td>To conceal, harbor
|·怨 harbor resentment</td><td>俗</td><td>mai^2</td><td>C</td></tr>
<tr><td>蠻^2</td><td>虫
142</td><td>䜌
888</td><td>Rude, barbarous 野|
|横^4 wild behavior
|夷 S. barbarians |人, |·子
|語 barbarous talk |話</td><td></td><td></td><td>F</td></tr>
<tr><td>滿^3</td><td>水
85</td><td>㒼
563</td><td>Full, entire, |足
|洲 Manchu
|處 everywhere
|服 expiration of mourning
|漢 Manchus and Chinese
|心 whole heart; so |臉, |面, |身
|意 satisfied (in mind or heart)
|地 all over the ground
|月 a full month, first month from birth of child</td><td>S.</td><td></td><td>A</td></tr>
<tr><td>墁^4</td><td>土
32</td><td>曼
849</td><td>To cover, pave |地
|磚 pave with bricks
|地板 to lay board floor
|甬路 to make a raised walk</td><td></td><td></td><td>F</td></tr>
</table>

幔^{4}	巾 50	曼 849	Curtain, screen |·子 |幃 to screen off, a curtain		E
慢^{4}	心 61	曼 849	Slow, rude, negligent |·着 slowly, gently | |^{1}·的 |性 easy disposition, chronic |待 to treat rudely		A
漫^{42}	水 85	曼 849	Overflowing, boundless, diffuse; wild, reckless |過 to rise above |說 I venture to say		H
鏝^{4}	金 167	曼 849	錢|兒 Obverse of a coin	man^{2}	K

Mang

忙^{2}	心 61	亡 646	Haste, busy, flurried |·了 |中有錯 an error through haste |·裏偸閒 snatch a little leisure |亂 flurried, confused | |碌碌 very busy |·得很 |·不過來 have no time for |甚麼 what is your hurry?		B
氓^{2} 甿^{2}	氏 83	民 358	Fugitives, gypsies; the people 流| vagabonds, tramps	meng^{2}	G
盲^{2}	目 109	亡 646	Blind, |眼 eyeball gone |於心 blindness of heart		F
芒^{2}	艸 140	芒 648	The awn, beard of grain; a point |種 bearded grain; a solar term 麥| awn or beard of wheat ·牛| a clay herdsman, |神		G
茫^{2}	艸 140	芒 648	Vast, vague, indistinct 渺| | | far and wide		H
鋩^{2}	金 167	芒 648	Edge, sharp point 鋒|		F
莽^{3}	艸 140	莽 461	Jungle; confused; rude, | | |∘撞 carelessly, rude 鹵|		G

蟒³	虫 142	莽 461	Python, boa 丨 蟲 丨 袍 ceremonial robes			I

Mao

貓¹ 猫¹	豸 153	苗 817	The cat; 夜丨·子 screech-owl 丨 兒眼 cat's-eyes, beads 丨 洞兒 hole in door for cat 野丨 wild cat, hare			C
摸¹	手 64	莫 453	To feel, grope, 丨·不着 can't get, can't find out, no clue	俗	ma¹ mo¹	C
毛²	毛 82	毛 375	Hair, fur, feathers, 丨 錢 fractional silver money 丨 兒窩 wadded shoes 丨 管 quills 丨 孔 pores of the skin 丨 驢兒 a young donkey 丨 筆畫 painting with brush 丨 邊紙 buff writing paper 丨·病 fault 丨 瑟鎗 Mauser rifle or pistol 丨 毯 hair or skin rugs 丨 頭紙 sort of cheap paper 發丨 to become mouldy	S.		A
矛²	矛 110	矛 115	Lance, spear; inconsistent 自相丨盾 self-contradictory			E
茅²	艸 140	矛 115	Thatched, poor 丨 房 reed hut, water-closet 丨·厠 丨 塞 obstructing rushes or weeds	S.		G
錨²	金 167	苗 817	An anchor. 下丨 drop anchor 丨 纜 an anchor cable			E
旄²	方 70	㫃 265	Yak-tail (as a banner) 丨 牛 Tibetan yak			I
卯³	卩 26	卯 309	5-7 a. m., to muster, sign on: a mortise 丨·子工 work done by the day			G

冒4	冂 13	冒 845	To risk, counterfeit, rash ｜充 to falsely act as ｜險 venture, risk danger ｜認 to claim falsely ｜∘昧 blindly, rashly ｜名 to assume a name (falsely) ｜·失 rash, heedless ｜烟 to smoke, emit smoke		E
帽4	巾 50	冒 845	Hat, cap ｜·子 ｜架 hat-rack. ｜·匠 hatter ｜盒兒 hat box. ｜舖 hat shop ｜紇繨 knot on top of cap ｜沿 the rim of a cap		A
⿰氵冒4	水 85	冒 845	To rise and overflow ｜漿兒 sap is oozing out		K
瑁4	玉 96	冒 845	A kind of jade	mei4	K
貌4 皃4	豸 153	皃 685	Form, appearance, likeness ｜醜 ugly in features ｜美 handsome 美｜ 容｜ mien, manner, face 面∘｜		D
茂4	艸 140	戊 341	Luxuriant, flourishing ｜生 ｜盛 to flourish, abound		D
貿4	貝 154	卯 309	To barter, trade ｜·易 to deal, trade 互｜		F
耄4	老 125	老 189	70-90 years of age, old 年紀垂｜ an octogenarian		I

Mei

沒2 没2	水 85	𠬛 536	Not, none of, gone 俗 ｜瞧∘見 never seen, didn't notice ｜見過面 never saw him before ｜錢 out of money 錢｜·了 ｜志·氣 without ambition ｜出·息 useless; of no promise	mo4 mu24	A

Mei

沒^{2}			︱法^{2}子 there is no help for it ︱想到 didn't think of it ︱·了 dead; used up, no more ︱臉見人 no "face" to see any one ︱毛病 has no defect ︱·哪 not yet. ︱念過書 have never studied ︱·甚麼 nothing, there is none ︱多少 not many ︱影兒 not a shadow of ︱∘有 not to have, there is not ︱有·了 there is none, all gone ︱有的話 (or 事) impossible! false!	
眉^{2}	目 109	眉 846	Eyebrows ︱·毛 ︱批 notes at top of page	B
楣^{2}	木 75	眉 846	Lintel over door 門︱	F
媒^{2}	女 38	某 509	A go-between (esp. for marriage) ︱·人 ︱柬 papers in engagement	D
煤^{2}	火 86	某 509	Coal ︱炸^{3}兒 small coal, cinders ︱廠 a coal yard ︱·氣 coal gas. ︱球 coal-balls ︱礦 a coal-mine ︱窰 ︱山 Coal Hill in Peking ︱油 kerosene 烟兒︱ soft coal 硬︱ anthracite, hard coal 紅︱	C
梅^{2}	木 75	每 572	Plum; arbutus; syphilis S. ︱花 plum blossom 酸︱湯 sour prune drink 楊︱ arbutus; venereal ulcer	D
枚^{2}	木 75	攴 548	Classifier of fingers, coins, etc., a shrub, cane 三︱ three coppers	D

Mei

Character	Radical	Phonetic	Meaning		Frequency
玫[2] 玟[2]	玉 96	攴 548	Red rose 丨·瑰		F
霉[2]	雨 173	每 572	Mildew, damp		I
美[3]	羊 123	羊 151	Beautiful, excellent, 丨好, 丨麗 丨景 a fine bit of scenery 丨學 esthetics, fine arts 丨術 丨以丨會 Methodist Episcopal Church 丨意 kindly intention 丨人 a beauty 丨女 丨感 artistic taste 丨術思想 丨·國 United States of America 丨貌 handsome countenance 丨色 丨事 a good thing 丨術館 art gallery 丨地 fine land 肥丨地土 丨才 great talent 丨味 luscious, delicious		B
每[3]	毋 80	每 572	Each, every, 丨回 each time; so 丨日, 丨天, 丨月, 丨年 丨一件事 each matter 丨人·一分 each man a share 丨到年·下 at each year-end 丨次 on each occasion		B
妹[4]	女 38	未 495	Younger sister 丨丨 丨丈 younger sister's husband 丨·夫		A
寐[4]	宀 40	未 495	To sleep, rest 丨息 寢而不丨 lie down but not sleep		H
昧[4]	日 72	未 495	Obscure, dark, 暗丨; to hide 丨·起來 to hide, secrete 丨良·心 ungrateful 丨心 蒙丨 ignorant		D
魅[4]	鬼 194	未 495	An ogre		I

媚⁴	女 38	眉 846	To smirk, flatter, fawn; love | 言 | 語 flattering words 諂 | flattery | 人 to flatter		F
袂⁴	衣 145	夬 482	Sleeve of robe. 攘 | roll sleeve 分 | to take leave of one		I
瑁⁴	玉 96	冒 845	Tortoise shell 玳 |	mao⁴	K

Men

們¹²	人 9	門 635	Sign of plural 我·| we, 俺·| 弟兄·| brothers; fellow soldiers		A
捫¹²	手 64	門 635	To lay hand on, grope; cover | 心 自問 to examine self		F
門² 门²	門 169	門 635	Gate, door; sect, school, family | 插關 bolt of a door | 風 family reputation | 下 in the family; a disciple | 壻 son-in-law | 戶 a door, a family | 環子 knocker of a door | 人 disciple, pupil |∘生, | 徒 | 檻 threshold of a door | 口兒 entrance, door | 框 door-frame | 簾 door-screens or curtains | 樓 rooms over city-gate |·路 an occupation; opening; clue |∘徑 | 楣 lintel of door |∘面 shop-front | 扇 a door, or leaf of door |·上 gate-keeper | 公, 看 |·的 |∘神 door gods | 閂 bar across door inside | 當戶對 a suitable marriage		A

Character	Radical	Phonetic	Meaning		
門²			｜墩 stone under door frame ｜外 out of doors		
悶⁴ 懣⁴ 懣⁴	心 61	門 635	Depressed, melancholy; cover ｜·氣 concealed anger, dumps ｜·作·了 puzzled; can't answer 納｜ ｜火 cover fire with ashes ｜熱 stifling hot, muggy ｜｜不樂 very melancholy 憂｜ ｜·得慌 dull, sad, ennui ｜坐 sitting in silence		D

Meng

Character	Radical	Phonetic	Meaning		
蒙¹	艸 140	蒙 289	To cheat, hoodwink｜蔽 ｜·哄人 to humbug a person	meng²³	D
濛¹²	水 85	蒙 289	Drizzle, mist ｜｜細雨 drizzling rain		H
朦¹²	月 74	蒙 289	Dawn. ｜｜亮兒 first glimmer of dawn		H
蒙²	艸 140	蒙 289	To cover, receive favor, dull, untaught child S. ｜情 receive favor from equal ｜恩 receive favor ｜學 infant education 啓｜,訓｜ ｜昧 grossly ignorant ｜童 pupil, untaught child ｜藥水 chloroform	meng¹³	D
幪²	巾 50	蒙 289	Covering, screen, awning 帡｜ ｜·上 to cover		K
矇²	目 109	蒙 289	Dim, dull, blind, ignorant 困眼｜朧		G
盟²	皿 108	明 796	Covenant, oath, swear contract, alliance ｜兄弟 sworn brothers ｜約 a treaty, a compact 聯｜ alliance 同｜國 Entente Powers		C

Meng

Character	Radical	Phonetic	Meaning			
萌²	艸 140	明 796	To sprout, bud ｜想 the first risings of thought ｜念 ｜芽 to put forth buds or shoots			F
氓² 甿²	氏 83	民 358	The people, vagrants, fugitives, gypsies 流｜ 編｜take census of people		mang²	G
蝱²	虫 142	亡 646	Horse-fly, gadfly 牛｜,瞎｜ 木｜bee-like fly in trees			H
蒙³	艸 140	蒙 289	Mongolia ｜·古		meng¹²	D
蠓³	虫 142	蒙 289	Sand-flies ｜蠛 ｜蚋 dung-flies			H
猛³	犬 94	孟 605	Fierce, violent, brave; hot ｜進 radical reform ｜◦撞 fiercely rush into ｜性 fierce disposition ｜虎 fierce tiger, ferocious ｜獸 ｜然 suddenly, rapidly ｜烈 ferocious, brave			E
蜢³	虫 142	孟 605	Grasshopper 草｜,蚱｜ ｜◦虫 small fly, midge			I
懵³ 懜³	心 61	夢 276	Stupid, dull; senile ｜◦懂 thick-headed, stupid ｜｜無知 stupid and ignorant			I
夢⁴ 梦⁴	夕 36	夢 276	Dream, obscure, phantasm; visionary ｜兆 prognostic in a dream ｜間 in a dream ｜·裏 ｜·見 to see in a dream ｜想 dreamy thoughts, reveries ｜醒 awake from dream ｜話 visionary language ｜魘 the nightmare			B
孟⁴	子 39	孟 605	Eminent, eldest; Mencius, ｜春 first month of spring ｜·夫子³ Mencius, ｜軻, ｜子³ ｜浪 careless, rough	S.		D

Mi

Character	Radical	Phonetic	Meaning		
迷^{2}	辵 162	米 517	To delude, lead astray, confused ｜·惑 be deceived, deluded ｜路 lose the road ｜途 ｜心 infatuation ｜信 superstition ｜·｜忽忽 absent-minded ｜失 to lose, stray		C
謎^{24}	言 149	米 517	A riddle, conundrum, ｜語,隱語 破｜ask or solve riddle -mer^{4}	mei^{4}	F
彌^{2}	弓 57	爾 564	Long, distant; very; to fill, full, close up ｜縫 to mend; fill up crack ｜勒佛 Maitreya, the expected Buddha ｜補 to fill up, mend ｜賽亞 Messiah, Christ ｜月 a full month after birth		D
糜^{2}	米 119	麻 494	Cooked soft, congee; dissolved S. ｜粥 rice-gruel		G
米^{3}	米 119	米 517	Hulled rice, grain, 白米 rice S ｜飯 cooked rice or millet ｜粉 rice flour ｜糠 rice husks or chaff ｜粒 rice grains ｜·湯 congee, gruel ｜店 a rice shop ｜莊 ｜°突 metre, 39.37 inches 小｜millet		C
眯^{32}	目 109	米 517	Blinded ｜·了眼睛 blinded, as by dust		G
靡^{3}	非 175	麻 494	Extravagant, to waste; not ｜費 extravagant, wasteful ｜麗 luxurious		E

<table>
<tr><td>弭^{3}</td><td>弓
57</td><td>耳
626</td><td>To remove, stop; put down
| 兵會 Peace Society</td><td></td><td>I</td></tr>
<tr><td>密^{4}</td><td>宀
40</td><td>必
378</td><td>Close, dense, thick; secret
| 切 close connection, intimate
| 事 a secret affair
| 言 secrets, private talk
| 約 a secret treaty
| 友 an intimate friend</td><td></td><td>C</td></tr>
<tr><td>秘^{4}
祕^{4}</td><td>禾
115</td><td>必
378</td><td>Secret, occult, private
| 訣 the secret, "mysteries"
|·密 secret, private
| 書 private secretary</td><td>pi^{4}</td><td>C</td></tr>
<tr><td>蜜^{4}</td><td>虫
142</td><td>必
378</td><td>Honey 蜂 |
| 餞 comfits, preserves
| 房 the honey-comb
|∘蜂 the honey bee
|·蠟 bees-wax
| 語 "sweet talk", flattery</td><td></td><td>D</td></tr>
<tr><td>覓^{4}
覔^{4}</td><td>見
147</td><td>見
865</td><td>To seek, hunt for | 索
| 訪 inquire after, search out
| 人 search for person, hire</td><td></td><td>G</td></tr>
<tr><td>冖^{4}</td><td>冖
14</td><td>冂
556</td><td>To cover</td><td></td><td>K</td></tr>
<tr><td>糸^{4}</td><td>糸
120</td><td>糸
886</td><td>Floss silk, delicate; used for 絲</td><td></td><td>K</td></tr>
</table>

Miao

<table>
<tr><td>喵^{1}</td><td>口
30</td><td>苗
817</td><td>| | mew of cat</td><td></td><td>H</td></tr>
<tr><td>苗^{2}</td><td>艸
140</td><td>苗
817</td><td>Sprouts, shoots S.
| 裔 descendants
|·子 Miao tribes</td><td></td><td>D</td></tr>
<tr><td>描^{2}</td><td>手
64</td><td>苗
817</td><td>To trace, draw, paint, depict, copy
| 寫 to sketch, trace, describe
| 畫 paint a picture
| 字 to copy writing</td><td></td><td>F</td></tr>
</table>

杪[3]	木 75	少 122	Tip, end 丨末, limit 枝丨 tip of branch			I
渺[3]	水 85	少 122	Vast, vague, doubtful 丨◦茫 丨丨 boundless, indistinct			G
眇[3] 緲[3]	目 109	少 122	Small, insignificant; one-eyed 丨一目 having but one eye 丨微 small, minute			C
秒[3]	禾 115	少 122	Least mite, a second, a ten-thousandth 一丨鐘 a second of time			D
藐[3]	艸 140	皃 685	To slight, disdain, despise 丨法 in contempt of law 丨視 treat with contempt			E
杳[3]	木 75	木 484	Obscure, dark, distant 丨遠 in the obscure distance		yao[3]	H
廟[4] 庙[4]	广 53	朝 16	Temple shrine; temple fair 丨主 manager of temple ·丨宇 temple, Taoist temple 逛丨 to visit temples 祖丨 ancestral temple			A
妙[4]	女 38	少 122	Admirable; mysterious, subtle 丨計 a capital plan 丨法, 丨術 丨訣 abstruse, occult 奧◦丨			D
謬[4]	言 149	翏 283	Error 丨悞, misleading 丨言 lies, falsehood	S.	miu[4] niu[4]	D

Mieh

咩[1] 哶[1]	口 30	羊 151	Bleating of sheep 丨丨 丨羊 the cry of a sheep 羊丨 a kid, lamb			H
乜[14]	乙 5	乙 297	Eyes crossing, to squint 丨斜着眼 squint-eyed	S.	nieh[1]	I
滅[4] 威[4]	水 85	戌 342	To destroy, extinguish, cut off 丨種 race extinction 丨息 to extinguish 丨·了			C

<table>
<tr><td>滅^{4}</td><td></td><td></td><td>|火 extinguish a fire; so |燈
|國 destroy a country
|·不了^{3} unable to extinguish
|·亡 exterminated, perished</td><td></td><td></td></tr>
<tr><td>蔑^{4}</td><td>艸
140</td><td>蔑
343</td><td>Without, not, small; throw away
|有 there is none</td><td></td><td>I</td></tr>
<tr><td>篾^{4}</td><td>竹
118</td><td>蔑
343</td><td>Bamboo splints, strips, laths
竹| splints for basket-work</td><td>nieh^{4}</td><td>I</td></tr>
<tr><td>衊^{4}</td><td>血
143</td><td>蔑
343</td><td>To defile, pollute 汚|
血| stain with blood</td><td></td><td>K</td></tr>
</table>

Mien

<table>
<tr><td>棉^{2}</td><td>木
75</td><td>帛
806</td><td>Cotton, downy; spreading
|襖 wadded coat
|·花 raw cotton
|·花線 cotton thread |線
|衣·裳 cotton clothes |衣·服
|布 cotton cloth
|子^{3} cotton seed</td><td></td><td>C</td></tr>
<tr><td>綿^{2}
緜^{2}</td><td>糸
120</td><td>帛
806</td><td>Downy, soft; continuous, lasting; ripening; weak
|長^{2} lasting, perpetual
|紙 coarse paper
|綢 silk and cotton mixture
|軟 soft, pliant, flexible
|羊 the sheep. |羊絨 wool</td><td></td><td>D</td></tr>
<tr><td>眠^{2}</td><td>目
109</td><td>民
358</td><td>To close eyes, sleep
|睡 to sleep 睡|, 安|
催|術 hypnotism</td><td></td><td>F</td></tr>
<tr><td>宀^{2}</td><td>宀
40</td><td>冂
556</td><td>A roof, shelter</td><td></td><td>K</td></tr>
<tr><td>免^{3}</td><td>儿
10</td><td>免
384</td><td>Avoid, remit, forgive
|戰 to avoid a battle
|戰旗 flag of truce |戰牌
|見 to decline seeing
|除 remit (as charges or penalty)</td><td></td><td>B</td></tr>
</table>

Mien

免[3]
- |職 put out of office
- |·去 to avoid, reject
- |課 excuse from lesson
- |禮 omit ceremony
- |票 a pass on railway
- |稅單 exemption certificate
- |·得 to avoid, lest
- |租 (糧) remit rent or taxes
- |罪 forgive an offence 赦|

勉[3] — 力 19 — 免 384 — Earnest effort, to arouse — B
- |强[3] to force, compel
- |·勵 urge to activity
- |勵會 Christian Endeavor Society

冕[3] — 冂 13 — 免 384 — Cap, crown, diadem |旒 — D
- 冠| crown, coronet

娩[3] — 女 38 — 免 384 — To bear a child — wan[3] — H
- 分| child-birth

愐[3] — 心 61 — 面 766 — To consider; bashful, modest — H
- |㥏 shy, timid, bashful

面[4] — 面 176 — 面 766 — Face, side, surface; honor — A
- |見 to visit; see face to face
- |∘前 before; in front of
- |謝 thank personally
- |議 discuss verbally |講, |商
- |軟 bashful, sheepish
- |·貌 the countenance 臉|, |·目
- |·上 the surface
- |生 a strange face
- |·子 face; social standing

麵[4] 麪[4] — 麥 199 — 面 766 — Wheat flour, vermicelli — C
- |案 trencher, kneading-board
- |酵 yeast, leaven
- |粉 flour. |包 bread
- |條 strips of dough boiled
- 切·| noodles
- 掛| fine vermicelli

Min

民[2]	氏 83	民 358	People, citizens, ｜人 ｜氣 public sentiment ｜間 among the people ｜質 national characteristics ｜情 popular feeling ｜主 democracy ｜主國 a Republic ｜權 power, or rights, of people ｜法 civil law. ｜庭 court ｜房 private houses ｜風 popular disposition, custom ｜變 rebellion of the people ｜黨 people's party ｜族主義 nationalism		B
珉[2] 砇[2]	玉 96	民 358	A stone resembling jade, alabaster ｜石 ｜玉 a white stone of fine texture 白｜ pure white alabaster		I
閩[3]	門 169	門 635	Kind of serpent; Fukien ｜省 ｜江 Min River		G
閔[3]	門 169	閔 635a	To feel for, grieve for; urge 痛｜ sorely grieved	S.	G
憫[3]	心 61	閔 635a	Sympathize, pity, grieve 憐｜ ｜恤 to compassionate ｜惜		C
皿[3]	皿 108	皿 604	Utensil, vessel 器｜ plates, dishes, etc.		D
敏[3]	攴 66	敏 573	Clever, diligent, active, quick ｜捷 quick, acute ｜慧 perspicuity, sharpness ｜愼 careful, attentive		E
抿[3] 㨉[3]	手 64	民 358	To feel, smooth, stroke ｜頭 to brush the hair ｜·子 woman's hair-brush		H

泯³	水 85	民 358	Confused, to destroy | 滅 | 沒 to obliterate		H
脗³	肉 130	勿 233	To join, match, blend |·着嘴笑 pucker lips in smiles	wen³	K
黽³	黽 205	黽 316	A toad; to strive for | 勉 to use effort		K

Ming

明²	日 72	明 796	Bright, plain; understand; dawn; a dynasty, A.D. 1368-1644 S. |∘朝 the Ming dynasty | 知故犯 intentionally transgress | 知故問 quiz to embarrass | 兒個 to-morrow | 日, |·天 | 顯 self-evident | 信片 post card | 夥 daring robbers | 溝 an open sewer | 亮 bright, splendid | | 白白 clear, evident, | | |·年 next year 來年 |·白 to understand, | 了³ | 說 to state openly or frankly |·天見 good bye 再見		A
名²	口 30	名 270	Name, |·字; fame, reputation | 稱 name, called | 叫 |·分 fame, position, duty | 號 epithet, designation | 賢集 sayings of wise men | 醫 a famous physician | 人 famous men | 利 fame and profit |·目 name, reputation | 片 a visiting card |·聲 fame, reputation |·譽, |·望 | 詞 noun, terminology | 譽會長 honorary chairman		B

茗²	艸 140	名 270	Tea-leaves ｜茶 tea of any sort		H
酩²	酉 164	名 270	Spirit made from barley 麥｜ ｜酊 very drunk		G
銘²	金 167	名 270	To engrave, carve｜刻 ｜記在心 engraven on the mind		H
鳴²	鳥 196	鳥 253	Cry of bird; to cry; sound ｜鑼 to strike a gong ｜砲 fire a salute ｜冤 call attention to wrongs		F
冥²	冖 14	冥 797	Dark, deep, Hades ｜府 the grave, Hades｜間 ｜衣 paper clothes		G
溟²	水 85	冥 797	Vast sea; fine rain｜｜ 北｜Arctic regions		I
瞑²	目 109	冥 797	To close eyes, death; dim ｜目而去 closed eyes in death		I
命⁴	口 30	令 438	To command; decree; life, fate ｜案 a case of murder ｜長² long life, old age; so｜短 ｜好 a good fortune ｜該如此 it is fated ｜·令 orders, mandates 誡｜ ｜薄 a "thin fate", ill-fated ｜∘運 destiny, cycle of life 性｜life 生·｜		B

Miu

謬⁴	言 149	翏 283	False, random, mistake, error (see niu⁴)	miao⁴ niu⁴	D

Mo

摩¹	手 64	麻 494	To feel, rub ｜·索 stroke gently; grope for	mo²	C

Mo

Character	Radical	Phonetic	Meaning	Other reading	Grade
麽^{1} 庅^{1}	麻 200	麻 494	Interrogative, a sort, also ironically 甚·｜ what? 他來·｜ will he come? –·me	ma^{1}	A
摸^{1}	手 64	莫 453	To feel, grope ｜·着黑走 grope way in dark ｜·不着^{2} nonplussed; can't find ｜·不清 can't make out ｜·索 feel with hand, stroke ｜·得着 can make it out ｜魚 feel about for fish	ma^{1} mao^{1}	C
糢^{1}	米 119	莫 453	Indistinct, confused ｜·｜ 糊糊, ｜·糊不清		C
蟆^{14}	虫 142	莫 453	Frog 蛤·｜ 文	ma^{12}	F
摩^{2}	手 64	麻 494	To feel of; rub, polish 揣｜ feel after, estimate	mo^{1}	C
磨^{2}	石 112	麻 494	Grind, rub, sharpen, polish ｜光 to burnish 打｜, ｜明 ｜鍊 to work or study hard ｜難 afflictions, distress ｜刀石 a whetstone ｜·蹭 to fumble; be lazy, fuss	mo^{4}	B
蘑^{2} 藦^{2}	艸 140	麻 494	Mushrooms ｜·菇		H
饝^{2}	食 184	麻 494	Feed infant by hand ｜·｜ steamed bread		H
魔^{2}	鬼 194	麻 494	Devil, demon ｜鬼 ｜力 fascination, magnetism ｜羅 Buddhist Evil One—Mara		C
摹^{2}	手 64	莫 453	Write over a copy, to copy ｜寫 ｜仿 copy a pattern	mu^{2}	G
模^{2}	木 75	莫 453	A model, pattern ｜範, ｜·子 ｜範監獄 model prison ｜·糊 blurred, indistinct 規｜ rules and regulations ; scale of an undertaking	mu^{2}	D

Mo

Character	Radical	Phonetic	Meaning	Other readings	Class
謨^{2}	言 149	莫 453	To plan; practise, imitate 嘉 | a capital plan	mu^{2}	G
抹^{3}	手 64	末 496	To rub out, efface, obliterate |·去 to abolish | 粉 apply face powder | 零 to forego (collecting) the change |·上點油 rub on a little oil	mo^{4}	C
邈^{34}	辵 162	皃 685	Deep; high; far off, abstruse 遙 | far off, distant		I
墨^{4}	土 32	黑 831	Black, ink; obscure | 黑 jet black | 西哥 Mexico | 水 ink, | 水壺 ink stand | 斗兒 carpenter's marking box		A
默^{4} 嘿^{4}	黑 203	黑 831	Retired, secret, silent, quiet | 記 inwardly remember | 想 contemplate, meditate | 念 | 寫 write out from memory | 許 a silent assent | 認 | 感 inspiration | 示 revelation | 禱 secret prayer		E
𠬛^{4}	又 29	𠬛 536	To dive under water		P
歿^{4}	歹 78	𠬛 536	To die, perish | 於陣 died in battle	mu^{24}	G
沒^{4}	水 85	𠬛 536	To submerge, set; die |·過腿·了 more than knee-deep |·了人·了 higher than a man | 藥 myrrh 沉 | sunk, perished 日 | the sun sets 淹 |·了 drowned, kept in obscurity	mei^{2} mu^{24}	A
末^{4}	木 75	末 496	End, branches, last; dust | 章 the last chapter; so | 節		B

Mo

末[4]
| 後 afterwards, at last |·| 了兒[3]
| 日 last day, end of world | 時
| 世 the last age; one's end
|·子 dust of any kind
| 次 last occasion, near end
| 尾 the rear, hind part

抹[4] 手 64 末 496 To rub on, color — mo[3] — C
| 角 to go round a corner
| 灰 rub on some lime
|·子 a trowel

沫[4] 水 85 末 496 Froth, foam |·子 — E
唾·| spittle t'u[4]-

茉[4] 艸 140 末 496 |·莉 white jasmine — H

磨[4] 石 112 麻 494 A mill-stone | 盤 (石) — mo[2] — B
|∘房 a mill-room
|·過來 to turn round
| 麪 to grind flour
|·不開臉 can't avoid loss of "face"

脈[4] 脉[4] 衇[4] 肉 130 血 143 𠂢 350 Veins, arteries; pulse; grain of wood; water-course; line of thought; mt. system 山 | — mai[4] — D
| 氣 constitution
診 | feel the pulse 號十, 看 | 評 |

莫[4] 艸 140 莫 453 Not, do not, if, perhaps S. — mu[4] — E
| 非 isn't it? certainly is |·不是
| 若 much better, nothing like
| 怪 don't be angry, don't blame
| 大之恩 unbounded grace
| 談國事 don't discuss politics
| 作 do not do it | 爲

寞[4] 宀 40 莫 453 Still, quiet, solitary 寂 | — H
| 落 fallen into decay

漠[4] 水 85 莫 453 Sandy plain, sandy — H
沙 | a desert, Gobi

Character	Radical	Phonetic	Meaning	Alt.	
膜[4]	肉 130	莫 453	Filmy skin, membrane ｜視 ignore, disregard 膈｜separation, misunderstanding		E
陌[4]	阜 170	百 805	Street, road, market-place 街｜market street		K

Mou

Character	Radical	Phonetic	Meaning	Alt.	
謀[2]	言 149	某 509	Scheme, plot; to plan ｜反 treason, plot rebellion ｜害 to plot mischief ｜畫 sketch out, a plan ｜衣食 to plan for a living ｜生 ｜略 military strategy, plot ｜殺 plot murder; to murder ｜士 a counsellor of state ｜事 to seek employment		D
牟[2]	牛 93	牛 38	To usurp, encroach; barley ｜尼 Buddha, Shakyamuni		K
眸[2]	目 109	牛 38	Eye-pupil ｜子[3] 凝｜fix the eye, stony gaze		H
某[3] 厶[3]	木 75	某 509	A certain one, "so-and-so", ｜｜ ｜處 a certain place ｜人 a certain person, so-and-so ｜日 a certain day	mu³	B
畝[3] 畆[3]	田 102	田 809	Chinese acre ─ ｜地 一百｜爲一頃 100 mou = 1 ch'ing³ 地｜acres, land	mu³	C
牡[3]	牛 93	牛 38	Male of quadrupeds	mu³	F
丘[3]	一 1	丘 213	Confucius' name	ch'iu¹	G
拇[3]	手 64	母 571	Thumb, great toe 大｜指	mu³	H
懋[4]	心 61	矛 115	Great, energetic, exert self 功｜｜賞 great reward to great merit		K

Mu

<table>
<tr><td>歿^{24}</td><td>歹
78</td><td>𠬛
536</td><td>To die (see mo^4)</td><td></td><td>mo^4</td><td>G</td></tr>
<tr><td>沒^{24}
没^{24}</td><td>水
85</td><td>𠬛
536</td><td>Not, none, has not</td><td>俗</td><td>mei^2
mo^4</td><td>A</td></tr>
<tr><td>摹^2</td><td>手
64</td><td>莫
453</td><td>To copy, follow, write over copy
描 | copy a drawing</td><td></td><td>mo^2</td><td>G</td></tr>
<tr><td>模^2</td><td>木
75</td><td>莫
453</td><td>A model, pattern, |·子, | 範
| 樣 manner, fashion, pattern</td><td></td><td>mo^2</td><td>D</td></tr>
<tr><td>謨^2</td><td>言
149</td><td>莫
453</td><td>Consult; imitate; a plan
謀 | to plan, scheme</td><td></td><td>mo^2</td><td>G</td></tr>
<tr><td>母^3</td><td>毋
80</td><td>母
571</td><td>Mother |·親, female
| 雞 hen, | 猪 a sow
| 校 alma mater
| 音 a vowel
祖 | paternal grandmother</td><td></td><td></td><td>A</td></tr>
<tr><td>姆^3
姥^3</td><td>女
38</td><td>母
571</td><td>Matron, dame, elderly widow</td><td></td><td>lao^3</td><td>G</td></tr>
<tr><td>拇^3</td><td>手
64</td><td>母
571</td><td>Thumb, great toe 大 | 指
| 戰 to play mora—a game of guessing fingers</td><td></td><td>mou^3</td><td>H</td></tr>
<tr><td>某^3</td><td>木
75</td><td>某
509</td><td>A certain one</td><td>文</td><td>mou^3</td><td>B</td></tr>
<tr><td>畝^3
畆^3</td><td>田
102</td><td>田
809</td><td>Chinese acre一 | 地
| 數 acres 地 |
一百 | 爲一頃 100 mu=1 ch'ing^3</td><td></td><td>mou^3</td><td>C</td></tr>
<tr><td>牡^3</td><td>牛
93</td><td>牛
38</td><td>Male of animals; peony
| 牝 male and female of animals
|·丹花 the tree-peony</td><td></td><td>mou^3</td><td>F</td></tr>
<tr><td>木^4</td><td>木
75</td><td>木
484</td><td>Wood, |·頭, tree; stupid
| 廠子 a timber yard
|·器 wood-ware
|·匠 a carpenter | 作</td><td></td><td></td><td>B</td></tr>
</table>

Mu

木^{4}

| 掀 wooden shovel | 杴
| 星 the planet Jupiter
| 蘭花 magnolia
| 料 timber, | 板 a plank
| 偶 wooden image; blockhead
|·梳 a large wooden comb
| 炭 charcoal
| 桶 a barrel, commode
| 曜日 Thursday

沐^{4} — 水 85 — 木 484 — F
To wash, bathe | 浴
| 恩 receive favors

目^{4} — 目 109 — 目 841 — B
Eye; class, index; perception
| 前 before eyes; at present |∘下
| 力 strength of sight, vision
|·錄 index, inventory
|∘的 object, aim, purpose -oti^{4}
|∘的達到 attain one's object -oti^{4}-
| 次 table of contents

苜^{4} — 艸 140 — 目 841 — G
Clover, alfalfa | 蓿

莫^{4} — 艸 140 — 莫 453 — 俗 — mo^{4} — E
Shady; evening, late
歲 | the close of the year

募^{4} — 力 19 — 莫 453 — D
To invite, enlist, solicit
| 捐 solicit contributions
| 兵 raise troops

墓^{4} — 土 32 — 莫 453 — C
A grave, tomb 墳 |
| 碑 a tombstone
掃 | sweep graves at Ch'ing Ming

幕^{4} 幙^{4} — 巾 50 — 莫 453 — F
Screen, tent, curtain, 帳 |
| 府 military headquarters
| 賓 a private secretary 作 |
黑 | ways that are dark

慕^{4} — 心 61 — 莫 453 — D
Long for, love, fond of 愛 | S.
| 容 double surname S.
| 道 long to find the Truth
羨·| long for, desire greatly

Character	Radical	Phonetic	Meaning		Other readings	Grade
暮^{4}	日 72	莫 453	Sunset 日 |, evening, end | 年 old age, declining year | 歲			G
牧^{4}	牛 93	牛 38	Shepherd, to pasture, | 師 pastor (Protestant) | 童 shepherd's boy, herd boy | 羊 to keep sheep, so | 牛 | 養 to feed, nourish	S		C
睦^{4}	目 109	坴 47	Friendly, harmonious 和∘| 親 | cordial, neighborly			C
穆^{4}	禾 115	禾 510	Solemn, profound, reverent | 罕默德 Mahomet, | 迦 Mecca	S		F

Na

Character	Radical	Phonetic	Meaning		Other readings	Grade
那^{1}	邑 163	那 143	Surname also see nai^{3}, nei^{34}, no^{2}	S	na^{34}	A
哪^{1}	口 30	那 143	Interrog, particle; final sound 沒·| not yet.Char. also used for 那^{3}		no^{2}	A
拿^{2} 拏^{2} 挐^{2}	手 64 減	合 708	To take, seize, grasp, carry | 茶當酒 look on tea as wine |·住 to take, grasp firmly |·出來 to take out, abstract |·去 take away |·開 | 獲 to apprehend, seize 捉 | |·來 bring, |·過來 bring here |·不着^{2} cannot seize, get hold |·不出 can't get it out |·不下 can't take down |·不上 can't take up |·不得 should not be taken |·不動 can't lift off ground | 定主^{2}意 to come to a decision | 賊 to apprehend a thief			A
那^{3}	邑 163	那 143	Where? what? which? |·個 | 兒呢 how is that? where is it? | 兒的 where? whence? | 裏的		na^{14} nai^{34} nei^{34} no^{2}	A

那^{3}

| 兒的話 what sort of talk! nonsense!
|·一個 which one? |·個
|·裏 where? whence?
|·裏知道 how do you know?
| 怕 no matter if

那^{4} 邑 163 那 143 There, that, |·個 — na^{13}, nai^{3}, nei^{34}, no^{2} — A
| 兒 there |·邊, |·裏
| 何用說 that goes without saying
|·些 those |·些個
|◦塊 that one, that piece; there
|·麼 thus |·麼着 — ne(m)^{4}
|·麼樣 in that way, thus, then — ne(m)^{4}
|·樣 that sort or style
| 也好 that is all right too

內^{4} 入 11 内 444 Insert in, receive 文 — nei^{4} — B

納^{4} 糸 120 内 444 To receive; pay tax — D
| 福 to enjoy happiness
| 貢 to pay tribute
| 粮 pay taxes, | 稅 pay duties
| 悶 sorrowful, melancholy
悅 | receive with approval

衲^{4} 衣 145 内 444 To patch, line, quilt — F
| 鞋底子 quilt soles of shoes
| 衣 robe of Buddhist priests

捺^{4} 手 64 大 451 To press with the hand; a stroke to the right in writing — H
|·着氣 to suppress wrath
按 | to press firmly down

Nai

那^{3} 邑 163 那 143 Which? what? |·一個, |·一位 俗 — na^{134} — A

乃^{3}	丿 4	乃 216	But, is, also, then, however ｜若是 but as it is ｜可 it will then do ｜是 but is, yes		D
奶^{3} 嬭^{3} 妳^{3}	女 38	乃 216	Breasts; milk; to suckle ｜茶 tea with milk in it ｜·着孩子 suckling a child ｜媽子 a wet-nurse ｜名 milk-name, given at 1 mo. ｜·｜ paternal grandmother ｜捲 cream roll ｜皮 cream ｜餅 cheese. ｜油 butter		A
那^{4}	邑 163	那 143	There, that ｜·邊，｜·個 俗 ｜·樣兒 that sort or style	na^{134}	A
耐^{4}	而 126	而 612	To endure, bear, patient 忍｜ ｜·着 patiently endure ｜煩 put up with annoyance ｜·性兒 patient disposition ｜冷 to stand the cold ｜不住 cannot put up with		C
奈^{4}	大 37	大 451	Remedy; alternative, what, how ｜何 what remedy? how can I? 無可｜何 without resource 無｜ no help for it, unfortunately		C
褦^{4}	衣 145	能 324	Stupid, gross; defiled	lai^{1}	I

Nan

男^{2}	田 102	田 809	Male, man, son ｜兒^{2} a male child ｜子^{3} ｜·人 a man; a husband ｜女 male and female ｜女平權 equality of sexes ｜女同校 co-education ｜色 sodomy		A

Nan

Character	Radical	Phonetic	Definition	Other readings	Grade
南[2]	十 24	南 591	South 丨方 丨極 the South Pole 丨·京 Nanking 丨蠻 southern barbarians 丨門 south gate 丨北 north and south 指丨針 compass 定丨針		A
喃[2]	口 30	南 591	To chatter, gabble 呢丨 丨丨吶吶 muttering		G
楠[2] 枏[2]	木 75	南 591	A fine grained, west China wood like cedar 丨·木 伽丨 fragrant bead wood		G
難[2] 难[2]	隹 172	難 108	Difficult, to distress 丨成 hard to accomplish, so 丨忍, 丨明白, 丨辦, 丨說, 丨測, 丨做 丨·處 difficulties 丨容 inexcusable 丨堪 intolerable 丨看 grievous to look at 丨過 sad, in straits 丨保 cannot guarantee 丨·不住 cannot embarrass 丨事 a difficult affair 丨受 hard to bear, distressed 丨當[1] hard to bear, or to do 丨∘道 you can't mean to say 丨得 difficult to obtain; rare 丨聽 disagreeable to hear 丨走 bad travelling, hard to go 丨·爲 to trouble, vex (one) 丨聞 disagreeable to smell	nan[4]	A
暖[3] 煖[3]	日 72	爰 187	Warm, mild 丨·和 -·huo 俗	nang[3] nuan[3]	A
蝻[3]	虫 142	南 591	Immature locust 丨·子, 蝗丨		H

赧^{3}	赤 155	赤 423	To blush | 顏, redden 驚 | redden on detection		I
唵^{3}	口 30	奄 810	To gobble up, hold in mouth 俗	an^{13}	K
難^{4}	隹 172	難 108	Calamity, trouble 災 |, 苦 | | 民 distressed people, refugee 患 | misfortunes	nan^{2}	A

Nang

囊^{2}	口 30	襄 369	Bag, sack, purse | 袋 錢 | purse, wallet, 行 | traveling bag, baggage		E
囔^{2}	口 30	襄 369	To speak indistinctly 嘟·| grumble and mutter		I
暖^{3} 煖^{3}	日 72	爰 187	Warm, mild |·和 --huo 俗	nan^{3} nuan^{3}	A
攮^{3}	手 64	襄 369	To fend off, push from; stab |·死人 stab to death 推 | to ward off		I
曩^{3}	日 72	襄 369	Of old, formerly | 昔, | 日 | 者 old times and events		I
儾^{4}	人 9	襄 369	Slow, dull, irresolute 倭·| slovenly, squalid; weak		I
灢^{4}	水 85	襄 369	Muddy, muddy water | 泥 精 | extremely muddy		I
齉^{4}	鼻 209	襄 369	A stoppage of the nose | 鼻 a nasal twang		K

Nao

㤮^{1}	心 61	柔 117	Worthless, inferior, trashy		I
撓^{2} 㧻^{2}	手 64	堯 391	To vex, scratch, disturb, pervert | 亂 to pervert; disturb | 破 scratch and tear open		E

Nao

撓^{2}			| 頭 scratch the head | 癢 scratch an itch		
鐃^{2}	金 167	堯 391	Hand-cymbals | 鈸 | 鈎 a double pronged hook		K
𡿺^{3}	川 47	𡿺 428	The brain		P
惱^{3}	心 61	𡿺 428	Vexed, irritated, resentful 煩 | | 恨 spite, hate; bother | 怒 extreme anger, indignation		E
瑙^{3} 碯^{3}	玉 96	𡿺 428	Agate, carnelian, jasper, etc. 瑪 | veined, colored stones of quartzose group | 威 Norway 挪威		F
腦^{3}	肉 130	𡿺 428	Brain, mind |·子, | 髓 | 筋 brain, (as organ of mind) | 系 nerves, | 蓋 the cranium, top of skull | 力 brain power | 病 brain-trouble | 門·子 the forehead |·袋 "brain-bag", the head | 瓜·子 |·袋疼 the head-ache 潮 | camphor		A
鬧^{4} 閙^{4}	門 191	門 638	Row, noise, disturb, bustle, scold | 飢荒 make disturbance | 亂子 |·着玩 play the fool, trifling |·出事來 create trouble | 風潮 | 鬼 to play tricks; haunted by ghosts | 脾氣 to exhibit temper | 嗓子 sore-throat | 天氣 unseasonable weather | 肚子 bowel trouble		B
𣨨^{4}	歹 78	𡿺 428	To poison		I

Nei

Character	Radical	Phonetic	Meaning			
那3	邑 163	那 143	Where? what? which? 丨·個 在丨兒 where?	俗	na134	A
那4	邑 163	那 43	There, that 丨·個 丨·邊 over there	俗	na134	A
內4	入 11	內 444	Within, inside, inner, native 丨政 home administration 丨姪 nephews on mother's side 丨親 wife's relations 丨中 in the midst, among them 丨行 versed in a business 丨心 the heart 丨人 my wife 丨容 contents 丨科 medical practice 丨裏 within; the particulars 丨病 internal disease 丨地 the interior, inland 丨政 (or務) 部 Board of Interior 分4丨 within one's prerogative 不在丨 not included 在丨 inclusive, included		na4	B

Nen

Character	Radical	Phonetic	Meaning			
嫩4 嫰4 嫩4	女 38	束 501	Tender, delicate, soft 丨肉 tender meat 丨芽 delicate shoots	俗	nun4	E

Neng

Character	Radical	Phonetic	Meaning			
噥1	口 30	農 357	Irrelevant talk		nung1	H

Character	Radical	Phonetic	Meaning		Variant	
能² 䏻²	肉 130	能 324	Ability, talent, to be able ｜以 able to ｜彀 ｜人 an able person ｜手 ｜·幹 power, ability ｜·耐 able to, enduring, ability ｜說 able to talk ｜言; so ｜算 全｜ almighty 無所不｜	S		A
農²	辰 161	農 357	To cultivate	俗	nung²	C
膿²	肉 130	農 357	Pus, matter ｜水 ｜瘡 an abscess ｜血 purulent sore, ulcer	俗	nung²	F
齈²	鼻 209	農 357	Nose-mucus	俗	nung²	G
弄⁴	廾 55	王 71	To toy with, do	俗	lung⁴ nung⁴	C
濘⁴	水 85	丁 2	Muddy, sloppy 泥｜		ning⁴	I

Ni

Character	Radical	Phonetic	Meaning		Variant	
呢¹	口 30	尼 725	Interrog. part., usually pronounced ·nê 他有甚麼病·｜ what is his disease?		ni²	A
尼²	尸 44	尼 725	To stop, ｜其行 ｜·姑 a Buddhist nun ｜·姑庵 nunnery 仲｜ Confucius			F
呢²	口 30	尼 725	To chatter ｜喃 ｜絨線 woollen yarn		ni¹	A
妮²	女 38	尼 725	Slave-girl 小｜·子			H
泥² 埿²	水 85	尼 725	Mud, miry ｜土 ｜牆 mud wall; to plaster walls ｜濘 muddy, sloppy ｜水 thin mud, muddy water ｜塑的 formed of clay, modeled ｜胎 mud idol, clay image ｜刀 a brick layer's tool		ni⁴	A

Ni

怩^{2}	心 61	尼 725	To blush 忸 | to blush with shame			H
倪^{2}	人 9	兒 684	Surname	S	i^{2}	G
霓^{2}	雨 173	兒 684	Rainbow 虹 |, variegated 彩 | colored, variegated			I
你^{3} 伱^{3}	人 9	小 121	You, thou (to inferiors & intimates) |·這個人 you fellow! | 個人 you yourself | 老 my good sir | 老人·家, |·們 you (plural) |·們倆 you two |·的 your, yours | 們的 plural | 我 you and I			A
擬^{3}	手 64	疑 479	To resemble, compare; propose, decide | 定 to decide, determine | 妥 比 | to compare			E
泥^{4}	水 85	尼 725	Bigoted, mulish 拘 | | 於風水 firm faith in geomancy		ni^{2}	A
屰^{4}	屮 45	屰 660	Disobedient			P
逆^{4}	辵 162	屰 660	Rebellious, disobey, contrary | 風 a contrary wind | 料 to anticipate, foresee | 流 against the stream | 子^{3} a disobedient son			C
搦^{4}	手 64	弱 245	To grasp, seize | 戰 provoke a battle			H
溺^{4}	水 85	弱 245	To drown | 死, sink | 愛 to dote upon		niao^{4}	F
匿^{4}	匸 23	匿 183	To hide, conceal; clandestine | 名帖 anonymous placard | 名書 anonymous book			F
暱^{4} 昵^{4}	日 72	匿 183	Approach, familiar | 近 親 | familiar, intimate 私 |			K

Character	Radical	Phonetic	Meaning		
䵑[4] 䵒[4]	黍 202	刄 222	Putty, |·子; cement, glue 上 |·子 put on some putty		G
膩[4]	肉 130		Greasy, unctuous |·子 油 | thickened grease, oily		H
疒[4]	疒 104		Sickness		K

Niang

Character	Radical	Phonetic	Meaning		
娘[2]	女 38	良 361	Mother, woman, girl |·家 wife's family | 兒倆 mother and daughter | 兒們 women, a woman |·子 |·| 廟 Temple of Chinese "Lucina"		A
孃[2]	女 38	襄 369	Oppressed with care; mother (for the preceding)		I
釀[24]	酉 164	襄 369	To brew, ferment; foment; cause, excite; produce | 酒 fermented wine, make wine |·出事來 resulted in trouble | 蜜 (bee) makes honey		H

Niao

Character	Radical	Phonetic	Meaning		
鳥[3]	鳥 196	鳥 253	A bird 飛 | | 鎗 a fowling piece | 叫喚 the cry of a bird | 鳴 | 哨 the singing of a bird | 窩 a bird's nest		C
尿[4] 溺[4]	尸 44	水 520	Urine, to urinate 撒 | | 壺 chamber pot, urinal | 盆 | 炕 to wet the bed | 床	sui[1]	H F

Nieh

Character	Radical	Phonetic	Meaning		
圼[1]	臼 134	圼 686	To fill up, a hole		P

揑^{1} 捏^{1}	手 64	圼 686	To knead; trump up; fabricate |·着 holding in the fingers | 弄 to mould, knead | 造 to forge, trump up | 做		D
捻^{14}	手 64	念 436	To pinch up, pick |·一·| | 花 to gather flowers | 果子 |·不住 cannot hold in fingers	nien^{3}	E
乜^{1}	乙 5	乙 297	Squint-eyed, to squint	mieh^{14}	I
孼^{4} 孽^{4}	子 39	辟 158	Retribution, ills; sin, crime, bastard | 障 retribution for one's evil (as bad children) 罪 | sin; retribution 自作 | evil brought on self		B
聶^{4}	耳 128	聶 633	To whisper, lisp; mix; S. used for 攝 | 許 co-ordination		H
鑷^{4}	金 167	聶 633	Forceps, nippers |·子 | 毛 pull out hairs		G
篾^{4}	竹 118	蔑 343	Bamboo splints, strips, laths 竹 | splints for basket-work	mieh^{4}	I
囓^{4}	口 30	㓞 147	Gnaw, bite; crunch in teeth | 牙 bite on something hard		K
臬^{4}	自 132	自 852	Provincial judge, limit, law | 限 boundary, impediment		K

Nien

年^{2}	干 51	午 37	Year | 分^{4}, age | 長^{3} the elder |·成 the year, crops, | 景, | 頭 |·紀 years, time, age | 歲 | 假^{4} New Year holidays | 節 | 前 previous year | 輕的 young in years | 少, 少 |, | 幼		A

Nien

年[2]
| 久 in the course of time | 深日久
| 初 first of the year | 頭
| 號 designation of the year
|·下 close of year | 底
| 限 limit of years
| 老 one advanced in years
| |.every year, annual
| 半 a year and a half
| 表 chronological table
| 月 year and months
前·| year before last
今·| this year 本 | , 現 |
去·| last year 頭 |
新 | New Year
明·| next year 來 |
拜 | to make New Year calls

拈[2] 手 64 占 720 — To pick out, pick up, draw lots — E
| 鬮 to draw lots
| 香 burn incense in hand
| 花 to pick flowers

粘[2] 米 119 占 720 — Glutinous, paste, to stick — chan[1] — B
| 住 to adhere
| 糕 a kind of pudding

鮎[2] 魚 195 占 720 — Cat-fish, sheat | 魚 — K

黏[2] 黍 202 占 720 — Glutinous rice, paste, sticky — E
| 米 glutinous rice
| 補 paste over wrong character

捻[3] 手 64 念 436 — To twist, spin | 線 — nieh[14] — E
|·不動 can't be twisted

趁[3] 走 156 念 436 — To pursue, run after 步 | — I
|·不上 can't catch up to

輦[3] 車 159 夫 465 — Imperial chariot; court — I
| 路 way through palace

攆3	手 64	夫 465	To expel, drive out 丨·出去 丨跑·了 driven out, ran away 丨·不動 can't budge him 丨走·了 expelled and gone		E
碾3	石 112	展 354	Upper millstone; to grind, roll, triturate 丨房 milling room 丨穀·子 thresh millet by rolling 丨米 husk rice by milling 丨磨·子 a mill-stone		F
輾3	車 159	展 354	To roll, crush by rolling	chan3	G
撚3	手 64	然 459	To twist in fingers, roll up 紙丨 twisted paper		F
念4	心 61	念 436	To reflect, study; read aloud 丨經 pray or chant prayers 丨咒 to recite charms 丨珠 count beads, a rosary 丨佛 recite the O-mi-to-fo 丨會 to memorize 丨熟·了 丨一遍 read once over 丨詩 to recite verses 丨書 to study, read books 丨誦 recite; chant, read aloud 丨·頭 cogitations, thoughts 紀丨 remember, anniversary		A
廿4 卄4	廿 55	十 13	Twenty, a score; also written 念	ju4	G

Nin

您2	心 61	小 121	Thou, you (polite form) ·丨·納 you, sir		C

Ning

<table>
<tr><td>寧^{2}
寗^{2}</td><td>宀
40</td><td>丁
2</td><td>To repose, peace; rather
| 靜 rest, tranquillity
| 肯 better, rather | 可
| 不 rather not, prefer not to
| 死 rather die, better die
| 願 I would rather</td><td></td><td></td><td>C</td></tr>
<tr><td>嚀^{2}</td><td>口
30</td><td>丁
2</td><td>To charge, enjoin 叮 |</td><td></td><td></td><td>I</td></tr>
<tr><td>擰^{2}</td><td>手
64</td><td>丁
2</td><td>To wring, to twist
| 乾了 twisted till dry
| 燈籠 make lantern of wire</td><td></td><td>ning^{34}</td><td>F</td></tr>
<tr><td>凝^{24}</td><td>冫
15</td><td>疑
479</td><td>To freeze, congeal, consolidate
| 結 to congeal, to freeze | 聚</td><td></td><td></td><td>F</td></tr>
<tr><td>甯^{2}</td><td>用
101</td><td>用
593</td><td>Peaceful
| 波 Ningpo</td><td></td><td>ning^{4}</td><td>G</td></tr>
<tr><td>擰^{3}</td><td>手
64</td><td>丁
2</td><td>To turn about, turn away
| 脚 sprain the foot, so | 手
| 壞 spoil by tampering</td><td></td><td>ning^{24}</td><td>F</td></tr>
<tr><td>擰^{4}</td><td>手
64</td><td>丁
2</td><td>Obstinate, perverse</td><td></td><td>ning^{23}</td><td>F</td></tr>
<tr><td>甯^{4}</td><td>用
101</td><td>用
593</td><td>Rather, would that</td><td>S</td><td>ning^{2}</td><td>G</td></tr>
<tr><td>佞^{4}</td><td>人
9</td><td>女
552</td><td>Eloquent, specious, artful
| 口 plausible, oily-mouthed
奸 | treacherous, cunning</td><td></td><td></td><td>I</td></tr>
</table>

Niu

<table>
<tr><td>妞^{1}</td><td>女
38</td><td>丑
676</td><td>A girl (Manchu) | 兒, 小 | 兒
二 | 兒 the second daughter</td><td></td><td></td><td>H</td></tr>
<tr><td>牛^{2}</td><td>牛
93</td><td>牛
38</td><td>Cow, ox, bull, cattle
| 角 buffalo horns, cow horns
| 圈 a bullock pen | 棚
| 庄 Newchuang, Manchurian port</td><td>S.</td><td></td><td>A</td></tr>
</table>

Character	Radical	Phonetic	Meaning		Other readings	
牛^{2}			| 尾巴 ox-tail, | 肉 beef | 乳 cow's milk | 奶 | 奶皮 cream | 舌頭 ox-tongue; dock-weed | 崽 a calf | 犢 | 油 beef-tallow, suet 水 | water-buffalo			
扭^{3}	手 64	丑 676	To twist, seize, wring |·—·| | 結 to twist; grapple | 乾 to wring dry |·了脖子 twisted neck | 頸 | 歪 to distort, twist awry			D
鈕^{3}	金 167	丑 676	Knob, button |·子, | 扣 | 口 a button hole | 襻子 a button loop | 絆兒	S.		B
謬^{4}	言 149	翏 283	False, random, error | 誤, 錯 | | 言 falsehood, lies | 傳 false reports		miao^{4} miu^{4}	D
忸^{4}	心 61	丑 676	Stubborn, mulish 憋·| obstinate, morose			G
拗^{4}	手 64	幺 876	Obstinate, perverse | 煞 | 性 perverse disposition | 頸 |·子 refractory child, follow		yao^{3}	H

No

Character	Radical	Phonetic	Meaning		Other readings	
哪^{12}	口 30	那 143	Final particle		na^{1}	A
那^{2}	邑 163	那 143	Ancient state in Kansu		na^{134}	A
挪^{2}	手 64	那 143	To move, divert, remove |·—·| | 借 to borrow, to embezzle | 移 to shift, to remove |·開 to move, set aside |·不開 unable to remove			D
諾^{4}	言 149	若 182	Answer, promise; yes | | 應 | respond, answer call			I

Character	Radical	Phonetic	Meaning		
懦^{4}	心 61	需 613	Weak, infirm 丨弱		G
糯^{4} 稬^{4}	米 119	需 613	Glutinous rice, old man's rice 丨米 丨米酒 sweet spirit from rice		I
訥^{4} 吶^{4}	言 149	內 444	Cautious or slow of speech 丨舌 tongue-tied, impediment 口丨 stuttering, stammering		I

Nou

Character	Radical	Phonetic	Meaning		
耨^{4} 鎒^{4}	耒 127	辱 356	To hoe, weed 丨草 丨耕 to hoe and plow 筆耕舌丨 to be a schoolmaster		G

Nu

Character	Radical	Phonetic	Meaning		
奴^{2}	女 38	奴 553	A slave, servant, 丨僕; abject 丨籍 slavery 丨·隸 a slave 丨·才 丨婢 a female slave		C
孥^{2}	子 39	奴 553	A child, weakly 妻丨 wife and children		G
駑^{2}	馬 187	奴 553	Broken-down old horse 丨馬		I
努^{3}	力 19	奴 553	Te make great effort, exert 丨力 exert one's strength 丨傷 over-exertion		E
帑^{32}	巾 50	奴 553	Legal wife's children	t'ang^{3}	G
弩^{3}	弓 57	奴 553	A crossbow 丨弓 丨箭 a crossbow arrow 丨彈 a crossbow pellet		I
怒^{4}	心 61	奴 553	Anger, rage, incensed 丨氣 丨恨 angry, hatred, resentment 丨惱 anger, rage 惱丨 丨色 angry countenance		D

Nuan

Character	Radical	Phonetic	Meaning	Variant	Group
暖3 煖3	日 72	爰 187	Warm, mild 丨·和 丨風 a warm wind 丨爐 a radiator	nan3 nang3	A
餪3	食 184	食 363	Present of food, house-warming 丨席 bridal feast		H

Nun

Character	Radical	Phonetic	Meaning	Variant	Group
嫩4 嫰4	女 38	束 501	Tender, delicate 丨肉 tender meat 丨芽 delicate shoots	nen4	E

Nung

Character	Radical	Phonetic	Meaning	Variant	Group
噥1	口 30	農 357	Irrelevant talk, gabble 唧丨 to mutter	neng1	H
農2	辰 161	農 357	Farm, agriculture, to cultivate S 丨家 farm laborers 丨夫, 丨人, 丨丁 丨界 farmer class 丨學 agricultural science 丨工部 Board of Agriculture and Industry 丨事 agricultural affairs 丨業 agricultural industry	neng2	C
儂2	人 2	農 357	I (Foochow)		I
濃2	水 85	農 357	Strong, thick, rich 丨厚 thick, as fluids 丨眉 heavy eyebrows		E
膿2	肉 130	農 357	Pus, matter 丨水 丨瘡 abscess. 放丨 let out pus	neng2	F
齈2	鼻 209	農 357	Nose-mucus, cold-in-head 丨涕 to snivel	neng2	G

弄^{4} — 廾 55 — 王 71 — lung^{4}, neng^{4} — C

Play with, handle; do, make
| 錢 make money dishonestly
| 飯 to cook rice; so | 菜
| 好·了 got ready, all done
| 壞·了 spoil by meddling with
| 玩意兒 play with a toy

Nü

女^{3} — 女 38 — 女 552 — A

Female, girl, woman
| 界 womankind, woman's world
| 權 rights of women
| 中丈夫 a woman hero
|·兒 a girl 閨·| , | 孩兒, | 子^{3}
|·兒經 The Girls' Classic
|·婿 a son-in-law
|·人 a woman, a wife
| 巫 a witch, sorceress

Nüeh

虐^{4} — 虍 141 — 虐 205 — E

Tyrannical, to oppress, maltreat
| 政 tyrannical government
| 待人 to oppress people
暴 | to tyrannize, violent

瘧^{4} — 疒 104 — 虐 205 — 文 — yao^{4}, yüeh^{4} — E

Fever
|·疾 remittent fever

謔^{4} — 言 149 — 虐 205 — H

To jest, ridicule 戲 |
笑 | laugh and jest

O,e

阿^{1} — 阜 170 — 可 699 — a^{1234} — C

Name, prefix, final particle, exclamation
| 彌陀佛 Amida Buddha
| 娘 a mother

O

痾[1]	疒 104	可 699	Sickness, pain, diarrhoea	k'o[41]	K
俄[24]	人 9	我 338	A moment, suddenly, ｜然 ｜頃 in a moment, presently ｜·國 Russia ｜羅斯		E
哦[2]	口 30	我 338	To chant, hum over ｜詩 吟｜ to hum, chant		I
蛾[2]	虫 142	我 338	A moth, silkworm ｜·子, ｜虫 蠶｜ silkworm moth		F
鵝[2]	鳥 196	我 338	A goose, crane 草｜ ｜掌 goose feet ｜絨 goose down, ｜毛 feathers ｜翎筆 quill pens 天｜ wild swan		D
額[24]	頁 181	客 712a	Forehead; fixed number; suddenly ｜角 the temples ｜頭 forehead ｜數 a fixed number ｜頂 top of the head ｜外 beyond the fixed number		E
訛[2] 譌[2]	言 149	化 327	False, erroneous; extort, cheat ｜詐 cheat, extort money ｜索 ｜傳 propagate error ｜言 unfounded declaration ｜語		F
我[3]	戈 62	我 338	I, myself (local)	wo[3]	A
惡[3]	心 61	亞 247	｜·心 nauseated	o[4] wu[4]	C
餓[4]	食 184	我 338	Hungry ｜·了, ｜極·了, 飢｜ ｜瘦·了 thin from want of food ｜·死 starved to death		A
惡[4]	心 61	亞 247	Bad, evil, depraved, ｜劣 ｜感 ill feeling ｜貫滿盈 cup of iniquity full ｜名 a bad name ｜念 evil thoughts ｜事 a wicked business ｜俗 an abuse, corrupt custom	o[3] wu[4]	C

Character	Radical	Phonetic	Definition		
惡4			丨毒 cruel, brutal 丨言 abusive, coarse language 丨有丨報 evil has its reward		
厄4	厂 27	厄 196	Distress, cramped 困丨 危丨 in danger		H
扼4	手 64	厄 196	To grasp, seize 丨守 to hold, as strategical position		I
阨4	阜 170	厄 196	A defile, distress, difficulty 窮丨 in great distress 艱丨		K
軛4	車 159	厄 196	Yoke, restraint, collar 丨制 to restrain, curb		E
噩4	口 30	噩 76	Grave, serious, startling		K
鱷4 鰐4	魚 195	噩 76	Crocodile, rapacious, cruel 丨魚 crocodile, alligator		G
咢4	口 30	咢 243	To beat a drum. Used for 愕, 諤		P
愕4	心 61	咢 243	To shudder, startled 丨然 丨顧 look suspiciously		I
鄂4	邑 170	咢 243	Ancient State in Hupei　S. 丨博 a Mongol boundary marker: "Obo"	ao4	H
遏4	辵 162	曷 239	To check, stop, terminate 丨禁 丨慾 curb lusts		I

Ou

Character	Radical	Phonetic	Definition		
嘔13	口 30	區 696	To vomit, disgorge 丨吐 丨心 sick feeling, nausea	ou4	E
歐1	欠 76	區 696	Europe; to vomit, retch　S. 丨風 European customs 丨化 European civilization; Europeanize 丨羅巴 Europe 丨洲 丨亞種 Eurasians 丨陽 double surname　S		F

Ou

漚[1]	水 85	區 696	Frothy bubbles, foam 泡 | ,浮 |	ou⁴	I
毆[13]	殳 79	區 696	To beat, maul, fight, brawl 鬥 | | 傷 wound by beating | 殺 | 打 beat, fight with fists		H
甌[1]	瓦 98	區 696	A bowl, 茶 | ; Wenchow-river 木 | wooden bowl		I
謳[1]	言 149	區 696	Ballads; to sing, chant | 唱 to sing | 吟, | 詠 | 歌頌讚 sing hymns of praise		H
鷗[1]	鳥 196	區 696	A sea-gull		I
偶[3]	人 9	禺 575	Image, mate; unexpectedly | 爾 suddenly, by chance | 然 | 合 to unite, union | 像 an image 木 | | 數 even numbers | 遇 to meet by chance		C
耦[3]	耒 127	禺 575	Mate, pair, together 配 |		F
藕[3]	艸 140	禺 575	Lotus-root | 粉 lotus-root flour, (like arrow-root) | 荷色 boiled lotus-root color, pale lilac | 絲 fibres of the lotus root		G
熰[3]	火 86	區 696	Heat and drought; to fire | 烟 to smoke (as a stove, k'ang, etc)		I
嘔[4] 慪[4]	口 30	區 696	To stir a quarrel, excite | 氣 constantly venting anger, (often on a third party)	ou¹³	E
漚[4]	水 85	區 696	To soak, steep | 柔 | 透了 soaked through | 糟了 rotten through steeping | 爛	ou¹	I

Pa

八[1] 捌[1]	八 12	八 392	Eight (before tones 1, 2, 3) |°十 |成 eight in ten, probably |分 |旗 Eight Banners at Peking |方 the points of compass |仙 the eight immortals |仙桌 square table for eight |音 sounds from 8 kinds of instrument 金石絲竹匏土革木	pa[2]	A
叭[1]	口 30	八 392	Open-mouthed 喇[3]·| trumpet		F
扒[1]	手 64	八 392	To pull out; climb; catch hold |衣·裳 strip off clothes |皮 peel, pare |·手 pickpocket		H
巴[1]	己 49	巴 312	Name of ancient state in Szechuen; Chungking S. |·掌 the open hand, palm |·結 to exert one's self, curry favor ||結結 |黎 Paris |·不得 would that! |·不能 嘴| a slap on the mouth		D
吧[1]	口 30	巴 312	Dumb; wide mouthed 啞·| |狗 Peking lap-dog		E
杷[1]	木 75	巴 312	Loquat fruit 枇·|		K
把[1]	手 64	巴 312	To take, take hold of	pa[34]	A
疤[1]	疒 104	巴 312	A scar, a cicatrix |·瘌		G
笆[1]	竹 118	巴 312	A kind of bamboo 籬·| bamboo hedge, fence		G
芭[1]	艸 140	巴 312	Banana, plantain |蕉扇 a palm leaf fan |蕉葉 palm leaves		H

Pa

琶[1]	玉 96	珏 77	Guitar 琵·|	p'a[1]	G
叭[1]	口 30	另 224	Cry of birds |·哥兒 myna (a black bird)		H
八[2] 捌[2]	八 12	八 392	Eight (before 4th tone) |·箇 | 卦 the eight diagrams | 面 on every side |·月 August, eighth moon	pa[1]	A
犮[2]	又 29	犮 188	To pull up		P
拔[2]	手 64	犮 188	Pluck up, raise, draw up, out |·出 to extract, draw out | 根 to root up, eradicate | 麥·子 pull wheat out by roots |·上來 to pull up | 刀 to draw a sword | 萃 exceed all, superior		D
跋[2]	足 157	犮 188	Tail-piece in book, colophon	po[4]	G
魃[2]	鬼 194	犮 188	Demon of drought 旱 |	po[4]	I
把[3]	手 64	巴 312	To grasp, keep; guard; a handful; C. of chairs, knives, etc. | 持 to monopolize, control | 門 to act as gatekeeper ∘| 門關·上 shut the door | 勢 athletic exercises | 守 to guard, hold fast | 握 security, guarantee	pa[14]	A
靶[3]	革 177	巴 312	Target, mark |·子 |·子場 rifle-range		G
弝[4]	弓 57	巴 312	Part of bow grasped 弓 |·子		K
把[4]	手 64	巴 312	A handle, handles | 兒 | 柄 to handle, grasp, a hold 話 | a handle for talk 話柄	pa[13]	A

Character	Radical	Phonetic	Meaning	Variant	Class
爸⁴	父 88	巴 312	Father, |·| ,阿| ; mollah		D
耙⁴ 鈀⁴	耒 127	巴 312	Drag, harrow |·子	p'a²	F
罷⁴	网 122	罷 325	To finish; sign of mild or strong imperative, and suggestion |休 to cease |手, |息 |工 quit work, strike; so |市, |學 or |課 |了 enough! |了|了 -liao³, -·le 去·| be off! begone! 這麼着·| let us do this way		A
霸⁴	雨 173	革 105	To usurp, rule by force; tyrant |占地土 to usurp land |權 tyranny, dictatorship |·道 encroach, rule of might		E
壩⁴ 垻⁴	土 32	革 105	Dike, breakwater 打| make embankment 築|		I
鮁⁴	魚 195	犮 188	The bonito fish		K

P'a

Character	Radical	Phonetic	Meaning	Variant	Class
趴¹	足 157	八 392	To fall prostrate |·下 on hands and knees, crouch	p'a²	F
琶¹	玉 96	玨 77	Guitar 琵|	pa¹	G
趴²	足 157	八 392	To creep, crawl, climb |城 scale the city-wall |·起來 get up, climb up |·上去 |虫 a creeping insect; reptile |行 to crawl along |珊瑚 "climbing coral", Virginia creeper |山虎	p'a¹	F

<table>
<tr><td>爬^{2}</td><td>爪
87</td><td>巴
312</td><td>To climb, creep; scratch, rake
|·着走 a child's creeping
| 癢 scratch an itch</td><td></td><td></td><td>D</td></tr>
<tr><td>耙^{2}
鈀^{2}</td><td>耒
127</td><td>巴
312</td><td>A rake, harrow; crockery-rivet
| 地 to rake the ground</td><td></td><td>pa^{4}</td><td>F</td></tr>
<tr><td>帕^{4}</td><td>巾
50</td><td>白
804</td><td>Kerchief, veil |·子, 頭 |
手 | a handkerchief</td><td></td><td></td><td>D</td></tr>
<tr><td>怕^{4}</td><td>心
61</td><td>白
804</td><td>To fear 害 |, dread, lest
| 羞 to feel shame, blush
| 甚麽 what are you afraid of?
| 死 to fear death
|·得很 extremely afraid
恐 | to be afraid, lest
不 | don't be afraid!</td><td></td><td></td><td>A</td></tr>
</table>

Pai

<table>
<tr><td>擘^{1}</td><td>手
64</td><td>辟
158</td><td>To break, split
|∘開 break open, or in pieces
| 兩半 to break into two
| 餅 to break a cake</td><td>俗</td><td>po^{4}</td><td>E</td></tr>
<tr><td>白^{2}</td><td>白
106</td><td>白
804</td><td>White, pure; freely, vainly
| 契 unstamped deed
| 鉛 spelter, zinc
| 晝 day-time, broad day |·天
| 去·了 went to no purpose
| 種 the white race, Caucasian
| 礬 alum. | 灰 lime
| 費工夫 useless waste of time
| 話 colloquial
| 饒 to take trouble in vain; to give a surplus free (in trade)
| 給 to give for nothing | |·的
| 露 "white dew" a solar term
| 米 white rice; | 麪 white flour
|∘事 a funeral</td><td>S</td><td>po^{24}</td><td>A</td></tr>
</table>

Pai

Character	Radical	Phonetic	Meaning		
白[2]			丨薯 sort of yam, sweet potato 丨水 plain water, so 丨開水 丨說 talking in vain 丨糖 white sugar, 丨菜 cabbage 丨銅 white brass 丨字 wrong word but same sound		
伯[23]	人 9	白 804	Father's elder brother	po24	D
百[3]	白 106	百 805	Hundred 一丨, many, all 丨靈 Mongolian lark 丨十來 somewhat less than 100; about 100	po42	A
擺[3]	手 64	罷 325	To arrange, set in order, spread out; move to and fro; pendulum 丨齊 arranged evenly 丨好 丨棹的 a waiter, or table boy 丨飯 spread table for meal 丨∘開 to set out, arrange 丨·上 丨·弄 to play with 丨·不開 not room to spread 丨·設 to arrange, an ornament 丨手 to warn with hand (as to "shake the head") 丨臺 set the table 丨攤 spread out wares for sale 丨·渡 a ferry		B
柏[3] 栢[3]	木 75	白 804	Cypress, cedar, 丨樹, 丨木 S. 香丨樹 the cedar, used for incense 黃丨 yellow cedar	po4	F
拜[4]	手 64	手 141	To honor, worship; visit 丨·見 to pay a visit 丨望, ·丨客 丨佛 worship Buddha 丨賀 to congratulate 丨謝 return a compliment 丨會 to make a call 丨年 New Year congratulations		A

拜[4]			| 偶像 to worship idols |·| to salute (as women) | 別 to take leave, farewell | 上帝 worship God 敬 |, 禮 | | 壽 visit on birthday | 帖 a visiting card | 天地 worship heaven and earth in weddings		
敗[4]	攴 66	貝 856	Defeat, ruin, to destroy | 仗 defeat, lose battle 打 | 仗 | 家 ruin one's family | 家子[3] spendthrift son |∘壞 corrupt; destroy | 落, | 盡 | 露 to be ruined by being discovered | 事 to ruin an affair | 亡 destroyed, dead		C
稗[1]	禾 115	卑 807	Tares, darnel, weeds | 草, |·子 | 說 a novel; careless chat		E
憊[4]	心 61	備 596	Exhausted, used up | 倦 | 累 wearied, exhausted 疲 |		H

P'ai

拍[1]	手 64	白 804	To clap, rap, slap, pat 俗 | 掌 to clap, applause | 手 | 照 snap-shot, to photograph | 花子 kidnappers | 賣 to sell by auction | 門 knock at a door | 巴掌 to hit a slap	p'o4	D
牌[2]	片 91	卑 807	Sign, tablet, card, arch |·坊 a memorial arch |·樓 | 示 a notification |·子 a check, label, bamboo slip |·位 ancestral tablet		A

Character	Radical	Phonetic	Meaning		
徘[2]	彳 60	非 418	To walk to and fro ｜徊 walking irresolutely		I
排[2]	手 64	非 418	Arrange, dispose; a rank, set ｜齊 all arranged in order｜列 ｜鎗 a volley of guns ｜斥 to oppose, exclude ｜球 volley ball ｜行第幾 what is your number among the brothers ｜骨 ribs, mutton or pork chops ｜隊 draw up troops in order ｜字 to set up type ｜外 anti-foreign		C
𠂢[4]		𠂢 350	To branch		P
派[4]	水 85	𠂢 350	To branch off; depute, appoint; a "school" ｜差 to send, appoint 差｜,｜出 ｜出所 police station ｜分 assign, distribute 分｜ ｜官 appoint an official ｜功課 to assign lessons ｜兵 to dispatch troops ｜定 to settle 支｜to branch, a tribe 學｜"school", "ism"		C

Pan

Character	Radical	Phonetic	Meaning		
般[1]	舟 137	般 569	Sort, kind, way｜樣 一｜ alike, similar, same size 一｜大		D
搬[1]	手 64	般 569	To move, transport, remove｜移 ｜家 change one's residence ｜·出去 carry out of room or place ｜·下來 take down from above ｜來｜去 to carry to and fro		A

Pan

搬[1]			｜挪 to shift, remove ｜·不倒 a self-righting doll ｜運 to transport, convey	
瘢[1]	疒 104	般 569	Scar, mark 瘡｜	H
班[1]	玉 96	玨 77	Rank, class; C. of students S. ｜別 to distinguish ｜次 gradation, order of service ｜位 a rank, row 插｜生 scholars added to class 一｜一｜ group (or class) by group	A
斑[1]	文 67	玨 77	Spotted, striped, variegated｜點 ｜鳩 turtle dove ｜文 streaks, mottled	F
頒[1]	頁 181	分 395	To bestow; make known, proclaim ｜發 to bestow, confer｜送,｜賜 ｜行 publish by authority	G
板[3] 版[3]	木 75	反 215	Board; stiff; register ｜廠 wood yard, lumber yard ｜墻 wooden fence or wall ｜橋 a foot bridge of wood ｜權 copyright on books, etc. ｜·櫈 a stool, or bench ｜·子 bamboo to beat offenders. 鉛｜ lead type 發｜ grow stiff, awkward	A
半[4]	十 24	半 144	Half｜·個,一·｜ ｜截 a half ｜斤 (or 觔) half a catty ｜新不舊 worn ｜信｜疑 half-believe, half-doubt ｜懸空 in mid-air ｜開化國 half-civilized land ｜路 half-way｜道兒 ｜死不活 neither dead nor alive ｜島 a peninsula ｜天 half-a-day, long time｜晌	A

Pan

Character	Radical	Phonetic	Definitions	Alt.	Freq.
半4			｜塗而廢 to break down halfway ｜夜 midnight 一｜一｜ half and half 多｜the majority 大｜		
伴4	人 9	半 144	Companion, partner, attend on ｜宿 a wake over a corpse ｜侶 an associate 同｜,夥｜ 陪｜to bear company		C
拌4	手 64	半 144	To mix. ｜勻 to mix evenly ｜嘴 to wrangle, quarrel		H
絆4	糸 120	半 144	To fetter, hinder, lasso, trip ｜住 ｜脚 to trip up ｜馬索 a lasso, a hobble ｜倒·了 to stumble; to trip one up		G
辦4 辦4	辛 160	辛 157	To manage, transact, do ｜案 to deal with lawsuits ｜成 successful, accomplished ｜·了 ｜喜事 manage a marriage ｜紅事 ｜貨 buy or import goods ｜公事 transact official business ｜理 to manage, administer ｜事 ｜白事 manage a funeral ｜喪事 ｜·不成 unsuccessful ｜·不起 can't afford to do it ｜·不到 can't do, impracticable ｜·得來 able to do, practicable ｜妥 manage satisfactorily ｜完·了 finished, transacted		B
瓣4	瓜 97	辛 157	Petals; section (as of orange) 花｜the petals of a flower		I
辯4	辛 160	辛 157	To dispute, to debate ｜論 ｜嘴 to wrangle, quarrel	pien4	C
扮4	手 64	分 395	To dress up, costume 打·｜ ｜戲 dress in character ｜作 to personate ｜演 theatrical "make-up"		E

P'an

攀[1] 扳[1]	手 64	樊 493	Pull down; drag in; climb ｜·不起 can't afford (to be his friend) ｜援 climb up to anything 高｜honor of his acquaintance	H
潘[1]	水 85	番 811	River in Honan S.	H
磐[2]	石 112	般 569	Rock, bedrock, ｜石; firm	D
盤[2]	皿 108	般 569	Plate, platter ｜·子; expenses; to turn, examine ｜查 to examine, to search ｜問 ｜·纏 travelling expenses ｜·川, ｜∘費 ｜球 billiards ｜香 coiled incense ｜繞 to wind or circle round ｜槓子 horizontal bar exercise ｜·上 to wind up, coil round	A
[illegible][2] 蹣[2]	足 157	般 569	To sit cross-legged ｜膝 ｜·着 squatting, crosslegged ｜腿	H
蟠[2]	虫 142	番 811	To coil up, ｜居; squat ｜·着 coil up, as a snake ｜桃 the flat peach ｜桃會 festival on 3rd of 3rd moon	I
盼[4]	目 109	分 395	To look at, hope for ｜想, ｜·望 ｜頭 something to hope for	B
判[4]	刀 18	半 144	To judge, divide ｜決 to decide a case ｜定 to sentence ｜·斷 to determine, to decide ｜斷力 decision of character ｜詞 the sentence after decision 審｜to judge, decide	B

Character	Radical	Phonetic	Meaning	Other readings	Grade
叛[4]	又 29	半 144	To rebel, revolt ｜亂, ｜逆, 反｜ ｜匪 rebels ｜賊 謀｜ plot rebellion		C
畔[4]	田 102	半 144	Path, boundary, land-mark 河｜ river-bank, tow-path		K
拚[4]	手 64	厶 868	Reject, disregard ｜財 to speculate recklessly	fan[1] pien[4] p'in[1]	F
襻[4]	衣 145	樊 493	Loop, band, strap 帽｜ 鈕｜ button-loop		H

Pang

Character	Radical	Phonetic	Meaning	Other readings	Grade
邦[1]	邑 163	邦 142	A state, country, nation ｜國 ｜交 international relations 聯｜政體 federal government 友｜ friendly power		C
幫[1] 幇[1] 帮[1]	巾 50 俗	邦 142	To bind edge, shore up; help; company, flock; C. of groups ｜錢 to assist with money ｜·助 to help, assist, relieve ｜忙 help, especially when busy ｜辦 assist in managing ｜·手 an assistant		A
梆[1]	木 75	邦 142	Watchman's rattle ｜·子, 更｜ ｜｜sound of rattle or clapper ｜鼓 kettle-drum		G
傍[1]	人 9	旁 262	王事｜｜king's business is urgent	pang[4] p'ang[2]	C
綁[3]	糸 120	邦 142	To bind, tie, ｜·上, ｜·起來 ｜結實 to bind securely ｜緊 to tie fast, tied tightly ｜·住 ｜票 to seize for ransom		C
榜[3]	木 75	旁 262	Example; placard; list; to beat ｜°樣 example, model, pattern ｜文 a notice, proclamation 開｜ publish list of successful graduates		D

Character	Radical	Phonetic	Meaning	Other readings	Freq.
髈^{3}	骨 188	旁 262	Shoulder 肩｜ ｜·子骨 shoulder bones 翅｜wings, fins		D
傍^{4}	人 9	旁 262	Near. ｜明 near dawn ｜晚 near evening	pang^{1} p'ang^{2}	C
謗^{4}	言 149	旁 262	To slander, vilify 毀｜ ｜讟聖道 revile Holy Religion ｜言 slander. ｜書 libel		C
鎊^{4}	金 167	旁 262	An English £, 金｜pound 過｜to weigh, be weighed	p'ang^{3}	E
棒^{4}	木 75	奉 470	A stick, staff, cudgel ｜球 baseball ｜°槌 beater for washing ｜·子 Indian corn, maize; cudgel		E
蚌^{4}	虫 142	丰 145	Oysters, mussels ｜蛤 ｜殼 oyster shells	peng^{4}	H

P'ang

Character	Radical	Phonetic	Meaning	Other readings	Freq.
磅^{1}	石 112	旁 262	A crash; a pound		B
胖^{1}	肉 130	丰 145	Bloated, dropsical ｜脹, ｜腫		K
旁^{2} 傍^{2}	方 70	旁 262	Side, lateral, side-wise; other ｜處 another or near place ｜人 bystander ｜觀 to look on, an observer ｜立 stand by the side ｜門左道 heretical sects ｜邊 the side; by the side of ｜道兒 a diverging road ｜聽者 (°的) auditors at assemblies or classes in schools	 pang^{14}	A C
螃^{2}	虫 142	旁 262	A crab ｜·蟹		E
龐^{2}	龍 212	龍 315	Great house; confused; large S. 面｜facial expression ｜°貌		K

Character	Radical	Phonetic	Meaning	Other readings	Class
鎊[3]	金 167	旁 262	To hoe, | 地, scrape	pang[4]	E
胖[4]	肉 130	半 144	Fat, corpulent, stout 肥 | | 人 a stout person |·子 | 瘦 fat and lean		B

Pao

Character	Radical	Phonetic	Meaning	Other readings	Class
勹[1]	勹 20	勹 225	To inclose		K
包[1]	勹 20	勹 225	To wrap up, contain; contract S. | 車 contract cart, private car |·起來 to wrap up | 金的 gilded | 兒 a small parcel | 飯 to contract for food |·袱 a cloth bundle, wrapper |·袱皮 |∘含 to contain; enduring |∘涵 | 廂 boxes, stalls in theaters | 容 bear with patiently |∘管 to guarantee | 工 to work by the job | 活 | 裹 wrap up or round; parcel | 攬 to monopolize | 辦 undertake, transact 承 | | 賠 guarantee compensation | 探 to detect, detectives | 藏 to store up |·子 dumpling		A
炮[1] 炰[1]	火 86	勹 225	To fry, roast | 肉 to roast meat	p'ao[24]	F
胞[1]	肉 130	勹 225	The womb; bladder 尿 | | 衣 the placenta	p'ao[1]	E
齙[1]	齒 211	勹 225	Teeth exposed | 牙		I

Pao

剝^{1}	刀 18	彔 525	To peel, flay; kill; extort |·去 | 殼 remove husk or shell | 栗子 to shell chestnuts | 皮 to peel, skin, pare | 羊 to flay a sheep	po^{14}	E
褒^{1} 襃^{1}	衣 145	保 758	Long robes; to praise | 奬 |°貶 to criticize; fault-finding		H
薄^{2}	艸 140	溥 599	Thin, poor, shabby; coldly | 紙 thin paper | 厚 thin and thick, thickness | 禮 poor presents, trifling | 餅 very thin cakes | 待人 treat people slightingly	po^{24}	B
雹^{2}	雨 173	勹 225	Hail |·子 | 冰 hail-stones	po^{2}	D
飽^{3}	食 184	勹 225	Satiated, satisfied 吃 | | 飯 to eat to fullness | 滿 | 學 well read, learned | 暖 fed and clothed | 食 a full hearty meal		A
保^{3}	人 9	保 758	To guard, protect. guarantee |·護 | 障 a defence; to defend |·證 a surety | 證金 bail | 結 a contract, bond, guarantee | 持 hold fast; keep intact | 舉 to recommend | 全 to preserve entire | 好 | 狀 security at law | 票, | 單 |·重 "take care of yourself" | 險 assurance, insurance | 火險 | 人 a security, a bail | 家 | 管 guarantee | 定 guaranteed | 留 to retain (as an official) |·不住 cannot guarantee |·不定 | 守 to defend, protect | 守黨 conservatives		C

Pao

Character	Radical	Phonetic	Meaning	Variant	Freq.
保³			｜存 to preserve, to maintain ｜存國粹 preserve national treasures and excellencies ｜養 to nourish ｜·佑 to bless		
堡³	土 32	保 758	Low walls, earthwork; city ward ｜障 defence, rampart	pu^{34} $p'u^{34}$	H
褓³ 緥³	衣 145	保 758	Swaddling clothes 襁｜		H
寶³ 寳³ 宝³	宀 40 减	貝 856	Precious, honorable, "your", jewel ｜器 precious articles ｜物 ｜劍 double-edged sword ｜局 a gambling saloon ｜眷 your wife; your family ｜號 name of your firm ｜星 a decoration ｜貴 precious, valuable ｜∘貝 ｜∘石 precious stone, 珍｜ jewels ｜座 the throne		C
報⁴ 报⁴	土 32	幸 159	To requite, report, a periodical ｜償 to avenge ｜仇, ｜怨, ｜·復 ｜界 the press-world ｜知 to inform, report ｜道 ｜紙 press, newspapers 日｜ ｜恩 to requite favors ｜喜 to announce birth ｜信 tell news, announce ｜告 to make a report 回｜ ｜官 inform magistrate ｜館 newspaper offices ｜明 to report clearly ｜名上冊 register name ｜喪 announce a death ｜稅 to declare goods ｜·答 to recompense ｜·應 retribution		A

Pao

<table>
<tr><td>抱^4</td><td>手
64</td><td>勹
225</td><td>To enfold, cherish, carry in arms
懷 |
| 屈 aggrieved, indignant |·不平
|·住 to embrace, hold fast
| 孩兒 to carry a child
| 恨 to harbour resentment |·怨
| 愧 to feel ashamed
| 養 to bring up another's child</td><td></td><td>C</td></tr>
<tr><td>菢^4</td><td>艸
140</td><td>勹
225</td><td>To incubate, brood | 窩</td><td></td><td>H</td></tr>
<tr><td>鉋^4
刨^4</td><td>金
167</td><td>勹
225</td><td>To plane, a plane |·子
| 床子 the frame of a plane
| 平 to plane. | 花 shavings</td><td>p'ao^2</td><td>C</td></tr>
<tr><td>暴^4</td><td>日
72</td><td>暴
99</td><td>Violent, cruel, scorching S.
| 風 a violent wind; so | 雨
| 烈 terrific—as a storm
| 民 rioters | 烈份子^3
| 虐 tyrannical, savage 兇 |
| 怒 fierce anger
| 病 sudden illness; so | 亡
|·躁之人 a bully. | 徒 ruffian
| 動 insurrection, riots</td><td>pu^4</td><td>D</td></tr>
<tr><td>曝^4</td><td>日
72</td><td>暴
99</td><td>To sun, to dry</td><td></td><td>G</td></tr>
<tr><td>瀑^4</td><td>水
85</td><td>暴
99</td><td>Water-fall | 布, 飛 |</td><td>p'u^4</td><td>G</td></tr>
<tr><td>爆^4</td><td>火
86</td><td>暴
99</td><td>To scorch, parch; snap; crack
| 煒 fire-crackers | 竹
| 火 crackling fire
| 裂 cracked, chapped</td><td></td><td>G</td></tr>
<tr><td>豹^4</td><td>豸
153</td><td>勺
231</td><td>Leopard, panther
金錢 | the North China panther</td><td></td><td>F</td></tr>
<tr><td>趵^4</td><td>足
157</td><td>勺
231</td><td>To leap</td><td>po^2</td><td>I</td></tr>
</table>

P'ao

<table>
<tr><td>抛^1</td><td>手
64</td><td>力
223</td><td>To throw down, cast off |·去
|棄 to cast away, reject |捨
|錨 to cast anchor
|撒 to separate, distribute</td><td>p'ou^1</td><td>D</td></tr>
<tr><td>胞^1</td><td>肉
130</td><td>勹
225</td><td>The womb; bladder 尿|
|兄 an elder brother
同| fellow countrymen</td><td>pao^1</td><td>E</td></tr>
<tr><td>脬^1</td><td>肉
130</td><td>孚
408</td><td>Bladder 尿|</td><td></td><td>F</td></tr>
<tr><td>刨^2
鉋^2</td><td>刀
18</td><td>勹
225</td><td>To dig up the ground |地; deduct
|·出 to dig up |挖
|·去零兒 throw off fraction
|根兒 dig out the root; ferret out the details
|坑 to dig a hole
|皮 deduct weight of container</td><td>pao^4</td><td>C</td></tr>
<tr><td>咆^2</td><td>口
30</td><td>勹
225</td><td>To roar, bluster |哮</td><td></td><td>E</td></tr>
<tr><td>庖^2</td><td>广
53</td><td>勹
225</td><td>Kitchen |厨. |人 a cook</td><td></td><td>H</td></tr>
<tr><td>炮^2</td><td>火
86</td><td>勹
225</td><td>To roast, mix
|製 to compound (medicines)</td><td>pao^1
p'ao^4</td><td>F</td></tr>
<tr><td>袍^2</td><td>衣
145</td><td>勹
225</td><td>Long robe |·子
|褂 outer coat
道| Taoist priest's robe</td><td></td><td>E</td></tr>
<tr><td>麅^2</td><td>鹿
198</td><td>勹
225</td><td>Small deer, roebuck |·子</td><td></td><td>G</td></tr>
<tr><td>跑^3</td><td>足
157</td><td>勹
225</td><td>To run, gallop; abscond
|賬的 debt collector
|·出來 to rush out |·出去
|信的 a messenger
|一身汗 all sweat with running
|∘開 run from. |·不開 unable to get away</td><td></td><td>A</td></tr>
</table>

跑[3]			| 馬 to race horses; so | 車 | 馬塲 a race-course | 不了喇 cannot escape |·不動 unable to run, exhausted | 堂兒的 eating-house waiter |·得快 to run fast		
泡[4]	水 85	勹 225	A blister; bubble | 兒, |·子; soak | 茶 make tea | 米 soak rice | 濕 to moisten | 透 soaked thoroughly		D
炮[4]	火 86	勹 225	Cannon, fire-cracker | 仗	pao[1] p'ao[2]	F
皰[4] 疱[4]	皮 107	勹 225	Pustule, blister, 燙·了一個 | I have made a blister		G
砲[4] 礮[4]	石 112	勹 225	Cannon, great gun; fire-works | 車 a gun carriage 迫擊 | trench mortar | 局 arsenal | 船 a gun-boat | 壘 a fort, fortress | 臺 | 手 a gunner, an artilleryman | 隊 a company of artillery | 子兒[3] shot, cannon balls 高射 | anti-aircraft gun		C

Pei

杯[1] 盃[1]	木 75	不 120	Cup, glass 玻璃 | tumbler. 酒 | wine-cup | 盤 tray for carrying cups		A
背[1]	肉 130	北 321	To carry on the back |·着, | 負 |·子 a back-load	pei[4]	B
悲[1]	心 61	非 418	To grieve, pity, sympathy | 哀 to compassionate, sad | 傷 | 凄 mournful, sad | 切, | 愁 | 觀 (主義) pessimism | 嘆 to sigh sadly | 慘 melancholy. | 痛 慈 | mercy, kindness, sympathy		C

Pei

卑[1]	十 24	卑 807	Base, low, humble, plebeian 丨賤 abject, base, lowly 丨微, 丨下 丨陋 mean, vile, base 丨劣 謙丨 humble, humbly decline 自丨 to humble oneself		C
俾[1]	人 9	卑 807	To cause; enable 丨得 enable to obtain or do 丨知 for information of	pi[4]	F
碑[1]	石 112	卑 807	Stone-tablet, monument 石丨, 一通丨 丨樓 pavilion over tablet 丨文 inscription on tablet 丨記 墓丨 tombstone		D
北[3]	匕 21	北 321	North 丨方, 丨極 North Pole 丨辰 North Pole Star 丨極星 丨京 Peking 丨·邊 north side, in the north 丨冰洋 Arctic Ocean 丨戴河 Peitaiho, Hopei 丨斗 Charles's Wain, The Dipper	po[4]	A
被[4]	衣 145	皮 537	Sign of passive, by; a coverlet 丨屈 wronged. 丨累 harassed 丨情所感 moved by circumstances 丨選舉權 eligible for election 丨·褥 cover and bed, bedding 丨告 defendant in a case 丨擄 to be made captive 丨保護國 protectorate 丨單 a sheet, a coverlet 丨·窩 upper covering of bed, quilt		A
背[4]	肉 130	北 321	Back, behind, turn the back on; repeat; oppose 丨教 to apostatize 丨道 丨景 background 丨後 behind the back 丨地裏 丨巷 a retired lane 丨逆 oppose to, resist 違丨	pei[1]	B

背[4]			｜叛 to revolt ｜反 ｜書 repeat by heart ｜念 ｜熟 recitation learnt well ｜陰兒 place that sees no sun ｜約 to break a treaty		
褙[4]	衣 145	北 321	To paste paper, paper for shoesoles 裱｜ to paste paper; paste-board		H
備[4] 俻[4]	人 9	備 596	To prepare, provide, complete ｜·下 prepare, make ready 預·｜ ｜馬 to saddle and bridle a horse ｜辦 get ready to do a thing ｜兵 to prepare troops 全｜ perfect, provided, complete		B
倍[4]	人 9	咅 89	Double, times, increase; revolt ｜利 double profit, 十｜ tenfold 加｜ twice as much; to add to		C
焙[4]	火 86	咅 89	To dry over fire ｜乾 ｜糊·了 burnt, scorched ｜卵 incubate eggs ｜熟·了 properly cooked		I
貝[4]	貝 154	貝 856	Shell, cowries, precious 寶∘｜ precious, treasure, gems	S	C
狽[4]	犬 94	貝 856	Jerboa; embarrassment 狼｜不堪 in distress		I
輩[4] 輩[4]	車 159	非 418	A generation; class; plural ｜長[3] superiors, seniors 長[3]｜, 前｜ ｜兒大 seniors 上｜, 下｜ seniors and juniors 吾｜ we, us, 我｜ 一｜·子 lifetime, through life		C
悖[4]	心 61	孛 113	To rebel, contrary, perverse ｜理而行 contrary to right ｜逆 refractory ｜謬父母 rebel against parents ｜叛 revolt, to rebel		C
臂[4]	肉 130	辟 158	The arm, fore-arm 肐｜ 膀｜ shoulders and arms		D

婢⁴	女 38	卑 807	Slave girls, maid servant | 女 僕 | male and female domestics	pi⁴	E
裨⁴	衣 145	卑 807	To aid, benefit, useful | 益 | 補 to assist, support		I

Pe'i

披¹	手 64	皮 537	To throw on, unroll, open | 甲 to put on armor | 髮 dishevelled hair | 衣裳 to wear clothes over the shoulders without using sleeves | 掛 in full uniform | 帶 put on clothing; carry at belt	p'i¹	D
丕¹	一 1	不 120	Unequalled, first; great | 運 great luck	p'i¹	I
呸¹	口 30	不 120	To hoot, snort, sputter; tush! | 啐 to spit at		I
胚¹ 肧¹	肉 130	不 120	Embryo, unfinished | 胎 month embryo, early growth	p'i¹	H
醅¹	酉 164	音 89	Unstrained liquor, must		K
培²	土 32	音 89	To bank up, | 土, strengthen | 養 to nourish, support | 補 栽 | to aid, nourish, cultivate; to patronize		C
賠²	貝 154	音 89	To compensate, make good, indemnify; lose money | 償 pay as surety, repay | 還 | 錢的事 a losing affair | 款 indemnity | 禮 to make an apology | 不是 | 本兒 lose in trade, lose capital | 補 to compensate, make up | 墊 |·不起 unable to indemnify		B

P'ei

陪[2]	阜 170	咅 89	To accompany, entertain 丨伴 丨行 accompany on journey 丨°客 keep visitor company 丨坐 丨審員 a juryman 丨送 accompany guest when leaving 失丨 excuse my leaving		B
裴[2]	衣 145	非 418	Long robes	S.	H
配[4]	酉 164	酉 781	To mate, match, a mate; worthy 丨·着 to match, 丨·不上 no match 丨·合 to join together 合丨 丨婚姻 to make a match 成婚丨 丨偶 husband and wife 丨·把鑰匙 fit a key to lock 丨色 match colors 丨對 couple, mate, copulate 答丨 丨藥 make up medicines 丨製 不丨 unworthy, not a match for		B
佩[4]	人 9	巾 557	To wear at waist; to respect 丨·服 to regard, respect 丨帶 things attached to girdle 丨刀 to gird on a sword		E
沛[4]	水 85	市 558	Copious, sudden 丨然 丨澤 fertilizing, enriching		I
霈[4]	雨 173	市 558	Soaking rain 滂丨		I
轡[4]	車 159	糸 886	Reins, bridle 丨頭 執丨 to hold the reins		K
旆[4] 斾[4]	方 70	㫃 265	Pennon, streamer; to journey 行丨 go on a journey 返丨 turn homewards		K

Pen

奔[1] 犇[1]	大 37	卉 416	To flee, hasten, 丨走, 丨跑; urgent 丨馳 to run out or abroad 丨忙 busy, hurried, bustling 丨逃 run away and disperse 丨散	pen[4]	C
捹[1]	手 64	卉 416	To fumble things over, mix up		I
錛[1]	金 167	卉 416	An adze 丨·子 丨·子·去 to cut away with adze		F
賁[1]	貝 154	賁 417	Energetic S. 丨怒 anger, rage	pi[4]	K
本[3]	木 75	本 485	Root, source, capital, native: C. of books 丨·錢 capital; prime cost 丨兒, 丨銀 丨∘分 duties of one's station 丨性 the natural disposition 丨人 proper person, in person 丨該 it ought 丨當, 丨須 丨國 one's country; so 丨家 丨來 original, originally 丨是 丨利 capital and interest 丨末 root and branch; first and last 丨能 instinct. 丨心 intention 丨意 丨色 unbleached, indigenous 丨身 I, myself. 丨書 a volume 丨·事 ability, skill 丨領 丨地 native place, local 丨位 standard, standing 丨源 cause, source, origin 丨月 this month; so 丨年, 丨處 根丨 root, source, fundamental		A
畚[3]	田 102	田 809	Dust basket, hod 丨斗, 荷丨		K
笨[4] 𢘆[4]	竹 118	本 485	Clumsy, stupid, dull, sluggish 丨人 clumsy person, stupid 丨才 丨·得很 very stupid 粗丨		C

Character	Radical	Phonetic	Meaning	Other readings	Group
奔⁴	大 37	卉 416	To run; urgent, hasten to ｜命 run for one's life ｜頭 worthy of pursuit ｜投 to repair to, resort to 投｜	pen¹	C
逩⁴	辵 162	卉 416	To hasten for or to (＝奔) ｜衣｜食 scramble for a living 投｜fly to for refuge		I

P'en

Character	Radical	Phonetic	Meaning	Other readings	Group
噴¹	口 30	賁 417	To blow out, spurt｜水; snort ｜氣 to puff and blow｜·出來 ｜壺 a watering pot ｜衣裳 sprinkle clothes ｜水管 garden hose ｜勻·了 to sprinkle evenly	fen⁴ p'en⁴	E
盆²	皿 108	分 395	Bowl, basin 水｜ 洗臉｜wash-basin 花｜a flower-pot 澡｜a bath-tub		B
噴⁴	口 30	賁 417	A puff, to puff out; emit ｜香 fragrant	fen⁴ p'en¹	E

Peng

Character	Radical	Phonetic	Meaning	Other readings	Group
崩¹	山 46	朋 622	To collapse, emperor's death 駕｜ ｜裂 to break open ｜坍 collapse of bank or wall		G
弸¹	弓 57	朋 622	A stiff bow; complete; swelled out ｜緊 stretched tight ｜弓·子 arched front of cart		K
痭¹	疒 104	朋 622	Menorrhagia｜症		K
帲¹	巾 50	幷 35	Screen, awning, shelter｜幪	p'ing²	K
弸¹	弓 57	幷 35	Pulled taut ｜騙 dwindle.｜·子手 swindler		K

絣[1]	糸 120	幷 35	To unite, baste. Used for 骿		K
蚌[4]	虫 142	丰 145	Oyster, mussels, | 蛤	pang[4]	H
迸[4]	辵 162	幷 35	To split, burst; jump | 跳, very | 散 flee in all directions 逃 | | 脆 brittle (as glass)		I
踭[4]	足 157	夆 148	To jump, bound, used for 迸		I

P'eng

烹[1]	火 86	亨 742	To boil, fry, decoct | 魚 etc. | 茶 to make tea; so | 湯 | 宰 work of cook, boil and kill		F
匉[1]	勹 20	平 36	Noise of waves | 訇		G
怦[1]	心 61	平 36	Eager, earnest, impulsive 急 | 忠 | loyal and earnest		I
砰[1]	石 112	平 36	Crash of falling rocks | 然如雷 crash like thunder		H
朋[2]	月 74	朋 622	Friend, companion |·友 良 | a good friend 好 | 情 very friendly		A
棚[2]	木 75	朋 622	Awning, shed, tent 天 | |·匠 mat-shed builders | 鋪 a mat-shop. 涼 | awning		B
硼[2]	石 112	朋 622	Borax | 砂		H
鵬[2]	鳥 196	朋 622	Monstrous fabulous bird, roc | 鳥		I
篷[2]	竹 118	逢 149	Mat cover, awning, tent, sail; ceiling | 帆 sail cloth, canvas, sail | 繩 rigging | 桅 a mast |·子 an awning; a sail 帳 | tent, mat-shed 車 |·子 awning of cart		D

Character	Radical	Phonetic	Meaning		
蓬2	艸 140	逢 149	Tangled, weed-grown S. 丨鬆 dishevelled hair 丨首 丨萊山 fairyland 丨島		G
彭2	彡 59	彡 280	Strong and handsome S. 丨祖 Chinese Methusaleh 老丨		I
膨2	肉 130	彡 280	Dyspepsia, bloated 丨脹 丨脹力 power of expansion		H
弆3	大 37	弆 469	Folded hands		P
捧3	手 64	奉 470	To hold up in both hands, offer respectfully 丨·着; promote 丨場 promote the success (of an artist, actor etc.) 丨水喝 drink out of the hands 丨碗 carry bowl with two hands		F
碰4 搒4	石 112	并 35	To hit, collide, meet unexpectedly; a thump; chance 丨機·會 hit upon opportunity 丨巧·了 occasionally, very likely 丨·見 to meet, encounter 丨壞 break by collision 丨碎 smashed to bits 丨釘子 to get into trouble 丨運氣 to run the risk		A

Pi

Character	Radical	Phonetic	Meaning		
逼1 偪1	辵 162	畐 816	To press, to compel 强丨 丨取 to extort 丨勒 丨迫 press, constrain, persecute 催丨 to press, urge		D
鼻2	鼻 209	自 852	Nose 丨·子 丨翅兒 lobes of the nostrils 丨孔 the nostrils 丨·子眼兒 丨樑兒 bridge of the nose 丨塞 nose stuffed with cold 丨·涕 snivel, snot. 丨煙 snuff 丨祖 first ancestor; founder		A

Pi

荸^{2}	艸 140	孛 113	Edible tuber, water chestnut |·薺		K
筆^{3}	竹 118	聿 669	Brush, pencil; to write, compose; style; composition ; stroke; penmanship; an item |跡 handwriting |記 to write, record with pen |尖 point of pen or pencil |法 style of handwriting |管 handle of pen or pencil |帽兒 cap to protect pen-point |墨 composition, pen and ink |述 written, dictated |算 calculate with the pen |筒 cylindrical holder for pens 鉛| a lead pencil 鋼| steel pens 毛| (Chinese) writing brush		A
匕^{3}	匕 21	匕 317	Ladle, spoon |首 a dagger		K
比^{3}	比 81	匕 317	To compare |◦較, |·一·|, |·|, 較| |這更大 still larger than this |·方 analogy, for instance |如 |國 Belgium |利時 |例 to compare, ratio |·不起 not to be compared |·不過 |賽 competition |武 contest in strength and skill |喻 a simile	pi^{4}	A
妣^{3}	女 38	匕 317	Deceased mother 先|		I
粃^{3} 秕^{3}	米 119	匕 317	Blasted grain, chaff, |糠		K
彼^{3}	彳 60	皮 537	He, it, that; as |時, |人 etc. |此 reciprocal, mutual		B

Pi

彼3			|此相愛 to love one another |此|此 the same to you		
壁3	土 32	辟 158	Next door, close by 街4|兒	pi4	F
啚3	口 30	啚 767	Low, mean		K
必4	心 61	必 378	Certainly, must, necessary |竟 must be so, must do 務| |須 must, it is sure to |然, |定 |不能 absolutely impossible |要 must do, essential |有 there must be, assuredly is 何| why must? what necessity? 不| it is not necessary 未| not certain, not necessarily		A
秘4 祕4	禾 115	必 378	Secret, private	mi4	C
敝4	攴 66	敝 561	Mean, poor, ruined |處 my place, |人 I myself |國 my country		A
幣4	巾 50	敝 561	Silk, present, wealth |帛 |制 monetary system 輔| subsidiary coins 納| to send silk as a betrothal present 銀| silver money, so 金|, 紙|		H
弊4 獘4	廾 55	敝 561	Used-up; malpractices |端 |病 fraud, abuses, corruption 私| bribery, corruption 作| to commit fraud 舞|		E
蔽4	艸 140	敝 561	To conceal, shade; include; dull 遮| to hide, screen, mislead 蒙|		F
斃4	攴 66	敝 561	To kill; die violent or bad death |命 be killed, die in prison 鎗| executed by shooting 倒| fall down and die		G

Pi

比^{4}	比 81	匕 317	To harmonize, equal; as to ｜匪 associate with criminals	pi^{3}	A
庇^{4}	广 53	匕 317	To screen, protect, shelter 護｜ ｜佑 protection and support 託｜"thank you"		D
篦^{4}	竹 118	匕 317	To comb, fine comb ｜·子 ｜髮 comb the hair 鐵｜·子 gridiron, grating		K
陛^{4}	阜 170	匕 317	Steps of throne ｜見 to have audience ｜下 the emperor; your majesty		I
閉^{4}	門 169	才 22	To close, stop up, shut ｜會 close a meeting, adjourn ｜口無言 complete silence ｜關自守 closed to trade ｜門 shut door; so ｜目 or 眼 ｜幕 close of era or event ｜塞 to close, stop up		B
畢^{4}	田 102	甲 825	To end, finish, 完｜; whole of S. ｜竟 at last, finally ｜業 graduate ｜業生 graduates ｜業式 graduation exercise		C
嗶^{4}	口 30	甲 825	｜嘰 English long cloth		B
辟^{4}	辛 160	辟 158	Sovereign, prince; laws 復｜ restoration of monarchy	p'i^{4}	G
壁^{4}	土 32	辟 158	Wall, screen, partition ｜壘 military wall; breastwork ｜·子 a wall 牆｜	pi^{3}	F
璧^{4}	玉 96	辟 158	A jewel, jade, princely gem ｜謝 declined (present) with thanks		F
避^{4}	辵 162	辟 158	Avoid, flee, shun, evade ｜風 avoid wind, draughts ｜雨 ｜邪 avoid uncanny influences ｜嫌疑 avoid suspicion		B

避[4]			|◦諱 avoid use of personal name | 禍 avoid calamity | 難 | 暑 avoid summer heat | 瘟球 naphthaline balls | 蚊香 mosquito-killer		
鄙[34]	邑 163	啚 767	Low, mean, | 劣; vulgar, rustic | 陋 | 人 I myself		E
俾[4]	人 9	卑 807	To cause, enable, so that | 益 to benefit | 得 enable to obtain	pei[1]	F
婢[4]	女 38	卑 807	Maid servant	pei[4]	E
痺[4]	疒 104	卑 807	Rheumatism, numbness 脚 |		I
睥[4]	目 109	卑 807	To glance around, spy | 睨 to look upon with disdain		I
愎[4]	心 61	复 544	Perverse, self-willed 剛 | | 諫 resist remonstrances	p'i[4]	F
碧[4]	石 112	白 804	Green jade | 玉 | 綠 dark green of jade | 色		H
賁[4]	貝 154	賁 417	Beautiful, elegant; to adorn | 臨 the arrival of a visitor	pen[1]	K

P'i

劈[1]	刀 18	辟 158	To split open |◦開 | 破 split in two, speak plainly | 碎 split up small	p'i[3]	C
霹[1]	雨 173	辟 158	The crash of thunder | 雷 | 靂 rapid claps of thunder		G
披[1]	手 64	皮 537	To unroll, open | 展 unroll, as a scroll	p'ei[1]	D
批[1]	手 64	匕 317	Order of court; rescript, contract; to criticize, revise | 准 to grant a petition | 貨物 buy goods to arrive | 定		E

P'i

Character	Radical	Phonetic	Meaning	Other reading	Grade
批^{1}			｜駁 reverse a judgment or deny a petition ｜°評 to criticise, censure ｜註 ｜點 criticise and mark		
砒^{1} 磇^{1}	石 112	匕 317	Arsenic ｜霜, ｜信, ｜石 ｜末 powdered arsenic		I
丕^{1}	一 1	不 120	Great, vast, first, unequalled ｜時 time of great prosperity	p'ei^{1}	I
坯^{1} 坏^{1}	土 32	不 120	Unburnt bricks (sun-dried) 土｜ ｜模·子 a brick-mould ｜場 brick yard		E
胚^{2} 肧^{2}	肉 130	不 120	Embryo, foetus; unformed ｜胎 a pregnant womb, foetus	p'ei^{1}	H
皮^{2}	皮 107	皮 537	Skin, fur, leather ｜·子; container S. ｜襖 a fur coat; so ｜靴子, ｜衣, ｜褥·子, etc. ｜夾·子 small hand-bag ｜包 valise ｜·匠 a worker in leather ｜箱 a leather trunk ｜帶·子 leather girdle, harness ｜貨 skins, furs. 書｜ book-cover		A
疲^{2}	疒 104	皮 537	Lassitude, fatigue, exhausted ｜倦 tired, fatigued ｜乏		D
啤^{2}	口 30	卑 807	Beer ｜酒		G
脾^{2}	肉 130	卑 807	Spleen, stomach; disposition ｜·氣 disposition, temper ｜病 enlargement of the spleen ｜胃 the stomach, appetite		D
琵^{2}	玉 96	珏 77	Balloon, guitar ｜·琶		G
枇^{2}	木 75	匕 317	Biwa, loquat ｜·杷		I

毘2 毗2	比 81	匕 317	Contiguous (fields) | 連		I
匹31	匸 23	匚 645	Mate, fellow, pair; C. of animals | 偶 a pair; husband and wife | 配 一 | 馬 a horse. 馬 | horses		C
劈3	刀 18	辟 158	|·柴 Kindlings, firewood	p'i1	C
癖3	疒 104	辟 158	Indigestion; craving; weakness 錢 | avarice 食 | craving for food		H
疋3	疋 103	疋 137	Piece, roll of cloth; C. of bolts 一 | 布 a bolt of cloth 成 |		D
否3	口 30	不 120	Obstructed; hard lot 命 | | 世 an evil world	fou3	F
痞3	疒 104	不 120	A stoppage, constipation; swelling | 積 indigestion, constipation		I
辟4	辛 160	辟 158	To punish; perverse 大 | capital punishment	pi4	G
僻4	人 9	辟 158	Mean, secluded, rustic; depraved 偏 | depraved, mean 邪 | 乖 | dissolute 放 |		G
譬4	言 149	辟 158	Compare, like, if, suppose | 如, | 若 |·喻 metaphor, for instance		C
闢4	門 169	辟 158	To burst forth, to open up | 地 open the earth, creation 開 |		G
愎4	心 61	复 544	Perverse, self-willed 剛 | stubborn, self-opinionated	pi4	F
屁4	尸 44	匕 317	To break wind 放 | |·股 the buttocks |·股 眼 the anus		H

Piao

標1	木 75	票 777	Signal, publish, exhibit; prize; troops; fine		D

Piao

Character	Radical	Phonetic	Meaning	Other readings	Grade
標[1]			｜記 marks—as in navigation ｜旗 a signal flag ｜識 sign, emblem, symbol ｜準 an example, standard ｜様 ｜桿 a beacon pole, goal ｜本 model, specimens ｜示 to publish; ｜語 slogans		
臕[1]	肉 130	鹿 319	Fat, corpulent, sleek 肥｜ ｜満 sleek and fat 脂｜		G
鑣[1]	金 167	鹿 319	Bridle and trappings 扣｜to rein in		I
杓[1]	木 75	勺 231	Handle of a dipper 斗｜	shao[2] shou[4]	G
彪[1]	彡 59	虍 203	Tiger cat; veins; ornate ｜柄 elegant clear style 文｜		I
髟[1]	髟 190		Bushy hair 垂｜		K
表[3]	衣 145	表 372	To manifest; clock, watch ｜章 a statement. ｜題 motto ｜記 a keepsake, souvenir ｜匠 a watch-maker ｜姐妹 female first cousins of other S., so ｜兄弟 male first cousins. ｜∘出 to manifest abroad ｜揚 ｜決 manifest opinion, take vote ｜鍊 a watch-chain ｜面 exterior, veneer ｜明 to state clearly ｜白 ｜∘示 sign, emblem; to express ｜様 an example		A
婊[3]	女 38	表 372	Harlot, prostitute ｜·子		I
裱[3]	衣 145	表 372	To paste; mount, paper ｜·糊 ｜·糊匠 a paper-hanger ｜畫 post or mount pictures		D

Character	Radical	Phonetic	Meaning	Variant	Grade
鰾4	魚 195	票 777	Fish bladder 魚丨 丨膠 fish-glue 魚丨		H

P'iao

Character	Radical	Phonetic	Meaning	Variant	Grade
漂1	水 85	票 777	Tossed about, drifting 丨流 drift about 丨來丨去 丨·在水面 float on the water	p'iao34	E
飄1	風 182	票 777	Blown about; floating 丨雪 whirl of snow falling 丨流 hither and thither, float 丨颻 丨灑 graceful, airy 丨·帶 a pennant 丨蕩 to swagger, rock, roll		E
嫖2	女 38	票 777	Profligate, wanton, to visit prostitutes 丨客 a debauchee 丨婊·子 to consort with prostitutes		F
瓢2	瓜 97	票 777	Calabash, gourd, ladle 水丨 calabash water dipper 椰丨 cocoanut-shell dipper		E
漂3	水 85	票 777	To bleach 丨白 丨布 to bleach linen	p'iao14	E
瞟3	目 109	票 777	To look askance, squint 丨眇		K
票4	示 113	票 777	Ticket, bank-note, check, bills 丨决 decide by ballot, vote 丨選 elect by ballot 丨·子 money order, note 錢丨,銀丨		A
漂4	水 85	票 777	Bright, fresh, smart 丨·亮	p'iao13	E

Pieh

Character	Radical	Phonetic	Meaning	Variant	Grade
瘷1	疒 104	敝 561	Suppurating ulcer; to restrain 丨·不住 unable to hold in 丨·子 a urinal 尿丨·子		I

Character	Radical	Phonetic	Definition		Freq.
憋[1] 懒[1]	心 61	敝 561	Sad, lonely, irritable 丨氣 draw or hold the breath 丨·悶 sad, melancholy, lonely 丨·扭 obstinate, unwilling		F
鼈[1] 鱉[1]	黽 205	敝 561	Turtle. 大沙丨 sea-turtle 丨蛋 a bastard 丨魚 tortoise		I
別[2]	刀 18	別 224a	To separate, distinguish; another; do not S. 丨針 clasp-pin, brooch 丨急 don't fret, or get excited 丨·家 do not 丨見笑 do not laugh at it 丨·處 elsewhere, another place 丨去 don't go! gone elsewhere 丨·人 another person, others 丨怪 don't blame me 丨忙 not so fast; don't hurry 丨名 another name, an alias 丨生氣 don't be angry 丨·的 another, different 丨動 don't disturb; don't stir! 丨樣 another kind 丨有 else, other, beside 分·丨 difference, distinguish		A
癟[3]	疒 104	侖 439	Shrivelled, limp, 乾丨 丨嘴子 a toothless person 皮帶丨·了 tire deflated		F

P'ieh

Character	Radical	Phonetic	Definition		Freq.
撇[13] 撆[13]	手 64	敝 561	Skim off, cast away; left stroke in writing 丨棄 to cast away 丨脫, 丨∘開 丨·下·了 abandon entirely 丨沫子 to skim off scum 丨油 to skim off fat		D

Character	Radical	Phonetic	Meaning			
潎[14]	水 85	敝 561	Rippling, pure | 淨·了			K
瞥[14]	目 109	敝 561	To glance at; to blink | 一眼, | 觀			I
丿[1]	丿 4	丿 166	Down stroke to the left			K

Pien

Character	Radical	Phonetic	Meaning			
邊[1] 边[1]	辵 162	方 261	Side, bank, edge, margin; place; frontier | 疆 a frontier, a border | 界 這·| this side, here. 那·| there 旁 | the side; by the side of 裏·| inside. 外·| outside	S		A
鞭[1]	革 177	更 834	A whip, |·子; to whip | 炮 fire-crackers in string | 梢 the lash of a whip | 撻 beat with a whip			C
編[1]	糸 120	扁 566	To plait | 髮; enroll; compile |∘輯(人) editor, compiler |∘輯部 editorial staff | 制 devise plans, methods | 造 compose, write, compile | 纂 | 物 crochet work			C
蝙[1]	虫 142	扁 566	The bat |·蝠			G
砭[14]	石 112	乏 300	Stone probe; to pierce 針 | acupuncture and probing			K
扁[3]	戶 63	扁 566	Tablet; flat, thin | 的 |·食 meat-dumpling |·担 a porter's pole | 簪兒 flat hair-pins | 方兒		p'ien[1]	F
匾[3]	匸 23	扁 566	Flat, horizontal; tablet | 額 honorary tablet			F
藊[3]	艸 140	扁 566	Trailing bean | 豆 green peas, kind of bean			F

Pien

貶3	貝 154	乏 300	To censure, cashier, dismiss ｜官 discharge official ｜退		G
便4	人 9	更 834	Convenient, ready; then ｜飯 common every-day food ｜衣 undress, not in uniform ｜易 convenient ｜∘利, ｜·當, 方｜ ｜可 then you may do it ｜門 side door, ｜道 side road ｜是 that is, then it is 隨｜ at your convenience	p'ien2	B
變4 变4	言 149	䜌 888	To change, alter, turn in affairs; mutiny ｜遷 variations; to change, (intransitive v.) ｜法 reform ｜戲法兒 sleight of hand ｜化 to change- ｜易, ｜更, 改｜ ｜賣 sell off, turn into money ｜兵 mutinying soldiers ｜色 to change color ｜天 weather changes ｜∘通 accommodating ｜様兒 change form or style 兵｜·了 the soldiers mutinied		B
辨4	辛 160	辛 157	To discriminate, discuss ｜別, ｜明, 分｜ ｜好歹 distinguish good and bad ｜論 to discuss, dispute ｜白 establish innocence		C
辮4	糸 120	辛 157	To plait; the queue ｜·子 ｜髮 to plait the hair		C
辯4	辛 160	辛 157	To discuss, dispute ｜∘論 ｜學 logic ｜護 plead case. ｜護士 lawyer ｜理 argue the right or wrong ｜駁 to contradict; dispute	pan4	C

Character	Radical	Phonetic	Meaning	Other readings	
辯4			丨士 an orator 丨才 ability to argue, eloquence		
遍4 徧4	辵 162	扁 566	Everywhere; a time; whole 丨街 the whole street 丨處 every place 丨地 丨告 to inform everyone 丨身 the whole body	p'ien4	D
弁4	廾 55	厶 868	Military cap, to rub hands 丨兵 petty officers and privates		H
拚4	手 64	厶 868	To tap, lay hand on	fan1 p'an4 p'in1	F
騈4	馬 187	幷 35	A pair of horses, joined 丨字 two-word phrases	p'ien2	I
釆4	釆 165		To sort out, discriminate		K

P'ien

Character	Radical	Phonetic	Meaning	Other readings	
扁1 艑1	戶 63	扁 566	A skiff, barge 丨舟	pien3	F
偏1	人 9	扁 566	Onesided, prejudiced, selfish, determined; leaning, partial 丨愛 strong partiality for 丨疼 丨巧 unexpectedly 丨見 view partially, prejudice 丨房 a concubine 丨室 丨向partiality, bias 丨私, 丨心眼兒 丨斜 inclined, oblique, slanting 丨過了 "I have eaten before you" 丨勞 thanks for your trouble! 丨離 to diverge, incline away 丨理 forced, onesided argument 丨·僻 depraved, eccentric 丨 丨 especially, certainly 丨待 treat unfairly, partiality 丨要 bent on having		C

篇[1]	竹 118	扁 566	A slip, leaf, book, section 一|書 |章 page and chapter 翻| turn over the leaves		B
翩[1]	羽 124	扁 566	Fluttering, bustle | |		I
便[2]	人 9	更 834	|·宜 Advantage, cheap 佔|·宜 take advantage of	pien[4]	B
駢[2]	馬 187	幷 35	A pair of horses, joined |字 two word phrases	pien[4]	I
諞[3]	言 149	扁 566	Artful, plausible |言 |嘴 deceitful lips		K
片[4]	片 91	片 164	A splinter, slip, card, leaf; few; C of sheets, slices |紙 a visiting card |·子, 名| |刻 a little time |時 |言 reticent; a few words 切|(兒) cut in slices		B
劘[4]	刀 18	扁 566	To pare, slice off |·下·去 |果·子 to slice fruits |刀 a carving-knife		K
徧[4] 遍[4]	彳 60	扁 566	Everywhere, whole, a time 俗 |地 everywhere |處 |遊 make pleasure tour	pien[4]	D
騙[4]	馬 187	扁 566	To cheat, deceive, swindle |人 |·去 to inveigle from |馬 to leap on horse |·子 a swindler |·子手 哄| cheat, humbug 誆|, 欺|		D

Pin

賓[1] 賔[1]	貝 154	賓 860	A guest; to submit, entertain |主 guest and host |服 to respect; submit |客 guests, visitors |朋 |位 predicate of sentence; guest's seat		B

<table>
<tr><td>嬪1</td><td>女
38</td><td>賓
860</td><td>Imperial concubine | 妃,妃 |, wife
| 婦 a wife</td><td></td><td>H</td></tr>
<tr><td>檳1
梹1</td><td>木
75</td><td>賓
860</td><td>The betel-nut | 榔
|·子 a tart apple</td><td>ping1</td><td>H</td></tr>
<tr><td>濱1
瀕1</td><td>水
85</td><td>賓
860</td><td>Shore, brink, beach 海 |
| 死 on brink of death</td><td></td><td>E</td></tr>
<tr><td>彬1
斌1</td><td>彡
59</td><td>林
492</td><td>Refined, elegant | 媚
文質 | | substantial and elegant</td><td></td><td>I</td></tr>
<tr><td>擯4</td><td>手
64</td><td>賓
860</td><td>To expel, reject | 逐
| 棄 to reject | 斥</td><td></td><td>K</td></tr>
<tr><td>殯4</td><td>歹
78</td><td>賓
860</td><td>To encoffin, a funeral 出 |
| 殮 to bury | 葬</td><td></td><td>F</td></tr>
<tr><td>鬢4
鬂4</td><td>髟
190</td><td>賓
860</td><td>The hair on the temples | 髮
|∘角兒 the temples
白 | white hair (from age)</td><td></td><td>I</td></tr>
</table>

P'in

<table>
<tr><td>拚1</td><td>手
64</td><td>厶
868</td><td>To risk; reject, disregard
| 命 I'll risk my life for it!</td><td>fan1
p'an4
pien4</td><td>F</td></tr>
<tr><td>貧2</td><td>貝
154</td><td>分
395</td><td>Poor, impoverished | 窮, | 寒, | 乏
| 賤 poor and mean
| 富 poverty and riches
| 人 poor person | 戶 the poor</td><td></td><td>D</td></tr>
<tr><td>頻2</td><td>頁
181</td><td>步
131</td><td>Unceasing, hurry, urgent | 速
| 催 incessantly urging</td><td></td><td>I</td></tr>
<tr><td>櫇2</td><td>木
75</td><td>步
131</td><td>The apple | 菓</td><td>p'ing2</td><td>E</td></tr>
<tr><td>品3</td><td>口
30</td><td>品
695</td><td>Series, rank, kind, character
|∘級 grade, rank | 職
|·出來 to form an estimate
|∘行4 conduct, actions, behavior</td><td></td><td>C</td></tr>
</table>

品[3]			丨格 mien, manner; disposition 丨性 丨類 sorts; things classified 丨物 丨德 character 丨詞 part of speech 物丨 things		
牝[3]	牛 93	牛 38	Female animals 丨雞, 丨馬, 丨羊 丨牡 male and female		F
聘[4]	耳 128	由 818	To betroth, engage, espouse 丨娶 marry a woman 丨姑娘 betroth a daughter 丨定的 (a girl) betrothed	p'ing[4]	E

Ping

兵[1]	八 12	丘 213	Soldier, military 丨丁, 丨卒, 丨士 丨車 a war-chariot or car 丨·器 military weapons 丨械 丨甲 armor, 出丨 go to war 丨船 a man-of-war 丨餉 pay, rations of troops 丨力 military strength 丨亂 mutiny of troops 丨變 丨額 fixed number of soldiers 丨營 military camp 馬丨 cavalry, 步丨 infantry		C
氷[1] 冰[1]	水 85	水 520	Ice, icy; to freeze 丨·激凌 ice-cream 丨水 ice water 丨窖 an ice pit, ice-house 丨床 an ice sledge, sled 丨箱(·子) ice-chest, refrigerator 丨鞋 skates, 丨凉 cold as ice 丨雹 hail. 丨山 iceberg 丨糖 rock candy, (sugar-crystal) 丨點 freezing point 丨洋 the Arctic Ocean 北丨洋		C

Ping

冫^{1}	冫 15	水 520	Ice		K
檳^{1} 梹^{1}	木 75	賓 860	The betel-nut | 榔 俗	pin^{1}	H
屏^{3}	尸 44	幷 35	To reject; expel | 去, | 逐, | 除 | 棄 to reject, dismiss	p'ing^{2}	H
餅^{3}	食 184	幷 35	Cakes, pastry, (many kinds) | 食 | 乾 biscuits, crackers 月·| cakes for 8 mo., 15 day 中秋 |		B
丙^{3}	一 1	丙 445	The third stem; fire, south		F
柄^{3,4}	木 75	丙 445	A handle, authority, power 權·| 把 | a handle, words that give a hold on one 話 |		C
炳^{3}	火 86	丙 445	Bright, luminous | 然 evident		I
稟^{3}	示 113	稟 769	To announce, petition, report; disposition | 知 to state as a report | 報 | 請 to ask from a superior | 賦 receive from heaven | 性 disposition | 質 | 告 petition of accusation | 帖 petition, report | 書, 遞 |		E
秉^{3}	禾 115	禾 510	To grasp, hold, uphold | 持 | 性 natural disposition | 公辦理 act with justice		F
病^{4}	疒 104	丙 445	Illness, defect, disease, vice | 症 | 重 sickness is severe | 犯·了 return of old disease | 好·了 cured. | 人 sick man | 根 root of a disease | 故 to die of disease | 死 | 源 cause of disease		A

並[4] 幷[4] 并[4] 竝[4]	一 1 干 51 立 117	幷 35	Two together, and, moreover; at once; also; really ｜∘且 moreover, besides ｜非 by no means ｜不是 ｜合 to unite, amalgamate ｜力 ｜行 to walk together ｜馬雙行 ride side by side 一｜ the whole together, all		B
併[4] 倂[4]	人 9	幷 35	Even, together; reduce, to equalize ｜進 to advance together		G

P'ing

平[2]	干 51	平 36	Even, level, tranquil; to weigh; uniform, equitable ｜安 peace, tranquillity ｜安無事 ｜常 common, ordinary ｜日, ｜素, ｜時 ｜治 to regulate ｜靜 still, quiet ｜權 equal rights. 公·｜ just ｜均計算 general average ｜分 to divide equally ｜·復 restored to health or tranquillity ｜和 harmonious, moderate ｜西 westering (sun) ｜心 calmly ｜行 to go side by side ｜行線 parallel lines ｜民 the ordinary people ｜輩 the same generation ｜生 all one's life ｜聲 the even tones of words (1,2) ｜臺 a terrace, level roof ｜坦 level, even, smooth ｜等 equal rank, equality		A

平²			｜地 level ground; plain ｜原 ｜◦定 steady, sober; just		
萍²	艸 140	平 36	Duckweed 浮｜, 水｜; drifting ｜草 water lichen or moss		I
評²	言 149	平 36	To criticise, discuss ｜議, ｜論 ｜脈 to feel the pulse ｜判 to decide, arbitrate, ｜定 批·｜ criticise, censure		D
屏²	尸 44	幷 35	To screen, cover 帷｜, ｜帳 ｜◦風 a screen ｜門	ping³	H
瓶² 缾²	瓦 98	幷 35	Pitcher, jar, vase, bottle ｜·子 ｜塞 a stopper, cork 花｜ a flower vase 水｜ water pitcher		A
憑² 凴² [illegible]²	心 61 减	馬 255	Proof; rely on, according to ｜仗 lean against; depend on ｜證 proof, evidence ｜·據 ｜心 obey conscience ｜良·心 ｜信 trustworthy, reliable ｜空 foundationless, no proof ｜理 depend on right ｜·你 as you please ｜票 bearer note ｜單 certificate		D
馮²	馬 187	馬 255	To rely on, evidence; to mount ｜氣 confidence; to boast	feng²	H
檳²	木 75	步 131	Apple ｜菓	p'in²	E
聘⁴	耳 128	由 818	To betroth, engage, espouse 俗 ｜姑娘 to betroth a daughter	p'in⁴	E

Po

玻¹	玉 96	皮 537	Vitreous glass ｜·璃 ｜·璃磚 plate glass ｜·璃盃 drinking glass, tumbler ｜·璃瓶 glass bottle or vase		A

Po

波[1]	水 85	波 537a	A wave, ripple, ∣ 浪 ∣ 瀾 waves; random talk ∣·稜蓋兒 the kneecap, knee ∣·羅菓 pineapple ∣·羅蜜 —jack-fruit ∣ 斯國 Persia			C
菠[1]	艸 140	波 537a	Winter cabbage, spinach ∣ 菜			G
撥[1]	手 64	發 246	To open out, scatter, transfer; revise; expel ∣ 正 to correct, regulate ∣ 錢 transfer money; so ∣ 兵 ∣ 去 to reject, expel ∣∘開 ∣ 船 lighters for cargo ∣ 給 give out, appropriate ∣ 用			D
剝[14]	刀 18	彔 525	To peel, flay ∣ 皮; kill; extort		pao[1]	E
餑[1]	食 184	孛 113	Baked cakes, biscuits ∣ ∣			F
蔔[1]	艸 140	畐 816	Carrot, turnip, radish 蘿 ∣			F
舶[14]	舟 137	白 804	Junk, ocean-going ship ∣ 來品 foreign things			I
鉢[1]	金 167	本 485	Bowl, alms-bowl ∣ 盂 priest's alms dish			I
渤[14]	水 85	孛 113	Arm of sea; mist ∣ 海 Gulf of Hopei			I
白[24]	白 106	白 804	White, pure	S.	pai[2]	A
伯[24]	人 9	白 804	Father's elder brother; earl ∣ 爵 3rd rank nobility, earl ∣·父 father's elder brother ∣ 母 paternal uncle's wife ∣ 叔 uncle on father's side 叔 ∣ 方 ∣ commissioner, deputy		pai[23]	D

Po

⿰口白^{2}	口 30	白 804	Sound for transliteration			G
泊^{24}	水 85	白 804	Shore; ripple; moor, anchor | 船			E
博^{24} 愽^{24}	十 24	尃 598	Widely-read; ample, spacious; to gamble; barter | 愛 philanthropy | 而不精 wide but shallow knowledge | 學 extensive learning | 聞 | 奕 to play at Chinese chess | 古家 archaeologists | 覽會 exhibition, exposition |∘士 holder of Doctor's degree | 物院 a museum			C
搏^{2}	手 64	尃 598	To strike, seize | 取 | 擊 to strike			I
膊^{24}	肉 130	尃 598	Shoulder 胳 | arm 轉 | change shoulders carrying			B
薄^{24}	艸 140	溥 599	Thin, poor, shabby; coldly |^{4}·荷 peppermint | 弱 weak, unstable | 待 to treat shabbily	S	pao^{2}	B
駁^{2} 駮^{2}	馬 187	爻 529	To argue against, disapprove; trans-ship; diverse | 價 object to the price | 回 to contradict 辯 | |·不倒^{3} cannot be disproven | 倒^{3} overthrow in argument			D
脖^{2}	肉 130	孛 113	The neck, |·子, | 頸子; navel | 帶兒 necktie 領帶			E
帛^{24}	巾 50	帛 806	Wealth; silk 財 | money, wealth			G
趵^{2}	足 157	勺 231	Noise of tramping		pao^{4}	I

Po

Character	Radical	Phonetic	Meaning		Reading	
簸^{3}	竹 118	皮 537	To winnow grain ｜米 ｜揚 to winnow		po^{4}	E
跛^{3}	足 157	皮 537	Lame, ｜足, ｜腿; favoritism			G
播^{34}	手 64	番 811	To sow, publish, winnow ｜種 scatter or sow seeds ｜弄 to deceive, cheat			F
百^{42}	白 106	百 805	Hundred, many, all ｜家姓 the Book of Surnames ｜合花 lily flower pai^{3}- ｜·姓 the people	文	pai^{3} pai^{3} pai^{3}	A
北^{4}	匕 21	北 321	North	•文	pei^{3}	A
擘^{4}	手 64	辟 158	To break, split		pai^{1}	E
簸^{4}	竹 118	皮 537	Winnowing fan ｜·箕		po^{3}	E
柏^{4} 栢^{4}	木 75	白 804	Cypress, cedar	文	pai^{3}	F
箔^{4}	竹 118	白 804	A splint door-screen, frame 蠶｜ frame for silkworms			K
跋^{4}	足 157	犮 188	Heel; summary; to travel ｜倒 stumble and fall		pa^{2}	G
鈸^{4}	金 167	犮 188	Small cymbals 鐃｜			E
魃^{4}	鬼 194	犮 188	Demon of drought 旱｜		pa^{2}	I
孛^{4}	子 39	孛 113	Plants shooting up; a comet ｜星			K
勃^{4}	力 19	孛 113	Suddenly, flurried ｜然大怒 sudden burst of passion			I
癶^{4}	癶 105		Back to back, to progress			K

P'o

Character	Radical	Phonetic	Meaning	
坡[1]	土 32	皮 537	Slope, declivity 山 | hillside. 平 | gentle slope	C
陂[1]	阜 170	皮 537	Uneven, inclined	G
頗[1]	頁 181	皮 537	Quite, very; somewhat, partial | 久 a very long time | 好 extremely good; fond of | 可 it will do very well | 多 very many or much | 有 well supplied, good deal	E
潑[1]	水 85	發 246	To throw out | 水, spill; waste |·出去 spill it out |·| 院子 sprinkle court-yard 撒 | create disturbance	F
婆[2]	女 38	波 537a	Wife, old lady, crone 老 |·子 |·家 husband's mother's family | 羅門教 Brahmanism | 母 a mother-in-law | |	C
鄱[2]	邑 163	番 811	District in Kiangsi	I
叵[3]	口 30	匚 640	Not; forthwith | 信 unworthy of belief	K
笸[3]	竹 118	匚 640	Feed-basket |·籮	H
破[4]	石 112	皮 537	To break, ruin; solve, detect |∘綻 a hole, fault | 產 bankrupt, bankruptcy | 解 to explain clearly | 船 a shipwreck | 風水 to spoil the luck | 壞 smash, destructive | 碎 | 壞名譽 to libel | 爛 torn, ragged | 裂 | 謎 ask or solve riddle -mer[4]	A

破^4			丨天荒 supply long-felt want 丨財 to squander wealth		
拍^4	手 64	白 804	Clap, rap, slap	p'ai^1	D
珀^4	玉 96	白 804	Amber 琥丨		H
粕^4	米 119	白 804	Grains in liquor, 糟丨 dregs		K
迫^4 廹^4	辵 162	白 804	To press, harass, persecute 强丨 丨切 hurried, urgent 急丨 逼丨 to constrain, persecute	po^4	C
魄^4	鬼 194	白 804	The animal soul; form 丨力 physical vigor, courage 魂丨 soul's two divisions		G

Pou

不^1	一 1	不 120	Not, no 俗	pu^{124}	A

P'ou

抛^1	手 64	力 223	To throw down, cast off 俗	p'ao^1	D
剖^{13}	刀 18	音 89	To halve, split, lay open; explain, decide 丨開 解丨 dissect. 解丨學 anatomy 丨心 to open one's heart 丨心瀝膽 丨判 to decide in judgment 丨斷		E

Pu

不^1	一 1	不 120	No, not (final or before interrogative), 是·丨 去·丨 will you go? 偏丨^4 won't 好·丨 is it good? will it do?	pou^1 pu^{24}	A
逋^1	辵 162	甫 597	Abscond, flee; to owe; defaulter		K

Pu

<table>
<tr><td>不²</td><td>一
1</td><td>不
120</td><td>No, not (before 4th tone)
|愛 averse to, do not like
|礙 unimportant, no harm |礙事
|見 to lose, invisible
|至於 not to the extent of
|住的 incessantly, constantly |斷
|中 won't do, no use
|像樣 inferior, disgraceful
|信 to disbelieve
|幸 unluckily; mishap
|會 unable to, unskilled
|幹 will not undertake
|彀本 a losing proposition
|顧 to disregard
|◦過 not exceeding; only, just
|料 unexpectedly
|論 no matter
|怕 don't be afraid
|必 it is not necessary
|◦是 fault; it is not so |◦是的
|◦是麼 is it not?◦是·|·是
|·是道理 unreasonable |^{4}合理
|送 (I will) not escort you
|大離 not far off, all right
|但 not only
|在 not at home or here; dead; does not depend upon
|錯 it is so, no mistake
|對 not agree, incorrect
|對勁兒 not congenial
|動產 real estate
|要 don't, don't want
|要緊 unimportant, no matter
|用 don't use; useless</td><td>pou¹
pu¹⁴</td><td>A</td></tr>
<tr><td>醭²</td><td>酉
164</td><td>菐
156</td><td>Mother of vinegar; mould 白|兒</td><td></td><td>K</td></tr>
</table>

Pu

Character	Radical	Phonetic	Meaning	Other readings	Code
哺^{34}	口 30	甫 597	To feed by hand, suckle | 乳 張口受 | birds receiving food	fu^{3}	I
捕^{34}	手 64	甫 597	To arrest, catch, hunt | 獲 to seize, arrest | 拿 | 役 constables, police | 盜 to apprehend robbers | 賊 | 魚 to catch fish 巡 | constable, policeman		F
補^{3}	衣 145	甫 597	To patch, repair; billion | 助 to help, assist | 缺 to fill a vacancy | 習科 supplementary class | 路 mend roads; so | 鞋, | 衣 | 品 tonic (medicine) | 藥 |·上 to add to or on |·靪 a patch on clothes | 足 make up deficiency 賠 | make good a loss | 還	p'u^{3}	B
卜^{3}	卜 25	卜 119	To divine, foretell, 占 | , | 卦 S. | 課 divination by diagrams		D
堡^{34}	土 32	保 758	Low walls, | 障; a city ward	pao^{3} p'u^{34}	H
不^{4}	一 1	不 120	No, not (before tones nos. 1, 2, 3) | 成 incomplete; eh? what? won't do | 成文 unwritten, poorly worded | 及 not in time, not up to mark | 彌 bad, not superior | 好 | 見其 not likely, hardly think | 知足 dissatisfied | 久 not long, before long | 拘 no matter which or what | 妨 there is no objection | 服 to differ with, object | 好意思 to feel diffident about | 合式 to disagree, misfit | 行 will not do or answer	pou^{1} pu^{12}	A

Pu

不4			丨然 not so; on the contrary 丨如 not so good as 丨該 ought not, owe nothing 丨敢當 thank you; you flatter me 丨可 ought not, should not 丨可知 agnostic; unknowable 丨管 to disregard, neglect 丨管事 inefficient, neglect affairs 丨管他 let him alone 丨理他 丨能 unable to, impossible 丨能丨 cannot but 丨得已 unavoidable 丨通 no thoroughfare, not current 丨由的 without cause		
布4	巾 50	佈 171	Cotton cloth; to spread, arrange 丨衣 cotton clothes, a commoner 丨告 disseminate, publish 丨疋 cloth, cotton fabrics 丨舖 a linen draper's shop, 丨店		B
佈4	人 9	佈 171	To spread, diffuse 丨·置 to place (troops etc.) 丨告 to publish. 丨道 to preach 丨散流言 spread idle rumors 丨道團 preaching band		C
怖4	心 61	佈 171	Afraid, alarmed 恐丨		I
步4	止 77	步 131	A step, pace; infantry S. 丨戰 to fight on foot 丨行 go on foot. 丨丨 step by step 丨兵 infantry 丨隊		B
部4	邑 163	咅 89	Class, section; board; a radical 丨·分 member, section, fraction 丨類 a class, tribe 丨首 head of category; radical		C
簿4	竹 118	溥 599	Account book, note book, tablet, register, record 丨賬 an account book 賬丨		F

簿⁴			| 記 book keeping 日記 | diary, journal		
暴⁴	日 72	暴 99	To dry in the sun	pao⁴	D
埠⁴	土 32	阜 752	A port, a mart		G

P'u

鋪¹	金 167	甫 597	To spread out, arrange | 陳 | 床 to make the bed | 席 spread mat, give feast |·盖 bedding. |·開 spread out	p'u⁴	A
仆¹	人 9	卜 119	To fall, prostrate | 倒在地 俗	fu⁴	D
撲¹ 扑¹	手 64	菐 156	To bang, rush against, a blow | 擊 to strike | 蝴蝶 to catch butterflies | 空 go on fruitless errand | 滅 exterminate, extinguish | 鼻 to affect the nose | 到臉·上 strike against the face		F
攴¹ 攵¹	攴 66	攴 548	To tap, rap		K
僕²³	人 9	菐 156	Servant, subject | 人, 臣 | | 隸 lictors in a yamen | 婢 men and women domestics | 從 attendants		D
樸²³ 朴²³	木 75	菐 156	Natural, plain, honest, simple | 實 plain, honest, sincere | 厚 | 素 simple, plain		E
匍²	勹 20	甫 597	Prostrate, to creep | 匐		H
浦³	水 85	甫 597	A creek, tributary S. | 邊 the bank of a creek 黃 | the river at Shanghai		G

P'u

葡[2]	艸 140	甫 597	The vine, grape |·萄 |·萄汁 the juice of grape |·萄酒 grape wine |·萄乾兒 raisins |·萄樹 the grape vine		E
蒲[2]	艸 140	甫 597	Rushes, cat-tail, | 草 S. | 蓆 a rush mat | 包兒 a rush basket | 扇 rush fan | 團 rush hassock | 墊子		F
菩[2]	艸 140	咅 89	Pusa, Bodhi tree or pipul |·薩 Buddhist idol | 提樹 Buddhist pipul tree		E
普[3]	日 72	幷 35	Universal, all, large, general | 通 | 及教育 general education | 通教育 | 救衆生 save all living beings | 遍 on all sides; full | 天下 the world universal | 通知識 general information		C
譜[3]	言 149	幷 35	Chronicle, register, genealogy | 籍 a list, genealogy | 系 family record, genealogy 家 |		E
堡[34]	土 32	保 758	Low wall; a city ward	pao[3] pu[34]	H
圃[34]	口 31	甫 597	Vegetable garden, orchard 農 | farmers and gardners 老 | gardener		H
溥[3]	水 85	溥 599	Vast, pervading, universal | 滿 in all parts | 遍		K
菐[3]		菐 156	A thicket		P
舖[4]	舌 135	甫 597	A shop, store |·子, | 店 | 戶 shop people, merchants | 家 | 櫃 shop cash-box | 保 tradesman's guarantee		C

舖4			丨底 shop fixtures, "good-will" 當丨 pawn-shop, 丨面 shop-front		
鋪4	金 167	甫 597	Store, (commonly 舖)	p'u1	A
瀑4	水 85	暴 99	A waterfall	pao4	G

Sa

三1	一 1	一 1	Three. 丨倆 two or three 俗 丨人 three persons	san14	A
撒1	手 64	散 800	To let go, let loose 丨∘開 丨歡 to frisk, play, (as animals) 丨謊 to tell lies, falsehood 丨尿 make water, urinate 丨潑 create a disturbance 丨手 loosen the hand, let go 丨帖 send out invitations	sa3	C
薩14	艸 140	生 41	Pusa 菩丨		G
趿14	足 157	及 218	To tread; slip-shod, 丨·着鞋, 丨·拉		H
[目+散]2	目 109	散 800	To glance at, catch sight of 丨·着		H
洒3 灑3	水 85	西 775	To sprinkle, scatter, spill over 丨水 to sprinkle water 丨∘脫 careless, free and easy 水丨·了 water spilt in carrying		B
撒3	手 64	散 800	To scatter, sow, spill 丨種 to scatter seed 丨花使者 flower girls 丨網 cast a fishing net	sa1	C

Sai

塞1	土 32	𡨄 100	To stop up, cork 丨·上, 丨·住 丨兒 a stopper, a cork 丨·子 丨口 to stop a hole	sai4 se4	A

顋[1] 腮[1]	頁 181	思 379	The cheeks, jaws, jowl, gills | 頰 the cheeks, the jaws | 膀子脹起 | puff out the cheeks		F
揌[21]	手 64	思 379	To move, shake, choose		I
塞[4]	土 32	実 100	A pass, northern and eastern frontiers | 外 Mongolia | 北 要 | strategic point	sai[1] se[4]	A
賽[4]	貝 154	実 100	To compete, rival, emulate | 珍會 exposition, exhibition | 船 boat-race; so | 馬, | 跑 比 | competition		D

San

三[1] 叁[1]	一 1	一 1	Three | 個, so |°十, | 百, etc. | 角 triangular; three-quarters | 角術 trigonometry | 教 Confucianism Buddhism Taoism, = 3 religions | 界 (Budd.) desire, form, formlessness | 清 "The Three Pure" (Taoist trinity) | 九 27 days after winter solstice | 伏 3 ten-day periods of summer heat | 心二意 undecided, hesitating | 綱 3 bands of society = prince minister, father son, husband wife | 光 sun, moon and stars | 兩個 two or three | 板 "three planks", a sampan | 寶 "Three Precious" (Buddhist) | 色版 chromo, colored picture	sa[1] san[4]	A

Character	Radical	Phonetic	Meaning	Other readings	
三^{1}			｜才 heaven, earth, man ｜位一體 The Christian Trinity ｜言兩語 a few words		
散^{3}	攴 66	散 800	Miscellaneous; to fall apart ｜·着腰兒 with the loins ungirt ｜文的 prosy. ｜·了 gone to pieces ｜藥 medicinal powder	san^{4}	C
傘^{3} 繖^{3}	人 9	人 429	Umbrella 雨｜ 旱｜ sun umbrella, parasol		D
三^{4}	一 1	一 1	Three, reiterate ｜思 think thrice, be careful	sa^{1} san^{1}	A
散^{4}	攴 66	散 800	To separate, disperse ｜○開 ｜·給衆人 give to multitude ｜錢 to scatter cash ｜學 dismiss school ｜會 break up an assembly ｜悶 dispel melancholy ｜·不開 can not be scattered ｜隊 order to disperse	san^{3}	C

Sang

Character	Radical	Phonetic	Meaning	Other readings	
喪^{1}	口 30	喪 352a	Mourning, to mourn ｜服 mourning clothes ｜○事 funeral. ｜禮 funeral rites	sang^{4}	B
桑^{1}	木 75	桑 533	Mulberry; mulberries ｜椹 S. ｜葉 mulberry leaves		D
嗓^{3}	口 30	桑 533	The throat, larynx ｜門 ｜·子啞·了 hoarseness ｜·子眼兒 the gullet 食｜		E
搡^{3}	手 64	桑 533	To push over or back 推｜ ｜·在地·下 tip onto the ground		I
顙^{3}	頁 181	桑 533	Forehead, 廣｜ broad brow		H

喪4	口 30	喪 352a	To lose, destroy, ruin, despond |·氣 ill-omened, down-hearted | 盡 to lose entirely | 父 lost his father | 良心 lose virtue or conscience | 命 to lose one's life | 亡 | 失 to lose, fail, e.g., | 失自由 | 胆 afraid, disheartened	sang1	B

Sao

臊1 [illegible]1	肉 130	喿 697	Rancid, rank, tainted |·的慌 | 氣 rank smell of fox, skunk etc. | 肉 tainted meat	sao4	F
搔1	手 64	蚤 787	To scratch, irritate | 首 scratch the head		F
騷1	馬 187	蚤 787	To stir up; sad, poetic | 擾 to harass, fidget | 人 a poet 勞·| grieved, miserable		I
繅1	糸 120	巢 508	To reel off cocoons | 絲		K
掃3 埽3	手 64	帚 674	To sweep, clean up 打·|, |·| | 淨·了 swept clean | 乾淨 | 除 to sweep away | 房 to clean house | 地 sweep ground or floor	sao4	B
嫂3 嫎3	女 38	叟 681	Elder brother's wife, matron |·子 家 | my elder brother's wife 大 | wife of eldest brother		D
掃4 埽4	手 64	帚 674	A broom |·箒 | 興4 bad fortune, dispirited | 箒星 a broom star—comet	sao3	B
喿4 噪4	口 30	喿 697	Chirp of birds, hum of men 蟬 | chirping of cicadas	tsao4	I

臊⁴	肉 130	喿 697	Ashamed 害 | 俗	sao¹	F
髞⁴	高 189	喿 697	High, lofty 高 | 亮 | light and roomy		K
彗⁴	彐 58	彗 673	Comet |·箒星 俗	hui⁴	H

Se

塞⁴	土 32	寒 100	To stop, obstruct | 住 文 | 責 evasion of responsibility	sai¹⁴	A
色⁴	色 139	色 313	Color, beauty; lust; sort | 彩 color, style, also used of art, politics etc. 好(hao⁴) | addicted to debauchery 顏·| color, countenance 五 | red, yellow, blue, white, black	shai³ —·shai	B
瑟⁴	玉 96	玨 77	Large lute; pure; chilly | | 琴 | music, conjugal harmony		D
嗇⁴	口 30	嗇 770	Stingy, sparing, miserly | 刻,吝 |		E
澀⁴ 澁⁴ 澀⁴	水 85	嗇 770	Rough, acrid, astringent 發 | | 味 acrid to the taste | 藥 astringent medicine		F
穡⁴	禾 115	嗇 770	Ripe grain, husbandry | 事 the harvest 斂 | gather in the harvest		G

Sen

森¹	木 75	林 492	Dense, forest-like, luxuriant | 林學 forestry | | deep, dense, umbrageous | 嚴 severe, dignified, rigorous	shen¹	G

Seng

僧[1] 人 9 曾 832 Buddhist priest | 家, | 人 — F
| 衣 Buddhist priest's robes
| 門 Buddhism
| 俗 priests and laymen

Sha

挱[1] 挲[1] 手 64 少 122 To open (flower) — so[1] — F
挓 | expand, open out

桬[1] 木 75 少 122 Various trees, | 果 sour apple — H
| 果梨 a sourish pear

沙[1] 水 85 少 122 Sand, gravel, granulated | 土 S. — C
| 雞 sand-grouse
| 河 a. sandy river, often dry
| 鍋 coarse earthenware kettle
| 漠 Gobi desert, any desert
| 布 very thin gauze
| 石 pebbles, small stones
| 灘 a sand bank
|·子 sand; small shot

痧[1] 疒 104 少 122 Cholera, diarrhoea | 眼 trachoma — H
絞腸 | Asiatic cholera

粆[1] 米 119 少 122 Coarse. | 糖 coarse sugar — H

紗[1] 糸 120 少 122 Gauze, lace, yarn — F
| 窗 gauze window; so | 燈 etc.
| 衣裳 crepe clothes

砂[1] 石 112 少 122 Gravel, sand |·子, used for 沙 — D
硃 | cinnabar

鯊[1] 魦[1] 魚 195 少 122 A shark | 魚 — H
| 綠色 a bright slate blue
| 魚皮 shagreen, shark's skin

殺[1] 殳 79 殳 399 To kill, slay, | 害, |·死 — sha[4] shai[4] — C
| 盡 exterminate. | 戮 slaughter

Character	Radical	Phonetic	Meaning	Other reading	Class
[illegible]14	衣 145	殳 399	To make smaller, fit; seam		I
杉1	木 75	彡 280	Fir, deal, pine | 松, | 木 | 高 fir scaffold-pole	shan1	F
傻3 儍3	人 9	夋 542	Foolish, simple, idiot |·子 | 笑 silly laugh, or giggle | 樂 | 說 to talk foolishly		F
殺4	殳 79	殳 399	To death, very | 氣 blood thirsty, ferocious | 緊 very tight	sha1 shai4	C
霎4	雨 173	妾 85	An instant, sudden, passing | 時 | 時間 a moment, momentarily		E
廈4 厦4	广 53	夏 854	Mansion; front room | 門 Amoy 大 | mansion	hsia4	G
煞4	火 86	彐 667	Baleful, kill by influences | 氣 noxious influences, malaria		I
[illegible]4	刀 18	少 122	To make eyelet hole | 眼; small cavities (as in porous iron)		K

Shai

Character	Radical	Phonetic	Meaning	Other reading	Class
篩1	竹 118	師 753	Sieve, to sift, strain |·子 | 米 to sift rice 草 |·子 sieve to clean straw		E
揌1	手 64	思 379	To strike, beat; roll; to beat a gong | 鑼		K
色3	色 139	色 313	Color, beauty; lust 俗	se4	B
骰3	骨 188	殳 399	Dice |·子, | 盆子 dice-bowl 擲 | 子 to throw dice		H
曬4 晒4	日 72	麗 320	To sun-dry, air | 衣裳 | 黑·了 sun-burnt | 乾 to dry in the sun |·的慌 too sunny		B
殺4	殳 79	殳 399	To reduce, clip, pare	sha14	C

Shan

Character	Radical	Phonetic	Meaning	Other reading	
山[1]	山 46	山 655	Mountain, hill; wild; loud S. ｜珍海味 (or 錯) rare delicacies ｜雞 a pheasant. ｜羊 a goat ｜墻 end walls of a house ｜尖 summit of a hill ｜頭 ｜峰 a peak. ｜口 a pass ｜海關 Shanhaikuan (Hopei) ｜·西 Shansi province ｜右 ｜谷 hills and valleys; a valley ｜·裏紅 species of hawthorn ｜林 a mountain forest ｜嶺 hills and mountains ｜路 a mountain road ｜道 ｜門 the gate of a temple ｜坡 mountain slopes ｜水 scenery. ｜洞 a cave ｜·東 Shantung province ｜左 ｜藥 the yam. ｜藥豆 potato		B
彡[1]	彡 59	彡 280	Feathers, long hair		K
杉[1]	木 75	彡 280	Fir, deal ｜木	sha[1]	F
衫[1]	衣 145	彡 280	Shirt, 汗｜; garments ｜裙 women's clothes		B
删[1]	刀 18	册 565	To cut, excise; reject; amend ｜改 ｜除 to cut out, expunge ｜開, ｜去 ｜削 pare off ｜訂 revise		E
珊[1]	玉 96	册 565	Coral ｜瑚 ｜瑚島 coral island		G
搧[1]	手 64	扇 295	To fan ｜·一·｜, ｜扇·子; strike ｜∘開·了 to brush aside ｜打 to flog		F
煽[1]	火 86	扇 295	To agitate, excite ｜火; delude ｜惑 delude, excite suspicion		G

Shan

Character	Radical	Phonetic	Meaning		
羶[1] 羴[1]	羊 123	亶 768	Rank, strong, goatish ｜氣 ｜腥 smell of meat or fish ｜羊 frowzy, musty, rank		G
芟[1] 刈[1]	艸 140	殳 399	To mow, cut grass or herbs ｜除 to cut down ｜刈 ｜刀 scythe		H
閃[3]	門 169	門 635	Flash; shun, evade, dodge ｜°開 to get out of the way ｜身 ｜光 a gleam, flash ｜道 get out of the ro .d ｜電 flash of lightning 打｜ ｜·在一邊 to slip aside, avoid ｜緞 "shot" satin. ｜綢 silk		D
陝[3]	阜 170	夾 455	Shensi province ｜·西 ｜甘 Shensi and Kansu		F
單[4]	口 30	單 826	Surname. S. ｜縣 district in Shantung ｜于 double surname S.	tan[1]	A
禪[4]	示 113	單 826	To abdicate; sacrifice to hills and fountains	ch'an[2]	H
闡[4]	門 169	單 826	To enlarge, explain ｜明, ｜達 ｜註 explain by notes	ch'an[3]	I
鱓[4] 鱔[4]	魚 195	單 826	The eel ｜羹 soup of stewed eels 非蛇即｜ very slippery		H
善[4]	口 30	善 152	Good, benevolent, skillful ｜政 good government ｜舉 virtuous deed, beneficence ｜勸 exhort to good deeds 勸｜ ｜終 good end, easy death ｜法 a good plan ｜策 ｜後 reconstruction, rehabilitation ｜行 good actions ｜德 ｜性 good disposition ｜良 mild, virtuous 良｜ ｜惡 virtue and vice ｜於 skillful in or at		B

繕^{4}	糸 120	善 152	To write out, 丨寫, copy 丨抄 丨修 put in repair		F
膳^{4} 饍^{4}	肉 130	善 152	Food, an imperial meal 丨房 imperial kitchen 丨宿費 board and lodging 丨宿生 boarding-pupils		G
蟮^{4} 蟺^{4}	虫 142	善 152	Earth-worm 蛐丨 蛐丨唱歌, 有雨無多 when the earth worm sings, not much rain		K
扇^{4}	戶 63	扇 295	A fan 丨·子 丨股·子 ribs of a fan		B
騸^{4}	馬 187	扇 295	To geld 丨馬, 丨羊, etc.		K
苫^{4}	艸 140	占 720	To thatch, straw mat 丨上油布 cover with oilcloth	chan^{1}	B
擅^{4}	手 64	亶 768	To usurp, assume, unauthorized 丨長^{2} skilled; versed in 丨權 on one's own authority 丨敢, 丨自 丨進 enter without leave		G
汕^{4}	水 85	山 655	Port of Swatow 丨頭		I
疝^{4}	疒 104	山 655	Hernia, rupture 丨氣		K
訕^{4}	言 149	山 655	To abuse, slander, backbite 丨謗		G
贍^{4}	貝 154	詹 741	To give, supply 丨補; enough 丨養 to rear, support		H

Shang

裳^{1}	衣 145	尚 584	Clothes 衣·丨	ch'ang^{2}	A
商^{1}	口 30	冏 578	To consult; merchant, commerce 丨戰 commercial competition		B

Shang

<table>
<tr><td>商^1</td><td></td><td></td><td>|·朝 the Shang dynasty 1766-1122 B.C.
|界 mercantile world
|情 commercial conditions
|酌 to deliberate |議, |·量
|辦 trade; act after consultation
|團 mercantile guards
|務 commerce |業</td><td></td><td></td></tr>
<tr><td>昜^1</td><td>日
72</td><td>昜
238</td><td>To injure</td><td></td><td>P</td></tr>
<tr><td>傷^1</td><td>人
9</td><td>昜
238</td><td>To wound, injure |害, |損, mourn
|情 to hurt feeling, hurt feelings, grieved |心
|處 an injured place
|風化 a breach of morality
|風敗俗 spoil a custom
|寒 typhoid; to catch cold |風
|痕 the scar of a wound
|和氣 injure cordial relations</td><td></td><td>C</td></tr>
<tr><td>殤^1</td><td>歹
78</td><td>昜
238</td><td>To die young 夭|</td><td></td><td>H</td></tr>
<tr><td>觴^1</td><td>角
148</td><td>昜
238</td><td>Goblet, cup 酒|
稱| to pledge</td><td></td><td>K</td></tr>
<tr><td>上^3</td><td>一
1</td><td>卜
119</td><td>To ascend, pay to
|官 double surname S
|聲 the third tone
不| not more than</td><td>shang^4

4</td><td>A</td></tr>
<tr><td>晌^3</td><td>日
72</td><td>向
579</td><td>Noon, midday |·午 --huo
|飯 the midday meal
|·午歪·了 past noon |·午錯·了
半| half-a-day, a long time</td><td></td><td>A</td></tr>
<tr><td>賞^3</td><td>貝
154</td><td>賞
588</td><td>Reward, bestow |給, |賜
|錢 to bestow money; |·錢 gratuities
|罰 to reward and punish
|臉 to give "face"
|善罰惡 reward good, punish bad</td><td></td><td>D</td></tr>
</table>

Shang

上[4]	一 1	卜 119	Above; upon; go up, go to; superior	shang[3]	A
			| 車 ascend cart; so | 轎		
			| 陣 go to battle; charge		
			| 將[4] a general		
			| 街 to go upon the street		
			| 京 to go to Peking		
			|·去 to go up. |·不去 unable to go up		
			| 船 to embark		
			| 房 chief room, | 座 chief seat | 位		
			| 海 Shanghai		
			| 好 very good. | 品 first-class		
			| 下 about, more or less		
			| 弦 to wind up (watch, etc.) | 絃		
			| 學 to go to school		
			|·回 the last time |°次		
			| 議院 Upper House, Senate		
			| 任 proceed to one's post		
			| 告 appeal to higher court | 訴		
			| 古 high antiquity		
			| 工 begin work, | 門 close door		
			| 流社會 upper classes of society		
			| 樓 go upstairs; so | 山, | 坡, | 樹		
			°|·面 on top, on surface |·邊, °|·頭		
			°| 那兒[3] where are you going?		
			|·半天 the forenoon | 午		
			| 輩 elders, older generation		
			| 膘 grow fat. | 凍 freeze		
			| 平 1st of the Chinese tones		
			| 生字 assign new characters (to students)		
			| 算 profitable, pay. | 當[4] cheated		
			| 腭 roof of the mouth		
			| 帝 Supreme Ruler; God		
			| 吊 to hang oneself		
			| 菜 put food on the table		
			|·月 the previous month		

Character	Radical	Phonetic	Definition	Freq.
尙4	小 42	尙 584	To esteem; aspire; still; superior S. ｜且 still, however, and if ｜姓 your esteemed name? ｜可 still possible. ｜有 still is ｜在兩可 matter still in doubt ｜武精神 militarism	C

Shao

Character	Radical	Phonetic	Definition	Freq.
弰1	弓 57	肖 124	End of bow 弓｜	I
捎1	手 64	肖 124	Take; select; send, carry ｜信 ｜帶 convey, include in party	D
梢1	木 75	肖 124	Tip, end, twig ｜末; stern of boat ｜公 boatman	H
稍1	禾 115	肖 124	Somewhat, slight, a little, wee ｜微; brief time ｜差點 slightly in error ｜好 rather better ｜緩 delay awhile ｜待, ｜停 ｜可 tolerable ｜｜gradually ｜坐坐 be seated for a little	B
筲1	竹 118	肖 124	Bucket, pail, 水｜; basket ｜箍 the hoop on a bucket	I
燒1	火 86	堯 391	To burn, bake, roast; feverish ｜雞 roast a fowl; so ｜肉 ｜焦·了 burnt ｜糊·了 ｜紙 burn paper at funerals ｜酒 whisky, ardent spirits ｜磚 burn bricks. ｜窰 fire kiln ｜香 burn incense ｜燬 burn up, ｜火 light fire ｜炕 warm the stove-bed ｜·餅 a round wheaten cake ｜水 heat water ｜點 ignition-point	C

Shao

勺[2]	勹 20	勺 231	Spoon, ladle ｜·子	俗	shuo24	E
杓[2]	木 75	勺 231	Spoon, ladle ｜·子; handle	俗	piao1 shuo4	G
灼[2]	火 86	勺 231	To cauterize; clear, brilliant ｜爛 badly burnt; ｜明 dazzling	俗	shuo24	I
芍[2]	艸 140	勺 231	Peony ｜·藥 peony; a medicine	俗	shuo24	I
韶[2]	音 180	召 715	Admirable; Shun's music ｜華 glorious, splendid	S.		I
少[3]	小 42	少 122	Few, seldom, briefly, wanting ｜見 have seen little of you ｜·些 a little less, too little ｜許 a very little, a few ｜給錢 give less money ｜·喇不賣 will not sell for less ｜陪 please excuse my going ｜·不了[3] unable to do with less ｜說話 speak less! be quiet! ｜停 wait a bit ｜等一等 ｜有的事 a rare thing		shao4	A
少[4]	小 42	少 122	Young, junior ｜年 ｜壯 a lusty young fellow ｜婦 a young woman ｜年中國 "Young China" ｜·爺 a son (honorable) 老｜ old and young		shao3	A
哨[4]	口 30	肖 124	Carol, whistle; patrol, outpost ｜兒 trumpet, whistle ｜探 a spy, scout 吹｜(兒) blow whistle			E
潲[4]	水 85	肖 124	Rain drives or spatters ｜濕·了 wet with rain, etc;			B
紹[4] 佋[4]	糸 120	召 715	To continue, hand down 介｜ to introduce			H

She

賒[1]	貝 154	示 514	To buy or sell on credit ｜賬 to give credit ｜出 ｜欠 to owe, debt; on credit ｜·的		E
奢[1]	大 37	者 192	Wasteful, extravagant ｜·侈, ｜華 ｜華品 articles of luxury		E
折[2]	手 64	折 210	To break in two ｜斷 俗 ｜·了本 to lose in business ｜損 to fail, to spoil	cha[3] che[2]	B
舌[2]	舌 135	舌 707	Tongue, ｜·頭; clapper ｜尖 tongue-tip, ｜本 palate 學｜ repeat what has been said		C
賒[2]	貝 154	舌 707	To lose money in trade ｜本		I
蛇[2]	虫 142	它 322	Snake, serpentine, subtle ｜行 snake-like movement ｜殼 snake-skin		D
捨[3]	手 64	舌 707	Let go, relinquish; give alms ｜己爲[4]人 sacrifice self for men ｜棄 to forsake, abandon ｜命 to give one's life ｜身 ｜·不開 unable to part with ｜·不得 ｜·不得去 reluctant to go		D
舍[4]	舌 135	舌 707	Shed, cottage, my ｜親 my relations; so ｜弟 etc. ｜下 my residence		A
葉[4]	艸 140	枼 110	Surname; name of place S	yeh[4]	A
社[4]	示 113	土 43	Gods of land; village, clan ｜長[3] president of news-paper ｜·稷壇 altars of land and grain ｜∘會 society, ｜∘會主義 Socialism ｜∘會學 sociology ｜∘會黨 Socialist Party		C

涉[4]	水 85	步 131	To ford 丨水; involve, concern 交丨intercourse, negotiation 干丨concern; to interfere with		C
赦[4]	赤 155	赤 423	To pardon, forgive 丨放, 丨免 丨過 to overlook faults 丨罪 法無可丨law knows no pardon		C
設[4]	言 149	殳 399	To set up, devise; if, supposing 丨計 to contrive, plan, 丨謀 丨教 instruct, open a school 丨法 institute law; scheme 丨席 to prepare a banquet 丨宴 丨或 if, provided 丨如, 丨若, 假丨 丨立 to erect, constitute 丨論 hypothesis 丨想 丨擺 to spread out, arrange 擺丨 丨下 丨身處地 put self in his place		D
瑟[4]	玉 96	玨 77	Large lute; pure; chilly 丨丨	se[4]	D
射[4]	寸 41	身 634	To shoot, dart, spurt 丨箭 shoot arrow 丨法 archery 丨光 luminous, shed light 丨影燈 magic lantern	shih[2]	E
麝[4]	鹿 198	身 634	Musk deer 丨鹿 丨香 musk		I
攝[4]	手 64	聶 633	To assist; act for; control 丨政 to assist government 丨政王 a regent, 丨影 photograph		F

Shei

誰[2]	言 149	隹 52	Who? whom? anyone	shui[2]	A

Shen

身[1]	身 158	身 634	Body, trunk; personal, I; lifetime 丨價 personal value		B

Shen

身[1]			｜軀 the body ｜·體, ｜·子 ｜·分 rank; quality ｜後的事 an affair after death ｜心 body and mind ｜量 height of the body ｜·上 on, about the person ｜◦段 physique. 渾｜whole body 起｜to rise, start journey 終｜whole life 分｜to get away (from duties)	
罙[1]	穴 116	罙 487	Deep	P
深[1]	水 85	罙 487	Deep, abstruse; intense, very ｜奧 abstruse, profound ｜查 to investigate thoroughly ｜淺 the depth of ｜厚 very intimate ｜信 believe profoundly ｜密 thick, dense, close ｜妙 admirable, capital ｜通 thoroughly understand	B
申[1]	田 102	申 824	To report, notify, explain; 3—5 p.m., S. ｜刻 3—5 o'clock p.m. ｜時 ｜明 to explain clearly ｜解 ｜命 to order, repeat command ｜命記 Deuteronomy ｜訴 state to a superior ｜屠 double surname S.	F
伸[1]	人 9	申 824	To extend, straighten, stretch ｜張 to extend, expansion ｜·着脖子 stretching out the neck ｜·出手 reach out the hand ｜·開腿 to stretch the legs ｜舌·頭 put out your tongue ｜縮 to expand and contract ｜寃 redress a grievance	D

Character	Radical	Phonetic	Meaning	Other readings	
呻[1]	口 30	申 824	To groan, recite, hum ｜吟 ｜欠 to yawn		I
紳[1]	糸 120	申 824	Sash, girdle; bind ｜束 ｜士 literary class, gentry ｜董		E
參[1] 蓡[1]	厶 28	參 282	Ginseng 人｜	ts'an[1] ts'en[1]	F
森[1]	木 75	林 492	Dense, forest-like	sen[1]	G
娠[1] 㛛[1]	女 38	辰 355	Pregnant ｜孕	chen[4]	K
甚[2]	甘 99	甚 104	What? ｜·麼 ·｜·麼的 and so forth, (etc.) 沒·有·｜·麼 nothing the matter	shen[4]	A
椹[24] 葚[24]	木 75	甚 104	Mulberry fruit 桑｜	chen[1] jen[4]	K
神[2]	示 113	申 824	Deity, divine, God; spirit, animal spirits; very ｜跡 "God's footsteps", miracles ｜·氣 expression, general effect ｜經過敏 nervous, sensitive ｜經病 nervous disorders ｜州 China. ｜聖 sacred ｜學 theology ｜道學 ｜學校 theological seminary ｜像 an idol. ｜仙 fairies, genii ｜鬼 spirits and devils ｜靈 spiritual, soul; the gods ｜秘教 mysticism ｜農 legendary Emperor B.C. 2838		B
審[3]	宀 40	番 811	To judge, examine, investigate ｜案 a judicial case, try case ｜事 ｜察 to judge and examine ｜計院 Board of Audit		B

Character	Radical	Phonetic	Definition			
審³			| 明 to decide | 判 to judge, try a case | 問 | 判官 judge, | 判廳 law-court			
嬸³	女 38	番 811	Aunt, father's younger brother's wife | 母, |·子			H
瀋³	水 85	番 811	Gravy, sap; to leak out			I
沈³	水 85	冘 176	Surname	S	ch'en²	C
哂³	口 30	西 775	To smile, sneering smile | 笑 微物見 | a trifling laughable present			G
甚⁴	甘 99	甚 104	Superlative, very | 至 to such an extent that | 好 extremely good; so | 大 etc. | 是 truly is, really are		shen²	A
愼⁴	心 61	眞 843	Careful, cautious; attentive |·重 heedful, circumspect | 思 carefully reflect on 謹 | cautious, careful	S.		C
腎⁴	肉 130	臤 643	Kidneys 內 | ; the testicles 外 | | 囊 the scrotum			H
滲⁴	水 85	參 282	To leak, soak through | 水, | 漏 |·下·去 to sink (as water into the ground)			H

Sheng

Character	Radical	Phonetic	Definition			
生¹	生 100	生 41	To beget, produce, birth; raw; strange; life, grow | 產 bring forth, produce |·出·來 | 長³ be born and grow up | 成 natural, innate, become | 機 a living germ, life |∘計 a livelihood, occupation | 氣 to be angry; breath | 前 during life			A

生[1]

| 殖力 fecundity, productivity
| 擒 to capture alive
| 瘡 to break out in sores
| 兒[2] to bear a son | 子[3], | 育
| 而知之 intuitional knowledge
|·活 living, work, life
| 火 to kindle a fire
|·意 trade, business, | 理
| 人 a stranger | 客
|·日 one's birthday | 辰
| 來的 naturally so, innate
| 理 trade, livelihood, physical
| 理學 physiology
| 利 profit, | 利者 producers
| 靈 living creatures
| 命 life. | 病 to fall ill
| 平 throughout life
| 事 make trouble. | 手 beginner
| 疎 to become estranged, distant
| 死 life and death.
| 鐵 cast iron. | 財 grow wealthy
| 菜 lettuce, salad greens
| 存競爭 struggle for existence
| 東西 raw things. | 銅 native copper
| 物學 biology

牲[1] — 牛 93 — 生 41 — B
Animals, sacrificial animals
|·口 cattle, beasts | 畜

甥[1] — 生 100 — 生 41 — D
Sister's child, daughter's child
外·| sister's son, so 外·| 女
外 ·孫 daughter's son

笙[1] — 竹 118 — 生 41 — I
Pandean pipe, small pipe organ

聲[1] 声[1] — 耳 128 — 殸 404 — A
Sound, note, tone, voice; reputation; to declare
|∘張 to noise abroad
| 稱 to declare. tell, state | 明

Sheng

<table>
<tr><td>聲¹</td><td></td><td></td><td>｜學 acoustics. ｜浪 sound waves
｜·名 reputation ｜聞 fame, report
｜·音 sound of any kind</td><td></td><td></td></tr>
<tr><td>升¹</td><td>十
24</td><td>廾
414</td><td>A pint; to ascend, promotion
｜級 to be promoted; so ｜班
｜降機 an elevator, lift
｜上 to ascend, rise 上｜
｜天 ascend to heaven
｜座 to take the chair
｜斗 dry pints and pecks</td><td></td><td>C</td></tr>
<tr><td>昇¹</td><td>日
72</td><td>廾
414</td><td>To ascend, rise; tranquil
｜平 tranquil. 日｜sunrise</td><td></td><td>C</td></tr>
<tr><td>陞¹</td><td>阜
170</td><td>廾
414</td><td>To ascend, raise, rise ｜上
｜車 please mount your cart
｜冠 to take off one's hat, (polite)
｜座 ascend throne or dais</td><td></td><td>D</td></tr>
<tr><td>勝¹</td><td>力
19</td><td>朕
468</td><td>To sustain; worthy of
不｜任 incompetent to hold post
不可｜言 words are inadequate</td><td>sheng⁴</td><td>C</td></tr>
<tr><td>繩²</td><td>糸
120</td><td>黽
316</td><td>String, cord, rope ｜·子, ｜索
｜墨 marking line; rule of life</td><td></td><td>C</td></tr>
<tr><td>省³</td><td>目
109</td><td>少
122</td><td>To save, frugal; a province
｜長³ governor of province ｜主席
｜城 provincial capital
｜儉 economical, saving 儉｜
｜錢 saving money ｜·下
｜心 worry saving, good
｜議會 provincial assembly
｜工夫 to save trouble
｜事 trouble-saving, efficient
｜用 frugal in expenditure</td><td>hsing³</td><td>A</td></tr>
<tr><td>聖⁴
圣⁴</td><td>耳
128</td><td>王
71</td><td>Sacred, holy ｜潔; sage
｜教 Confucianism
｜經 sacred books; the Bible ｜書
｜經會 American Bible Society
｜賢 saints and worthies</td><td></td><td>B</td></tr>
</table>

聖[4]			|·人 a sage; Confucius			
			| 公會 Holy Catholic Church			
			| 靈 The Holy Spirit			
			| 誕 Christmas			
			| 道 the holy doctrine			
			| 徒 saints, disciples			
			| 諭 "The Sacred Edict"			
剩[4]	刀 18	乖 25	Overplus, left over, residue			B
賸[4]			| 錢 surplus money; so | 飯, | 貨			
			|·下 there remains; left over			
勝[4]	力 19	朕 468	To conquer, 得 | ; excel		sheng[1]	C
			| 仗 a victory, to win a battle 打 | 仗			
			| 過仇敵 overcame enemies			
			| 敗 victory and defeat			
			|·似 superior to, better than			
盛[4]	皿 108	成 347	Abundant, flourishing 豐 |	S	ch'eng[2]	D
			| 京 Liao Tung, Mukden			
			| 恩 abundant kindness			
			| 行 flourishing, thriving | 興			
			| 世 a period of plenty			
			| 德 great virtue			

Shih

詩[1]	言 149	寺 46	Poetry, odes; 聖 | hymns			B
			| 家 poets, | 人			
			|·經 Book of Odes			
			| 曲 songs, verses | 歌			
			| 韻 rhyme, 唱 | to sing hymns			
施[1]	方 70	㫃 265	Bestow, grant, aid; expand	S.		B
			| 展 display, spread out | 張			
			| 敎 to teach, | 主 a donor			
			| 恩 confer favor, be kind			
			| 洗 to baptize			
			| 行 to grant, give effect to			
			| 醫院 a charity hospital			

Shih

<table>
<tr><td>施[1]</td><td></td><td></td><td>| 捨 bestow in charity | 濟
| 與 to confer upon</td><td></td><td></td><td></td></tr>
<tr><td>濕[1]
溼[1]</td><td>水
85</td><td>㬎
802</td><td>Damp, wet, moist 發 |
| 潮 wet 潮·|
| 生 generated by moisture
| 透 wet through. | 潤 moisten</td><td></td><td></td><td>B</td></tr>
<tr><td>師[1]</td><td>巾
50</td><td>師
753</td><td>Teacher; (military) division
| 長[3] teachers 老 |
| 長[3] division commander
| 範學校 normal school
|·傅 master, master workman
| 母 wife of one's teacher | 娘
京 | the capital</td><td>S</td><td></td><td>C</td></tr>
<tr><td>獅[1]</td><td>犬
94</td><td>師
753</td><td>Lion |·子
| 吼 the roar of a lion
睡 | sleeping lion, (as China)</td><td></td><td></td><td>C</td></tr>
<tr><td>螄[1]</td><td>虫
142</td><td>師
753</td><td>A spiral shell, whelk 螺 |</td><td></td><td>·ssu</td><td>I</td></tr>
<tr><td>失[1]</td><td>大
37</td><td>失
481</td><td>To lose, |·去, | 落; err, a fault
| 察 fail to examine
| 機會 miss an opportunity | 時
| 脚 make misstep, slip | 足
| 節 lose chastity | 身
| 敬 I beg your pardon
| 和 disagree (of men or nations)
| 信 breach of trust
| 火 to catch fire
| 意 disappointed
| 口 slip of the tongue | 言
| 禮 breach of etiquette
| 路 to lose the way
| 迷 lose possession; lost
| 明 to lose one's sight
| 敗 defeat, failure
| 陪 excuse my leaving you
| 散 scattered
| 神 absent-minded; to faint</td><td></td><td></td><td>C</td></tr>
</table>

失[1]			| 手 a slip of the hand | 望 to lose hope | 迎 sorry I was not at home 過·| a fault, error		
尸[1]	尸 44	尸 724	Corpse, |·首, | 身; effigy; useless | 位 impersonator; idler (in any post)		E
屍[1]	尸 44	尸 724	Corpse, especially of murdered one | 身 a corpse |·首, | 骨 驗 | post-mortem inquest		E
虱[1] 蝨[1]	虫 142	虫 785	Louse, parasite |·子 長 |·子 to have lice 摸 |·子 to feel for lice		E
筮[14]	竹 118	巫 12	To divine by plant-stalks | 人 a fortune teller		H
十[2] 拾[2]	十 24	十 13	Ten | 個; complete, perfect | 幾 how much over ten? | 幾個 above ten, in teens |·來·箇 | 誡 Decalogue | 指 the ten fingers | 全 complete, perfect | 分 | 分之一 one-tenth, tithe | 八省 18 provinces of China | 條誡 The Ten Commandments | 天半月 ten or fifteen days | 字架 a cross, The Cross | 字街 crossing of streets		A
什[2]	人 9	十 13	A file of ten. | 長[3] corporal | 器 household utensils | 物,家 | | 麼 what thing? what? shen[2]-		F
時[2] 旹[2] 时[2]	日 72 減	寺 46	Time, hour; period, season | 常 constantly, often |·辰 two hour division of time | 機 present opportunities | 期 time, period | 間, | 代 | 節 time, season | 令, 四 |	S.	A

時[2]			｜局 condition, present situation ｜·候 a time, 這｜·候 now, 那·｜·候 then ｜興[1] fashionable; seasonable ｜疫 epidemic ｜刻 incessantly ｜｜刻刻 ｜光 the times, state ｜勢 ｜派 prevailing fashion ｜事 current events ｜式 fashionable, a la mode ｜樣 ｜務 present times or conditions		
匙[2]	匕 21	匕 317	Spoon, key 鑰·｜ a key	ch'ih[2]	A
識[24]	言 149	戠 93	To know, recognize, understand ｜見 experience, observation 見·｜ ｜力 discernment ｜面 to know by sight ｜透 know thoroughly ｜破 ｜[2]字 know characters 知·｜ knowledge, experience 認·｜ to know, distinguish	chih[4]	A
實[2] 寔[2]	宀 40	貫 861	True, sincere; solid, verily, in truth, fruit of plants, filled ｜際 reality ｜情 facts of the case ｜據 proofs, facts ｜現 realization; to realize ｜行 carry through, practical ｜行家 practical man ｜話 truth ｜言 ｜利 of practical value ｜｜在在 truly, really ｜在 ｜事 facts, a fact 事｜ ｜說 to speak the truth ｜業 industries. ｜業學校 Technical School ｜驗 demonstrate, experiment		B

實^{2}			︱驗室 laboratory 結︱to form fruit; strong, firm 結·︱			
食^{2}	食 184	食 363	To eat; food; eclipse; retract ︱肉動物 carnivorous animals ︱管子 the aesophagus ︱道 ︱堂 dining hall ︱物 eatables ︱言 to eat one's words, to retract a promise			B
蝕^{2}	虫 142	食 363	To eat up gradually; eclipse 日︱solar eclipse, 月︱lunar eclipse			F
拾^{2}	手 64	合 708	To gather up, pick up; ten ︱·起來 to pick up, collect ︱取 ︱糞的 manure-gatherer ︱·掇 repair, put in order 收·︱			B
石^{2}	石 112	石 722	Stone, mineral, ︱·頭; firm ︱·匠 stone-mason, ︱灰 lime ︱·榴 pomegranate ︱碑 a stone tablet ︱·頭鑿的 chiseled out of stone ︱·頭子兒 pebbles ︱印 lithography	S.	tan^{4}	C
射^{2}	寸 41	身 634	To shoot (arrows) ︱箭		she^{4}	E
使^{3}	人 9	吏 170	To use, employ; cause that; a messenger, a commissioner ︱錢 to use money; squeeze ︱勁兒 to exert strength ︱者 person sent, messenger ︱壞·了 spoilt by using ︱·喚 to employ (servant), employed ︱役 a servant, ︱女 maid ︱館 legation or embassy ︱·不住 not durable ︱·不得 it will not answer ︱·得 it will do			A

Shih

Character	Radical	Phonetic	Definition		
使[3]			｜徒 Apostle ｜徒行傳 The Acts ｜完·了 finished, ended, used ｜用 to employ, expense		
史[3]	口 30	史 169	History 歷｜,｜記 S. ｜學家 historians, ｜書 histories		C
駛[3]	馬 187	史 169	To sail, drive 行｜; speedy ｜船 to sail a ship ｜馬 to drive a horse fast		H
始[3]	女 38	台 718	Beginning, first; then ｜初 beginning, at first 元｜,起｜ ｜終 first and last ｜末 ｜祖 first ancestor, founder		D
矢[3]	矢 111	矢 474	Arrow, arrange 弓｜bow and arrow, archery	shih[4]	F
豕[3]	豕 152	豕 285	A hog, swine; 牧｜swineherd		H
屎[3]	尸 44	尸 724	Ordure, night-soil ｜坑 a necessary, privy ｜·蝌螂[4] dung beetle ｜桶 closed-stool, commode 拉｜ease oneself, go to stool		H
弛[3]	弓 57	也 301	To unstring, relax 解｜; annul ｜力 relax strength; remiss		I
舐[34]	舌 135	氏 348	To lick, lap ｜窗 lick peep-hole in window		I
是[4]	日 72	是 139	To be; yes, correct; such, thus; this ｜·阿 just so, yes, to be sure。｜·的 ｜·非 right and wrong; gossip ｜非之心 i.e., conscience ｜非學 ethics, moral philosophy ｜非的人 a wrongdoer ｜否 yes and no; is it or no? ｜以 hence, so, therefore ｜故 on this account, therefore 。｜·不是 is it? is it not so?		A

Shih

事4 亊4	亅 6	彐 667	Affair, thing; to serve, manage ｜成·了 an affair completed ｜·情 affair, business, action ｜項 ｜·奉 to serve. ｜忙 very busy ｜半功倍 half the work, twice the results ｜實 reality of affairs, fact ｜｜everything, all affairs ｜·務 a matter, concern, affair ｜·務所 an office for business ｜◦業 employment, occupation		A
世4	一 1	世 109	Generation; world ｜·界, ｜間, ｜·上 ｜紀 century ｜家 an ancient family ｜·界 the world ｜·界語 world language (Esperanto) ｜情 customs of the age ｜俗 ｜人 mankind ｜面 state of things, the times ｜事 worldly affairs, events ｜道 ｜｜無窮 world without end ｜代 generations of men		B
式4	弋 56	式 329	Shape, fashion; to imitate ｜樣 manner, pattern 合｜ suitable, the very thing 格◦｜ ruled form as pattern		B
拭4 栻4	手 64	式 329	To wipe, rub clean ｜淨; brush ｜淚 to wipe away tears ｜刀 wipe a knife		G
弒4	弋 56	式 329	To murder a superior ｜君 regicide. ｜父 parricide		H
試4	言 149	式 329	To try, test, verify; trained ｜嘗 to taste and try 嘗｜ ｜金石 a touchstone ｜行 tentative, experimental ｜看 try, test a thing ｜煉 to test. ｜探 to tempt		B

試[4]
|·| 大小 to try the size
| 演 make trial, practice
|·驗 trial, examination

室[4] 宀 40 至 883 Room, house, office, dwelling B
| 家 a household, a family 家 |
正 | a legal wife | 人

士[4] 士 33 士 65 Scholar, officer, soldier, gentleman C
| 林 the learned generally
| 卒 a follower; infantry 甲 |
壯 | valiant soldier 勇 |

仕[4] 人 9 士 65 To hold office, serve F
| 官 an official
| 途 official career | 路

示[4] 礻[4] 示 113 示 514 Notify, proclaim, show, reveal D
| 知 to proclaim, declare | 明
| 意 to inform, 指 | direct
| 威 make a demonstration
| 諭 mandate 告 |
默 | revelation 啓 |
表 | sign, emblem, to typify
打手 | indicate by signs

視[4] 見 147 示 514 To look, see, regard D
| 線 line of vision
| 點 end in view, point of view
藐 | to despise, contempt

氏[4] 氏 83 氏 348 Family, clan, female, maiden name D
黃李 | Mrs. Huang, née Li

市[4] 巾 50 市 558 Market, trade, | 井; vulgar D
| 場 market for goods
| 政 municipality, city government
| 價 market price
| 口兒 a market | 上
| 儈 a market broker
| 面 state of trade
| 平 market weight

Shih

柿4	木 75	市 558	Persimmon ǀ·子 ǀ 餅 dried persimmon 西紅 ǀ the tomato		D
勢4	力 19	埶 305	Power, influence, authority ǀ·力; pomp; circumstances ǀ·力範圍 sphere of influence ǀ 壓 repress with authority		D
釋4	釆 165	睪 160	To let go; explain; Sakyamuni ǀ 迦牟尼 Sakyamuni Buddha ǀ 教 Buddhism ǀ 放 to release, discharge ǀ 手 ǀ 疑 to dismiss doubts ǀ 義 explanation of meaning ǀ 寃 remove ill-will or enmity		D
誓4	言 149	折 210	To take oath, an oath 起 ǀ, 發 ǀ ǀ 書 oath of office, vow ǀ 言 ǀ 願 to swear to do, a vow ǀ 約 to contract 盟 ǀ		D
逝4	辵 162	折 210	To pass away, die, ǀ 世; reach ǀ 亡 to depart this life		F
飾4 餙4	食 184	食 363	To adorn, ornament, 裝 ǀ; pretend 粧 ǀ 品 decorations, ornaments 修 ǀ to adorn, to polish up 首 ǀ women's head ornaments		D
侍4	人 9	寺 46	To attend, wait on 服·ǀ, ǀ。奉, ǀ 立 ǀ 臣 attendant courtiers ǀ 婢 female servants		E
恃4	心 61	寺 46	To rely upon, trust to 倚 ǀ, 仗 ǀ ǀ 强 trust to strength ǀ 力 ǀ 能 depend on ability ǀ 勢 rely on influence ǀ 財 depend on wealth		E
適4	辵 162	啇 590	To reach; suit; just now, to happen; marry ǀ 者生存 survival of fittest ǀ 宜 proper, fit, suitable ǀ 當	ti4	E

適[4]			｜然 suddenly, accidentally ｜用 suitable, sufficient ｜我願		
矢[4]	矢 111	矢 474	Take oath ｜誓, ｜志	shih[3]	F
螫[4]	虫 142	赤 423	To sting, to poison	che[1]	F
嗜[4]	口 30	老 189	To be fond of, greedy, given up to; weakness for ｜·好 ｜酒色 given to wine and lust ｜音 fond of music ｜慾 to lust after, desire		F
謚[4] 諡[4]	言 149	益 610	Posthumous title, ｜名; memoir		I
啻[4]	口 30	帝 88	To stop at, different, only 不｜ not less than, short of	t'i[4]	I
碩[4]	石 112	石 722	Great, ripe, eminent ｜彥 ｜士 a worthy scholar, M.A.	shuo[4]	I
鼫[4]	鼠 208	石 722	Long tailed marmot ｜鼠		I

Shou

收[1] 収[1]	攴 66	丩 161	To receive, accept, harvest; quit ｜賬 receive payment ｜·成 harvest gathered in ｜齊·了 received in full ｜淸, ｜足 ｜監 put in prison ｜莊稼 reap the crops ｜據 a receipt ｜條, ｜單 ｜取 collect together ｜·下 to receive ｜入 ｜心 keep the mind; reform ｜回 to receive back ｜工 quit work ｜留 retain, give hospitality ｜納 to receive, accept		B

Shou

收[1]			| 生婆 a midwife |·拾 mend, put to rights | 稅的 a revenue officer | 藏 to lay by, store up | 租 collect rents | 存 to keep, retain | 徒弟 receive pupils		
熟[2]	火 86	孰 744	Ripe, skilled; intimate |·識, | 人 | 主·戶 an old customer | 飯 cooked victuals | 習 conversant, acquainted | 手 an experienced hand | 鐵 wrought iron	shu[2]	A
手[3]	手 64	手 141	Hand; skill; person | 掌 palm of the hand | 心 | 抄 manuscript copy | 車 hand barrow, or cart | 鎗 a pistol, revolver |∘脚 hands & feet, assistants | 巧 skillful, ingenious | 節 knuckles of hand | 指 the finger | 指頭 |·巾 napkin, handkerchief | 搋·子 a muff | 法 sleight of hand |∘續 process, methods | 選 elect by show of hands |·藝 handicraft, manual | 工 | 背 back of the hand | 套兒 gloves, mittens |·段 handicraft, ability, skill, way | 足 "hands & feet", brothers | 腕·子 wrist. | 紋 lines of hand		A
首[3]	首 185	首 855	Head, chief, origin; C. of verses | 角花 the hollyhock | 先 the first. 元 | chief | 戶 the leading farmer in a village	shou[4]	C

Shou

Character	Radical	Phonetic	Meaning	Grade
首[3]			︱領 the head, leader	
			︱·飾 women's head ornaments	
			︱尾 head & tail, bow & stern	
			︱位 principal seat	
守[3]	宀 40	寸 18	To keep, guard, observe	
			︱齋 to fast, abstinence	C
			︱晨更 keep morning watch	
			︱城 to guard a city	
			︱家 care for family, at home	
			︱制 in mourning for parents	
			︱舊黨 conservatives ︱舊派	
			︱法 keep or obey the laws	
			︱(本)分 keep to one's duty 安分︱己	
			︱候 wait for; take care of	
			︱寡 widow not marrying again ︱節	
			︱規矩 observe the customs	
			︱身 to preserve chastity	
			︱·得住 able to maintain, so ︱·不住	
			︱業 care for one's patrimony	
			︱夜 to watch at night	
受[4]	又 29	受 410	To receive, bear, endure, ︱·着; sign of passive	B
			︱氣 subject to another's anger	
			︱教 receive instruction	
			︱戒 to fast, do penance	
			︱吃 nice, tasty, palatable	
			︱驚 have had a fright	
			︱窮 suffer poverty; so ︱害, ︱熱, ︱苦, ︱難, ︱傷, ︱屈, ︱寃	
			︱恩 receive favor	
			︱洗 to be baptized	
			︱人欺負 to be insulted by others	
			︱累 endure trouble; involved	
			︱·不得 unable to endure, etc.	
			︱(or 授)室 to take a wife	

Character	Radical	Phonetic	Meaning	Variant reading	Grade
受[4]			| 聽 pleasant to hear | 罪 to bear pain (as hunger, cold) | 業 to receive instruction		
授[4]	手 64	受 410	To give, transmit, confer; impart | 命 transmit ordinance | 受 to give and receive 教 | professor, teacher, to teach 教 | 法 teaching method		C
瘦[4]	疒 104	叟 681	Lean, thin, poor | 弱, | 小 | 衣 tight-fitting clothes | 肉 lean meat. | 地 barren | 馬 a poor horse		B
獸[4]	犬 94	吠 457	Animal, brute beast | 類 | 醫 a veterinary surgeon 走 | quadruped, 野 | wild beast		C
壽[4] 壽[4] 寿[4]	士 33 减	壽 66	Longevity, age, birthday S | 衣 grave clothes, | 木 coffin | 禮 birth day presents |◦數 age, old age; | 終 death | 誕 old person's birthday 高 | what is your age? 拜 | visit one on birthday		C
首[4]	首 185	首 855	To confess | 罪	shou[3]	C
售[4]	口 30	隹 52	To sell | 出, 出 | , | 賣 | 價 price, value of what is sold		G

Shu

Character	Radical	Phonetic	Meaning	Variant reading	Grade
書[1] [illegible][1]	曰 73	聿 669	Book, letter; to write, compose | 案子 a study table | 棹子 | 札 a letter | 信 | 齋 a study, library | 房 |·籍 books | 本, | 册 |·記 secretary | 架(子) book-shelves, | 櫃, | 槅子 | 簽 label on books		A

書^{1}			｜·經 The Book of History ｜名 a title of a book ｜目 the index of a book ｜篇 the leaf of a book ｜頁 ｜鋪 a book shop ｜店 ｜套 case, cover for books ｜衣 四｜ Chinese "Four Books"		
梳^{1}	木 75	㐬 871	Comb, to comb ｜篦 ｜洗打扮 wash and dress ｜·頭 comb the hair 木｜ large wooden comb		B
疏^{1} 疎^{1}	疋 103	㐬 871	To estrange; distant, lax, coarse ｜遠 distant, (as relatives) ｜·忽 careless, remiss ｜率	su^{1}	E
蔬^{1}	艸 140	㐬 871	Edible greens, vegetables ｜菜	su^{1}	F
紓^{1}	糸 120	予 114	Slow, remiss; to relax ｜民困 relax the people's burden		I
舒^{1}	舌 135	予 114	To extend, unroll; comfortable S. ｜展 open, expand, spread out ｜暢 cheerfulness, good spirits ｜·服 comfortable, easy ｜·坦 ｜散 open; get rid of; at ease		B
輸^{1}	車 159	俞 619	To lose, beaten; pay duty; report ｜錢 lose money in gambling ｜出 to export. ｜入 import ｜稅 pay duty, taxes, so ｜餉 ｜贏 to lose or win 捐｜ subscribe, contribute		E
樞^{1}	木 75	區 696	Pivot, axis, cardinal, gist ｜紐		G
殊^{1}	歹 78	朱 499	To kill, exterminate; very; unlike ｜異 very different ｜不知 don't you know? in fact		G
殳^{1}	殳 79	殳 399	A long spear, to kill S.		K

Shu

孰^{2}	子 39	孰 744	Who? which? what? ｜是｜非 who right and who wrong?		F
塾^{2}	土 32	孰 744	School-room, vestibule 家｜ 義｜ a free school		F
熟^{2}	火 86	孰 744	Ripe, skilled; intimate	shou^{2}	A
叔^{21}	又 29	叔 123	Father's younger brother ｜｜ ｜·父 an uncle, junior uncle ｜母 an uncle's wife, aunt ｜^{1}·伯兄弟 paternal cousins		D
淑^{24}	水 85	叔 123	Pure, virtuous, limpid, fine ｜女 a virtuous female ｜德 female virtue ｜秀		F
贖^{2}	貝 154	賣 864	To redeem, ransom, atone ｜·出來 ｜·不起 can't afford to redeem ｜當^{4} redeem pawned article ｜罪 pay ransom for crime, or sin		D
朮^{2}	木 75	朮 491	Medicine, plant 蒼｜ like an artichoke	chu^{2}	K
秫^{2}	禾 115	朮 491	Glutinous millet ｜秸 kaoliang stalks		H
暑^{3}	日 72	者 192	Summer heat, heat ｜假^{4} summer vacation ｜伏 the hot season ｜熱 小｜,大｜ calendar terms		A
曙^{3}	日 72	者 192	Bright, dawn ｜日		I
署^{3}	网 122	者 192	Public office, to write, court ｜任 provisional appointment ｜理 administer provisionally		F
薯^{3}	艸 140	者 192	Potato, tuber, bulb, yam ｜芋 a sort of yam 大｜ 白｜ sweet potato 紅｜		F
數^{3}	攴 66	數 791	To count ｜·｜, ｜·一·｜ ｜錢 to count money ｜九 winter solstice to spring	shu^{4} shuo^{4} so^{4}	A

Shu

Character	Radical	Phonetic	Definition		Other readings	
屬3 屬3 屌3	尸 44 減	蜀 788	To belong to, allied, dependency; sort, rank ｜下 dependents. 親｜relatives ｜性 attributes, qualities ｜國 dependent states ｜·不著2你 none of your business ｜甚麼的 what do you belong to? ｜誰管 under whose jurisdiction? ｜他大 he is the biggest or eldest ｜於 belong to ｜員 subordinate officers 連｜related, connected			D
黍3	黍 202	黍 527	Glutinous millet (growing) ｜·子, ｜米 ｜角 a three-cornered pudding			E
鼠3	鼠 208	鼠 689	Rat, mouse, rodent 老｜ ｜疫 bubonic plague ｜皮 squirrel skins 松｜皮			F
蜀3	虫 142	蜀 788	A tree-worm; tripod; tribe ｜葵 hollyhock 巴｜Szechuan			H
抒1	手 64	予 114	To strain, take out, scoop ｜恨 put aside hate			I
數4	攴 66	數 791	Number, amount, a few ｜兒 ｜學 mathematics 算學 ｜·目 numbers, an account ｜年以來 a few years since ｜十個 several tens of ｜次 several times ｜日 無｜numberless		shu3 shou4 so4	A
恕4	心 61	如 554	To forgive, indulgent, mercy ｜過 to forgive a fault 寬｜ ｜罪 to forgive sin 饒｜forgive sin or fault			A
尌4	寸 41	尌 738	Surname	S		P
樹4	木 75	尌 738	Tree; to erect, establish ｜杈 tree-fork, ｜枝 branch			B

Shu

Character	Radical	Phonetic	Definition		
樹⁴			丨膠 gum from trees, rubber 丨汁 sap. 丨幹 trunk 丨立 to plant; set upright 丨根 root. 丨林 a forest 丨·木 trees generally. 丨皮 bark 丨梢 twigs. 丨葉 leaves, foliage 丨陰 the shade of a tree 菓木丨 fruit trees		
豎⁴ 竪⁴	豆 151	臤 643	To erect, perpendicular; a menial 丨起 to set up, erect 丨立 丨直 perpendicular, upright 丨碑 to erect a tablet		B
術⁴	行 144	朮 491	To devise, art, trick, magic, plan 丨學 tricks, schemes 法丨, 邪丨		C
述⁴	辵 162	朮 491	Narrate, publish 陳丨 丨明 to narrate, make clear 丨說 to proclaim, relate		C
束⁴	木 75	束 501	To bind, restrain; salary S. 丨脩 stipend of a teacher 丨儀 presents to teachers 丨綑 to tie up, bind up 丨帶 to tie on a girdle, gird		D
庶⁴	广 53	庶 201	All; people; so that, but, nearly; concubine 丨幾 (chi¹) nearly, about 丨乎 丨人 the common people 丨∘務處 business office 丨∘務員 business manager		F
欶⁴ 㰫⁴	欠 76	欶 502	To suck in, 丨氣, imbibe 丨濕 absorb moisture		P
漱⁴	水 85	欶 502	To rinse, scour, wash 丨口 rinse the mouth; loquacity		G
倏⁴ 儵⁴	人 9	攸 549	Suddenly, hastily 丨忽	shua⁴	G

Character	Radical	Phonetic	Meaning	Variant reading	
墅[4]	土 32	里 827	Lodge in field, villa 別丨, 圃丨		I
俶[4]	人 9	叔 123	To begin, do, act; good	ch'u[4]	I
菽[24]	艸 140	叔 123	Edible pulse		K

Shua

Character	Radical	Phonetic	Meaning	Variant reading	
刷[14] 㕞[14]	刀 18	巾 557	A brush, to brush, ink blocks 丨洗 brush and wash, scrub 丨鞋 brush or black shoes 丨灰 to whitewash 丨白 丨鍋 to wash the kettle 丨馬 groom horse. 丨·子 a brush 丨顏色 to paint, color 丨印 to print books, etc.		B
耍[3]	而 126	而 612	To play, sport, 玩丨; fence 丨鎗 practise with a gun 丨錢 gamble for money 丨笑 to joke, banter 丨脾氣 create disturbance 丨手藝 to practise a craft		D
倏[4] 儵[4]	人 9	攸 549	Suddenly, hastily 丨忽 丨爾不見 suddenly vanished 起丨滅 rising and sinking	shu[4]	G

Shuai

Character	Radical	Phonetic	Meaning	Variant reading	
衰[1]	衣 145	衣 367	To decay, fade, decline 丨弱 weak, feeble, debilitated 丨老 old, worn out, decayed 丨敗 decay, decline, fail 丨微 dwindle away, decay		C
摔[1]	手 64	十 13	To tumble, wrestle 丨跤 丨·下來·了 thrown down 丨跟頭 fall heels over head 丨·了傢伙 smashed the dishes	shuai[3]	E

摔[1]			| 破 dash down and break | 碎 | 倒[3] dash down, overturn		
摔[3] 甩[3]	手 64	十 13	To whirl, throw away, throw about | 手就走 a hand-fling and off | 子[3] lay eggs, spawn	shuai[1]	E
率[4]	玄 95	十 13	To command, lead | 領; follow; all; quickly | 常 in general, generally | 爾 sudden, hasty | 然 | 性 follow one's disposition	lü[4]	D
帥[4]	巾 50	師 753	Leader, commander 將 | | 府 general's quarters 元 | commander in chief		E

Shuan

拴[1]	手 64	全 78	To fasten, tie, bind |·住 | 繫 to fasten |·上 | 馬樁 hitching post | 牲口 to hitch animals | 繩子 string for hitching		C
閂[1]	門 169	門 635	Door bolt or bar 門 | | 門 to bolt a door 竪 | upright for double door		E
涮[4]	水 85	巾 557	To rinse, wash | 洗, |·一·| | 乾淨 to rinse clean		F

Shuang

雙[1] 双[1]	隹 172	隹 52	A couple, both, double, pair, mate, twin S. | 親 parents. | 方 both sides | 喜 two auspicious events | 姓 double surname | 關 double meaning, pun |·生 twins.— | a pair | 手 both hands | 數 an even number	shuang[4]	C

霜[1]	雨 173	相 847	Hoar-frost; old, candied 丨降 "frost's descent", a solar term 丨兒 bloom		D
孀[1]	女 38	相 847	A widow 丨婦 丨∘居 to live alone, widowed		F
礵[1]	石 112	相 847	Arsenic shale 砒丨		K
爽[3]	爻 89	大 451	Lively, well, agreeable, cheerful; to fail, error 丨·快 brisk, happy, comfortable 丨神 in good health, hearty 丨言 fail in promise 丨信		E
雙[4]	隹 172	隹 52	丨棒兒 Twins 丨生子[3]	shuang[1]	C

Shui

誰[2]	言 149	隹 52	Who? whom? any one 丨知 to my surprise 丨料 丨能彀 who is able to? who can? 丨不知 who doesn't know that? 丨·的 whose? 不是丨·的 no one's 丨也不行 no one would do	shei[2]	A
水[3]	水 85	水 520	Water, fluid; discount 丨淺 water is shallow, so 丨深 丨車 water-wheel 丨車·子 water-cart 丨雞 snipe 丨膠 glue 丨池 pond, tank. 丨∘晶 crystal 丨·仙花 the narcissus 丨星 the planet Mercury 丨性 unstable, capricious 丨壺 kettle. 丨缸 water vat 丨溝 a canal, gutter 丨鼓 dropsy in abdomen 丨罐 water-pitcher 丨雷 submarine mine	S	A

水[3]			丨力 water-power 丨路 road by water 丨道 丨龍 a pump, fire-engine 丨牛 water buffalo; snails 丨泡 a bubble; a sponge 丨筆 pen which needs water 丨瓢 calabash dipper 丨瓶 water bottle, pitcher 丨平尺 a water-level 丨筲 a bucket. 丨賊 pirates 丨·手[2] sailors, seamen 丨災 water calamities, floods 丨彩畫 water-color drawing 丨土不服 climate disagrees 丨桶 a water cask; buckets 丨曜日 Wednesday 丨烟袋 the water pipe 丨銀 quicksilver 丨源 a spring, fountain 扣丨 to discount		
睡[4]	目 109	垂 26	To sleep, 丨覺; die -chiao[4] 丨着了 to fall asleep 丨醒 asleep or awake; wake up 丨晌覺[4] take a noon siesta 丨獅 sleeping lion, i.e., China 丨·不着[2](覺) unable to sleep 丨熟·了 slept soundly		A
稅[4]	禾 115	兌 756	Revenue, duty, taxes 丨契 register a deed 丨錢 revenue, duties 丨餉, 丨銀 丨局子 a revenue office 丨·務處 丨關 Custom House 丨吏 Customs' officer 丨單 a duty memorandum 收丨 collect taxes. 上丨 pay 納丨		D
說[4]	言 149	兌 756	To urge, persuade; stop 丨客 glib trouble-makers	shuo[1]	A

Shun

Character	Radical	Phonetic	Meaning	Other reading	Grade
隼3 鶽3	隹 172	隼 54	A kind of hawk, kestrel 茶 | | 發必中4 a hawk-strike hits	sun3	K
順4	頁 181	川 425	To obey; convenient, fair, favorable, easy, graceful | 情 agreeable to feelings | 風 a fair wind | 服 submissive, obedient |∘從 | 心 agreeable to wishes | 利 prosperous. | 便 convenient | 流 with the tide, or the nap | 路 to follow a road | 道 | 民 loyal people, law-abiding | 手 favorable, easy to do |·當 proper; going smoothly |·天府 Prefecture of Peking (old)		C
舜4	舛 136	舜 274	Emperor Shun, B.C. 2255; wise		E
瞬4	目 109	舜 274	To glance, blink; twinkling | 息之間 in twinkling of an eye		H

Shuo

Character	Radical	Phonetic	Meaning	Other reading	Grade
說1	言 149	兌 756	To speak, narrate, talk, scold | 長道短 criticize, gossip |·起來 to speak of, mention |·出來 to describe, express |·法 way of speaking, mood | 好 come and mediate |·合 | 媳婦 negotiate for a wife | 笑話 joking, tell stories | 話 to speak, talk, converse | 來 | 去 circumlocution, ramble | 媒 act as go-between | 明 explanation 解 |	shui4	A

Shuo

Character	Radical	Phonetic	Meaning		Other readings	
說[1]			| 明白 stated clearly, a bargain | 白·了 to mispronounce | 破 speak out, reveal secret |·不淸 unable to explain clearly |·不過 can't out-talk |·不上來 can't say, can't explain | 不得 not to be mentioned |·不出 | 是非 scandal-mongering |·他 speak to him, scold him | 道 he said; to say; it is said |·得好 you say well; truly | 錯·了 I spoke incorrectly | 走就走 to go at the word | 文 famous Dictionary of 80 B. C. 沒得 | nothing to say			
勺[24]	勹 20	勺 231	Spoon, ladle |·子	文	shao[2]	E
妁[24]	女 38	勺 231	A go-between 媒 |		cho[4]	K
灼[24]	火 86	勺 231	Lustrous, clear | 明	文	shao[2]	I
芍[24]	艸 140	勺 231	Peony |·藥 -yüeh	文	shao[2]	I
數[4]	攴 66	數 791	Worried, flurried 煩 |	文	shu[34] so[4]	A
朔[4]	月 74	朔 661	1st day of moon 月 |		so[4]	F
槊[4] 鎙[4]	木 75	朔 661	Large spear; chess-board		so[4]	H
溯[4]	水 85	朔 661	To trace source, go up stream		so[4]	G
杓[4]	木 75	勺 231	Spoon, ladle, handle	文	piao[1] shao[2]	G
爍[4]	火 86	樂 490	Bright, flashing 閃 | , 灼 | | 閃 to reflect light			I

鑠^{4}	金 167	樂 490	To melt, fuse; brilliant ｜目 bright eyes		K
碩^{4}	石 112	石 722	Great, eminent; ripe	shih^{4}	I

So

索^{14}	糸 120	糸 886	To search, demand ｜討 to demand, extort ｜取	so^{23}	D
縮^{1}	糸 120	百 805	To contract; confuse; shrink; draw back ｜小 ｜減 to shorten, abbreviate ｜短 ｜脖子 shrunk neck, short-necked		E
唆^{1}	口 30	夋 542	To incite stir up ｜挑, 挑｜ ｜事 incite a quarrel		E
梭^{1}	木 75	夋 542	Shuttle, to and fro; swift ｜布 narrow fabric, nankeen		F
挱^{1} 挲^{1}	手 64	少 122	To rub in hand, stroke 摸·｜ rub with hand, feel of	sha^{1}	F
蓑^{1}	艸 140	衣 367	Grass rain-coat ｜衣		I
索^{2}	糸 120	糸 886	Keep on, might as well ｜∘性	so^{13}	D
所^{3}	戶 63	戶 728	Place, building, office; relative pronoun, which; C. ｜^{2}∘以 therefore, accordingly, so ｜^{2}∘以然 the cause for which ｜說的話 what was said ｜得^{2}稅 income tax ｜在 a cause, place; wherever ｜從 derivation, source ｜爲^{4} for this or that reason ｜有 whatever there is ｜有權 ownership, copyright		A
𧴪^{3}	貝 154	𧴪 125	Fragments		P

瑣^{3}	玉 96	貨 125	Fragments, small, trifling, vexatious 繁｜ ｜事 minute, petty affair ｜碎 importunate, troublesome			E
鎖^{3}	金 167	貨 125	Lock, to lock, chain, fetters ｜·起來 to lock ｜·上, ｜·住 ｜港 blockade. ｜鍊 fetters ｜門 lock a door. ｜頭 a lock ｜拿 to capture and fetter			B
索^{3}	糸 120	糸 886	Cord, to cord; ask for ｜·子 string, rope. 纜｜ hawser	S.	so^{12}	D
數^{4}	支 66	數 791	Worried, flurried		shu^{34} shuo^{4}	A
素^{4}	糸 120	素 886	To search into	文	su^{4}	A
朔^{4}	月 74	朔 661	First day of moon; north ｜望 1st and 15th of moon		shuo^{4}	F
溯^{4} 泝^{4}	水 85	朔 661	To trace source, go up stream ｜源 trace source 追｜		shuo^{4}	G
槊^{4} 鎙^{4}	木 75	朔 661	Large spear 善｜者 skilled spearmen		shuo^{4}	H
⿰扌索^{43}	手 64	糸 886	To select, seek out			H
蟀^{4}	虫 142	十 13	House cricket 蟋｜			K

Sou

廋^{1}	广 53	叟 681	To conceal, search for ｜求			I
搜^{1} ⿰扌叜^{1}	手 64	叟 681	To search, search out ｜查, ｜檢, ｜˳索 ｜·出 search out, discover ｜尋 ｜根兒 investigate the root			E
溲^{1}	水 85	叟 681	To soak, steep, macerate ｜酒 to make spirits			I

Character	Radical	Phonetic	Meaning	Alt.	Freq.
艘[1]	舟 137	叟 681	Boat, junk, C. of vessels		I
颼[1] 颾[1]	風 182	叟 681	Cold blast; whirr | |·的風 sound of wind | 瑟 凉·| |兒的風 cold piercing wind		I
餿[1]	食 184	叟 681	Spoiled food | 飯, 飯 |·了 汗 | odor of sweat		E
蒐[1]	艸 140	鬼 808	To hunt, drill, search | 取 | 練 to drill		I
擻[3]	手 64	數 791	To arouse 抖 | 精神 to rouse energies	sou[4]	B
叟[3] 傁[3]	又 29	叟 681	Venerable, old man, sir 老 | 田 | an old rustic		H
嗽[4]	口 30	欶 502	Cough, to cough 咳·| , | 喘 乾 | a dry cough 痰 | cough up phlegm		B
藪[4]	艸 140	數 791	Swamp; resort, retreat 郊 | 盜 | robbers' retreat		I
擻[4]	手 64	數 791	To shake | 一 | |·下來 to shake and sift	sou[3]	B

Ssu, see Szu P. 479

Su

Character	Radical	Phonetic	Meaning	Alt.	Freq.
穌[1]	禾 115	穌 257	To revive 復 | 耶 | Jesus. 耶 | 教 Protestants		C
蘇[1]	艸 140	穌 257	To revive; thyme; Soochow |·州 S. | 格蘭 Scotland. | 聯 Soviet Union |·子 mallow, | 麻, | 打 soda		G
疏[1] 疎[1]	疋 103	㐬 871	To estrange, distant; coarse |·忽 careless, remiss | 率 | 遠 distant, (as relatives)	shu[1]	E
蔬[1]	艸 140	㐬 871	Edible greens, vegetables | 菜	shu[1]	F

Su

Character	Radical	Phonetic	Meaning	Variant	Grade
甦[1]	生 100	更 834	To revive, rise from dead ｜醒 to revive, resuscitate		E
酥[1]	酉 164	禾 510	Curd, cheese, crisp ｜油 butter		I
俗[2]	人 9	谷 710	Vulgar, common, plebeian ｜·氣 annoyance; commonplace ｜傳 vulgar tradition ｜話 vulgar dialect; sayings ｜人 common person, layman ｜事 common affair, secular ｜物 a commonplace thing ｜語 a common saying, proverb	hsü[2]	A
速[24]	辵 162	束 501	Haste, quick, urgent ｜｜,疾｜ ｜成科 a short and quick course ｜記法 shorthand ｜記生 stenographer		E
素[4]	糸 120	糸 886	Simple, plain; heretofore｜來 ｜常 habitually, usually ｜服 white or plain clothes ｜性 natural disposition ｜日 commonly, daily ｜不相識 previously unacquainted ｜菜 plain food, vegetables ｜因 predisposition	so[4]	A
嗉[4] 膆[4]	口 30	糸 886	Crop of bird ｜·子 狗攔｜Adam's apple		G
訴[4] 愬[4]	言 149	斥 214	To tell, make known 告｜ ｜呈 file answer to plaint｜詞 ｜狀 make an accusation｜稟 ｜訟費 costs of law suit ｜寃 tell one's grievances 分｜	sun[4]	A
宿[4]	宀 40	百 805	To pass the night; old, stale ｜·一·｜lodge at inn｜店, 住·｜ ｜命論 fatalism 星｜a star, constellation -hsiu[4]	hsiu[13] hsü[1]	D

蓿4	艸 140	百 805	Clover, alfalfa 苜 |	hsü4	G
肅4	聿 129	肅 164a	Respectful, severe; Kansuh | 敬 respectful | 靜 stillness, solitude 嚴 | stern, awful, severe		F
粟4	米 119	西 775	Rice in husk; maize; millet | 米 maize, Indian corn		F
塑4 塐4	土 32	朔 661	To model in clay, mold shape | 像 make a clay image 泥 | clay molded, a dolt		G
夙4	夕 36	歹 277	Dawn, early, previous existence | 昔 formerly | 慧 naturally intelligent		H
觫4	角 148	束 501	To tremble, start		I

Suan

痠1	疒 104	夋 542	Aching, painful muscles 骨 |, | 疼 腿 | aching legs		E
酸1	酉 164	夋 542	Sour, distressed, grieved | 狂 haughty, supercilious | 梅湯 drink of sour prunes		B
算4 筭4	竹 118	算 848	To estimate, plan, calculate | 賬 to reckon an account | 計 to calculate, plan |·起來 reckon up, enumerate | 法 counting, arithmetic | 術 | 學 mathematics | 卦 to calculate fortunes | 命 |·了 (·罷) that'll do, never mind |·盤 abacus, reckoning board | 甚麼 of what consequence?		A
蒜4	艸 140	示 514	Garlic | 頭 | 苗 shoots of garlic		E

Sui

Character	Radical	Phonetic	Meaning	Alt. reading	Grade
綏[12]	糸 120	妥 409	To tranquillize 撫｜; peace ｜合 peace and quiet ｜遠 Suiyüan		G
荽[14]	艸 140	妥 409	Coriander 芫｜, 胡｜		H
尿[1]	尸 44	水 520	Urine, to urinate	niao⁴	H
夊[1]	夊 35	夊 540	To walk slowly		K
雖[12]	隹 172	隹 52	Although; even if, even｜然,｜則		A
隋[2]	阜 170	隋 180	Sui dynasty, A.D. 581—618		G
隨[2]	阜 170	隋 180	To follow, succeed, accord with ｜長｜落 rising and falling ｜機應變 adapt self to circums. ｜衆 to do as the rest do ｜和 pliable, a trimmer ｜心 as you wish or fancy｜你 ｜護 to escort, accompany ｜便 follow convenience｜意 ｜身 with me, on my person ｜時 at once, at any time ｜勢 acc. to circumstances ｜手 easy, while the hand is in ｜地 anywhere, acc. to place ｜從 accompany, follow｜同, 跟｜		B
遂[24]	辵 162	豖 288	Comply, follow, then, presently ｜心 follow own way｜意 ｜即 at once, forthwith｜後		D
髓[3]	骨 188	育 179	Marrow 骨｜		F

Character	Radical	Phonetic	Meaning		
歲4 歳4 亗4 岁4	止 77 滅 滅	歲 132	Year, year of life 年 | | 出 yearly expenditure | 入 yearly income | 口 age of an animal | 首 beginning of the year |·數兒 years of a person's age 幾 | how old? 多大 |·數 辭 | bid the old year farewell 萬 | live for ever; Emperor		A
碎4	石 112	卒 14	Fragments, broken, petty 零 | | 貨 small miscellaneous goods | 嘴子 a chatterbox | 銀 broken bits of silver 打 | break in fragments 砸 |		B
穗4	禾 115	惠 840	Ear of grain, spike, head |·子 麥 | ear of wheat		D
繐4	糸 120	惠 840	Fine cloth, tassel		I
繸4	糸 120	家 288	Girdle-string, tassel |·子 珠 | knotted tassel		H
祟4	示 113	出 665	Calamity, evil; spirit, ghost 怪 | goblin, demon 鬼 |		I

Sun

Character	Radical	Phonetic	Meaning		
孫1	子 39	系 887	Grandson |·子 |·女 a grand daughter 子 | descendants 外·| daughter's son	S.	C
損3	手 64	員 760	To wound, injure, spoil | 害 | 處 injury, injured parts | 壞 to break, spoil | 人利己 injure others for gain | 傷 to bruise, wound, hurt |·失 damage, loss 虧 | injury, loss, failure		C

<table>
<tr><td>笋^{3}
筍^{3}</td><td>竹
118</td><td>尹
677</td><td>Bamboo shoots, sprout | 芽, 竹 | ;
tenon
| 尖 the tops of bamboo shoots
| 片 slices of bamboo shoots
|·頭 a dovetail, corner</td><td></td><td>H</td></tr>
<tr><td>榫^{3}</td><td>木
75</td><td>隼
54</td><td>A dovetail, tenon |·子, | 頭,
| 眼 tenon and mortise
鬥 | to mortise</td><td></td><td>I</td></tr>
<tr><td>隼^{3}
鶽^{3}</td><td>隹
172</td><td>隼
54</td><td>A kind of hawk, kestrel
| 發必中 a hawk-strike hits</td><td>shun^{3}</td><td>K</td></tr>
<tr><td>訴^{4}</td><td>言
149</td><td>斥
214</td><td>To tell 告 | 俗</td><td>su^{4}</td><td>A</td></tr>
<tr><td>巽^{4}</td><td>己
49</td><td>巽
97</td><td>A diagram; mild, gentle 卑 |
| 與之言 words of gentle advice</td><td>hsün^{4}</td><td>K</td></tr>
</table>

Sung

<table>
<tr><td>松^{1}</td><td>木
75</td><td>松
393</td><td>The pine, needle-leaf conifers S.
|·香 resin. |·香水 turpentine
| 木 pine, fir timber
| 鼠 pine squirrel. | 樹 fir-tree
| 子^{3} fir cones or seeds
| 油 pine tree oil</td><td></td><td>D</td></tr>
<tr><td>淞^{1}</td><td>水
85</td><td>松
393</td><td>Name of river 吳 | Wusung</td><td></td><td>H</td></tr>
<tr><td>鬆^{1}</td><td>髟
190</td><td>松
393</td><td>To slack, loose, easy
|·開 to slacken, loosen, free
| 手 to let go, drop it
| 點 loose it a bit, slacken
| 綁 to release, let go, unbind</td><td></td><td>D</td></tr>
<tr><td>嵩^{1}</td><td>山
46</td><td>高
582</td><td>Mountain in Honan | 山</td><td></td><td>H</td></tr>
<tr><td>聳^{3}</td><td>耳
128</td><td>從
135</td><td>To raise, excite, egg on | 動</td><td></td><td>E</td></tr>
</table>

竦[3]	立 117	束 501	Alarmed, trembling; to incite ｜然 horrified, terrified ｜動 be agitated, horrified	I
送[4]	辵 162	天 462	To escort; send; give ｜·給 present to. ｜∘回 send back ｜終 gather round death-bed ｜信 carry news or letters ｜信簿 a chit-book ｜行 farewell visit, escort ｜客 escort guest leaving ｜別 ｜官 send to the authorities ｜禮 to make presents 饋｜ ｜殯 to attend a funeral	A
訟[4]	言 149	八 392	Litigate, accuse, go to law ｜告 accuse before magistrate ｜師 a lawyer ｜事 litigation	D
頌[4]	頁 181	八 392	To extol, praise 稱｜ ｜美 to praise, extol ｜讚, ｜揚	C
誦[4]	言 149	甬 594	To intone, recite, chant, read, recitative ｜習 learn by heart, memorize ｜詩 to recite poetry ｜讀 to recite, read aloud	G
宋[4]	宀 40	木 484	Sung dynasty, A. D. 960-1127 ｜∘朝; to dwell S. ｜字 ordinary style of type	G

Szu, ssu

思[1]	心 61	思 379	To think, reflect; meaning ｜潮 popular opinion, flood of ideas ｜想 to think, theory, idea ｜想自由 freedom of thought ｜量 ponder, deliberate ｜慮 ｜慕 to long for, miss ｜戀	A

Szu

思[1]			丨念 thoughts; think, consider 丨索 to think out, reflect 意·丨 thoughts, ideas, meaning		
厶[1]	厶 28	厶 868	Private, selfish	mou[3]	K
私[1]	禾 115	厶 868	Private, selfish, personal 丨自 丨產 private property 家·丨 丨錢 illicit cash 丨訪 secret inquiry, incognito 丨孩子 a bastard 丨生子[3] 丨合 illicit intercourse; to privately condone 丨∘下 (·裏) privately, secretly 丨自 丨心 selfish, a selfish mind 丨刑 lynch-law 丨貨 smuggled goods, so 丨酒 丨意 private views 丨立 privately established 丨賣 secret sale 丨事 private affairs		C
斯[1]	斤 69	斯 103	This, these, then, such 丨人 this person 丨時 this time 丨事 this matter 丨文 polished, refined		C
厮[1] 廝[1]	厂 27	斯 103	Attendant, servant, serve; a forager; to feed 丨役 servants, menials 丨徒, 丨僕 丨殺 to kill in battle		G
撕[1]	手 64	斯 103	To rend, tear, tear apart 丨∘開 丨·下來 to tear down 丨破 tear up, spoil 丨打 to fight, struggle		C
絲[1]	糸 120	糸 886	Silk, thread, wire, fine 丨毫 the least, slightest 丨線 silk thread, sewing silk		C

Szu

Character	Radical	Phonetic	Meaning		
絲^{1}			|絛·子 silk edging, fringe		
			肉| shreds of meat		
噝^{1}	口 30	糸 886	A call to come; to hiss		H
鷥^{1}	鳥 196	糸 886	White heron, egret		I
司^{1}	口 30	司 701	To control, preside, board	S.	D
			|法界 judicial world		
			|法制度 legal system		
			|庫 treasurer		
			|空 double surname	S.	
			|令 officer in command		
			|馬 double surname	S.	
			|事 manager |理		
			|書生 clerk, copyist		
			|徒 double surname	S.	
			|獄官 governor of a jail		
			公| a public company		
死^{3}	歹 78	死 278	To die, death, |·了; fixed, closed		A
			|而復生 dead but alive again		
			|法·子 a fixed plan		
			|後 after death, future world		
			|心眼兒 very stupid, obstinate		
			|刑 capital punishment |罪		
			|人 a dead person, the dead		
			|·不了^{3} will not die		
			|屍 a corpse		
			|守 to maintain till death		
			|水 dead or stagnant water		
			|亡 dead, perish		
			|物 inanimate objects		
四^{4} 肆^{4}	口 31	四 773	Four |·個; all around		A
			|季 the four seasons |時		
			|肢 the limbs, arms and legs		
			|角 rectangular, 4 corners		
			|·川 Szechuen province		

Szu

四⁴			丨方 square; four points of compass; all around 丨下, 丨面 丨海 "four seas", everywhere 丨散⁴ dispersed in all directions 丨聲 the four tones (Peking) 丨十 forty. 丨百 four hundred 丨書 The Four Books (Classics)		
泗⁴	水 85	四 773	Mucus 丨涕 丨水 River in Shantung		I
駟⁴	馬 187	四 773	Team of four horses 丨馬難追 a four-horse team can't recall (a word spoken) 丨不及舌		I
似⁴	人 9	以 431	Like; as if, similar, seem 丨·乎 丨是 it appears right 丨是而非 specious, fallacious ·丨·的 like, colloquial enclitic ·shih-		C
姒⁴	女 38	以 431	Elder brother's wife 丨娣		K
巳⁴	巳 49	己 311	9-11 A.M. 丨時; 4th moon 丨月		F
祀⁴	示 113	己 311	To sacrifice 祭丨, 丨神 丨孔子³ sacrifice to Confucius 丨上帝 to sacrifice to heaven 丨祖 sacrifice to ancestors 丨先人		D
寺⁴	寸 41	寺 46	Council hall, monastery 丨人 eunuchs 宦丨 丨院 Buddhist monasteries 禮拜丨 Mohammedan mosque		E
廁⁴ 厠⁴	广 53	則 858	A privy, 茅·丨; to arrange 上茅·丨 go to stool	tz'u⁴	E
肆⁴	聿 129	聿 669	Four, (large writing); to set forth, reckless, although, thus 丨行無忌 dissolute 放·丨		E
伺⁴	人 9	司 701	To spy, examine	tz'u⁴	E

笥^{4}	竹 118	司 701	Trunk, box, hamper 箱丨		I
嗣^{4}	口 30	司 701	Heirs, posterity, succession 丨接 to inherit 丨後 hereafter, subsequently 丨續 posterity, heirs 後丨 丨子^{3} an adopted son		E
飼^{4} 飤^{4}	食 184	司 701	To feed, food, nourish 丨養 寄丨 to live on other people		H
俟^{4} 竢^{4}	人 9	矣 477	To wait upon; until, when 丨候 to wait for, expect 等丨 丨下月 wait till next month		H
涘^{4}	水 85	矣 477	River banks 河丨		K

Ta

荅^{1}	艸 140	荅 709	Kind of pulse; to undertake 奉丨天命 do the will of God		K
搭^{1}	手 64	荅 709	To add on, assist; raise, hang up, move, take passage 丨界 join boundaries, bound 丨橋 build bridge; so 丨棚 丨救 to help, save, rescue 丨·拉·着 hanging down 丨配 animal copulation 丨·上 add to. 丨手 assist		F
褡^{1}	衣 145	合 708	A wrap, purse 丨·子; drilling 丨·褳(布) drilling (cloth) 丨·包 a sash, girdle		H
答^{14}	竹 118	合 708	To comply, consent 丨·應	ta^{2}	B
耷^{1}	耳 128	大 451	To hang down, large ears 丨·拉着 hanging down, pendant		F
瘩^{12}	疒 104	荅 709	Boil; sore 疙·丨		F

Ta

<table>
<tr><td>答[2]</td><td>竹
118</td><td>合
708</td><td>To answer, recompense 回 |
|·覆 to answer; a reply 對 |
| 話 an answer; to parley
| 拜 to return a visit
| 報 to recompense 報 |
|·不上 can not answer
| 詞 response to address</td><td>ta[14]</td><td>B</td></tr>
<tr><td>達[24]</td><td>辵
162</td><td>達
155</td><td>To open, see through; inform
| 知 inform, notify
| 者 an intelligent person | 人
| 信 send letter
| 賴喇嘛 Dalai Lama</td><td></td><td>C</td></tr>
<tr><td>韃[2]</td><td>革
177</td><td>達
155</td><td>Mongols |·子</td><td></td><td>G</td></tr>
<tr><td>打[3]</td><td>手
64</td><td>丁
2</td><td>To whip, strike; do; play; make; from
| 柴 to cut firewood
| 戰 to tremble
| 仗 to fight, war. | 架 quarrel
| 場 to thresh grain
| 吵 to wrangle. |∘攪 stir up
|∘擊 to strike; a shock; injure a cause or plan
| 價 beat down the price
| 糨子 to make paste
| 結子 to tie a knot
| 尖 snack at noon on journey
| 前失 stumble, | 鞦韆 swing
| 更 to act as watchman
| 球 to play ball, (ten-pins, billiards etc.)
| 拳 to box. |·發 to send
| 哈息 to gape, yawn, gasp
| 硶 beat the ground firm
| 呼嚕 to snore. |∘開 to open
| 一下 to strike a blow
|·個盹兒 to nap, doze</td><td></td><td>A</td></tr>
</table>

Ta

打^{3}
| 鼓 beat drum. | 官·司 go to law
| 滾兒 to roll on the ground
| 雷 thunder. | 獵 hunting
| 冷顫 to shake with the cold
| 量 to measure, estimate
| 那·裏來 whence do you come?
| 敗仗 dafeated in battle
| 牌 to play cards
|·扮 to dress, costume
| 破 to tear, break
|·不過 can't thrash (him)
| 掃 to brush; sweep
| 勝仗 conquer in battle
| 水 draw water from well
|·算 suppose, guess, plan
| 算·盤 reckon on the abacus
| 碎 break to bits
|·死 strike dead
| 倒^{3} knock down; down with!
| 嚏·噴 to sneeze
|·點 look after, arrange
| 電話 ring up a telephone
| 電報 send a telegram
| 鐵的 blacksmith
|·聽 to inquire, listen
| 雜兒的 coolie
| 草稿 make a rough draft
| 字機 typewriter
| 印 to stamp | 戳·子
| 魚·的 a fisherman

撻^{3} 手 64 達 155 To beat, chastise 鞭 | ; quick 俗 t'a^{4} H
楚 | beat, cane in school

大^{4} 大 37 大 451 Great, noble, best; very tai^{4} A
| 丈夫 a great or good man
| 車 large cart, wagon
|·臣 a minister of state
|·起膽來 to brace up courage

大[4]

| 器 man of great ability | 才
|·家夥兒 all, every one of them
| 建小建 30 and 29 day months
| 襟 overlap of coat; a bib
| 淸國 China under Manchus
(|)主筆 editor-in-chief
| 局 public affairs, situation
| 衆 all, the whole crowd
| 發財 get very wealthy
| 凡 every, the whole
|·方 genteel, generous
| 寒 "great cold", a solar term
| 西洋 the Atlantic Ocean
| 學 university; 1st of "4 Books"
| 小 the size of
| 雪 "great snow", a solar term
| 戶 rich family. | 話 boast
| 會 Synod of Presb. Church
| 意 chief idea |·意 careless
| 人 adult; your excellency
| 概 generally, probably
| 開 wide open. | 褂 long coat
| 沽 Taku, port of Tientsin
| 工 master-workman
| 理院 Supreme Court
| 禮服 full dress suit, so | 禮帽
| 諒 most likely. probably
| 略 generally, general outline
| 陸 continent
| 麥 barley. | 米 rice
| 門 great gate, front door
|·拇指 the thumb
| 娘 paternal elder aunt | 媽, |·|
| 半 the greater part | 部分
| 便 evacuate, go to stool
| 伯 paternal elder uncle |·爺
|·不過 cannot be greater than

大[4]			丨不同 very unlike 丨·師傅 head-cook, steward 丨使 ambassador. 丨勢 condition 丨事 important affairs 丨暑 "great heat", a solar term 丨水 high water; an inundation 丨膽 bravery, courage 丨堂 principal hall 丨道 high way, true doctrine 丨總統 president of a republic 丨同社會 the ideal state, Utopia 丨同小異 only slightly different 丨慈丨悲 of great compassion 丨烟 opium 丨約 probably, nearly, about		
怛[2]	心 61	旦 793	Distressed 丨 丨; pity, afraid 惻丨 to commiserate		K

T'a

他[1]	人 9	也 301	He, she, it, other. 丨·的 his 丨方 another quarter; so 丨人, 丨日 丨兩個 they two 丨倆 丨·們 they, them. 丨·們的 theirs 丨·那個人 that person 丨動 reaction, outside influence 丨自己 he himself	t'o1	A
㒓[1]	羽 124	㒓 296	Sound of wings		P
塌[1]	土 32	㒓 296	To collapse, fall in ruin 丨·下 丨梁 main beam has fallen 坍丨 fall down, collapse 倒丨 遭·丨 (or·蹋) spoil, waste, defame		D
褟[1] 溻[1]	衣 145	㒓 296	Inner garment, sweat-shirt; to soak, moisten 丨透 soaked through, e.g., sweat 汗丨兒 a sweat-shirt		F

Character	Radical	Phonetic	Meaning	Variant	Grade
蹋[14]	足 157	㣛 296	To tread heavily; stamp, step 丨·躐着鞋 shoes down at heel		B
塔[3] 墖[3]	土 32	荅 709	Pagoda, dagoba, tower 一座丨 義丨 "baby tower" for dead babies 寶丨 pagoda of precious relic		D
獺[34]	犬 94	賴 503	An otter 水丨, beaver 山丨 the beaver, 海丨 sea otter		I
踏[4]	足 157	足 133	To tread, step 踐丨 to tread down, trample 脚丨車 a bicycle		E
搨[4]	手 64	㣛 296	To rub, take rubbing (of incised stone tablet) 丨板 a shelf 搥丨 apply paper for rubbing		H
榻[4]	木 75	㣛 296	Couch, bed 牀丨 上丨 to go to bed		F
撻[4]	手 64	達 155	To beat, chastise; quick 鞭丨 to beat with a whip	ta[3]	H
躂[4]	足 157	達 155	To slip 丨倒 蹧丨 spoil, waste; defame		H
闥[4]	門 169	達 155	Door of inner room 閨丨, screen 排丨直入 open door and go in		I

Tai

Character	Radical	Phonetic	Meaning	Variant	Grade
獃[1] 呆[1]	犬 94	豈 732	Silly, foolish 癡丨 丨笑 idiot laugh. 丨·子 simpleton 賣丨兒 to gaze in the doorway	ai[12]	F
歹[3]	歹 78	歹 277	Bad, perverse 作丨 好∘丨 good and bad; anyhow 不知好丨 no sense of fitness		E
大[4]	大 37	大 451	丨·夫 doctor 丨∘黃 rhubarb	ta[4]	A

Tai

帶^4 䌦^4 — 巾 50 — 帶 560 — A

Girdle, zone; to take, lead; close, connected, with; C. of land
|·去 to carry off, carry with
| 信 to carry a letter
|·來 bring. |·回來 bring back
|∘累 to encumber, impede
| 兵的 troop leader
|·子 a ribbon, sash, girdle
佩 | attached to girdle

戴^4 — 戈 62 — 𢦏 334 — A

To wear, bear, sustain S.
| 花兒 to wear flowers
| 帽子 wear hat or cap, put on
| 眼鏡 to wear glasses

代^4 — 人 9 — 代 328 — B

For, instead; generation; dynasty
| 價 compensation
| 求 intercede for, beg for
| 議制 parliamentary system
| 勞 do instead of one | 作
| 理會長 acting president
| 名詞 synonyms, pronouns
| 辦 a deputy; to depute
| 筆 a writer, amanuensis
| 表 representative, stand for
| 數 algebra
|∘替 acting as locum tenens

岱^4 — 山 46 — 代 328 — H

T'ai Shan | 宗, | 山, now written 泰山

玳^4 瑇^4 — 玉 96 — 代 328 — H

Tortoise-shell | 瑁 (殼)

袋^4 帒^4 — 衣 145 — 代 328 — B

Bag, sack, 口 | , pocket, purse
褡 | belt pocket. 烟 | a pipe

貸^4 — 貝 154 — 代 328 — F

To lend on interest 借 | ; pardon
寬 | pardon, show mercy

黛^4 — 黑 203 — 代 328 — K

Umber, black 青 |
畫 | pencilled eyebrows

待4	彳 60	寺 46	Wait for, wait on 等｜; treat ｜承 treat well 寬｜, 厚｜, 款｜ ｜·一會兒 wait a little while ｜客 entertain guests 接｜ ｜·兩天 wait a couple of days ｜·不住 can not remain here 對｜attitude or relation to 薄｜treat shabbily 慢｜, ｜·不好		C
怠4	心 61	台 718	Rude, remiss, idle 懈｜ ｜慢 to neglect; disrespectful ｜惰 indolent, lazy		E
殆4	歹 78	台 718	Perilous, 危｜; hazard, nearly ｜盡 nearly exhausted ｜死不活 half dead and alive		G
隶4	隶 171	隶 526	To reach to, surplus		K
逮4 迨4	辵 162	隶 526	To reach, until, catch up ｜今 until now 追｜pursue and seize	ti4	F

T'ai

胎1	肉 130	台 718	Womb｜胞; pregnant, congenital ｜衣 the after-birth ｜生 viviparous, womb-born 懷｜to be pregnant		E
苔1	艸 140	台 718	Moss, lichen 青｜, 蒼｜ ｜菜 edible sea-weed		I
臺2 台2	至 133	臺 885	Eminent; terrace, stage, table; your ｜階 steps to building, ascent ｜前 before the bench or throne ｜甫 your honored name, Sir? ｜灣島 Formosa. 燈｜lampstand 砲｜a fort, gun-mound		B
擡2 抬2	手 64	臺 885	To carry between two, elevate ｜·起來 carry, lift up, raise ｜價 raise the price		A

擡^{2}			｜轎 carry a sedan chair		
			｜·舉 to exalt, praise, advance		
			｜槓 carry on pole; dispute		
			｜·不起來 unable to raise		
			｜·不動 too heavy to carry		
			｜頭 raise the head, "look out!"		
太^{4}	大 37	大 451	Too, very; term of respect		A
			｜矮 too low; so ｜高, ｜長, ｜利害		
			｜極 eternal; first principle		
			｜∘監 eunuch. ｜古 very ancient		
			｜初 the first beginning		
			｜∘后 the empress dowager		
			｜過 excessive		
			｜·平 peaceful, tranquil		
			｜平洋 the Pacific Ocean		
			｜叔 double surname S.		
			｜·｜ old lady, mandarin's wife; Mrs.		
			｜子^{3} crown prince ｜·陽 the sun		
汰^{4}	水 85	大 451	To rinse, correct, scour 沙｜		K
			淘｜(natural) selection 天然淘｜		
態^{4}	心 61	能 324	Gait, air, behavior, bearing		D
			｜·度 attitude, behavior		
			小人｜ mean behavior		
泰^{4}	水 85	夫 469	Liberal; prosperous; exalted		E
			｜西國 Western, European nations		
			｜·平 great prevailing peace		
			｜山 famous mt. in Shantung		
			｜國 Thailand (Siam)		

Tan

單^{1}	口 30	單 826	Single, only, odd, thin; but; a list	shan^{4}	A
			｜純 simple, homogeneous 簡｜		
			｜衣 clothes without lining		
			｜日雙日 the odd and even days		
			｜·薄 thin, poor, weak		
			｜片兒 a tract, sheet of paper		
			｜衫 a single garment, shirt		

Character	Radical	Phonetic	Meaning	Other reading	
單^{1}			｜數 odd number, singular ｜｜one; only, merely｜｜·的 ｜套車 cart drawn by one animal ｜獨 alone, singly ｜·子 a bill, note, list ｜位 a unit of measure 清｜memo. of accounts, invoice		
襌^{1}	衣 145	單 826	Single, sheet. 被｜bed-sheet 汗｜an undershirt		E
躭^{1} 耽^{1}	身 158	冘 176	To delay, loiter, neglect ｜·擱 to loiter, delay｜·悞,｜延 ｜·悞工夫 hinder work, waste time		C
擔^{1} 担^{1}	手 64	詹 741	To carry on pole; undertake; sustain ｜承 undertake an affair ｜驚 to be frightened ｜負 bear burdens, sustain ｜險 stand danger, run risk ｜任 to take responsibility, bear｜當 ｜任義務 to undertake responsibility ｜保 go security for any one ｜水 carry water with pole ｜·待 to bear, put up with ｜代 take on oneself to do ｜^{1}｜·^{4}子 to carry a load ｜當不起（住）unable to endure ｜憂 bear sorrow, grieved	tan^{4}	G
丹^{1}	丶 3	丹 570	Carnation, red; drug, elixir, pill ｜青 colours; painting ｜硃 pure red｜紅,｜色 ｜國 Denmark｜麥 ｜丸 bolus, pill		E

Tan

膽³ 胆³	肉 130	詹 741	Gall, courage, daring ｜·子, ｜兒 ｜戰 afraid, fearful ｜怯, ｜虛 ｜氣 bravery, courage ｜兒, ｜◦量 ｜小 cowardly. ｜敢 intrepid ｜大 bold, daring, brave		C
撢³	手 64	覃 780	To dust, a duster ｜·子 ｜去塵土 to brush off the dust ｜·一·｜ to dust, give a dusting	t'an⁴	E
撣³⁴	手 64	單 826	To seize, hold lightly	t'an²¹	F
亶³	亠 8	亶 768	True, sincere; to trust ｜不聰 truly not discriminating		K
旦⁴	日 72	旦 793	Morning, dawn 平｜, day ｜夕 morning and evening ｜晚 小｜ actor of female parts 元｜ first morn of the year		F
但⁴	人 9	旦 793	But, only, merely; whenever ｜凡 whenever; whatever ｜不知 but I do not know ｜·是 but, but it is ｜有一件 but it must be remembered ｜願如此 would that it be so		B
擔⁴	手 64	詹 741	A load ｜·子. 重｜ a heavy load 扁｜ carry-pole	tan¹	C
蛋⁴	虫 142	虫 785	Egg, testes ｜卵 ｜青 the white af an egg ｜黃 the yolk of an egg ｜殼兒 the shell of an egg ｜白質 albumenoid, protoplasm 雞｜ hen's egg 雞子兒³ 下｜ to lay an egg		C
石⁴	石 112	石 722	A picul 133⅓ lbs.	shih²	C
誕⁴	言 149	延 128	Wide, boastful; birthday ｜辰 a birthday ｜日, ｜時, 生｜		D

誕4			丨妄 boast extravagantly 聖丨 Christmas		
淡4 澹4	水 85	炎 447	Weak, tasteless, dull; fresh 丨青 plain blue. 丨水 fresh water 丨而無味 insipid, tasteless 丨薄 thin, indifferent, tasteless 鹹丨 salt and fresh		E
彈4	弓 57	單 826	Bullet, shot, 丨∘子, pill 丨丸 丨藥 ammunition, ball and powder	t'an2	E
憚4	心 61	單 826	Dread, averse to, fear 丨煩 averse to taking trouble		I

T'an

探1	手 64	罙 487	To feel for; explore, try 丨天 to draw God's wrath	t'an4	C
攤1	手 64	難 108	Spread, apportion; stall or mat for small business 丨錢 to subscribe money according to a ratio 丨分4子 to contribute, to subscribe, divide up—as money for feast 丨∘開 to unfold, to open 丨還 to pay by instalments 丨·子 a stall		B
灘1 潬1	水 85	難 108	Sand-bank, a rapid 沙丨 shoals		E
癱1	疒 104	難 108	Numbness, paralysed, palsy 丨瘋, 丨瘓, 丨病 丨·子 a paralytic person		E
貪1	貝 154	今 434	To covet, greedy, desire 丨心, 丨·圖 丨愛 be fond of, desire 丨求, 丨慕 丨吃 gluttonous; so 丨酒 丨想 to long for, covetous 丨望 丨戀 avaricious, greedy 丨吝, 丨婪 丨名 ambitious of fame; so 丨財		D

T'an

貪[1]			| 便宜 to covet advantage -p'ien[2]·i | 色 lustful, lascivious | 睡 too fond of sleep |·頭 the object of desire | 贜 grasping, greedy of bribes		
坍[1]	土 32	丹 570	To collapse, fall in ruins 崩 | | 塌 broken, ruined, fall | 倒[3]		F
痰[2]	疒 104	炎 447	Phlegm, mucus | 涎 | 氣 asthma | 喘 | 盒 a spittoon | 罐		E
談[2]	言 149	炎 447	To talk, chat, converse | 話 S. | 話會 conversazione, social | 論 to converse, chat |·|, | 説 閒 | to chat, gossip		B
壇[2] 坛[2]	土 32	亶 768	Altar, arena | 社, 祭 | 築 | erect an altar 設 | 天 | Temple of Heaven, Peking		E
檀[2]	木 75	亶 768	Sandal wood | 香木 | 香 incense of sandal wood 紫 | red sandal wood		K
彈[2]	弓 57	單 826	To play, thrum, snap; mark | 琴 play the dulcimer or piano | 劾 to impeach | 絃子 to play on the lute or fiddle | 棉花 to fluff up cotton with bow | 壓 to keep down, to suppress	tan[4]	E
撣[21]	手 64	單 826	To thrum—used for 彈 動 | move about, just stir	tan[34]	F
覃[2]	襾 146	覃 780	Wide, spreading, to reach | 恩 clemency, an amnesty		K
潭[2]	水 85	覃 780	Deep, pool, extensive | 水 deep water 黑龍 | Black Dragon Pool		F
罈[2] 壜[2]	缶 121	覃 780	Earthenware jar, or jug |·子 酒 |·子 wine-jar; drunkard		F

T'an

譚^{2}	言 149	覃 780	To boast; gossip; extended S. 參｜chatter, talk		H
曇^{2}	日 72	云 875	Lowering, overcast		I
毯^{3}	毛 82	炎 447	Rug, carpet ｜·子 椶｜coir matting		B
坦^{3}	土 32	旦 793	Level place, quiet, peaceful ｜然 composed, comfortable ｜白 frankly ｜克車 tank 平｜level, smooth ｜平 舒·｜comfortable and happy		E
袒^{3} 襢^{3}	衣 145	旦 793	To strip; screen; bare ｜服 ｜護 to protect, screen 偏｜		K
忐^{3}	心 61	上 119	Nervous, fearful ｜忑 timid, vacillating		H
探^{4}	手 64	罙 487	To search out, investigate, spy, try, test, visit ｜見電燈 electric torch ｜知 to ascertain ｜聞 ｜親 visit one's relatives ｜悉敵情 to reconnoitre ｜險家 explorers, adventurers ｜病 inquire after sick man ｜水 try depth of water ｜深淺 ｜·｜口氣 'sound' the feelings ｜·聽 spy, inquire, listen ｜望 to inquire, ascertain ｜問 窺｜to peep, spy, pry 試｜try, essay, tempt, test	t'an^{1}	C
嘆^{4} 歎^{4}	口 30	𦰩 107	To sigh, moan, ｜息, ｜惜, regret ｜·一口氣 to heave a sigh ｜辭 an interjection 讚｜admiring praise ｜美 可｜how sad! what a pity!		D

Character	Radical	Phonetic	Meaning	Variant	Class
炭⁴	火 86	火 446	Charcoal, coal 木 | , 柴 | | 氣 carbonic gas | 質 carbon. | 精燈 arc light | 火 a charcoal fire		D
撢⁴	手 64	覃 780	To feel for, seek out | 癢 animal scratching	tan³	E

Tang

Character	Radical	Phonetic	Meaning	Variant	Class
當¹ 当¹	田 102	當 586	Ought, suitable; to bear; match, meet; at time of | 差 (使) employed officially | 家 "boss", head of house | 間兒⁴ in the middle | 中, | 中間兒⁴ | 今 now, the present time | 下 | 初 original; at first | 兒 point of time; opening | 先 in the front; formerly | 選人 candidate who is elected | 然 should, ought; of course | 日 today; on that day | 天, | 時 | 面 face to face, openly | 兵 to become a soldier | ·不起 unequal to responsibility | 時 at that or this time |⁴ 做 to represent, stand for 相 | proportionate; to suit, good 該 | ought, should, proper, 應 |	tang⁴	A
襠¹	衣 145	當 586	Crotch of trousers 褲 |		K
鐺¹	金 167	當 586	Lock, pedlar's gong | | sound of drum, gong		H
擋³ 攩³ 挡³	手 64 俗	當 586	To prevent, resist, stop 阻 | , 攔 | | 駕 decline to see visitor | ·着亮 to stand in the light | ·着道兒 stopping the road | 路 | ·住 stop, obstruct, so | ·不住 抵 | 不住 cannot resist		B

Character	Radical	Phonetic	Definition	Alt.	Grade
黨[3]	黑 203	尙 584	Party, faction, village, club 丨爭 party strife 丨人 a cabal, clique, party 丨◦派 party. 丨見 party idea 丨員 member of party		D
讜[3]	言 149	尙 584	Faithful words, counsel 忠丨		I
當[4]	田 102	當 586	To pawn; consider as, suitable 丨眞 it is a fact, deem it true 丨衣裳 to pawn clothes 丨票 a pawnbroker's ticket 丨·舖 a pawn-shop 丨十錢 Peking cash, 1 piece=10 丨丨 to pawn, pledge things 上丨 cheated in bargain 贖丨 redeem a thing from pawn	tang[1]	A
檔[4] 欓[4]	木 75	當 586	Cross-piece, rung, space between 丨房 registry department; 丨案 files 椅子丨 round of a chair, rung		G
盪[4]	皿 108	湯 237	To move, oppose, shove; bathtub 震丨 to startle, disturb	t'ang[4]	B
蕩[4]	艸 140	湯 237	Vast; profligate; to squander 丨費 squander wealth 丨產 放丨 heedless, reckless 飄丨 a swagger; to float		E
宕[4]	宀 40	石 722	Covered way, passage 跌丨 original, unique		I

T'ang

Character	Radical	Phonetic	Definition	Alt.	Grade
湯[1]	水 85	湯 237	Broth, soup, gravy; to scald S. 丨匙 soup ladle. 丨泉 hot spring 丨藥 medicine in draught		A
趟[1]	走 156	昜 236	To wade 丨水, get wet, mired 丨濕·了 have wet feet		E

T'ang

Character	Radical	Phonetic	Meaning		
鏜[12]	金 167	堂 585	Noise of gongs, drums etc. ｜口 a mouthpiece ｜·的響 loud drumming		K
堂[2]	土 32	堂 585	Hall, court, chapel — 座｜ ｜兄弟 cousins generally ｜會 Presbyterian Session ｜·客 female guests, women ｜·子 brothel; bath; bath-house 教｜church, meeting-house 禮拜｜ 福音｜preaching chapel 禮｜assembly hall 大｜principal hall in court		A
膛[2]	肉 130	堂 585	Breast, hollow, fat; capacity ｜兒 the centre, inside ｜·子 上｜roof of the mouth 上牙｜ 胸｜pit of the stomach, breast		F
螳[2]	虫 142	堂 585	A mantis ｜。螂		I
唐[2]	口 30	唐 723	Boasting, rude, wild, rash ｜突 S. ｜。朝 a dynasty, A.D. 620-907		F
塘[2]	土 32	唐 723	Dyke, pond, tank, post. 池｜a pond, pool, moat 蓮｜lotus pond, so 魚｜		F
搪[2]	手 64	唐 723	To parry, evade, presume ｜·不過去 unable to parry or put off ｜塞 make excuses, put off		G
糖[2] 餹[2]	米 119	唐 723	Sugar, candy. 沙｜granulated sugar ｜薑 preserved ginger ｜菓 preserved fruits ｜水 treacle, syrup		B
棠[2]	木 75	尙 584	Crab apple tree 海｜ ｜梨 name of kind of pear		G
倘[3] 儻[3]	人 9	尙 584	If, supposing, perchance ｜若 ｜或 if, but if, should it be		D
淌[3]	水 85	尙 584	To flow, drip ｜水 to drip, to leak		I

躺3	身 158	尙 584	To lie down, lie |·着, |下, |臥 |椅 a long chair |箱 a long clothes-box		A
帑3	巾 50	奴 553	Treasury 國| the national treasury	nu3	G
燙4	火 86	湯 237	Heat, scald; to iron; blister |熱·了 scalding hot |·得慌 |·個泡兒 scalded to a blister |手 to scald the hand |衣服 iron clothes. |斗 flat-iron		B
盪4 ⿺辶湯4 ⿰車尚4	皿 108 車 159	湯 237	A time; row; C. of journeys, acts, etc. |盤 a bath-tub 走·了一| went once 一|瓦 a row of tiles 一|字 a column of characters	tang4	B
鐋4	金 167	湯 237	A plane, to smooth		I
逿4	辵 162	昜 236	To fall, miss; C. of times		E

Tao

刀1	刀 18	刀 219	Knife, sword |劍; C. of cuts |鞘子 a sheath, scabbard |尖 point of knife. |刃 edge |護手 a sword hilt |口鈍 edge of knife is dull |快 the knife is sharp |把兒4 handle of knife. |背 back		A
叨1	口 30	刀 219	To gabble; mixed up |·| loquacious, prosy | |念念 嘮·| noisy, clamorous	t'ao1	G
倒3	人 9	到 220	To fall over, prostrate, topple |換 exchange, substitue for |·過來 turn over. 跌| stumble |斃 fell down and died |塌 to fall down; thrown 坍|	tao4	A

Tao

倒^{3}			｜店 to sell the business, ｜舖子 ｜臥 to lie down; drop dead ｜運 ill-luck; change of luck 顚｜ topsy-turvy, reversed		
道^{3}	辵 162	首 855	過｜兒 Narrow passage	tao^{4}	A
導^{34}	寸 41	首 855	To lead, guide, teach 教｜ ｜線 line of advance, guide ｜火線 a fuse 嚮｜ a local guide 引｜ to lead, guide		C
島^{3}	山 46	島 254	Island 海｜ 半｜ a peninsula		B
搗^{3} 擣^{3}	手 64	島 254	To pound ｜碓, beat, ram down ｜線 reel or wind thread ｜衣 beat clothes in washing ｜亂 to trouble, disturb ｜碎 to beat to pieces		F
禱^{3} 禂^{3}	示 113	壽 66	To entreat, prayer ｜·告, 祈｜, ｜祝 家｜ family prayer 默｜ silent prayer. 公｜ public		C
到^{4}	刀 18	到 220	To reach, come to 來｜; to ｜極處 to the last degree ｜·處 everywhere ｜·過 to have been to a place ｜·了 arrived. ｜·不了^{3} can't reach ｜了^{3}兒 at last, after all ｜手 come to hand, receive 收。｜·了 ｜底 to the bottom; at last, yet ｜頭 reach end, finally		A
倒^{4}	人 9	到 220	To pour out; on contrary, and yet ｜茶 pour tea; so ｜水 ｜車 to back up a vehicle ｜嚼 to chew the cud ｜·出 to pour out ｜·出來 ｜好 still it is good ｜換 to exchange	tao^{3}	A

<table>
<tr><td>倒4</td><td></td><td></td><td>|·過來 turned over
∘|·是 though (—yet); indeed, but
| 弔 suspend upside down | 懸
| 座 rooms facing main building
| 退 to step back, retire
| 有 still there is, there is yet</td><td></td><td></td></tr>
<tr><td>道4</td><td>辵
162</td><td>首
855</td><td>Road, way, passage; zone; doctrine; officer; to say
| 教 doctrine of Taoism
| 喜 congratulate
| 謝 thank | 之
| 學院 Bible Institute
| 心 spiritual nature
|·理 right principles, doctrine
|∘路 road, way, path | 途
| 袍 Taoist priest's robe
|·士 a Taoist priest
| 德 virtue, morals, ethics
| 德家 moralist
| 德經 Taoist classic (of Laotze)
| 德學 ethics 倫理學
| 尹 prefect, Taotai
官 | public road, highway 大 |</td><td>tao3</td><td>A</td></tr>
<tr><td>盜4
盗4</td><td>皿
108</td><td>次
442</td><td>Robber, highwayman; to plunder
| 竊 to steal, pilfer 偷 |
| 寇 pillager, thief, rebel
| 賊 a thief, thieves
强·| robbers, banditti</td><td></td><td>D</td></tr>
<tr><td>稻4</td><td>禾
115</td><td>舀
682</td><td>Growing rice, paddy | 米
| 皮·子 rice husks. | 草 straw</td><td></td><td>E</td></tr>
<tr><td>蹈4</td><td>足
157</td><td>舀
682</td><td>To trample, disregard 踐 |
| 法 to violate the law</td><td></td><td>F</td></tr>
<tr><td>悼4</td><td>心
61</td><td>卓
15</td><td>Grieved, afflicted, mourning
追 | 會 memorial service
| 哭 bewail, grieved 悲 |</td><td></td><td>F</td></tr>
</table>

T'ao

Character	Radical	Phonetic	Meaning		
搯[1] 掏[1]	手 64	舀 682	Draw out, clean out, pull out ｜錢 to hand out money ｜井 clean out a well; so ｜溝 ｜·出來 to pull out of ｜耳朵 to pick the ears		B
滔[1]	水 85	舀 682	To rush, roll, inundate ｜濫 ｜｜不斷 unceasing flow, roll ｜天大禍 an awful calamity		G
縚[1] 絛[1]	糸 120	舀 682	A band, silk edging ｜·子; sash 絲｜ a silk girdle		F
韜[1] 弢[1]	韋 178	舀 682	Sheath, case; strategy; liberal ｜弓 put a bow in its case ｜略 tactics, strategy		I
濤[1]	水 85	壽 66	Great waves, billows 波｜		D
叨[1]	口 30	刀 219	To enjoy, desire, addicted ｜擾 thanks at end of feast ｜光 solicit favor or custom ｜蒙 thanks for benefits ｜沐	tao1	G
饕[1]	食 184	虍 203	Gluttonous, ｜餮 covetous		I
咷[2]	口 30	兆 383	Cry of infants, to wail 號｜		F
桃[2]	木 75	兆 383	The peach. 扁｜ flat peach 蟠｜ ｜核 peach stones. ｜仁 kernels ｜園 a peach orchard 核·｜ walnut. 櫻·｜ cherry		C
逃[2] 迯[2] •	辵 162	兆 383	To flee, escape, abscond ｜·去 ｜犯 escaped prisoner ｜學 to play truant from school ｜荒 flee from famine ｜命 to fly for one's life ｜生 ｜難[4] escape from distress		D

Character	Radical	Phonetic	Meaning		
逃[2]			丨跑 to run, flee 丨脫, 丨走 丨避 to avoid, shun 丨兵 deserters (soldiers) 丨·不出 cannot escape 丨·不脫		
淘[2]	水 85	匋 226	To scour, wash in sieve, clean out 丨氣 mischievous; fidgetty 丨井 clean out a well 丨淨了 cleaned out 丨乾淨 丨米 to wash rice in sieve 丨汰 natural selection 丨陽溝 dig an open ditch 丨溝		D
萄[2]	艸 140	匋 226	The grape 葡·丨 丨乾 raisins, dried grapes 丨藤 the grape vine		D
陶[2] 匋[2]	阜 170	匋 226	Pottery, kiln, happy 丨器 earthenware, pottery 丨化 to melt, fuse 丨鎔 丨丨自得 happy frame of mind	S.	E
討[3]	言 149	寸 18	To ask for, seek, beg, demand; to punish, exterminate 丨戰 excite to war; go to battle 丨賬 to collect an account 丨債 丨情 to ask favors 丨求 ask, entreat. 丨要 demand 丨伐 to punish, to subject 丨飯 to beg for food or money 丨擾 bring trouble on self 丨人喜歡 seek to please people 丨人嫌 cause dislike 丨愧 to be ashamed, mortified 丨論 debate, discuss 丨論會 debating society 丨保 to seek bail, find security 丨賞 ask reward or gratuity 丨厭 dissatisfaction, dislike		C

套[4]	大 37	大 451	Envelope, wrapper; suit; to include; harness; C. of books ｜車 to harness, get cart ready ｜話 formal compliments ｜言 ｜褲 leggings, overalls 褥｜ bag for bedding 手｜ gloves, mittens 書｜ case for set of books		B

Te

得[2]	彳 60	㝵 794	To get, gain, attain ｜·着 --·chao ｜救 to be saved, rescued ｜意 to get one's wish ｜空兒[4] to have leisure for ｜便 ｜利 get profit, advantage ｜·了 enough! all right! ｜民心 to be popular ｜人意 ｜·不着[2] unable to obtain or succeed ｜勝 to vanquish, gain victory ｜時 in luck; in favor ｜手 to get an opportunity ｜道 discover true doctrine ｜罪 to offend; I beg pardon 不｜ must not. 不｜不 cannot but	tei[3]	A
悳[2]	心 61	悳 381a	Virtue		P
德[24] 悳[24]	彳 60	悳 381a	Virtue, goodness, principles in action; energy; conduct S. ｜∘行 virtuous conduct ｜·國 Germany, Prussia ｜育 moral culture		C
·的			Subordinating particle. See p. 509	.ti	

T'e

特[4]	牛 93	寺 46	Purposely, special, only ｜薦 specially recommend		B

特[4]

｜遣 specially despatch
｜質 idiosyncrasy
｜權 special power, privilege
｜許 patent, special permit
｜意 on purpose, specially ｜｜·的
｜任 special appointment
｜來 to come purposely
｜賣權 patent rights
｜班 special class in school
｜別 special, unique
｜別性質 individuality
｜色 peculiar, exceptional
｜點 peculiarities
｜此 only concerns this, especially this
｜·為 specially to, in order to

忒[4] 心 61 弋 328 To err; too, very, excess; error
不｜ makes no mistakes — F

忑[4] 心 61 卜 119 Down hearted, timorous, 忐｜ — t'u[42] — H

慝[4] 心 61 匿 183 Evil, vice, dissolute; 作｜ do evil
引｜ take the guilt on self — I

Tei

得[3] 彳 60 㝵 794 Must, ought, should 必∘｜，總∘｜ 俗
｜有 must be or have — te[2] — A

Teng

登[1] 豋[1] 癶 105 登 733 To mount, ascend; at once — D
｜岸 ascend bank; go ashore
｜基 to ascend a throne ｜位
｜記 to record, register; so ｜賬
｜·州 Tengchow in Shantung
｜·出 to publish ｜報

Teng

登[1]

| 高 ascend high; festival of 9th moon 9th day
| 告白 to advertise
| 錄商標 register trade-mark
| 門拜謝 I come to thank you
| 山 to ascend a hill
| 時 in a moment, at once | 卽
| 梯子 to mount a ladder

燈[1] 灯[1] — 火 86 — 登 733 — C

Lamp, light, lantern 一盞 |
| 罩兒 a lamp-shade
| 節 feast of lanterns, 1st moon 15th to 17th
| 心 the wick of a lamp
| 火 the light of a lamp | 光
|·籠 a lantern
| 塔 a light-house | 樓
| 臺 a lamp post or stand
|·草 reed used for lamp wick
| 語 light-signals
電 | electric lamp
洋取 |（兒）matches

蹬[1] — 足 157 — 登 733 — F

To steep; fail to get on
蹭·| dilatory, foiled; wearied

縢[1] — 肉 130 — 縢 468 — P

To progress, rise

等[3] 䒭[3] — 竹 118 — 寺 46 — A

To wait: sign of plural; a class, grade; equal to
|∘級 a rank, degree, caste
| 候 to wait for | 待
| 項 sorts, kinds | 樣
|·一會兒 wait a little |·一·|
| 類 and such like, et cetera | |
|·不得 cannot wait |·不上
| | 不一 different sorts
| 次 grade, place in series
| 語 and so on (end quotation) | 事

等^{3}			相｜alike, equal 不｜not wait; unlike, unequal 頭｜first class 上｜; so 中｜,下｜ 我｜we, us; so 爾｜,彼｜		
戥^{3}	戈 62	星 42	Small steelyard for silver, etc. ｜·子 ｜星 dots on beam of steelyard		H
凳^{4} 櫈^{4}	几 16	登 733	Bench, stool ｜·子, 板·｜,長^{2}｜ 梯｜a step-ladder 杌｜square stool	t'eng^{4}	C
澄^{4}	水 85	登 733	To strain, filter ｜乾了 ｜淸 to cleanse; limpid, clear	ch'eng^{2}	G
磴^{4} 嶝^{4}	石 112	登 733	A ledge, cliff, stone steps 趴石｜to scale a precipice		H
瞪^{4} 瞠^{4}	目 109	登 733	To stare at, gaze superciliously ｜眼 to stare ｜·着眼, ｜目 ｜·他一眼 have a stare at him		F
鄧^{4}	邑 163	登 733	District in Honan, ｜州 S.		I
鐙^{4}	金 167	登 733	Stirrup-irons, a stirrup ｜·子		F

T'eng

疼^{2}	疒 104	冬 541	To pain, ache ｜痛; love dearly ｜愛 to love tenderly, dote on ｜·不·｜ is it painful? ｜·得狠 very painful 怪｜·的		A
籐^{2} 藤^{2}	竹 118	朕 468	Creepers, cane, rattan, wistaria ｜器 rattan ware. ｜床 cane-bed ｜·蘿樹 the wistaria ｜牌 a cane shield, (soldiers')		F
謄^{2}	言 149	朕 468	To copy, transcribe ｜·出來, ｜寫 ｜淸 clearly copied out ｜寫板 manifolder, mimeograph		E

騰² 籐²	馬 187	朕 468	Mount, to rise | 起, run | 房 move out of a house | 空 rise to sky; gain leisure | 挪 to transfer, remove 飛 | soar aloft, rise in air		E
凳⁴ 櫈⁴	几 16	登 733	Bench, stool 板·| 俗	teng⁴	C

Ti

的	白 106	勺 231	Subordinating particle. A few current writers distinguish: 的 adjectival 的, e.g., 紅·的花 地 adverbial 的, e.g., 快快地 底 possessive 的, e.g., 我·底書	.tê	A
堤¹	土 32	是 139	Dyke, bund, barrier | 岸 bank of a river or canal 築 | raise embankment	t'i²	F
提¹	手 64	是 139	Carry by handle | 溜 to lift, raise, carry	t'i²	B
隄¹	阜 170	是 139	Dyke, bank, to guard against |·防 watch against, defences	t'i²	D
滴¹	水 85	啇 590	To drop, drip, a drop, mite 一 | | 溜 | 溜 go round and round |·溜圓 perfectly round |·水 the dripping of water | 打 (or 搭) to drop, to drip | |		C
低¹	人 9	氐 349	To hang down, lower, low, base | 價 low in price | 處 a low place, inferiority | 聲 a low tone of voice | 頭 bend or hang the head |·微 humble, mean		D
啇²	口 30	啇 590	Stem, base, origin 根 |		K

Ti

嫡[2]	女 38	啇 590	Wife (legal), consort | 室, | 妻 | 母 concubine's child's name for legal wife | 子[3] children of legal wife		G
敵[2]	攴 66	啇 590	To oppose, enemy, 仇 | ; match for | 住 oppose, withstand | 擋 | 軍戰地 the firing line | 國 enemy nation, equal nation | 兵 the enemy's troops |·不過他 unable to oppose him | 手 an equal, a match for		C
笛[2] 篴[2]	竹 118	由 818	A fife, flute 吹 | (·子) play the flute		E
迪[2] 廸[2]	辵 162	由 818	To follow footsteps, lead forward, right path 啓 | instruct and guide		H
狄[2]	犬 94	火 446	Northern barbarians S. | 國 northern countries 北 |		E
翟[2]	羽 124	翟 57	Tartar pheasants, plumes	chai[2]	K
糴[24]	米 119	翟 57	To buy grain, lay in grain | 粮		F
覿[24]	見 147	賣 864	Face to face, have audience | 面 to see face to face		I
氐[3]	氏 83	氐 349	Bottom; fundamental; on the whole 大 |		K
底[3]	广 53	氐 349	Bottom, under; end; sediment; modern adjectival 的 |·細 in detail, the details 細 | |·下 below, at last, in future |·下·人 servants, menials | 稿 a rough draft, copy | 根 at root, originally | 起根 | 欵 reserve fund		B

Ti

底^{3}			｜·子 rough draft; foundation; sole; commission or squeeze		
抵^{3}	手 64	氏 349	Substitute; resist; arrive; knock ｜至 to arrive at ｜到, ｜達 ｜制外貨 boycott foreign goods ｜·換 substitute, exchange ｜抗力 power of resistance ｜命 to forfeit one's life ｜償 ｜·不住 unable to bear, sustain ｜擋 to oppose, hinder ｜◦押 to mortgage		E
詆^{3}	言 149	氏 349	Slander, blame, defame ｜毀 誣｜ wilfully misrepresent		H
邸^{3}	邑 163	氏 349	Prince's lodgings at capital 京｜ the capital ｜舍 a lodging place 旅｜		K
地^{4}	土 32	也 301	The earth; place, position; adverbial 的 ｜◦基 foundation. ｜契 deed ｜震 earthquake. ｜氣 climate ｜界 boundary. ｜質 geology ｜球 the globe. ｜主 owner ｜·方 a place, territory, space ｜·方官 the local officials ｜方自治 local self-government ｜·下 on the ground ｜雷 military mines ｜理 geography, geomancy ｜理圖 a geographical map ｜圖 ｜爐子 ground stove, furnace ｜面 place, locality, area ｜·畝 land, acres. ｜板 wood floor ｜·步 footing, place, situation ｜勢 physical geography ｜毯 carpet. ｜道 sub-way ｜壇 Temple of Earth, Peking		A

Ti

<table>
<tr><td>地4</td><td></td><td></td><td>| 點 location, position
| 丁 land-tax. | 租 ground rent
| 土 earth, territory
|·位 place, situation, rank
| 窖子 cellar. | 獄 hell, prison</td><td></td></tr>
<tr><td>弟4</td><td>弓
57</td><td>弟
249</td><td>Younger brother 兄·|
|·兄 brothers—young and old
| 妹 younger brother's wife
| 子3 a pupil, a disciple</td><td>A</td></tr>
<tr><td>娣4</td><td>女
38</td><td>弟
249</td><td>Younger sister</td><td>H</td></tr>
<tr><td>第4</td><td>竹
118</td><td>弟
249</td><td>Series, rank, ordinal; house; a degree; but, only
| 一 number one, the first
| 一名 first, best, first rate
| 三者 a third party</td><td>A</td></tr>
<tr><td>的24</td><td>白
106</td><td>勺
231</td><td>Really, truly; bull's eye
|2確 true; certain
| 然 clear, easily perceived
目 | motive, aim, purpose</td><td>A</td></tr>
<tr><td>遞4
遆4</td><td>辵
162</td><td>虒
204</td><td>To hand to | 給, forward, transmit, hand in; exchange |
| 解 to send, forward
| 名 to hand in name
| 禀帖 to hand in a petition
傳 | pass from one to other</td><td>B</td></tr>
<tr><td>帝4</td><td>巾
50</td><td>帝
88</td><td>Ruler, Emperor 皇 | , | 王
| 國 empire
| 國主義 imperialism
上 | Supreme Ruler, God</td><td>C</td></tr>
<tr><td>締4</td><td>糸
120</td><td>帝
88</td><td>A knot, close connection
| 結 make treaty, betroth
| 造 to construct
| 約 alliance, treaty
取 | to regulate, control</td><td>H</td></tr>
<tr><td>蒂4</td><td>艸
140</td><td>帝
88</td><td>Stem, stalk 花 | ; foundation</td><td>I</td></tr>
</table>

Character	Radical	Phonetic	Meaning	Other reading	Grade
諦[4]	言 149	帝 88	To judge, examine into 審｜ ｜視 to scrutinize		G
適[4]	辵 162	啇 590	Heir; to direct, take lead	shih[4]	E
逮[4]	辵 162	隶 526	Affable, agreeable	tai[4]	F

T'i

Character	Radical	Phonetic	Meaning	Other reading	Grade
梯[1]	木 75	弟 249	Ladder, stairs, steps ｜·子 樓｜a staircase 板｜step-ladder. 軟｜rope-ladder		B
剔[1]	刀 18	易 235	To pick out, scrape off ｜∘出 to reject, pick out ｜骨頭 pick bones from meat ｜篦子 to clean a fine comb ｜牙 to pick the teeth		E
踢[1]	足 157	易 235	To kick, kick up ｜·着 ｜球 to play foot-ball, etc. ｜∘開 to kick open		D
提[2]	手 64	是 139	To raise; mention; summon ｜案 summon case in court ｜倡 advocate cause, promote ｜∘過 to pick up, mention ｜∘到 ｜交 submit for discussion ｜∘出 proposals, demands ｜携 to lead by hand, aid ｜鞋 to pull on shoes ｜醒 to put one in mind of ｜議 to make a suggestion ｜·拔 to prefer, raise ｜燈會 torchlight procession	ti[1]	B
題[2]	頁 181	是 139	Theme, text, title, to discuss ｜綱 a theme, subject, text ｜·目 ｜名 get degree, nominate		B
啼[2] 嗁[2]	口 30	帝 88	To wail; caw, crow; scream ｜叫 ｜哭 to cry, lament, weep 悲｜weep silently, wail		E

T'i

蹄² 蹏²	足 157	帝 88	A hoof of horse, ox, pig, etc. 前 | fore-feet. 失前 | stumble 馬 | horse's hoof; so 牛 |, etc.	D
鵜²	鳥 196	弟 249	The pelican | 鶘	H
體³ 体³	骨 188	豊 735	Body 身·|; substance. form; limbs | 恤 to pity. |·面 respectable |∘格 physique | 力 strength |·諒 put self in his place | 貼 | 操 gymnastics. | 操場 drill ground. | 操室 gymnasium | 統 pomp, show, dignity |∘育 physical culture 赤 | the naked body 露 | 全 | all, whole |∘裁 form, style	B
替⁴	曰 73	夫 465	To substitute, change, act for |·換 to substitute, exchange |∘工 do another's work for him |∘身兒 a substitute | 代 instead of, in place of 代 |	A
屜⁴ 屧⁴	尸 44	世 109	Buffer, pad, tray, drawer 抽·| drawer 籠 | bamboo steamer	A
剃⁴ 鬀⁴	刀 18	弟 249	To shave. | 頭 shave head | 頭棚 a barber's shop 理髮舘 | 頭刀 a razor	C
悌⁴	心 61	弟 249	To act brotherly 孝 | duty to parents & brothers	G
涕⁴	水 85	弟 249	To snivel, mucus, weep, tears | 泣 to weep silently 哭 |	K
薙⁴	艸 140	隹 52	To shave; clear off weeds, root up | 草 clear ground of grass	D
嚏⁴	口 30	疋 137	To sneeze 打 |·噴	F

Character	Radical	Phonetic	Meaning		
惕[4] 愁[4]	心 61	易 235	To respect, stand in awe | |		H
倜[4]	人 9	周 730	Noble, courteous, free | 儻 masterful, energetic		H
啻[4]	口 30	帝 88	To stop at, different, only 不 | no less than, short of	shih[4]	I

Tiao

Character	Radical	Phonetic	Meaning		
凋[1]	冫 15	周 730	To fade; wither, fall | 謝, | 落 | 零 scattered,—as leaves, rare | 殘 declining,—as trade		G
雕[1] 彫[1]	隹 172	周 730	To carve, engrave | 刻; polish | 匠 a carver, engraver, | 工 | 像 to carve an image | 刀 an engraving tool 木 |·的 carved in wood		E
鵰[1]	鳥 196	周 730	Sea-eagle, eagle | 翎 eagle feathers (for arrows)		I
刁[1]	刀 18	刀 219	Perverse, depraved, rascality S. | 詐 perverse and crafty | 風俗 evil customs | 婦 a vixen, virago | 野 savages, barbarians		F
叼[1]	口 30	刀 219	To seize with mouth or bill |·去了 carried off in mouth		E
貂[1]	豸 153	召 715	Sable, sable skin | 皮 | 尾 sable tails		H
掉[4]	手 64	卓 15	To fall |·下; adjust, move |·換 to exchange | 溝裏 fall into the ditch |·過來 to turn round | 轉 | 色 to fade (of dyes) -shai[3] 丟·| to lose. 失·| put awav 去·|		A
吊[4]	口 30	巾 557	To hang; string of cash 一 | 錢 "1000 cash", ten coppers		B

弔⁴	弓 57	弔 248	Condole; hang; withdraw; a string of cash │·起來 to hang up │·上 │橋 draw or suspension bridge │孝 condole on parent's death │死 to die by hanging 上│, │頸 │問 make kind inquiries		D
調⁴	言 149	周 730	To transfer, move; tune, air │查 to investigate facts │查表 chart of results, record │遣 transfer to other office │∘換 exchange. │兵 move troops │度 to calculate, tactics │·動 agitate, issue orders 腔∘│ in tune; tunes, airs │兒, 曲│	t'iao²	D
釣⁴	金 167	勺 231	Hook, to angle, to fish │魚 │竿 a fishing rod │鈎 fish hook		E
佻²	人 9	兆 383	To provoke, act furtively │巧 tricky ways	t'iao²	I
銚⁴	金 167	兆 383	Sauce pan │·子		H
窵⁴	穴 116	鳥 253	Deep, distant, secluded │角 │∘遠 a great distance		I

T'iao

佻¹⁴	人 9	兆 383	Weakly, unsteadily │ │ │脫 frivolous, unsteady	tiao⁴	I
挑¹	手 64	兆 383	Bear on shoulder-pole; to mix, stir; choose; a load │揀 to choose, select │選 │斥 to censure, reprove │·出來 pick out │取, │ │ │·不動 too heavy to carry │·不是 to find fault │錯 │水 carry water. │担 carry load	t'iao³	A

T'iao

<table>
<tr><td>挑1</td><td></td><td></td><td>|·子 a load carried on a pole
| 眼 fault-finding, provoking</td><td></td><td></td></tr>
<tr><td>祧1</td><td>示
113</td><td>兆
383</td><td>Ancestral shrine or hall 宗 |</td><td></td><td>K</td></tr>
<tr><td>條2</td><td>木
75</td><td>攸
549</td><td>Branch, twig; strip; C. of streets, ropes, dogs, snakes, etc.
|°件 articles, e.g. of treaty
| 欵 rules, conditions | 規, | 例
| 目 a list, an index
| 約 a treaty. |·子 a strip</td><td></td><td>A</td></tr>
<tr><td>調2</td><td>言
149</td><td>周
730</td><td>To harmonize, blend, mix; sport; instigate
| 和 mix, harmonize, mediate
| 合 to mix, compound
| 絃 tune stringed instrument
| 羹 soup-spoon. | 治 to cure
|°理 to repair, heal, arrange
| 說 to mediate and settle
|°唆 to instigate, egg on
|·停 arrange, modify, mediate
| 味 blend flavors, season
| 養 to nurse, to look after
| 匀 to moderate, equally blended</td><td>tiao4</td><td>D</td></tr>
<tr><td>笤2</td><td>竹
118</td><td>召
715</td><td>Broom, besom |·箒</td><td></td><td>D</td></tr>
<tr><td>髫2</td><td>髟
190</td><td>召
715</td><td>Children's hair tufts | 髮</td><td></td><td>H</td></tr>
<tr><td>挑3</td><td>手
64</td><td>兆
383</td><td>To open; irritate, provoke
|°開 open out, spread out
| 弄是非 to stir up trouble
| 唆 to sow discord, instigate</td><td>t'iao1</td><td>A</td></tr>
<tr><td>窕3</td><td>穴
116</td><td>兆
383</td><td>Refined, attractive 窈 |</td><td></td><td>K</td></tr>
<tr><td>䠷3</td><td>身
158</td><td>兆
383</td><td>A tall, slender man 細高 |</td><td></td><td>I</td></tr>
</table>

Character	Radical	Phonetic	Definition		Alt.	Group
跳[4] 趒[4]	足 157	兆 383	To jump, dance, skip over |·過去 | 墻 to leap over a wall | 河 leap into river, suicide | 高 high jump. | 遠 long jump | 板 a plank, gangway | 迸 jump, skip. | 繩 skip-rope | 舞 to dance, caper			A
糶[4]	米 119	翟 57	To sell grain | 糧			F

Tieh

Character	Radical	Phonetic	Definition		Alt.	Group
跌[12]	足 157	失 481	To slip, stumble, fall |·下, | 倒[3] | 打損傷 injured by a fall		tsai[1]	B
爹[1]	父 88	多 269	Father, papa, daddy | | | 媽 father and mother | 娘			F
疊[2] 叠[2]	田 102	畾 814	Layer, fold, double, reiterate | 句 chorus of a hymn | | in many folds or layers | 次 repeatedly			B
攂[2] 撘[2]	手 64	畾 814	To pile on; fold over 摺 | |·起來 to fold up | 衣裳 to fold up clothes 整 | put in order and fold			G
堞[2]	土 32	枼 110	Battlement, parapet 城 |			H
牒[2]	片 91	枼 110	Tablets, records, archives, 簡 | 譜 | genealogies			G
碟[2]	石 112	枼 110	Saucer, plate |·子 四 | 一碗 a small dinner			D
蝶[2] 蜨[2]	虫 142	枼 110	Butterfly 蝴[2] |	文	t'ieh[3]	E
迭[2]	辵 162	失 481	To alternate, repeatedly | 次 | 興[1] | 廢 now prosper, now fail			G
垤[2]	土 32	至 883	Hillock, ant-hill 丘 |			H

耋[2]	老 125	至 883	Aged (70—80), infirm		H
凸[4]	凵 17	凵 650	Protuberent, in relief |·上來 | 字 characters in relief	ku³	G
瓞[4]	瓜 97	失 481	Melons just set; posterity		I
跕[4]	足 157	占 720	To dart down | |	tien³	I

T'ieh

貼[1]	貝 154	占 720	To stick, attach; make up, add | 已 intimate, private | 近 to stick close to, near |·出告示 post a proclamation | 膏藥 put on sticking-plaster | 報子 post an announcement | 身 next to the body, personal | 水 pay discount on money | 對子 post antithetic couplets	t'ieh⁴	D
帖[31]	巾 50	占 720	Card, placard; slip, document; settled 賬 | 兒 a bill, an account 請 | an invitation 謝 | card of thanks 賞 | notice of reward	t'ieh⁴	B
鐵[3] 鉄[3] 銕[3]	金 167	金 79	Iron, iron-like; metal; firm | 案 irrevocable decision | 證 incontrovertible evidence | 器 iron-ware. |·匠 blacksmith | 甲汽車 armored car | 甲船 iron-clad, war-ship | 銑 a shovel, spade | 血主義 Bismarkian policy | 管子 iron pipes. | 鍊子 chain | 路(道) a railway. | 絲 iron wire | 板 sheet-iron | 葉子		C

鐵^{3}			| 紗窗 wire window-screens | 條 rod or bar iron | 裁縫 sewing-machine 縫紝機		
蝶^{3}	虫 142	枼 110	Butterfly 蝴‡| 兒 俗	tieh^{2}	E
餮^{3}	食 184	㐱 281	Gluttonous 饕 |		I
帖^{4}	巾 50	占 720	A "rubbing" from an inscription	t'ieh^{13}	B
貼^{4}	貝 154	占 720	To sympathize 體∘|	t'ieh^{1}	D

Tien

巔^{1}	山 46	眞 843	Peak of hill		H
搷^{1}	手 64	眞 843	To beat, jolt, knock |·採 estimate weight, heft	t'ien^{2}	H
癲^{1} 瘨^{1}	疒 104	眞 843	Mad, deranged, infatuated | 癇 epileptic fits |·狂 insane, deranged 瘋 | 瘋瘋 | | delirious, crazy		E
⿺走眞^{1}	走 156	眞 843	To jolt in trotting, |·的慌; jog | | 跑跑 to run about		F
顛^{1}	頁 181	眞 843	To overturn; forehead, top | 頂 | 覆 to turn upside down |·倒 | 險 misfortunes, dangerous | 馬 trotting horse | 三倒四 bungling, awkward |∘倒是∘非 to confound right and wrong		B
掂^{1} 敁^{1}	手 64	占 720	To weigh in hand; jolt | 量 to weigh, estimate |·採 | 搭 shake up and down		E
踮^{3}	足 157	占 720	To limp, on tiptoe | 脚 (兒) |·着脚 standing on tiptoe	tieh^{4}	I

Tien

Character	Radical	Phonetic	Meaning		
點^3 点^3	黑 203	占 720	Speck, mite, dot, point, comma; to nod; to light; o'clock |·心 cakes, sweetmeats | 畫 marks & strokes (writing) | 名 roll-call | 卯. | 名單 (冊) roll |·不着 lamp or fire will not light |·上燈 light the lamp | 燈 | 書 punctuate book | | 兒 | 頭 nod head, assent |·子 a spot or dot 優 | point of superiority, so 劣 |		A
典^3	八 12	曲 819	Canon, rule, records; to mortgage | 主 mortgagee, 恩 | grace, favor |∘故 episodes, quotations 故∘| | 賣 mortgage, pawn | 當, | 押 經 | canon. | 禮 rites		B
電^4	雨 173	雷 813	Lightning, electricity, electric | 車 electric trams or cars |∘氣 electric current |∘氣燈 an electric light | 燈 | 學 science of electricity | 學家 electricians | 線 electric wires | 線杆 telegraph poles | 話 telephone. | 鈴 electric bell | 光照像 picolography | 碼 telegraphic code | 報 telegram, despatch | 信 | 報局 telegraph office | 閃 flash of lightning 閃 | | 扇 electric fan | 影 cinema		A
店^4	广 53	占 720	Shop, inn. 酒 | wine-shop | 主 innkeeper. 住 | stop at inn | 戶 shop, inn; rooms in an inn 客 | inn, hotel 旅 |		B

惦⁴	心 61	占 720	To think of, remember ｜念 ｜·記 to be anxious ｜懷, ｜掛	E
玷⁴	玉 96	占 720	Flaw, blemish, defect ｜缺 ｜辱 to disgrace, debauch ｜汚	E
墊⁴	土 32	執 304	To fill in, wedge-up; advance money ｜錢 advance money for another ｜平了 fill up and make even ｜·上 make up, fill up, advance ｜·子 a cushion ｜·頭 ｜穩了 make steady (table, etc.) ｜債 pay another's debts ｜賬	B
殿⁴	殳 79	共 95	Palace 宮｜; hall, temple ｜下 heir-apparent ｜宇 temple-buildings. 聖｜	D
奠⁴	大 37	酋 782	To settle; offer libation ｜茶 libation of tea; so ｜酒 ｜祭 libation 祭｜ ｜敬 "with condolences" ｜儀 ｜定 settle, determine	F
淀⁴	水 85	定 138	Shallow water 海｜ town N.W. of Peking; a.w. 海甸	I
靛⁴	青 174	定 138	Indigo, indigo color 藍｜, ｜青 ｜池 indigo tank. ｜缸 vat ｜色 indigo blue. 洋｜ foreign or chemical dye	G
佃⁴	人 9	田 809	To till; lease; hunt ｜田 ｜戶 a husbandman, laborer ｜字 a lease. ｜批 lease to	I
甸⁴	田 102	田 809	The imperial domain; to rule, cultivate	H
鈿⁴	金 167	田 809	Filagree, enamel, inlaid work ｜·子 Manchu head ornament	H

T'ien

天[1] 靝[1]	大 37	天 462	Heaven, sky; day; celestial, Supreme Ruler, emperor; natural |·氣 the weather | 職 calling, duty |·津 Tientsin | 津衞 | 晴·了 fine day; the day is fine | 竺國 India. | 窗 skylight | 主 God | 主堂 Rom. Cath. Church | 主教 Roman Catholic religion |∘分 natural ability | 才 | 旱 drought, dry weather | 黑·了 after dark. 白·| daytime | 河 the Milky Way | 橋 | 下 the world 普|下 | 仙 a fairy. | 心 the zenith | 性 natural disposition | 資 | 花 the small-pox | 然 natural. | 然界 nature | 然淘汰 natural selection | 擇 | 空 the sky, the air, space 藍| | 理 heavenly principles | 良 conscience, nat'l good 良·心 | 亮 break of day, daylight | 明 |·靈顳 cranium, top of head | 倫 one's father, natural relationships of a man | 棚 an awning. |∘平 scales | 邊兒 the horizon | 涯 |·上 in heaven. | 生 natural | 神 heavenly spirits, angels | 使 angel; imperial messenger | 壇 Temple of Heaven in Peking |∘堂 heaven, paradise | 道 heaven's truth, weather		A

T'ien

<table>
<tr><td>天^{1}</td><td></td><td></td><td>| 地 heaven and earth; nature
|。| every day, daily 每 |
| 庭 the forehead
| 子^{3} "son of heaven", Emperor
| 文 astronomy. | 文鏡 telescope
| 演進化 theory of evolution</td><td></td><td></td></tr>
<tr><td>添^{1}</td><td>水
85</td><td>天
462</td><td>To add, increase 加 | , |·上
|·些兒 to add a little |·一點兒
|·個小孩 to have a child born
| 病 to grow worse (in sickness)
|·頭 an addition, hope of more</td><td></td><td>B</td></tr>
<tr><td>甜^{2}</td><td>甘
99</td><td>甘
101</td><td>Sweet, agreeable 甘 |
|·瓜 sweet melons
| 水 sweet, i.e., good water
| 言蜜語 sweet words, flattery</td><td></td><td>B</td></tr>
<tr><td>田^{2}</td><td>田
102</td><td>田
809</td><td>Field, land S.
| 產 lands, possessions |·地, | 土
| 雞 frog. |·家 husbandman
| 作 husbandry | 功
心 | the heart, moral field</td><td></td><td>C</td></tr>
<tr><td>塡^{2}
寘^{2}</td><td>土
32</td><td>眞
843</td><td>To fill up, fill in, complete | 補
| 滿 fill up or entirely
| 平 to fill up, level off
| 塞 to stuff up, close up</td><td></td><td>E</td></tr>
<tr><td>搷^{2}</td><td>手
64</td><td>眞
843</td><td>To beat, jolt, knock</td><td>tien^{1}</td><td>H</td></tr>
<tr><td>滇^{2}</td><td>水
85</td><td>眞
843</td><td>Lake in Yünnan | 池
| 省 province of Yunnan</td><td>tien^{1}</td><td>H</td></tr>
<tr><td>恬^{2}</td><td>心
61</td><td>舌
707</td><td>Peaceful, still | 靜, | 淡</td><td></td><td>H</td></tr>
<tr><td>忝^{3}</td><td>心
61</td><td>天
462</td><td>To disgrace, unworthy | 辱</td><td></td><td>K</td></tr>
<tr><td>舔^{3}
餂^{3}</td><td>舌
135</td><td>天
462</td><td>To lick, taste, try with tongue
| 乾淨 to lick clean
| 舌 to lick. | 一 | taste it</td><td></td><td>C</td></tr>
<tr><td>㥏^{3}</td><td>心
61</td><td>曲
819</td><td>Bashful, to blush | 愧</td><td></td><td>H</td></tr>
</table>

Character	Radical	Phonetic	Meaning		
腆³	肉 130	曲 819	Plenty, prosperous; rich food 不｜ unworthy gift		I
殄³	歹 78	㐱 281	To exterminate, end, waste ｜滅 ｜絕 put an end to		I
靦³ 覥³	面 176	面 766	To blush, ashamed 靦｜; see face to face ｜着臉 shameless ｜色 very bashful		K

Ting

Character	Radical	Phonetic	Meaning		
丁¹	一 1	丁 2	An individual, person; to sustain S. ｜香 cloves. ｜香花 lilac ｜稅 poll-tax ｜捐 ｜憂 to mourn for parents 成｜ become an adult 人｜ a man, people ｜口		C
仃¹	人 9	丁 2	Alone 孤｜｜, 冷孤｜的		H
叮¹	口 30	丁 2	To enjoin, strict order ｜囑, ｜嚀		F
玎¹	玉 96	丁 2	Jingling noise ｜玲 ｜璫 hand gong, ding-dong		K
疔¹	疒 104	丁 2	Felon; pox-sores, a boil ｜瘡 ｜毒 venereal poison		H
酊¹	酉 164	丁 2	Drunk 酩｜		H
釘¹	金 167	丁 2	A nail, spike ｜子 (see 4th tone) ｜鞋 shoes with nails 螺絲｜(子) screws, bolts 碰｜子 to get into trouble	ting⁴	B
頂³ [illegible]³	頁 181	丁 2	Top, head; very; to wear on head; oppose head to; C. of hats, etc. ｜針 a thimble ｜撞 to contradict		A

頂[3]			|風 head-wind, to face the wind	
			|好 the best; so |大, |上, |多	
			|棚 the ceiling of room	
			|·不住 can't hold up against	
			|水 against tide or current	
1			|∘到現在 down to the present	
			|嘴 contradict impertinently	
鼎[3] 鼑[3]	鼎 206	片 164	Tripod; firm; then; new; dynasty, power; 立| set up new state	G
			|立 to establish firmly	
定[4]	宀 40	定 138	To fix, stop; determine; tranquil	B
			|案 to decide a case	
			|期 a fixed time, set a time	
			|期存欵 fixed deposit	
			|·錢 earnest money, |銀	
			|志 to make up one's mind	
			|親 make marriage engagement	
			|更 watch-setting at 9 p.m,	
			|·下 to settle, |明, |準, |妥	
			|然 positively, undoubtedly	
			|∘規 decide, settle, for certain	
			|南針· the mariners' compass	
			|額 fixed quantity, number |數	
			|妥 fixed safely, satisfactorily	
			|做的 made to order |·着做的	
			|罪 to condemn, convict	
			|∘要 to insist, demand	
			|約 a contract; to contract	
錠[4]	金 167	定 138	Ingot, "shoe", C. of silver	F
			銀| a silver ingot 一|銀·子	
			一|墨 a cake of ink	
訂[4]	言 149	丁 2	To settle, fix, edit	F
			|正 to revise, to edit |書	
			|盟 take oath, make treaty	
			|問 examine, come to agreement	
			|約 to make a treaty	

釘[4]	金 167	丁 2	To nail (also read 1st tone) │住 to nail fast │鈕子 to sew on buttons │馬掌 to shoe a horse │·上 to nail up, sew on │書 to bind a book │∘死 nailed fast; crucified │[4]│[1]·子 to drive a nail	ting[1]	B
靪[4]	革 177	丁 2	A patch, to patch 打補·│ │底 to mend a sole		I

T'ing

聽[1] 听[1]	耳 128	壴 381a	To hear, listen, obey; smell │差 office boys, messengers │講 attend instruction │覺 sense of hearing │·見 to hear, heard │·見·了 │勸 give heed to advice │候 to await │戲 to attend a theatre │信 hear and believe, hear news │話 to be obedient │從 │·不真 can't hear distinctly │·不見 unable to hear │·不進去 can't understand │·不明·白 to misunderstand │錯·了 │·不得 unfit to hear │說 listen, heed advice; hear say │·│ listen, do you hear? │·頭 worth hearing 打│ inquire, listen 打·│·打·│ 探│ spy, inquire about; listen	t'ing[4]	A
廳[1]	广 53	壴 381a	Hall, parlor, a court │房 a hall, drawing-room 客│ │堂 principal hall of college 飯│ a dining-room		A

T'ing

Character	Radical	Phonetic	Meaning		Tone
廷[12]	廴 54	廷 70	Court, 朝◦｜; audience hall ｜臣 a courtier, a minister		F
庭[12]	广 53	廷 70	Court, hall, family ｜舍 a house ｜堂 家｜ family, home, domestic		D
梃[13]	木 75	廷 70	Stalk ｜兒, stick, cudgel ｜立 upright, perpendicular		G
蜓[12]	虫 142	廷 70	Dragon fly 蜻◦｜		I
汀[1]	水 85	丁 2	Sandspit, low level beach 沙｜ ｜江 river in Fukien		K
亭[2]	亠 8	亭 3	Arbor, pavilion, ｜·子; level, even 涼｜ summer arbor 花｜		D
停[2]	人 9	亭 3	To stop, settle, delay, rest ｜·着 ｜戰 armistice, truce ｜止 stop, discontinue ｜息, ｜·住 ｜·一·｜ stop a bit. ｜刋 suspend publication ｜版 ｜課 to stop lessons ｜工 to leave off work ｜靈 delay burial of coffin ｜·當 satisfactorily settled		C
婷[2]	女 38	亭 3	Beautiful, ladylike 娉｜		I
霆[2]	雨 173	廷 70	Thunder, loud noise 雷｜		H
挺[3]	手 64	廷 70	To stretch, strain; stick out; very ｜緊 to pull tight ｜嚴 ｜胸 expand or thrust out chest ｜高 very tall; so ｜好 etc. ｜身 stretch oneself up ｜立		E
艇[3]	舟 137	廷 70	Boat, barge, canoe, dug-out 潛水｜ a submarine 飛｜ aeroplane, air-ship 魚雷｜ torpedo-boat, destroyer		E
聽[4]	耳 128	𡈼 331a	To receive, comply with ｜受	t'ing[1]	A

Tiu

丟[1] 一 1 去 44 To throw, cast away, lose B

| 棄 cast aside |·開, |·去, |·掉
|·下 to leave behind
|·下去 to throw down
|·了 lose, lost | 失
| 臉 lose reputation or "face" | 人
|·不了[3] unable to lose
一 | 點兒 a trifle, mere nothing

To

多[1] 夕 36 多 269 Many, much, how many? how much? mostly, too much; more A

| 住幾天 stay a few days longer
| 重 very heavy; how heavy? 2
so | 高, etc. 2
| 謝 many thanks | 蒙
| 心 to be suspicious | 疑
|·會兒 when? whenever
| 寡 many or few; how many?
| 虧 very fortunate that
| 禮 overpolite. |∘半 probably
|·麼好 how good! 2
|∘少 how many? a good many
| 神教 polytheism
| 事 officious. | 數 majority
| 說話 to talk much
| 大 how big? how old? 2
|·咱 when? what time? | 早晚兒
| 嘴 very loquacious | 言
| 次 often. 許 | a great many
|·餘的 the remainder

奪[2] 大 37 大 451 To snatch, carry off | 取 D

| 佔 to grasp, seize 搶 |
|·過來 take from another |·去
| 標 carry off the prize | 錦標

To

Character	Radical	Phonetic	Meaning	Other reading	
鐸^{2}	金 167	睪 160	Bell with clapper, 木| |德 incite to virtue		H
朶^{3} 朵^{3}	木 75	朶 216a	A cluster; head; lobe; C. of pendants 一|花 a bunch of flowers 耳·| lobe of ear, ears --t(')ou		A
垜^{3} 垛^{3}	土 32	朶 216a	Battlement |·子; target; pile up |柴火 stack up fire wood |口 embrasures		K
躲^{3}	身 158	朶 216a	To shun, avoid, slip away |。開 withdraw, out of the way! |懶 to loiter, delay |難^{4} to avoid difficulty |避 to avoid, to shun |·|, |身 |閃 to dodge away from |藏 to lie concealed |雨 take shelter from rain		C
⿱左月^{3}	肉 130	⿱左月 179	To fall		P
度^{4}	广 53	度 200	To guess, calculate 揣| 量| to measure, estimate	tu^{4}	A
⿰忄度^{4}	心 61	度 200	To estimate, calculate		H
惰^{4}	心 61	⿱左月 179	Idle, lazy, 懶|; heedless 怠| careless, remiss		B
馱^{4} 駄^{4}	馬 187	大 451	Pack animal, pack-load |·子 |(t'o^{2}) |·子 carry a load	t'o^{2}	D
掇^{24}	手 64	叕 534	To collect; pluck |採; arrange |弄 to arrange, look after 拾·| to repair, put in order --tou		D
敠^{24}	攴 66	叕 534	To weigh by lifting, heft 掂·| estimate weight, heft		K
柁^{4}	木 75	它 322	Rudder 俗	t'o^{2}	E

舵^{4}	舟 137	它 322	Helm, rudder | 工 the helmsman 掌 |·的 | 把 tiller, handle of tiller 裏 | port helm 推 | ,左 | 外 | starboard helm 右 |		E
剁^{4}	刀 18	朵 216a	To chop fine, | 碎, cut off | 爛 to mince very small		G
䅳^{4}	禾 115	朵 216a	Heap of grain, stack, pile 柴火 | stack of fuel		I
跺^{4}	足 157	朵 216a	To stamp | 脚; knock off		F
堕^{4}	土 32	隋 180	To fall down, fall | 落 | 馬 fall off a horse		F
沰^{4}	水 85	石 722	To drip 滴 |		I

T'o

脫^{1}	肉 130	兌 756	To undress; avoid; remove | 節 interrupted, disjointed |·出 escape | 除 remove. | 卸 unload |·下來 to take off (as clothes) | 鞋 take off shoes; so | 衣裳, | 帽 |∘開 to withdraw, retire | 身 | 離兇惡 escape from evil | 免 avoid. |∘生 transmigrate | 逃 to escape, desert | 走	t'o^{3}	A
他^{1}	人 9	也 301	He, she, it, other 文	t'a^{1}	A
拖^{1} 拕^{1}	手 64	也 301	To tow, tug; delay; implicate | 欠 to defer payment | 累 to involve; drag | 拉		F
托^{12} 拓^{12}	手 64	乇 373	To carry on palm; entrust (used for 託); pretext | 付 entrust to the care of | 人 to request a person		B

T'o

Character	Radical	Phonetic	Meaning	Other reading	Grade
托^{12}			丨。盤 a tray 丨·子 丨腮 to lean face on hand 推。丨 make excuses, shirk		
託^{1}	言 149	乇 373	Entrust, request; pretext 丨情 appeal to feelings, favor 丨。付 to entrust to 丨人 丨庇 "thank you" 丨福, 丨賴 丨辭 invent an excuse 丨言, 丨故		B
毻^{1}	毛 82	育 179	To molt, shed 丨毛		G
它^{1} 佗^{1}	宀 40	它 322	He, she, it, that, another 丨如 besides, again 丨·子 a humpback		K
柁^{2}	木 75	它 322	Tie-beam, girder 丨樑 large and small beams	to^{4}	E
砣^{2} 鉈^{2} ⿰石育^{2}	石 112	它 322	Stone roller, weight 秤丨 steelyard weight 打飛丨 throw stone for exercise		E
跎^{2}	足 157	它 322	To slip, miss, misstep 蹉丨		H
酡^{2}	酉 164	它 322	Flushed, red 顏丨 醉丨 flushed with wine		K
陀^{2}	阜 170	它 322	Steep bank, declivity 陂丨		G
駝^{2}	馬 187	它 322	Camel 駱·丨; to bear pack 丨轎 mule litter 丨背 hump backed 丨馱子 a beast's load 丨鳥 emu, ostrich		B
馱^{2} 駄^{2}	馬 187	大 451	To lade on back, bear as pack 背丨 丨·不動 unable to carry it	to^{4}	D
橐^{2}	木 75	石 722	Sack open at ends 丨·子 丨籥 a bag, wallet		H

Character	Radical	Phonetic	Definition	Variant	Key
鼉²	黽 205	黽 316	Large water lizard, iguana ｜更 strike watch in Drum Tower		K
脫³	肉 130	兌 756	To escape, e.g., ｜難 ｜·不開身 cannot get away from	t'o¹	A
妥³	女 38	妥 409	Safe, secure, satisfactory, ready ｜寔人 a trustworthy person ｜·當 satisfactory, safe ｜寔辦｜ transact satisfactorily		B
庹³	广 53	度 200	Full stretch of arms ｜·不過 too big to embrace		K
唾⁴ 涶⁴	口 30	垂 26	To spit, expectorate, saliva ｜·沫 spittle, saliva ｜·沫盒 a spittoon	t'u⁴	E
乇⁴	丿 4	乇 373	To depend on, trust to		P

Tou

Character	Radical	Phonetic	Definition	Variant	Key
都¹	邑 163	者 192	All, the whole 俗	tu¹	A
兜¹	儿 10	兜 693	Helmet, hood; pocket, bag; to keep ｜盔 a kind of helmet ｜·子,(兒) bag, mason's hod, pocket		B
挽¹	手 64	兜 693	To seize, grasp, gather in ｜攬 grasp after, engross		G
斗³	斗 68	斗 23	A peck, 10 pints, dipper (水｜) ｜柄 peck-handle, dipper-handle 北｜ Charles's Wain, Dipper, Ast. 升｜ dry measure ｜斛		C
抖³	手 64	斗 23	To shake off, tremble 發｜ ｜·下去 to shake up, so as to settle down ｜·一·｜ to shake up or out ｜·摟 ｜胆 pluck up courage ｜擻		E
蚪³	虫 142	斗 23	Tadpole 蝌｜		I

陡^{3}	阜 170	走 134	Sluice; precipitous; suddenly | 然 suddenly, unexpectedly | 坡兒 a steep hill		H
豆^{4}	豆 151	豆 731	Beans, peas; wooden platter | 角 bean pods. | 稭 bean stalks |·腐 bean curd. | 餅 cake | 芽 bean sprouts. | 油 oil		C
痘^{4}	疒 104	豆 731	Small pox, | 疹 | 種 vaccine lymph 牛 |		F
荳^{4}	艸 140	豆 731	Beans, pulse, peas—see 豆 | 蔻 cardamom, nutmeg		G
逗^{4}	辵 162	豆 731	To loiter, dawdle | 遛; excite |·弄 to fidget, disturb		G
讀^{4}	言 149	賣 864	Half stop, comma, clause 句 | sentences	tu^{24}	C
讟^{4}	言 149	賣 864	To slander, murmur, sedition 俗	tu^{24}	F
鬥^{4}	鬥 191	鬥 638	To fight, play, wrangle		K
鬭^{4} 鬪^{4}	鬥 191	鬥 638	To fight, contest 爭 | ; play at, make sport with | 紙牌 to play cards | 牌 | 笑 to provoke a laugh | 毆 fight with fists or sticks |·不過 can't thrash in fight | 嘴 to wrangle, to squabble		D
竇^{4}	穴 116	賣 864	Hole, drain; corrupt, error S 狗 | dog-hole in door		K

T'ou

偷^{1}	人 9	俞 619	To steal, pilfer, secret, stealthy | 竊 to steal, pilfer | 盜, | 東·西 | 閒 to waste time, idle | 看 look by stealth; so | 聽, | 作 | 空兒 to steal leisure | 跑 skulk off. | 稅 smuggle		C

T'ou

偷[1]			| 私 clandestine, illicit | 嘴 surreptitious eating | 營 surprise enemy's camp	
頭[2]	頁 181	豆 731	Head, top, chief, end, in front; C. of wide use, animals, etc. | 兒 a head, chief | 目 |·髮 the hair of the head |∘緒 way, clue, opening, means |·一件 above all, first thing |·一回 the first time |·一次 | 盔 helmet. |·裏 at first, in front | 名 first-rank, excellent | 品 | 年 last year. | 本 first book |·半天 forenoon | 晌 | 生兒子 first born son | 繩兒 string for hair | 等 the first class, best | 頂 crown of the head | 暈 head giddy, headache | 昏 | 尾 head and tail, first and last	A
投[2]	手 64	殳 399	To throw into; surrender, tender; join, thrust, plunge; to go to | 案 give oneself up to the law | 審 | 機 agree; to speculate | 親 to take refuge with relatives | 井 suicide in well; so | 河 | 軍 enlist in army | 降 (hsiang[2]) surrender | 稿 contribute to paper | 奔 fly to for refuge | 票 cast a vote, ballot | 票權 suffrage | 票匭 (kuei[3]) ballot-box | 宿 find place for night | 遞 to take to; hand to | 緣 suited, congenial (of persons)	C

亠[2]	亠 8	亠 80	Above		K
透[4]	辵 162	秀 217	To pass through, penetrate, understand, thoroughly ｜徹 penetrate; intelligent 通｜ ｜氣 permeable to air｜風 ｜·過 to pass through｜越 ｜·亮 clear, transparent｜光,｜明 ｜·了 penetrated through 濕｜·了 ｜雨 a penetrating rain 看｜see through, understand 測｜		C
咅[4]	口 30	音 89	To spit out		P

Tsa

咂[1] 咘[1]	口 30	巾 557	Nipple; suck, lick ｜·一·｜ taste with tongue, suck ｜∘｜兒 suck breast nipple		F
紮[1] 紥[1]	糸 120	乙 297	To bind, tie up, wind｜綁 ｜裹 to dress up, mend ｜綵匠 decorators at weddings, etc.	cha[1]	G
腕[1]	肉 130	兒 684	Nipple, pap,—see 咂		I
咱[2] 偺[2]	口 30	自 852	We (you and I); I, me (dial.) ｜·家 I, me, myself ｜·們 we, us.｜·們倆 we two ｜(tsa[3]) 的 why? how's that?	tsan[2]	A
雜[2] 襍[2]	隹 172	隹 52	Confused, mixed, heterogeneous ｜記賬 miscellaneous accounts ｜誌 a miscellany, magazine ｜居 live in non-treaty ports ｜·種 a bastard, hybrid ｜費 sundry expenses ｜∘貨 miscellaneous goods ｜亂 jumbled together ｜俎 miscellanea in paper 攙｜to mix up, blend		B

砸2	石 112	巾 557	To strike, rap, knock | 壞·了 smashed by a blow | 碎·了 |·開 to smash open		E
			Ts'a		
擦1	手 64	祭 515	To rub, brush, wipe, clean | 抹 mo3 | 傢伙 to wipe the dishes | 汗 wipe off perspiration | 亮·了 rubbed bright | 臉 rub face. | 牙 brush teeth | 油泥 to wipe away oily dirt	ch'a1	A
			Tsai		
跌1	足 157	失 481	To tumble down |·下來 俗 | 跟頭 to tumble down | 倒3	tieh12	B
災1 灾1 烖1 菑1	火 86 艸 140	火 446	Misfortune, calamity, suffering | 害 calamity, misfortune | 難4 | 禍 misery, Heaven-inflicted | 民 calamity-stricken people | 病 a dangerous disease | 殃 danger, calamity 招 | to invite disaster 旱 | drought. 水 | flood		C
哉1	口 30	𢦏 334	An interjection, exclamation 哀 | alack! alas! 大 | How great!		F
栽1	木 75	𢦏 334	To plant, transplant, set out |·上 | 種 to plant and sow | 花 to plant flowers; so | 樹 | 跟頭 tumble down; lose face |·培 plant & earth up; nourish		D
宰3	宀 40	辛 157	Minister, ruler, steward; to slaughter S. | 制 to rule, direct 主 | |°相 chief or prime minister | 牲口 to kill animals 屠 眞 | first cause, God 大主 |		D

載^{3}	車 159	戈 334	A year 三｜ three years	tsai^{4}	D
崽^{3}	山 46	思 379	Puppy, cub, young ones ｜·子		H
再^{4}	冂 13	冉 600	Again, a second time, then ｜者 further, what is more; P.S. ｜見 to see again; goodbye ｜一次 once again ｜過幾天 a few days hence ｜來年 year after next ｜不敢·了 never venture to again ｜三｜四 again and again ｜｜·的 ｜說 to mention again ｜題 ｜搭·上 in addition, moreover ｜添一點 add a little more ｜造 give second lease of life		A
在^{4}	土 32	丿 166	At, in, present, at home; living; involved in, consist in ｜這邊 on this side, here ｜這·裏(兒) ｜其內 in it, included ｜內 ｜家 at home, to be at home ｜教 to be a Mohammedan or a Christian ｜前(·頭) before. ｜後(·頭) behind ｜中間 in the middle ｜行 (hang^{2}) en rapport, an expert ｜下 below; I. ｜上 above ｜先 before (time); so ｜後 ｜心 in the heart ｜·乎 depends on, consists in ｜一塊兒 in or into one place ｜意 to notice, bear in mind ｜任 at his post. ｜理 reasonable ｜禮 Chinese secret Total Abstinence Society ｜目前 before one's eyes ｜眼前 ｜那兒^{3}住 where do you live?		A

在^{4}			| 那 na^{3}·裏 (or 兒) where? | 那 (na^{4}) ·裏 (or 兒) there | 你身·上 depends on you | (·乎)你 | 不 | is he at home? is he living? | 世 alive, in the world | 地·上 | 手 in one's hand, or power | 底·下 under, beneath | 地·下 (or ·上) on (or above) the ground | 座 to be seated, all present | 此 here, at this place | 外 outside, not included | 我 it rests with me | 我身·上 | 我看 in my opinion, I think 不 | not here; dead 沒 | 家 not at home		
載^{4} 儎^{4}	車 159	戋 334	To contain; load; record | 脚 freight | 貨 carry or load goods | 客 to carry passengers | 運 to convey, transport 記 | to record in history	tsai^{3}	D

Ts'ai

猜^{1}	犬 94	靑 82	To guess, suspect, doubt |∘着·了 to guess right | 中^{4}·了-∘chao^{2}- | 拳 guess fingers held up | 想 to imagine, guess | 疑 to doubt, suspect | 謎 to guess riddles |·得着^{2} can guess |·不着^{2} can't guess | 度 (to^{4}) to conjecture, suppose		C
纔^{2} 才^{2}	糸 120	毚 386	Then, and then, just now | 知道 just made aware of | 好 then it will be well | 是		A

<table>
<tr><td>纔[2]</td><td></td><td></td><td>| 剛 just now 剛 | , 方 |
| 到·了 just come | 來·了; so | 去·了
這∘| at last
這∘|∘是 then O.K.; enough!</td><td></td><td></td></tr>
<tr><td>𢦏[2]</td><td>戈
62</td><td>𢦏
334</td><td>To wound</td><td></td><td>P</td></tr>
<tr><td>裁[2]</td><td>衣
145</td><td>𢦏
334</td><td>To cut out, cut off; plan, decide
| 撤 do away with, cashier | 革
| 減 diminish, cut down
| 紙 cut paper. | 布 cut cloth
|·縫 cut and sew, a tailor
| 判 to hear cases, decide
| 判所 a court-house</td><td></td><td>B</td></tr>
<tr><td>才[2]</td><td>手
64</td><td>才
22</td><td>Talent, ability, genius |·幹, | 能
(often used for 纔)
| 智 wisdom, knowledge
| 學 learning, knowledge
| 子[3] talented person, genius | 士
人 | man-force
三 | Heaven, Earth and Man</td><td></td><td>C</td></tr>
<tr><td>材[2]</td><td>木
75</td><td>才
22</td><td>Materials |·料; abilities
不成 | useless, good for nothing</td><td></td><td>C</td></tr>
<tr><td>財[2]</td><td>貝
154</td><td>才
22</td><td>Wealth, riches, property
| 產 property. 錢 | wealth
|∘政學 science of finance
|∘政部 Ministry of Finance
|∘主 a wealthy person | 東
| 禮 betrothal presents
| 迷 infatuated with wealth
| 寶 precious things, valuables
|·神 (爺) the god of wealth</td><td></td><td>C</td></tr>
<tr><td>采[3]</td><td>釆
165</td><td>采
488</td><td>Gay; applaud; gather
| | 衣服 gay clothing</td><td></td><td>I</td></tr>
<tr><td>彩[3]</td><td>彡
59</td><td>采
488</td><td>Variegated, brilliant; lucky
| 氣 luck, good fortune
| 轎 wedding sedan-chair
| 衣 gay coloured clothes</td><td></td><td>A</td></tr>
</table>

Character	Radical	Phonetic	Definition		Other reading	Freq.
彩3			丨票 a lottery ticket 丨色 variegated colours			
採3	手 64	采 488	To pick, gather, select, sip 丨取 to choose out 丨用 丨掘權 right to exploit mines 丨訪 to listen, inquire 丨花 gather flowers; deflower 丨辦 to buy up 丨桑 pluck mulberry leaves			E
睬3	目 109	采 488	To notice, pay attention, greet 不丨 pay no attention to			I
綵3	糸 120	采 488	Variegated silk 丨緞			H
跴3 跐3	足 157	西 775	To tread on, step 丨壞·了 spoiled by trampling 丨·了一·脚 to stamp the foot		ch'ai3 tz'u3	E
菜4	艸 140	采 488	Vegetables 丨蔬, herbs; food 丨牀子 vegetable stand 丨攤 丨市 vegetable market 丨刀 a chopping knife 丨園子 a vegetable garden 海丨 edible sea-weed			A
蔡4	艸 140	祭 515	Weeds, herbs	S.		K

Tsan

Character	Radical	Phonetic	Definition		Other reading	Freq.
簪1	竹 118	朁 801	Hair clasp, pin 丨·子 丨花 stick flowers in hair			G
咱2 偺2 喒2	口 30	自 852	I, me, we (speaker and addressed) 丨們 we, us 丨們的 our, ours 多喒 when?		tsa2	A
儹3	人 9	贊 40	To hoard up 積丨			D

攢³	手 64	贊 40	To hoard up | 錢, gather | 聚 | 湊 to subscribe	tsuan⁴ ts'uan²	D
趲³	走 156	贊 40	To urge, hasten, get on | 勁 make strenuous effort | 路 travel hastily | 行, | 程		H
贊⁴	貝 154	贊 40	To assist, second, praise | 成 approve, second motion | 助 to aid, assist, approve | 同 join in advocating | 揚 to praise; extol; acclaim		B
濽⁴	水 85	贊 40	To spatter, splash, scatter | 濕身 spattered and wet me		I
讚⁴	言 149	贊 40	To praise, commend 誇 | | 美 to praise 頌 | , 稱 | | 嘆 praising and lamenting		C
鏨⁴	金 167	斬 212	To chisel, engrave, cut out | 花 to carve flowers, so | 字 | 子 chisel. | 刀 graving-tool		H

Ts'an

餐¹	食 184	食 363	A meal, to eat; C. of meals | 飯 to take a meal 聖 | The Lord's Supper 晚 | 大 | foreign meal 西 |		B
參¹ 叅¹	厶 28	參 282	To reflect on; impeach; visit a superior, consult; mixed | 政院 Political Council | 加 to take part in | 與 | 見 to visit a superior | 拜 | 酌 to consult, deliberate | 議院 the Senate | 考 to compare authorities | 看 | 觀 make tour of inspection | 謀總長 chief of general staff | 透 think out, see through | 贊 deputy minister, attaché	shen¹ ts'en¹	F

殘^{2}	歹 78	戔 332	To spoil, injure; cruel 丨忍, 丨暴 丨疾 a cripple 丨廢 丨缺 deficient, injured 丨害 to injure 丨燈 an expiring lamp		D
慚^{2} 慙^{2}	心 61	斬 212	Mortified, ashamed, 丨愧 丨悔 penitence, remorse 羞丨 to feel ashamed 發丨		D
蠶^{2} 蚕^{2}	虫 142	朁 801	Silk worm, attend silk worms 丨繭 cocoons. 丨種 silkworms' eggs 丨子^{3} 丨蛾 the silk worm moth 丨桑 silkworm mulberry 丨豆 broad beans		E
譖^{2}	言 149	朁 801	To slander, libel 誣丨 丨言 slanderous words		I
讒^{2}	言 149	毚 386	To slander, traduce 丨謗 to calumniate 丨說		F
慘^{3}	心 61	參 282	Grieved, sad; cruel, inhuman 丨悽 grieved, pained 丨然, 悽丨		G
燦^{3}	火 86	粲 518	Lustrous, brilliant 丨爛		G
朁^{3}	曰 73	朁 801	Nevertheless, if, suppose		K
儳^{3}	人 9	毚 386	Mulish, obstinate, stupid	ts'an^{4}	H
儳^{4}	人 9	毚 386	Vile, worthless 丨頭 blockhead, poor-looking	ts'an^{3}	H
粲^{4}	米 119	粲 518	Fine rice; beautiful, brilliant; a feast; 丨 丨 elegant, stylish		K

Tsang

髒^{1}	骨 188	死 278	Obese, dirty 骯丨 丨症 venereal disease, so 丨瘡		A

Character	Radical	Phonetic	Definition		Other readings	Freq.
臧[1]	臣 131	臧 644	To commend; good, right, 丨善	S.		H
贓[1] 贜[1] 賍[1]	貝 154 减	臧 644	Stolen goods, plunder; bribes 丨官 a corrupt official 丨物 stolen goods, loot 認丨 identify stolen goods 貪丨 greedy for bribes			E
駔[3]	馬 187	且 623	Fine horse 丨駿 丨儈 broker, middleman		ts'ang[3] tsu[4]	K
藏[4]	艸 140	臧 644	Storeroom, strong-box, 庫丨 丨經 Tibetan classics 西丨 Tibet. 丨香 Tibetan incense		ts'ang[2]	C
臟[4]	肉 130	臧 644	Chief viscera 五丨 丨腑 internal organs			F
葬[4] 塟[4]	艸 140	死 278	To bury, inter 丨埋, 埋丨 火丨 to cremate 殯丨 inter with decorum			C

Ts'ang

Character	Radical	Phonetic	Definition		Other readings	Freq.
倉[1]	人 9	倉 679	Granary; hurried; box, bin 丨房 a granary 丨廩 (public) 丨卒 (ts'u[4]) flurried, excited 丨惶 開丨 dispense grain			E
傖[1]	人 9	倉 679	A reckless fellow, outcast 丨父 an old reprobate		cheng[1]	H
艙[1]	舟 137	倉 679	Ship's hold, cabin 丨房, 船丨 丨口 hatchway of vessel			B
蒼[1]	艸 140	倉 679	Azure, green, grey, old 丨穹 dark heavens, God 穹丨 丨海 the ocean 丨天 azure heavens, God	S.		F
蒼[1]	虫 142	倉 679	The fly, the housefly 丨·蠅 丨·蠅紙 fly-paper			D
藏[2]	艸 140	臧 644	To hide, conceal, store 丨奸 to hide away traitors		tsang[4]	C

藏²			| 匿 to hide. | 躲 abscond | 收 to store up 收 | | 書樓 library		
駔³	馬 187	且 623	Strong horse; dirty | 兒貨 shoddy goods |·子 rascal. |·子錢 poor cash	tsang¹	K

Tsao

𣴓¹	小 42	曹 820	Worn out, spoiled | 壞 | 朽 rotten, decayed | 爛·了 worn out, e.g., clothing	ts'ao²	E
糟¹ 醩¹	米 119	曹 820	"Grains", dregs; to waste | 朽 rotten, decayed | 肉 meat cured in grain |·了 rotten, decayed; too bad!		B
遭¹ 蹧¹	辵 162	曹 820	To endure; meet with; waste; a revolution; occasion; C. of turns | 禍害 meet with calamity | 難⁴ encounter misfortune |·塌 (or·蹅) throw about; defame |·塌東·西 to waste things |∘遇 to meet with 一 | a turn, a time		B
鑿²	金 167	金 79	To chisel |·子; bore; a punch 俗 | 冰 to saw ice blocks	tso⁴	D
早³	日 72	早 795a	Early, morning, soon; long ago |·晨 morning |·上, 淸 |, |·起 | 起晚睡 rise early, retire late | 知·道 knew before; almanac | 飯 breakfast. |·半天 forenoon |³·些兒 a little earlier |²·點兒 | 已 previously, already | 先, | 日 | | 兒的 early; soon | 晚 early and late; eventually 趁 | be beforehand, prompt		A

澡^3	水 85	喿 697	To bathe, cleanse 洗｜ ｜盆 a bath-tub ｜堂子 a bath, bathhouse ｜塘子		B
藻^3	艸 140	喿 697	Graceful, elegant; water grass 詞｜elegant composition		H
棗^3	木 75	朿 500	"Dates", jujubes ｜兒 ｜核兒 date-stones -hur^2 酸｜wild dates. 黑｜wild persimmon		D
蚤^3	虫 142	蚤 787	A flea, to scratch; spoke-mortises ｜·起 early in the morning 虼·｜a flea 跳｜		F
造^4	辵 162	告 717	To make, build 蓋｜,建｜, create, do ｜成 made; finished; to perfect ｜·就 accomplish, develop ｜房子 build a house ｜·化 create; a boon, good luck ｜幣廠 a mint ｜作 to compose, form, make ｜罪 sin and be punished ｜次 be reckless, make trouble ｜謠言 to fabricate rumors 製∘｜to make, form, invent 創｜to invent, to create 修｜to build, to repair		C
燥^4	火 86	喿 697	Dry, parched 乾｜ ｜熱 intensely hot, fiery ｜烈 fierce, raging		E
躁^4 趮^4	足 157	喿 697	Hasty, irascible, cruel ｜動 noise, disturbance 急｜impetuous, hasty ｜急 浮｜volatile, frivolous 暴∘｜cruel, bad temper		E
竈^4 灶^4	穴 116	黽 316	Kitchen-stove, furnace ｜頭 ｜馬 the cricket ｜神 god of the kitchen ｜·王爺 打｜put up a range 搭｜		F

皁[4] 皂[4]	白 106	早 795a	Black; yamen runners; soap; early 丨隸 police runners 丨班 胰丨 soap 香丨		F

Ts'ao

操[1]	手 64	喿 697	To grasp, hold fast; drill; manage 丨場 drill ground 丨持 manage, control, hold firm 丨心 anxious care 丨行[4] deportment (school) 丨•練 to drill, discipline 丨演 丨守 to guard, maintain 丨作 to do manual work		C
糙[1]	米 119	告 717	Hulled paddy; rough, common 粗•丨		G
曹[2]	曰 73	曹 820	Plural; a class; state S. 爾丨 you all. 陰丨 next world		F
嘈[2] 譜[2]	口 30	曹 820	Noise, row, clamor, wrangling 丨鬧, 丨雜 丨耳 to deafen		H
䵦[2]	小 42	曹 820	Worn-out, spoiled 丨奮	tsao1	E
槽[2]	木 75	曹 820	Trough, manger, groove; C. of wood partitions, windows, etc. 丨牙 grinders (teeth) 馬丨 manger. 水丨 water-trough		E
漕[2]	水 85	曹 820	To transport 丨運; millrace 丨河 Grand Canal		I
草[3] 艸[3]	艸 140	早 795a	Grass, weeds; careless; running hand; rough draft; mean 丨案 draft copy of document 丨紙 rough paper 丨房 a thatched house 丨席 straw-mat. 丨鞋 straw shoes 丨寫 running hand, scrawl 丨字 丨稿 a rough draft, sketch		B

草3			｜料 forage. ｜帽兒 straw hat ｜木 the vegetable kingdom ｜率 carelessly			
騲3	馬 187	早 795a	Female (of donkey) ｜驢 a she-ass			F

Tse

則2	刀 18	則 858	And so, then; pattern, rule ｜就 then in consequence ｜已 that is the end of it, so be it ｜例 rule, custom, regulation ｜是 then it will be right ｜可 準｜ rule, standard, normal 一｜; 二｜ firstly; secondly			C
賊24	貝 154	戎 336	A thief	文	tsei2	C
責24	貝 154	責 83	Reprove, punish; responsibility ｜罰 to chastise, to punish ｜打 ｜·任 duties, responsibilities ｜·備 to reprove, rebuke 斥｜ 自｜ reprove, blame oneself		chai2	D
擇24	手 64	睪 160	Choose, select, pick out ｜選,選｜ ｜吉日 to choose a lucky day ｜交 select one's associates ｜要 choose important points		chai2	D
澤24	水 85	睪 160	To soak, enrich, benefit; marsh; fertile; sleek ｜民 to benefit the people 恩｜ favor, kindness 潤｜ fertilize, agreeable		chai2	F
窄4	穴 116	乍 150	Narrow, contracted	文	chai3	A
摘4	手 64	啇 590	To pluck	文	chai1	A
謫4	言 149	啇 590	To reproach; fault	文	chai1	K

仄4 人 9 人 429 Oblique tone, oblique, slanting 文 chai3 che4 G
| 聲 oblique tones, i.e. 上,去,入聲
| 韻 oblique tone rhymes

嘖4 口 30 責 83 To cry; quarrel; praise H
| | 不已 unceasing praise

簀4 竹 118 責 83 Splints, slips; a mat H
易 | change the mat,—to die

Ts'e

坼4 土 32 斥 214 To crack, chap; burst, slip I
| 裂 to chap (hands)

拆4 手 64 斥 214 To skip over (chess) ch'ai1 B

策4 竹 118 朿 500 Treatise, book; plan, scheme; examination questions; whip; slip D
| 論 questions and themes | 問
| 馬 to whip horse
| 士 clever strategist
政∘| government policy
計∘| plan; stratagem

册4 冂 13 册 565 Register, list |·子; tables 文 ch'ai3 D
| 籍 records, archives | 簿,書 |

側4 人 9 則 858 Side, sideways, on one side; perverted, prejudiced chai1 F
| 耳聽 apply the ear and listen
| 立 stand by the side of
| 室 a concubine
| 臥 to lie on one side

惻4 心 61 則 858 To sympathise, pity | 隱 G
痛 | feel deep pity for

測4 水 85 則 858 To fathom, estimate |∘量, | 度
| 繪 to draw a map
|·不透 cannot fathom 不可 |
| 字 tell fortunes by words

Tsei

賊[2]	貝 154	戎 336	A thief, robber ｜匪 brigands, rebels ｜星 shooting star, meteor ｜盜 robbers 盜｜ ｜窩 a nest of thieves	俗	tse[2]	C

Tsen

怎[3]	心 61	乍 150	How? why? what? ｜·麼 ｜·麼呢 how is it? ｜·麼樣 in what way? how?			A

Ts'en

參[1] 叅[1]	厶 28	參 282	Irregular, uneven ｜差 (tz'u[1]) confused, uneven ｜差 (tz'u[1]) 不齊 same		shen[1] ts'an[1]	F
岑[2]	山 46	今 434	Lone peaks, lofty	S.	ch'en[2]	K

Tseng

曾[1]	曰 73	曾 832	Great; to add to ｜孫 great-grandson ｜元 ｜祖 great-grandfather ｜祖父 ｜子[3] a disciple of Confucius	S.	ts'eng[2]	B
增[1]	土 32	曾 832	To add to, increase ｜給 additional amount ｜加 add to. ｜廣 enlarge ｜價 to raise the price ｜減 modify, more or less ｜光 to add brilliancy to ｜補 recompense, increase			C
[illegible][1]	矢 111	曾 832	Arrow for crossbow			I

憎4	心 61	曾 832	To hate, dislike, abominate ｜嫌 bear a grudge ｜惡, ｜恨可｜ hateful		D
甑4	瓦 98	曾 832	A steamer 飯｜, to steam	ching4	H
贈4	貝 154	曾 832	Souvenir, parting present; posthumous honors ｜品 presents, gifts ｜送 present on departure ｜別		G

Ts'eng

曾2	曰 73	曾 832	Already, past, done ｜。經 ｜記得 don't you remember? ｜有人說 it was once said 不｜ not yet; have not; eh? what? 未｜ had not yet, before he had	tseng1	B
層2	尸 44	曾 832	Layer, story, stratum; degree; paragraph; C. of layers ｜｜ layer upon layer 一｜·一·｜ ｜次 regular order, series 一｜ a turn, time, matter		B
蹭4	足 157	曾 832	To rub; shuffle, dawdle ｜·蹬 ｜楞子 to shilly-shally		F

Tso

作1	人 9	乍 150	Manufactory ｜坊; workman, bring to pass ｜揖 fold hands and bow 木｜ carpenter; so 泥｜, 瓦｜	tso24	C
嘬1	口 30	最 628	To suck, ｜乳 suck breast	ch'uai4	I
撮1	手 64	最 628	A pinch, handful 一｜	ts'o14	G

Tso

昨²	日 72	乍 150	Yesterday, recently | 兒個, | 日, |·天 | 兒晚·上 yesterday evening | 夜 last night		A
作²	人 9	乍 150	Condiments |·料	tso¹⁴	C
左³	工 48	左 177	Left hand; deputy; error; east S | 證 to verify | 傳⁴ Spring and Autumn Commentary or Annals | 翼 left wing or flank (army) | 脾·氣 a cantankerous temper |·邊 left side. | 手 left hand | 道 false doctrine | 右 left and right; near to; in any case | 右爲難 in a dilemma		B
佐³	人 9	左 177	To aid, assist, assistant | 助 | 理 assist in managing 輔 | to assist, second		G
坐⁴	土 32	坐 432	To sit |·下, |·一·|; a seat, place | 車 ride on cart; so | 轎·子 | 監 be confined in prison |·住(·了) to sit still, so |·不住 | 兒 a seat, a passenger, e. g., in car or bus etc. | 席 be present at a feast | 褥 cushion. | 穩 sit firmly | 落 situation of a house |·不下 not room for all to sit | 堂 to sit in judgment |·位 a seat | 月·子 a woman's confinement		A
座⁴	广 53	坐 432	A seat, throne; place, C. of houses, temples, cities, hills |·位 a seat 上 | seat of honor. 寶 | throne 一 | 城 a city, city wall; so 一 | 塔		B

Tso

Character	Radical	Phonetic	Meaning	Other reading	Class
做^4	人 9	古 702	To do, act; make; be in action	tsou^4	A
			｜成 to complete an affair		
			｜親 to get married		
			｜·法 form a plan, method		
			｜飯 make food. ｜聲 speak		
			｜活 work for living, to sew		
			｜官 to be an official		
			｜·不來 unable to do		
			｜·不得 can't be done; ought not		
			｜甚麼 what are you doing?		
作^4	人 9	乍 150	To make; work, act; be	tso^{12}	C
			｜証 act as witness, testify		
			｜成·了 accomplished. ｜好 do good		
			｜工 to work. ｜工的 laborer		
			｜夢 to be dreaming		
			｜孽 to commit sin		
			｜惡 to do wickedly		
			｜伴(兒) act as companion to		
			｜詩 to make verses		
			｜事 to transact business		
			｜書的 an author		
			｜得 done, made, able to do		
			｜對 to act as an enemy		
			｜爲 actions, conduct		
			｜文章 to compose an essay		
			｜·用 use, process, purpose		
			著·｜ make books, compose		
怍^4	心 61	乍 150	Shamefaced, confused		H
			｜于人 ashamed before men		
柞^4	木 75	乍 150	Kind of oak tree or lumber ｜木		F
祚^4	示 113	乍 150	Dignity, honor; to bless		H
			福｜ happiness and dignity		
胙^4	肉 130	乍 150	Sacrifices (ancestral); reward		I
			｜肉 sacrificial food		
鑿^4	金 167	金 79	To chisel stones, punch 文	tsao^2	D

Ts'o

<table>
<tr><td>搓[1]</td><td>手
64</td><td>差
178</td><td>To roll between hands, twist by rubbing | 揉, 揉 | , | 手
| 線 twist thread; so | 繩子</td><td></td><td>D</td></tr>
<tr><td>磋[1]</td><td>石
112</td><td>差
178</td><td>To rub | 磨, polish; correct
| 商 to deliberate, discuss</td><td></td><td>H</td></tr>
<tr><td>蹉[1]</td><td>足
157</td><td>差
178</td><td>Slip | 跌, miss, go by
| 跎 to stumble, to let slip</td><td></td><td>H</td></tr>
<tr><td>撮[14]</td><td>手
64</td><td>最
628</td><td>To pinch, pick, gather; make; résumé
| 合 to join, make agree
| 土 to shovel earth
| 要 make an abstract
| 影 to photograph, a photo</td><td>tso[1]</td><td>G</td></tr>
<tr><td>矬[2]</td><td>矢
111</td><td>坐
432</td><td>Short, dwarfed | 小, 短 |
| 人 short man. |·子 dwarf</td><td></td><td>H</td></tr>
<tr><td>厝[4]</td><td>厂
27</td><td>昔
799</td><td>To carve; bury; tombstone
浮 | bury temporarily</td><td>ts'u[4]</td><td>I</td></tr>
<tr><td>措[4]</td><td>手
64</td><td>昔
799</td><td>To put, place, arrange; collect; publish
| 手 set hand to, prepare
| 詞 arrange phraseology</td><td></td><td>G</td></tr>
<tr><td>錯[4]</td><td>金
167</td><td>昔
799</td><td>Mistake, error, wrong | 失, |·悞
| 縫[4]子 fault, crevice; weak point
| 想 a mistaken thought
| 寫 to mis-write
| 認 to mistake (a person)
| 骨縫[4] bones out of joint
|·過 mistake, pass by, except
| 亂 confused
|·不了[3] unable to mistake; good
| 字 wrong characters</td><td></td><td>A</td></tr>
<tr><td>剉[4]</td><td>刀
18</td><td>坐
432</td><td>To lop off, file, trim
| 折 to file in two
| 角 to file off corners
| 平·了 filed smooth</td><td></td><td>G</td></tr>
</table>

挫[4]	手 64	坐 432	To dislocate, upset, resist, push down; try 丨磨 to force, compel, bully		H
銼[4]	金 167	坐 432	A file, rasp; iron pan		F

Tsou

謅[1]	言 149	芻 663	Jesting, raillery, banter 文 胡丨talk wildly, at random	chou[1]	G
諏[1]	言 149	取 627	To consult, choose 擇丨 丨吉 choose a lucky day		I
走[3]	走 156	走 134	To go, travel, depart, warp 丨岔 part ways; go astray 丨氣 to escape, as steam 丨·着 on foot, to walk 丨路兒, 丨道兒 丨乏·了 weary with traveling 丨後 after (he) went away 丨·開 to walk or step apart 丨快 hurry up 快丨; so 慢丨 丨來丨去 going back and forth 丨了水了 a fire has started! (water has escaped) 丨馬 a pacing horse 丨·不開 unable to pass or let pass 丨·不了 unable to go 丨·不得 road is impassable 丨·不動 unable to walk from age 丨獸 quadrupeds, animals 丨錯·了 take a wrong road 丨肚·子 diarrhoea		A
做[4]	人 9	古 702	To make (see tso[4]) 俗	tso[4]	A
奏[4]	大 37	奏 471	To memorialize; make music 丨章 a memorial to the throne 丨摺 丨任 to recommend for office 丨樂 to make music, play		F

<table>
<tr><td>驟^{4}</td><td>馬
187</td><td>取
627</td><td>A racer, fleet, suddenly
| 然間 abruptly. | 行 instantly</td><td></td><td>G</td></tr>
</table>

Ts'ou

<table>
<tr><td>湊^{4}
凑^{4}</td><td>水
85</td><td>奏
471</td><td>To collect, make up, come together
| 集 collect, assemble | 聚, |·合
| 齊 all collected together
| 巧 by a lucky chance
| 錢 collect money | 繳
|·不出 can't raise the amount
|·在一塊(處) gather in one place</td><td></td><td>F</td></tr>
<tr><td>輳^{4}</td><td>車
159</td><td>奏
471</td><td>Centre of wheel, focus</td><td></td><td>H</td></tr>
</table>

Tsu

<table>
<tr><td>租^{1}</td><td>禾
115</td><td>且
623</td><td>To rent, lease; a tax
| 價 amount of rent |·錢
| 借地 leased territory
| 界 Foreign Concessions
|·出去 to let or rent out
| 房住 live in rented house
| 約 a lease</td><td></td><td>B</td></tr>
<tr><td>足^{2}</td><td>足
157</td><td>足
133</td><td>Foot; enough | 彀, | | ; pure
| 跡 foot print. | 指 toes
| 球 foot-ball. | 下 you, sir
| 意 satisfied. 滿 | complete full
知 | content. 失 | slip, stumble</td><td>ts'u^{4}</td><td>B</td></tr>
<tr><td>卒^{24}
卆^{24}</td><td>十
24</td><td>卒
14</td><td>Retainer, soldier; to finish, die,
| (ts'u^{4}) 然 hastily, suddenly
|·子 soldiers 兵 |, | 伍
| 業 to graduate
禁 | jailer, turnkey 監 |</td><td></td><td>D</td></tr>
<tr><td>族^{2}</td><td>方
70</td><td>㫃
265</td><td>Tribe, clan, relatives 宗 |
| 長^{3} eldest man of family
| 類 a class, clan, tribe 種 |
| 譜 genealogical register</td><td>ts'u^{4}</td><td>D</td></tr>
</table>

鏃[24] 金 167 族 265 — Barb, point, head of javelin — H

俎[3] 人 9 且 623 — Sacrificial bowl | 豆 — K

徂[3] 彳 60 且 623 — To advance, to go to — I
| 東 proceed to the east

殂[3] 歹 78 且 623 — To fall and die | 落 — H

祖[3] 示 113 且 623 — Ancestor, founder |·宗, | 先 — S. — C
| 產 ancestral property
| 傳[2] family heirlooms
| 父 paternal grandfather, so | 母
| 國 the fatherland
| 廟 ancestral temple | 先堂

組[3] 糸 120 且 623 — Cord, girdle, fringe; to organize — G
| 成 achieve, convene, organize
|·織 organize, systematic | 立
| 合 unite, confederated

詛[3] 言 149 且 623 — Oath; to curse, imprecate — E
| 誓 take an oath
咒 | to curse, imprecate

阻[3] 阜 170 且 623 — To hinder, stop, oppose | 止, | 擋 — C
| 礙 an obstruction
|·住 to interrupt, hinder
| 隔 impassable, cut off from
| 力 opposition, friction, reaction
| 擾 obstruct, hinder | 撓, 攔 |

椊[3] 木 75 卒 14 — Plug, cork — I

Ts'u

粗[1] 麤[1] 觕[1] 米 119 且 623 角 148 — Rough, coarse, rude, gross, vile; partially; heedlessly — B
| 茶淡飯 plain food, homely fare
| 風暴雨 a sudden storm
| 細 coarse and fine; quality
| 心 careless, coarse

Character	Radical	Phonetic	Meaning	Alt. reading	Class
粗[1]			| 工 heavy work; unskilled | 活 | 鹵 coarse salt; rude, stupid | 暴 coarse, rough, boisterous | 布 coarse native cloth | 率 (shuai[4]) rough in action | 糙 | 俗 vulgar, commonplace | 大 large, coarse | 野 wild, rough		
厝[4]	厂 27	昔 799	Inter coffin; carve 安 | place a coffin in a shelter	ts'o[4]	I
醋[4]	酉 164	昔 799	Vinegar 黑 |, 白 | 吃 | eat vinegar,—be jealous		B
足[4]	足 157	足 133	Treat with respect | 恭	tsu[2]	B
促[4]	人 9	足 133	To press, urge, contracted | 進 to expedite, promote | 迫 urge, stimulate, be quick		F
齪[4]	齒 211	足 133	To grate teeth 齷 | paltry, mean, dirty		I
族[4]	方 70	㫃 265	Tribe, clan, relatives 文	tsu[2]	D
簇[4]	竹 118	㫃 265	Cocoon frame; group | 新 brand new, just appointed		H
蹴[4]	足 157	尤 175	To tread on, kick | 蹋 | 然 uneasy in manner		H
蹙[4]	足 157	叔 123	To hasten, urgent, anxious | 然 incontinently, suddenly		H
猝[4]	犬 94	卒 14	Abrupt, hurried, urgent | 急 | 然間 suddenly, unexpectedly		H

Tsuan

Character	Radical	Phonetic	Meaning	Alt. reading	Class
躦[1]	足 157	贊 40	To jump with two feet 好跳好 | fond of hops and jumps		F
鑽[1]	金 167	贊 40	To bore, pierce | 窟窿 | 入 to bore or creep into	tsuan[34]	E

鑽[1]			|·不動 cannot be bored into |◦營 to intrigue, lobby		
鑽[3]	金 167	贊 40	To bore a hole |眼	tsuan14	E
纂[3]	糸 120	算 848	To compile, edit; invent |定 |輯 to compile a book |書 |修 revise book; compile		F
⿰火雋[3] 臇[3]	火 86	隹 52	To make chowder 醋|小魚 make fish chowder	ts'uan1	H
賺[4]	貝 154	兼 671	To cheat |人, |哄	chuan4	B
攢[4] 揝[4] 撍[4]	手 64	贊 40	To grasp, hold |·着 |拳頭 close the fists |乾·了 to wring dry |·不住 cannot keep hold |手 grasp the handle	tsan3 ts'uan2	D
鑽[4]	金 167	贊 40	An awl, gimlet |·子 |石 a diamond 金剛|	tsuan13	E

Ts'uan

攛[1]	手 64	鼠 689	To fling; stir up, excite |掇 to excite to evil		H
⿰火雋[1] 臇[1]	火 86	隹 52	To stew |丸子 to stew meat-balls |魚 a fish stew	tsuan3	H
攢[2]	手 64	贊 40	To collect, assemble |錢 |湊 collect, make up	tsan3 tsuan4	D
竄[4]	穴 116	鼠 689	To skulk off, sneak; pilfer; seduce 逃| sneak away and hide		B
躥[4] ⿰馬竄[4]	足 157	鼠 689	To leap, jump, prance 一| a start or leap forward		G
篡[4]	竹 118	算 848	To rebel, |逆; usurp |位 to usurp the throne		F

爨[4]	火 86	同 580	Furnace; to cook; a mess, table 丨飯 to cook victuals		I

Tsui

堆[1]	土 32	隹 52	Pile, group 俗 歸拉包丨the whole lot	tui[1]	C
嘴[3]	口 30	此 129	Lip, mouth-piece, bill; nozzle 丨強 obstinate, contradictory 丨唇 lips, mouth 丨·裏 in the mouth 丨巴子 lower jaw 丨不好 foul-mouthed person 丨損 to vilify, slander 丨硬 firm language		C
醉[4]	酉 164	卒 14	Intoxicated, drunk 丨酒, 丨·了 丨·漢 a drunken man 丨話 a drunkard's talk 丨鬼 habitual drunkard 丨眼朦朧 drunkard's bleary eyes		A
最[4]	曰 73	最 628	Very, most, extreme; e.g., 丨大 丨初 the very first 丨先 丨好 extremely good, best 丨後 the very last 丨要 most important		B
罪[4] 辠[4]	网 122	非 418	Fault, sin; retribution 丨孽 丨愆 crime, guilt 丨輕 light offence; so 丨重 丨犯 a culprit, criminal 丨人 offender, sinner 丨辜 sin, guilt 丨·過, 丨惡 丨魁 chief offender 丨·名 reputed guilt, misdeeds		B

Ts'ui

Character	Radical	Phonetic	Definition		Code
崔[1] 磪[1]	山 46	崔 53	High, precipitous 丨嵬 rock-covered height	S.	H
催[1]	人 9	崔 53	To urge, hasten 丨逼, 丨迫, 丨促 丨賬 press payment of account 丨請 send and urge guest to come 丨馬 to urge on a horse 丨眠術 hypnotism 丨討 require urgently, dun 丨租 to press for rent 丨·丨·他 to importune him		B
摧[1]	手 64	崔 53	To repress, force, break 丨折 丨抑 repress, restrain		I
脆[4] 脃[4]	肉 130	危 197	Delicate, brittle, crisp 丨骨 gristle, cartilage 丨快 quick, decided 爽丨 乾丨 decidedly, definitely		E
啐[4]	口 30	卒 14	To spit, spit out 丨吐沫 to spit saliva		H
悴[4]	心 61	卒 14	Sad; distressed 哀丨 困丨 in straits, distressed		I
瘁[4]	疒 104	卒 14	Distress; worn out, diseased 殄丨 torn with distress		H
粹[4]	米 119	卒 14	Pure, unmixed 純丨		F
翠[4]	羽 124	卒 14	Kingfisher, blue 丨雀兒[3] kingfisher, 丨雀花 larkspur 丨花 feather flowers 丨毛 kingfishers' feathers 翡丨		G
萃[4]	艸 140	卒 14	Grassy, thicket; to congregate 丨聚 collect together 丨集		H
毳[4]	毛 82	毛 375	Down, nap; asbestos; fragile 丨布 cloth with a nap		K

Tsun

Character	Radical	Phonetic	Meaning	Alt.	Class
尊^{1}	寸 41	尊 783	Honorable, to honor, you; C. of cannon 丨長^{3} an aged person, elder 丨駕 you, sir. 丨敬 to reverence 丨∘重 to esteem, to respect 丨崇 丨姓 what is your name? 丨榮 high rank, to honor 丨·貴 of honorable rank 丨卑 high and low 自丨自大 high esteem for self		B
樽^{1} 墫^{1} 罇^{1}	木 75 缶 121	尊 783	Vase, goblet, bowl, decanter; C. of drinks 一丨酒 花丨 a flower-vase		H
遵^{1}	辵 162	尊 783	To obey, accord with 丨從 丨法 to obey the law 丨奉 to venerate, obey 丨行, 丨依 丨命 to obey orders 丨令 丨守 observe a law or treaty		B
夋^{1}	夊 35	夋 542	To dawdle	chün^{1}	K
吮^{3}	口 30	允 869	Suck, lick; lickspittle 丨味 test the flavor	shun^{3}	H
撙^{31}	手 64	尊 783	To adjust, hoard up 丨節 to economise 丨省 丨·出來的 saved up by economy		I
俊^{4}	人 9	夋 542	Beautiful, fine 俗	chün^{4}	D
竣^{4}	立 117	夋 542	Finished	chün^{4}	G

Ts'un

Character	Radical	Phonetic	Meaning	Alt.	Class
村^{1} 邨^{1}	木 75	寸 18	Village, hamlet 丨·子, 丨∘莊, 鄉丨 丨夫 villager, rustic 丨戶 丨話 rustic talk; coarse language		B

Character	Radical	Phonetic	Meaning		Level
皴[1]	皮 107	夋 542	Rough, chapped; to draw 丨法 the art of drawing 丨裂 rough and cracked 丨皮 chapped skin 涷丨·了		H
存[2]	子 39	丿 166	To preserve; continue; deposit 丨案 a case preserved in records 丨錢 savings 丨財 丨據 to preserve a proof 丨項 balance in hand 丨欵 丨心 keep heart; inner man 丨活 maintain life 丨貨 store goods, stock 丨根 stub, counterfoil 丨留 detain, keep in charge 丨·不住 unable to keep a thing 丨水 spot collects water 丨在 remain present, exist		B
忖[3]	心 61	寸 18	To consider, ponder, surmise 丨想 consider, think over 丨思 丨量 to suppose 丨度 (to⁴) to conjecture, reflect		H
寸[4]	寸 41	寸 18	Inch, a very little, small 丨心 the heart 丨衷 丨口 place to feel pulse 丨脈 丨步 a step. 丨陰 a moment 方丨 square inch, heart		B

Tsung

Character	Radical	Phonetic	Meaning		Level
宗[1]	宀 40	宗 516	Ancestor, clan, a kind; honor 丨政 double surname 丨教 religion 丨教思想 religious interest 丨教自由 religious liberty 丨旨 scope; chief idea, purpose 丨派 family & branches, sects 丨譜 a family register	S. S.	B

Tsung

宗[1]			| 社黨 royalist party |·室 the Imperial kindred | 族 kindred generally | 家, | 親 | | 樣樣 all sorts. 一 | a kind		
棕[1] 椶[1]	木 75	宗 516	Palm tree, coir palm |·色 dark brown | 繩 coir rope; | 毯 coir mat		E
豵[1]	豕 152	宗 516	Pig, a litter		H
踪[1] 蹤[1]	足 157	宗 516	Vestige, footstep, trace | 跡 | 影 sign, trace, clue | 緒 追 | follow up a clue		D
鬃[1]	髟 190	宗 516	Wig, high head-dress 假 | a chignon, false hair		H
縱[1]	糸 120	從 135	Perpendicular, vertical | 生者人 man alone erect	tsung[4]	D
總[3] 摠[3] 捴[3]	糸 120 减	悤 380	To unite in one, sum up; all, generic, generally; still; certainly | 賬 account totals only | 機關 headquarters | 稽查 general inspector | 結 to combine; all completed | 之 but, the upshot is | 而言之 in a word, to sum up | 會 guild, general assembly | 管 a general manager | 辦 | 理 to superintend, premier | 領事官 consul-general | 目 contents of a book | 簿 a ledger. | 不 never |·是 always; probably | 司令 Commander-in-chief | 算 add together, reckon up |°得[3] must, should |°要 | 督 a governor-general | 統 President of a Republic 共 | altogether, the whole 攏 |		A

Character	Radical	Phonetic	Meaning	Other readings	
從^{4}	彳 60	從 135	Clan, family; following 丨者, 丨人	ts'ung^{12}	A
縱^{4}	糸 120	從 135	To allow, indulgent; although 丨性 follow inclinations 丨然 although, even if 放丨 to tolerate, be lax	tsung^{1}	D
粽^{4} 糉^{4}	米 119	宗 516	Dumplings of glutinous millet or rice wrapped in reed leaves 丨·子 丨葉 leaves to wrap dumplings 三角丨 3-cornered dumplings 丨·子		F
綜^{4}	糸 120	宗 516	To inquire into, collect 丨合 synthesis, to combine 丨核 to make general estimate or grading		I

Ts'ung

Character	Radical	Phonetic	Meaning	Other readings	
從^{1} 从^{1}	彳 60	從 135	丨丨容容 Easy, unembarrassed	tsung^{4} ts'ung^{2}	A
聰^{1} 聦^{1}	耳 128	悤 380	Astute; acute hearing; clever 丨慧 cleverness, wise 丨·明, 丨敏 天丨 natural cleverness		B
怱^{1} 匆^{1} 悤^{1}	心 61	怱 234	Agitated, hurried, excited 丨猝 丨忙 hurried, in a great hurry		H
葱^{1}	艸 140	怱 234	Onion 丨頭 丨心綠 pea-green 丨白兒 the heart of an onion		F
叢^{12} 樷^{12}	又 29	取 627	Bushy, a grove; crowded 丨林 a dense wood; Buddhist monastery 丨生 many growing together 丨書 collection of reprints		G

從[2] 从[2]	彳 60	從 135	To follow, agree with, obey; from, by, since S. ｜前 formerly ｜先 ｜今以後 from henceforth ｜·着 follow, obedient 依｜，順｜ ｜權 act acc. to circumstances ｜中 between, within this ｜衆 follow the multitude ｜小 from child-hood ｜新再辦 begin afresh and do ｜人 to follow a person ｜寬 give way, yield, lenient ｜來 hitherto ｜俗 to follow custom ｜死復活 a resurrection ｜頭至尾 beginning to end ｜此 from this place or time ｜無 never ｜無生有 fabrication ｜優 liberal, considerate ｜豐	tsung[4] ts'ung[1]	A

Tu

都[1]	邑 163	者 192	Capital; all, everyone S. ｜城 a capital city 京｜ ｜會 town or city ｜來·了 all came, all have come tou[1]- ｜督 military gov. of province	tou[1]	A
嘟[1]	口 30	者 192	Bunch of grapes ｜·嚕 ｜∘噥 to mutter		H
督[1]	目 109	叔 123	To superintend, admonish, lead ｜軍 military gov. of province ｜會 Session or Presbytery ｜管 to superintend ｜辦 ｜理 to govern, rule ｜責 admonish, reprove ｜過 監·｜ to superintend, a bishop		B

Tu

纛^{2}	糸 120	毋 571	Banner, standard	tao^{4}	G
獨^{2} 独^{2}	犬 94	蜀 788	Alone, only 單丨; widow 丨唱 a solo 丨處^{3} live alone, solitary 丨門丨院 丨一眞神 the only true God 丨一無二 absolutely unique 丨立 stand alone, independent 丨立精神 spirit of independence 丨立主義 independency 丨坐 sit alone. 丨自 one self 惟丨 the exception, only		B
毒^{2}	毋 80	毋 571	Poison, virulent; to hate 丨氣 foul air; poison gas 丨虫 venomous insect, reptile 丨害 to poison; injure foully 丨恨 to abominate 丨心 malicious, spiteful 丨蛇 poisonous snake 丨手 malicious, inhuman man 丨死 to kill by poison 丨斃 丨藥 poison		C
牘^{24}	片 91	賣 864	Records, documents, tablet 尺丨 letters, collected letters		G
犢^{24}	牛 93	賣 864	A calf 牛丨, 丨·子		F
讀^{24}	言 149	賣 864	To read aloud, study 丨書 丨書人 (or 的) literati, students 誦丨 to recite, read aloud	tou^{4}	C
讟^{24}	言 149	賣 864	To slander, murmur; sedition 謗丨 to revile, slander	tou^{4}	F
堵^{3}	土 32	者 192	To block, obstruct, fill up 丨塞 丨·住門口 block up doorway 丨窟·窿 to stop up a hole 丨嘴 to stop the mouth 丨口		C

Character	Radical	Phonetic	Meaning		
睹^{3} 覩^{3}	目 109	者 192	To look at, see, observe 目丨眼見 see with own eyes 丨而不見 gaze at but not see		D
賭^{3}	貝 154	者 192	To gamble, wager, bet, risk 丨氣 angrily to insist out of spite 丨錢 to gamble 丨博 丨局 gaming table or house 丨·個東兒 to bet 打丨 丨棍 a gambler 丨鬼 丨賽 to compete with		C
肚^{3}	肉 130	土 43	Stomach, tripe 丨·子 丨量 capacity for food 羊丨 mutton tripe	tu^{4}	C
篤^{34}	竹 118	馬 255	Sincere, serious, pure; stable 丨志 determined, resolution 丨信 firmly believe 丨信無疑 丨實 true, sincere, really		E
度^{4}	广 53	度 200	To measure, degree; limit, capacity; to pass 丨日 pass the days, make a living 丨·量 consideration, capacity 丨·數 number of degrees 程·丨 grade, qualification, degree 法丨 rules, method, pattern 過丨 extravagance, excess	to^{4}	A
渡^{4}	水 85	度 200	To ford, cross 丨河; a ferry 丨船 a ferry boat 擺丨 丨口 ferry landing. 丨°過 cross over		B
鍍^{4}	金 167	度 200	To plate, gild e. g. 丨金, 丨銀 丨金作 a gilder's shop		F
杜^{4}	木 75	土 43	Printing-block wood i.e. wild pear; stop up, prevent S. 丨撰 bogus, fictitious 丨弊 stop corrupt practices		H

肚[4]	肉 130	土 43	Belly, temper ｜脹 swelling of the belly ｜臍 (眼) the navel ｜腹 the abdomen, belly ｜·量 bigness or smallness of mind ｜飽 a stomachful of food ｜帶 girth for saddle or harness ｜·子 the belly ｜·子疼 to have the belly ache 走｜to have diarrhoea 跑｜, 瀉｜	tu³	C
妒[4] 妬[4]	女 38	戶 728	Jealous, envious 忌·｜, 嫉·｜, ｜·嫉 ｜婦 a jealous woman 生｜心 give way to envy		D
瀆[2]	冫 15	賣 864	Trouble, profane ｜聽 importune to listen ｜請		E
匵[2] 櫝[2]	匚 22	賣 864	A case, sheath, coffin 啓｜to open a casket 劍｜a scabbard		H
瀆[2]	水 85	賣 864	Foul, ditch, drain, to profane 褻｜to profane, blaspheme		H
蠹[4] 蠧[4]	虫 142	虫 785	Worms in books, clothes, or wood ｜毛虫 hairy caterpillar ｜·魚 book-worm ｜虫; also fig.		H
碡[4]	石 112	毋 571	A stone roller 碌｜		H

T'u

禿[1]	禾 115	禾 510	Bald, bare, blunt ｜頭 ｜尖兒 a blunt point ｜·子 bald-headed person		D
嗸[1]	口 30	禾 510	Thick, tongue-tied, lisping		I
瘏[1]	疒 104	禾 510	Scald-head, head sores ｜瘡		I
吐[1]	口 30	土 43	Pout out the lips ｜·嚕嘴	t'u³⁴	D

T'u

圖[2]	囗 31	啚 767	Chart, plan, map; seal; to scheme, covet, reckon on |·章 seal | 記, |·書 | 强 ambition; make an effort | 像 likeness of any thing | 畫 picture, illustration; draw | 利 scheme after gain; so | 名 | 謀 to plan, plot | 書館 library |∘樣 a plan, a design 貪 | greedily desire, covet		B
徒[2] 迲[2]	彳 60	走 134	Disciple, apprentice; vainly | 刑 banishment | 罪 | 然 in vain, uselessly | 事 | 勞 to labor in vain |·弟 a pupil, an apprentice 匪 | vagabonds, banditti 門 | pupil, disciple, follower 使 | an Apostle		B
塗[2]	土 32	余 31	Daub, smear, erase, blot out | 抹 | 改 to blot out and alter 糊·| dull, stupid (read tu)		B
荼[2]	艸 140	余 31	A bitter herb, sowthistle | 毒 bitter and poisonous		G
途[2]	辵 162	余 31	Road, way, path, pursuit | 程 a road, route 路 | 前 | the future		E
纛[2]	糸 120	毋 571	Banner, standard	tu[2]	G
屠[2]	尸 44	者 192	To kill, butcher | 宰 S. |∘戶 a butcher | 人 | 戮 to exterminate | 滅		H
土[3]	土 32	土 43	Earth, soil; place, local | 產 products of the soil | 耳其 Turkey. | 紅 dull red | 匪 local robbers, banditti | 星 the planet Saturn		A

土[3]
| 話 local dialect, patois
| 人 native of a place
| 岡 rising-ground. | 塊 clod
| 木工程 civil engineering
| 坏 unburnt brick. | 山子 mound
| 坡 bank, slope
|∘地神 guardians of the soil
| 作 a navvy. | 腰 isthmus
| 曜日 Saturday
| 音 local sounds, dialect
黃 | clay, loess
地 | earth, territory

吐[3] 口 30 土 43 To vomit up; blossom — t'u[14] — D
|·出來 spit out. | 花 blossom
| 咕朶兒 to bud (as flowers)
| 實話 divulge the truth
| 痰 expectorate phlegm

吐[4] 口 30 土 43 To vomit, spit — t'u[13] — D
| 血 to spit blood

唾[4] 口 30 垂 26 To spit, spittle, saliva |·沫 俗 — t'o[4] — E
|·沫盒 spittoon

兔[4] 兎[4] 儿 10 兔 385 Hare, rabbit, | 兒 — E
|·子 a catamite, sodomite
家 | domestic rabbit 白 |
山 | wild hare 野 |

突[4] 穴 116 穴 394 To rush out, run against; protrude; rude, suddenly — F
| 然 suddenly, abruptly
衝·| rush against, variance

忑[42] 心 61 卜 119 Timorous 忐 | 俗 — t'e[4] — H

Tuan

耑[1] 而 126 耑 614 Origin, cause — chuan[1] — H

端[1] 立 117 耑 614 Origin, head; upright, correct — A
|∘正 correct, upright | 方

Tuan

<table>
<tr><td>端[1]</td><td></td><td></td><td>| 莊 modest, coy, dignified
| 飯 bring on the food | 菜, |·上
| 然 smoothly, evenly
| 盆 carry dish with hands
| 午 dragon boat festival (5th of 5th Moon) | 陽節
造 | make beginning 開 |</td><td></td></tr>
<tr><td>短[3]</td><td>矢
111</td><td>豆
731</td><td>Short, brief; few, deficient
|·處 shortcomings, faults
| 禮 impolite, discourteous
| 命 short life. |·不了[3] frequently
| 數 short in count; e.g., cash
| 刀 dagger. | 促 early death
| 少 less than, too few | 缺</td><td>A</td></tr>
<tr><td>斷[4]
断[4]</td><td>斤
69</td><td>㡭
882</td><td>To break, cut off |∘開, discontinue, decide, surely
| 案 to decide a case
| 氣 breathe one's last
| 交 break off intimacy | 來往
| 酒 break off wine, so | 煙, | 癮
| 絕交通 cut off communication
| 絕關係 break off relations
|·乎 certainly; e.g., |·乎不可
| 然 undoubtedly
| 乳 to wean a child | 奶
| 不肯 absolutely refuse
| 事 to decide affairs
| 定 to decide, to give a judgment 決 |
公 | a just decision</td><td>B</td></tr>
<tr><td>段[4]</td><td>殳
79</td><td>段
401</td><td>Piece, section, paragraph; C. of sections S.
一 | 地, 一 | 水, 一 | 書
手·| workmanship, method</td><td>D</td></tr>
<tr><td>煅[4]
鍛[4]</td><td>火
86</td><td>段
401</td><td>To forge; practice, make perfect
| 灰 to calcine, make lime
| 鍊 work metal; make perfect</td><td>H</td></tr>
</table>

Character	Radical	Phonetic	Definition	Alt.	Group
緞4	糸 120	段 401	Satin ｜·子, 花｜brocade 綢｜silk and satin		D

T'uan

Character	Radical	Phonetic	Definition	Alt.	Group
團2	口 31	專 839	Round; a mass, group, guard ｜結 collect, affiliation ｜結力 united strength, unity ｜體 organization, group ｜｜conglomerated ｜·圓 circle; united; full moon		B
摶2	手 64	專 839	To roll into ball, pat, model ｜成丸子 roll into pills ｜土爲人 model men of clay		F
糰2 糐2	米 119	專 839	Dumpling of flour or glutinous rice; doughnut ｜粉 paste for thick gravy		H
疃3 畽3	田 102	童 829	Village, alley ｜怨 reckless, regardless		K
彖3	彐 58	彖 287	A hog running, "definitions" of the "I Ching" classic		K

Tui

Character	Radical	Phonetic	Definition	Alt.	Group
堆1 自1	土 32	隹 52	Heap, pile, to heap; C. of piles ｜積 to pile together ｜·房 warehouse. ｜·子 sentry-box 土｜子 dust-heap, mound	tsui1	C
對4 对4	寸 41	寸 18	To front, suit; a pair, to oppose; reply; to add to (as fluids) ｜陣 to fight; opposing armies ｜·證 to prove, verify ｜襟 single-breasted coat ｜勁兒 to one's liking, to agree ｜·着 facing, opposite｜過, 相｜ ｜鐘表 set clock or watch		A

對[4]			| 縫兒[4] fit closely at edges |·付 match, agree, suitable; make the best of | 心思 to one's mind | 人說 to speak to a person | 稿 to correct proof 較 | | 光 (spectacles) fitted to the eyes | 聯 antithetical sentences |·子 |·不起 offend a person |·不住 | 手 a match for, one's equal | 數兒 to check figures | 說 to reply to | 答 |∘待 attitude or relation to |∘頭 opponent. | 敵 join battle | 調 officers exchange posts |·於 in relation to, regarding 反 | oppose. 相[1] | agreeing		
兌[4]	儿 10	兌 756	To exchange, pay, barter | 換 | 賬 to pay on account | 換券 draft, bill of exchange | 銀子 weigh silver, cash draft 匯 | "exchange" on other place		C
㒸[4]	八 12	㒸 288	Company		P
隊[4]	阜 170	㒸 288	A company of 50, regiment 兵 | | 長[3] lieutenant. | 官 captain | 球 volley-ball |·伍 rank and file, ranks		C
碓[4]	石 112	隹 52	Foot-pestle | 頭; pound | 臼 pestle and mortar | 搗 to pound in mortar		I

T'ui

推[1]	手 64	隹 52	To push; decline | 讓, shirk | 車 push wheelbarrow | 己及人 put self in his place |·進去 push in		B

推[1]			｜進力 momentum	
			｜究 scrutinize. ｜求 investigate	
			｜舉 recommend, nominate	
			｜拒 to dismiss, decline	
			｜却 to decline, refuse ｜辭	
			｜翻 to overthrow ｜倒[3]	
			｜·開 push away or open, evade	
			｜故 make excuses ｜∘脫, ｜諉	
			｜廣 extend, enlarge upon	
			｜類 analogy. ｜理 reasoning	
			｜論 to reason, conclusion ｜定	
			｜磨 (mo[4]) turn the mill stone	
			｜·事 judge, justice	
			｜·子 clippers	
			｜原 search original cause	
頹[2]	頁 181	禾 510	To collapse; ruin, dilapidated	H
			｜壞 destroyed, collapsed	
			｜然 drooping, relaxed	
			衰｜(also read t'ei[2]) decayed	
腿[3] 骽[3]	肉 130	艮 359	Leg, thigh, ham	B
			｜快 good walker	
			｜瘦 leg-ache	
			｜帶子 garters	
			｜肚子 calf of leg	
			｜腕子 the bend of the knee	
			火｜hams. 大｜the thigh	
退[4]	辵 162	艮 359	To retire, withdraw; decline	B
			｜職 resign, retire, abdicate ｜位	
			｜親 break off engagement ｜婚	
			｜學 give up study	
			｜化 decadence, deterioration	
			｜回 to retire, withdraw ｜·去	
			｜讓 to yield, abdicate	
			｜皮 cast skin. 辭｜refuse	
			｜縮 recede, shrink, draw in	
			｜伍 disband soldiers	
			倒[4]｜to step back, retire ｜∘步	

Tun

蹲^{1}	足 157	尊 783	To squat on heels |·着; reside |居 to be detained in an inn 狗| dog sitting on its hams		E
敦^{1} 惇^{1}	攴 66	敦 746	Honest; to urge; generous; substantial |厚 honest, generous, staunch |篤 strongly built, consolidate		F
墩^{1}	土 32	敦 746	A mound, beacon; stand; ton |堡 a beacon mound, tower |台 |布 a mop, scrub-cloth		I
撴^{1}	手 64	敦 746	To strike, thump, jolt |的慌 jolting unpleasantly		I
橔^{1}	木 75	敦 746	A coffin cover |·子 a wooden chopping block		K
不^{1}	木 75	不 120	A stump, 樹|·子, block, hillock		K
盹^{3}	目 109	屯 376	Dim sight; to doze, nod |睡 to nod, doze 瞌|, 打|兒	tun^{4}	F
躉^{3}	足 157	萬 576	Store, wholesale, warehouse |貨 to buy up goods, "corner" |賣 to sell wholesale		I
囤^{4}	口 31	屯 376	A bin for grain; monopolize |積 store up; hoard 米| a rice-bin		G
扽^{4}	手 64	屯 376	To shake |掣, move, bob		H
沌^{4}	水 85	屯 376	Turbid, chaotic 混|		G
鈍^{4}	金 167	屯 376	Blunt, dull, obtuse |角 an obtuse angle |尖 blunt & sharp, blunt point |刀 a blunt knife 遲| slow in thought or action		D

飩^4	食 184	屯 376	餛 | boiled meat-balls wrapped in dough		K
頓^4	頁 181	屯 376	To bow; a pause, time; meal; prepare; suddenly; a ton | 脚 to stamp the foot | 足 | 首 to bow the head | | 飯 at every meal 打·了·一·| gave a beating		E
噸^4	口 30	屯 376	A ton		F
盾^4	目 109	盾 844	A shield, buckler | 牌		D
遁^4	辵 162	盾 844	Retire, vanish, skulk, hide |·去 | 藏 to conceal 隱 | | 走 skulk off, run away 逃 |		F
燉^4	火 86	敦 746	To stew, heat, boil; as | 肉		G
遯^4	辵 162	豕 285	To hide, concealed | 跡		H

T'un

吞^1	口 30	天 462	To swallow, gulp; appropriate | 佔 to usurp, engross | 金 gold leaf suicide | 下 swallow, bolt; so |·不下 | 聲 repress one's feelings | 氣 | | 吐吐 stutter, stammer		D
屯^2	屮 45	屯 376	A camp, village, assemble | 聚 encamp, encampment | 紮 | 糧 to store grain | 兵 troops quartered out |·子 a village | 兒	chun^1	E
豚^2	豕 152	豕 285	Sucking pig, porker 肥 | | 柵 pig-sty | 蹄 pig's feet		H

Character	Radical	Phonetic	Definition		Tone
臀[2]	肉 130	共 95	The seat, buttocks or nates		I
褪[4]	衣 154	艮 359	To draw in, retractile; take off ｜骨雞 a boned chicken ｜衣裳 put off clothes ｜手 draw hands into sleeves ｜頭 draw in head, as tortoise		G

Tung

Character	Radical	Phonetic	Definition		Tone
東[1] 东[1]	木 75	東 504	East, eastern S. ｜·家 a master, host ｜人 ｜京 Tokio, capital of Japan ｜方 eastern regions, east; double surname S. ｜·西 east and west; a thing ｜南西北 E.S.W.N. (fixed order) ｜陵 eastern mausoleum ｜南 the south-east; so ｜北 ｜跑西奔 run hither and thither ｜·邊 east side, east of here ｜三省 Manchuria ｜倒[3]西歪 reeling drunk, toppling ｜·道 a spread, a treat ｜兒 ｜亞 Eastern Asia ｜°洋 eastern sea; Japan (｜)洋車 a jinriksha		A
冬[1]	冫 15	冬 541	Winter, ｜·天, ｜日, ｜景天 ｜至 the winter solstice ｜節 ｜·瓜 a kind of pumpkin ｜筍 edible bamboo shoots ｜·月 the 11th month ｜·子月 過｜ pass the winter 立｜ beginning of winter		A
董[3]	艸 140	重 27	To regulate, lead, manage; firm; store up S. ｜·事 a manager, trustee		C

Tung

董[3]
| 事部 Board of Managers
紳 | gentry and elders

懂[3] 心 61 重 27 To understand |·得 — A
| 人情 understand human nature
|·不·| do you understand?
懵 | bewildered, demented

動[4] 力 19 重 27 To move, influence, shake; excite — A
| 產 chattels, movable effects
| 機 motive, inducement
| 氣 to be angry | 火, | 怒
|·靜 motion and rest, conduct
| 心 to move the heart
| 工 to commence work
| 力 personal or polit. influence
| 兵 to move troops | 刀兵
|·不∘| constantly; for nothing
| 身 to make a move, start
| 手 put hand to anything
|·揮 move, shake. | 詞 a verb
|∘作 behavior, process
| 土 go to work (as digging)
|∘物界 animal kingdom
|∘物學 zoology
|∘物園 zoological gardens
| 搖 unsteady, wavering 搖 |
| 員令 order to mobilize
別 | don't move! don't touch it!

凍[4] 冫 15 東 504 To freeze | 冰; cold; stiffen — C
|∘著[2] caught cold. | 破 chap
| 瘡 frost sores, chilblains
|·死 to freeze to death

棟[4] 木 75 東 504 Roof-beam; able man, chief — F
| 梁 pillars of state

洞[4] 水 85 同 580 Hole, cave; see through, know — D
| 徹 deeply clever, see through
| 房 bridal-chamber

洞[4]			丨穴 a cavern, cave 丨兒, 山丨 丨明 to comprehend 丨悉	

T'ung

通[1]	辵 162	甬 594	To go through; perceive; succeed; pervade; general, all of S. 丨常 regular, customary 丨鑑 univ. mirror, famous history 丨知 to inform, acquaint 丨縣 Tunghsien (near Peking) 丨信 send letter, correspond 丨信所 address of letter 丨信處 丨信員 reporter, correspondent 丨行 current, general use 丨·融 to accommodate; to compromise 丨告書 a circular, a notice 丨共 whole, all 丨 丨·的 丨過 passed through, motion passed 丨理 to understand reason 丨報 to announce. 丨商 commerce 丨商口岸 treaty ports 丨身 whole body. 丨·事 interpreter 丨書 an almanack 丨俗 popular, suiting public 丨俗教育 simple educ. for adults 丨俗語 colloquial speech 丨達 thorough understanding 丨·條 poker. 丨用 in common use 交丨 intercourse, communication	B
鼕[1]	鼓 207	冬 541	Rattle of drums	H
恫[2]	心 61	同 580	To moan 呻丨; dissatisfied 哀丨 alas! alas!	I

T'ung

Character	Radical	Phonetic	Definition	Class
同^{2} 仝^{2}	口 30	同 580	Together, united; all; and, with; identical; (used for 衕) ｜志 united in aim, comrades ｜治 Emperor before 光緒 1862-75 ｜情 fellow-feeling, sympathy ｜居 fellow-lodgers; cohabit ｜窗 fellow-student ｜學 ｜種國 lands of kindred race ｜房 in the same room ｜行 (hang²) of same class or trade ｜席 a fellow-guest ｜鄉 natives of same region ｜心 of the same mind ｜心合意 ｜行 cooperate, go together ｜姓 same surname; so ｜名 ｜一 unity, identity ｜意 same idea, to confirm ｜人 associate, companion ｜伴 ｜類 of the same species ｜等 ｜力合作 cooperation ｜盟 brotherhood, confederacy ｜盟國 allied nations ｜謀 to plot together ｜年 same year; fellow-grads. ｜胞 same mother, same race ｜輩 same class or generation ｜時 contemporary. ｜·他 with him ｜事 same affair. ｜歲 same age ｜在 at same place, company with ｜坐 to sit together ｜文｜種 of same language and race	A
峒^{2}	山 46	同 580	Islands off Shantung	H
桐^{2}	木 75	同 580	Paint tree ｜樹, 梧｜樹 ｜油 oil of the dryandra tree seeds	F

T'ung

筒[23]	竹 118	同 580	A pipe, tube, duct |·子 煙·| chimney, tobacco-pipe		E
銅[2]	金 167	同 580	Copper (紅 |), brass(黃 |), bronze |·器 copper or brass ware |·匠 brazier, coppersmith | 錢 copper coin | 像 bronze statue | 礦 copper mine. | 綠 verdigris | 板 copper type, copper cent | 片 sheet copper. | 絲 wire | 子兒[3] copper cent | 元		A
童[2]	立 117	童 829	Boy, girl, virgin; student S. | 貞女 a virgin. | 女 girl, maiden | 蒙[3] a youth; a dolt, | 男 a boy | 子軍 Boy Scouts 孩 | a child, boy		C
潼[2]	水 85	童 829	A river and pass in Shensi		I
瞳[2]	目 109	童 829	Pupil of eye | 人 or | 仁		F
佟[2]	人 9	冬 541	A sorcerer S.		H
統[3]	糸 120	充 870	All, general; to gather; control | 計 statistics; to estimate | 治權 administrative control | 轄 to govern the whole | 系 a system 系 | | 緒 a clue; succession | 一 to unify, centralized | 一黨 union party | 共 altogether, total — | 宣 | last Ch'ing Emperor 1908-11 總 | President of Republic		B
捅[3]	手 64	甬 594	To strike against, punch into | 破 break a hole through		I

桶[3]	木 75	甬 594	Bucket, tub, pail, cask 水 | a water cask; buckets 子孫 | midwife's tub	C
痛[4]	疒 104	甬 594	Pain, ache; extremely | 恨 bitter hatred | 悔 bitter repentance | 哭 to cry bitterly |·快 delighted, outspoken 疼 | in pain; love tenderly	A
衕[42]	行 144	同 580	Street, lane 衚 |[4] (同[4] also used)	A
慟[4]	心 61	重 27	Moved, affected, to grieve 心 | | 切 the feelings stirred | 哭 to be moved to tears 哀 | extreme grief	E

Tzu

咨[1] 諮[1]	口 30	次 442	To deliberate, plan, report; a dispatch; sigh, ah! | 嗟 to sigh, lament | 訪 write to inquire about | 稟 state to a superior |·謀 to plot, plan	H
姿[1]	女 38	次 442	Beauty; manner, disposition | 質 endowments, talents | 色 beautiful; a beauty | 容 性 | disposition, temper	H
恣[14]	心 61	次 442	Licentious; rude; dissipation | 意 licentious feelings | 縱 loose, dissipated 放 |	H
資[1]	貝 154	次 442	Property, funds; fees, aid, subscriptions; to help, trust |·質 natural disposition | 稟 | 助 to help | 貨 goods, commodities |·格 ability, character	E

資[1]			｜本 capital. ｜本團 syndicate ｜本家 capitalists, financiers ｜財 property, funds ｜產 捐｜to contribute money	
貲[1]	貝 154	此 129	Property; a ransom, fine ｜贖 家｜family property	E
髭[1]	髟 190	此 129	Moustache	I
齜[1]	齒 211	此 129	Projecting teeth; to show teeth ｜牙 ｜·着牙 teeth which show	I
茲[1] 玆[1]	艸 140	玆 880	A mat; this, it; now, here ｜者 now, at present moment 今｜ ｜因 now because of	F
孳[1]	子 39	玆 880	To breed, bear ｜生; diligent ｜｜indefatigable diligence	I
滋[1]	水 85	玆 880	Fertile, to enrich; stir up; moisten; sap ｜潤 ｜補 supply what is wanting ｜生 to produce, increase ｜事 to pick a quarrel ｜味 taste, flavor	E
輜[1]	車 159	田 809	Baggage-wagon ｜重隊 army service corps	I
孜[1]	子 39	子 112	Unwearied effort, diligent ｜｜爲善 diligence in virtue 喜｜｜·的 covered with smiles	I
子[3]	子 39	子 112	Child, son; seed; sir; noun-ending ｜粒 a grain, seed ｜民 the people ｜女 sons and daughters ｜時 11 to 1 o'clock, midnight ｜嗣 children, offspring ｜系, ｜∘孫 ｜彈[4] cartridges. 兒·｜ son, boy ｜∘弟 sons and young brothers ｜財 income, interest	A
仔[3]	人 9	子 112	To bear, carry as a nurse; careful ｜·細 careful, minutely	F

Tzu

籽[3] 米 119 子 112 Seeds of cereals | 粒 H

紫[3] 糸 120 此 129 Purple, dark red, brown | 色 D
| 禁城 Imperial City, Peking
| 竹林 foreign city at Tientsin
| 檀 red sandal wood
| 菜 agar-agar, seaweed

朿[3] 丿 4 朿 250 To stop P

姊[3] 姉[3] 女 38 朿 250 Elder sister D
|·妹 sisters, a sister
| 弟 sister and brother

滓[3] 水 85 辛 157 Sediment, dregs | 泥, 埿 |
渣 | sediment, remnants F

自[4] 自 132 自 852 Spontaneous, naturally; from; self, personally A
| 己 oneself | 己各 (ko[3]) 兒
| 己的 one's own
| 欺 self-deceived. | 謙 humble
| 節 self-control | 治, | 持
| 知 or 覺 conscious of, to know oneself
| 治權 autonomy
| 治團體 self-governing body
| 今以後 from this time forth
| 盡 to commit suicide
| 主 free-willed, independent
| 主權 sovereignty, free will
| 取其禍 calamity self-inflicted
| 專 self-opinionated, "bossy"
| 傳 autobiography
| 重 self-respect
| 覺心 self-consciousness
| 發 spontaneous
| 費生 self-supporting students
| 信 self-confidence

自^4

|∘行車 a toy; a bicycle
| 省 (hsing^3) self examination
| 修 self-culture
| 以為是 self-opinionated
|∘然 certainly; spontaneous, naturally. | 然界 nature
| 然而然 certainly, naturally
| 然神學 natural theology
| 然淘汰 natural selection
| 高 proud | 大. | 誇 to boast
| 古以來 from ancient times
| 顧 | look out for oneself
| 來水 waterworks
| 立 | 養 self-support (of churches)
| 滿 self-satisfied | 足
| 便 convenient to oneself
|·在 be one's self, composed
| 在畫 free-hand drawing
| 作 | 受 it is your own fault
| 從 since, from that time
| 動 automatic. | 衛 self-defense
| 問 to examine oneself
| 言 | 語 to soliloquize
| 由 have way, liberty, freedom
| 由權 freedom
| 由行動 freedom of action
| 由言論 freedom of speech
| 幼 from youth up
| 用 use own discretion

字^4 子 39 子 112 To shelter, love; a written Chinese word, name 名·| , style — A

| 跡 hand-writing
| 據 written proof, a license
|·號 mark; style; sign; name, firm
| 彙 a dictionary (small) | 典
| 母 the alphabet; initials
| 部 the Chinese radicals

字[4]			| 帖 (t'ich[4]) copy-slip | 眼 meaning and use of characters		
牸[4]	牛 93	子 112	A cow | 牛. | 馬 a mare		I
漬[4]	水 85	責 83	To soak, stain, damage 浸 | soak through 水 | water-soaked		K

Tz'u

差[1]	工 48	差 178	Uneven 參 (ts'en[1]) |	ch'a[14] ch'ai[1]	A
疵[12]	疒 104	此 129	Flaw, blemish, fault | 病, 瑕 | 吹毛求 | fault-finding		E
辭[2] 辤[2] 辞[2]	辛 160 减	𤔔 535	Words, expression, phrase; to refuse; resign; excuse, take leave | 呈 letter of resignation | 職 resign office | 官 | 謝 to decline with thanks | 館 throw up position as teacher | 別 to separate, leave | 行 | 世 to die. | 退 refuse 推 | | 典 a dictionary | 脫 to decline, avoid 告 | take leave; resign		B
慈[2] 慈[2]	心 61	兹 880	Kind, gentle, compassionate | 愛 kindness, love, mercy 仁 | | 心 tender-hearted | 惠 love, kindness. |。悲 mercy | 善 sympathy, compassion 恩 | | 善家 philanthropists 令 | your mother		C
磁[2] 瓷[2]	石 112	兹 880	Porcelain, crockery |·器 | 瓶 porcelain vase | 石 loadstone, a magnet		B
鷀[2]	鳥 196	兹 880	Fishing cormorant		H

Tz'u

祠^{2}	示 113	司 701	Ancestral hall; tablet; spring |堂 hall of ancestors		H
詞^{2}	言 149	司 701	Word; phrase, style; statement; to ask (used for 辭) |句 wording, text |曲 (ch'ü^{3}) songs, ballads, etc. 言| an expression, language		D
雌^{2}	隹 172	此 129	Female of birds; weak |雄 female and male birds		H
茨^{2}	艸 140	次 442	Thatch, to thatch 茅| a thatched cottage		H
此^{3}	止 77	此 129	This, here. |人 this man |處 this place, here |地, 在| |後 after this |刻 at present, just now |時 |等 this class, kind, sort		B
跐^{3}	足 157	此 129	To tread on, step, trample |蹈 |穩 to tread firmly	ch'ai^{3} ts'ai^{3}	E
賜^{4}	貝 154	易 235	To give, confer, bestow |予, 賞| |爵 confer rank of nobility |恩 to bestow favor |惠 |福 to bestow blessings 恩| gracious gift		B
次^{4}	欠 76	次 442	Second, inferior; next; a time |·序 regular order |∘第 |日 next day. 依| in order |等 second quality |子^{3} second son. 一| once 其| the next. 下·| next time		B
朿^{4} 莿^{4}	木 75	朿 500	A thorn; sarcastic |玫花 the prickly rose		G
刺^{4}	刀 18	朿 500	Thorn; prick, stab; tablet, card; lampoon |綉 embroider. |刀 a bayonet |∘客 assassin. |殺 assassinate		C

Character	Radical	Phonetic	Meaning	Alt. reading	
刺4			|撓 to itch, tingle |透了 pierced through 激| incitement, stimulus, |激		
伺4	人 9	司 701	To wait upon; spy, examine |查 to examine into szu4 |·候 to wait on, serve |應 |探 to spy out, find out 窺| szu4	szu4	E
廁4 厠4	广 53	則 858	A privy; to arrange |所 water closet	szu4	E
蠀4	虫 142	茲 880	Spiny-haired caterpillar |◦蝟 hedge hog		K

Wa

Character	Radical	Phonetic	Meaning	Alt. reading	
挖1	手 64	穴 394	To dig out, gouge, pick |掘 |井 dig well- 挑| clear out |坑 scoop out a hole in ground |窟窿 to dig through (as a wall, floor, board) |◦補 to erase and patch up		C
哇1	口 30	圭 48	Wanton; to coax; vomit |喇 a sound (cry of baby) |吐 to spit out, vomit		H
窪1	穴 116	圭 48	A puddle, low ground |地 |凹 hollow collecting rain		E
蛙1 鼃1	虫 142	圭 48	Green frog; wanton 井底| narrow-visioned		F
凹1	凵 17	凵 650	A hollow, dug-out cavity 俗 |地 a hollow place |凸 concave and convex |字 in-cut characters	yao12	G
呱14	口 30	瓜 407	To cry as a child |·的一聲哭了 打| |groan with distress	ku1	I
窊1	穴 116	瓜 407	Depression, low (used for 窪, 凹) 草| grassy plateau, Mongolia		H

Character	Radical	Phonetic	Meaning	Alt.	Class
娃^2	女 38	圭 48	A girl baby, doll 丨·丨, 丨·子 丨·丨臉兒 "baby-faced", rosy		E
瓦^3	瓦 98	吾 763	Tiles, pottery earthenware 丨器 丨碴 fragment of pottery 丨片 丨·匠 mason; brick-layer 丨解 (fig.) separation, collapse; scattered 丨房 a tiled house 丨屋 丨罐 common earthen jar 丨隴 channels of tiled roof 丨盆 an earthen bowl 丨窰 tile kiln		C
搲^3	手 64	瓜 407	To grasp, pull to		I
襪^4	衣 145	蔑 343	Stockings, socks, hose 丨·子 丨·子肥 stockings too big 一雙丨·子 a pair of stockings		B

Wai

Character	Radical	Phonetic	Meaning	Alt.	Class
歪^1	止 77	不 120	Awry, aslant 丨斜, 丨扭; wicked 丨心 a depraved heart 丨脖子 wry-necked 丨頭 丨嘴 a distorted mouth		E
舀^3	臼 134	舀 682	To bale, dip, ladle 丨水 to bale water, or dip out	yao^3	F
外^4	夕 36	夕 267	Outside, foreign; extra 丨債 foreign loans 丨交家 diplomats 丨交部 Foreign Office 丨務部 丨交團 diplomatic body 丨僑 foreign settlers 丨行 (hang^2) not an expert, amateur, layman, amateur(ish) 丨號 nick-name. 丨·人 outsider 丨感 outside influence; a cold 丨科 surgery. 丨褂 outer coat		A

外^{4}
|∘國 a foreign country | 邦
| 貌 external appearance
|·面 the outer surface |·邊
|·甥 a sister's son, nephew, so |·甥女
| 省 (sheng^{3}) other provinces
|·頭 outside
| 財 illegitimate gain
| 祖 maternal grandfather
| 祖母 maternal grandmother

Wan

剜^{1} 刀 18 宛 272 E
To scoop out, pare, cut down
| 補 shape hole for patch
| 菜 cut vegetables by root
| 削 cut away, pare

豌^{1} 豆 151 宛 272 D
The garden pea | 豆
| 豆糕 pastry of peas

彎^{1} 弓 57 䜌 888 E
To bend, curve; draw a bow
| 曲 (ch'ü^{1}) curved, winding, bend
| 弓 to bend a bow, a curve
|·過來 to crook, bend, curve
| | 曲曲 very winding, crooked
| 腰 to stoop, hunch-backed

灣^{1} 水 85 䜌 888 F
Bend of a stream, bay; tortuous
| 船 to lie at anchor
海 | a bay

完^{2} 宀 40 完 389 A
To finish, completed, all done
| 整 completed | 成, 做 |·了
| 結 to complete, wind up | 畢
|∘全 complete, preserved entire
|∘全責任 full responsibility
| 固 strong and well made
|·備 fully prepared, ready

玩^{2} 玉 96 元 388 B
To enjoy; play; test; a toy; to examine into; rare

Character	Radical	Phonetic	Meaning		
玩^{2}			丨巧 perform clever tricks 丨兒 to play 丨耍, 丨弄 丨戲法兒 jugglers 丨笑 to quiz, jest. 丨話 jesting 丨意兒 playthings, toys, 丨物, 丨器 丨·不得 not to be fooled with 丨索 turn over in mind 丨·頭 amusement 古丨^{4} curios, antiques		
頑^{2}	頁 181	元 388	Stupid, obstinate, mulish; fun 丨·固 conservative, reactionary 丨皮 mischievous; obstinate 丨梗		F
丸^{2}	丶 3	丸 303	Pill, ball, pellet. 丨藥 pills 肉丨·子 balls of meat		E
紈^{2}	糸 120	丸 303	White silk. 丨扇 silk fans		I
宛^{3}	宀 40	宛 272	To give way, yield, obliging 丨轉 bring things round to point 丨平縣 Peking's western district		H
婉^{3}	女 38	宛 272	Obliging, kind, docile, winning 丨言 courteous words		G
碗^{3} 盌^{3} 椀^{3}	石 112 木 75	宛 272	Cup, bowl, deep dish 一丨飯 丨盞杯盤 crockery-ware 飯丨 rice-bowl, living 火丨 bowl with heater		A
夗^{3}	夕 36	夗 271	To give way; turn in bed		K
娩^{3}	女 38	免 384	Winning, complaisant, obliging 丨順 accommodating, obliging	mien^{3}	H
挽^{3}	手 64	免 384	To lead, pull; lay hold; draw back; restore, regain 丨回 丨袖 to roll up the sleeves 丨回利權 recover lost privilege 丨留 detain by gentle force, retain		D

Wan

Character	Radical	Phonetic	Definition		
晚³	日 72	免 384	Evening; late, tardy 丨間 in the evening 丨·上 丨莊稼 second crop. 丨飯 supper 丨·了 late. 丨年 late in life 丨輩 juniors, inferiors 丨餐 the evening meal; the Lord's Supper 早丨 sooner or later		A
輓³	車 159	免 384	Draw a hearse; rope for hearse 丨詩 funeral ode, elegy 丨言		I
萬⁴ 万⁴ 卍⁴	艸 140	萬 576	A myriad, 10,000; many S. 丨福 innumerable blessings 丨幸 immense felicity 丨花筒 kaleidoscope 丨花鏡 丨一 just a possibility 丨古 from remotest antiquity 丨古流芳 famed for ages 丨國和平會 Hague Conference 丨國公法 International Law 丨里長城 Great Wall of China 丨民 masses. 丨能 all-powerful 丨不可 on no account 丨不能 丨不得已 to be obliged to do 丨牲園 zoological gardens 丨事 everything. 丨物 all things 丨壽 everlasting old age 丨·壽山 The Summer Palace near Peking 丨歲(爺) myriad years; Emperor 丨無一失 perfectly safe 丨物之靈 most intelligent, man 千。丨 by all means; don't fail		C
腕⁴ [illegible]⁴	肉 130	宛 272	The wrist, universal joint, 手丨 丨力 capacity, ability 肘丨 the elbow		F
蔓⁴	艸 140	曼 849	Tendril, vine; to creep, spread 爬丨·子 a climbing plant	man²	G

Wang

Character	Radical	Phonetic	Definition	Alt.	Group
汪[1]	水 85	王 71	Expanse of water; watery ｜｜ S. ｜水 vast expanse of water ｜洋 the open sea		H
尢[1] 尣[1]	尢 43	尢 174	Lame, weak; crooked		K
王[2]	玉 96	王 71	King, prince ｜子[3], ｜·爺; ruler; royal S. ｜爵 rank of a prince ｜位 ｜法 laws, royal laws ｜府 palace of a prince ｜化 civil. influence of good gov't ｜·八 a bastard, tortoise		B
亡[2] 亾[2]	亠 8	亡 646	Destroyed, gone, lost, dead ｜種 (chung[3]) race extinction ｜故 dead, perished 死｜ ｜國 national extinction ｜國奴 slave without a country ｜羊 a lostsheep 滅｜ exterminated, dead 敗｜ defeat; 陣.｜ killed in battle	wu[2]	C
往[3] 徃[3]	彳 60	王 71	To go past; proceed toward ｜常 hitherto, usual ｜者不追 let bygones be bygones ｜返 to go and come ｜復 ｜[4]好裏學 study that which is good ｜古 of old, in ancient times ｜來 to and fro; intercourse 來｜ ｜年 last year, formerly ｜日 ｜｜ repeatedly, frequently 前｜ to proceed to, advance	wang[4]	B
枉[3]	木 75	王 71	In vain ｜然; oppression, wrong ｜費 expend in vain, waste 寃·｜ wrong, grievance		D

Wang

罔^{3} 网^{3}	网 122	罔 647	To deceive; not, without; net ｜然 undecided, irresolute ｜談 don't speak of it		E
網^{3}	糸 120	罔 647	A net, web, ｜·子, ｜羅; to entrap ｜球 tennis. 撒｜ cast net 設｜ set a net 張｜, 布｜		B
魍^{3}	鬼 194	罔 647	Undine, a sprite, elf		I
妄^{4}	女 38	亡 646	Reckless, wild; false, absurd ｜證 false evidence ｜取 to steal, misappropriate ｜費 to squander, waste ｜想 indulge in vain hopes ｜告 to accuse falsely ｜殺 put to death unjustly ｜誕 unfounded stories ｜爲^{2} disorderly behavior		D
忘^{42}	心 61	亡 646	To forget, absent-minded ｜·記 ｜恩 ungrateful ｜本 ｜·不了^{3} I can not forget		G
望^{4}	月 74	亡 646	To look at; towards; hope, expect 盼·｜, 希｜ ｜·見 look toward, be visible ｜日 15th of moon ｜月 ｜日蓮 the sun-flower ｜看 to visit 探｜ ｜道的 a religious inquirer ｜遠 to look to a distance 指·｜ to desire, hope 想｜		A
往^{4}	彳 60	王 71	To go toward; look toward ｜前 to go forward ｜後 to go behind, hereafter ｜下 henceforth. ｜東 go east ｜那兒^{3}去 where are you going?	wang^{3}	B

旺[4]	日 72	王 71	Vigorous; prosperous; bright |地 a prosperous place |運 good fortune, luck 興[1]◦| to prosper, prosperous 火| a blazing fire		B

Wei

微[12]	彳 60	徵 550	Small, minute; subtle, obscure |敬 a trifling present |蟲 microbes, bacteria |生物 |笑 smile. |弱 sickly, feeble |妙 abstruse, minute, subtle |末 very small |小, |細 |點 small particle |物 an insignificant thing		B
威[1]	女 38	女 552	Pomp, majesty, awe-inspiring |權 authority, power, pomp |勢 |·風 grandeur, majesty |逼 browbeat, tyrannize |嚇 |◦武 martial. |嚴 grave, stern		C
蝟[1] 猬[1]	虫 142	胃 617	Hedge hog, porcupine 螆| hedge hog		F
倭[1]	人 9	委 512	To yield, bend	wo1	G
萎[1]	艸 140	委 512	To wither, dry |落		K
巍[1]	山 46	委 512	Lofty, exalted, eminent | |		K
煨[1]	火 86	畏 352	To bake in ashes |炭 burn coal or charcoal		
爲[2] 為[2]	爪 87	爲 260	To do; be; make; cause |非 to act wickedly |惡 |人 act as a man; character |難[2] to be in difficulties	wei4	A

Character	Radical	Phonetic	Meaning	Other reading	Class
爲[2]			丨善 to do good. 行·丨 conduct 丨是 be right, correct		
韋[2]	韋 178	韋 764	Leather, hide; refractory S. 丨陀 the Vedas		G
圍[2]	囗 31	韋 764	To surround, besiege, enclose 丨城 surrounding wall, besiege 丨棋 chess. 丨·屏 folding screen 丨·着 surrounded, beset 丨·住 丨繞 to wrap round, besiege 丨·子 mud ramparts, cart hood 打丨 to hunt or shoot game 範丨 sphere, environment		D
幃[2]	巾 50	韋 764	Curtain, women's room 丨帳		G
違[2]	辵 162	韋 764	To disobey, disregard, oppose 丨背 丨禁 disregard a prohibition 丨理 contrary to reason		B
唯[2]	口 30	隹 52	But, only (used for 惟, 維) 丨心論 idealism 丨理論 rationalism 丨物主義 materialism 丨物論	wei[3]	F
帷[2]	巾 50	隹 52	Curtain, screen, veil 丨帳 丨·裙 apron. 丨幕 screen 丨屏		F
惟[2]	心 61	隹 52	Only, but, just so, and; namely 丨一 unity, single, unique 丨恐 I fear, lest, perchance 丨。獨 the exception, only 丨有 there is only, but		D
維[2]	糸 120	隹 52	Carriage curtain; to tie; maintain; but, only 丨持 to help; maintain 丨持治安 to maintain the peace 丨持人道 work for human uplift 丨新 new, novel; reform 四丨 4 cardinal virtues 禮,義,廉,恥		C
濰[2]	水 85	隹 52	River in Shantung		I

Wei

危[2]	卩 26	危 197	Dangerous, peril, hazard S. ｜機 crisis, danger-point ｜險 danger, peril, hazard ｜急 ｜病 dangerous illness ｜言 bold words		E
桅[2]	木 75	危 197	A mast. ｜·杆, 船｜		E
薇[2]	艸 140	徵 550	Herbs; a fern 紫｜花 the crepe myrtle		I
囗[2]	囗 31	囗 765	An enclosure		K
尾[3]	尸 44	毛 375	Tail, end, stern; C. of fish ｜末 fag end, utmost ｜底 首｜beginning and end 頭｜	i[3]	C
娓[3]	女 38	毛 375	To comply with ｜順 ｜勉 to exert oneself		I
委[3]	女 38	委 512	To commission, depute; throw away; a wrong; give up ｜·曲 (ch'ü[1]) oppression, wrong ｜屈 ｜人 entrust to a person ｜任 to commission (gov't) ｜辦 depute manager; committee ｜託 to commission an underling ｜·員 officer deputed		D
痿[3]	疒 104	委 512	Weak, lame; paralysis ｜痺		H
諉[3]	言 149	委 512	To shirk, decline; excuse 推｜ ｜託 shift to some one else		E
偉[3]	人 9	韋 764	Admirable, powerful, giant ｜人 remarkable person, hero ｜大 great, remarkable		F
緯[3]	糸 120	韋 764	Parallels of latitude; fringe ｜道 parallels of latitude ｜度	wei[4]	G
葦[3]	艸 140	韋 764	A hollow rush, reed ｜·子, 蘆｜ ｜蓆 mats made of reeds ｜簾 a reed screen ｜箔		E

Wei

唯^3	口 30	隹 52	Yes, to answer promptly | |	wei^2	F
未^4	木 75	未 495	Not (past), not yet; 1 to 3 p.m. | 甞 not in any case, never | 甞不可 allowable, no objection | 成 not yet completed | 完 | 見 not seen. | 然 not so | 可 not yet suitable | 可知 cannot know, uncertain | 來 not yet come | 免 cannot avoid or prevent |∘必 improbable | 必然 not necessarily so | 便 not convenient | 時 1 to 3 p.m. | 月 6th moon | 定 uncertain, unresolved | 曾^2 not yet, not so, have not		B
味^4	口 30	未 495	Taste, flavor, smell; interest | 氣 flavor, odor | 道, 滋 | , | 兒 | 料 condiments, spices 滋∘| agreeable flavor 一 | one flavor, persistently 意·| meaning, interest 趣·| 五 | five flavors, 甜,酸,苦,辣,鹹		A
位^4	人 9	立 84	Seat, throne; a post, trust; person, C. of persons |·置 to station; position | 格 personality | 次 in order, a position | 分 諸 | all present 列 | 座·| a seat, throne		A
爲^4 為^4	爪 87	爲 260	Because, for, on behalf of | 這個 on account of this | 己 for oneself. | 利 for gain | 何 why? wherefor? | 甚麼 |·的是 the purpose, in order to 因·| because, on account of	wei^2	A

Wei

<table>
<tr><td>僞[43]</td><td>人
9</td><td>爲
260</td><td>False; 'puppet-' (government, etc.)
| 詐 to deceive, deceit
| 神 a false god | 裝 camouflage
| 做 counterfeit, forge | 造</td><td></td><td>E</td></tr>
<tr><td>緯[4]</td><td>糸
120</td><td>韋
764</td><td>The woof; to weave
| 線 silk tassel, the woof</td><td>wei[3]</td><td>G</td></tr>
<tr><td>衛[4]
衞[4]</td><td>行
144</td><td>韋
764</td><td>To guard, escort; a garrison; Tientsin S
|·護 to escort, protect 護 |
| 生 hygiene; | 生術 sanitation
| 生球兒 naphthaline balls
| 生局 Board of Health
| 戍 garrison. 天津 | Tientsin
| 嘴子 the talkative Tientsinese</td><td></td><td>B</td></tr>
<tr><td>尉[4]</td><td>寸
41</td><td>尉
727</td><td>To pacify, calm, quiet
上 | captain; 中, 少 | lieutenants</td><td>yü[4]</td><td>H</td></tr>
<tr><td>慰[4]</td><td>心
61</td><td>尉
727</td><td>To comfort, soothe 安 |
| 問 make kind inquiries</td><td></td><td>C</td></tr>
<tr><td>熨[4]
㷉[4]</td><td>火
86</td><td>尉
727</td><td>To iron | 衣服; a flat-iron yün[4]-
|·開 iron out creases "
|·斗 a flat-iron "</td><td>yün[4]</td><td>B</td></tr>
<tr><td>蔚[4]</td><td>艸
140</td><td>尉
727</td><td>Luxuriant, elegant | 茂</td><td>yü[4]</td><td>G</td></tr>
<tr><td>畏[4]</td><td>田
102</td><td>畏
352</td><td>To dread, respect; awe
| 懼 fear, dread | 怕
| 敬 to venerate 敬 |
無 | without dread,—Buddha</td><td></td><td>C</td></tr>
<tr><td>穢[4]</td><td>禾
115</td><td>歲
132</td><td>Unclean, to defile 汚 |</td><td>hui[4]</td><td>C</td></tr>
<tr><td>餧[4]
喂[4]</td><td>食
184</td><td>委
512</td><td>To feed, rear | 養
| 孩子 to feed a child
| 牲口 to feed animals
| 飽 give a full feed | 足</td><td></td><td>D</td></tr>
<tr><td>魏[4]</td><td>鬼
194</td><td>委
512</td><td>Lofty; a state; a dynasty S.
| 紀 Wei dynasty A. D. 220-264
| 國 Wei state 403-241 B. C.</td><td></td><td>G</td></tr>
</table>

胃⁴	肉 130	胃 617	Stomach, digestion | 寒 "cold" in the stomach | 火 biliousness, indigestion |·口不淸 have no appetite 反 | turn the stomach 翻 | 對 | agrees with stomach		E
渭⁴	水 85	胃 617	River in Shensi		H
謂⁴	言 149	胃 617	To say, be called; said, speak | 何 how is it? how styled? 此 | 之 this is called 此之 |		E
遺⁴	辵 162	貴 862	To send a present	i²	E

Wen

𥁕¹ 昷¹	皿 108	𥁕 606	Compassionate; to feed a prisoner		K
溫¹	水 85	𥁕 606	Warm, mild, to warm up; to review S |◦泉 hot springs |·和 warm, genial | 煖 | 厚 amiable, bland, gentle |◦柔 | 習 to practise, review | 書 | 水 warm water, boil water |◦存 to cherish, mild, gentle | 度 Temperate Zone		B
瘟¹	疒 104	𥁕 606	Epidemic; plague; malaria | 氣 | 疹 rash, measles, etc. |◦疫 contagion, pestilence | 災 | 病 pestilence, epidemic | 症		D
聞²	耳 128	門 635	To hear, smell; fame S. | 人 double surname S. | 名 famous, hear of by repute | 聽 to hear, heard | 味 to smell an odor	wen⁴	A

Wen

文^{2}	文 67	文 546	Literary; elegant; veins, lines; civil; form. C. of cash S ｜·章 literary essays ｜籍 books. ｜∘具 stationery ｜法 book style, grammar ｜話 classical language ｜化 civilize. ｜人 literary man ｜科 liberal or arts course ｜庫 library. ｜理 literary style ｜官 a civil officer ｜理不順 style not smooth ｜理不通 style unintelligible ｜∘明 illustrious, civilized ｜∘明結婚 foreign style wedding ｜∘憑 diploma. ｜士 scribes ｜·書 official despatches ｜才 literary talents ｜彩 elegant style, adorned ｜字 writing ｜武 civil and military ｜∘雅 polite, genteel, elegant 斯｜ ｜約 a contract, agreement ｜苑 literary dep't (newspaper)	wen^{4}	B
紋^{2}	糸 120	文 546	Lines, pattern, figures; pure ｜兒 streaks, lines. ｜跡 trace		G
蚊^{2}	虫 142	文 546	Mosquito ｜·子. 花｜ striped mosquito ｜帳 mosquito net or curtains 避｜香 mosquito-ridder		E
穩^{3} 穏^{3}	禾 115	㥯 381	Firm, secure, stable ｜固 ｜∘健 firm of purpose, stable ｜重 modest, reserved, coy ｜·婆 a midwife ｜·當 firm, safe, steady ｜妥		C
吻^{3} 脗^{3}	口 30	勿 233	Corners of mouth, lips; to kiss ｜合 lips fit; agree, the same 接｜ to kiss, join the lips 口｜ lips, speech		G

Character	Radical	Phonetic	Definition		Ref.
脗3	肉 130	勿 233	To join, match; blend ｜合 unite in wedlock	min3	K
問4	口 30	門 635	To ask, examine; a question, problem; hold responsible ｜案 try cases. ｜·一·｜ inquire ｜·住·了 cannot answer ｜倒·了 ｜好 inquire after ｜安, ｜·候 ｜訊 salutation of priest ｜話 an interrogation ｜詞 ｜明·白·了 inquire clearly ｜知 ｜·不出 cannot find out ｜答 question and ans., catechism ｜題 theme, question, problem ｜罪 to condemn ｜定 不｜ no matter whether		A
聞4	耳 128	門 635	To state to, heard 奏｜	wen2	A
文4	文 67	文 546	Gloss over, hide ｜飾 ｜致其罪 impute guilt to innocent	wen2	B
紊4	糸 120	文 546	Raveled, involved, tangled ｜亂 in confusion, anarchy		G
慍4	心 61	昷 606	Irritated, wroth, hurt ｜怒	yün4	H
璺4	玉 96	同 580	Crack in crockery, flaw 碎｜		I

Weng

Character	Radical	Phonetic	Definition		Ref.
翁1	羽 124	八 392	Old man, venerable 老｜ S. ｜婿 father and son-in-law ｜姑 husband's parents		F
嗡1	口 30	八 392	Lowing, humming ｜｜		K
甕4 罋4 瓮4	瓦 98	雍 62	Jar, pot ｜圈 enceinte of city gate ｜缸 a wine or water jar ｜洞兒 archway of city gate		H

Wo

Wo

Character	Radical	Phonetic	Meaning	Other reading	
渦[1]	水 85	咼 581	Whirlpool, eddy 漩｜; dimple 酒｜ dimples in the cheeks		K
窩[1]	穴 116	咼 581	Nest, hollow, nook, den; to harbor ｜巢 a bird's nest, home 巢｜ ｜主 receiver of stolen goods ｜心 to feel put out, annoyed ｜·過來 bend around inwards ｜棚 a shanty, shed, shack ｜藏 shelter. ｜·子 den, nest ｜(·｜)頭 cakes shape of bird's nest 肐肢｜ the arm-pit 毛兒｜ wadded shoes 被·｜ upper covering of a bed		D
萵[1]	艸 140	咼 581	Lettuce, salad plants ｜苣 ｜筍 dried stems of lettuce		H
倭[1]	人 9	委 512	Dwarf; Japanese ｜人 ｜·瓜 a kind of pumpkin	wei1	G
踒[1]	足 157	委 512	To sprain ｜腿; curly ｜脚 to sprain the ankle ｜足		F
窠[1]	穴 116	果 507	Nest, hole	k'o1	G
我[3]	戈 62	我 338	I, myself ｜一個人 俗 ｜兄弟 I, in polite address 兄弟｜ ｜國 our country ｜·們 we, us ｜輩, ｜等, ｜曹, ｜儕 ｜·們各人 each of us ｜·的 my, mine. ｜·們的 ours	o3	A
臥[4]	臣 131	臣 642	To lie down, to rest ｜床 a bed; lie on a bed ｜榻 ｜房 a bed-chamber ｜佛寺 famous temple near Peking 倒[3]｜ to lie down; drop dead		B
握[4]	手 64	屋 884	To grasp, 掌｜; hold fast; handful ｜兵權 have military power	wu14	E

握[4]			| 手 (禮) to shake hands | 定 grasp firmly | 固 把·| something to grasp		
渥[4]	水 85	屋 884	Soak, enrich; benefit 恩 |		I
齷[4]	齒 211	屋 884	Teeth crowding; small; narrow-minded | 齪		I
沃[4]	水 85	夭 463	To wash; fertilize, reform S. | 手 wash hands 灌 | 心 fertilize the mind		I

Wu

屋[1]	尸 44	屋 884	House, room |·子 | 舍 a house, cottage 房 | houses, buildings 一間 |·子 a room in a house		B
握[14]	手 64	屋 884	To grasp, handful 俗	wo[4]	E
汚[1] 汙[1] 洿[1]	水 85	夸 242	Unclean, filthy, impure; defile | 濁 foul, dirty, filthy | 穢 | 辱 to dirty, insult | 吏 avaricious official | 泥 mire. | 淫 to ravish | 點 blemish, stigma		C
巫[1]	工 48	巫 12	A witch; magic. divination S. | 婆 a witch. 男 | a wizard | 術 sorcery, magic		I
誣[1]	言 149	巫 12	To slander, malicious | 証 false evidence | 告 to accuse falsely | 控 | 賴好人 falsely accuse the good		E
烏[1]	火 86	烏 253	The crow, black; not; alas! how? S | 黑 black, dark. | 木 ebony | 合 unorganized gathering | 乎 alas! alack! | 鴉 a crow, rook, raven		F

無[2] 无[2]	火 86	無 259	Not, without, wanting; initial character ｜礙於事 it does not interfere ｜差 accurate, correct ｜常 to die, death ｜政府 anarchy. ｜機 inorganic ｜價寶 a priceless treasure ｜疆 boundless. ｜恥 shameless ｜知 ignorant, stupid ｜中生有 fabrications ｜妨 of no consequence ｜關緊要 ｜∘非 merely, truly; is it not? ｜效 unsuccessful, fruitless ｜限 unlimited, boundless ｜線電報 wireless telegraph ｜線電台 wireless station ｜形 invisible. ｜益 useless ｜用 ｜花菓 flowerless fruit, fig ｜疑 without doubt or suspicion ｜干 no connexion, no part in ｜可如何 in straits. ｜可奈何 ｜辜 inoffensive. ｜故 causeless ｜過 no faults. ｜禮 rude ｜賴 rowdies ｜量 immeasurable ｜論 no discussion, no matter ｜名指 the fourth finger ｜名氏 anonymous person ｜能 incapable, inability ｜惡不作 execrably bad ｜比 incomparable ｜邊 boundless, e.g., a flood ｜不 invariably, always ｜神派 atheists ｜神主義 atheism ｜事 disengaged, no trouble ｜數 innumerable		A

Character	Radical	Phonetic	Meaning	Alt.	Group
無²			｜所不知 omniscient ｜所不好⁴ he likes everything ｜所不能 omnipotent ｜所不在 omnipresent ｜所不爲² does everything evil ｜思｜慮 free from anxious care ｜膽 cowardly ｜道 without principle ｜敵艦 a dreadnought｜畏艦 ｜底坑 bottomless pit, hell ｜味 tasteless, insipid ｜影 without a shadow of truth ｜有 without and with; have not ｜緣｜故 without cause｜因		
蕪²	艸 140	無 259	Thick undergrowth; weedy, jungle; neglected, abundant ｜茂 luxuriant growth ｜湖 Treaty port on Yangtze		G
亡² 亾²	亠 8	亡 646	Without, not ｜而爲有 affecting to have ｜何 in a little while	wang²	C
吾²	口 30	吾 763	I, my, me.｜輩 we, us｜等 ｜兄 you, sir		E
梧²	木 75	吾 763	Paint tree｜·桐 (oil from its seeds) Aleurites cordata		F
吳²	口 30	吳 761	Wu dynasty, A. D. 229-280,｜紀; Soochow; to bawl, brag S. ｜淞 Woosung, on Shanghai river		F
蜈²	虫 142	吳 761	The centipede｜·蚣		H
毋²	毋 80	毋 571	Do not, not, or not S. ｜必 don't positively have to ｜違 do not disobey!		F
五³	二 7	五 762	Five, perfect number｜·個, 第｜ ｜常 5 constants: 仁 義 禮 智 信 benevolence, justice, courtesy, wisdom, fidelity		A

Wu

Character	Radical	Phonetic	Meaning		
五³			｜金 5 metals; gold, silver, copper, iron, lead ｜經 5 classics: Books of Changes, Poetry, History, Rites, Annals ｜福 5 blessings: long life, wealth, health, love of virtue, natural death ｜行 5 elements: water, fire, wood, metal, earth ｜穀 5 grains: millet, hemp, rice, wheat, pulse ｜官 5 senses: ears, eyes, mouth, nose, heart ｜倫 5 relations: king & subject, father & son, husband & wife, brothers, friends ｜色 5 colors; blue, yellow, red, white, black ｜臟 5 viscera: heart, spleen, liver, lungs, kidneys ｜族共和 fed. of the five races ｜毒 5 poisons: snake, toad, lizard, scorpion, centipede ｜味 5 flavors: bitter, sweet, sour, acrid, salt ｜色旗 flag of the Republic ｜∘十 fifty. ｜百 500. ｜千 5000 ｜大洲 the five continents ｜台山 famous mt. in Shansi ｜音 the five Chinese tones ｜·月｜日 Dragon-Boat Festival		
伍³	人 9	五 762	Five, fives, a squad S. 行｜rank & file, ranks 隊·｜ (行 hang²) 營｜the army		F
午³	十 24	午 37	11 a.m. to 1 p.m., noon ｜正, 晌·｜ ｜飯 dinner [-·huo 上｜forenoon. 下｜afternoon		A

忤^{3}	心 61	午 37	Obstinate, froward ｜意 ｜逆 perverse, disobedient		G
武^{3}	止 77	武 330	Military, martial, violent 威◦｜ S. ｜器 military weapons ｜裝和平 armed peace ｜藝 military arts, tactics ｜官 military officers ｜◦力解決 settle by appeal to arms ｜◦力干涉 military question ｜廟 military temple ｜備 military strength		D
鵡^{3}	鳥 196	武 330	A large parrot 鸚｜		I
塢^{3} 隖^{3}	土 32	烏 253	Low wall; barracks; walled village; entrenchment 村｜ 船｜ a dry dock	4	I
摀^{3}	手 64	烏 253	To cover with the hand ｜耳朵 to muffle the ears ｜·了 spoilt by mildew, faded ｜^{2}·死 smothered to death		D
熓^{3}	火 86	烏 253	To smother, put out, go out	wu^{4}	I
舞^{3}	舛 136	無 259	To posture, brandish; urge ｜劍 sword exercise ｜刀 ｜臺 modern theatre 跳｜ to dance, caper		E
侮^{3}	人 9	每 572	To insult, be rude to, ridicule ｜慢 to despise, be rude to ｜弄 to deceive, humbug		G
勿^{4}	勹 20	勿 233	Do not, not. ｜謂 do not say— ｜能 inability, unable ｜用 don't use ｜事		B
物^{4}	牛 93	勿 233	Article, thing; matter, substance ｜產 natural productions ｜·件 things. ｜◦質 matter ｜競天擇 natural selection by struggle		B

物^4			| 類 classes, categories		
			| 理(學) physics		
			萬 | all things, nature		
務^4	力 19	務 116	Devote attention to; must; duties, function		B
			| 須 must, is sure to |·必		
			| 本 attend to the main thing		
			| 要 must, indispensable		
			家 | household affairs		
			義 | duty, voluntary service		
霧^4	雨 173	務 116	Fog, mist, vapor | 氣, 雲 |		D
			| 燥 damp and muggy		
惡^4	心 61	亞 247	To hate, dislike | 恨, 憎 |	o^{34}	C
			| 惡 (o^4) abominate the evil		
			可 | detestable, abominable		
			厭·| to hate, detest		
悞^4	心 61	吳 761	To neglect; hinder; deceive		C
			| 車 cart stuck, train late | 點		
			| 犯 unintentional fault		
			|·了 neglected, delayed | 事		
			| 殺 kill by accident; so | 傷		
誤^4	言 149	吳 761	To mistake; hinder; wrong		C
			|·會 misconceive		
			| 認 mistakenly recognize		
			錯·| mistake, wrong		
悟^4	心 61	吾 763	To awake, apprehend 自 |, 醒 |		D
			|·性 natural quick perception		
			| 透 thoroughly understand		
			覺 | roused to a sense of | 會		
			省 | to understand, to perceive hs-		
晤^4	日 72	吾 763	Clear, to meet 面 |; perceive		H
			| 商 discuss at interview | 言		
寤^4	宀 40	吾 763	To awake, rouse up 驚 |		I
兀^4	儿 10	兀 387	To cut off feet | 趾; determined		K
			| 然不動 very determined		

杌⁴	木 75	兀 387	A square stool | 櫈子 (or 兒)		H
戊⁴	戈 62	戊 341	Flourishing, fifth stem		H
迕⁴	辵 162	午 37	Conflicting, confused, to oppose, resist 相 |		I
熓⁴	火 86	烏 253	To warm, steam	wu³	I

Ya

呀¹	口 30	牙 165	Final particle, to gape 啰 | alas! oh dear!		A
犽¹	牙 92	牙 165	Very young child | 兒梨 a winter pear		H
鴉¹	鳥 196	牙 165	The crow, raven 烏 | | 雀無聲 not a sound heard |³·片烟 opium		F
押¹	手 64	甲 825	To sign; pawn; arrest; press, imprison; give or keep as security | 解 (chieh⁴) to escort prisoners |·住 to keep in custody | 送 convey under arrest | 當 (tang⁴) to pawn, mortgage | 字 sign document | 誌, 簽 | | 韻 to ryhme 按 | to press down, crush 花 | a device for a signature	ya³	D
鴨¹	鳥 196	甲 825	A duck |·子 | 蛋 ducks' eggs | 卵		D
壓¹⁴	土 32	猒 195	To press down, repress |·住 | 制 repress, keep subject | 驚 calm fears, pacify | 壞 to crush. |·死 crush to death | 力 oppression, tyranny; pressure | 平 flatten, roll level		D

Character	Radical	Phonetic	Meaning	Alternate	Grade
壓[14]			|·不下去 cannot crush down | 塌·了 break down by weight | 倒[3] overthrow; intimidated		
丫[1]	丨 6	丿 111	Fork, crotch | 叉 手 |·巴 spaces between fingers | 鬟 a slave-girl | 頭		E
牙[2]	牙 92	牙 165	Tooth, serrated, ivory |∘齒 |·碜 gritty. | 籤 a tooth-pick | 床子 gums, jaw-bone | 關 | 粉 tooth-powder | 醫生 dentist. | 科 dentistry | 疳 gum-boil. | 刷子 tooth-brush |∘疼 tooth-ache 蟲吃 |		B
芽[2]	艸 140	牙 165	To bud 發 | ; a bud, shoot, germ | 菜 bean sprouts 豆 | |·子 shoots, sprouts, buds		E
衙[2]	行 144	吾 763	Public office, tribunal, yamen | 役 constables, runners |·門 mandarin's office, court		C
耶[2]	耳 128	耶 632	Empty character	yeh[1]	C
亞[3]	二 7	亞 247	Second, inferior; ugly; a prefix | 非利加 Africa. | 西 | Asia | 如 like, similar | 似, | 賽 | 聖 2nd class sages (Mencius)		C
啞[3] 瘂[3]	口 30	亞 247	Confused; hum; dumb | 巴, |·子 | 鈴 dumb-bells | 謎 an enigma, riddle | 嗓子 hoarseness of throat		E
押[3]	手 64	甲 825	Make one's mark 畫 |	ya[1]	D
雅[3]	隹 172	牙 165	Elegant, refined; your |·致 genteel, stylish | 趣 refined pleasure | 意 your fine idea; so | 教, | 論 | 觀 elegant in appearance 文 | polite, cultured, elegant		E

Character	Radical	Phonetic	Definition	Alt.	Freq.
訝4	言 149	牙 165	Surprised; to object 驚 丨 startled, surprised		G
迓4	辵 162	牙 165	To go to meet, welcome 迎 丨		I
軋4	車 159	乙 297	To creak; crush, grind 磨 丨 丨 碾 to hull small grains		H

Yai

Character	Radical	Phonetic	Definition	Alt.	Freq.
崖2 厓2	山 46	厓 50	Cliff, bank, ledge, precipice 山 丨 丨 岸 a steep bank 懸 丨 overhanging cliff		F
捱2	手 64	厓 50	To endure 丨 苦; to put off 丨 一會3 delay a moment	ai2	H
涯2	水 85	厓 50	A shore 水 丨, limit 天 丨 horizon, far regions 無 丨 boundless	ya2	G

Yang

Character	Radical	Phonetic	Definition	Alt.	Freq.
央1	大 37	央 483	The middle; to solicit; ample, 丨 丨 vast 丨·求 to entreat, beseech 丨 請, 丨 告 中 丨 the centre, middle, central		F
呋1	口 30	央 483	To vomit; a sound, echo 丨 奶 overfed baby vomits		K
殃1	歹 78	央 483	Divine judgment; calamity; retribution, mishap 災 丨, 禍 丨 丨 害 to injure 遭 丨 suffer misfortune		F
秧1	禾 115	央 483	Shoots, sprouts, young plants 丨 歌 songs of stilt-walkers 丨 苗 rice shoots, sprouting grain 丨·子 first shoots, rich child		F
鴦1	鳥 196	央 483	Hen of mandarin duck 鴛·丨 the mandarin duck		H

羊²	羊 123	羊 151	Sheep, 綿 | ; goat 山 | S. | 角 ram's horn. | 角瘋 epilepsy | 圈 sheep-fold. | 羣 a flock | 肉 mutton. | 絨 fine wool | 肉床子 butcher's shop | 肉舖 | 羔 sheep and lambs, lambs 羔 | | 毛 wool. | 皮 sheep-skin		A
佯²	人 9	羊 151	To feign, pretend | 爲, ruse | 笑 to pretend laughter | 不知 pretend not to know		F
洋²	水 85	羊 151	Ocean | 海 vast 汪 | ; foreign | 錢 foreign coins, "Mexicans" | 鎗 foreign gun. | 裝 foreign dress. | 火 matches | 行 foreign firm -hang² | 貨 foreign goods | 人 foreigners | 鬼子 "foreign devil" | 布 foreign cloth. | 商 merchants | | 得意 highly elated		A
昜²	日 72	昜 236	To expand, glorious		K
揚²	手 64	昜 236	To raise; spread, display, publish; praise; scatter | 場 (ch'ang²) winnowing ground | 氣 conceited, supercilious | 帆 to set sail, depart | 眉吐氣 very comfortable | 名 to become famous | 子³江 the Yangtze River 宣 | to spread, proclaim		D
楊²	木 75	昜 236	Aspen, poplar | 樹 S. | 柳 the poplar and willow | 梅 arbutus; venereal ulcer		E

陽² 氣² 阳²	阜 170 減	昜 236	Male principle; sun; open; this life; front. 太·｜the sun ｜氣 the male principle ｜·間 among the living, alive ｜世 ｜春 the spring. ｜溝 open drain ｜∘曆 solar calendar 陰｜dual principle, pos. & neg.		B
颺²	風 182	昜 236	Tossed, whirled; to fly ｜塲 (ch'ang²) to winnow grain		I
養³	食 184	羊 151	To nourish; bear; raise, support S ｜氣 oxygen ｜兒²女 rear children ｜孩子 give birth to a child ｜心 nourish mind, cult. virtue ｜·活 to support, rear ｜老院 home for aged people ｜廉 means of living, salary ｜病 to rest and care for one's self in sickness, (at home or in hospital) ｜傷 treated for injuries ｜身 take care of health ｜生要素 necessaries of life ｜育 to rear, educate 教｜ ｜牧 to feed, nourish, shepherd	yang⁴	A
癢³ 痒³	疒 104	羊 151	To itch ｜｜ 痛｜pains and itches ｜酥酥的 to itch terribly		E
仰³	人 9	卬 308	Look up; respect ｜慕 S. ｜仗 look up to, trust ｜賴, ｜託 ｜面 upturned face, front ｜望 to look up with hope 久｜long desired to meet you		C
恙⁴	心 61	羊 151	Indisposition, ill 抱｜ 貴｜your disease 貸｜		H

樣[4]	木 75	羊 151	Sort, manner, model, style | 本 a sample copy; goods catalog | 式 fashion, pattern |·子, 模 | | | 俱全 all complete 一 | the same, alike 一個 | 不是 |·子 not "the thing"		A
養[4]	食 184	羊 151	Support parents 供 | 父母	yang[3]	A
怏[4]	心 61	央 483	Uneasy, dissatisfied | |		H

Yao

要[1]	襾 146	要 776	Seek for, force; agree |∘求 insist on having | 勒 | 約 make an agreement	yao[4]	A
腰[1]	肉 130	要 776	The waist, loins, middle; isthmus |∘帶(子) sash, girdle, waistband | 刀 short sword, dagger |·子 loins, animal kidneys | 眼 small of the back		C
褄[1]	衣 145	要 776	Overlap, plait 裙 | 壓 | make folds or plaits		I
幺[1] 么[1]	幺 52	幺 876	Small, tiny, tender | 小 | 豚 last pig of a litter		K
吆[1]	口 30	幺 876	To cry out, call to, call wares |·喝 to scold, cry out |·呼 call wares, cry goods |·喚		E
邀[1]	辵 162	敫 551	To invite, seek, engage, request | 請 to invite, request 相 | | 客 to invite a guest | 賓		F
夭[1]	大 37	夭 463	Winning; tender, young; calamity | 亡 premature death | | young and beautiful		G
妖[1]	女 38	夭 463	Phantom, sprite, magical |·精 uncanny, weird		G

Yao

Character	Radical	Phonetic	Meaning		
妖[1]			|·怪 ghost, unnatural appearance |魔 |術 magic spells		
凹[12]	凵 17	凵 650	Hollow, cavity	wa[1]	G
䍃[2]	缶 121	䍃 658	A jar, vase, pitcher		K
搖[2]	手 64	䍃 658	Shake, wave, sway to and fro |車 hammock, swing, cradle |旗 wave flag. |·幌 shake; jolt |鈴 a pedlar, ring the bell |櫓 to scull. |手 wave hand |頭 wag head. |·動 move, shake		B
瑤[2]	玉 96	䍃 658	Green jasper, gem |函 "your valued favor" |箋		K
窰[2] 窯[2]	穴 116	䍃 658	A kiln, pottery-furnace 燒| |·匠 potter, burner of bricks |貨 pottery, earthenware |·子 a brothel		D
謠[2]	言 149	䍃 658	Rumour, invented tale |·言 造|·言 make or spread false tales		E
遙[2]	辵 162	䍃 658	Far, remote, distant |遠		E
颻[2]	風 182	䍃 658	Floating; roaming |颺 飄| floating, self-satisfied		H
堯[2]	土 32	堯 391	Lofty; Emperor Yao, 2356-2258 B.C. |舜之世 the golden age of Yao[2] and Shun[4]		F
淆[2]	水 85	有 184	Mixed, confused; Shansi river |混 muddy water; mixed up		G
殽[2]	殳 79	有 184	Viands; mixed, confused |雜 嘉| dainty viands		I
餚[2]	食 184	有 184	Meats, delicacies |饌 prepared food, victuals		H
姚[2]	女 38	兆 383	Handsome, elegant |冶 S.		H

Yao

爻^{2}	爻 89	爻 529	To blend, crosswise, intertwine | 卦 divining symbols, 六 |		K
齩^{3} 咬^{3}	齒 211	交 531	To bite, gnaw, masticate 俗 | 人 to bite a person |·不動 can't bite into it | 傷 wound from a bite | 舌兒 clip words in speech | 斷 bite off or in two |開 | 牙 grind or gnash the teeth		C
舀^{3}	臼 134	舀 682	To ladle, bale out | 水 |·不乾 can't bale it dry |·子 a ladle, dipper	wai^{3}	F
拗^{3}	手 64	幺 876	To drag, pull; break | 折 -she^{2} |·出禍來 bring on trouble	niu^{4}	H
窈^{3}	穴 116	幺 876	Retired, profound, refined 幽 | retired, secluded | 窕		H
杳^{3}	木 75	木 484	Obscure, distant | 冥 | 遠 in obscure distance	miao^{3}	H
殀^{3}	歹 78	夭 463	Premature death | 命, | 亡		G
要^{4}	西 146	要 776	To want, need; intend; important, abstract; shall, will | 賬 collect debts | 錢 to want money | 緊 important. | 略 abridgment | 求 wish to ask | 犯 ringleader. | 飯的 beggar | 害 vital spot; strategic point | 塞 [sai^{4} | 義 main thought | 命 to take life, deadly | 甚麼 what do you want? |·是 if it is, should it be | 事 an important matter | 死 at the point of death | 素 requisite, essential | 點 chief points, essential	yao^{1}	A

Yao

要4			| 做 about to do | 言 important words		
樂4	木 75	樂 490	Surname S.	le4 yüeh4	A
藥4 葯4	艸 140	樂 490	Medicinal herbs, medicine | 酒 medicated spirits | 局 drug factory | 方 medical prescription | 房 dispensary; shop for proprietary medicines, (especially foreign) | 料 medicines |·材 | 舖 a retail chemist's shop | 散 (san3) medicinal powders | 面 | 水 liquid medicines |·死 to poison. | 丸 a pill | 店 a wholesale drug house | 引子 help to take medicine 一服 | a dose of medicine	yüeh4	A
鑰4	金 167	龠 567	Bolt of lock, a key |·匙	yüeh4	B
曜4	日 72	翟 57	Brilliant, illustrious 照。| 日 | rays of sun; Sunday	yüeh4	H
耀4 燿4	羽 124	翟 57	Bright, glorious, to illumine | 眼 to dazzle the eyes 榮 | glory, illustrious	yüeh4	B
瘧4	疒 104	虐 205	Fever, ague |·子 俗 發 |·子 have fever and ague	nüeh4 yüeh4	E
靿4	革 177	幺 876	Leg of boot 靴 |·子		H
鷂4	鳥 196	䍃 658	Harrier, falcon; paper kite |·鷹 the black-eared kite 放 |·子 fly kites		K

Yeh

Character	Radical	Phonetic	Meaning	Alt.	Tone
噎[1]	口 30	壹 734	To choke, hiccough | 嗝 | 住 something stuck in throat		I
耶[1]	耳 128	耶 632	A final interrogative particle | 教 Protestantism | 穌教 | 和華 Jehovah. | 穌 Jesus 是 | 非 | is it so or not?	ya[2]	C
椰[12] 梛[12]	木 75	耶 632	Cocoanut tree |·子樹 | 肉 flesh of cocoanut |·子瓢 cocoanut shell as ladle		G
爺[2]	父 88	耶 632	Grandfather; gentleman; title | 兒倆 father and son or daughter |·們 men | 娘 father and mother |·| paternal grandfather		D
也[3]	乙 5	也 301	Also; final particle | 好 also well, will do | 行, | 可 | 可以 also do; still answer | 不行 that will not do either | 曾[2] already. | 許 possibly 未之有 | there never has been		A
野[3] 埜[3]	里 166	里 827	A desert; rude, wild, savage, rustic | 鷄 pheasant | 心 extravagant ambition | 人 countrymen, barbarians | 蠻 | 蠻手段 barbarous methods | 貓 wild-cat, hare. | 獸 wild animals | 地 uncultivated ground 曠 | wilderness, the country		B
冶[3]	冫 15	台 718	To fuse, smelt; fascinating | 金家 assayers | | fascinating 妖 |, | 容 銷 | to smelt 鎔 |		G

Yeh

Character	Radical	Phonetic	Meaning		Other readings	
夜⁴	夕 36	夜 268	Night, darkness. |·裏 at night | 靜 the stillness of night | 行 travel by night | 巡 night patrol, rounds | 壺 the chamber utensil | 貓子 "night cat" i.e. the owl | 深 late at night 晝 | day and night 白天黑 | 打 | 工 (or 作¹) to do night work			A
掖⁴¹	手 64	夜 268	To raise up, palace side-room |·起衣裳 tuck clothes in girdle 扶 | support, uphold			H
液⁴	水 85	夜 268	Juices, secretions; moist 潤 | | 體 liquids			G
腋⁴	肉 130	夜 268	Arm-pit, under fore-leg 集 | 成裘 collect fur under fox legs for a robe			H
枼⁴	木 75	枼 110	A slip, tablet, leaf; slate			K
葉⁴	艸 140	枼 110	Leaf, 樹 |·子; lobe, hinge, slip |·子菸 tobacco in leaf	S	she⁴	A
鍱⁴	金 167	枼 110	Thin plate of iron 鐵 |·子			G
業⁴	木 75	業 156	Patrimony, estate; a profession, trade; to entice; already | 經 past and done, already | 已 | 主 a man of property 職 | profession, office 事·| employment, affairs 營 | to do business, trade			C
曳⁴ 拽⁴	曰 73	曳 835	To trail, drag, pull, haul	文	chuai¹⁴ i⁴	E
頁⁴	頁 181	頁 866	A leaf, page 書 | ; head 百 | 窗 venetian blinds			F
謁⁴	言 149	曷 239	To visit superior | 見 拜 | visit a friend, pay a call			H

Yen

<table>
<tr><td>咽^{1}</td><td>口
30</td><td>因
771</td><td>The throat
｜喉 the throat; a narrow pass</td><td>yen^{4}</td><td>D</td></tr>
<tr><td>烟^{1}
煙^{1}
菸^{1}</td><td>火
86
艸
140</td><td>因
771</td><td>Smoke; tobacco, opium
｜鎗 opium pipe. ｜捲兒 cigaret
｜煤 "smoke coal", bituminous
｜袋 a pipe. ｜土 opium 大｜
｜·台 Yent'ai, Chefoo
｜·筒 pipe, chimney. 紙｜ cigaret
｜·子 soot, lamp-black 黑｜·子
｜葉 leaf-tobacco
｜癮 the craving for opium
抽｜ to smoke tobacco</td><td></td><td>B</td></tr>
<tr><td>胭^{1}
臙^{1}</td><td>肉
130</td><td>因
771</td><td>Throat; cosmetics, like rouge ｜·脂
｜粉 rouge and powder
｜喉 throat, key to position</td><td></td><td>H</td></tr>
<tr><td>燕^{1}</td><td>火
86</td><td>北
321</td><td>A feudal state S.
｜都 (tu^{1}) Peking ｜京, ｜市</td><td>yen^{4}</td><td>D</td></tr>
<tr><td>淹^{1}</td><td>水
85</td><td>奄
810</td><td>To soak, drown; delay ｜久
｜沒·了 drowned ｜·死 (沒 mo^{4})
｜濕 soaking wet
｜消 dissolved by water action</td><td></td><td>E</td></tr>
<tr><td>醃^{1}</td><td>酉
164</td><td>奄
810</td><td>To salt, pickle ｜製
｜火腿 to salt ham
｜肉 salt meat, corned beef
｜菜 salt vegetables; so ｜魚</td><td></td><td>E</td></tr>
<tr><td>閹^{13}
剦^{13}</td><td>門
169</td><td>奄
810</td><td>To castrate, ｜割, eunuch
｜雞 a capon
｜·子 eunuch ｜人, ｜宦, 內｜</td><td></td><td>F</td></tr>
<tr><td>焉^{1}</td><td>火
86</td><td>正
127</td><td>How? why? final affirmative
｜知 how do I know? I don't know
｜敢 how dare I? dare not
｜能 how able to? not able to</td><td></td><td>E</td></tr>
</table>

Yen

蔫[1]	艸 140	正 127	Droop, decay, fade 色丨		I
			丨舊 old, wanting freshness		
言[2]	言 149	言 740	Word, a saying; language; speak	yüan[2]	B
			丨其 that is, as much as to say		
			丨論機關 the press		
			丨論家 praters, talkers, critics		
			丨論時代 age of propagandism		
			丨論自由 freedom of speech		
			丨明 to state distinctly		
			丨不二價 only one price		
			丨定 positively, absolutely		
			丨詞 an expression		
			丨語 words, conversation		
			語丨學 science of language		
鹽[2] 塩[2]	鹵 197	鹵 654	Salt, saltish, saline		B
			丨政 the Salt Gabelle		
			丨井 salt-wells. 丨滷 block lye		
			丨商 salt merchant. 丨稅 salt tax		
			丨店 government salt office		
			丨務署 Salt Bureau		
			丨運使 salt comptroller		
顏[2]	頁 181	彥 284	Color 丨·色; face S.		B
			丨料 colors, paints, dyes		
			容丨 the countenance 丨面		
嚴[2]	口 30	嚴 630	Stern, strict, dignified; father; tight S.		B
			丨整 austere; imposing, close		
			丨緊 severe, strict 丨厲		
			丨禁 strictly prohibit		
			丨重 grave, stern 威丨		
			丨罰 severe punishments		
			丨防扒手 beware pickpockets!		
			丨寒 extremely cold		
			丨令 strict orders 丨命		
			丨密 private, retired (room)		
			丨守中立 strict observance of neutrality		

Character	Radical	Phonetic	Definition		Other reading	Group
嚴²			丨守秘密 strictly confidential 家丨 my father			
巖² 岩²	山 46	嚴 630	Cliff, crag; steep, hazardous 丨谷 mountain gorge			G
延²	廴 54	延 128	To allow; delay, prolong; invite 丨長² extended, long delay 丨遲 to delay 遲丨, 丨擱 丨請 to invite 丨年 advanced in years 丨壽			D
涎²	水 85	延 128	Saliva	文	hsien²	F
筵²	竹 118	延 128	Bamboo mat; banquet, feast 丨席 banquet 丨宴 設丨 prepare a feast 擺丨			C
姸²	女 38	开 34	Beautiful 丨美; skilled 鮮丨 fresh and pretty			H
研²	石 112	开 34	To grind, rub; fine; investigate 丨∘究 investigate minutely 丨審 丨∘究所 research institute 丨磨 (mo⁴) to turn a hand-mill 丨墨 to rub Chinese ink			F
檐² 簷²	木 75	詹 741	Eaves of a house, 房丨 丨下 under the eaves 帽丨 brim of hat			E
沿²	水 85	㕣 719	To skirt, by; hand down 丨城 run along city wall 丨海 (places) on sea coast 丨路 follow road, along road 丨道兒		yen⁴	E
炎²	火 86	炎 447	To blaze, flame; ardent, hot 丨丨 丨天 hot season. 火丨 blaze			F
芫²	艸 140	元 388	Coriander 丨荽	俗	yüan²	G
閻² 閆²	門 169	臽 683	Gate to a village, hamlet 里丨 丨·王 the Chinese Pluto, Yama 見丨·王 see Yen Wang—to die	S		H

眼[3]	目 109	艮 359	Eye, opening, hole; C. of wells, etc. ｜睜睜的 in plain sight, before eyes ｜睫毛 eye lashes ｜毛 ｜界 mental horizon, view-point ｜見 to see with one's own eyes ｜·睛 the eyes ｜目 ｜鏡 spectacles, eye-glasses ｜球 ball of eyes, so ｜珠 iris ｜中無人 conceit, supercilious ｜下 at the moment ｜斜 squint-eyed. ｜熱 covetous ｜花·了 the eyes dim (with age) ｜看 evidently, on point of ｜科 ophthalmology ｜光 eye sight; vision; outlook ｜眶 socket of the eye ｜淚 tears ｜力見兒 quick to notice wants, observant ｜亮 clear-sighted ｜眉 eyebrows. ｜皮 eyelids ｜皮·子淺 fig.=greedy ｜色 discernment; a wink ｜痛 sore eyes. ｜暈 dizziness ｜藥 eye medicine 近視｜ short-sighted eyes, so 遠視｜ far-sighted		A
演[3]	水 85	寅 821	To practice; perform; lecture; extend, long ｜講 speak on a subject, lecture ｜習 to practice ｜戲 to play, to rehearse ｜繹法 deductive method in logic ｜禮 to practice rites ｜兵 to exercise troops		B

Character	Radical	Phonetic	Meaning		
演³			｜說 discourse. ｜說家 lecturers ｜說臺 lecture platform ｜說團 lecture bureau ｜武 military exercises ｜樂 (yüeh) to practice music		
奄³	大 37	奄 810	To remain, stop; a long time; forthwith; entirely ｜留 remain a long time		K
掩³ 揜³	手 64	奄 810	Cover, conceal; shut, screen ｜耳 to shut one's ears ｜蓋 cover over, screen ｜蔽 ｜護 to cover (military) ｜面 cover or shade the face ｜藏 to hide, conceal 遮｜		E
衍³	行 144	行 5	Ample, amplify, abundant 推｜make widely known		G
兗³	儿 10	兗 756	City in Shantung ｜州府		G
儼³	人 9	嚴 630	Majestic, dignified; like, ｜然 ｜若 very like, resembling		H
偃³	人 9	安 555	To bend, lie down; desist, cease ｜仆 fall flat. ｜臥 lie down		K
蝘³	虫 142	安 555	Lizard ｜蜓; cicada		I
魘³	鬼 194	厭 195	Bad dreams, nightmare 夢｜		K
广³	广 53	广 198	Roof, shelter		K
㕣³	口 30	㕣 719	A march		P
㫃³	方 70	㫃 265	Streamer		P
硯⁴	石 112	見 865	Ink slab ｜台 ｜水壺（盒）small vessel holding water to use on the ink-slab		B

Yen

驗4 騐4	馬 187	僉 436	To examine, verify 考 | ; fulfill | 查 to examine | 看, | 視 | 貨 examine goods at Customs | 尸 post-mortem examination | 單 a customs permit 效。| results. 試·| test, experiment 應 (ying4) | come true, fulfill		D
厭4	厂 27	猒 195	To dislike, loathe | 惡; wearied -wu4 | 棄 reject, disdain |·氣 disgust, aversion | 煩 to annoy, bother | 悶 | 世家 pessimist; cynic | 世觀 pessimistic views		D
饜4	食 184	猒 195	Satiated, satisfied | 飽 | 口 agreeable to taste | 腹		I
燕4	火 86	北 321	The swallow, a feast, easy | 安 at rest, peaceful | | |·子 swallow. 土 | sandmartin | 窩 edible birds' nests	yen1	D
咽4 嚥4	口 30	因 771	To swallow, gulp down |·下去 | 氣 to breathe his last	yen1	D
沿4	水 85	㕣 719	Shore, coast, edge | 邊 河 | the banks of a river	yen2	E
宴4 讌4	宀 40	安 555	Banquet, repose, merriment | 會 assemble at banquet | 樂 merry-making		F
晏4	日 72	安 555	Quiet; late; splendid S. | 安 quiet and peaceful | 駕 death of an emperor 早 | early and late		G
焰4 燄4	火 86	臽 683	Brilliant; flame, blaze 火 | 放 |·口 release from Hades 烈 | a roaring blaze		F

釅^{4}	酉 164	嚴 630	Strong tea or spirits ｜茶 strong tea. 茶太｜ tea too strong		F
贗^{4} 贋^{4}	貝 154	貝 856	Counterfeit, false, spurious ｜僞 ｜製 make imitation goods ｜手 forger, counterfeiter 作｜ play the hypocrite		H
雁^{4} 鴈^{4}	隹 172	隹 52	Wild goose, ｜鵝, 水｜ ｜陣 flight of wild geese 嫁｜ the wedding goose 奠｜ libation to the goose		G
彥^{4}	彡 59	彥 284	Handsome 俊｜; accomplished ｜士 a refined scholar		G
諺^{4}	言 149	彥 284	Proverb, common saying, ｜語, 俗｜ ｜云 the proverb says		G
豔^{4} 艷^{4} 豓^{4}	豆 151	豐 736	Beautiful, fascinating; wanton ｜妻 a handsome wife ｜粧 handsomely dressed ｜麗 handsome, beautiful 嬌｜ charming, fascinating		H
讞^{4}	言 149	鬲 589	To decide; a judge 成｜ a precedent		K

Yin

因^{1}	口 31	因 771	Cause, reason, for, because ｜其 because of his (its, etc.) ｜而 and so, and hence ｜小失大 lose greater for less ｜循 remissness, perfunctory ｜果 cause and effect ｜罪而死 died on account of sin ｜此 therefore, for this reason ｜∘爲 (wei^{4}) because, on account of ｜由 origin, cause 原｜, ｜緣		A

Character	Radical	Phonetic	Meaning		Grade
姻¹ 婣¹	女 38	因 771	Marriage, betrothal 婚 | | 戚 a wife's relatives | 親 | 緣 marriage affinity		D
茵¹	艸 140	因 771	Cushion, padded, mat | 蔯 artemisia, medicine for jaundice		H
陰¹ 隂¹	阜 170	陰 435	Female principle; negative; shade, dark, secret; Hades; cloudy |·間 among the dead, Hades | 曹 | 氣 female principle, negative | 險 treacherous, hid danger | 溝 hidden drain, covered ditch | 功 secret merits |∘歷 lunar calendar |·涼兒 shady, in the shade | 天 cloudy day or weather | 毒損壞 to secretly injure | 陽 heaven and earth, positive and negative, male and female | 陽學 the geomantic art 光 | light and shade, time 太 | moon		A
音¹	音 180	音 90	Sound, musical tone, news | 鍵 key of piano | 信 news, tidings | 聲 sound, noise 聲·| | 調 accent. 口·| local accent |∘樂 musical instrument; music |∘樂家 musician. |∘樂會 concert |∘樂隊 band, orchestra 福 | Gospel (of Christ)		A
殷¹	殳 79	殷 402	Many, full; very rich |∘朝 Yin dyn., 1766-1122 B.C. | 實 affluent, substantial | 富	S.	F
慇¹	心 61	殷 402	Anxious, careful, earnest |·懃 diligent, attentive (also 殷勤)		D

湮[1]	水 85	西 775	To soak; stain; drown; spread ｜沒 (mo⁴) to be drowned; lost 墨｜·了 the ink has spread	G
銀[2]	金 167	艮 359	Silver, money, wealth ｜錢 ｜硃 powder used for red ink ｜行 (hang²) a bank ｜號 ｜行 (hang²)團 bankers' syndicate ｜庫 a silver treasury ｜礦 a silver mine ｜兩 cash, money. ｜元 dollar ｜幣局 silver mint ｜元局 ｜鼠 ermine or Siberian weasel ｜錠 ingots of silver	A
淫[2]	水 85	壬 67	Licentious, lewd; excess; to soak ｜瘡 venereal ulcers ｜婦 an adulteress ｜風 fashion of dissipation ｜戲 lewd plays. ｜心 lustful desire ｜亂 lewdness, incest ｜蕩, ｜艷 ｜書 obscene books ｜文	C
寅[2]	宀 40	寅 821	Respectful, reverent; 3-5 a. m. ｜時 3-5 a.m. ｜月 1st moon ｜畏 to regard with awe 同｜ fellow-officer ｜兄	G
吟[2] 唫[2]	口 30	今 434	To hum, chant, mutter, sigh ｜詩 hum verses—composing ｜｜ tittering, giggling	H
冘[2]	冂 14	冘 176	To move on	P
引[3]	弓 57	弓 244	To lead, draw out; quote; a preface 小｜, ｜言 ｜荐 to introduce ｜薦 ｜近 to bring near to one ｜進 lead in, introduce ｜號 quotation marks	B

Yin

引[3]			|線 to furnish a clue |行 to lead the way |路 |領 to expect; guide, lead |導 |書作證 quote a book as proof |得 index 索| |典故 make historical or mythical allusion |渡 extradition |·子 the gist; dry yeast |誘 to entice, seduce 吸| attraction			
㥯[3]	心 61	㥯 381	To care for			P
隱[3] 隠[3]	阜 170	㥯 381	To avoid, conceal, hidden, retired |◦去 to retire. |瞞 deceive |名 nom de plume |匿 to conceal, screen |藏 |蔽 to obscure, cover over |士 a retired scholar or officer |語 elliptical sentence, riddle			C
癮[3]	疒 104	㥯 381	Craving, habit; eruption |疹 eruption on the body 上| to have formed the habit 有| 煙| the craving for opium			F
飲[3]	食 184	欠 441	To drink, swallow |水; drink |器 drinking vessels |酒 drink wine. |湯 take soup |◦食 eat and drink; food		yin[4]	D
尹[3]	尸 44	尹 677	To rule, oversee; true 道| prefect, taotai	S.		G
廴[3]	廴 54		To move on, journey			K
印[4]	卩 26	巳 306	To seal, print; a seal, stamp |章 seal, token, emblem |記 a seal mark |跡 |象 mental impression |花票 revenue stamps	S		B

印^4			| 板 block type | 花稅 stamp duty |·色 ink used for seals | 泥 | 書 to print books, printing 刷 | | 刷所 (or 局) press-works |·度 India. |∘度洋 Indian Ocean		
飲^4	食 184	欠 441	To water (animals) | 牲口	yin^3	D
窨^4	穴 116	音 90	Cellar 地 |·子, store-room		E
蔭^4 廕^4	艸 140	陰 435	Shade, shadow, shelter | 涼兒 shade, in the shade | 庇 protect		F
䌥^4 縯^4	糸 120	㥯 381	To sew, stitch, quilt, "run", baste 先 |^{3}後緝 first run then fell		I

Ying

䧹^1	隹 172	䧹 202	A hawk		K
應^1	心 61	䧹 202	Ought, must | 當, | 該, proper, right | 承 promise, acquiesce in | 諾 | 許 to promise | 時 seasonable, at right time | 允 consent to, allow | 用 available for use, applied	ying^4	A
膺^1	肉 130	䧹 202	The breast; undertake; receive | 親 to do personally | 胸 breast. | 受 receive		H
鷹^1	鳥 196	䧹 202	A hawk, kite, falcon | 膦 hawk-eyed (bad sense) | 洋 the Mexican dollar		E
英^1	艸 140	央 483	Eminent, brave, superior |∘雄 hero, man of noble char. | 豪 |·國 England. | 民 Brit. subjects | 才 splendid talents		B

Ying

Character	Radical	Phonetic	Meaning	
英[1]			丨威 majestic, dignified 丨偉 extraordinary, great	
瑛[1]	玉 96	央 483	Luster of gems, quartz 石丨	I
嬰[1] 孾[1]	女 38	嬰 859	Infant, baby 丨孩, 丨兒 抱丨 carry baby in arms 育丨堂 foundling hospital	C
櫻[1]	木 75	嬰 859	Cherry 丨·桃 丨桃口 cherry lips 丨脣	E
瓔[1]	玉 96	嬰 859	Fine pebble; jewel; necklace 丨珞	H
纓[1]	糸 120	嬰 859	Tassel, fringe, throat-band 丨帽 red-tassel hat	H
罌[1] 甖[1] 罃[1]	缶 121	嬰 859	Jar with small mouth and ears, vase, jar 丨粟花 the opium poppy,(so) 丨·子·果 水丨 a water-jar	I
鸚[1]	鳥 196	嬰 859	A parrot, cockatoo 丨·鵡, 丨鵡 白丨鵡 a cockatoo	G
鶯[1] 鸎[1]	鳥 196	𤇾 448	Oriole, i.e. mango-bird 丨花 a courtesan 黃丨 Chinese oriole	G
迎[2]	辵 162	卬 308	To go to meet, welcome 丨·接 丨親 go to meet the bride 丨娶 丨春 welcoming spring; forsythia 丨祥 may you be fortunate 丨客 to receive guests 丨敵 encounter in fight 歡丨會 a welcome reception	B
盈[2]	皿 108	乃 216	Full, to fill, surplus, abundant 丨豐 full, abundant 丨滿, 豐丨 丨餘 a surplus	D
蠅[2]	虫 142	黽 316	A fly, house-fly 蒼丨, 丨·子 丨刷子 a fly-brush 丨甩子 a fly swatter 丨拍·子	D

Ying

塋²	土 32	𤇾 448	A grave, cemetery ｜地 ｜墳 a grave ｜穴, ｜窟 祖｜ one's family tombs			F
營²	火 86	𤇾 448	A camp, regiment; to scheme, plan ｜寨 a camp. ｜壘 a fort ｜口 port of Newchwang ｜利 profit making ｜·盤 cantonment, barracks ｜兵 soldiers. ｜伍 the army ｜生 profession; work ｜業 ｜業所 place of business 經｜ carry through, plan, trade			D
瑩²	玉 96	𤇾 448	Lustrous, clear, pebble 琇｜ whitish jade ear-plugs			H
螢²	虫 142	𤇾 448	Glow-worm ｜虬, firefly ｜火虫			G
贏²	貝 154	亡 646	Surplus, full; to win, profit ｜錢 win money. ｜利 profit			E
影³	彡 59	景 748	Shadow, image ｜像; effect ｜兒 a trace, a shadow ｜戲 magic lantern, cinema ｜·響 tidings, effect, influence ｜格 copy-slips			B
穎³ 頴³	禾 115	頁 866	Full head of grain; sharp point; writing-brush ｜悟 clever, sharp 聰｜, ｜慧			H
應⁴	广 53	鴈 202	To respond, fulfill, answer ｜·酬 intercourse, return ｜募 to enlist, join the colors ｜聲 echo, responding sound ｜試 go up to examination ｜答 to respond, reply 答·｜ ｜驗 to verify, fulfill	S	ying¹	A
硬⁴	石 112	更 834	Hard, strong, obstinate 剛｜ ｜·氣 positive, peremptory ｜搶 to take by force			B

硬[4]			｜壯 strong, powerful ｜心 hard-hearted 心｜ ｜留 to detain by force ｜煤 hard coal, anthracite ｜·木 hard wood ｜逼 compel	
暎[4] 映[4]	日 72	央 483	Sunlight, shine, dazzling, reflection; to favor; apparent ｜照 shining, bright ｜日 brightness of the sun ｜眼 dazzling to the eye	G
㷛[4]	火 86	㷛 448	Brilliant	P

Yu

憂[1]	心 61	憂 412	Sad, anxious, grief ｜愁, ｜心 ｜恤 to sympathize ｜患 distressed, sad ｜傷, ｜悶 ｜慮 anxiety, sorrow ｜勞 ｜思 think over with concern 担｜ to be grieved	C
優[1]	人 9	憂 412	Superior, fully, to excel ｜先 precedence, predominant ｜先權 preferential rights ｜禮 extremely polite ｜美 excellent, superb ｜勝劣敗 survival of fittest ｜勢 victory, advantage ｜待 special treatment, complimentary ｜待室 reception room ｜點 excellency, fine points	D
幽[1]	幺 52	幺 876	Dark, gloomy; secluded; occult ｜暗 dark, obscure ｜閉 imprisoned, confined ｜深 deep, profound. ｜默 humor ｜微 minute, abstruse ｜雅 secluded, quiet	E

攸[1]	攴 66	攸 549	Whereby; which, what, who; distant 丨歸 thereby accrue 丨丨 distant, far away		G
悠[1] 滺[1]	心 61	攸 549	Grieved; distant, far-reaching 丨丨 glidingly, long time 丨遠 distant, far		G
鞦[1]	革 177	秋 450	To swing, a swing 丨·韆	ch'iu[1]	H
呦[1]	口 30	幺 876	Bleating of deer 丨丨		H
麀[1]	鹿 198	匕 317	Roe, doe		H
由[2]	田 102	由 818	From, by; permit; cause, origin, follow 丨淺而深 from shallow to deep 丨近而遠 from near to far 丨·不得人 not depend on man 丨∘他 rests with him, let him 丨·得我 it depends on me; I can 丨天 from or depends on heaven 丨此 from this 丨此觀之 from which it follows 自丨 free, liberty		B
油[2]	水 85	由 818	Oil, oily, fat, greasy; paint 丨炸[2]鬼 a kind of twisted cake 丨榨 oil press. 丨紙 oil paper 丨漆 oil color; varnish, lacquer 丨漆匠 painters, varnishers 丨坊 an oil manufactory 丨畫 oil paintings 丨簍 oil baskets. 丨泥 dirt, oily 丨布 oil cloth. 煤丨 kerosene		A
郵[2]	邑 163	垂 26	Post-office, lodge, error 丨政 (or 務 or 便) 局 Government Post Office		A

Yu

Character	Radical	Phonetic	Meaning	Code
郵[2]			｜件 articles of mail matter ｜局匯票 postal money-order ｜費 postage ｜資. ｜差 postman -chai[1] ｜票 postage stamp	
猶[2] 犹[2]	犬 94	酋 782	Yet, still; like as, as if ｜且 still more, further ｜疑不定 doubtful, suspicious ｜豫 ｜然 as if; just like ｜若, ｜如 ｜可 it may yet do ｜太國 Judea. ｜太人 Jews ｜有 there is still; still more	C
猷[2]	犬 94	酋 782	A scheme, to plan; ho! oh! 有｜ to be wise in counsel	F
斿[2]	方 70	斿 266	Dog-tooth border to flag	P
游[2]	水 85	斿 266	To ramble, travel; swim ｜水 S. ｜民 homeless people (see 遊)	E
蝣[2]	虫 142	斿 266	Ephemera fly, water fly	H
遊[2]	辵 162	斿 266	To wander, travel, saunter ｜◦戲 recreation, amusement ｜◦戲場 place of amusement ｜◦戲體操 athletics, gymnastics ｜學 to go abroad to study ｜藝 regulated play ｜逛 to stroll, travel, ramble ｜◦玩 ｜覽 sight-seeing. ｜·歷 travel ｜牧世代 pastoral or nomadic age ｜手好[4]閒 loafer fond of idling ｜蕩 dissipated. ｜惰的 tramps	D
尤[2]	尢 43	尤 175	Still more; fault, blame S. ｜其要緊 still more important ｜加 still more, excessive ｜甚 ｜重 set extreme value on ｜異 passing strange 不｜人 I do not blame mankind	E

Yu

疣² 肬²	疒 104	尤 175	A swelling, wen 皮上結丨		H
囮² [illegible]²	口 31	化 327	To inveigle, decoy 丨·子 a decoy bird 鳥丨 作丨人 a decoy man, a tout		K
繇²	糸 120	䍃 658	Follow, resemble		K
有³	月 74	有 184	To have, be; yes 丨得衞生 unsanitary 丨機 organic 丨求必應 "ask and ye receive" 丨趣 agreeable, interesting 丨福 happy, blessed 丨限 limited, not much, few 丨限公司 a limited company 丨心 intentionally. 丨形 visible 丨·一天 on a certain day 丨益 profitable, beneficial 丨利 丨人緣 popular 丨過 have, had, has faults 丨理 reasonable, sensible 丨·了 there is, have, has 丨·沒·丨 have you? Is there any? 丨名望 men of reputation 丨名無實 name without reality 丨憑丨據 certain, incontestable 丨不是 culpable, at fault 丨時 sometimes, there are 丨始無終 unfinished, abortive 丨數 not many, limited 丨·的 some; there are some 丨·的是 plenty of, lots of 丨多麼重 how heavy is it? 丨多少 how much is there? 丨罪 guilty, excuse me	yu⁴	A

Yu

有^3
｜味兒 savory, tasty
｜餘 a superabundance
｜用的 useful, some use it
萬｜the universe

友^3 又 29 友 186 — A
Friend｜人, 朋·｜, friendly
｜愛 the affection of friends
｜誼 friendly feeling
｜邦 friendly state or country

酉^3 酉 164 酉 781 — G
Ripe, complete; 5-7 p.m.
｜時 5 to 7 o'clock p.m.
二｜堂 fancy name for book-store

莠^3 艸 140 秀 217 — H
Weeds, tares; vicious
｜民 disloyal people

又^4 又 29 又 532 — A
Also, and, again, moreover
｜飢｜渴 both hungry and thirsty
｜加上 and besides 況｜, 且｜
｜·一天 still another day
｜來 came again
｜·是 still it is, again it is
｜添了 added still more
｜有 still have, there is more

有^4 月 74 有 184 — 文 — yu^3 — A
Also, and

侑^4 人 9 有 184 — I
To wait on; press to eat, urge
｜食 press to eat; so｜酒

囿^4 囗 31 有 184 — G
Park, garden,｜苑, 園｜; enclose
淺｜shallow and limited

宥^4 宀 40 有 184 — F
To pardon, forgive; lenient
｜罪 remit offence, reprieve
原｜to forgive 寬｜, 恕｜, 赦｜

右^4 口 30 右 181 — B
Right hand, on right; to honor
｜翼 right wing of army
｜·邊 the right hand side
｜手 the right hand

佑^4 祐^4 人 9 右 181 — C
Protect, aid, divine care
｜民 to protect the people
保·｜to protect 庇｜

Char.	Radical	Phonetic	Meaning		
誘⁴	言 149	秀 217	Allure, induce, encourage 丨獲 to abduct, inveigle 丨惑 to tempt, beguile 引丨		C
幼⁴	幺 52	幺 876	Young 丨年, tender, immature 丨稚 young, jejune 丨小, 丨少⁴ 丨∘稚時代 period of childhood 丨∘稚園 kindergarten 丨童 a young boy 丨子³ 長³丨 seniors and juniors 老丨		C
牖⁴³	片 91	甫 597	A window, lattice; to lead 天之丨民 God enlightens people		G
柚⁴	木 75	由 818	Pomelo 丨·子 丨·木 teak wood		K
釉⁴	采 165	由 818	Glossy, glazed		H
鼬⁴	鼠 208	由 818	North China pole-cat, Siberian weasel		K

Yung

Char.	Radical	Phonetic	Meaning		
雍¹ 邕¹	隹 172	雍 62	Affable, harmonious, union S. 丨和宮 Lama Temple at Peking 丨睦 friendly, cordial		K
壅¹³	土 32	雍 62	To block, dam; put on 丨塞 (se⁴) stop, close up, obstruct		G
擁¹	手 64	雍 62	To crowd, press 丨擠 丨·上來 push ahead 丨·上前 一丨 with one rush,—a crowd	yung³	D
癰¹	疒 104	雍 62	A malignant boil, abscess 丨瘡 丨疽 a running sore, cancer		H
庸¹	广 53	庸 595	To employ; ordinary, constant; merit 丨常 common, ordinary 平丨, 凡丨 丨醫 stupid doctor, quack 丨人 simple, common person 丨碌 incapacity 丨劣		E

Yung

傭[1]	人 9	庸 595	To employ, hire, serve, hired ｜工 hire for labor, workmen ｜賃 to be let out for hire		D
墉[12]	土 32	庸 595	Adobe wall, redoubt		K
容[2]	宀 40	容 711	Contain; endure; manner, face, looks (see jung[2])	jung[2]	A
永[3]	水 85	永 521	Eternal, long, always ｜不 never; as ｜不止息 ｜生 eternal life ｜活 ｜世無窮 for ever, everlasting ｜遠 eternal, everlasting ｜久		B
咏[3] 詠[3]	口 30	永 521	Sing, chant, hum 唱｜ ｜詩班 choir, chorus 歌｜ sing, chant		G
泳[3]	水 85	永 521	To swim, dive		H
勇[3]	力 19	勇 594a	Brave, daring, braves ｜氣 martial ｜壯 ｜猛 bold, intrepid, fierce ｜敢 ｜士 a brave person ｜人 ｜往直前 resolutely advance		C
湧[3] 涌[3]	水 85	勇 594a	To well up, rush, rise ｜泉 bubbling up of spring ｜流 rippling streams		E
擁[3]	手 64	雍 62	To hug, embrace, clasp ｜抱 ｜護 protect, preserve 蜂｜ gather in crowd like bees	yung[1]	D
甬[3] 埇[3]	用 101	甬 594	Middle; burst forth; measure ｜路 raised pathway, paved walk ｜東 Ningpo. ｜河 Ningpo River		I
俑[3]	人 9	甬 594	Puppets buried with the dead 作｜ to start evil customs		G
踊[3]	足 157	甬 594	Exult, to leap ｜躍 jump about for joy		C

用[4] 用 101 用 593 A

To use, employ; expenses; with, by
| 計 contrive. | 勁 use effort
| 錢 to expend money
|·處 use; service, function 功 |
|·法 use, manner of using
| 飯 to take a meal
| 項 expenditure
| 心 to apply the mind
| 人 employ men
| 工 work hard
| 力 to use strength
|·不着[2] of no use, not required
|·不慣 unaccustomed to
| 完·了 finished using, used up
|·度 expenses, living
應 | useful. practical 合 |

Yü

淤[1] 水 85 於 263 F

Mire, mud, silt | 泥
| 漲 to silt up | 積

瘀[1] 疒 104 於 263 H

Extravasated blood
| 氣 sort of melancholia
| 血 local accumulation of blood
| 肉 gangrenous flesh

迂[1] 辵 162 于 30 I

Distant; distorted; very
| 見 distorted view, prejudice
| 滯 stupid, obstinate

魚[2] 魚 195 魚 256 A

Fish, fishy, 一條 | or 一尾 | S.
| 池 fish-pond. | 鈎 fish hook
| 翅 sharks' fins; fish fins
| 竿 a fishing rod
| 缸 a fish-globe or jar
| 雷 torpedo. | 雷艇 torpedo-boat
| 鱗 fish scales. | 鰾 fish-glue
| 食 fish-bait. | 子[3] fish roe
| 網 a fishing net

Character	Radical	Phonetic	Meaning		
魚^{2}			｜眼 "fish—eyes" warts, corns ｜鷹 the fish-hawk or osprey		
漁^{2}	水 85	魚 256	To fish; seize upon ｜取 ｜翁 fisherman ｜·夫, ｜戶, ｜人 ｜業 the fishing industry		F
余^{2} 予^{2}	人 9	余 31	I, me, myself, we	S	F
餘^{2}	食 184	余 31	Remnant, overplus, balance ｜錢 surplus, balance ｜銀, ｜欵 ｜力 superabundant strength ｜利 earnings, profit ｜剩 surplus, remainder 有｜ 其｜ the rest, the others		A
於^{2}	方 70	於 263	With, at, to, in; in reference to S. ｜今 now, at present time ｜人有益 beneficial to men ｜是 thereupon, at that ｜此 here, at this 問｜我 learnt from me		B
于^{2}	二 7	于 30	In, at, with, as to (as 於) ｜歸 the marriage of a girl ｜是 as to, as far as	S	G
盂^{2}	皿 108	于 30	A bowl, tub, basin, large cup ｜蘭會 "All souls' Day" 15-7 mo. 鉢｜ priest's alms-dish		B
竽^{2}	竹 118	于 30	Reed organ of 36 tubes 濫｜充數 a pretender		K
禺^{2}	内 114	禺 575	A monkey; to begin 端｜		K
愚^{2}	心 61	禺 575	Silly, stupid; to befool ｜見 my stupid opinion ｜拙 rustic, simple, stupid ｜人 ｜兄 "stupid brother", I; so ｜弟 ｜弄 to deceive, befool ｜昧 simple, stupid ｜蒙, ｜鈍, ｜笨		B

Yü

Character	Radical	Phonetic	Meaning	Other reading	Grade
隅²	阜 170	禺 575	Corner, angle 角｜ 方｜right angle		G
俞² 兪²	入 11	兪 619	To assent, yes, ｜允 S. ｜｜quiet and respectful air		K
愈²	心 61	兪 619	More; better, surpass, increase ｜久｜好 the longer the better ｜甚 much more	yü⁴	B
楡²	木 75	兪 619	The elm ｜樹, ｜·木 ｜·錢 "elm cash," i.e. elmseeds		F
瑜²	玉 96	兪 619	Luster, excellence		H
逾² 踰²	辵 162	兪 619	To pass over, exceed; cross, omit ｜分 exceed one's functions ｜過 pass beyond, exceed ｜于 ｜越節 Passover of the Jews		D
與²¹ 欤²¹	臼 134	與 691	Particle of query, exclamation	yü³	C
譽²	言 149	與 691	To eulogize, flatter; reputation 面｜praise to one's face	yü⁴	D
輿²	車 159	與 691	To sustain, carriage; the world; basis; many, the public ｜情 public sentiment ｜論 public opinion ｜地 topography, geography 地理		G
娛²	女 38	吳 761	To rejoice, pleasure, relaxation ｜樂 pleasure, joy -le⁴ 歡｜to rejoice, be pleased		G
虞² 驉?²	虍 141	吳 761	Provide for; anxious; danger; Emperor Shun, to appease S. 防｜guard against dangers		G
舁²	臼 134	臼 680	To lift, carry, offer ｜拱, ｜舉 ｜扛 carry on a pole		H
臾²	臼 134	臼 680	A moment 須｜		H

Yü

諛²	言 149	臼 680	To flatter, adulate 面 | | 色 a toadying expression		I
雨³	雨 173	兩 562	Rain, 下 | to rain | 具 waterproof articles | 星 rain drops. | 靴 rain boots | 衣 waterproof clothing | 帽 rain cap. | 傘 umbrella | 水 rain water; a solar term	yü⁴	A
圄³	囗 31	吾 763	To detain, imprison, prison		I
敔³	攴 66	吾 763	To stop the music		K
語³	言 149	吾 763	To converse, language, words | 調 the tune, or style of language | 言 an expression; language | 云 the proverb says 言 | words, speech 成 | ready-made phrases 不言不 | not saying a word	i⁴ yü⁴	A
與³ 与³	臼 134	與 691	Give; with, by; than; and |∘其 rather than | 人物 give a person anything | 理不合 inconsistent with reason | 料 data | 物 | 你何干 what concern of yours?	yü²¹	C
宇³	宀 40	于 30	Canopy of heaven; vast; eaves | 宙 space & time, universe | 文 double surname S. 廟 | temples		D
羽³	羽 124	羽 293	Wings, plumes, feathers | 翼 wings; to assist | 毛緞 English camlets | 布 bunting, stuff, alpaca | 扇 feather fans | 族 feathered tribes, birds		E

禹^{3}	内 114	内 574	Emperor Yü (｜王) B.C. 2205-2198; loose, full S. ｜步 barefoot		G
傴^{3}	人 9	區 696	Hunchbacked, stooping ｜僂		H
窳^{3}	穴 116	瓜 407	Filthy; useless, flawy, weak ｜惰 weak and indolent		I
雨^{4}	雨 173	兩 562	To rain, fall from the sky	yü³	A
語^{4}	言 149	吾 763	To speak, tell to ｜人	i⁴ yü³	A
寓^{4}	宀 40	禺 575	To dwell, lodge; at home, residence ｜∘處 a lodging ｜所 ｜居 reside at 寄｜ ｜言 a fable. 公｜apartments		C
遇^{4}	辵 162	禺 575	To meet, happen ｜∘着, ｜·見, 遭｜ ｜險 to meet with danger ｜難⁴ to fall into misfortune ｜·不見 can not meet ｜事 when something happens		B
豫^{4} 預^{4}	豕 152	予 114	Prearranged, beforehand, already, prepare ｜兆 a presage, premonition, omen ｜計 estimates, budget ｜算 ｜知 aware of, presentiment ｜防 to provide against ｜先 beforehand, anticipate ｜科 preparatory course ｜·備 to prepare, ready ｜·備不及 can't be ready in time ｜表 a presage, fore-type ｜算表 a budget statement ｜定 fix beforehand ｜言 to predict, prophecy		B
喻^{42}	口 30	俞 619	To understand, illustrate, a parable S.		C

喩[42]			｜言 metaphor; allegory 敎｜to instruct 比｜an illustration, for instance 不言而｜it goes without saying		
愈[4] 瘉[4]	心 61	兪 619	Healed, recovered 全｜cured, recovered 痊｜	yü[2]	B
諭[4]	言 149	兪 619	Edict, proclaim; instruct ｜旨 edict, rescript 上｜, 聖｜ ｜示 proclaim, proclamation 曉｜to notify publicly｜知		F
育[4]	肉 130	育 872	To rear, nurture, nourish 養｜ ｜嬰堂 a foundling home 敎｜education. 德｜moral educ. 生｜bear children, rear 產｜		C
峪[4]	山 46	谷 710	Pool in ravine, gully		I
欲[4]	欠 76	谷 710	Desires; to desire, long for ｜°望 desire, longing｜求 ｜要 if I want, to wish to 私｜private aims, selfish desires		D
慾[4]	心 61	谷 710	Passion, lust, desire 情｜, 嗜｜ ｜想 wanton thoughts｜念 ｜火 the fire of lust		C
浴[4]	水 85	谷 710	To bathe, cleanse 洗｜, 沐｜ ｜盆 a bathing-tub ｜室 a bath-house		E
裕[4]	衣 145	谷 710	Abundant; generous, enrich 富·｜ ｜後 enrich one's successors 豐｜abundant 寬｜open handed		F
玉[4]	玉 96	王 71	Jade, gem; imperial; you ｜成 bring to perfection ｜·器 jade ware.｜石 jadestone ｜璽 imperial jade seal ｜皇 Taoist Pearly Emperor｜帝 ｜工 jade workmanship		D

Yü

Character	Radical	Phonetic	Meaning		Other reading	
玉4			|·米 Indian corn |女 a lovely girl			
獄4	犬 94	獄 460	Litigation, law case; prison; Buddhist hell |官 prison officials 監| prison 牢|. |吏 jailor 地| hell—Buddhist and Christian			D
譽4	言 149	與 691	Fame, praise |人 to flatter a person 名◦| reputation, honorary		yü2	D
御4 馭4	彳 60	卸 307	To drive, manage; imperial; censor; to wait on |車 drive carriage; imperial car. |前 imperial attendants |服 imperial robes |衣; so |路 |河 Grand, or Imperial Canal |事 to manage affairs			F
禦4	示 113	卸 307	To resist, ward off 防|, 抵| |止 to stop, hinder |寇 to oppose banditti			H
域4 [illegible]4	土 32	或 333	Frontier, limit; country |中 in the world or universe 西| western foreign regions			F
澳4	水 85	奥 519	Bay, cove, dock		ao4	F
龥4 籲4	龠 214	龠 567	To pray, implore, invoke |禱 to pray to		yüeh4	
尉4	寸 41	尉 727	Surname |遲 double surname	S. S.	wei4	H
蔚4	艸 140	尉 727	City in N. W. Hopei |縣	S.	wei4	G
鬱4 鬰4	鬯 192	鬯 653	Anxious; oppressed, sullen; dense |氣 pent-up feelings |結 melancholy, depressed |悶	S.		H

Character	Radical	Phonetic	Definition	Variant	Code
鬻4	鬲 193	鬲 589	To sell, barter, nourish 丨女 sell one's daughters		I
芋4	艸 140	于 30	The taro; flourishing 丨·頭 species of potato; taro		I
圉4	囗 31	幸 159	Stable; prison; frontier 疆丨 丨守 guard the frontier		K
矞4	矛 110	矞 118	Felicitous; your; fear 丨座 your house		K
聿4	聿 129	聿 669	Pen; thereupon; to narrate 丨求 then I sought for—		K

Yüan

Character	Radical	Phonetic	Definition	Variant	Code
寃1 冤1	宀 40	兔 385	Ill-usage, grievance, wrong 丨·家 avenger, one oppressed, enemy 丨錢 "squeeze" money 丨情 aggrieved, injured 含丨 丨讎 enmity, hatred 丨仇 丨·屈 wronged, oppressed 丨·枉 伸丨 to avenge wrong 報丨		A
淵1	水 85	片 164	Abyss, deep gulf 深丨 丨海 the ocean, the deep 丨博 deep and wide, profound 丨深 deep, profound		E
鴛1	鳥 196	夗 271	The drake of mandarin duck 丨·鴦 mandarin ducks, conjugal fidelity		G
鳶1	鳥 196	鳥 253	Black-eared kite, kites; paper kite 紙丨		K
肙1	肉 130	肙 759	A worm; to surround; twist		K
員2	口 30	員 760	Officer, round 官丨 officer of government 委·丨 officer deputed	yün2	D

Yüan

圓^{2}	口 31	員 760	Round, circle, sphere, dollar 丨徑 diameter of a circle 丨球兒 round ball. 長丨oval 丨圈 a circle. 丨月 full moon 丨全 complete, thorough 丨∘滿 rounded out; complete; satisfactory 丨夢 to interpret dream 丨明園 (site of) palace near Peking, east of 頤和園 丨通 versatile, tactful 銀丨silver dollars		B
言^{2}	言 149	言 740	To speak 丨·語 (i^{4}) 俗	yen^{2}	B
元^{2}	儿 10	元 388	First, original, head; dollar; Mongol, a dynasty S. 丨∘朝 the Mongol dynasty, A. D. 1206-1333 丨氣 constitution, health 丨質 elementary substance 丨·宵 Lantern Feast; rice flour-balls 丨勳 great distinction, patriot 丨日 first day of the year 丨年 first year of any reign 丨∘寶 large ingot sycee of 50 taels 丨始 the very beginning 丨首 the chief, a sovereign 丨∘帥 commander-in-chief 丨素 original elements 丨點 atom, corpuscle 丨祖 the first ancestor		C
芫^{2}	艸 140	元 388	Coriander 丨荽 sui^{1}	yen^{2}	G
阮^{2}	阜 170	元 388	A pass in Kansu 五丨關	juan^{3} yuan^{3}	K

Yüan

黿²	黽 205	元 388	Great sea turtle | 鼈 老 | turtle; also abusive term		I
原²	厂 27	原 194	Origin; truly, actually; to forgive; plateau, plain | 案 the original case | 籍 one's birth place | 起 originally, at first | 先 | 價 prime or original cost | 質 element | 舊 the same as before | 意 original intent, motive | 議案 the original motion | 該如此 naturally should be so | 稿 original copy | 底·子 | 告 a plaintiff. | 來 in first instance, in fact | 理 first principles, reason |·諒 to make allowance for; excusing | 料 original materials | 本 the origin, originally | 始 in the beginning, primitive |·是 as before; in fact, indeed | 作 original copy or model | 動力 motive. | 子³ atom | 文 original text | 因 cause, origin | 宥 to forgive		C
源²	水 85	原 194	Spring, source, fountain 泉 | | 流 source and history of		D
緣²	糸 120	彖 287	Affinity, connection; because |·分⁴ providential opportunity | 何 why? wherefore? |·故 a cause, a reason | 此 on account of this | 由 a cause or origin		C

櫞²	木 75	彖 287	Palm-like tree 香 |		K
袁²	衣 145	袁 370	A long robe S.		G
園²	口 31	袁 370	Garden, park |·子; enclosure | 夫 a gardener | 丁 花 |·子 flower garden; so 菜 |·子 公 | public park		C
轅²	車 159	袁 370	Cart shafts; palisades before yamen; general's office | 門		H
爰²	爪 87	爰 187	Therefore, then; onto, thereupon | 既 and thereupon		H
媛²	女 38	爰 187	Winning, beautiful, flighty 名 | famous beauty, Hebe 淑 | chaste and beautiful		G
援²	手 64	爰 187	To pull out; rescue, assist; quote | 救 to rescue. | 助 help; aid | 拔 to pull out from | 兵 reinforcement of troops 後 | backing, reliance		D
垣²	土 32	亘 795	A wall 牆 | . 城 | city wall		E
遠³ 远³	辵 162	袁 370	Distant, far, remote 遙 | | 近 far and near, distance | 親 distant relations | 族 | 來的 come from a distance | 路 long road | 足會 touring society | 東 Far East. 永 | forever | 因 remote cause | |·的 far away, distant	yüan⁴	A
阮³	阜 170	元 388	A mountain, ancient Kansu	juan³ yuan²	K
願⁴ 愿⁴	頁 181	原 194	To wish, desire; be willing; a vow |·意 to wish, desire, willing | 力 will power		B

願^4 (continued)
| 書 pledge, bond of scholars
|∘望 to hope, desire
| 欲 to desire, to wish
志∘| resolution
情∘| quite willing, voluntarily
請 | petition
許 | make a vow

遠^4 — 辵 162 — 袁 370 — yüan^3 — A
Keep aloof from, keep at a distance
| 小人 aloof from mean men
| 離 keep aloof from, avoid

院^4 — 阜 170 — 完 389 — B
Hall, college, court yard
|·子 a courtyard; attendants
書 | college, library 學 |

怨^4 — 心 61 — 夗 271 — D
To grumble, murmur; hate, ill-will; grievance
|∘氣 ill-will, dissatisfaction
|∘恨 to abhor, detest
|·不得 not to be blamed; no wonder
| 誰 whose fault is it?
| 天 murmur against heaven
| 言 words of dissatisfaction
埋 (man^2)·| bear grudge, resent 抱·|

苑^4 — 艸 140 — 夗 271 — G
A collection; imperial park S.
翰林 | Hanlin Academy

Yüeh

約^{14} — 糸 120 — 勺 231 — yüeh^4 — B
A covenant; restrain; about, in general; a treaty; frugal 儉 |
| 期 appointment, engagement
| 契 an agreement, treaty 契 |
| 法 provisional constitution
| 會 to arrange to meet
|·摸着 surmising, probably 大 |
| 束 restrain, keep in order

<table>
<tr><td>約[14]</td><td></td><td></td><td>| 條 contract, treaty 條 |
新舊 | Old and New Testaments
立 | make covenant agreement</td><td></td><td></td></tr>
<tr><td>曰[14]</td><td>曰
73</td><td>日
792</td><td>To speak, call, say. 答 | reply
詩 | it is said in the Odes</td><td></td><td>F</td></tr>
<tr><td>噦[1]</td><td>口
30</td><td>歲
132</td><td>To retch, vomit 乾 |</td><td></td><td>I</td></tr>
<tr><td>月[4]</td><td>月
74</td><td>月
621</td><td>Moon |·亮; month, lunar
| 季花 the monthly rose
| 經 the menses | 水
|·分[4]牌 almanac, calendar
| 黑天 moonless night
| 薪 teacher's salary
| 光 moonlight
| 滿 the full moon | 盈, | 圓
|·餅 cake for 8 mo. 15 day festival
| 蝕 an eclipse of the moon
| 臺 veranda, rwy. platform
| 臺票 platform-ticket
| 底 the end of the month
| 牙 moon's quarters
| 曜日 Monday
|。| every month, monthly
| 暈 halo round the moon | 闌</td><td></td><td>A</td></tr>
<tr><td>樂[4]</td><td>木
75</td><td>樂
490</td><td>Music. 奏 | strike up music
| 隊 band of musicians
音 | musical instruments, music</td><td>le[4]
yao[4]</td><td>A</td></tr>
<tr><td>藥[4]
葯[4]</td><td>艸
140</td><td>樂
490</td><td>Medicinal herbs, medicine | 材 文
| 王 Chinese god of medicine
| 線 a fuse yao[4]-</td><td>yao[4]</td><td>A</td></tr>
<tr><td>戉[4]
鉞[4]</td><td>戈
62</td><td>戉
340</td><td>A halberd with crescent blade
秉 | grasp a halberd</td><td></td><td>K</td></tr>
<tr><td>越[4]</td><td>走
156</td><td>戉
340</td><td>To exceed, overstep, pass over S.
| 級 to pass over, overstep
| 墻 to get over a wall</td><td></td><td>B</td></tr>
</table>

越⁴			|。發 more and more, still more | 國 the ancient state of Yüeh | 禮 overstep propriety | 南國 Annam | 早 | 好 the earlier the better 超 | surpass, excel 卓 |			
曜⁴	日 72	翟 57	Effulgence	文	yao⁴	H
耀⁴ 燿⁴	羽 124	翟 57	Bright, glorious, to illumine 榮 | glory, illustrious, glorify 光 | bright, brilliant	文	yao⁴	B
躍⁴ 趯⁴	足 157	翟 57	Skip, leap, caper, quickly | 然 plainly 跳 | dance and skip			G
龠⁴	龠 214	龠 567	A flute, fife, measure			K
鑰⁴	金 167	龠 567	Bolt of lock, a key	文	yao⁴	B
籲⁴ 龥⁴	竹 118	龠 567	To invoke, implore 呼 |, | 懇 | 天 cry to God | 禱 to pray to		yü⁴	F
悅⁴	心 61	兌 756	Pleasing, pleased, gratified | 服 submit with pleasure | 從 | 心的 pleasing, acceptable | 口 please the taste | 目 gratify the eye 喜 | pleased, rejoice			D
閱⁴	門 169	兌 756	To examine, review, inspect | 者注意 readers, take notice! | 歷 view in order, experience | 報所 public reading room | 兵 view troops | 操			E
岳⁴	山 46	丘 213	A mountain peak; a wife's parents |。父, | 母			E
瘧⁴	疒 104	虐 205	Fever | 疾 remittent fever	文	nüeh⁴ yao⁴	E

嶽[4]	山 46	嶽 460	Lofty peak. 五 | 5 sacred mountains i.e. 泰山, 衡山, 華山, 恒山, 嵩山		G

Yün

云[2]	二 7	云 875	To say, speak; an expletive | 爾 in this way, thus | | etc., etc., and so on 有 | there is a saying that		F
耘[2] 秐[2]	耒 127	云 875	To weed, hoe | 草 pull up weeds		G
芸[2]	艸 140	云 875	Fragrant herb, rue; to weed |·香 rue; a kind of resin | 豆 French bean		I
雲[2]	雨 173	云 875	Clouds |·彩, fog; numerous S. | 氣 vapour, fog; mist | 霞 red clouds |·南 province of Yünnan | 散[4]·了 the clouds dispersed 浮 | a passing cloud		A
勻[2]	勹 20	勻 232	Equal, even, divide equally |·淨 uniform, even |·分 divide equally 均 | impartial, equally | 和		D
筠[2]	竹 118	勻 232	Bamboo splints or skin 青 | | 籃 splint baskets		K
員[2]	口 30	員 760	To speak, add to, of use to	yüan[2]	D
允[3]	儿 10	允 869	To grant, assent, allow; sincere | 准 to consent, sanction | 行 | 許 to promise, assent | 肯, | 從 |·了 promised, sanctioned 應[1] | consent to, respond to	jun[3]	D
殞[3]	歹 78	員 760	To die, perish | 滅, | 命		H

隕^3 磒^3	阜 170	員 760	Fall from height, ｜落, crash ｜石 an aerolite ｜墮 fall in ruin, collapse		H
暈^4	日 72	軍 838	Dizzy 頭｜; mist, halo ｜車 feel motion of cart ｜船 to be sea-sick ｜海 ｜過去 to faint		B
鄆^4	邑 163	軍 838	Ancient city in Shantung		I
運^4	辵 162	軍 838	To revolve; transport; luck [strength ｜·氣 fortune, luck. ｜氣^4 concentrate ｜轉^3 to revolve, circulate ｜費 freightage. ｜送船 a transport ｜河 The Grand Canal ; canal ｜行 to come and go ｜∘動 to move, to exercise; to work for private ends; a campaign ｜∘動家 an athlete ｜∘動選舉 election campaign ｜∘動會 athletic meet, sports ｜用 to make use of, apply		D
熨^4 尉^4	火 86	尉 727	To iron, to smooth ｜衣服 to iron clothes ｜·斗 a smoothing iron	wei^4	B
孕^4	子 39	乃 216	To be pregnant 懷｜ ｜婦 a pregnant woman ｜育 conceive and bring forth		E
韻^4 韵^4	音 180	員 760	A rhyme, chord, dulcet ｜調 to tune; rhyme and tune ｜書 rhyming dictionary ｜文 poetry, rhyming compositions		G
慍^4	心 61	𥁕 606	Irritated, hurt, wroth ｜怒	wen^4	H
熅^4	火 86	𥁕 606	To smooth out, iron ｜衣服 ｜平·了 ironed smooth		H

Yün

藴[4]	艸 140	𥁕 606	To collect, bring together; abstruse 丨蓄 contained within 含丨		F
韞[4]	韋 178	𥁕 606	To contain, conceal, keep close 丨秘 secrete, 包丨 contain.		H

RADICAL INDEX

(1) Stroke (2) Strokes

2 Strokes (con't.)

人 亻

儿

低	509	侯	157	倪	360	偶	372	傾	82	僻	404
佃	522	係	163	倚	220	偪	398	僂	317	儍	433
佗	532	俠	164	個	251	偏	410	傲	5	儎	539
佟	582	俅	86	俱	112	偸	534	傷	437	儕[14]	10
佐	552	俚	295	倨	114	停	528	僊	177	儔	92
作	553	俐	297	倔	121	偈	41	僉	63	㒚	602
位	599	俄	370	倦	117	偺	541	催	561	儒	231
佚	224	保	386	倆	300	倂	415	傴	646	儘	75
佑	639	侶	324	埶	239	側	549	傭	641	償[15]	17
余	643	便	409	們	335	傁	473	僑[12]	52	儡	292
侈[6]	72	信	183	倫	322	做	553	僭	62	優	635
侖	321	俗	474	俺	3	偹	392	僱	261	儭[16]	27
依	216	俟	483	俾	391	偵	24	僚	303	儲	98
侃	240	俏	53	倍	392	偉	598	僕	425	㒺[17]	139
佳	42	侵	77	俻	392	偃	626	僧	432	儳	543
侔	45	俎	557	倭	604	傅[10]	145	像	169	儷[19]	299
供	277	促	558	併	415	傖	28	㒋	480	儹	541
來	284	俊	123	倏	465	傚	172	僞	600	儼[20]	626
侚	196	侮	609	倐	465	傢	41	僥	50	儻	499
例	299	俓	80	修	186	傑	55	儀[13]	218	儾[22]	356
佩	394	俑	641	倘	499	傀	274	價	43	**10 儿**	
佬	290	倡[8]	18	倒	501	傍	384	僵	44		
侍	456	倈	285	倜	515	備	392	儌	50	儿	227
侅	235	値	67	倉	544	傘	429	儉	59	兀[1]	610
使	452	倣	131	借	55	傁	473	億	221	兀[2]	295
侊	516	俯	142	俶	465	債[11]	10	儆	80	元	650
佯	614	俸	139	假[9]	43	傳	102	儈	266	允	656
侑	639	候	157	偕	174	傻	433	儊	99	充[3]	110
俘[7]	141	倖	186	健	61	僅	75	儂	368	兄	188

2 Strokes (con't.)

力 勹 匕 匚 匸 十 卜 卩巳 厂 厶 又 口

口

3 Strokes (con't.)

号	151	吱	66	咐	143	咩	340	哺	142	唯	597
叫	50	呈	29	呵	154	哀	1	唇	107	[illegible]	319
可	253	吹	106	呼	197	品	412	哨	440	唫	630
古	259	吩	135	和	154	哂	445	唆	471	喳[9]	6
句	113	吠	134	咕	258	咲	172	唐	499	喞	32
另	313	否	139	咎	85	咷	503	[illegible]	418	喘	102
叭	373	含	147	命	345	咱	541	員	649	喊	148
叵	420	吼	157	呢	359	哉	537	唀	569	喜	161
史	453	吸	159	咆	389	咠	38	唱[8]	18	啣	179
司	481	告	244	呸	393	咢	371	啤	403	喝	154
台	490	呌	50	呻	444	咨	583	啄	89	喧	192
叨	500	君	123	咂	536	哇	589	啜	89	喚	204
叼	515	吝	310	呱	259	咬	618	唬	171	喙	210
叮	525	呂	324	味	599	咽	627	啃	247	喬	52
右	639	吶	367	咉	613	哲[7]	22	啓	40	喫	71
后[3]	158	吧	373	呦	636	哮	171	啌	46	喉	157
向	169	吞	577	音	536	哼	124	唳	300	喵	339
合	154	吣	78	咏	641	哰	289	唵	3	喇	283
吁	190	吮	562	哎[6]	1	哥	249	啊	1	喪	429
吉	34	[illegible]	536	咫	68	哽	248	商	436	善	435
吃	71	吻	602	响	168	哭	262	售	460	喃	355
各	251	吾	607	咸	178	哩	294	啡	132	啻	457
吏	299	吳	607	哈	145	哶	340	啐	561	單	491
名	344	呀	611	哄	213	唚	78	啇	509	啼	513
吊	515	吟	630	咳	253	哪	352	啚	400	喂	600
吐	571	听	527	咵	264	唉	1	唾	533	喈	541
吆	616	周[5]	90	咼	263	唻	464	啞	612	喻	646
同	581	咋	7	咧	305	哦	370	唼	58	嗔[10]	25
吵[4]	21	呪	90	咯	316	唎	374	問	603	嗤	72

口 口 土

3 Strokes (con't.)

Character	Page
嗐	147
嗅	188
嗎	326
嗓	429
喿	430
嗇	431
嗜	457
嗣	483
嗁	513
嗦	474
嗆	47
嗟	121
噏	603
嘗[11]	17
嘛	326
嘉	42
嘁	38
嘇	31
嘔	371
嗶	401
嗽	473
嘆	496
嘈	547
嘖	549
嗹	306
嘲[12]	21
嘱	95
嘎	235
嘬	551
嘟	566
嘷	150
嗡	159
噐	40
嘩	200
嘮	288
噘	120
嘿	347
嘰	30
噍	48
嘴	560
噓	190
噝	481
噎	620
噫[13]	217
噙	77
嚧	291
器	40
噤	76
噸	577
噯	1
嚕	319
噩	371
噥	368
噴	396
噪	430
噦	654
嚎[14]	150
嚀	365
嚇	156
嚙	179
嚏	514
嚕[15]	318
嚮[16]	169
嚨	323
嚥	627
嚷[17]	225
嚵	13
嚴	623
嚼[18]	49
囂	171
囊[19]	356
囉	315
囑[21]	95
囓	362
囔[22]	356

31 囗

Character	Page
囗	598
囚[2]	87
四	481
回[3]	208
囘	208
囟	186
因	628
囬[4]	208
囫	197
国	280
困	276
囤	576
囮	638
固[5]	262
囹	311
囿[6]	639
圅[7]	148
圃	426
圄	645
圈[8]	118
國	280
圇	322
圉	649
圍[9]	597
圓[10]	650
園	652
圖[11]	570
團	573
圔	638
圞[19]	321

32 土

Character	Page
士	570
圭[3]	272
地	511
在	538
址[4]	68
坊	131
坎	240
坑	248
均	122
坍	495
坏	403
坛	495
坆	135
坐	552
垂[5]	106
坰	87
坤	275
坭	359
坴	320
坯	403
坡	420
坼	549
坦	496
型[6]	185
垜	530
垛	530
垢	256
垤	518
垣	652
埋[7]	327
城	29
埃	2
垻	375
埇	641
執[8]	67
基	31
埽	430
堅	58
堇	75
堃	275
培	393
埠	425
埶	222
堂	499
堆	573
埜	620
埳	240
域	648
場[9]	18
堪	240
堦	54
堡	387
報	387
堤	509
堞	518
堵	567
堿	60
堯	617
堭	206
塊[10]	266
塚	109
塞	431
塑	475
塐	475
塌	487

Character	Page
塔	488
塘	499
塡	524
塟	544
塗	570
塢	609
塋	634
塵[11]	26
塲	18
墈	241
境	81
墓	351
墅	465
墁	329
塾	462
墖	488
墊	522
墉	641
墜[12]	105
墳	135
墰	495
墨	347
墩	576
墮	531
墫	562
增	550
墾[13]	247
壁	401
壇	495
墻	47
壅	640
壕[14]	150
壑	157
壓	611
壙[15]	271
壘	292
壞[16]	202
壤[17]	225
壩[21]	375

33 士

Character	Page
士	455
壬[1]	226
壯[4]	104
壳	253
声	446
壺[9]	197
壻	191
壹	216
壽[11]	460

34 夂

Character	Page
夂	71
夅[3]	46
夆[4]	137

35 夊

Character	Page
夊	476
夋[4]	123
夌[5]	312
复[6]	142
夏[7]	165

36 夕

Character	Page
夕	163
外[2]	590
夗	592
夙[3]	475
多	529
夜[5]	621
夠[8]	256
够	256
梦	337
夢[11]	337
夥	215

37 大

Character	Page
大	485
夫[1]	139
夬	120
太	491
天	523
夭	616
夯[2]	149
失	449
央	613
夫	398
夷[3]	218
夸	264
臾	184
夾[4]	42
奉[5]	138
奇	38
奈	354
奄	626
奐[6]	204
契	41
奎	274
奔	395
奏	555
奕	223
奘[7]	104
奚	159
套	505
奢[9]	441
奠	522
奧[10]	5
奪[11]	529
奬	45
奩	308
獘[12]	400
奮[13]	136

38 女

Character	Page
女	369
奶[2]	354
奴	367
妁[3]	89
妃	133
好	150
如	231
奸	59
妄	595
妝[4]	103
妨	131
妓	36
妗	76
妙	340
妞	365
妣	399
妥	533
妒	569
妖	616
妍	624
妯[5]	90
姑	258
妹	334
姆	290
妳	354
妮	359
始	453
姤	569
妻	37
姐	55
妾	57
姊	585
姉	585
委	598
姒	482
姓	186
姪[6]	68
姨	218
姜	45
姦	59
姥	290
姿	583
娃	590
威	596
姚	617
姻	629
娌[7]	295
娭	36
娘	361
𡟰	444
娓	598
娣	512
娠	444
娩	342
娛	644
娼[8]	16
婦	143
婚	211
婪	286
婁	317

3 Strokes (con't.)

Character	Page
婢	393
婊	405
婆	420
娶	116
婉	592
媧	629
媍[9]	143
媛	652
媒	333
媚	335
媆	358
嫂	430
婷	528
婿	191
嫌[10]	178
嫁	43
媿	274
媽	326
嫪	430
媳	160
嫉	36
媼	5
嫠[11]	295
嫩	358
嫰	358
嫖	406
嫦	17
嫡	510
嬉[12]	160
嫺	178
嬌	48
嬭[14]	354
嬪	412
嬰	633
嬸[15]	445
孃[17]	361
孀	467
孌[19]	325

39 子

Character	Page
子	584
孔[1]	280
孕[2]	657
存[3]	563
字	586
孚[4]	141
孝	172
斈	194
孛	419
孜	584
季[5]	34
孤	259
孟	337
孥	367
孩[6]	145
孫[7]	477
孰[8]	462
孳[10]	584
學[13]	194
孺[14]	231
孼[16]	362
孽[17]	362
孾	633

40 宀

Character	Page
宀	341
宁[2]	96
它	532
宄	234
安[3]	3
守	459
宅	9
宇	645
宏[4]	213
宋	479
完	591
宙[5]	91
宜	218
官	267
宝	387
宕	498
定	526
宗	563
宛	592
宦[6]	205
客	254
室	455
宣	192
宥	639
害[7]	146
家	41
宮	278
[illegible]	164
宵	170
宰	537
宴	627
容	233
寄[8]	36
寇	258
密	339
宿	474
寂	37
寅	630
寃	649
富[9]	143
寒	147
寐	334
寗	365
寔	451
寓	646
寘[10]	70
察[11]	8
寨	10
寡	263
寥	303
寞	348
寧	365
實	451
寢	78
寤	610
寬[12]	269
寮	303
審	444
寫	175
寰[13]	203
寵[16]	111
寶	387
寳[17]	387

41 寸

Character	Page
寸	563
对[2]	573
寺[3]	482
㝵[5]	2
封[6]	137
将[7]	44
尅	255
尃	140
射	442
專[8]	100
將	44
尉	648
尋[9]	195
尌	463
尊	562
對[11]	573
導[13]	501

42 小

Character	Page
小	171
少[1]	440
尔[2]	125
尖[3]	58
尚[5]	439
尞[9]	304
尠[12]	547

43 尢

Character	Page
尢	594
尣	594
尤[1]	637
就[9]	85

44 尸

Character	Page
尸	450
尺[1]	73
尹	631
尼[2]	359
尻	245
尽[3]	76
局[4]	112
尿	361
屁	404
尾	598

3 Strokes (con't.)

屆[5] 56
届 56
居 112
[illegible] 112
屈 115
[illegible] 463
屍[6] 450
屋 605
屎 453
展[7] 11
屑 176
屏[8] 416
屜 514
属[9] 463
屧 514
屠 570
屢[11] 324
屣 162
履[12] 324
層 551
屬[18] 463

45 屮

屮 23
屯[1] 577
屰[3] 360

46 山

山 434
[illegible][2] 477
岔[4] 8
岑 550
岐 39
岁 477
岡[5] 241
岱 489
岸 4
岩 624
岳 655
峒[6] 581
峯[7] 137
峰 137
峻 123
峪 647
島 501
崇[8] 111
崎 38
崑 275
崙 322
崩 396
崔 561
崖 613
嵌[9] 65
崽 538
嵗[10] 477
嵩 478
嶂[11] 16
嶇 115
嶗[12] 289
嶝 508
嶺[14] 312
嶽 656
巍[18] 596
巔[19] 520
巖[20] 624

47 川

川 102
巛 102
州[3] 89
巡[4] 195
巠 78
[illegible][6] 357
巢[8] 21
巤 306

48 工

工 276
左[2] 552
巧 52
巨 114
巫[4] 605
差[6] 7

49 己

己 34
已 219
巳 482
巴[1] 373
㠯[3] 219
巷[6] 169
巽[9] 197

50 巾

巾 74
市[2] 455
布 424
帆[3] 128
帆 128
帋[4] 68
希 159
帚[5] 90
帙 70
帘 307
帕 376
帛 418
帒 489
帑 500
帖 519
帥[6] 466
[illegible] 454
帝 512
帮[7] 383
師 449
席 161
帳[8] 15
帡 396
常 17
帶 489
帷 597
幅[9] 140
帽 332
幇 383
幏 51
幃 597
幌[10] 207
幔[11] 330
幕 351
幙 351
幣[12] 400
幟 69
幡 127
幠 200
幨[13] 307
幫[14] 383
幪 336

51 干

干 238
平[2] 415
年[3] 362
幵 64
开 64
并 415
幷[5] 415
幸 186
幹[10] 239
[illegible] 60

52 幺

幺 616
么 616
幻[1] 204
幼[2] 640
幽[6] 635
幾[9] 34
鹽[11] 36

53 广

广 626
庄[3] 103
広 346
床[4] 104
庇 401
序 191
府[5] 142
庚 248
庙 340
庖 389
底 510
店 521
度[6] 568
庠 168

广 廴 廾 弋 弓 彐彑 彡 彳 心忄⺗

3 Strokes (con't.)

(4) Strokes

庫[7] 262
庭 528
座 552
康[8] 242
庵 3
庶 464
庹 533
庸 640
廂[9] 167
廁 482
廈[10] 165
廊 288
廋 472
廉 307
廏[11] 5
廕 632
廠[12] 18
廛 13
廚 97
廢 134
廣 270
廟 340
廩[13] 310
廬[16] 318
廳[22] 527

54 廴

廴 631
廵[3] 195
廷[4] 528
延[5] 624
廼 510
廹 421
廻[6] 208
建[6] 61

55 廾

廾 278
廿[1] 364
弁[2] 410
弄[4] 369
弈[6] 223
弊[12] 400

56 弋

弋 224
弌[1] 216
弍[2] 125
式[3] 454
弒[9] 454

57 弓

弓 278
弔[1] 516
引 630
弗[2] 141
弘 213
弛 453
弝[4] 374
弟 512
弦[5] 178
弩 367
弢 503
弭[6] 339
弸 396
弱[7] 230
弰 439
張[8] 14
強 47
弸 396
强[9] 47
彀[10] 256
彈[12] 495
彊[13] 47
彌[14] 338
彎[19] 591

58 彐

彐 37
彑 37
旧[2] 271
彔[5] 320
彖[6] 573
彗[8] 209
彙[10] 210

59 彡

彡 434
形[4] 185
彥[6] 628
彫[8] 515
彪 405
彩 540
彬 412
彭[9] 398
彰[11] 14
影[12] 634

60 彳

彳 73
彷[4] 131
役 223
彿[5] 141
征 27
彼 399
往 594
徂 557
徃 594
很[6] 153
後 157
徊 208
律 324
待 490
徇 196
徑[7] 80
徐 190
徒 570
徘[8] 379
徠 285
徙 162
得 505
從 566
徜 17
御 648
復[9] 144
徤 61
徧 410
徨 206
循 196
微[10] 596
徹[12] 23
徵 28
德 505
徽[14] 207

61 心

心 181
必[1] 400
志[3] 70
忍 227
忌 35
忙 330
忒 506
忐 496
忑 506
忖 563
忘 595
忠[4] 109
忻 182
忿 136
怀 202
忽 197
快 265
念 364
忱 26
忸 366
忝 524
忤 609
怙[5] 199
怵 99
怡 219
怩 360
怳 207
怯 57
急 33
怪 265
怒 367
怌 395
怕 376
怦 397
怖 424
性 186

4 Strokes (con't.)

怛	487	悍[7]	149	悼	502	惰	530	慝	506	懍	310
思	479	患	204	悳	505	惻	549	慙	543	懋	349
怠	490	悋	310	惪	505	愁	92	慚	543	懊	5
怎	550	悔	208	惦	522	愠	657	慘	543	懂	579
怍	553	悃	275	⿰忄典	524	愚	643	慼	38	憶	221
怱	565	您	364	惕	515	愈	647	慣	268	應	632
怏	616	悖	392	惇	576	慌[10]	205	慽	38	懣[14]	336
怨	653	悉	160	悽	37	愰	207	慰	600	懞	337
恥[6]	73	悌	514	情	82	愿	652	憂	635	懦	367
恨	153	悐	515	悴	561	愧	274	慾	647	懲[15]	30
恆	153	悄	52	惟	597	慄	299	憤[12]	136	懸[16]	192
恒	153	悤	565	惡	370	愽	418	憿	18	懷	202
恍	207	悆	587	惶[9]	206	慎	445	憩	41	懶	286
恪	122	悟	610	惽	211	愬	474	憨	147	懵	337
恰	44	悞	610	意	220	愻	196	憲	181	懺[17]	14
恐	279	悠	636	惹	229	態	491	憍	121	懾[18]	23
恋	308	悅	655	愯	530	慈	587	憐	307	懼	114
恭	278	悵[8]	15	感	239	慇	629	憫	343	懽	203
恠	265	惝	18	愜	58	⿱雲心	631	⿰忄敝	407	懿	223
恢	207	惑	215	愆	63	慧[11]	209	憋	407	戀[19]	308
恩	124	惠	210	愐	342	慨	237	憑	416	**62 戈**	
恃	456	惚	197	惱	357	慊	243	憚	494		
恕	463	惧	114	愛	2	憩	41	憎	551	戈	250
息	160	惛	211	愕	371	慶	83	憊	378	戊[1]	611
恤	191	悶	336	愎	402	慮	324	憔	51	戉	654
恬	524	⿰忄門	336	想	168	慢	330	懈[13]	175	戎[2]	234
恫	580	悲	390	惺	184	慕	351	憾	149	戌	199
恣	583	惜	158	⿰忄者	184	慪	372	懇	247	戔	540
恙	615	惩	30	⿰忄柔	356	慟	583	懃	77	成[3]	56

4 Strokes (con't.)

成	29
我	604
或[4]	215
戕	46
戔	59
戚[7]	38
戟[8]	34
戛	235
戥[9]	508
戢	66
截[10]	55
戮[11]	320
戰[12]	12
戲[13]	162
戳	89
戴	489

63 戶

戶	199
房[4]	131
戾	300
所	471
扁[5]	408
扇[6]	436
扉[8]	132

64 手

手	458
才[1]	540
扎	5
扔[2]	228
扒	373
扑	425
打	484
扠[3]	8
执	67
扞	149
扛	243
托	531
扣	257
抓[4]	99
找	20
抄	21
折	22
扯	23
抍	28
承	30
扶	140
扻	240
抗	243
抅	255
技	36
扼	371
报	387
抛	421
扭	366
把	374
扮	381
扳	382
批	402
抒	463
抖	533
投	535
扽	576
抑	223
招[5]	19
抽	91
拙	88
拄	95
拚	412
拊	143
拂	145
拃	7
拑	65
拘	112
拒	114
拐	265
拉	283
抹	347
拇	350
抿	343
拏	352
拈	363
拔	374
拜	377
拌	381
抱	388
披	393
拍	378
抬	490
抵	511
担	492
拕	531
拖	531
拓	531
拆	10
押	611
拗	366
挓[6]	6
指	68
持	72
拯	28
拽	100
拷	245
挈	58
拳	119
[illegible]	356
拱	278
挂	264
括	282
拿	352
挐	352
按	4
拾	452
拭	454
拴	466
挑	516
挖	589
挨[7]	1
振	25
捉	88
捍	149
挾	42
捐	117
捆	275
挪	366
捌	373
捕	423
捎	439
挱	432
挲	432
挺	528
捏	362
捅	582
挫	555
[illegible]	91
挽	592
捵[8]	26
掌	15
掙	27
掣	23
捶	106
捧	398
掀	177
掯	247
掐	43
捡	77
掘	121
捲	117
掬	112
控	280
掛	264
掠	325
掄	321
捫	335
捺	353
捻	363
排	379
捹	395
掃	430
捨	441
授	460
探	496
掏	503
掉	515
掎	142
掂	520
掇	530
推	574
採	541
接	53
捷	55

4 Strokes (con't.)

措	554	援	652	摀	609	撓	356	擘	376	攘	225
捱	613	搽[10]	8	搖	617	撚	364	擅	436	攔	286
掩	626	搌	11	摺[11]	22	撇	407	撻	485	攜[18]	174
掖	621	搘	67	摳	256	撆	407	擔	492	攝	442
插[9]	8	搥	106	摟	317	播	419	擋	497	攛	559
揰	111	搋	100	摞	317	撥	417	操	547	攣[19]	325
揣	100	[illegible]	124	摩	346	撲	425	擇	548	攤	494
換	204	携	174	摻	472	撒	427	擁	641	攢	542
揮	207	搆	256	摸	346	[illegible]	433	擢[14]	88	攪[20]	49
揉	230	搦	360	[illegible]	304	撕	480	擦	537	攩	497
揩	57	搬	379	摎	304	撣	495	擤	185	攬[21]	286
揀	60	搏	418	摹	346	撢	493	擰	365	攮[22]	356
揆	274	搡	429	摔	465	撮	554	擬	360	[illegible]	518
揭	53	搔	430	[illegible]	533	撙	562	擱	249	**65 支**	
揦	283	搧	434	摶	573	撴	576	擯	412		
描	339	搰	262	摘	9	撍	559	擡	490	支	66
捪	343	[illegible]	472	摧	561	擉[13]	89	擣	501	攲[8]	38
揘	362	損	477	摠	564	撼	149	擠	34	**66 攴**	
揌	428	搭	483	撑[12]	29	[illegible]	239	擲[15]	67		
[illegible]	398	搨	488	撐	29	[illegible]	518	擾	225	攴	425
搜	472	[illegible]	497	撦	23	撿	60	擴	282	攵	425
提	513	搪	499	撤	23	擖	252	攆	364	攷[2]	245
揪	84	搗	501	撞	104	擊	31	擺	377	收	457
揔	564	搯	503	撰	101	擒	77	攀	382	改[3]	235
揝	559	搷	520	撫	142	擎	83	擻	473	攸	636
握	604	搊	91	撬	53	據	113	攉[16]	215	攻	276
揚	614	搓	554	撅	120	[illegible]	265	攋	283	政[4]	28
揜	626	搶	47	撈	288	擂	292	攏	323	放	132
揖	217	[illegible]	590	撩	303	擄	316	攙[17]	13	故[5]	261

4 Strokes (con't.)

敁	520
效[6]	172
敕[7]	73
敎	50
救	85
敏	343
敖	5
敗	378
敔	645
敘	191
敞[8]	18
[illegible]	23
敢	239
敝	400
散	429
敪	530
敦	576
敬[9]	81
敫	32
敲[10]	51
敷[11]	140
敺	115
數	463
敵	510
整[12]	28
斂[13]	308
斃[14]	400
[illegible]	111
斆[16]	173

67 文

文	602
齐[2]	39
斉[3]	113
斎[6]	9
斍[7]	120
斐[8]	133
斌	412
斑	380

68 斗

斗	533
料[6]	304
斜[7]	174
斛	199
斟[9]	24

69 斤

斤	73
斥[1]	73
斧[4]	142
斬[7]	12
斷	572
斯[8]	480
新[9]	182
斷[14]	572

70 方

方	130
㫃[2]	626
於[4]	643
施[5]	448
旆	394
斿	637
旆[6]	394
旅	324
旁	384
旄	331
旋[7]	192
族	556
旌	80
旗[10]	39
旘[12]	69
旛[14]	127

71 无

无	606
旡[1]	606
既[7]	34

72 日

日	229
旦[1]	493
旨[2]	68
旬	196
旭	191
早	545
旱[3]	149
时	450
昂[4]	4
旹	450
昌	16
昊	152
昏	211
易	221
昆	275
明	344
昔	161
昇	447
旺	596
昭[5]	19
春	107
昧	334
昵	360
是	453
星	184
昨	552
昜	614
映	635
晁[6]	21
晃	207
晒	433
晌	437
時	450
晉	76
晋	76
晏	627
晨[2]	26
晝	91
晦	210
[illegible]	437
晚	593
晤	610
智[8]	69
景	80
晷	272
晾	302
普	426
晶	80
晴	82
晳	160
晰	160
暇[9]	164
暎	635
暗	4
[illegible]	157
暖	368
暑	462
暌	274
暈	657
暢[10]	18
㬎	179
暮[11]	352
暱	360
暴	388
暫	12
曉[12]	172
曁	34
曆	299
曇	496
曙[14]	462
曜	619
曠[15]	271
曝	388
曩[17]	356
曬[19]	433

73 曰

曰	654
曳[2]	100
曲	115
更[3]	247
曷[5]	156
書[6]	460
曼[7]	329
曹	547
替[8]	514
朁	543
曾	550
最	560
會[9]	209

74 月

月	654
有[2]	638

4 Strokes (con't.)

服[4]	140	杏	186	枉	594	株	93	梅	333	棱	293
朋	397	杆	238	杳	340	荣	234	梆	383	棚	397
朕[6]	25	杠	242	查[5]	8	核	156	梹	412	森	431
朔	470	李	297	柴	10	桓	204	桬	432	棲	38
朗[7]	288	呆	1	柘	23	根	246	梢	439	棠	499
望	595	杉	433	柵	7	校	172	梳	461	棵	252
朝[8]	21	東	464	枳	68	桀	55	梭	471	棟	579
期	37	杜	568	柱	95	格	250	梯	513	棗	546
朢[10]	595	材	540	枵	171	框	271	條	517	椒	48
朦[14]	336	村	562	染	224	桂	273	桶	583	棕	564
朧[16]	323	杌	611	柑	238	栛	297	梃	528	椊	557
75 木		枕[4]	24	柔	230	栗	299	梛	620	椀	592
		枝	66	枷	42	案	4	梧	607	楂[9]	6
木	350	杼	96	架	43	栢	377	棧[8]	12	椹	228
朩	576	杵	98	柬	60	桑	429	棹	88	楮	98
札[1]	6	果	281	柩	84	栖	38	植	67	楚	98
末	347	林	309	柯	253	桃	503	椅	220	椿	107
本	395	杴	177	枯	262	桐	581	棋	39	椽	102
朮	94	枚	333	枴	265	栽	537	棊	39	楥	193
未	599	杪	340	柳	315	桅	598	棄	41	楦	193
朱[2]	93	枏	355	某	349	梵[7]	130	棘	36	樺	238
朽	187	杷	373	柄	414	械	176	極	33	楷	237
朴	425	板	380	柏	377	梔	67	棐	133	楞	293
朶	530	枇	403	柁	532	梟	171	棃	294	楣	333
朵	530	杯	390	柒	37	桿	238	棺	267	楠	355
束	588	柿	456	枼	621	梗	248	椁	282	椶	564
杈[3]	9	析	160	柞	553	桼	38	棍	275	楫	36
杖	16	松	478	柚	640	梨	294	棉	341	楸	86
杓	440	東	578	桌[6]	88	梁	300	棒	384	楊	614

木 欠 止 歹歺 殳 毋 比 毛

4 Strokes (con't.)

業 621
椰 620
榆 644
榨[10] 7
榛 24
槌 106
槁 244
構 256
榾 260
榔 288
榧 133
榴 314
槙 242
榜 383
槊 470
榭 175
槐 202
榫 478
榻 488
槍 46
榮 234
榕 234
樟[11] 15
樞 461
樁 103
樊 129
槩 236
槪 236
樛 282
樓 317
樂 291
模 346
標 404
槽 547
槳 45
樣 616
橕[12] 29
橙 26
橫 153
樺 201
橄 239
機 31
橇 51
橡 169
橋 52
橜 121
橛 121
橘 112
樸 425
樹 463
橐 532
橔 576
樵 52
樽 562
蘂 565
檄[13] 32
檢 60
檜 273
檁 310
檀 495
檔 498
檣 47
檐 624
櫂[14] 20
檻 62
檾 83
櫃 273
檳 412
櫈 508
櫓[15] 319
櫝 569
櫞 652
櫇[16] 412
櫬 27
欄[17] 286
櫻 633
權[18] 119
欒[19] 321
欓 498
欖[21] 286
鬱[22] 648

76 欠

欠 65
欢[2] 203
次 588
欣[4] 182
欬[6] 253
欮 120
欵[7] 269
欸 1
欶 464
欲 647
欼[8] 89
欻 99
欺 37
欽 77
款 269
歇[9] 173
歆 182
歉[10] 65
歌 249
歐[11] 371
歎[15] 496
歠 89
歡[18] 203

77 止

止 68
正[1] 28
此[2] 588
步[3] 424
歧[4] 39
武 609
歪[5] 590
歱[9] 109
歲 477
歷[12] 299
歸[14] 271

78 歹

歹 488
死[2] 481
歿[4] 347
殀 618
殆[5] 490
殄 525
殂 557
殃 613
殊[6] 461
殉 196
殖[8] 67
殘 543
殙 211
[illegible][9] 357
殞[10] 656
殤[11] 437
殨[12] 274
殮[13] ·309
殯[14] 412

79 殳

殳 461
段[5] 572
殷[6] 629
殻 253
殼[7] 83
殹 216
殺 432
殽[8] 617
殼 253
轂[9] 35
毀 209
殿 522
毅[11] 223
毆 372

80 毋

毋 607
母[1] 350
每[3] 334
毒[5] 567

81 比

比 399
毗[5] 404
毘 404
毚[12] 13

82 毛

毛 331
毡[5] 11
毧[6] 234
毫[7] 150

4 Strokes (con't.)

毛
氏
气
水氵

4 Strokes (con't.)

水氵 火灬

湧	641	滿	329	潛	65	濘	359	灼	440	烖	537
準[10]	107	漫	330	潜	65	濱	412	灴	212	烏	605
滑	201	漠	348	澁	431	濕	449	灸	84	烟	622
滙	210	漚	372	澇	290	濤	503	灵	311	烽[7]	137
溷	212	漂	406	潘	382	濰	597	災	537	烹	397
溝	255	滲	445	潎	408	濟	35	灾	537	焉	622
溪	38	漱	464	潑	420	濾[15]	325	灶	546	焚[8]	135
溜	313	漩	192	澀	431	瀑	388	炒[4]	21	然	224
滅	340	滴	509	潲	440	瀋	445	炙	71	焙	392
溟	345	滷	319	潬	494	瀉	176	炊	106	焦	48
溺	360	漕	547	潭	495	瀆	569	炕	243	無	606
溥	426	漿	44	潼	582	濺	62	炉	318	焰	627
溼	449	漸	61	潤	233	瀕[16]	412	炎	624	熨	657
溯	470	滬	199	濁[13]	88	瀝	299	炸[5]	6	照[9]	20
溻	487	漆	38	澥	175	瀾[17]	286	炷	95	煠	6
滔	503	漎	636	澣	204	灌[18]	268	炫	193	煅	572
滇	524	演	625	激	32	灑[19]	427	炰	385	煮	95
滋	584	漁	643	澳	5	灘	494	炮	385	煑	95
滓	585	漊	287	濃	368	灒	542	炳	414	煩	128
溢	223	漬	587	濇	431	灣[22]	591	炭	497	煕	159
源	651	潮[12]	21	澹	494	灢	356	点	521	煳	198
漲[11]	16	澈	23	澡	546	**86 火**		烝[6]	28	煥	204
滯	71	澄	30	澤	548			烛	94	煇	207
漢	148	潰	133	濯[14]	89	火	214	烘	212	煌	206
漑	236	潰	274	濠	150	灮[1]	6	烤	245	煖	368
滾	275	澆	48	濡	231	灰[2]	207	烈	305	煉	308
漏	317	潔	54	濶	283	灰	207	烙	290	煤	333
漓	294	澗	61	濫	287	灯	507	烕	340	煞	433
漣	306	潦	290	濛	336	烄[3]	73	烾	635	煍	52

5 Strokes (con't.)

玉王 瓜 瓦 甘 生 用 田 疋 疒

Character	Page
珊	434
玷	522
玳	489
珠[6]	93
珥	125
珞	291
珪	272
班	380
現[7]	179
球	86
琅	288
理	295
琉	314
琢[8]	89
琥	199
琴	77
琨	275
琳	309
琶	374
琵	403
瑕[9]	164
瑚	198
瑁	335
瑇	489
瑙	357
瑟	431
瑞	233
瑛	633
瑜	644
瑰[10]	273
瑯	288
瑠	314
瑪	327
瑣	472
瑤	617
瑩	634
璋[11]	15
瑾	75
璃	294
璉	306
環[13]	203
璧	401
璽[14]	162
璺	603
瓅[15]	294
瓔[17]	633

97 瓜

Character	Page
瓜	263
瓞[5]	519
瓠[6]	199
瓢[11]	406
瓣[14]	381
瓤[17]	225

98 瓦

Character	Page
瓦	590
瓮[4]	603
瓶[6]	416
瓷	587
甎[11]	101
甌	372
甑	551
甕[13]	603
甖[14]	633
甗[17]	14

99 甘

Character	Page
甘	238
甚[4]	444
甜[6]	524

100 生

Character	Page
生	445
產[6]	13
甥[7]	446
甦	474

101 用

Character	Page
用	642
甩[1]	466
甫[2]	142
甬	641
甯[7]	365

102 田

Character	Page
田	524
甲	43
由	636
申	443
男[2]	354
甸	522
画[3]	201
甾	314
甿	330
畐[4]	140
畊	248
界	56
畆	350
畏	600
畜[5]	99
留	314
畝	350
畚	395
畔	383
畦[6]	39
異	222
畧	325
略	325
畢	401
番[7]	127
畫	201
畱	314
畺[8]	44
[illegible]	648
當	497
畽[9]	573
畿[10]	31
畾	292
疃[12]	573
疇[14]	92
疆	44
疊[17]	518

103 疋

Character	Page
疋	404
疎[7]	461
疏	461
疑[9]	218

104 疒

Character	Page
疒	361
疔[2]	525
疙[3]	250
疚	85
疝	436
疥[4]	56
疤	373
[illegible]	129
疫	223
疣	638
痄[5]	7
疹	25
症	28
痡	133
疴	255
疳	238
疲	403
病	414
疼	508
疱	390
疾	33
疵	587
痔[6]	71
痕	152
痍	218
痊	118
痒	615
痣[7]	70
痤	569
瘌	297
痧	432
痠	475
痘	534
痞	404
痛	583
痮[8]	15
痴	72
痳	326
痭	396
痹	402
痰	495
瘁	561
痿	598

5 Strokes (con't.)

Character	Page
痙	612
瘀	642
瘌[9]	283
瘋	137
瘊	157
瘉	647
瘓	204
瘡[10]	104
瘤	314
瘠	34
瘧	619
瘩	483
瘢	380
瘦	460
瘨	520
瘟	601
瘴[11]	16
瘈	122
癝	316
癇[12]	178
癈	134
癀	205
療	303
癆	289
[illegible]	406
癖[13]	404
癡	72
癟[14]	407
癥[15]	28
癤	54
癢	615
癨[16]	215
癧	299
癩	285
癬[17]	193
癮	631
癰[18]	640
癱[19]	494
癲	520

105 癶

Character	Page
癶	419
癸[4]	272
登[7]	506
發	125

106 白

Character	Page
白	376
百[1]	377
皃[2]	332
皂	547
皁	547
的[3]	512
皇[4]	206
皆	54
皈	272
皕[5]	49
皎[6]	49
皓[7]	152
皖	204
皦[13]	49

107 皮

Character	Page
皮	403
皰[5]	390
皴[7]	563
皻[9]	8
皷	260
皺[10]	91

108 皿

Character	Page
皿	343
盂[3]	643
盅[4]	109
盇	156
盆	396
盃	390
昷	601
盈	633
盍[5]	156
盌	592
𥁕	601
益	218
盒[6]	155
盖	236
盔	274
盗	502
蓋	236
盛[7]	448
盜	502
盞[8]	12
盟	336
塩	623
監[9]	59
盡	76
盤[10]	382
盬[11]	260
盥	268
盧	318
盪[12]	500

109 目

Character	Page
目	351
直[3]	67
直	67
盲	330
盼[4]	382
眢	197
看	241
眉	333
眇	340
盻	163
省	447
相	167
眈	492
盾	577
盹	576
眨[5]	7
眞	24
真	24
眖	194
眠	341
眩	193
看	241
眵[6]	72
眾	110
眷	118
眶	271
眸	349
眯	338
眼	625
䀹[7]	57
睏	276
着	19
睚[8]	3
睜	27
睘	88
睖	293
睦	352
睥	402
睡	468
督	566
睧	211
睬	541
睫	57
睛	78
睪	221
睿[9]	233
睹	568
瞅	92
瞋[10]	26
瞎	163
瞌	253
瞑	345
[illegible]	92
[illegible][11]	327
瞠	508
瞞	329
瞟	406
瞘	256
瞭[12]	304
瞥	408
[illegible]	427
瞬	469
瞶	274
瞪	508
瞰	240
瞳	582
瞧	52
瞻[13]	11
瞽	260
矁	92
瞿	116
矇[14]	336

5 Strokes (con't.)

Character	Page
稾[10]	244
稿	244
稽	32
稼	42
穀	260
稻	502
穉[11]	71
穅	243
穆	352
穌	473
積	31
穎	634
穗[12]	477
穚[13]	431
穢	209
穪[14]	29
穤	367
穩	602

116 穴

Character	Page
穴	195
究[2]	83
穹[3]	87
空	279
穿[4]	101
突	571
穼	443
窃	57
穽	80
窄[5]	10
窊	589
窈	618
窐[6]	70
窓	104
窕	517
窗[7]	104
窖	51
窘	87
窠[8]	252
窟	262
窩[9]	604
窨	632
窪	589
窮[10]	87
窯	617
窴	524
窰	617
窳	646
窺[11]	274
窻	104
窵	516
窿[12]	323
竅[13]	53
竄	559
竆[14]	87
竇[15]	534
竈[16]	546
竊[17]	57

117 立

Character	Page
立	297
竒[4]	38
站[5]	12
竚	96
竑	415
章[6]	14
竟	81
竦[7]	479
竢	483
童	582
竣	123
竪[8]	464
靖	81
竭[9]	54
端	571
競[15]	81

118 竹

Character	Page
竹	94
竺[2]	96
竿[3]	238
竽	643
笊[4]	20
笆	373
笑	172
笋	478
笞[5]	72
笥	483
符	141
笨	395
笸	420
笙	446
第	512
笠	298
笤	517
笛	510
筓[6]	33
筹	245
筋	74
筏	127
筐	270
筆	399
筍	478
答	484
等	507
筒	582
策	549
筯[7]	96
筠	656
筷	266
筲	439
筳	450
筭	475
筵	624
箚[8]	6
箄	20
箒	90
箏	27
箕	31
箇	251
箍	259
管	267
箛	259
箔	419
算	475
箋	59
箴[9]	24
箸	96
篆	101
範	130
節	54
篋	58
箬	230
篇	411
箱	167
箭	62
築[10]	94
篡	559
篙	244
篦	401
篩	433
篤	568
篴[11]	510
簍	317
簏	320
篱	294
簀	549
篾	341
簇	558
篷	397
簣[12]	206
簡	60
簫	171
簪	541
簾[13]	307
簸	419
簿	424
簽	63
簷	624
籌[14]	92
籃	286
籍	33
籐[15]	508
籠[16]	323
籟	285
籤[17]	64
籬[19]	294
籮	316
籲[26]	655

119 米

Character	Page
米	338
籼[3]	177
籽	585

6 Strokes (con't.)

米

糸 糹

粉[4]	136	糐	573	紥	5	絛	503	練	308	繃	489
粃	399	糢	346	紓	461	統	582	緲	340	縱	565
粒[5]	298	糟	545	純	108	絕	120	緜	341	總	564
粘	11	糧[12]	301	索	472	經[7]	78	緥	387	縯	632
粕	421	糯[14]	367	素	474	絹	118	編	408	繇	638
粗	557	糰	573	紋	602	綑	276	線	180	織[12]	67
粥[6]	90	糴[16]	510	紊	603	綁	383	緒	191	繈	45
粧	103	糶[19]	518	紮[5]	5	綉	188	締	512	繙	128
粦	309	[illegible][23]	321	紬	92	綏	476	緞	573	繞	225
粟	475	**120 糸**		終	109	綻[8]	13	緝	41	繚	303
粳[7]	79			紘	178	綢	92	緯	600	繖	429
粮	301	糸	339	累	292	綽	89	緣	651	繕	436
粆	432	系[1]	163	絆	381	綴	106	緻	70	繡	188
粱	300	糺	84	紳	444	緋	132	縋[10]	105	繐	477
粲	543	糾[2]	84	紹	440	綱	242	縛	142	繫[13]	35
粹[8]	561	紂[3]	91	細	162	緊	74	縣	180	繪	209
精	79	紇	250	組	557	綾	312	縊	224	繳	50
粽	565	紅	212	紫	585	綹	315	縚	503	繭	60
糊[9]	198	紁	227	絨[6]	234	綠	325	縐	91	繮	45
糉	565	紈	592	絳	46	綸	322	縉	76	繩	447
糕[10]	244	紀	35	絞	49	綿	341	縈	234	繸	477
糗	87	約	653	結	54	絣	397	繁[11]	128	繹	221
糓	260	紙[4]	68	経	78	綫	180	縫	138	繼[14]	36
糖	499	紛	135	給	246	綵	541	縴	65	辮	409
糞[11]	136	紡	131	絖	270	綜	565	縲	292	纂	559
糠	243	級	33	絡	291	網	595	縷	324	纓	632
糙	547	納	353	絏	176	維	597	繅	430	纏[15]	13
糡	46	紷	74	絮	191	緩[9]	204	縮	471	纊	270
糜	338	紗	432	絲	480	緘	59	績	31	纍	292

6 Strokes (con't.)

6 Strokes (con't.)

6 Strokes (con't.)

芹	77	荔	297	萊	285	葺	41	蔴	326	薪	182
芭	373	茫	330	菱	312	蔥	565	蔑	341	薙	514
芟	435	茗	345	莽	330	萬	593	蓬	398	薔	47
芽	612	荅	483	萌	337	葦	598	蔔	417	薦	62
芫	650	䓁	507	菴	388	萵	604	蔬	461	[illegible]	444
芸	656	草	547	萍	416	葉	621	蓿	191	薇	598
苧[5]	96	茲	584	菠	417	葯	619	蔡	541	薰[14]	195
苛	253	茨	588	菩	426	蒸[10]	28	蔣	45	藍	286
苴	219	茵	629	菽	465	蒭	98	蔓	593	藐	340
若	230	莊[7]	103	萄	504	蓄	191	蔚	648	藊	408
苡	219	莖	78	菜	541	蒿	150	蔦	623	薯	462
苟	255	荷	155	菑	537	蒦	215	[illegible]	83	藏	544
茄	57	莢	43	菁	78	蓋	236	蔭	632	藿	268
苦	262	莉	297	萃	561	蒞	298	蕃[12]	128	藉	56
茅	331	莅	298	菸	622	蒙	336	蕎	52	藩[15]	129
茂	332	莧	348	萎	596	蒲	426	蕭	171	[illegible]	21
苗	339	莩	399	著[9]	96	蒐	473	蕙	210	藝	222
茉	348	荽	476	葫	198	蓆	161	蕊	233	藜	295
苜	351	荳	534	葷	211	蕐	200	蕋	233	藦	346
苫	436	莆	328	葭	42	蓑	471	蔽	406	藕	372
苔	490	荼	570	葁	45	蒜	475	蕩	498	藪	473
英	632	莠	639	葛	251	蒼	544	蕉	49	藤	508
苑	653	萇[8]	17	葵	274	蒺	33	蕪	607	藥	619
茶[6]	8	菲	133	落	290	蓉	234	蕁[13]	150	蘑[16]	346
荒	205	華	200	葡	426	蔯[11]	26	薊	37	蘆	318
茴	208	莿	588	葚	228	蔗	21	薑	45	蘇	473
茹	231	菇	258	蒂	512	蓺	222	薛	194	藻	546
荐	62	菊	113	董	578	蔻	258	薄	386	蘊	658
荊	79	菓	281	葬	544	蓮	307	薩	427	蘭[17]	286

6 Strokes (con't.)

艸 艹 丱 虍 虫 血 行 衣 衤

6 Strokes (con't.) (7) Strokes

7 Strokes (con't.)

言 谷 豆 豕 豸 貝

誶	154	謎	338	譯	221	豌	591	負	144	賃	310
調	516	謗	384	護[14]	199	豐[11]	137	貢[3]	279	賍	544
諏	555	謚	457	譽	648	豔[20]	628	貣	471	賊	548
請	83	謝	175	讀[15]	567	豓[21]	628	財	540	資	583
諛	645	謄	508	讎[16]	92	**152 豕**		販[4]	129	賑[7]	25
諸[9]	93	謅	90	讐	92	豕	453	貨	215	賔	411
諷	138	謠	617	變	409	豖	94	貫	268	賓	411
諠	192	謹[11]	75	讌	627	豚[4]	577	貧	412	賖	441
諧	174	[illegible]	547	讒[17]	543	象[5]	169	貪	494	賬[8]	16
諼	192	謾	329	讓	225	豦[6]	113	責	548	賙	90
諻	209	謬	340	讖	14	豪[7]	150	貯[5]	96	質	70
諱	210	謨	347	讚[19]	542	豵[8]	564	費	134	賦	145
諫	62	謳	372	讜[20]	498	豬[9]	93	賀	156	賢	178
謀	349	謫	9	讞	628	豫	646	貺	207	賚	285
諳	3	證[12]	28	讟[22]	567	**153 豸**		貽	219	賣	328
諾	366	譁	200	**150 谷**		豸	10	貴	272	賫	32
諞	411	譏	31	谷	260	豺[3]	11	買	327	賠	393
諡	457	譎	121	豁[10]	213	豹	388	貿	332	賞	437
諦	513	䜌	321	**151 豆**		貂[5]	515	貶	409	賜	588
諮	583	譌	370	豆	534	貍[7]	295	貰	395	賤	62
謂	601	譖	543	豇[3]	44	貌	332	貳	125	販[9]	129
諣	621	識	451	豈	40	貓[9]	331	貸	489	賴	285
諺	628	譚	496	䜶[6]	44	貛[18]	203	貼	519	賭	568
諭	647	譙	53	豐	296	**154 貝**		貲	584	賺[10]	101
謔[10]	369	譭[13]	209	登	506	貝	392	賄[6]	210	購	256
謊	206	議	222	豎[8]	464	貞[2]	24	賅	235	賽	428
講	45	警	80					賒	441	賸	448
謙	63	譬	404					賈	43	贃[11]	101
謌	249	譜	426					賂	320	贄	71

Strokes (con't.)

Character	Page
贅	105
贊12	542
贈	551
贋	628
賺13	101
贍	436
贏	634
贒14	178
贓	544
贖15	462
贗	628
贛17	239
贜18	544

155 赤

Character	Page
赤	73
赦4	442
赧	356
赫7	156
赭9	22

156 走

Character	Page
走	555
赴2	144
赶3	238
起	40
趁5	27
趂	27
超	21
趄	58
趋	116
越	654
趔6	306
趒	518
趙7	20
趕	238
趝8	363
趣	116
趤9	498
邅10	520
趨	116
趮13	546
趯14	655
趲19	542

157 足

Character	Page
足	556
趴2	375
趷3	250
趵	418
趾4	68
趿	427
距5	115
跑	389
跛	419
跋	374
跌	518
跎	532
跕	520
跙	58
跐	541
跴6	541
跤	48
跩	100
跟	246
跨	264
跪	273
路	319
跳	518
跺	531
跡	36
踉7	287
踊	641
踝8	202
踦	38
踞	114
踡	119
踏	488
踢	513
踫	397
踐	61
踪	564
踜	293
踒	604
蹅9	6
踹	100
踵	109
蹂	230
蹄	514
踰	644
蹇10	60
蹣	382
蹣	382
蹋	488
蹈	502
蹏	514
蹉	554
蹌	46
蹝11	162
蹧	545
蹟	36
蹩	558
蹤	564
蹻12	51
蹺	51
蹶	121
蹷	121
蹬	507
蹭	551
蹴	558
蹲	576
躇13	98
躉	576
躂	488
躁	546
躋14	32
躍	655
躚15	13
躕	97
躐	306
躘16	323
躥18	559
躦19	558

158 身

Character	Page
身	442
躬3	278
躭4	492
䠷6	517
躲	530
躳7	278
躴	287
躷8	2
躶	316
躺	500
軀11	115
躿	243

159 車

Character	Page
車	23
軋1	613
軍2	123
軌	272
軒3	192
軔	228
軟	232
軛	371
軸5	90
軻	253
輩	392
軲	259
較6	49
[illegible]	100
載	538
輒7	23
輔	142
輕	81
輓	593
輙8	23
輝	207
輥	275
輛	302
輦	363
輪	322
輩	392
輜	584
[illegible]	500
輻9	141
輵	252
輭	232
輳	556
輸	461
輯	36
輾10	11

轄	164
轂	259
輿	644
轅	652
轉[11]	101
轇	48
轆	320
轍[12]	22
轎	51
轕[13]	252
轟[14]	212
轡[15]	394
轤[16]	318

160 辛

辛	182
辜[5]	258
辟[6]	401
辠	560
辞	587
辣[7]	284
辤[8]	587
辦[9]	409
辨	381
辭[12]	587
辯[14]	409

161 辰

辰	26
辱[3]	231
農[6]	368

162 辵

辵	89
辶	89
边[2]	408
达[3]	22
迄	40
过	282
迅	196
迲	570
迁	63
迂	642
这[4]	22
返	129
还	203
近	75
迕	611
迓	613
迎	633
远	652
迦[5]	42
迥	87
迫	421
述	464
迨	490
迯	503
迭	518
迪	510
追[6]	105
迴	208
迻	218
逆	360
迷	338
迸	397
送	479
逃	503
退	575
迹	36
這[7]	22
逞	30
逐	94
逢	138
逕	80
遆	512
逛	270
連	306
逋	421
逝	456
逍	170
速	474
逗	534
透	536
途	570
通	580
造	546
週[8]	90
逮	490
進	75
逬	396
逸	223
遐[9]	164
遑	206
過	282
遏	371
遍	410
逼	398
遂	476
遢	500
達	484
道	502
遁	577
違	597
遊	637
逾	644
遇	646
運	657
遣[10]	65
遛	313
遜	196
遞	512
遙	617
遠	652
遮[11]	21
遲	72
適	456
遯	577
遭	545
遺[12]	219
暹	177
遶	225
遼	303
遴	309
選	193
遷	63
遵	562
還[13]	203
遽	113
邁	328
避	401
邀	616
邇[14]	125
邈	347
邋[15]	284
邊	408
邏[19]	316

163 邑

邑	223
邕[3]	640
那[4]	352
邦	383
邪	173
邮	562
邱[5]	86
邸	511
郊[6]	48
郇	196
郝[7]	151
郡	123
郎	287
郭[8]	280
部	424
郵	636
鄂[9]	5
都	533
鄆	657
鄉[10]	166
鄙[11]	402
鄭[12]	29
鄰	310
鄱	420
鄧	508
酆[18]	137

164 酉

酉	639
酋[2]	84
酊	525
酌[3]	88
配	394
酒	84
酖[4]	25
醇	108

Character	Page
酣[5]	147
酥	474
酡	532
酬[6]	91
酧	91
酪	345
酵[7]	51
酷	263
酸	475
醅[8]	393
醇	108
醋	558
醉	560
醃	622
醒[9]	185
醡[10]	7
醜	92
醫[11]	217
醩	545
醪	289
醬	45
醭[12]	422
醮	49
醺[14]	195
醻	91
釀[17]	361
釁[18]	184
釅[20]	628

165 釆

Character	Page
釆	410
采[1]	540
釉	640
釋[13]	456

166 里

Character	Page
里	295
厘[2]	295
重	110
野[4]	620
量[5]	301
釐[11]	295

167 金

Character	Page
金	74
針[2]	24
釜	142
釘	525
釧[3]	103
釵	10
釦	257
釬	149
釣	516
鈔[4]	21
鈎	255
鈐	64
鈞	123
鈕	366
鈀	375
鈍	576
鉤[5]	255
鉏	98
鉗	65
鉈	532
鈴	311
鉋	389
鉢	417
鈸	419
鉄	519
鈿	522
鉞	654
鉛	63
銃[6]	111
銜	179
鉿	252
鉸	49
銘	345
銚	516
銁	123
銕	519
銅	582
銓	118
銬	246
銀	630
鋤[7]	98
鋒	138
鋩	330
銲	149
銷	170
銳	233
鋏	42
鋪	425
銹	188
鋟	64
銼	555
鋑	59
錐[8]	105
錚	27
錘	106
鋼	242
錦	75
錮	262
鋸	114
錁	254
錄	320
錛	395
錫	161
錠	526
錢	64
錯	554
鍤[9]	8
鍼	24
錨	331
鍾	109
鍵	61
鍋	280
鍊	308
鍍	568
鍛	572
鍪	51
鍬	51
鍱	621
鎮[10]	25
鎡	26
鎒	367
鎚	106
鎧	237
鎌	308
鎊	385
鎙	470
鎖	472
鎗	46
鎔	234
鏟[11]	14
鏡	81
鏤	318
鏈	307
鏝	329
鏊	5
鏇	193
鏜	499
鏨	542
鏃	557
鐘[12]	109
鏵	200
鐙	508
鐝	121
鐐	305
鐃	357
鐋	500
鏽	188
鐶[13]	203
鐲	88
鐓	50
鐮	308
鏴	319
鐺	497
鐵	519
鐸	530
鐫	59
鑄[14]	96
鑊	215
鑑	62
鑒	62
鑛[15]	271
鑞	284
鑣	405
鑠	471
鑭[16]	6
鑪	318
鑱[17]	13
鑲	168
鑰	619
鑵[18]	268

金 長镸 門 阜阝 隶 隹 雨 青

8 Strokes (con't.)

8 Strokes (con't.) (9) Strokes

非
面
革
韋
韭
音
頁
風
飛
食飠
首
香

187 馬

馬	326
馮^{2}	138
馭	648
馳^{3}	72
馴	195
馱	532
馿^{4}	324
駁	418
駄	532
駐^{5}	96
駕	43
駒	112
駑	367
駛	453
駟	482
駝	532
駔	545
駭^{6}	176
騖	509
駱	317
駮	418
駢	411
隲^{7}	67
駿	123
騎^{8}	38
騍	254
騐	627
騙^{9}	411
騭^{10}	67
騷	430
騸	436
騖	509
騲	548
驅^{11}	115
騾	316
驕^{12}	48
驚^{13}	79
驉	644
驗	627
驛	221
驟^{14}	556
驢^{16}	324
[illegible]^{18}	559
驩	203
[illegible]^{21}	14

188 骨

骨	259
骯^{3}	249
骯^{4}	4
骰	433
骶^{5}	245
骸^{6}	174
骽^{7}	575
髈^{10}	384
髏^{11}	317
髓^{13}	476
體	514
髑	262
髒	543

189 高

高	243
髙	243
髞^{13}	431

190 髟

髟	405
髮^{5}	127
髯	224
髫	517
髦	584
髻^{6}	32
髽^{7}	99
鬀	514
鬂	412
鬆^{8}	478
鬃	564
鬍^{9}	198
鬒^{10}	25
鬚^{12}	190
鬟^{13}	203
鬢^{14}	412
鬣^{15}	306

191 鬥

鬥	534
鬧^{5}	357
鬨^{6}	213
鬩^{8}	163
鬮^{10}	84
鬪	534
鬭^{14}	534
鬮^{17}	84

192 鬯

鬯	19
鬱^{19}	648

193 鬲

鬲	300
鬻^{12}	649

194 鬼

鬼	272
魂^{4}	211
魁	274
魃^{5}	374
魅	334
魄	421
魎^{8}	302
魍	595
魏	600
魑^{11}	72
魔	346
魘^{14}	626

195 魚

魚	642
魯^{4}	319
魦	432
鮎^{5}	363
鮁	375
鮮^{6}	177
鯊^{7}	432
鯉	296
鯨^{8}	79
鯗	169
鰕^{9}	164
鰉	206
鰐	371
鰍	86
鯽	36
鰥^{10}	267
鰲^{11}	5
鰾	406
鱗^{12}	310
鱉	407
鱔	435
鱑	206
鱓	435
鱸^{16}	318
鱷	371

196 鳥

鳥	361
鳩^{2}	83
鳳^{3}	139
鳴	345
鳶	649
鳮	31
鴆^{4}	25
鴉	611
鴈	628
鴟^{5}	72
鴞	171
鴒	312
鴨	611
鴦	613
鴣	258
鴛	649
鴻^{6}	213
鴽	228
鴿	250
鴰	263
鵝^{7}	370
鵜	514
鵠	261
鵡	609
鵪^{8}	3
鵬	397

NUMERICAL LIST OF RADICALS

	0	10	20	30	40	50	60	70	80	90	100	110	120	130	140	150	160	170	180	190	200	210	
0		儿	勹	(3) 口	宀	巾	彳	方	毋	爿	生	矛	糸 (糹)	肉 (月)	艸 (艹 䒑)	谷	辛	阜 (阝)	音	髟	麻	齊	0
1	(1) 一	入	匕	囗	寸	干	(4) 心 (忄 㣺)	无 (旡)	比	片	用	矢	缶	臣	虍	豆	辰	隶	頁	門	(12) 黃	(15) 齒	1
2	丨	八	匚	土	小	幺	戈	日	毛	牙	田	石	网 (罒 㓁)	自	虫	豕	辵 (辶)	隹	風	鬯	黍	(16) 龍	2
3	丶	冂	匸	士	尢 (兀 尣)	广	戶	曰	氏	牛	疋	示 (礻)	羊	至	血	豸	邑 (阝)	雨 (⻗)	飛	鬲	黑	龜	3
4	丿	冖	十	夂	尸	廴	手 (扌)	月	气	犬 (犭)	疒	内	羽	臼	行	貝	酉	青	食	鬼	黹	(17) 龠	4
5	乙	冫	卜	夊	屮	廾	支	木	水 (氵 氺)	(5) 玄	癶	禾	老 (耂)	舌	衣 (衤)	赤	釆	非	首	(11) 魚	(13) 黽		5
6	亅	几	卩 (㔾)	夕	山	弋	攴 (攵)	欠	火 (灬)	玉 (王)	白	穴	而	舛	襾 (西)	走	里	(9) 面	香	鳥	鼎		6
7	(2) 二	凵	厂	大	巛 (川 巜)	弓	文	止	爪 (爫)	瓜	皮	立	耒	舟	(7) 見	足	(8) 金	革	(10) 馬	鹵	鼓		7
8	亠	刀 (刂)	厶	女	工	彐 (彑)	斗	歹 (歺)	父	瓦	皿	(6) 竹	耳	艮	角	身	長 (镸)	韋	骨	鹿	鼠		8
9	人 (亻)	力	又	子	己	彡	斤	殳	爻	甘	目 (罒)	米	聿	色	言	車	門	韭	高	麥	(14) 鼻		9
	9	19	29	39	49	59	69	79	89	99	109	119	129	139	149	159	169	179	189	199	209